MECHANICS' INSTITUTE

MECHANICS'

MERCANTILE LIBRARY

RISING TO THE LIGHT

RISING TO THE LIGHT

A Portrait of Bruno Bettelheim

Theron Raines

ALFRED A. KNOPF   *New York*   2002

THIS IS A BORZOI BOOK
PUBLISHED BY ALFRED A. KNOPF

www.aaknopf.com

Knopf, Borzoi Books, and the colophon are registered trademarks of Random House, Inc.

Due to limitations of space, permissions to reprint previously published material can be
found following the index.

Library of Congress Cataloging-in-Publication Data

Raines, Theron.
Rising to the light : a portrait of Bruno Bettelheim / Theron Raines. — 1st ed.
p.   cm.
Includes bibliographical references and index.
ISBN 0–679–40196–2
1. Bettelheim, Bruno.   2. Psychoanalysts — United States — Biography.   I. Title.
BF109.B48 .R35 2002
618.92'89'0092 — dc21
[B]
2001054536

Manufactured in the United States of America

First Edition

TO THOSE WHO TEACH

&

TO THOSE WHO LEARN

THIS BOOK

IS

RESPECTFULLY

DEDICATED

The truly virtuous man, desiring to be established himself, seeks to establish others. . . . To find in the wishes of one's own heart the principle for his conduct toward others is the method of true virtue.

—Confucius

Wherefore I perceive that there is nothing better, than that a man should rejoice in his own works; for that is his portion: for who shall bring him to see what shall be after him?

—Ecclesiastes, 3:22

Sownynge in moral vertu was his speche,
And gladly wolde he lerne and gladly teche.

—Chaucer

CONTENTS

ACKNOWLEDGMENTS

MY FIRST thanks to those named in the interviews—and to those not named. If they were connected with the Orthogenic School, they showed Bruno (and themselves) in action, in a small and unique setting whose workings nevertheless have lessons for the world at large.

For their comments on portions of the manuscript, special thanks are due to Karen Zelan, Alvin Rosenfeld, Raul Hilberg, "Wyatt," and "Betsy." Also to Rabbi David J. Meyer, whose insightful Talmudic eulogy led me to the ending for this book. Early on, Gayle Janowitz offered creative and crucial advice, most of which I took.

A large and many-faceted thanks to the team at Knopf:

—to George Andreou, editor, who had to ask me, "Why don't you focus the narrative more on Bruno?" before I saw what I had to do;

—to Robin Reardon, George's assistant, who transferred her growing dedication to the fate of my manuscript;

—to Ashbel Green, for making a priceless editorial suggestion so long ago that he has surely forgotten it;

—to Kathleen Fridella, the production editor, who seems to have borrowed a device from *Star Trek* to transform a stack of typed pages into a handsome book;

—and, most gratefully, to Sonny Mehta, whose benign idiosyncrasy let me arrive on Knopf's doorstep with a book almost ten years late. And, of course, thanks to many others, unnamed, whose efforts turn the wheels and propel the forward movement of the publishing juggernaut.

My thanks also to Rebecca Lubin and Barbara Barrett-Bolster of the Rensselaerville Library for chasing down many books in the Mid-Hudson Library System, and to Regenstein Library at the University of Chicago; also to Dr. Karl Fallend of Vienna for his admirable long-distance research, and to Mary Shapiro.

Most of all, I have to thank the two persons closest to me, Joan Raines and Keith Korman, for all the reasons they know and perhaps one or two I haven't mentioned to them.

BECAUSE this book is about learning and teaching, I also want to set down the names of a few teachers from whom I learned more than I realized at the time:

—Mrs. Schneider in the sixth grade, who got angry at the class because she misspelled a word on the blackboard and none of us corrected her;

—Mr. Elder, my Latin teacher in Pine Bluff High School, who was the first person to suggest that I should consider going to college, and whose enthusiasm for the measured beat of Latin verse gave me a feeling that the way we say things might be important;

—Miss Jobelle Holcombe, a silvery-haired, independent-spirited seventy-year-old spinster who came out of retirement in my freshman year at the University of Arkansas because male teachers were going off to war. Her inspired teaching of Keats gave me an unforgettable introduction to English poetry, but even more memorable was the sadness that filled her face—she was pink and white like Mrs. Santa Claus—at the moment I told her I had been notified to report for the service. The recollection of this moment became a lesson in itself, showing that a teacher may feel deeply about a naïve teenager;

—my Air Force instructor at Hondo navigation school a little over a year later, a warrant officer who squinted fruitlessly in the bright Texas morning sun at my last five flight logs and then surrendered to a monumental hangover. If he had been able to look, he would have seen written evidence that on my first night mission I had missed the target by at least fifty miles, but his whiskey-blind approval made me a navigator and a second lieutenant, an officer and a gentleman with a rank just higher than his own. He showed me that human frailty sometimes has harmless results.

In the years right after the war, Columbia College had a magnificent cadre of professors, assistant professors, and instructors, and I wish to acknowledge the ones from whom I benefited: Quentin Anderson, Andrew Chiappe, Charles Everett, Charles Frankel, Moses Hadas, Richard Rowland, Maurice Valency, and Mark Van Doren. They would probably not remember me, but I remember them because they mysteriously decided I should be granted $4000 for two years at Oriel College, Oxford. However, their most lasting mark on an impressionable learner was imprinted through my awareness of their integrity, their complex interest in learning and teaching, and occasional hints of the depths of their inner life. There were others whose names and faces I cannot summon up, and although the passage of time is no excuse, memory fades.

As for Oxford, if a good teacher is like fresh water, then Oxford was a desert for me. It had many able scholars of well-deserved repute, but their minds made me think of dry bones drifted over with sand. My favorite example of literary scholarship came down from the previous century: the professor who spent his life proving that Anglo-Saxon has no dative case. As teachers, the dons slowly taught me that I did not want the academic life; with the moral inertia typical of ambivalence, I continued to wish I could bend myself in that direction but could not—a valuable lesson to have learned. My happiest memory of two years at Oxford is how well I slept there; although, to be fair to the place and the people, I should add that the lectures of Lord David Cecil were a delight.

Finally, a belated thanks to my mother and father, whose affection for each other after eight children gave the gift of life to the ninth, myself. I now see they did much else of value in making a family, because I could not have had kinder and better brothers and sisters.

A NOTE ON THE TEXT

ALL NAMES followed by an asterisk* are pseudonyms.
Where necessary, I have edited interviews to ensure brevity, correct syntax or grammar, and avoid repetition; I have also sometimes changed the order in which memories were related, so as to fashion a smoother narrative. In the first years, Bruno complained that some of his quotes made him sound too wordy, and he asked me to trim them, but I checked the passages with my wife/partner/first reader/best friend, who said that I had captured Bruno's voice, and so I told him I did not want to make him more succinct. He dropped the subject.

Although the Orthogenic School had both male and female workers and students, when speaking generally I chose to refer to counselors as "she" and students as "he." This is a narrative convenience and intends no disrespect for male counselors or girl students.

I have preferred not to name certain persons connected with the Bettelheim story—the "American mother," for instance. Although she is long dead and has been identified in other books, it felt better for me to leave her unnamed, on the grounds that if our situations were reversed, this is what I would have wanted. In making the point I do not imply criticism of anyone else. It's merely personal.

As for the possibility of mistakes, which most writers are right to acknowledge, I'm sure I've made them and so beg the reader's forgiveness in advance, with a promise to rectify inaccuracies if an opportunity arises at a later time. However, I do not expect to rectify my opinions even though they may be mistaken in some respects, because I have tried them out endlessly in my own mind until they have at last taken on the status of essential truths—for me. The reader who does the same for his own opinions perhaps will not be too troubled by mine.

INTRODUCTION

A Personal Note

MY INTEREST in Bruno Bettelheim began at least ten years before he asked me to represent him as a literary agent. A *New York Times* review of *The Informed Heart* caught my attention, and I bought and read the book when it was published in 1960. It made such a powerful impression that after I had turned the last page, I started at the beginning and read it again.

Bettelheim subtitled the book *Autonomy in a Mass Age*, and in it he analyzed the Nazi concentration-camp policies that led to personality disintegration among prisoners. He did not retell the horrors of camp life except as relevant to his theme; instead, he aimed to remind us of how social pressures can weaken personality in a mass society, and that protecting our inner self and achieving personal growth is our most important task in life.

In Bettelheim's view, the wisdom and warning embodied in "Know thyself" was never more needed than in our time of new technologies and swiftly moving events. Rapid social change gives us little chance to develop or test new attitudes and leaves the individual confused, perhaps more uncertain than he can acknowledge even to himself. If he watches others and copies them to meet the challenge of new ideas or situations, the copying renders his integration vague and shallow, because copying is not truly in line with one's impulse to develop in a unique way. The copier responds to events and social change not with genuine autonomy but with the illusion of autonomy.[1] Bettelheim foresaw

> a mass society in which people no longer react spontaneously and autonomously to the vagaries of life, but are ready to accept uncritically the solutions that others offer.[2]

It used to be that life-stabilizing attitudes and certainties passed from one generation to the next, in personal ways and by common tradition; people understood what they owed the world and what they could expect from it. Life might be hard, but they knew their place because they had been guided to it by family and community, and they accepted it. Now possibilities have proliferated as time-honored certainties have faded. Bettelheim felt that we need to cultivate an attitude that asks, What can *I* afford to give to the group, and what do I owe myself? What should I do in any given situation where group pressures encroach? He recognized that by joining a group we shed some of the burdens of individuality in our need to find safety in solidarity with others; but the person who submerges himself in group opinion also curbs his spontaneity when he shuns views not shared by his peers.

To strengthen the dignity our parents nurtured in us (if they did), we must tune out the clamor of a mass society that tells us in a thousand voices what we should do and feel. In this context I have come to see one sentence as the moral of Bettelheim's book:

Our hearts must know the world of reason, and reason must be guided by an informed heart.[3]

Putting it another way: *Know what you feel, and feel what you know; examine your attitudes and actions, which embody the values by which you live*. Of course, this is easier said than done, and *The Informed Heart* resists quick understanding. It is dense, ambitious, and far-reaching in its critique of the modern human condition, in which we now need to resist the subtle coercions of a huge and noisy world, where some groups declare all values relative while others seem intent on reducing everyone except themselves to the status of ants. At times the book is cryptic, even though Bettelheim strove for clarity in analyzing what happened to the inner life of men forced to cope with extreme pressures. The book has no set of reassuring certainties to replace those our culture has undeniably lost, but Bettelheim believed we can learn to find personal certainties through the honest and stubborn interplay of reason and feeling—the "informed heart."

Somehow his book stirred me to think about myself as only a few others (writings of Freud among them) have ever done. Several times I have come back to it over the years, always finding fresh insights in the rereading. The book's jacket called it "an answer to those who fear the loss of self in modern society," a claim too pointed to be true for Bettelheim, who did not mean to give "answers" but to remind us of the kind of questioning attitude useful in finding our own answers about ourselves, if we want to.

In 1963 I happened to read Bettelheim's review of Hannah Arendt's *Eichmann in Jerusalem*, and I wrote him a letter arguing that it had been a mistake to execute Eichmann, that Israel should have deported him to Germany instantly after the guilty verdict, forcing the new German nation to deal with him in its own way. It seemed to me that a second trial, one with German prosecutors in Eichmann's homeland, in his own language and under German law, would have engaged the attention and perhaps the conscience of a whole generation of those indirectly responsible for the systematic destruction of Jews under German rule, whereas the execution in Israel gave many European "bystanders" an easy way out, a sense that matters had been brought to a close, with no need for them to look at the evidence or at themselves. Bettelheim surprised me with an immediate one-sentence reply, saying in effect, "I wish things had been done the way you said."[4]

We corresponded three or four times over the years, and at one point I offered him a book project that did not work out. In 1970, when he decided to change publishers, he called me to talk about what he should do. We had not spoken for at least a year, but at the end of the conversation he asked if I would care to represent him, which I did for the next twenty years, until his death in 1990.

We did not become friends quickly, though I soon found he had a real gift for friendship. Gradually, and to a degree, we became close, mostly by discussing his writing and the business related to it. He did not say much about family matters, nor did I. Bruno met my wife, Joan, in 1971 and exchanged some letters with her, but for many years his wife, Trude, was simply a name to me and occasionally a pleasant voice on the telephone. Eventually I met Trude and their son, Eric, but in the course of our conversations Bruno and I still did not talk much about those nearest to us.[5] This may have been due in part to circumstance and distance, but also he had a longtime habit of keeping his private and professional lives quite separate. As for myself, people have told me I'm unusually quiet and reserved, so any relationship with Bettelheim was likely to develop slowly; but it did develop, and we had a friendship in addition to our professional relation.

I BEGAN this project intending to write a long profile that I hoped would be suitable for a magazine.[6] It would be a short-term effort, fifteen or twenty thousand words, written over a couple of months of nights and weekends, much of it in Bettelheim's own voice. It would either be published or not; and if not published, at least I would have satisfied myself in learning more about someone I liked very much, a man of deep mind and exotic background. Coming from a small southern town, I found Bettelheim's personal history (what I knew of it) fascinating. Also, despite my readings of *The Informed Heart*, I had not quite grasped how he had survived the camps, and I wanted to talk with him about this.

In 1983 I asked Bruno if I could come to California for a visit to interview him for a profile, and he said very forcefully, "You'll be wasting your time. No one will be interested." I told him he might be right but that I wanted to take the chance. He paused, then said in his characteristic way, "Let me think about it. I call you." The next day he called and said, "Well, if you want to waste your time . . ."

In August 1983 I interviewed him for five days, in the back bedroom of the home in California where he and Trude had retired after leaving Chicago in 1974. They had bought a single-level house on a hillside up a fairly steep drive, in a gardenlike setting. They liked the mild California climate and also the nearness of a major university, Stanford. The town, Portola Valley, was not far from San Francisco, and at night one could see the lights of the city from the north side of the living room. Many times in the course of a day I caught the flash of brightly colored birds in trees nearby, and now and then during our sessions a lone rabbit hopped about peacefully just outside the window.

The house was built of cedar, in the style of an A-frame chalet. On one side of the living room, a lofty wall held paintings, books, and LP records. On the other side, floor-to-ceiling glass walls angled out like the prow of a ship and pointed west over a valley, toward the Santa Cruz Mountains. The place had been Trude's choice to escape Chicago's raw weather, which aggravated her arthritis. Bruno missed the convenience and liveliness of the big city but hoped Trude would feel less pain in a warmer climate.

AFTER we talked for the better part of a week, I still envisioned a long magazine article. On rereading the transcript (which my wife had kindly offered to type) I finally saw that there was just too much material; it had to be a book. I began to think of a modest volume having some of the features of a profile, yet not a formal biography in which the reader would expect a fuller and more methodical account. However, even after I switched my sights, I failed to realize how far beyond the profile approach I would have to go in order to do justice to Bruno. I hoped first to capture his voice, the steady manner in which he developed and pursued an idea, circling his subject and finally running it to ground; to show his seriousness and poise, his knack for finding fresh ways to express familiar concepts. And the questions, always the questions.

In the midst of the interview, the realization came to me that I had actually set out upon this inquiry by thinking of Bruno as a teacher. He had often spoken of himself as a teacher, but I had caught only a hazy glimpse of the depth of this self-description before seeing what made it so. Bruno believed that genuine learning comes slowly, that we are reluctant to give up what we imagine we know. "We are really very simple," he liked to say. "Only our defenses are complex." And he knew that most students came with strong defenses against the simple truths they might learn in the teaching environments he created. Bettelheim understood that many little things and a great deal of time would go into a teaching-and-learning enterprise where the teacher's self-knowledge tracks his deepening insight into his students and their growing knowledge of themselves. But this was the kind of enterprise he tried to create.

I KNEW that Bettelheim's own voice and words would tilt the book toward autobiography, an idea I liked so much that several times I had urged him to write a book about himself. However, he steadfastly refused; he distrusted the form and said so both in conversation and in the introduction to his last volume of essays, *Freud's Vienna*. Anyone who wrote about himself would put his own case too one-sidedly, and he was determined not to do that. On the other hand, if I asked questions, he would answer them and then I would be free to make whatever I wanted out of the information he had given me. Also, I was free to talk to others or not, according to my wish. When I still imagined I was writing a magazine article or a short book, I thought a few telephone calls would do the job; but in the end I talked at far greater length with others than with Bruno.

As it turned out, speaking with former staff members and students filled many gaps he had left. For instance, he told me not a single vivid anecdote about life at the Orthogenic School, yet this was exactly the kind of story that came up at once when I talked to others. Since these anecdotes come from many sources, they tilt the book's balance away from autobiography by showing the man as some coworkers and students saw him. His words, their words, and my words will combine, I hope, into a portrait of the whole man.

AS I LEARNED more about Bruno during the 1983 interviews and realized that I wanted to understand him as a teacher, I came to see that I had no desire to write a conventional account of his life, but instead wanted to make a kind of portrait. When a painter stretches canvas for a portrait, he usually works swiftly with charcoal or brush to outline his subject's head, neck, and shoulders. After this, he often turns to layering: a slightly more detailed sketch brings in the features—eyes, nose, mouth, hairline, ears; the next layer may be color, the tones of skin, hair, and shadows; then the creases and wrinkles that give a face its unique cast. More layers create definition, mood, the look in the eyes; and final brush strokes modulate the smoothness or roughness of texture. The hints of the subject's inner life, the portrait's depths, come together little by little on canvas, until at last we see the person *as the painter saw him.*

Such a layered portrait is my aim, but only in part. I also want the reader to be able to imagine a gifted teacher in action over a long span of time, a man who at first lived a privileged life but then met with extreme circumstances, which he surmounted in ways that served him well when he had to make a new life. To present this aspect of my friend Bruno, I hope for some of the effects of a fresco, a mural that shows many events of a man's life in scenes depicting his active influence on others.

Frescoes are painted swiftly on wet-lime plaster while the wall is drying, but they are not decoration or something merely superimposed: since the plaster absorbs the pigment, the fresco turns into part of the structure that houses it. The central scene of Bettelheim's teaching life was the Orthogenic School, which became for him a kind of secular cathedral; he created the form in which the School grew, and he was a key element in its structure. We may guess his motive, why he came to this life task with so much energy and enthusiasm, although we can hardly know; but *how* he did it can be described and may prove instructive to others who want to learn about helping emotionally disturbed children. To such readers, this book may also be informative by showing aspects of Bettelheim that he left out of his own books about the School.

SOME will view Bettelheim with fascination, perhaps mingled with wonder because he did so much in his life. But he antagonized many people by his self-assured independence, his attitudes and ideas, his often prickly manner; and those he angered will probably not care for features in him that I find admirable, which is to be expected. "If everyone agreed with me," he sometimes said, "I know I would be doing something wrong."

At one point I said that some of his observations would never be popular, and he laughed and replied, "I *like* to be unpopular!"

He enjoyed the renown his books and lectures brought him but was not impressed by it, and he accepted recognition as it came, without reaching for it. Once when I felt personally aggrieved by reviews that were skimpy, shallow, and condescending, I asked, "Bruno, do you care about your reviews?"

"Yes," he said, after a moment's thought. "I care, but not very much."

The work itself counted for more than immediate public acclaim, and by the time a book was published, he had usually moved on to his next project, at least in his ruminations about it. He found much to do, and he did it in his own way and as best he could, no matter what the world might say or think.

For a man who in his own time was called a maverick and a crank by some, and a pariah by others, Bettelheim seemed, to me at least, untroubled as he went his way in a long and busy life as teacher, clinician-administrator, writer, and psychologist. He liked to paraphrase Freud on replying to critics: "If I did that, I would do nothing else."

Many months after my week in California, when I saw that I was going to write a book rather than a magazine profile, I called to tell Bruno this. He said, forcefully, "Now you will *really* be wasting your time!"

"Let me worry about that," I said. "And besides, Bruno, you're not always right."

"Well," he said, in a voice suddenly mild, "that's certainly true."

RISING TO THE LIGHT

CHAPTER 1

Young Bruno — Infancy, Background, and Early Adolescence

I N 1980 my wife and I were having dinner at the apartment of a prominent analyst, and in the course of conversation he said, "I want you to hear something by your friend Bruno." The analyst knew that I represented Bettelheim, who at that point had been a client for about ten years. After dinner our host played an audiotape made several years earlier at a conference where Bettelheim was a featured speaker. Bruno had begun with a story of his infancy and early childhood, material well suited for an audience of analysts and other professionals. In the speech he revealed that like many children in his time and circumstances, he had been reared by a wet nurse.

In speaking personally Bettelheim sounded modest, confessional, and charming, and yet I detected notes of impudence and irreverence as he began to imply a disagreement with conventional psychological attitudes toward raising children. He made the wet-nurse episode sound scandalous, an outrageous way of treating an infant. However, since the product of this upbringing, a genuine celebrity, was standing there on the podium in a sober business suit, speaking with a heavy Viennese accent, with an innocent manner and an artless delivery, the audience murmured at some remarks, laughed at others, and sent him off at the end with a good round of applause.[1]

After we listened to the tape, our host (also Viennese but younger than Bettelheim) said thoughtfully and perhaps a bit wistfully, "We [the psychoanalytic establishment] should have reached out to him and taken him in. We shouldn't have left him isolated all those years." I believe the sentiment was genuine, and I know it was remarkably generous, because Bettelheim had written a damning review of this man's book a few years earlier.

WHEN I interviewed Bettelheim three years later, I asked him to tell the wet-nurse story again, and he obliged. "First, I think it has an important lesson, because my mother was a very Victorian lady. But she was also enlightened for her time and quite cultured, and she had every intention of being a good mother. On the one hand, it would not have occurred to her to do something as vulgar as to breast-feed her children, but on the other hand, she would never deprive her infants of being nursed at the breast. So, when I was almost ready to be born—this was in the summer of 1903—she made inquiries to find a wet nurse. In Vienna these were girls from the country, young girls from the farm. They were examined by doctors to make sure they were clean and healthy. Naturally, one such wet nurse was found for me, someone who would be on hand from the moment I was born.

"Now, what were the qualifications of such a wet nurse? Firstly, she had to have an illegitimate child. Most girls who had children born out of wedlock were hired as wet nurses. So we start out with a girl who is a 'sex delinquent,' if we use the kind of term you find in textbooks. But not only is she a sex delinquent, she is so deprived of all natural motherly instincts that she leaves her own child behind on the farm for somebody else to take care of, and she goes to the city for purely monetary gains.

"But that was not all: everyone believed that a wet nurse should drink a lot of beer in order to have a good supply of milk, so my wet nurse—like all of them—was encouraged and advised to drink beer. While she wasn't necessarily an alcoholic, most of the time she was slightly inebriated. So my entire care for the first three years of my life—because that was how long a wet nurse stayed with her job (of course, there was supplementary feeding, too)—was entrusted to a not particularly well educated and rather uncultured teenager of questionable morals who was also a sex delinquent, however you want to call it, and a person devoid of natural motherly instincts, with a tendency toward alcoholism."

When he was speaking to a psychologically oriented audience, at this point in the story Bettelheim summed up his case: he shrugged helplessly and said, "So you see the result," and everyone burst out laughing. However, there was more to the story as he told it to me.

"That girl, of course, was anxious to preserve her employment as long as possible, so she had no interest in weaning the child. Also, the child must seem to thrive, he shouldn't cry too much, should sleep well, should grow appropriately. In other words, he should develop normally and with a minimum of anxiety and trouble for the mother. Since the nurse knew she had to keep the child happy, whenever he cried, a typical wet nurse would sexually stimulate the baby to quiet him down. And this certainly made him happy."

I interrupted: "You may be describing the perfect childhood."

"That's what I'm trying to say," Bettelheim replied. "Why? Why did she do that? It's really very simple. While these girls were paid by present standards what we would call a pittance, or barely a pittance, the arrangement was, if she did a good job and the baby developed well, that at the end of the nursing period she would be given a fairly large sum of money as a dowry. That made up for her small wage and at the same time assured that she would take good care of the child. And out of this dowry, she could then go home and buy a little farm and marry the father of her own child, or even somebody else. That was the customary arrangement, but in my case it didn't work out that way, because Mitzi didn't want to go back to the farm or to take care of her child. I don't know, maybe the child died. Interestingly, I never asked. But she married an upholsterer and bought him a shop, and they lived in Vienna. I kept in touch with her as long as I was in Vienna. Naturally, I was very attached to her.

"But why did it work? Why did this 'outrageous,' if you go by the textbooks, system work so well? First, there were no distractions for a wet nurse. She concentrated strictly on the infant. She didn't have to take care of the house, she didn't have to cook, she didn't have to clean—all the tasks we think of as 'mother's work.' She only had to care for the infant and see that he was healthy. That was all, that was *it*.

"She didn't care about world politics, she didn't care if I went to college or whether I learned to talk early, or how soon I learned to walk. She wanted only that I should nurse well and not cry too much, that I should develop well in general. She had a vital interest in those elements of my life up to the age of three—her whole future depended upon it! Her attention made me happy, and it made my parents happy, and the result made Mitzi happy. Nobody talked about delinquency or about rehabilitating anybody, but Mitzi became a good citizen, very responsible, and when she married she had five children, who she naturally brought to see us. It was a good arrangement."

But wouldn't he really rather have been nursed by his mother?

"Sometimes I think I might have liked it better, but then I know that this couldn't be true in reality because my mother didn't want to, and if she did the nursing only out of a sense of duty, which she would naturally resent, then it wouldn't have been good for either of us.

"Incidentally, I don't believe the British nanny was nearly as good an arrangement for children, because she was much too concerned that the child should be 'decent.' Farm girls in Austria, maybe you would think they were oversexed drunken immoral teenagers, but thank god they were not concerned with 'decency' or anything rigid like that. These girls had only a concern that the child should be happy and that their masters and mistresses should be satisfied."

Was there any danger that the wet nurse would take the mother's place?

"No, I knew who was my mother from an early age. Practically every day my sister and I were brought in to play with her, at least that's how I remember it from the age of two. And during this hour or two (at the most) that we were with our mother, she played with us and wasn't distracted by anything else. She enjoyed us fully at that moment, which is important. It's amazing, but a French study I read when I was writing the book on the kibbutz showed that mothers who were all day at home actually spent only about two hours with their children. So you see, maybe there's a natural limit to how much you can be interested in a baby, or how much time you can spare from other tasks. Most of all, our mother could enjoy the time with us because it was limited time. When we became restless, there was a sacred formula my mother used—as many other mothers did, I'm sure. She said, 'I guess the little darling is getting tired,' which meant, 'I want to get rid of him now.'

"Then Mitzi took us back to the nursery, where we would be rambunctious or do whatever we wanted. So we had a marvelous time with our mother, nothing but play. It was usually teatime, and we had some cookies or other goodies, and we were played with. My mother had no need to criticize or reprimand us. That was done by the nurse, but because she was a servant we could take it or leave it. The nurse was not as powerful and important to us as the parent. Remember, in Shakespeare, it's Juliet's nurse who takes care of her and indulges her, makes it possible for her to be with Romeo. But all this was only possible in a servant culture.

"Psychologically, the most important thing of all was that the criticism and reprimanding was not done by the all-important person, the parent. All the petty education was from the servant, and the parents were reserved for really major issues. The child was superior to the servant and soon realized it. Also, there was a much freer atmosphere in the servants' quarters of the house. This was not a nuclear family as we think of it now, but it was a very strong family, and the child knew his place in it. Yes, it was very reassuring, very secure."

BETTELHEIM told me that his family name dated back at least to the mid–eighteenth century, where it probably originated in the town of Bratislava, now in southwest Slovakia. Bratislava lies downstream on the Danube about forty miles east of Vienna, and Budapest is about a hundred miles farther downstream to the southeast. Bratislava was first a Slovak capital, but when the Turks occupied the lower Danube basin, the Magyars who ruled Hungary took the city, changed its name to Pozsony, and made it their capital. Later, the city was named Pressburg by German-speaking traders who dominated this crossroads of commerce where Austria, Hungary, and Slovakia met. Long before Jews were welcome in Vienna or Budapest, Bratislava was noted for its busy ghetto.

Early in the eighteenth century, Bruno said, a *Bettelheim*, or "beggar's home" for Jews was established on land leased from the bishop of Bratislava. Poor vagrant Jews, Jewish peddlers, and students who traveled to study with prominent rabbis all stayed there, and at some point it was also an orphanage for Jewish children. Late in the eighteenth century, when Jews were ordered to take surnames, the owners of the *Bettelheim* chose to name themselves after their trade (as many Jews did), and by the end of the nineteenth century several distinct branches of Bettelheims lived in Bratislava.

Jews needed a toleration permit to live in Vienna, and Emperor Ferdinand, who came to the throne in 1835, gave a permit to the banker Salomon Rothschild. In 1843 Salomon also got permission to buy real estate that could be passed on by inheritance, but in 1848 both he and Ferdinand fled Vienna because of the revolution. Salomon's son Anselm stayed behind to take care of the family's interests, and when things stabilized under the new emperor (the eighteen-year-old Franz Josef), Anselm worked to gain favor at the Imperial Court. Salomon's death in 1855 gave Anselm full control of the Rothschild Bank in Vienna, and in 1861, when the emperor made him a baron, he became the first Jewish member of the Imperial House of Lords.

In the family legend that Bruno retold, his grandfather Jacob Moritz Bettelheim left Bratislava for Vienna (probably in the 1840s) because he had been chosen from perhaps a thousand candidates to tutor the sons of Anselm Rothschild. At that time wealthy employers brought tutors to live in the household, where they came into daily contact with all members of the family. Moritz, who had studied to be a rabbi, lived with the Rothschilds, made a lasting impression, and formed a lofty connection; eventually he became overseer of the Rothschild estates—as Bruno said, the *Forstmeister*. Moritz also had a lumber business and worked effectively in it, doing well enough to be awarded the title of *Kommerzialrat* ("counsellor of commerce"). Austria's pervasive class system put a high premium on titles as adding luster to one's reputation, and *Kommerzialrat* was more than a modest prize, since the monarchy conferred the title to prominent businessmen at its own discretion, as a special state honor.

Another fragment of family lore says that Baron Rothschild suggested to the emperor that the brilliant former tutor was himself worthy of a title in the aristocracy, and the emperor asked how many sons Moritz Bettelheim had. Eleven children, he was told—ten sons. Impossible, Franz Josef replied. A noble title was out of the questions; the man had too many sons. He would have to make do with *Kommerzialrat*.

LONG after Moritz Bettelheim had made his fortune in Vienna, he heard that he had inherited property in Egypt. To collect his inheritance he needed only to furnish proof of his birth, which he refused to do. His sons asked permission to go to Bratislava for the documentation, but Moritz, a firm autocrat, said no, and his dutiful sons left the question of their parent's parents a family mystery. For reasons known only to himself, Moritz never revealed which branch of the Bettelheims in Bratislava he came from, and apparently none claimed him, despite his rise to prominence.[2]

CONSCIENTIOUS assimilation did not keep Viennese Jews from being viewed with suspicion as a people apart, whose very presence somehow threatened the culture and traditions of the majority. Anti-Semitic organizations flourished in the second half of the nineteenth century, and Jew-baiting was openly tolerated.

In the 1870s, as Bruno recalled the story, Moritz Bettelheim's oldest son, then at the University of Vienna, became angry at a fellow student's remark about Jews. He challenged the young man to a duel, a practice outlawed almost everywhere else but still legal in Germany and Austria, where personal combat could settle a question of honor. The parties usually fought with sabers, and so duels rarely proved fatal; in fact, they left valuable scars on a man's face or body, marks of virility and high character.

The young man who was challenged had the right to choose weapons, and he chose not sabers but pistols; he upheld his honor by killing the Bettelheim son with a single shot. Moritz Bettelheim then forbade his other sons to attend the university and hired tutors for all nine boys; they lived in his home as he had lived with the Rothschilds. As his sons came of age, Moritz set them up in business or steered them to jobs of the sort available to the sons of a man connected to the Rothschilds. Bruno said that two went into banking, others into the civil service, and still others into business after marrying wives with good dowries. For instance, when Bruno's father, Anton, married Paula Seidler, her father gave her a dowry equivalent to $50,000, a handsome sum in 1898 Vienna, and the money financed Anton's first business venture.

Adolf Seidler, Bruno's maternal grandfather, was born in Bohemia (about a hundred miles from Vienna) and came with a family legend somewhat different from that of the Bettelheim side.[3] Bruno said that Adolf's father was a poor peddler whose wife died when Adolf was an infant. The next wife did not want her children to share their meager patrimony with the child of another woman, and after Adolf's bar mitzvah she told her husband that the boy had to leave home. His father gave him a large silver coin and said that he must find his own way in life, perhaps with distant relatives.[4] At thirteen Adolf hung his only pair of shoes over his shoulder and walked barefoot to Vienna, where the distant relatives owned a small machine shop. He became an apprentice, learned the trade well, married, and eventually bought the shop. By the time Bruno's mother, Paula, was born, Adolf Seidler was on his way to making a substantial fortune in a variety of businesses.[5]

Moritz Bettelheim died shortly before his son Anton married Paula Seidler in what both families saw as a good match. Her father's sharp and not too scrupulous business practices had enabled him to amass great wealth, which he began to invest in real estate. Bruno estimated that before the First World War, his grandfather Seidler owned between twenty and thirty houses and apartment buildings in Vienna. At home Seidler showed the face of an absolute tyrant to his children but was delightful with his grandchildren and overindulgent toward his wife, whose hairdresser came to the house every day. Bruno thought she was the first in her circle to bob her hair in the new style.

Seidler robbed his sons of ambition even as he planned a good education for each. "Nice people, my three uncles," Bettelheim said, "but unfortunately they didn't amount to anything. Often you see that, when the father is too autocratic and has to keep on proving himself, even against his sons."

ANTON BETTELHEIM made costly mistakes in bringing timber from forest to sawmill, and in a few years he had lost everything. Seidler staked him again to the dowry amount, $50,000, but insisted that one of his sons become Anton's partner. A lesson learned, Anton ran the second company quite profitably despite the dead weight of a feckless brother-in-law. Young Bruno heard words pass between his father and mother about her brother but failed to catch the drift of the veiled references until much later in life.

After Moritz's death, his widow, Eleanor ("Grandmother Laurie"), kept the huge old apartment where she had raised eleven children, and Bruno spent long Sunday afternoons there when the whole family visited. The adults ate and talked in the dining room and parlor, while the young cousins played quietly under the table, hidden by a low-hanging tablecloth, or less quietly many rooms away, out of earshot. As the afternoon wore on, maids and governesses came to take the youngsters home, while their parents either stayed for supper or went out to a restaurant.

"I was the first male Bettelheim born after my grandfather's death," Bruno wrote me, "and I was given his Jewish middle name, Jacob, as my Jewish middle name."[6] Bruno never called himself Jacob and could not recall his father's Jewish name, saying, "In an assimilated family such as ours, one's Jewish name was accorded no importance."

DESPITE good care in infancy and as a toddler, young Bruno had serious illnesses. Shortly after he was weaned (at about three) the family took a vacation in the mountains, where they planned to spend July and August at a country inn. There Bruno came down with severe dysentery, he thought probably from polluted water. However, his sister Margarethe ("Grete"), who was seven at the time, believed that green elderberries from a hedge in the inn's yard had made him sick. "I loved unripe fruit," Grete told me, "and he saw me eat them, and he ate them. He got dysentery, and I didn't."

Bruno developed a fever that night, and his mother became alarmed. She would not trust her sick child to a local country doctor and so took him in her arms on the next train to Vienna. At the train station she hired a horse-drawn carriage and hurried to the home of their family doctor.

The doctor saw the three-year-old was deathly ill and thought he should not be moved; he ordered a couch prepared in his living room. Grete said, "The doctor's family was away for the summer, so his apartment in Vienna was empty, and he put my mother and Bruno there. Not in a hospital."

The experience of recovering in the milieu of the doctor's home for a week or more made a deep impression on Bettelheim. When I asked about it, he pointed to the advantages of his continual care in a home environment with pleasant surroundings and the instant availability of the doctor, who came in between patients at all hours of the day and so could catch any nuances or changes in his condition. One of Bettelheim's earliest memories was the fragrance of strong black coffee, which the doctor fed him regularly to stimulate his heart and replace body liquids drained by the dysentery.

"This careful treatment in his own house saved my life," Bettelheim said, "and I always remembered it. As long as I lived in Vienna, I maintained a close relationship with this physician."

Bettelheim also survived diphtheria and caught scarlet fever twice, the latter disease at a time when many people did not realize that bright light would damage the eyes of a child with scarlet fever. Conventional wisdom told parents to keep a sickroom bright and cheerful, and Bettelheim's mother flooded his room with sunlight. Her intentions were good, but before he was five years old, his eyes had been irreparably damaged.

As THE well-loved son in an upper-middle-class family, Bruno knew that his parents wanted the very best for him. They made him feel he had been born into a safe world where progress was certain, as exemplified by his diligent and successful grandfathers, who had attained distinction and importance in one of the great capitals of Europe. "All that was part of our family lore, and when I was very young I took it all for granted, I didn't have to think about it. I was already the third generation in Vienna and so got all the benefits—maybe they were benefits, I'm not so sure—without the same kind of struggle. My father and grandfather did not go to the university, but it was always assumed that I would go.

"Maybe in some ways it's like—I haven't really thought about this— the experience of a successful immigrant family in America, where each generation goes through something quite different as life becomes easier. Of course, there were so many children that no great fortune could be left to any one child, but everyone was comfortable. The whole Jewish group in which I moved also understood and shared this spectacular rise in affluence."

He saw his family's progress as due in part to the nineteenth century's growing tolerance and assimilation of Jews, who were allowed to leave behind the persecutions of the past and advance into the middle class.

"We saw the ghetto Jew as hemmed in by the world's prejudice and by the strict regimentation that religion imposed on him," Bruno said. "We whose families had succeeded in Vienna all believed we had gained an intellectual scope not available in the ghetto. In hindsight, it's very easy to see the shadows in this bright picture, but despite the class restrictions in Vienna, there was an air of freedom, an expectation of real happiness, an anticipation of success. It's quite astonishing when I look back on it now."

Despite signs of prejudice against *all* Jews, despite having been bullied in school (if they were) and blind to the implications of their own rejection of the ghetto Jew, assimilated Jews in Vienna felt socially secure. It was as easy as breathing to accept conventional wisdom, the group belief about the future's bright promise. "Whatever hardships or injustices might exist, we felt they were merely temporary and would soon disappear. Someone like the charismatic Dr. Lueger, who ran for mayor of Vienna on a platform of open anti-Semitism, would eventually lose office or die, and then he would not be a threat anymore." Bettelheim singled out this overarching optimism in parents, supported by the atmosphere of the extended family, as a source of deep inner security in assimilated children, at least about their place in society. "We knew that the world was good, and we believed people were good."

BETTELHEIM had little memory of his first home in the district near the Schönbrunn palace, but one impression, probably from age four, remained vivid — that of his mother and father in formal dress, about to depart for the opera. Caruso would be singing that evening, and Anton wore a tuxedo, Paula a long black lace gown, heavily corseted in the style of the day, with a black plumed headdress and a dazzling string of pearls. The Bettelheims no doubt sat in a box with friends for the performance, unconcerned about whether Paula's feathers would block anyone's view.

Later, Anton moved the family to an apartment nearer the center of the city because Paula needed to be closer to her aging parents. The Seidlers had never assimilated as wholeheartedly as the Bettelheims, and while at first Paula hoped to keep a kosher home, she abandoned the idea when she saw how much it displeased Anton. Although Mitzi was long gone, the household ran smoothly with two in help, cook and maid. Paula always inspected the crystal chandelier after the maid cleaned it and often polished it again herself. One day while bringing it to perfection, she fell off a ladder and permanently injured her knee. "She was a *balabusta*," Bettelheim said.[7]

He remembered the new apartment as only a short walk from the Ringstrasse, the busy beltway that encircles the old heart of Vienna. The city had been the last walled capital in Europe, and officials in the mid–nineteenth century wanted to ease traffic and bring new grandeur to the seat of an ancient empire.[8] In 1857 the heavy wall that had kept the Turks at bay two centuries earlier began to be leveled to make way for a handsome boulevard lined with parks, museums, spacious apartment houses, and massive public buildings. Those who planned the ambitious urban renewal modeled the Ringstrasse's grand new structures in neo-Gothic, baroque, Greek, and Renaissance styles, but the overall impression in our time is perhaps less grand than grandiose.

Even before the buildings were finished, many Viennese began to enjoy evening strolls along the four-mile path of the former wall. Toward the end of the century, a thinker like Freud, walking briskly with his stick and cigar and a head full of fantastic notions about dreams and syndromes, could work out his ideas about the human psyche while retracing the ghostly outline of the archaic defense the city had given up in order to grow.

Bruno's mother often took him to the museums on the Ringstrasse, cultivating an interest in art that lasted the rest of his life. At six he went to a *Volksschule* within walking distance of the new apartment, and when his teacher realized he couldn't see the blackboard, she told his parents he needed glasses. Young Bruno's eye damage had at last been noticed.

Most upper-middle-class Viennese took summer vacations either in the mountains or at the seaside; the Bettelheims always chose the mountains, except for one summer on the shores of the Baltic. Also, they had a family ritual in which they all talked endlessly for weeks about where to go on vacation (although Grete and Bruno understood that they were expected to be delighted with whatever their parents decided). For several summers the family went to Velden in Carinthia, in the south of Austria, where they rented a floor in a villa near a lake. In 1911, when Bruno was eight, they stayed at a large resort hotel in the Tirol, near the Brenner Pass. Hotels such as this arranged for all the children to eat together at eleven o'clock, and thirty or forty would sit down to a noisy lunch that allowed their parents to enjoy a quiet meal an hour later. Dinner followed the same pattern. "The children had a jolly good time eating together," Bruno said, "and it would never have been so jolly if we sat with our parents and had to behave."

The clientele of this hotel came mostly from Austria, with some families from Germany and a few from Italy. Bettelheim said that he knew of no restrictions against Jews, because before the First World War only the well-to-do could afford to stay in large Austrian family resort hotels, and nobody seemed to care about anyone's background as long as he could pay. After the war, restrictions were "according to the wishes of the owner of the establishment," he said, adding that the owner drew the clientele he wanted by advertising the restriction.

LIKE MANY boys of his time and class, Bruno had a set of toy soldiers in full-dress Hungarian uniforms that were authentic, gorgeously colored, and very dashing. The real army also had an almost make-believe aura and took the spotlight in Vienna chiefly as a theatrical presence. Never mind that the military had been driven out of Vienna by rebel students in 1848 and had lost a war to Prussia in 1866 that left Prussia free to create the German state and dominate it; Vienna loved the marching bands, the rainbow of regimental colors from all corners of the empire, the clattering cavalry, the horse-drawn weapons on parade. Until the beginning of the First World War, the people of Vienna responded warmly to this glory on display; also, Franz Josef, the ruler since 1848, had come to be revered as the ever-present father of an empire embracing fifty million people: a sovereign dignified, benevolent, stern, remote.

"The emperor's reign spanned the industrialization of the country," Bettelheim said. "He was associated with the increase of well-being for everybody, so his birthday was a holiday and a celebration that made people feel good about their country and their government." America has nothing like it, he said — "but at any rate, that's what the emperor's birthday did for people."

The emperor made a habit of riding in an open carriage from the Hofburg (his palace in the inner city) to Schönbrunn (his summer palace) when the weather warmed up. He always made this trip in early afternoon at the same time and by the same route, and the Bettelheim maid often took the children for a walk to see him ride through their neighborhood.

BEFORE the age of nine, Bruno became an avid reader of newspapers, and the first headline he could recall told of the *Titanic* disaster in 1912. In June 1914, when a Bosnian Serb assassinated Archduke Ferdinand at Sarajevo, Bruno and Grete were staying with their Seidler grandparents, who always started summer vacations a month earlier than the rest of the family. The murder of the heir to the Habsburg throne had a stunning impact, the kind that fixes the moment in a person's memory. "On that afternoon I was attending a performance of an operetta, *The Dollar Princess*, which was interrupted at the end of the first act by the shocking news. I never saw the rest of this operetta," Bettelheim said, "and I felt cheated, so I remember very well what led to World War I."

Anton Bettelheim's forests and sawmills were in Galicia, near the Russian border. In the first weeks of war, the Austrian army quickly lost most of Galicia to the Russian "steamroller," as the czar's huge army was called by the press, and Anton's business virtually collapsed. Bruno, eleven, and Grete, fifteen, heard their parents discussing the loss but did not feel the impact of it or understand what it might mean, especially since the family's way of life continued with little change, obviously supported by Anton's reserves.

Bruno had entered a *gymnasium* at about this time, and he and his friends read the newspaper closely every day.[9] With two uncles in the Austrian army, he felt personally involved and followed the war news anxiously. Street vendors shouted headlines about a great fortress that had fallen on the Russian border, but when Bruno read of the sweeping early victories on the western front, the news reassured him that the war would come out all right.

CHAPTER 2

Gymnasium *and Wandervogel*

IN GERMAN-SPEAKING countries at the turn of the century, the *gymnasium* was the school of choice for upper-middle-class families. It was comparable to an American prep school but was state-sponsored; Austrian *gymnasiums* had government funding and genuine local control, and they also charged tuition. Academically rigorous and highly competitive, they prepared students for entry into the upper ranks of society. Passing the *gymnasium's* final exam sent a student out into the world having already earned a measure of respect, and because of the schools' high standards, their graduates were guaranteed admission into any Austrian, German, or Swiss university. All able-bodied Austrian males had to enter the Imperial army for three years, but the *gymnasium* graduate would become a "volunteer" for only one year and then get a promotion to *Fahnrich.* With more training he would become a lieutenant in the reserves, after which he was free to pursue his career. Only about 10 percent of school-age children got into *gymnasiums,* but those who did left with an education roughly equivalent to two years of college. Understandably, young Bruno and his parents were extremely serious about his attending a *gymnasium* and doing well there.

In September 1914 he entered the Realschule und Reform Realgymnasium, which was near enough to his home for him to walk to school. In the early nineteenth century, *gymnasiums* emphasized Greek and Latin studies, and in fact the name *gymnasium* was chosen to suggest a kinship with classical Greece. However, the name of the *Realschule* indicates that it did not follow a strict classical tradition but had reformed its curriculum to be more modern—for instance, offering studies in contemporary languages. A more important difference was that traditional *gymnasiums* required a student to choose the direction of his life at age eleven; that is, whether he would read classics and go to the university or concentrate on technical studies and go to a technical university, or *Hochschule*. In the *Realschule* this decision could be put off until the student was fifteen.

The entering class of 1914 had a little over fifty students, for some of whom the school soon became an educational obstacle course that led them to transfer elsewhere.[1] Young Bruno, however, did his homework conscientiously and had no problem with grades. One of his closest friends in the *Realschule* was Hans Willig; the two met as schoolboys and saw each other until both men were into their eighties. I asked Bruno about the long friendship.

"Friendship is quite different in this country," he said, "where few keep up with childhood friends, or even college friends. Our lives fly apart, we cease to feel comfortable with people to whom we thought we were once very close. Americans socialize easily on the surface, but there's often an obvious practical motive for it—it's good for business, or for one's profession, and so on. There's a hard core hidden inside that is very difficult to penetrate.

"It was different for us. When you became a friend, you got to know each other quite well and were always friends; you didn't have to prove anything or gain anything beyond this. The friendship was always there when you got together, and you got together because you enjoyed your friends. Three of us became especially close in the *gymnasium*—myself, Hans Willig, and Walter Neurath. Oh, there were many others I thought of as friends, but we three were somehow a group. Walter became a very successful publisher in England. He founded Thames & Hudson, so naturally when I began to write books, he published them there."

Besides teaching habits of academic diligence, the *gymnasium* expected to carry on the building of character that had begun in the family. "The teachers in the *gymnasium* were committed to the idea that if you became a cultured individual with a classical education, you would also become a good person," Bruno said. "That is, your own self-image would be such that you would not do anything beneath what you considered as the dignity of man. And I think the concept of dignity is very important here. Revisionist history has made us doubt that this classical ideal was ever a reality, and people in classical times may have been just as inhuman as people today, but still it was a good idea, a good way to teach children."

In every classroom a portrait of the emperor hung on one side, a crucifix on the other. Hans Willig spoke to me of the *gymnasium*'s obligatory religious instruction: at a fixed hour, Catholic boys went to a priest, Jewish boys to a rabbi, and Protestants to a minister. Willig learned a little Hebrew in this way, but, he said, "My family was not religious at all, did not keep any rituals or holidays. Bruno went through the same religious instruction as I did, and his family didn't keep any religious ties either."

A crisis came to the *gymnasium* in 1914 because of feelings aroused by the war. Should French, the language of the enemy, continue to be taught? The professors acknowledged the paradox but argued that French was an important linguistic and historical fact; they refused to drop it and taught it throughout the war. As a teenager Bettelheim became fluent in French—"It's easier than English," he said—and he remained fluent to the end of his life.

The Austrian public's hopes for the war gave way to a more somber mood by Christmas of 1914, and in 1915 disillusionment began to set in. When food rationing was imposed, Bettelheim's parents sent him at age twelve to stand in lines for bread and coffee. However, with Anton's connections out in the countryside (through the lumber company), the family's food supply did not suffer. In 1916 Bruno's parents sent him away for a few weeks to stay on a small farm with the parents of his wet nurse, Mitzi. He had plenty to eat there but became desperately unhappy with sanitary conditions on the farm. He hated having to use the outhouse, and he asked his parents to bring him back to Vienna.

Later that year, the old emperor died. Bruno stood with Grete in the street all afternoon and into a late November evening waiting to see Franz Josef's elaborate funeral cortège pass by. He had come to the throne in 1848, a date so far in the past that the eighty-six-year-old monarch almost seemed beyond the reach of time. Now, for his last parade, buildings and monuments had been draped in black crepe, and glass globes had been removed from the lampposts along the path of the procession so that gas flames would flicker in the night breeze. A new emperor, Karl, had succeeded to the throne, and at thirteen, young Bruno could not have imagined that the six-hundred-year-old empire would not go on as it always had.

Anton Bettelheim was a stout, well-built man with heavy-lidded eyes, a ruddy complexion, close-cropped hair, and a neat mustache over full lips. Bruno said he was gentle in manner most of the time, quite happy that his son did well in the *gymnasium*. He would have liked to go to the University of Vienna himself, but this was not possible after the duel that killed his older brother.

Hans Willig spoke of Anton as a shy man, friendly but distant, whereas Bruno's mother was warm and outgoing, at least to him. "She would say, 'Come have dinner with us,' which was unusual in Vienna. People did not invite other people for dinner—family, yes, but not outsiders. But she took me in as an old friend of Bruno's when I was maybe fourteen or fifteen."

Bruno characterized his father as self-contained, ready to make a joke at the right moment, but "definitely on the quiet side." He felt that his father showed some of the features seen in the kibbutz, "which come from being raised by one's peers. He was brought up by his four elder brothers and a tutor, the tutor being like a *metapelet*.[2] His parents were distant figures to him, because there were so many children in the family." Bettelheim contrasted this atmosphere with that of Jewish ghetto families, with all their quarreling and hurt feelings, where "intimacy could thrive because people depended on each other not only for warmth and security but also as targets for anger. That is, someone on whom you could safely discharge your frustrations. This ghetto characteristic would be too disruptive in the kibbutz, and also it was not possible in an upper-middle-class Viennese Jewish home."

Bruno's bar mitzvah ceremony at age thirteen was pro forma; relatives on his mother's side of the family expected it, and she did not want to disappoint them. His father remained indifferent to the idea, and Bruno himself was never drawn to religion, either formally or informally, at any time in his life.

BRUNO'S parents never spanked him; however, when he was about fourteen, one aptly worded threat made a lasting impression. Something had irked him and he spoke brusquely to his mother, with words like, "Let me alone." He did not know any genuine obscenities at that time, but his abruptness shocked her. When Anton came home she told him, and he became quietly angry and upset. The way Bruno had spoken carried only the mildest hint of early teenage defiance, but it was too much for his father, who confronted him and said, "Do I have to slap you to make you mind the way you speak to your mother?"

The question in fact felt like a slap; it made him stop and think. Even at that moment he understood that the threat of punishment did not disturb him as much as the realization that he had upset his father. "Showing disrespect for a parent put the family honor in question, and one just didn't speak like that in our family." His quiet father had taught him a lesson with "a rhetorical question which most effectively achieved its purpose." He wrote about this incident in *A Good Enough Parent*, implying praise for his father for the verbal slap:

> A warning . . . rather than a punishment, was enough to make me feel
> I had done wrong. . . . Punishment would not have had this effect;
> probably it would only have aroused my resistance.[3]

In 1917 many Austrians doubted that the Central Powers (Germany and Austria) could win the war; officialdom and the press put the best possible face on things, but skeptics read between the lines. In the spring of 1917, when Bruno was about thirteen and a half, he heard of the youth organization called Jung Wandervogel. Restless adolescents discontented with the world in which they were growing up could join the local Wandervogel club to talk about many subjects, including the war and society's need for radical reform. Meetings were spontaneous and free-flowing, with gentle leadership from an older member.

Bettelheim explained the Wandervogel by characterizing the stifled mood of his youth. "You see the baroque everywhere in Vienna," he said, "and it is beautiful and even magnificent. But when you live with it every day, when you grow up surrounded by a baroque world, it can be overpowering. Young people of my generation felt suffocated. Maybe there was too much order, too much stress on the value, and values, of the past. At any rate, that was how a great many young people felt in my circle." Once a boy like Bruno was in the *gymnasium*, it was rare for him to feel free; he lived under the shadow of the school director, the masters, his parents, and the whole authority structure of the state. However, he had one socially acceptable way to escape—the Wandervogel.

Teenagers could meet for a few hours after school to avoid well-meaning supervision and to associate freely with other teenagers. The movement had started in a suburb of Berlin near the turn of the century, when a group of young people got together, at first to study shorthand. However, they soon began to go on weekend hikes and outings. The movement spread quickly throughout Germany, Austria, and Switzerland, mostly by word of mouth. In Germany the inspiration was at least partly nationalistic, but some members also let their hair grow long, bought guitars, and played folk songs. During the week they often went to the clubroom,[4] where they could converse in a lighter atmosphere than in their bourgeois homes and on subjects that might raise parental eyebrows. On weekends parents permitted them to leave the city for day trips, or to go off on outings to the mountains, the forests, or the shore of a lake, where they would camp out overnight. They were "wandering birds": well-behaved, repressed teenagers free of adult expectations for the moment.

The Wandervogel club had no regular supervision, but on most occasions a young man, perhaps four to eight years older than the rest, took part in the meetings. The younger members voluntarily accepted him as the leader, and as the movement grew, young women also provided this casual leadership.

Bruno's cousin Edith Buxbaum, the daughter of his mother's sister Jenny, invited him to join her club. Edith was one year older than Bruno, just enough age difference to leave them more or less equals but make the relationship stimulating. In fact, he got on much better with Edith than with his sister, Grete, where the age difference was greater. The Buxbaum family lived in an apartment only a few minutes away from the Bettelheims, and Edith and Bruno had played and spent time together since infancy. Parents and children alike benefited from the orderly support of a nuclear family, combined with the conveniences, freedom, variety, and unstressful friendliness of the extended family.

All through his teenage years, Bruno would go to the Buxbaum home on most afternoons for an hour or more, and he said of Edith, "We became not just good friends but extremely close friends." The Buxbaum apartment was a second home to him, and he and Edith had a brother-sister relationship without the anger, jealousy, or rivalry that siblings often feel.

By coincidence Hans Willig joined the same Wandervogel at about the same time as Bruno. Edith's best friend, Annie Pink, also belonged, and although these four were Jewish, the membership of their club was mostly gentile. Willig told me the Vienna group had adopted the name Jung Wandervogel to distinguish itself from the more nationalistic German organization, and since the movement had no central authority, nobody objected to the change.

"The Wandervogel was a good escape valve," Bettelheim said. "It made us feel freer, and in my case it really changed many of my ideas about society. We have nothing analogous to it in this country, certainly not the protest movements in the sixties. Wandervogel was completely nonviolent, we were against violence altogether. You see, Wandervogel was more of an exploration than a protest. Nobody said, 'Let's smash it all!' Maybe we thought we were more revolutionary than we were." He added that there was always one student around who was a communist, "but this was before the Russian Revolution took its course, so it wasn't the same as if he were trying to justify a totalitarian system, which he couldn't have done in the Wandervogel."

Although the spontaneous and somewhat anarchical Wandervogel influenced young Bruno's attitudes and ideas in a lasting way, he felt the work habits, relationships, and systematic efforts to deal with reality in the *gymnasium* had greater significance. Both the Wandervogel and the *gymnasium* provided peer groups, "but we didn't know it. I don't think the concept had come forward in sociology at that time." Of the *gymnasium* he said, "It wasn't just the masters who were important. There were many crosscurrents between students, and as I have already said, friendships were formed that would last a lifetime. We walked to school every day with the same friends and discussed the teacher and the classwork. That was part of the effort to master the school for ourselves, and this went on after school, on weekends, and so forth."

Bettelheim did not see peer groups as beneficial per se and commented that many peer groups nowadays are gangs of delinquents, "children left to their own devices to learn from the tougher kids in the streets. They are exposed to what I believe are the most dangerous aspects of a young peer group without a mature influence. I can't overstress the importance of peer groups having a congenial adult who helps to mold the young people and in whose image they can model themselves." He also remarked on the misuse of the term *peer group* in schools when children are simply grouped by age and come from very different family and social backgrounds. "I believe we do this in a vague effort to say that there is some social ideal created between these children, which I doubt is actually the case in the long run."

He said that there was a ferment of ideas in the *gymnasium*, "because of the effect of the peer group, and in the Wandervogel even more so. It was the youth of the present against the world of the past. We imagined a new beginning, a better world . . . that we could help make the world better. Very idealistic, and very naturally so. However, at the same time we understood that since we were making a new world for ourselves, we had to explore our thoughts and ideas and find out just what we would like to have for ourselves in the future. In other words, self-knowledge. What do *I* want?"

JUNG WANDERVOGEL members could take a trolley from the center of Vienna to the end of the line, and when they stepped out they were in the Vienna Woods. "Every Sunday we went out there," Bettelheim said, "and that was the first time I had a crush on a girl, puppy love you might call it. We developed more slowly in those days, so maybe I came to it a little late by our modern standards, but I was very fond of one girl in the group and she seemed to like me, so we always walked together when we got out in the woods. It was very exciting for a thirteen-year-old from a proper Jewish household.

"Finally one Sunday a young soldier joined us, a man a few years older who had been in the Wandervogel earlier but had to report to the army. Now the army gave him leave to finish his medical studies, and he came along with us. He wasn't an adult leader but simply one of us who had been in the Wandervogel longer, and so we accepted him as being more knowledgeable than we were. That Sunday he seemed to take an interest in my girl—she was about my age but more mature in appearance—and he began to talk in a fascinating way about a man named Freud."

The young soldier was Otto Fenichel, later prominent in psychoanalysis in the generation after Freud.[5] Bruno feared losing his girl to Fenichel, and so after a sleepless night he went to the Deuticke bookstore, which specialized in psychoanalysis, and "bought whatever I could of Freud's writings, from my limited funds," including *The Psychopathology of Every-day Life* and some journals. "*The Interpretation of Dreams* was too heavy for me, but, oh yes, there was also the book *Three Essays on Sexuality*, and of course I got that one right away.

"I took it all home and immediately began to read, and it was terribly exciting. I realized that this was pornography—that is, pornography if I considered it in the light of everything I had been led to believe up to that point." He read Freud all week but hid the books where his parents wouldn't see them. By the weekend he felt well versed in psychoanalysis, ready to hold up his side of any conversation.

His girlfriend surprised him by not wanting to talk about analysis, but the books had made a convert. "I didn't know it then, but I was a young Freudian, and as the years passed I could never stop reading Freud. So that's how I became interested in psychoanalysis. I was jealous and angry,

but when I got over being jealous and wanting to compete, I was still fascinated with psychoanalysis."

BRUNO and his Wandervogel friends could hear about a new development like analysis long before they would have encountered it at home or
in school. This gave them a foretaste of independence, and for some the
experience may even have been a rite of passage into the adult world. In
Young Germany Walter Laqueur says that the "average male Wandervogel
was shyer, less confident, less mature than other young men his age," a
description that fit young Bruno, who, like many of his fellow members,
needed to explore mildly rebellious impulses and interests with no danger
of being carried away or taken to task.[6]

   "Above all," Bettelheim said, "it was a relief from the family setting
and family pressures, and because it was such a reaffirmation of the dignity of the young person who joined, I have to believe it was most beneficial." He also said that the Wandervogel motto that meant most to him
was *Gegen den Strom*, "Against the stream." "That was the basic idea, to
encourage young people to let their minds go against received opinions
and conventional wisdom, to weigh everything for themselves and not be
afraid to say something different. That idea, that encouragement, had a
big influence on the way I have lived and thought about life. I suppose my
colleagues in analysis regard me as being outside the mainstream of psychoanalysis, psychology, whatever, and that's fine with me. I may have
been 'against the stream' from someone else's point of view, but not from
my own."

IN THE following year, 1918, just after his fifteenth birthday, Bruno joined
the Academic Legion, an organization of *gymnasium* students who did
real work on the home front. "We were only schoolboys, but we met the
trains and helped unload the dead and wounded from the front. Three or
four afternoons a week we went to the railroad station after school and
waited for the trains to come in. There were perhaps forty of us from my
gymnasium. When a train pulled in with several hundred dead or
wounded soldiers, we carried the bodies and men who couldn't walk and
got them into ambulances. It was a bloody mess, horrible. Seeing these
men when I was only fifteen, I got a notion of what the war was like, and I
became violently opposed to it."

Also at about this time, Bruno's father collapsed with a sudden illness that showed some of the symptoms of a stroke. He became completely helpless and paralyzed on one side of his body for a week, and he could not speak. Bruno's mother kept the rest of the family in the dark about the nature of the illness, but they saw the gravity of it. "From that moment, I was terribly worried that he might die," Bettelheim said, and at fifteen he knew he could not take charge of everything in the way he had been told men were expected to do. Family legends about heroic grandfathers only told him that he was not prepared for what had just happened to him.

SHORTLY after his father became ill, Bruno got into trouble at the *gymnasium*. He had always been an excellent student—quiet, self-absorbed, "almost subdued"—and he suddenly flared up in a way that seemed utterly out of character. He has written at some length about what happened in his mathematics class, so I will give only a brief account here.[7]

"I got out of my chair and from behind my bench," Bettelheim said, "and grabbed the teacher by the collar. I started to push him, and suddenly two of the other boys came out and put hands on him for reasons I don't know." They pushed the teacher out of the classroom; Bettelheim later described the man as a "simpering fool who spoke with the voice of a eunuch."

Why did the adolescent Bruno, almost a model student, suddenly assault the teacher? At the time he could think of no reason, could not even make up an excuse; he simply did not know why he had done it. At home that afternoon he told his parents. (His father had recovered enough to be able to speak but was still in bed.) Anton and Paula were anxious but did not criticize him or ask the reason for his astonishing behavior; instead they discussed where he could go to school if he was expelled. Bruno did not sleep that night, thinking of the enormity of what he had done, and he went back to school the next morning certain he would be punished.

Dr. Anton Rebhahn, an austere and forbidding figure, ran the school with a firm hand.[8] He came into the math classroom, and the students jumped to their feet and stood at attention for the expected reprimand. Bettelheim writes:

As we all stood at attention, he blistered us verbally . . . particularly myself as leader. . . . [After a screaming tirade] he suddenly fell silent

for a while, and then added in the quietest voice . . . words I have
never forgotten. He said: "Of course I know that if Dr. X had behaved
as I expect all masters of this institution to behave, nothing like this
could ever have happened."

Then he turned to Bruno and said,

> "Bruno Bettelheim, tomorrow you will stay for two hours after school,
> working on your own studies, which Dr. X should have made so inter-
> esting that there would have been no place for such misbehavior."[9]

Without explaining or excusing himself, Rebhahn showed he understood he had given the students a poor teacher. The school had lost many
of its staff to the army, and wartime conditions made it hard to find good
teachers. Because Dr. X was not of the caliber the school usually hired,
Rebhahn dismissed him; but since Rebhahn could not tolerate a breach
of discipline, he punished the worst offender. However, young Bruno was
right about the teacher, so Rebhahn made the punishment light.

The point of Bettelheim's story was that a child's unconscious pressures may be too urgent to resist, and self-control vanishes: he knows only
that he *felt like* doing something. "I had not the slightest idea why I did it,"
Bettelheim told me. "This is why I hope the story is a good example of
how children often do things, not without reason but without knowing
why they do it. You shouldn't press the child, because it's destructive if he
is forced to confront the fact that he does something without knowing
why." Years later Bettelheim realized that he acted against the teacher
because his father's illness terrified him, and he doubted his own masculinity and assertiveness. It angered him to see a weak and silly teacher
in school every day, and he said he had to rid himself of this unacceptable
model for masculine behavior.

The incident occurred just after Anton Bettelheim's illness in the fall
of 1918, when the war had only a few months to run its course. Bruno's
self-doubts could not have been relieved by his assault, but perhaps his
useful and serious duties in the Academic Legion added a touch of maturity that fall.

Near the war's end, the legion had more to do than carry the dead
and help the wounded, Bettelheim said. "When it was clear that everything was collapsing, the authorities used schoolboys to disarm the demobilized soldiers as they came into Vienna. Most had demobilized

themselves—they didn't wait to be told, nobody could stop them from leaving the army and going home. There was a great fear in the city, well justified, that the Czechs and Hungarians and Croats would get off the trains and pillage Vienna. That would have been very easy to do. The Academic Legion had maybe two thousand boys altogether, and we disarmed several hundred thousand soldiers. Myself, I know I disarmed many thousands. So how did we do it?

"We were only boys, and they were fighting soldiers, men who had endured terrible things. When they came off the trains, streams of them, with rifles, bayonets, pistols, we young boys stood there waiting for them, holding bread and other food. We had to exchange bread for weapons, and we did it. I don't know who got the idea, but it worked. We were told to call the police if we had trouble, but the police wouldn't have gotten anywhere with these men, this was a situation in which children could do more than adults. We were not threatening in any way, and we offered to help anyone however we could. We told the soldiers how to get from one train station to another, or we escorted them across town so they could get home."

ANTON BETTELHEIM had hoped that his forests and sawmills would be restored after the war, but with the fall of the empire he had to find other resources for his business. "My father had recovered, more or less, from the illness of 1918," Bettelheim said, "and was ready to build up the family fortunes again, though it was difficult."

During the war, Paula's father, Adolf Seidler, had become more and more frightened. With a fortune Bruno estimated at more than $5 million, and wishing to protect it, Seidler had sold everything: his businesses, his real estate, even the houses he had given to his sons, away in the army. He put everything into the safest investment he could think of, Austrian government bonds, but on November 12, 1918, when Emperor Karl was dethroned, these became worthless.

"He never understood what happened," Bettelheim said. "The whole thing was beyond his grasp. His children were able to take care of him, and of course my father helped a bit, but he simply didn't understand what had hit him."

CHAPTER 3

The University;
the Business; Gina

B RUNO'S SISTER, Grete, had always wanted to become an actress, and when she graduated from the lycée in 1917, an offer for a stage part was waiting for her. The idea of such a thing caused a great stir in the Bettelheim family, and the brothers met to demand that Anton put a stop to it. According to Bruno, however, he said, "She does what she does," and he signed the contract for her because she was still underage. Grete took the stage name of Roederer (after the champagne) and moved quickly into the adult world.

Young Bruno's course was not so clear-cut. Hans Willig said that he and Bruno took the "technical" part of the *gymnasium* (math, science, French, and English) so they could go to a technical university, which in Austria at that time could be compared to our outstanding institutes of technology, like MIT or Caltech. It had great prestige, but instead of the humanities it stressed physics, chemistry, and the other sciences.

After finishing the *gymnasium* in June 1921 (a few months before he was eighteen), Bruno enrolled in a business school for a year while also attending the University of Vienna.[1] A second year at the school would have given him the right to add a title under his name on all business letters: *Diplom Kaufman*, or Businessman with a Diploma. This sounds faintly comic to American ears, but titles were still taken seriously in Austria despite the monarchy's demise.

Bettelheim decided against the *Diplom Kaufman*. I believe that by spending a year on accounting, trade law, economics, and other subjects that no doubt bored him, he was being a dutiful and prudent son because the year would give him a useful background if he had to go into his father's business. However, in not committing to a second year he was showing the limits of his sense of duty. As one requirement for *Hochschule* accreditation, he also had to work in a business, which he did for a time in an insurance company.[2] Again, I believe he was a good son, following the rules, meeting the expectations of family and society. He was, of course, still financially dependent on his father. However, by going to the University of Vienna, he began to enlarge his horizons. In his reformed *gymnasium* he did not study Latin, and Hans Willig said that he and Bruno added an *examen* in Latin and philosophy, without which they could not have attended the university. As yet, Bettelheim had no clear and committed direction in life, but he had turned away from the technical university for which the *Realschule* had prepared him.

FROM TIME to time after grade school, Bruno had gone to an eye doctor for a new prescription and was invariably told that with the new glasses he would have perfect vision. Nevertheless, something was wrong. In the *gymnasium* he liked soccer and was anxious to excel at it, but he played so poorly that as a goalie he could never seem to stop the other team from scoring. Sometimes he thought he was stupid, and at other times he tried to live with the idea that he was clumsy by nature, born with poor reflexes and coordination. Later, he played tennis, but with no better luck.

As a student at the university he went to a different ophthalmologist, who happened to say in an offhand way, "Of course, with your eyes, nobody can correct your vision." The comment startled him. He had lived for years under the illusion that he had perfect vision with glasses, and in fact it was twenty-twenty, but the doctor went on to explain that he had no depth perception.

"From this," Bettelheim said, "I learned never to say anything that was not exactly true if I am trying to reassure someone. Everybody had said, 'You have perfect vision,' and so when I couldn't play football or tennis as well as everybody else, I thought I was naturally incompetent. Of course, my parents sent me to the best specialists, who didn't tell me the *whole* truth. I suppose they saw I hated the glasses and were trying to make me feel better."

BETTELHEIM did not want to go into the family business and began to think of becoming a teacher, a professor in the history of art. "What I didn't realize at the time," he said, "was how swiftly the social atmosphere was changing, the increasing dislike of Jews, and the openness of it. It was always there — remember, I had an uncle killed in a duel long before I was born — but in the accepted class system in Vienna one's family could have a good life nonetheless. At about the time I began to plan to be a professor, this career, which had always been difficult for a Jew, became almost impossible."

With the loss of empire, Austria's population suddenly dropped from fifty million to about six million. "This shrinking of power gave nationalism an ugly twist. All the ethnic minorities Austria had dominated after a fashion were now able to have their own countries, so the German-speaking Austrians didn't have to consider their interests or feelings anymore. The people who disliked the minorities in the first place were strengthened and thought it was good riddance. For a while Jews felt safe enough, because this was in the time of 'Red Vienna,' with a very liberal socialist administration. This was also the time of the Social Democrats, the party I chose to join for a while."

When the remnant of Austria became a federalized republic within new boundaries, the provinces had more power than Vienna. However, Vienna was the equivalent of a province, and its mayor held office like a governor. The new constitution gave wide local autonomy, which led to an odd body politic for the new republic: a very liberal capital surrounded by a ring of reactionary provinces. This yoking of opposites was an invitation to turmoil, especially since all three major political parties had private armed forces. I asked Bettelheim to characterize the mood after the empire fell, and he chose to speak more of psychological turmoil than politics.

"I believe I can say something about the zeitgeist, how it was for those of my background and position after the First World War and until the *Anschluss*.[3] How did we feel?" His first point was that it became hard psychologically for teenagers to rebel against their parents because the parents' world had been shattered when the war was lost and Emperor Karl resigned. "We spoke of this as the *Zusammenbruch*, the collapse. You didn't have to give your father's world a push, it had fallen apart, and the elaborate larger life reflecting our parents' values was suddenly fading. A sense of security was gone, and nobody was sure that the replacement would be better.

"I knew very well in the twenties that I was living in a different world from my father, but I also wanted to help him, so I went into the office the last couple of years before he died. And it was well that I did. When I had to take over, I already had some experience in buying timber, measuring a limited section of forest, counting the trees on that piece of land, and then estimating how much the whole forest was worth to us. That was not hard, and it got me outdoors and into the country. I was going to college then, and it was a good change."

Another point was Bruno's realization that the shattered world meant that his father was not as smart and powerful as he had seemed. This felt like a betrayal of sorts, even though Bruno also recognized that his father was not the oppressive and dominant figure of his younger impressions. "I might have been anxious to rebel as an adolescent—the Wandervogel allowed me to express those feelings—but when the social collapse came, I found I had counted on the stability of my parents' world." The moral support of his social milieu vanished with a suddenness that made him doubt the values his parents had instilled in him. If they had been so wrong about the realities of their society, he could not trust their values to guide him, and this at the very moment he was cautiously exploring his independence. It was unsettling, even frightening.

"The old order went up in smoke just when we needed it, and we felt we had to find another way to shape the security of the world we lived in. After the war, most young people either went left or right." Their disillusion was not simply at losing a war, a loss many Austrians had dreaded but seen coming. Rather, fifteen-year-olds like Bruno had been born into an empire eight times the size of the new Austria. "To see it changed into a minor middle-European country, that was a real shock. We young people wanted to keep on believing in permanent progress, and to do this we had to find a new way when the old way vanished."

The dissolution of the empire, he said, was like a play where the stage falls in and the scenery collapses; the political stage remained crowded with actors, but no one could approach the stature the emperor once possessed. "Karl never had a chance to become the autocratic and benign figure that Franz Josef had been for sixty years, and nobody else had any authority to speak of."

Another element in the zeitgeist was the nature/nurture dispute. "Our nature had been called into question by the events of history, and the modern among us—the forward-looking, or so we thought—were all for nurture and for forgetting about nature. Those were the ones most on the left, the Social Democrats and Communists. Two of my closest personal friends, people I enjoyed talking with, very exuberant, charming,

and outgoing types, were Willy Reich and Kurt Landau. And though I
liked them very much and continued to like them as long as we saw each
other, somehow I couldn't go so far in the controversy as to choose their
side." Also, it was clear to Bettelheim that as his sense of himself as an
individual grew stronger, his interest in politics faded.

"I think this is something fairly common in a situation where one feels
one cannot make a difference in the overwhelming social questions, or
dilemmas, or crises. I like [Erik] Erikson's term, the moratorium, because
it sums up what happens to people inside themselves when they realize
how complicated and difficult life turns out to be." Bettelheim eventually
dropped his membership in the Social Democratic Party. "I just wasn't all
that interested in politics, and besides, I could never convince myself to
follow a party line."

As I HAVE mentioned, Bettelheim's fascination with psychoanalysis
began at around age fourteen, when he met (and resented) the precocious
Otto Fenichel. In about 1920 his involvement deepened when his cousin
Edith Buxbaum went into analysis. She was eighteen and just out of
school: Bruno was seventeen, with another year at the *gymnasium*. She
and Bruno still saw each other almost every day, and she talked with him
about her analysis as it progressed. After a year Edith decided she wanted
to become an analyst herself. At about the same time, when Bruno was
still not quite eighteen, she brought him into the circle of her psychoanalytic friends.

Edith had been drawn to analysis, in part, by her closest friend, Annie
Pink, who was Edith's age and also in the Jung Wandervogel. At seventeen
Annie was very brilliant and ready to enter medical school, but she also
felt unhappy enough to seek analysis. In Vienna's small analytic world,
Otto Fenichel recommended her to his friend Wilhelm Reich, who was
just then beginning to make his reputation. Reich took her as a patient,
only to find that he was spellbound by her. They both understood that
they were deeply in love, and this presented a problem. Reich insisted
that she go to another analyst, and she went first to Hermann Nunberg
and later to Anna Freud. Once the two lovers were no longer analytically
involved, they married. The witnesses at their wedding in 1922 were Edith
Buxbaum and Otto Fenichel.

"So through Annie Reich I got to know Willy Reich," Bettelheim said.
"I was already friends with Otto Fenichel, and I was also very friendly with
Siegfried Bernfeld and a few analysts of the younger generation. But Willy

was so delightful and so extraordinary that I suppose I began to accept him as a kind of mentor, at least at first. We didn't think in those terms—we were just friends—but he was a fascinating person, so very persuasive in his explanations and extremely brilliant. He was a few years older than I, maybe in his late twenties, and he was taking on a few patients when we first met. I don't know for sure, but I have the impression that he hadn't finished his own analysis at that time. He was a glowing personality, very charming, lively, and open in his manner. Willy was lovable, he had a magnetism that drew people to him. In any event, he was important to me because of our friendship and the wonderful conversations about analysis, which we all took part in. Edith, Annie, and Willy were all analysts—I was the only outsider—and we talked for hours. However, it was somehow Willy who first brought me systematically to analysis.

"He was dazzling, he was surprising, but he was also very consistent. Certainly not so powerful a mind as Freud's, but there is no doubt in my own mind that Willy took psychoanalysis to its next stage with his ideas and his book on character analysis. Freudian analysis, as it is practiced now, is a result of the Reichian modification, although analysts in this country don't like to dwell on that fact so much nowadays, because Willy went to prison later, and lots of people thought he was crazy. In my opinion, he was a genius, and with a genius you always get a lot of things you don't like—the striking intuitions are there, but you also get very unpleasant aspects of character, flaws of character. When Willy was a teenager, about 1911 or 1912, he saw his mother making love to his tutor, and so he told his father, and then his mother committed suicide. It was terrible, horrible. Anyone who has a sense of the ambivalences he must have felt in that situation might find it remarkable that he did as well as he did in life."

BETTELHEIM at that time did not see himself as someone who might go into analysis; he had read a lot about it and was convinced of its validity— "from reading Freud and from experiencing the insights into myself which my limited acquaintance with analysis gave." However, an episode with his friend Willy prompted him in an indirect way. "We were so close in age that we communicated easily and understood each other quickly. I can't date it exactly, but as I recall he and Annie already had their first child."

One evening Bruno, Edith, and Annie were sitting in Edith's home, waiting for Willy. "We planned to do something together, go somewhere, I can't remember what. But when Willy came into the room, he was not his usual effervescent self, and we could see that he was upset. He showed his emotions readily, showed everything. That was one of the traits that made it fun to be with him, he let everything show on the surface. If he was holding anything back, you couldn't tell it. However, on this day he was not enjoying himself, he was deeply troubled and you could see it on his face, the way his features were twisting.

"He walked up and down the room without telling us what was bothering him, and he seemed agitated, which was unusual. So we waited, and he finally told us. He had already become a promising analyst, and I suppose he was getting referrals. That day a young medical student had come to see him, a refugee from Lithuania or Latvia, I don't remember which. But this young man asked to be analyzed, saying that he wanted very much to become an analyst himself. He was highly intelligent and personable, and Willy believed he would be a good candidate for analysis, maybe for the profession. But Willy had one problem: the young man was broke. He had barely enough income to live on and no money to pay for analysis. Willy had told him he would have to think it over. Now he paced the room in distress because he was so torn.

"At that time I believe Willy was already a communist, though maybe he had not joined the party. But he was a communist, idealistic, of course, not a party-liner, and he was distressed by the money question. Finally, he began to say, 'What's happening to me? What am I doing? Here was a young man of great promise, I liked him a lot, and just because he couldn't pay me I did not accept him as a patient. And I still don't know whether I will accept him or not.'

"At that time Willy was already prominent enough to have patients who paid very well, and he felt terribly upset that he did not say yes and take this young man for treatment. You understand, at that time in Vienna analysis was six days a week, appointments usually at the same hour, and the analyst could have a maximum of eight to ten patients. That was the *absolute* maximum. So if you had a nonpaying patient, it made a great deal of difference in your income, because each patient was easily an eighth to a tenth of your total income.

"Actually I don't know how he resolved his dilemma. Somehow I never asked. I wasn't curious about what happened, because I was so involved with myself at the time. But the meaning of that experience went very deep. It made me think about analysis, and I decided that if my friend Willy, whom I esteemed as a highly moral person, very socialist-minded and honorable, if Willy cannot make up his mind whether to take on someone who couldn't pay, then there is something questionable in doing analysis for money. I realized that if you do it for money you will never know, as Willy did not know, 'If I take a patient or do not take him, what is the true basis of my decision?'

"Surely, analysts have to live, and I know what Freud said about the necessity of payment, but I was uncomfortable with that particular dilemma. I couldn't resolve it in the way all practicing analysts do when they take private patients. You see, Willy spoke very feelingly of his own unsureness, about how easy it was to begin telling yourself the young man was not a worthwhile candidate because he could not pay, how easy it is to maintain to oneself that a patient is not worthy of analysis while actually you rejected him because he wouldn't pay, or couldn't pay, your full fee.

"So I said to myself, 'Look, somebody who is as moral a person as Willy cannot trust his own mind on this question.' " Reich's agitation and the reason for it affected Bettelheim so deeply that he told himself that if he should ever go into the field of analysis he would not do it in private practice because he could never be sure whether his motive was money or a true interest in the patient.

"I know analysts sometimes give reduced fees, but the dilemma is still there. That was a very early decision—maybe I was still nineteen—but when I went into the field of analysis many years later I never took payment directly. At Chicago I was paid by the university and got my salary each month, and therefore it never made any difference as far as my income was concerned whether or not anybody could pay. The parents of the children in the Orthogenic School might pay their bills or not pay. It might make a difference to the university, but it made no difference in my salary. The university never asked anyone to leave for nonpayment, though I suppose they could have, but they supported the School and didn't bother us.

"I saw students from the university in private practice—graduate students only, as part of my work for the School and university—but there was no payment from them to me. However, when you don't take money, it's not that there's no payment at all; in fact, the opposite. The payment, if you can call it that, is of a different sort. Frankly, when I analyzed students from the university and worked with the children in the School, I felt I was educating myself. I was always learning, not just about them but also about myself. That's the payment, or the reason to do analysis in that way—the deeper understanding, such as it is, of analysis and of oneself. I was lucky to get an institutional setting that allowed me to forget about money whenever I had to decide who to take for treatment and who not. Obviously, you cannot take everybody, and must choose those you believe for some reason, or have a hunch, you can help. Otherwise, you're wasting your time or maybe the patient's time."

WHEN BRUNO was nineteen, he went to the funeral of a man his family knew. At the graveside he noticed a strikingly beautiful sixteen-year-old girl dressed in black mourning attire. He could not take his eyes off her and later heard others speak of her as one of the most beautiful young women in Vienna. "Her father died of tuberculosis," Bettelheim said, "and I met her while she was in mourning, which was part of her attraction." He had studies to pursue, but he began to spend time with Regina Altstadt—"Gina," his future wife.

"She was the most beautiful, charming girl, but ours was a relation engaged in on questionable and neurotic basis on both our parts, as became very clear later," he said, willing to characterize the relationship between himself and Gina in this way but not to discuss it. He did not wish to talk with me about his most personal relations except in general terms. Clearly this was "love at first sight," a subject we once discussed, though not in relation to himself.

ANTON BETTELHEIM died in 1926, from an illness that probably dated back to a summer twenty years earlier when his family was vacationing. Typically, the wife and children withdrew from Vienna to the countryside for July and August, while the husband spent most of the summer city-bound; he worked at his business, then joined his family on weekends and for occasional weeks.

One evening that summer Anton had gone out for dinner with friends, followed by a visit to a brothel. Soon afterward Anton saw that he had contracted syphilis, which at that time had no certain cure, and for the rest of his life he and Paula did not sleep together. Life went on, but with a strain of silence that gave Bruno hints of deep family secrets and unmentioned miseries. Curiously, this incident seems to have occurred at about the time young Bruno fell ill with dysentery and had to be rushed back to Vienna.

The course and development of syphilis had caused Anton's collapse in 1918, with symptoms near enough to those of a stroke for Paula to keep the real cause secret. After the "stroke," Anton had been paralyzed and unable to speak for several days, and then he seemed to recover in an amazing way. Bruno and Grete heard the truth only in the last weeks of their father's life, when Anton had to be taken to a clinic and kept there. Their mother finally told them, and Bruno witnessed the last stages of his father's deterioration, all too aware of the foolish and shameful circumstances.[4]

"It was a shadow over my youth without my knowing it," he said, "and over my mother and father. It was really a shadow over my whole life and also part of why, as I said before, I'm a very private person."

EVERY semester at the university, students had to complete a form called the *Nationale* to list the lectures they wished to attend, although attendance was not mandatory. From the winter semester 1921–22 to winter 1925–26, Bettelheim took courses in art, literature, philosophy, and psychology. However, he did not file a *Nationale* for summer 1926. His father's death had left him, not yet twenty-three, head of the family and fully responsible for his mother and sister.

"It was fortunate I had been going into the office to help, because suddenly I had to take over. I knew how to buy trees, but in the lumber business that's the simplest thing. The big issue is what it costs to get them from the forest to the sawmill and then to bring the lumber into the city. Sometimes you had to build roads or small railroads, and this was important to know how to calculate. As I mentioned, that's where my father lost his first dowry—beautiful timber, but he figured it wrong, because the terrain didn't permit building a railroad. Too steep, too many ravines, too many tunnels would have been needed. We couldn't use rivers—we had big trees and small rivers."

Bettelheim skipped the summer 1926 semester and then signed up for only three lectures in winter 1926–27. Usually he registered for seven to twelve courses, but now he didn't have the time. Still, he wanted to work for his degree while running the business, which would not be easy because he had to write a dissertation. His father's partner was a man named Hanns Schnitzer, whom Bruno did not like, but with the family's capital still tied up, he had little choice. He hoped the compromise would not last for more than a few years, then he would sell the family's interest and follow the teaching career he truly wanted.

Around this time, he decided to see the head of the philosophy department to talk about becoming a teacher of art history.[5] He had been studying aesthetics and other subjects, preparing himself for this moment, and now he asked what his prospects would be if he completed his dissertation in the next year or two. His question brought an answer that showed him how naïve he had been. The department head said that he could not hope to become a full professor unless he converted to Christianity.

This was not out of the question for someone in Bruno's circle. Several relatives had married Christians, and Bruno's "conversion" would surprise those who knew him well but not make him an outcast. However, the professor's advice stunned him; the notion that he might cravenly seek a future by denying a truth about himself insulted him to the core. He did not need time to consider his position. He thanked the professor and said that he would not convert. In his heart he knew he was a Jew and would always be a Jew.[6] The professional reality in the academic world infuriated him, but there was no way around it.

Bettelheim turned his back on the university and devoted his energies to the lumber business. He began to build it up by specializing in woods for fine furniture, and from an office the size of a small shed in the midst of a large lumberyard, with a staff of perhaps a half dozen men, he made the business more profitable than his father had.

Meanwhile, the young woman in his life was not well. A few years after her father's death from tuberculosis, Gina Altstadt seemed to have developed the same disease. "I never believed it," Bettelheim said. "Actually, she never had it, but she had all the symptoms."

Gina went several times to the sanatoriums such as Arosa where she and Bruno could be together, and he visited her there and elsewhere as she sought a cure. He knew enough about analysis to suspect that her symptoms were psychosomatic, and after three years of medical treatment with no progress, she agreed to go into analysis. Bruno asked Wilhelm Reich to see her, but Reich refused.

"Since we were such close friends, Willy sent her to somebody else, someone whose name I don't want to mention, because she later became very well known." He said that six months with this analyst did nothing, and that years afterward, in the States, the analyst told him that Gina was the first patient treated for a psychosomatic disease.

"At that time," he said, "there was a great deal of doubt whether psychosomatic diseases, as distinguished from psychosomatic disturbances of other kinds, could be treated analytically." The analyst also told him that she had discussed the case with Freud, who had encouraged her to try, though he doubted it would work. "I tell you all this, the beginning of psychosomatic psychoanalysis, to show you how recent it is and how my own life history had been placed in relation to these things."

After a time Bettelheim asked Reich to suggest someone else, and he recommended Richard Sterba, who then analyzed Gina for three years. Bruno and Gina waited for the end of the analysis to get married, in 1930.

"I still hated the lumber business," Bettelheim said, "but when we got married we took up a very expensive lifestyle, one that no professor or even analyst could afford to maintain, so there I was, living very well, with a beautiful wife, with every reason for happiness so far as anyone could see, and yet I was not happy. I must have wanted that way of life or I wouldn't have done it—*ja?*—but I was unhappy, and not just with the lumber business. Within a year I realized that the marriage was a mistake and that I had to extricate myself from it, but somehow I couldn't. On the one hand I felt that I *had* to get out of the marriage, but at the same time I felt I *couldn't* do it, so this made me a good candidate for psychoanalysis. We were very young and inexperienced, just kids really, but that only adds to one's desperation in a situation like this."

Bettelheim did not wish to speak in detail about his first marriage, or about his apartment and lifestyle. However, he told me that they had ten rooms—an entire floor in a large house built almost two centuries earlier by a man famous in his own time, the court physician to Empress Maria Theresa. Dr. van Swieten had been a prominent medical figure in eighteenth-century Vienna, and the house was his country place near Schönbrunn palace.[7]

I asked Bruno's sister for an impression of the apartment, and she exclaimed, "Gorgeous!" Grete said it was on an upper floor, with a garden out back; the living room had a huge sectional couch in three parts, and the kitchen was on the other side of a landing, so that cooking smells did not come into the living and dining room areas. Bruno's own room had a very large desk, books on all sides, and a built-in daybed with indirect lighting above it.

Hans Willig, who visited many times, said that the apartment was furnished by a young architect named Wolf Adler and designed in modern style "with Scandinavian influence." An Egon Schiele painting hung on the living room wall, and Willig could see that everything seemed expensive. He suggested that perhaps Bruno and Gina hoped to have a salon, an intellectual center where they could hold open house for many interesting people; but, he said, "It did not develop in that direction. They did not have many visitors."

He remarked in passing that Bruno slept in the room with the desk and daybed, a "sitting room." The expression on Willig's face — raised eyebrows and wide-eyed innocence — told me he understood that Bruno and Gina were not sleeping together and that Bruno, as a friend, had confided in him.

PSYCHOANALYSIS fascinated Bettelheim, but he resisted it as an option for himself, arguing that he could see no real difference in the lives of friends who had gone into analysis. Reluctantly, after a year of marriage, he came to feel he had no better way to approach his unhappiness.

"So I said to my wife several times, 'I'm going into analysis,' and we talked about it; but somehow this was very threatening to her, and she insisted that if I did it, I must go to her analyst, Richard Sterba. I had mixed feelings about it, but I went. He was a good and decent man, and I had a thorough analysis, six or seven years, but it was probably a mistake for me to go to him and a mistake for him to accept me.

"The reasons are obvious. In analysis you want somebody completely objective insofar as this is possible, so this means an analyst who has no connections with anyone related to you, so that his interest is in you and not in anyone around you. That was not always possible in Vienna, because there were so many family and social connections in a particular circle, through the *gymnasiums* and the university and so on, but I suppose I could have done it if I had wanted to make the effort. It was, as I said, a mistake, but we live with our mistakes, or rather the results, and try to make the best of things. At some level, despite my misgivings, the arrangement suited me, at least as I was at that period of my life. Fortunately, Sterba was a remarkably honest man, and I respected him, and he was helpful to me."

Richard Sterba was a few years older than Bettelheim, and he was not Jewish; in fact, he was the only gentile on the board of the Vienna Psychoanalytic Association in 1938, when Freud was forced to leave. He could have succeeded Freud as head of the association but instead chose to uproot his life and go to another country. Bettelheim found him lively, sympathetic, and insightful, with an openness about himself that helped take the edge off a patient's distrust.

When talking about analysis, Bettelheim commented that gentiles got on well with Jewish analysts, in part because of traditional cultural prejudices. A Jewish analyst would be far removed from a gentile patient's

circle of friends, and many gentiles, he said, still believed Jews were so different that one could safely tell them shameful secrets. Of course, the
problematic element between Bettelheim and Sterba had nothing to do
with Jew and gentile but everything to do with Sterba and Gina. Both
men had already heard perhaps too much about each other, but to a
degree they overcame it.

"I had an experience with Sterba in my analysis which in a way speaks
very well for him. One day I came to my hour as usual, and I saw a pair of
binoculars on his desk. And I lay down on the couch, and it came to my
mind, what are those binoculars doing here? So, being a good patient—
you're supposed to say whatever comes into your mind spontaneously—I
said, 'What are the binoculars doing on your desk?' And he said, 'They're
for looking into the window across the way, where there's a beautiful
young woman. I observe her dressing and undressing.' And then he
added, 'Wouldn't you?'

"And that made a very deep impression on me. Firstly, that he readily
admitted to such a weakness, and then that he expected me to have similar weaknesses, you know? You can call it general human weakness or
similar masculine interests, whatever you like. But he wasn't afraid of
being discovered by me, and this was helpful to me, because I felt there is
not all that great a gap. We're all human. And if we all have these desires,
I can open up my own feelings. He doesn't hide his, I don't have to hide
mine. I believe he said this quite spontaneously and not with any therapeutic intention. It confirmed to me that he was an honest man.

"Nevertheless, I should never have gone to the man who had been the
analyst of my wife. But not only that, to make it even more complicated,
after I got into analysis, this was very hard for her to take, and she said she
had to have more analysis. Since Richard was my analyst at that time, we
of course both conferred with him, and he did something that was very
unethical, as I now know. He sent Gina to be analyzed by his wife."

Editha Sterba worked primarily as a child analyst but occasionally took
adults, and she shared office space with her husband. "My wife and I
more or less decided to stay together until both our analyses were finished, at which time we thought we would both know whether we really
wanted to stay together. It was not a good situation, and perhaps I
shouldn't talk about it at this late date, but I don't know—so much has
happened since then that it doesn't seem as momentous as it used to.

"Everybody has a life history with many things in it that he wishes
hadn't happened just the way they did, and as I look back, this episode

seems not high on the scale of troubles I have faced. I tell you all this to show you, or to suggest to you, that even analysts make mistakes. Very *good* analysts, I should say."

EARLY in his marriage Bettelheim bought a sports coupé, a small car with a convertible top, a cramped rumble seat, and a powerful motor. However, before he could buy the car, he had to go to driving school and learn not only how to drive but also how to take the motor apart and put it back together. Not being quick on such things, Bruno needed two months of lessons to pass the test for his license, which he had to do before he could get a permit to buy the car.

The little car made good sense for his business: he could get around the countryside quickly to look at timber, visit sawmills, and do other jobs out of the office. Late one afternoon when he was hurrying back to get home in time for dinner, he was driving much too fast along a rutted country road and suddenly hit a pothole. The jolt threw him against the steering wheel and broke ribs on both sides of his chest. Flung out of the car and knocked senseless, he lay unconscious for an hour or more, and as he came to, he heard voices. Two farmers were talking to a policeman. They had found the wreck and taken Bettelheim for dead; he heard them telling the policeman that the body should be carried off to the morgue rather than wasting someone's time at a hospital. Bettelheim struggled to speak, to let them know he was alive, but the broken ribs had left him unable to make a sound.

"I was in terrible pain but I couldn't get a word out. I couldn't even groan to call their attention. Perhaps others have had the same experience, I don't know, but fortunately for me the policeman decided on the hospital. They saw I was alive, and after they taped my ribs, I could talk."

He learned later that the farmers had walked to the nearest village and reported the accident to the only policeman in those parts, who was having a drink in a local tavern. Since he was off duty, he was not wearing his hat, and since he would have to write a report of the accident, it was unthinkable that he should do so while out of uniform, and so he went home for his hat.

"That's what we mean when we say of someone, 'He's an Austrian, you know!' At least this is one of the meanings—the crazy little formality that someone rigidly observes even though someone else may be dying while the ritual goes on. Maybe I was lucky that the man's sense of proper form told him to take me to the hospital first, where somebody saw I was alive. But being locked inside my body that way, in terrible pain but unable to speak to save my life—that total misery and helplessness is something I will never forget."

AT THE same time Bettelheim was seeing Richard Sterba, Editha Sterba had a psychotic boy as a patient. Bettelheim wrote of his encounter with the boy in an essay in *Freud's Vienna,* but in his conversation with me a special passion came through, a passion he still felt half a century later about the insight he gained into himself from the boy's words.

Bettelheim saw the boy now and then, whenever both sat in the Sterbas' waiting room at the same time. Several cactus plants grew on the windowsill, and sometimes the boy would come into the room, walk over to the window, pull a spiny leaf from a cactus, and chew it.

"I tried not to look, but I couldn't help myself," Bettelheim said. "It was too grotesque." One day he blurted out something about the boy having been in analysis for two years, but here he was, still chewing cactus leaves. Most of the time the pathetically thin boy had a cowering manner, but as Bettelheim spoke, the boy suddenly seemed to grow in stature. "He turned to me and pulled himself very erect and somehow managed to make me feel he was looking down at me. And he said with a disdainful tone that I can still hear in my mind, 'What are two years compared with eternity?' "

Bettelheim sat in shock for a few moments, until Sterba invited him into the office. As he lay down on the couch he realized he had been shamefully selfish, and he thought the incident through in silence. He saw he was guilty of using the boy to try to solve an acute problem of his own—whether or not to stay in analysis. Unable to face the question, he had projected it onto the boy.

"This was not a nice thing to do, but you must remember that the unconscious doesn't care who it steps on—it's a cunning but very primitive part of our psyche. However, I realized that the boy had told me just what I wanted to know: Yes! Analysis was doing him some good! In fact, he told me much more, and this encounter proved in retrospect to have been one of the most important ever to happen to me in psychoanalysis. He saw through my pretense, and his question induced me to open a door in my mind at the very moment I was ready for it. I saw I had to have patience about my own status as a patient. You can't force the issue.

Internal resistance dissolves gradually; you don't beat it down by brute power or get around it with your intellect."

The boy had offered him the insight that calendar time is not the same as emotional time; his mental suffering felt like an eternity, so that two years in analysis was merely a beginning. Bettelheim also learned how easily we all tell ourselves that we are motivated by a concern for the other person. "We want to think nicely of ourselves and so fail to notice the continuing motive of our self-involvement. We can't face the selfish core in most of our thoughts, and to the extent that you don't account for your own motives in an honest way, you go on projecting those motives in disguised form onto the behavior of others. In my view, a deep understanding of one's selfishness is necessary before you can have a true concern for the other person."

Bettelheim also saw the boy's purpose in torturing himself with the cactus: severe physical pain drove out his mental anguish. Further, if pain is self-inflicted, the self controls it. "I can start it and stop it. The psychotic's mental pain is just the opposite; he's at the mercy of tortures over which he had no control. In the boy's frame of reference, chewing cactus leaves was an act of sanity, but his act horrified me so deeply that I couldn't think about it until he had given me the key."

Bettelheim believed that this incident and the much earlier encounter with Fenichel in the Vienna Woods were the two experiences (besides the endless discussions with Reich) that brought him most strongly into analysis. "In both instances I saw that real understanding can only come from personal experience. Obviously, many psychologists, including analysts, disagree with me about this, and they try to keep their scientific inquiries apart from their personal experiences for the sake of something they call objectivity. However, I have grave doubts about the objectivity of 'objectivity,' if you see what I mean."

Bettelheim said that those who strive to separate themselves from their own experiences, especially psychologists, have good personal reasons to do so, even if they don't understand the reasons. "I always end up putting everybody somewhere on the same continuum — myself, other psychologists, and the boy with the cactus leaves."

I asked whether he knew how the boy's treatment with Editha Sterba turned out, but he could summon up no details, only an impression that the analysis had helped the boy a great deal. He also recalled having heard later that the family did not leave Vienna and that the boy and his parents died in Auschwitz.

BRUNO said that in the course of her second analysis, Gina decided she wanted to be a child therapist; Editha Sterba also thought it was a good idea. "Since I had this rather profitable business, though it was in the depression and not doing as well as before, she and her analyst agreed that I should finance a small psychoanalytic nursery on a private basis. My wife needed an occupation, and it seemed like a reasonable idea to me as well, so we did it. I had been in analysis maybe two years, and she had been with Editha Sterba probably a year at that point.

"Then something very significant in my life happened, quite fortuitously. An American lady from a prominent New York family came to Vienna with a child who was very sadly disturbed. We later called this disturbance autism, but there was no name for it then. [Leo] Kanner had not yet described and named infantile autism, which he did some years later in various papers."

The "American lady" had first gone to analysts and psychiatrists in New York, and later she took her daughter to visit experts in other cities. Everyone told her the child was hopeless: at the age of five she had not talked, and her behavior was usually withdrawn. As Bettelheim recalled, various American authorities had pronounced her feebleminded, a misfit, a vegetable, and so on; and they said that permanent institutional care would be needed when she got older. Even Kanner had been consulted, and he agreed that the girl was not treatable.

Someone suggested that the mother try Jean Piaget in Geneva, and she brought her child there in 1931. Piaget studied the psychology of children but did not treat them, and he advised her to take the girl to Freud in Vienna.

"I don't know why he didn't recommend Jung right there in Switzerland," Bettelheim said, "but he didn't. I suspect he told her to try Freud so she would leave the country and he wouldn't see her again. Many years later, when I met Piaget, I asked him, but he had no recollection. It couldn't have been important to him, though it turned out to be critical in my own life. Anyway, she went to Vienna and got an appointment with Freud and asked him to help her. Freud said, as he could have been expected to say, 'I don't treat children. I know nothing that can help you.' But she was persistent, she wouldn't take no for an answer, and finally Freud said, 'Look, my daughter Anna is interested in what psychoanalysis can do for children. Why don't you take your child to her?' "

Bettelheim said that she went to see Anna Freud, who told her that a regular analysis, an hour a day, would do nothing for such a child. She would have to live in a psychoanalytically oriented environment, which could be provided only by persons who were analyzed and would have the understanding to create a proper setting. The woman would not be put off, and at last Anna Freud suggested that she come to a meeting on child analysis later that day.

"My first wife happened to be a part of this group, and when the American lady came into the room, for no particular reason she approached my wife and sat down beside her. They began to talk. The woman was feeling very distressed, and immediately she told my wife the history of the child, how she herself was at the end of her rope, that if she couldn't find someone to help the child she would kill herself and kill the child, and that would be the end of it."

Bruno said that Gina was shocked and tried to say something helpful, but then Anna Freud came and the meeting started. Afterward, Gina invited the woman to come home and have dinner. (The girl was staying in a sanatorium because she could not be alone.)

"In the next few days, the mother spent quite a bit of time with us and in our house, and I found myself becoming interested in her story and also in the effect on this girl, which I won't go into. My wife felt the same way. We talked about it and said to the woman, 'Next Sunday, bring your daughter—we would like to meet her.' The girl came the following Sunday, a completely nonspeaking psychotic child. We tried to entertain her and talk to her, but what can you do with such a child? My psychoanalysis didn't help me on that point.

"But after a while I went into my study, where I was working from time to time on my thesis. I had a huge desk there with a typewriter and reference books on art history and all my papers, and somehow the girl followed me into the room and began to look at what I was doing. And to entertain her I pushed some big sheets of paper and crayons over to her, which I happened to have there.

"The desktop was very wide, and she was on the other side. I'm not sure why I did it, it was simply an impulse on my part. I had it in mind that I ought to entertain her, see that she was occupied in a nice way. I don't know what I expected, maybe that she would make marks on the paper with the crayons. But to my astonishment, she picked up the crayons and began to draw, and at once I realized that she was fabulously gifted! She drew sketches of animals in movement exactly like the beautiful cave art in France and Spain. It was one of the most exciting things I ever saw. I was absolutely fascinated, I couldn't get over it; her artistic gifts were magnificent. She wouldn't talk, but her drawings were precise, lovely, and eloquent."

The girl was then only about seven. "I tell you this to emphasize how shocked and delighted I was, when my casual effort to be friendly in giving her the paper and crayons resulted in this amazing response. At that moment I wanted to work with her to see if I could help. She was an artist but didn't talk. Extraordinary!"

After the girl and her mother left that evening, Gina and Bruno talked things over and decided to try bringing the child into their home for a few months. The next morning they called the mother, who then went back to Anna Freud to see whether she approved. "Anna Freud knew us and said it was a good idea, but she also suggested the girl should go into analysis with Editha Sterba. The mother later went into analysis with Richard Sterba, and this, I think, complicated things very badly—the girl being in analysis with my first wife's second analyst, the mother being in analysis with my analyst and my wife's first analyst. But in any event the girl came to live with us."

The Bettelheims had help, so there was always someone to take care of the girl when both Gina and Bruno could not be there. Bruno said he was going to the office every morning but came at noon for a few hours—"a long Austrian lunch hour, and then I was with her again in the evening until she went to bed, at which time I often stayed up and worked on my studies." In short they provided care around the clock.[8]

BESIDES contributing to the nursery school in which Gina was a partner, Bruno later financed another place, a summer home for delinquent children in a castle at Schallerburg. "I was able to rent it inexpensively because I had done some lumber business with the baron who owned it, and we knew each other fairly well." Gina ran the summer home in partnership with Fritz Redl, a *gymnasium* teacher and friend of Bruno's who was also in training to become a child analyst.

"The girl also spent some time in the camp at Schallerburg during the summer, but most of the time she was simply living with us. For a while we had a second child with us, a Canadian girl, an autistic child, but she did not stay with us as long. It was principally through this American girl living in our house that I first became deeply preoccupied with child analysis and with the treatment of extremely disturbed children."

ABOUT a year and a half after the girl came to live with the Bettelheims, an incident took place, which Bettelheim described in *A Good Enough Parent*.9 He often played with the girl in the evening, hoping to draw her out of her placid-passive state as a "virtual mute." She was spoken to only in German at the Bettelheims, but she had begun to seem somewhat less withdrawn, perhaps because Gina and Bruno had given her steady care and had found things she liked to do. One game she seemed to like was hide-and-seek, when she hid in the drapes that closed off Bettelheim's study from the rest of the house. One Sunday evening, as he recalled it, they were playing and he had just "found" her, and he said something like, "I found you—what would you like now?"

"I cannot recall the exact words, they were not terribly important, but what she did next was indeed very important"—she said a complete sentence in English (which Bruno had studied in the *gymnasium*): "Give me the skeleton of George Washington." Bruno saw that her answer was both metaphoric and symbolic, framed so as to go to the heart of what was troubling her: not knowing who her father was. "Since the unknown father was the 'skeleton in the closet' of her life, she asked for his skeleton"10—referring to him obliquely by naming George Washington, "the father of his country."

Bruno's marriage to Gina was already troubling enough to bring him into analysis, and the girl's presence was an additional impediment. However, he said, "In another way, the girl provided a stability or center that we didn't have on our own. Not that I blame her or my first wife for anything that happened in the marriage—that's only the way things were bound to turn out at that moment." He said that her sentence in English left him "completely bowled over," and he thought of it as a breakthrough, because "she began to talk more, and then she learned to read and write." Her question showed him that "she knew what her problem was and that it was important to her. This sentence came like a bolt from the blue and focused my mind on her problem in a way that had not occurred previously." The girl was eight at the time. "She became a remarkably charming, very sweet girl. We really loved her dearly."

DURING the late 1920s and early '30s several psychoanalytically oriented schools (or nursery schools) started up in Vienna. Perhaps the best-known place was a small private Montessori school that used Montessori meth-

ods but also looked to psychoanalysis for a coherent point of view in dealing with children.[11] Gina had volunteered to work in this school, and ultimately she got a degree in the Montessori method. In one of Gina's
Montessori classes she met Gertrude Weinfeld. Trude, as everyone called
her, was about seven years younger than Gina, and the two women got to
know each other without ever quite becoming friends.

Trude had graduated from a *gymnasium* and intended to go to the
University of Vienna, but then changed her mind and enrolled in a two-
year course at the School of Social Work. When she finished her studies
and fieldwork, she had no luck finding a job. Prejudice against Jews, perhaps made worse by the depression, had shut many doors against young
persons like herself. However, Trude had visited a Montessori nursery as
part of her fieldwork, and what she saw there intrigued her—the freedom
in the classroom and the way in which teachers encouraged the children's
creativity. She decided to learn to be a Montessori teacher, and she and
Gina met in a class in Montessori theory.

Trude's training led to a job in the Montessori school mentioned
above, which rented two classrooms in a public school. The atmosphere
was friendly and informal: children and teachers wore blue and green
smocks, and two mothers who lived in the neighborhood cooked and
brought in the midday meal for everyone. The school also drew students
from families who wanted to get away from the strict *gymnasium* atmosphere, and Trude recalled that one student was Trotsky's nephew.

Trude first worked as an assistant to a young woman from Switzerland,
Emmi Vischer, who at that time was in analysis with Editha Sterba.
Emmi soon introduced Trude to her analyst, and Trude went into analysis
five times a week for three years and, she later said, "never told my parents
about it."[12]

The girl living with the Bettelheims was able to go to the Montessori
school after about two years, by which time Trude had been promoted
from assistant to teacher. At a party for the girl, probably in 1934, Trude
and Bruno met for the first time.[13] "After that birthday party," Trude said,
"Bruno asked me occasionally to go out with him when Gina was gone
or otherwise occupied. Once, he and the girl and I went to the Prater,
the amusement park of Vienna, and I was quite taken with him, and
we became close friends." However, the relation was "fraught with difficulties" and "feelings of guilt," and she and Bruno became close only
very slowly: "It took me some time to realize what was really happening
with me."

VIENNA'S *Fasching*, or carnival season, runs from Epiphany on January 6 to Shrove Tuesday, just before the start of Lent. *Fasching* was not for Catholics only—anyone could enjoy the endless rounds of lavish balls and costume parties, often on elaborate themes. The Bettelheims once invited Trude to go to a *Fasching* ball with them, and she came to their apartment an hour early to put on her costume. "Gina and I were making up as little girls, I think, with long braids." Afterward they all came back to the apartment very late, and Bruno and Gina insisted that Trude stay overnight. She went to bed in a small room but found she couldn't sleep, and as she lay thinking, she began to realize that she "was really much in love with Bruno."

Trude knew Gina "was already involved with Peter Weinmann, whom she eventually married," and this knowledge eased her guilt about her love affair with Bruno. "Later, as I became involved with Bruno, I remember I would run down during my few free minutes and across the street, where there was a little school store with a telephone, and I would call him. In this way I could speak with Bruno in his office instead of calling his home, where Gina would be likely to answer the telephone. . . . Although, as I have said, analysis was very helpful to me and freed me from a lot of sexual repressions, among other things, I have always thought it rather funny that analysis also drove me into the arms of a married man."

GINA TOLD me that she knew of Bruno's involvement with Trude and he knew about hers with Peter Weinmann.[14] In their circle everyone shared the belief that to stay married despite infidelities was more moral than to break up a family by divorce. This held especially true for assimilated Jews, whose sense of family loyalty was a source of inner and social cohesion after religion had lost its authority over them. Gentile society in Vienna also disapproved of divorce, and Jewish couples could not dissolve a marriage without bringing shame to their families in the eyes of the world. If one's choice lay between divorce and a love affair, divorce was the greater scandal.

Bettelheim said to me (off the tape and unwilling to say more), "You know, it was permitted to find sexual satisfaction outside marriage." He loved Gina, but their failure to reach a steady emotional intimacy led him, and her, to look for it elsewhere. Neither wanted to consider divorce while in analysis, and both agreed not to have a child or to separate as long as the girl lived with them. However, Bruno insisted that he and Gina did what they did for their own reasons, of which the girl was only a part.

BETTELHEIM had grown up in a home polite to the point of suffocation. Ghetto families had very little of what assimilated families called decorum, and assimilated families like his had perhaps too much correctness because of secrets not shared with the children.[15] The silence of things left unsaid spoke volumes to a privileged and sensitive child like Bruno, who learned from decorous parents that it was unseemly to give vent to anger or to talk about sex. Some unhappy adults in Bettelheim's time and place were fortunate to be able to relieve the stifling effects of their early life by resorting to psychoanalysis; but if one had a joyless marriage, as Bruno and Gina did, they made the best of it in socially accepted ways, because everybody knew that marriage was permanent.

CHAPTER 4

A Bearable Moratorium;
a Ph.D.

BETTELHEIM HAD enough money in the early 1930s for his life to be very pleasant despite Austria's unsettled political climate. He could put aside his personal unhappiness and coast along in an existence that had the distractions of daily work, quiet pleasures, a few friends, and a vague sense of meaning but no real direction. He could also put politics out of his mind most of the time, except perhaps for a few afternoon hours in a coffeehouse, where everyone read newspapers, drank coffee, and talked with friends.

Vienna's coffeehouses gave an illusion that reassured many of that time, the feeling of a safe and warm place in a disorderly world. Coffeehouses tended to have clienteles so faithful that the atmosphere was like that of a club. Hans Willig said that Bettelheim favored the Café Centrale, where one saw artistic and literary regulars like Karl Kraus, the best-known satirist and social critic of the time. The Herrenhof next door was primarily for a circle of Jewish intelligentsia, and Bruno would drop in there to see the Willigs, who disdained the Centrale and never set foot in it. Vienna, once the center of an empire, had been transformed into a city in some ways like a gossipy small town, with layers of class and wealth and with many loosely knit groups, each jealous of its own sense of belonging—and exclusion.

I asked Bruno what he thought of the Sacher Hotel, where my wife and I had a surprising experience in 1972.[1] "I went to the Sacher a few times," he said, "but it was not a place where I felt at home. I knew I wasn't welcome there—it was not my circle. I don't think Trude ever in her life went to the Sacher, she knew she wouldn't like it. In a closed society like Vienna, you would find the subgroups, the in-groups, the sub-societies, each of which got the idea they belonged in a certain place. You just knew when you were not in your place; nobody had to tell you. In an open society like America it's harder for such groups to form, at least in the numbers and with the sharp exclusiveness of Vienna before the second war."

Fifty years later, in the 1980s, the Austrian government tried to re-create some of the coffeehouses as they had been in the 1930s, but Bettel-heim found the results distressing. "The intellectual richness of Vienna was impoverished when they got rid of the Jews. Fixing up the Herrenhof was a terrible idea. I could only think of what happened to the people who used to go there."

ALSO IN the early 1930s the Austrian government was so unpopular and its grip so shaky that some parties waiting in the wings felt tempted to reach for power. In February 1934 the Christian Socialists (conservative heirs of Dr. Lueger) could barely maintain their dominance. In the absence of Parliament and with the support of the Catholic Church, they had ruled by decree for a year while permitting many attacks on the parties of the left, especially their main rivals for power, the Social Democrats.

Severely provoked, the Social Democrats and their allies on the left took up arms, hoping to topple the Christian Socialists. Another group, the Heimwehr ("Home Defense Forces"—conservatives from the outer provinces who also held a handful of seats in the suspended Parliament) made a quick alliance with the Christian Socialists to put down the leftist revolution. The Heimwehr patrolled the streets, and in short order the Austrian army's artillery could be heard all over Vienna shelling the Karl-Marx-Hof, a fortresslike block of workers' housing in which the Social Democrats had barricaded themselves. The bombardment easily crushed the leftist defenders.

Despite pockets of fighting in which perhaps a thousand people died, the brief revolution did not bring life in the city to a halt, and most Vien-nese went about their business uninvolved in the conflict. Once the fight-ing ended, the Christian Socialists promptly outlawed the Social Democratic Party and soon abolished all other parties not conservative or hard right. To underscore the new political reality, they removed the word *Republic* from the official name of the Austrian state.

"We were in sympathy with the Social Democrats, of course," Bettelheim said, "but we were also afraid of what might happen if they won." He and his friends feared that a leftist victory might cause Germany and Italy to intervene militarily and make things worse. However, the quick triumph was not enough for extremists on the far-right fringe. Five months after the leftist defeat, on July 25, 1934, a small group of Austrian Nazis seized government buildings and murdered Chancellor Engelbert Dollfuss, the Christian Socialist who had led the parties of the right to consolidate their power.

On the day Dollfuss was murdered, Bruno and Gina were on a short vacation with Hans and Wanda Willig in the Dolomites, a dramatic and beautiful range of mountains in the Italian Alps. (The Willigs rode in the bumpy rumble seat of Bruno's little car, which Hans recalled as quite uncomfortable.) The vacationers heard that martial law had been declared in Austria, but news reports did not say why. Bruno and Gina decided to return to Vienna at once to make sure things were all right at home with the girl and their immediate family. They left the Willigs in the Austrian Tirol to finish their vacation before going back to Prague, where Hans and Wanda had moved two years earlier. Just after crossing the border into Austria, "We saw the soldiers with rifles behind the trees when we were driving at night," Hans said, "but we didn't know exactly what had happened."

"Perhaps we were naïve or stupid," Bettelheim said of his judgment in those years, "in not leaving Austria sooner, but somehow it didn't seem immediately necessary. Nobody foresaw the weakness of England and France in the face of Hitler's Germany, which left the rest of Europe so exposed. Of course, the inner logic of the Nazi regime was developing, this one sees very clearly in hindsight, but the fears and reasons that kept people in place were also very powerful. When Kristallnacht came, by that time I was already in the camp at Buchenwald. If it had happened in thirty-six or thirty-seven, I think I would have said, 'Let's not take any more chances, let's clear out,' but it's not always possible to see ahead so clearly in life. People who have not familiarized themselves with the situation say very easily, 'Why didn't you leave sooner?' but this does not take into consideration all the real difficulties Jews had in going from one country to another, in giving up one life and starting another. You had to know somebody in another country who would help you, because there was nowhere that Jews were readily welcomed in large numbers, not even in the States, unfortunately."

AFTER finishing with Sterba, Bettelheim continued to look to psycho-analysis for a worldview that suited him. He remained unhappy in his marriage and at work, but he could find no system of thought that told him more than the insights of psychoanalysis had. "Freud always insisted that psychoanalysis did not have a weltanschauung—a view of the world from a particular position in the way, for example, the communists have in Marxism. And I now believe he was correct. As a method of observa-tion, psychoanalysis is enormously powerful, but it is only a therapeutic tool—it has no inherent strength as an ideology seems to have. The per-son must have the strength."

In this period of his life Bettelheim said he was "living in what Erik-son named and described decades later as a psychosocial moratorium," which is

> a period of delay granted to somebody who is not ready to meet an obligation or forced on somebody who should give himself time. By psychosocial moratorium, then, we mean a delay of adult commit-ments, and yet it is not only a delay.[2]

An adolescent typically has a moratorium phase before making adult commitments, but when the moratorium comes later, Erikson saw it as "marking time" before the person finds the ultimate direction of his life.[3] Moreover, the very absence of a crisis may overlie a deeper crisis, as was true for Bettelheim.

"With Erikson's moratorium," he said, "if you're in that state of mind or feeling, you don't change your marriage or your job or anything basic about yourself. If something bothers you, you just try not to think about it too much. I suspect a lot of people who are disappointed in life, but fairly successful, do this and don't tell anybody. Psychoanalysis is very accept-able to people in this frame of mind because it doesn't really seek to change the world, and my own analysis was like this. On the other hand, I invested a great deal of hope in the analytic point of view, I tried to use it as a weltanschauung, but that's simply what you do when you feel the need to distance yourself from your own recurring discomfort within the life you have built around you."

He went on living in deep unhappiness that no casual acquaintance would have noticed, and to most people he would have seemed to have everything. "Yet underneath it all, something continued to trouble me. I went on functioning, like a man with a low-grade fever. Perhaps if times had not changed, I might have gone on that way the rest of my life, though somehow I doubt it. I suspect my restlessness would have come to a head."

BETTELHEIM tried to overcome his unhappiness by escaping into "privatization"—literature, art, music, and a few good friends[4]—thus returning to interests that had occupied him before his analysis. With his business income he could enrich the life he already had and make things better for himself and those close to him. His interest in the American girl occupied him, but besides his relation with Trude, perhaps his closest friendship at that time was with a young man his own age named Kurt Landau, a wine merchant in a family business.

"He was a very dear friend," Bettelheim said, "and he also happened to be a Trotskyite communist, and so we had lots of conversations about the way society was organized—or misorganized—and we liked to go to the vineyards, the *heurigers*, and drink the fresh wine and have a good time. I wasn't involved in politics at the time, but Landau was what you might call a convinced idealist."

In 1936 Landau decided to fight on the Socialist side in the Spanish Civil War. His family couldn't talk him out of it and threw a farewell party for him and a dozen other Austrian volunteers. A few weeks later Bettelheim heard that when Landau and his friends got off the train in Barcelona they were arrested and shot by Russian secret police.

"It was shocking, he was really almost my best friend. Maybe I felt a little guilty that I didn't have the courage to do what he did, but it was a terrible and tragic thing."

Around the same time, Bettelheim went back to work on a doctorate. He had stopped taking courses years earlier, but his friend Fritz Redl (as well as Trude) urged him to go for a degree. A little later, it alarmed him when the police interrogated Edith Buxbaum about her leftist activities; she told him she was leaving Austria and would set up a practice in America, and he knew that as a practical matter he needed a degree if he wanted a teaching job elsewhere.

In 1936 he registered mostly for lectures in psychology and philosophy rather than art history, and worked on a dissertation. The psychology courses were not Freudian. "I was reading everything of Freud's, but actually Karl Buehler was my teacher, for whom I had the highest regard." Buehler was a brilliant theoretical psychologist, Bruno said, who came to

America but never got the recognition he deserved because his eclectic approach was "not in the fashion that prevailed here." He thought one reason Buehler had accepted the call to Vienna was that he hoped to work with Freud; also, unlike many theoretical psychologists, Buehler was introspective. "He could see things about himself that he couldn't quite account for in the schemata of his psychology."

However, Freud ignored Buehler. "I don't want to psychoanalyze Freud, but it's entirely possible that he was resentful that he himself never received proper acknowledgment of his very real distinction by being made a full professor of psychology at the university. That honor always went to people he felt were lesser men, which is probably true. Also, you have to remember that a great many very good people, well intentioned, who tried to establish relations with Freud were rejected. Partly, I believe, he was afraid that the wrong kind of adherent would water down psycho-analysis, so he tried to keep a circle of friends and followers who would see things his way. This is an understandable impulse but may be impossible in practice, though the core of literature he created certainly gives all ana-lysts a good deal in common even now."

Bettelheim found Buehler charming as a man and impressive as a scholar but could never mention his own interest in Freud and psycho-analysis. Buehler was establishment, and Freud was not. "I'm sorry Buehler and Freud could never talk to each other or have a working rela-tion, but that's how it was."

Many good Viennese doctors felt that Freud's writings on sex were dis-reputable and that psychoanalysis was shady. "But people in the field of analysis were very excited, and they associated with each other a lot, and there was a prevalent feeling that analysis was providing a kind of yeast in the social ferment that would result in a new sense of community for everybody. They saw themselves—or perhaps I should say 'we'—as the elect, the leaders. It was a little like in communist groups, the feeling that 'we have the answer.' "

ALSO IN 1936, Gina took the American girl to the United States so she could visit her family. While they were away, Bettelheim vacationed in France. By this time he had begun to use his money to help Jews who wanted to escape from Germany. "I didn't know the people I helped, didn't keep their names, most often didn't know their real names—that would have been too dangerous. But I did not think of this activity as anything special or unusual. I felt it was simply what anyone would do who was in my position and able to help. A great many Jews in Austria tried to help the Jews in Germany in the early years."

He said he had allowed his home address to be used as a letter drop and that his office was too public, with workers and customers coming and going all day. The envelopes would contain a coded message telling him how to proceed.

"I've forgotten the code now," he said, "but it told me whether to contact someone or send a package to someone else, and so on. Often I simply put the material inside another envelope and mailed it to another address. The most difficult thing was to get false passports into Germany—that was usually done by a courier. I would pay for the passport, receive it, and send it on to someone else, who would take it somehow to the person for whom it was intended. I didn't buy the passport directly but through a third or maybe a fourth party. You could buy an Austrian passport or a Czech passport and change the picture. It was easy to buy the passport for several hundred dollars, substitute a picture in it, and get out of the country. Smuggling papers into Germany—that was more dangerous than what I was doing, and I did not do that myself. I never knew who the passport was for; that would have been too dangerous, and there was no need. A friend would come to me and say, 'We need money for a ship's ticket,' or 'We need forged papers,' and so on. I would simply give the money to friends who knew how to get false passports. The real owner would report the passport lost or stolen."

BETTELHEIM began to send money to Switzerland. "In Vienna we took it for granted we would have trouble sooner or later, and most of my friends were already quite worried. But, of course, it was difficult to get money out of the country." He and his business partner, Schnitzer, agreed to cooperate in sending money out, and Schnitzer recommended a small private bank owned and staffed by Jews. Despite Austria's currency restrictions, he and Schnitzer managed to deposit a substantial amount (the equivalent today of several hundred thousand dollars, as Bruno recalled) in a Swiss bank, where they hoped to claim it later.

They also met an American journalist who offered to deposit money in an American account. The journalist needed money in Austria but promised to put the same amount in a bank in their names. They did not know the man well, but they talked it over and decided to take a chance. Each gave him $10,000 and hoped for the best.

IN THE spring of 1937 Bettelheim presented his dissertation,[5] and in July Professors Buehler and Robert Reininger examined him and suggested changes. In January 1938 two more professors examined him on the rewritten dissertation, and the university awarded him a Ph.D. on February 2, 1938. Work on the degree had used up most of his spare time and had also taken time from the lumber business.

When I interviewed him, he showed little interest in talking about his dissertation. "More importantly," he said, "I had a huge collection of notes about the child who lived with us. I intended to publish a book about her, with permission and with her identity concealed, of course. The book would have included a selection of her art, which was quite beautiful and which I had saved. I believe that such a book would have been a valuable contribution to the psychological literature, but after 1938 there was no way to save the notes or her drawings. They were confiscated with the rest of my papers."

AFTER getting his doctorate, Bettelheim took steps to prepare himself for a second profession. Despite misgivings about being paid by patients, he decided to train as an analyst, which would actually be easier than the doctorate because he would have more time for the lumber business and anything else. When he was ready, he would sell his share to Schnitzer and take his family out of Austria. I asked him when he had applied to the Vienna Psychoanalytic Institute but he could not recall— probably early 1938. He said that Anna Freud and Paul Federn interviewed him and that the examination took the better part of two afternoons. During one of the sessions Freud walked into the room and Anna introduced him to Bruno.

"He was very generous," Bettelheim said. "When he heard my name he said, 'A Bettelheim doesn't need any introduction to me.' Why? Because he had studied with another Bettelheim, my father's oldest brother, who was killed, and had visited the house of my paternal grandparents and was very friendly with my father's sister, the aunt I never knew. He was very generous, as I said, and he said a few words to the effect that I was welcome in his house. I met him a few other times when I came to see Anna Freud, but we never really talked."[6]

Starting in the late 1920s, those who wanted to become psychoanalysts had to undergo a "didactic"—a training analysis.[7] On my last visit with

Bettelheim, a few days before he committed suicide, I happened to ask the name of his analyst for the didactic, and he said that he did not go back to Sterba but to an analyst named Eduard Kronengold. He said that he had just started when the events of March 1938 intervened and that he doubted that Kronengold (who was still alive) would even remember him. "It was too short a time. The invasion of Austria, that was the end of it."[8]

CHAPTER 5

The Anschluss;
Dachau

IN FEBRUARY 1938 Kurt von Schuschnigg, the Austrian chancellor, went to Berchtesgaden to present Hitler with evidence of an Austrian Nazi plot; he expected Hitler to repudiate the plotters, as had been done in 1934, when Austrian Nazis staged a coup and murdered Dollfuss. Instead, Hitler exploded with a stream of harsh demands and an ultimatum. Schuschnigg went back to Vienna, and in the next month the maneuverings were constant but hopeless.[1] Schuschnigg's party, the Christian Socialists, had crushed and outlawed the Social Democrats four years earlier, but now Schuschnigg quietly contacted underground leftist leaders, who agreed to help in the crisis. On March 9 he called a surprise plebiscite to vote on March 13 as to whether or not Austria would remain an independent country. Hitler, sure that the Nazis would lose, demanded Schuschnigg's resignation and sent tanks and troops to the border.

Schuschnigg spoke to the nation on the evening of March 11 and resigned as of midnight. Early on the morning of the twelfth, German forces crossed the border without opposition, and the outpouring of greetings for Hitler later that day, when he went to Linz (where he had lived as a child), was so heady that he hurriedly ordered an *Anschluss* law drawn up. Instead of voting on its independence on March 13, Austria joined Germany by decree.

The mother of the American girl had called the American authorities in Vienna at once, to arrange for the girl to leave on the thirteenth with Gina and Bruno and come to the United States. "It was all arranged over the telephone, the visas and everything," Bettelheim said. "I was ready to go." He feared staying for obvious reasons, and he telephoned his mother and sister to say good-bye. "You see, it was always possible that somebody had some idea about me, and all they needed was a suspicion and then they could pick you up. Anybody who didn't like you could report you anyhow, whether it was true or not, once the Nazis were in control."

His mother said he should leave and help Grete and herself through the wealthy American woman's influence. "But when I talked to my sister, she began to cry and said, 'They know about you, and if you escape they will take revenge on me and your mother.' Well, I guess I felt guilty and thought maybe she had a case, so the next day at the last moment I decided not to go. I would stay and try to get them out of Austria. I still had my passport, and I had money abroad, and I thought I could manage it. I don't know whether my sister was actually right, but I thought about it all night and came to feel I couldn't leave."

Gina's recollection was slightly different. She said that she, Bruno, and Peter Weinmann and his wife spent a tense evening in the Bettelheim apartment talking over what they should do. She and the Weinmanns were ready to leave at once, and Gina said she argued that Bruno should go with them, but he wouldn't budge. "Bruno said he couldn't do that—I mean he had his mother, he had Margaret. So he said, 'I'll be much better off if you can take the girl. It would be easier for me.' "

Bettelheim stayed, and the next day the others went to the station and boarded the train for Paris. They had booked compartments in different cars and did not see one another after getting on the train, but when Gina and the girl got up for breakfast, they went to the Weinmann compartment and found it empty. Peter Weinmann and his wife had been taken off the train during the night and held at the border. "It was really very frightening in the morning," Gina said. "We woke up, and they were gone . . . taken by the Nazis."

Peter Weinmann later came to suspect he had been betrayed by one of his dental assistants, but in any event someone had called the police and made a report, which had led to his questioning. Since he had done nothing illegal and had made proper arrangements, the police soon permitted the Weinmanns to take another train to Paris, where Gina saw them again before she left for New York.

Back in Vienna, Bettelheim's troubles mounted. "The next day after Gina left, the Austrian police came to my house, took all my papers, including my passport, and told me not to go anywhere. I could go to the office, but I shouldn't leave Vienna. They said, 'You have sent your wife away, you must have something to hide.' It was logical from their point of view, but I just hadn't visualized how they would see it.

"As soon as the police left, I said to myself, 'This is it, I'd better do something,' and I got in my car and drove to the Czech border to see if I could bluff my way through. It was not even a two-hour drive from Vienna—to Bratislava, as a matter of fact—and I got through the Austrian side with a bribe, but the Czechs turned me back, so there was nothing to do."

The next day, when he went into the office, his partner told him the bad news about the small bank through which they had sent money to Switzerland. One of the Jewish partners had given his gentile brother-in-law a job as a clerk, and on the day of the *Anschluss* the clerk came in wearing his Nazi uniform and took control of the bank. He knew about the money in Switzerland and demanded that it be brought back.

"I saw now that I was not going to be as helpful to my mother and sister as I had believed, but I stayed at my job and hoped that the American lady and my wife in New York would somehow get us out. Of course, they tried, but this was not really possible at that moment. Everybody was trying to get out, I believe people were paying for visas, because by then everybody was terrified."

Bettelheim tentatively decided to make his way on foot through the mountains into Switzerland, but when he talked to his lawyer about it, the lawyer advised him not to. A border guard might shoot and kill him, whereas if he stayed in Vienna perhaps he would go to jail for a few weeks and then be released. The Nazis wanted the Jews to leave, and he had good chances for America. Also, if he were caught or shot at the border, his mother and sister would be arrested and interrogated. "The lawyer thought I should work to get out legally through our connections, so that's what I continued to do. I was hoping every day that my passport would be returned, and of course my wife and the American lady were doing everything that they could."

If only he could get his passport back, he could leave, because the *Anschluss* had given Austrian Jews an unexpected opening that many were quick to use. Anyone holding a German passport needed no visa to enter Switzerland, and Jews with Austrian passports suddenly found they had the equivalent of German passports. When Jews began to slip through this loophole, the Swiss authorities raised objections. In August they protested to Germany about the "Judaification" of Switzerland, and two months later the Germans began stamping all passports of Jews with a

large red J, which would allow Switzerland (or any other country) to identify Jews and deny them entry. Jews still crossed the border illegally, but
they needed a Swiss friend to help them stay in the country long enough
to get an exit visa to some other destination.

"I should not have waited, I should have left," Bettelheim said, "but I
didn't. It was a risk, yes, but I would have avoided going to Dachau. Everybody thought that any arrest in Vienna would only be for a few hours or
days, and this seemed reasonable to me. I don't want to blame him, the
lawyer, but of course it was a mistake not to try to escape."

About a year later I listened again to the tape on which Bettelheim
said this, and his words came so slowly, so heavy with pain that I felt he
was reliving and feeling all the terrible consequences of his mistake. And I
could detect no blame in his voice for anyone but himself.

Bettelheim also had another regret. "Sometimes in the camps I felt I
probably should have done more against the Nazis. After all, I gave some
money for false papers, and I probably could have done a lot more than
that. Compared to my income, it was relatively little."

JEWISH writers, artists, and thinkers had led the cultural renaissance that
brought world attention to Vienna in the decades before and after the
turn of the century. But Jewish success also inspired envy and gave new
life to Austria's traditional anti-Semitism, now for two decades uninflu-
enced by the benign model of the emperor. In 1938 more than 180,000
Jews lived in Austria, most of them in Vienna. Many felt uncomfortable
with their situation, but they knew things were worse in Hitler's Germany
next door, and most saw no immediate threat. Like others, Bettelheim
underestimated the danger.

In the first five years of Nazi rule in Germany, the government had
generated a steady flow of anti-Semitic laws, regulations, and policies that
took away, step by step, the rights of Jewish citizens. Now, at a single
stroke, these harsh measures fell like an avalanche on Austrian Jews, who
went to bed in Austria and woke up in Germany. Suddenly Jews could not
eat in public restaurants, visit public parks, or go to a theater; could not
own property; could not practice their professions. Of course, some doctors and lawyers went on working, but for other Jews only and at a serious
risk to themselves.

Since 1933 Nazi policy in Germany had pressured Jews to emigrate,
and by 1938 perhaps 150,000 were gone, leaving their possessions behind.

This policy, and more, descended upon the Jews Germany had just annexed. On the streets of Vienna, the SS and SA helped Austrian police harass and arrest Jews; troops painted *Jude* in red on Jewish shops, offices, and coffeehouses. Jews arrested at random might be ordered to scrub streets or to clean SS latrines; some were taken to the Prater and forced to eat grass like sheep. The message was clear: *Leave*; but it was not easy to leave.

In the face of Nazi terror, an Austrian Jew had several choices. He could try to escape across a border and risk being shot; he could apply for an exit permit and a visa, mark time while the bureaucratic wheels turned, and hope not to be arrested for one thing or another; he could simply wait and do nothing except hope for the best; he could go into hiding; he could lay hands on a gun and resolve not to die without a fight, which was suicidal; or he could dispense with all hope and kill himself. In the first month of Nazi rule, over five hundred Jews in Vienna committed suicide, some as individuals and others as families. Some families sent their children away, expecting that the parents would follow in a year or so. However, after the war intervened, many parents who had saved their children went to the death camps.

FROM THE beginning of the Nazi regime, Heinrich Himmler and the SS took control of the concentration camps, a responsibility Himmler used to augment his own power. The camps also made money for the SS, and their evil repute cowed the populace at large. In 1937 Adolf Eichmann, a clever young officer in the SS, drafted a new German emigration program to expel Jews in a methodical and "legal" way. His ideas lay untouched until after the *Anschluss*, when Reinhard Heydrich ordered him to organize and run the first emigration office in Vienna. Eichmann did the job along the lines of the memorandum he had written the previous year, aiming to rid Austria of Jews through bureaucratic diligence and terror. This would also speed up the looting of Jewish wealth, which was transferred to the SS, to the Nazi Party, and to other Germans and Austrians.

It was a job well rewarded, if we consider Eichmann's lifestyle in Vienna. Somehow he has achieved the reputation of a drab and banal bureaucrat, a faceless functionary who merely followed orders; however, when the SS posted him to Vienna he lived (with others) in a mansion confiscated from the Rothschilds, was chauffeured to work in the Rothschild Rolls-Royce, and drank wine from the superb Rothschild cellar. He also is rumored to have taken an elegant Austrian mistress, a liaison initiated during his wife's pregnancy. In short, he may have been a bureaucrat, but he had the tastes of a prince.

About half the Jews of Austria left the country or survived in some way. When we consider the fate of certain other European Jewish communities, a survival rate of 50 percent sounds almost reassuring—until we pause to reflect that the other 50 percent perished. Well-publicized SS actions put Jews on notice, and Jews fearing an impending pogrom lined up at the new emigration office, whose mere existence offered the hope that Jews could get away for a price—the price of leaving everything behind.

BETTELHEIM had a sponsor (the American mother), a quota number, and his visa for America; he needed an exit permit and his passport, which the police still held. In his affidavit to the Nuremberg Trial Counsel, he tells of being questioned for the first time when the police searched his home shortly after the *Anschluss*. He also says he was taken into custody "three or four weeks later," when the local police held and interrogated him for three days.

Bettelheim had tried to avoid giving me a clear reason for his first brush with the police, but Grete offered an unqualified and plausible explanation; as she put it, the police arrested him because they suspected that Gina had left with a lot of money.

"They said she took the money out. So he tried to explain she took the American child out, but you know—explain to Hitler! They wanted the business, but it was mainly because they said his wife got the money out."

Ultimately, Bettelheim reluctantly admitted to me that he and Gina had not realized how her flight would look to the police and how this would reflect on him. At first he would not say this, and when it finally came out, he did not mention the police accusation about money. To me he was speaking officially and on the record, and I believe he tried not to blame Gina. I see the same motive in his neglecting to tell me about the arrest several weeks later, when the police held him for three days, then released him with no action against him. He did not mention the second incident because it was probably prompted by a story about the arrival of Gina and the girl that appeared in a New York newspaper.

In the usual course of such investigations, Bettelheim's file would have gone to Gestapo headquarters in Berlin, with information about his business, his wealth, his absent wife, and the money sent to Switzerland, then reclaimed and confiscated. With more property to be disposed of, and having already aroused suspicion, he was probably marked for the camps, although he still assumed he would leave Austria legally, as his lawyer expected.

For about two months after the *Anschluss,* the SS made well-publicized mass arrests of Jews, whom they would brutalize, harass, and humiliate for a few hours, or a day or two, and then release. Some individuals disappeared, but for the most part Jews were taken into custody at random and then let go. Toward the end of May, however, the SS planned an action that required more subtlety. One morning two policemen came to Bettelheim's office at the lumberyard and politely told him that he had to report for questioning.

"They said, 'You have to come in to the police station not later than so-and-so'—a certain time in the afternoon, I can't remember just what time, but I had to be there. Also they said, 'We just want to ask you some questions.' Since they didn't detain me then and there, I thought it was best to go and see what they wanted. Just the day before, I had seen an old friend on the street, Karli Popper. We met by chance that day and talked of what we were going to do to get out of Austria. He told me he was going to New Zealand, and I said I was going to America. I was still hoping for the passport. So Karli and I wished each other luck, and he got to New Zealand not long after that, but I was taken into custody the next day.

"Frankly, they did not tell me what it was, because if they had, I probably would have tried to escape. But I phoned my lawyer and told him what was happening and he said not to worry, and then when I got to the police station I saw a couple of friends who had also been told to report on that day."

As he remembered it, everyone there had to sign a document, a red slip of paper requesting protective custody. The document had the legal effect of committing the signer to a concentration camp, though the paper had been carefully worded not to spell this out.[2] "We were really very naïve or stupid, or whatever. While I knew I was in danger for political reasons, I didn't anticipate they would move against Jews in this way. I thought I might be arrested, but then I would notify my lawyer and there would be normal legal procedures."

The police took everyone from the jail to a school building in another district, which had been turned into a temporary detention center. "Many of us were Jewish," he said, "but not all, and that was also confusing."

(Later, in Dachau, he heard that the SS called this operation an "Action Against International Trained Freemasonry, Leftists, and Jews.") "I could have been on the list in one or two categories, but you couldn't tell for sure. None of us knew what was wanted of us, but nobody interrogated or accused us of anything, so we weren't too worried. Also, we were still in the hands of the Austrian police, not the SS or Germans.

"We kept thinking we would be put on some kind of work detail for a few days and then let go. There was a flood in the south of Austria, and somehow the rumor started that they collected us to clean up this flood. You see, they had collected leftists and Jews before, to clean up the anti-Nazi slogans, and let them go after a few hours, so our assumption was not entirely unreasonable. I guess maybe it was the beginning of rounding up Jews and putting them into the camps. At any rate, I didn't hear of this kind of thing previously."

The atmosphere of the school–detention center seemed routine and nonthreatening; men waited to see what would happen next, not imagining that their lives might be at stake. On the third day, vans driven by Austrian police officers pulled up in front of the school, and everyone got in.

"Again, if we had known what was about to happen, a lot of us would have tried to escape, but we had not assumed the worst. I was still speculating whether they had found something in my papers, and that's why I was in trouble, or was it because somebody denounced me? Incidentally, I now believe that my main trouble was first that I was Jewish, and second that I had simply come to their attention, it didn't matter in what way. The vans took us to the railroad station, the Westbahnhof, and we were frightened but glad to be moving at last."

The SS had gained experience in controlling large groups of prisoners in Germany, and this action seems to have been planned to forestall resistance by keeping the eight hundred prisoners in the dark until the last moment. As the final step, the vans had to arrive in an orderly sequence so that men just coming into the station did not see the turmoil before they became part of it.

At the Westbahnhof, guards threw open the vans, and prisoners jumped down into chaos. "When we reached the station and came out of the vans," Bettelheim said, "we saw the SS men in their uniforms. Some had rifles with bayonets, others were hitting people with clubs and whips. They were screaming, cursing, and beating prisoners who had arrived just before us, driving them through the station and into the railway cars. We were totally helpless, and it was too late to run away. Anybody who did that would have been shot, and some were.

"The vans pulled up close to the platform, and there was a train lined up. The SS screamed 'Run!' and they had guns and whips. They made it into a stampede."

TO THE end of his life, Bettelheim remained unwilling to go into detail about what had happened to him as a prisoner, except perhaps when he spoke to someone he trusted totally, like Trude. At one point shortly before he died, I suggested that his silence might make the unknown details seem more monstrous then they were, and he put me in my place with a polite but weary glance that said, "You don't know what you're talking about."

He worried that a fuller knowledge of this experience would disturb his children, who had asked him about it many times. "If you go into this material too deeply it becomes a burden to them, and I don't wish to burden them. Enough has been published about the horrors of the camps without my making it something my children feel personally. There is nothing that happened to me that didn't happen to millions of others, so the cruelty of it is known, widely known. I don't have to add to it, but I will talk to you a little."

AT THE Westbahnhof, SS guards lunged furiously to hit anyone within reach, and the prisoners ran in the only direction left open to them, into the train. The cars were third class, their compartments lined with wooden benches that seated eight, although the guards pushed ten or twelve into each compartment. With the prisoners isolated in small groups, the guards (outnumbered perhaps ten to one) dealt with one compartment at a time.

Bettelheim heard them hitting people in the next compartment, and besides punching and cursing the prisoners, the SS forced them to hit and curse each other, to curse their god, to call their wives and mothers whores. This went on all through the night, and he saw one man dragged out into the corridor, where "two SS played football with him, one kicking him to the other, kicking him with heavy boots."

Bright ceiling lights had been installed in each compartment, and guards ordered everyone not to move but to sit and stare at the lights.

"They were tremendously strong lights, and I think the whole thing was planned to hypnotize." Bettelheim did not mean to hypnotize literally, but to blind, exhaust, and immobilize the prisoners. When the train was under way, the guards stayed in the corridors and watched the compartments. If a prisoner looked away or closed his eyes, a guard would reach in and club the man or drag him out and beat him. However, the SS did not have to wait for an excuse; they brutalized prisoners at random and for hours.

A truncheon blow to the head had broken Bettelheim's glasses, turning everything into a blur. He sat dazed and bleeding but kept himself upright, determined not to fall over or faint. "I wanted to faint, but I knew that if I did, the SS would finish me off, so I didn't. Also it was dangerous not to know what was going on. Actually, it was too crowded to fall over. Looking at the lights was an order, but sometimes the guard's attention was somewhere else, so you didn't obey. But if he saw you with your eyes closed, he hit you."

In the melee, Bettelheim had been stabbed twice with bayonets. "They pushed the bayonet onto you, and it went through the clothes, and if it went through the flesh, they didn't care." With gashes on his left side and right shoulder, he lost a great deal of blood in more than a day on the train. Prisoners could not help each other if wounded, nor could they go down the corridor to the bathroom and relieve themselves, all of which added to their demoralization. Before the trip ended (it lasted about thirty hours), all had been forced to soil themselves.

GUARDS beat Bettelheim about the head more than once, not always for a clear reason, but probably (as he thought later) because they saw him already wounded and bleeding and thus marked as a troublemaker. "From time to time," he said, "they would grab a prisoner and drag him out into the corridor and give him a beating. You could see this through the windows of the compartment, and they would threaten: 'We're going to finish you all off,' 'None of you is going to come alive out of this train.' Screaming, cursing."

At moments he wondered whether he could endure all this without killing himself or going insane; but he also had other, more complex reactions, the most significant of which was to become detached from his panic, his pain, and his overwhelming rage. Caught between the urge to flee and the impulse to fight back, he could do neither. A mood of detachment set in, where everything seemed to be happening to someone else, with himself observing but not feeling.

In another odd reaction, he felt a kind of lofty amusement about how the guards sometimes threatened prisoners. They had a formula, saying over and over that they intended to beat the prisoners to death, because "a bullet costs six pfennigs" and a prisoner wasn't worth it.[3] His amusement at this banality gave him a secret sense of superiority to the SS guards; but he could not react openly without risking death, and in his first hours of crisis, this spontaneous detachment was perhaps the most positive and least destructive response he could make. It denied the reality of the torture he was suffering, a response he saw later as a mechanism that protected personal integration.[4] This reaction to an extreme situation (Bettelheim's term) protected him at first but would not do so for long. Schizophrenia is often defined as a denial of and withdrawal from a reality with which the person cannot cope, a condition that Bettelheim recognized as closely parallel to his involuntary response to SS brutality. He wrote that his split

> into one who observed and one to whom things happened couldn't be called normal, but was a typical psychopathological phenomenon.[5]

The prisoners did not know that their destination was Dachau and could hardly have guessed how long their ordeal would last. Whipping and screaming went on for hours, but then the guards slackened their pace and became less violent. After about half a day an order came down to stop mistreating the prisoners, and the guards stopped. "They found they had intimidated us enough," Bettelheim said.

The train carried almost eight hundred prisoners, of whom Bettelheim estimated about twenty were either killed or had died during the trip. Even in the less brutal atmosphere after the guards eased off, prisoners were still forbidden to tend their own wounds or help one another. Strangely, as the excitement of the guards ebbed, a few of them began chatting with the prisoners, and on the whole they left the prisoners in peace for the rest of the trip; but when the train arrived at Dachau, a fresh contingent of guards beat the prisoners with truncheons and whips to establish their own authority.

The trip had taken all night and most of the next day. On June 3, 1938, that first afternoon in Dachau, a weak and bleeding Bettelheim felt almost grateful to be ordered into a cold shower. "They took all our clothing and put it in a bag, and we were given uniforms after the shower. The uniform was underpants and a shirt and pants, socks, and a jacket. No coat." The bags went into storage in the camp's personal-property room, to be returned to anyone lucky enough to get out; or if the SS shipped a prisoner to another camp, the property bag was shipped along with him.

The prisoners stood in a line at the camp office to get their numbers. Bruno Bettelheim became 15029, to which he answered at roll call or mail call, the number he gave instead of his name when speaking to an SS guard or to anyone in authority.[6] Prisoners wore colored triangles to show the category of their offense, and Bettelheim had two categories: red for his politics (leftist) and yellow for Jewish. On the left breast of his jacket, he sewed the red patch on top the yellow, making the triangles form a Star of David. His number appeared below the patches and on his right trouser leg.

New prisoners also had their heads shaved and got a brief medical exam. The medical officer noticed he was weak from loss of blood and thought he might also have a concussion. Luckily, his injuries were not serious, but he was ordered to the hospital for three days of bed rest and medical attention, such as it was. "I mostly slept," he said. "I was completely exhausted under the shock, and I slept practically all the time." After the hospital he got a week of preferred treatment that let him stay in the barracks instead of going out on a labor detail. He stayed inside for a week, rested, and "did a little easy cleaning." Much later he came to see the beatings and loss of blood as having given him a reprieve to regain his strength, especially his mental strength. He wrote in *Surviving,*

> Had I been projected immediately into the dreadfully destructive grind of deadly mistreatments and utterly exhausting labor, as were my comrades, I do not know whether I would have succeeded equally well in reestablishing some parts of my psychological protective system.[7]

Bettelheim had also lost some teeth, making it painful for him to eat, but his state of mind was worse than his wounds—a deep despair and a revulsion for all food. He loathed the sight and smell of camp food and so ate practically nothing. In the barracks all day, he soon fell into conversation with the *Blockaltester* (barracks commander, or foreman), who noticed the new prisoner's condition and tried to help him. "He showed me the ropes," Bettelheim said, "though as I look back I think I might have figured it out."

The barracks foreman had been in Dachau for four years, almost since the camp's beginning, and as a German socialist he had no prospect of getting out. Jewish prisoners in 1938 could be released when they gave up their property and left the country, but political prisoners like the foreman had little hope. He was part of the leftist prisoner elite that ran Dachau and decided who got the easier jobs. As an old-timer he gave Bettelheim crude but cogent advice: "Eat when you can, sleep when you can, shit when you can."

Bettelheim became convinced both of the soundness of this advice and that he had to find some freedom of action and freedom of thought if he were to survive. He wrote that activity and passivity are the two most basic human attitudes and that the dualities of intake and elimination and of mental activity and rest are the two most basic physiological activities. Even though he could have only a token experience of these freedoms in the camps, he felt the token helped him survive.

> By contrast, it was the senseless tasks, the lack of almost any time to oneself, the inability to plan ahead because of sudden changes in camp policies, that was so deeply destructive. By destroying man's ability to act on his own or to predict the outcome of his actions, they destroyed the feeling that his actions had any purpose, so many prisoners stopped acting. But when they stopped acting they soon stopped living.[8]

In his few days of bed rest and preferred treatment, Bettelheim had reflected on his reactions: What did his spontaneous feelings tell him about himself? And what could he learn from the changes he saw taking place in his fellow prisoners? It didn't happen all at once, but he gradually fell into a pattern of behavior that sustained him in the camps.

"The first experience," he said, "was so overwhelming that you just do nothing but learn the ropes of the camp and try to survive. And after a while you get to learn the routines, you have a little free time, so it's a question of how to spend your free time." Many prisoners seemed delusional, with childlike fantasies and attitudes.

"I felt that if it could happen to them, then it was only a question of time before it happened to me, and I wondered how I could protect myself against it. Could I see how this came about? Then it occurred to me that the very fact I thought about it and observed what was going on was a step toward protecting me against falling into it, and I thought, 'I've got to do more of that.' "

As he did "more of that," he came ultimately to what he later spoke of as a "plan." His first steps were not consistent or coherent, but within two or three months he grasped his unconscious or instinctive purpose, and his strivings became a conscious means of personal survival. He resolved to learn what he could about prisoners, about guards, and about himself; the camp controlled his body, but his mind could keep a small nook of freedom to itself as he explored the psychology of camp behavior.

"When I determined to collect information and analyze what was going on around me," he said, "I was really trying to demonstrate something about myself *to* myself. In order to be autonomous, you really have to demonstrate something to yourself, and that is more important than what you demonstrate to others. Reputation is fine, but your own sense of worth is crucial. Most crucial because what other people think of you may change through no fault of your own, and you still have to live with yourself. That's easier to do if you've demonstrated something to your own satisfaction."

It became clear to Bettelheim that precisely because a prisoner could not act with genuine independence, he had to nurture his sense of himself as still possessing the power to judge and choose some action (or nonaction) with personal meaning, even though the action might be a small one known only to himself. Bettelheim did not claim either that other survivors had taken this approach or that he was the only one to do it, but he believed it worked for him.

"An intellectual defense through understanding firstly gives one the feeling you haven't been completely beaten to a pulp. The less you can act, the more incompetent you feel, and so it becomes even more important to have independence of judgment. This is not a special quality or ability but a willingness, in a way, to swim against the stream. It can develop in a person early on, but I think it's also something nurtured later in life."

Bettelheim later tried to apply the lessons he learned in the camps both to his work and to the tasks of living in society. Given a mass society like ours, where traditions have weakened and opinions push in from all sides to influence behavior, he felt that in order to foster our autonomy we need to avoid an unexamined submission to pressures of the group. Coercion in the camps was an extreme situation, and social coercion is not, but Bettelheim put all such coercive pressures on a continuum insofar as we let them limit the exercise of our autonomy.

"It's so easy to fall in with the crowd, or with the dominant tendency, and going against the stream requires each time a rather complicated decision, as I've tried to describe in writing about the effect of the Hitler salute.9 Each time you go against the stream, it's a tremendous expenditure of mental energy, and at the same time — each time — also a buttressing of your autonomy if you are clear and firm on the grounds of your decision. You risked your life if you didn't give the salute, so it was much simpler merely to do it. But then you felt terrible if you did it simply because you were coerced. On the other hand, if you *decided* to do it each time, knowing you did not mean it but doing it out of your own decision to save your life, then you demonstrated your independence of judgment to yourself. So you do it in that way, unless you are willing to risk your life not to give the salute, which I consider not all that smart."

IN THE spring of 1938 Dachau was a detention and labor camp where many prisoners died from exhaustion, beatings, and other punishments. I asked Bruno's sister, Grete, about her efforts to get him out, and she said that one of her cousins, a lawyer, had advised sending a telegram to the camp commander. Her telegram pointed out that Bettelheim was charged with no political offense and that he had been taken into custody only for protection. She sent the telegram "reply paid" so that the camp commander would have no expense for a return telegram acknowledging Bettelheim's status.

With the commander's answer in hand, Grete and a distant relative (who also had a relation in Dachau) took a night train to Berlin. Jews were forbidden to stay overnight in Berlin hotels, but the two women could go to Gestapo headquarters during the day and take a train back to Vienna that evening.

In Berlin, Grete telephoned the Gestapo and managed to get the right office, but the man (his name was Adler) refused to see her. Her relative had more success; she got an appointment, and Grete decided to take a chance and go with her to Gestapo headquarters. "The guard at the door stopped us, and she gave her name and it was on a list, so he let her in. He looked at me and said, 'Who are you?' and I said, 'I'm with her,' so he let me go in."

Once again Adler refused to see her, but she waited in the hall outside his office. She wanted to speak to him simply to push along the paperwork that would get Bruno out of the camp. He had his exit visa, he had "sold" his property, he had a sponsor in America, and the camp commander's telegram confirmed that there was no political charge against him. If she could say all this to Adler, perhaps he would take Bruno's case out of file and act on it.

As she sat on a bench in the hallway, she noticed two Gestapo officers walking down a flight of stairs from the floor above. They were laughing and talking, and finally they paused and said, "Heil Hitler!" One went back up the stairway, and the other came down to the floor where Grete waited.

"I got up and went to him and said, 'May I talk to you for a moment?' He looked me up and down and said, 'What is it?' He probably knew I was Jewish. Anybody who didn't say 'Heil Hitler!' was Jewish." She told him her story and said she hoped to see the official who was her brother's referee. "So the officer looked me up and down again and said, 'Wait here.' He went into the office and then came out and said, 'He'll see you.' That's how I got in. I showed the referee the telegram, and he said, 'I see what I can do.' He had Bruno's file there, and that was it. I went back to Vienna."

THE FIRST wave of prisoners sent to Dachau in 1933 had been criminals and men with outlawed political views, such as communism and socialism. The "politicals" became the prisoner elite, a network of communists and their friends who controlled the best jobs and any favors that might be done for a prisoner. No Jew could hold a position of power among the prisoners or become a barracks foreman or the *kapo* of a detail. Usually he could not get an office or kitchen job, or any assignment that did not require hard labor, unless he had a close gentile friend in the system who would help keep him off work details that were exhausting or dangerous.

From time to time, the power of German political prisoners declined, and the criminals took over. Eugen Kogon says in his book about Buchenwald that the SS actually preferred criminals holding power, because they were more brutal toward their fellow prisoners.[10] But sooner or later the criminal elite would create a scandal, and then power would revert to the politicals, who would dispense jobs and favors once again—and, also, rough treatment.

"The prisoner's worst enemy is the prisoner" became a common saying in the camps.[11] SS violence struck unexpectedly and passed quickly, but the menace of the prisoner elite remained a constant.

Prisoner foremen exerted pressure without letup; one felt it continuously—during the day at work, and all night in the barracks.[12]

For example, a barracks foreman might roust prisoners out of bed in the middle of the night and order double-time laps around the barracks for some real or imagined infraction—harshness that served the ends of the SS very well.

In cold weather only elite prisoners could wear overcoats. They also enjoyed extra food, as a result of helping friends get jobs in the kitchen. On the other hand, if something went wrong in the barracks or on a work detail, the barracks foreman or the *kapo* would be flogged. The other prisoners felt grateful that one person bore the punishment for all, but the SS took care not to let heroes emerge from the mass of prisoners, who might lead an uprising.

Not many of the prisoner elite managed to resist the chances for bribery that their limited powers offered, but

> a few outstanding persons used their positions with daring and unselfishness to better the lot of common prisoners. There were a few super-kapos who successfully interfered with an SS private mistreating prisoners, but they were the exception, since their action called for extraordinary courage.[13]

The German politicals remained in power at Dachau while Bettelheim was there, and his background as a Social Democrat helped him with the friendly barracks foreman, whom he suspected was actually a communist afraid to identify himself as such, because it was relatively safer to be thought a socialist.

Being in the power network had both benefits and drawbacks, but Bettelheim believed that in the long run the system worked mainly to the advantage of the SS, that only the SS

> benefited from the inner warfare among prisoners for survival and positions of power. In the fully developed oppressive mass state even the victim's efforts to organize in self defense seemed to work toward personality disintegration.
>
> It is relatively easy to show why this had to happen when a single overwhelming organization, the SS, was pitted against a very weak one whose members felt they could only succeed by cooperating with the

powerful opponent. It may be harder to realize that the same held true
for the individual prisoner's psychological defenses.[14]

I asked Bettelheim to be more specific about what he had in mind in
this passage, and he replied, "I wanted to establish a parallel between
what goes on in the individual and what goes on amongst the groups. The
groups I had in mind were the socialists and the communists. They
should have made common cause, and occasionally they did make common cause against the criminals. But the communists did battle against
the socialists when the criminals were not dominant, and I was trying to
make this conflict compare to inner processes. I had friends in both
camps, of course, but I didn't identify myself with either one of them. My
position was that the camp was not the place where we should argue
against each other—we had to cooperate to survive."

The idea that individual mental processes are in some ways similar to
group processes is an insight I wish Bettelheim had pursued in his writings. He saw that prisoners had to cooperate for their best chance to survive but wasted energy fighting each other; likewise, a prisoner could
spend great energy on violent fluctuations of feeling when his impulses
were in conflict and out of control. Panicked by extreme events he could
not escape, such a prisoner might fall apart, and to Bettelheim this was the
greatest danger in the camps. The overwhelming pressures of the environment, made worse by the malice of the SS, were terrifying enough; but to
Bettelheim the loss of psychological defenses and the crumbling of personal integration—the loss of self—finally seemed decisive in bringing
the prisoner to grief.

EACH BUNK in the barracks at Dachau had a coverlet of blue and white
squares. Two rows of double bunks had to line up exactly, with the coverlet pattern repeating perfectly from one end of the barracks to the other.
Prisoners smoothed their straw mattresses to the same height; if an SS
guard wished, he could fire a bullet that would skim just over a row of
bunks and not muss a coverlet. Straw pillows had to be squared off
neatly; the whole barracks could be punished for sightlines that deviated
noticeably.

A siren woke the prisoners, usually between four and five a.m.,
although in summer they could be roused as early as three-fifteen if the
camp commander felt like it. They had about forty-five minutes to shave,

get dressed, use a crowded toilet, have a piece of black bread and a cup of cheap coffee, make their bunks, and clean up their area. Mornings were a frantic scramble as men rushed to do what they had to do; fistfights broke out when prisoners bumped into each other or when newcomers could not get the hang of things and made mistakes. Sixty men had to use a handful of washbasins, and they wasted precious time waiting in line. Lines also formed at the latrines, and tempers flared when those waiting urged those using the latrines to hurry up.

The barracks foreman assigned Bettelheim to an upper bunk, and this presented a problem in the mornings. The upper bunk could be made only by standing on the lower bunk, and if the lower bunk had been made first, making the upper could ruin the neatness of the lower. If the new-comer could not make his bed perfectly, somebody else had to, or every-one else might suffer. Old-timers earned a little money by offering to make a new prisoner's bed. "I was very clumsy," Bettelheim said. "I paid until I learned it. Eventually, you learn it, but it took me a long time." (Prisoners could get small sums of money from home to use in the camp.)

Austrians like Bettelheim who came to the camps in 1938 had an extra problem: older prisoners (mostly German and gentile) hated them and ridiculed them for the polite manner of speech typical of Austrians at that time. It was only verbal harshness, but the cursing and ridicule made things feel worse.

THE MOST serious offense one prisoner could commit against another was to spy for the SS. When prisoners caught one of their number spying, they warned him he would be killed if he did it again; if he was caught a second time, they beat him to death. The SS did not punish such acts.

The offense next in seriousness was to steal bread. "We were given a loaf of bread every three days," Bettelheim said, "and it was quite nourish-ing—black, very coarse black bread. That was still in peacetime, and the bread was most important to us. When someone stole bread he was hardly ever denounced to the SS, because he would be punished so severely that he was practically finished off. But the other prisoners beat him—if they caught him—because bread was a matter of life and death."

Prisoners ate in the barracks, or wherever they happened to be work-ing at noontime; a huge bucket of soup was carried from the camp kitchen, and they stood in line with a metal bowl and a spoon. The barracks commander or his assistant ladled out the soup. "There could be a difference in what you got," Bettelheim said, "depending upon whether or not the prisoner who dished it out stirred the soup each time so that everyone got about the same amount of meat or vegetables, maybe potatoes. But he could skim from the top where the soup was watery. An honest one stirred each time, but there were others.

"Somebody could come along that they didn't like, they would take it from the top, and there was nothing you could do. Usually there was something left over, so that for a few there was a second serving. Again, it depended on the prisoner who dished it out, whether he gave it to those who were weak and needed additional food, or whether he gave it to his friends."

Shocked, depressed, with a battered mouth and broken teeth, Bettelheim did not want to eat. "In Dachau they started to use whale meat, which at first I found disgusting but later found nourishing," he said, referring not only to the unpleasant oiliness and smell of whale meat but to his aversion to food, which he had to overcome by forcing himself to eat.

The conscious choice to live made eating more bearable as a personal decision. The SS controlled everything, including the camp food, but a prisoner could choose to eat or not to eat. If he chose to eat, then the act of eating was not in fact imposed by the SS, who could not care less if the prisoner starved to death. For Bettelheim, eating became a "self-chosen act of freedom."

After he got over his revulsion, Bettelheim thought the food in Dachau was "all right." He added that "they had a canteen where the prisoners could buy things. There was a wide variety of excellent food, and as a matter of fact the SS liked that, because they made profits, selling at a price several times what it would cost outside. You could go there for coffee and doughnuts, and all kinds of foods, delectable foods you could buy there. And the same SS men when they were taking your money in the canteen, or served you, they were perfectly polite. They would joke, 'Oh, that's real good,' and whatnot. No mistreatment in the canteen, never. But when you went out, it was the other way around. Completely schizophrenic."

Not everyone had money to buy food at the canteen, and many prisoners were still hungry after a grueling day. "In Dachau the camp commander was an uneducated crude fellow," Bettelheim said, "and on Sundays we had to march in review and sing the camp songs. One day the commander said, 'Why don't these guys sing with more gusto?' An SS man said, 'They're hungry, and you can't sing with much gusto if you're hungry.' So the commander ordered a second serving, which we got, an ample serving for three days. Then it came back to what it was. You know, these things were so without rhyme or reason."

BETTELHEIM said that he battled consciously against depression. "To be depressed was such a natural reaction that you had to make special efforts to pull yourself out of it. You just wanted to crawl into a corner and give in. For me, some of the most depressing moments—well, not the only ones—were when you had to stand at the assembly place for hours. You couldn't talk—talking with others was forbidden—and you couldn't move much. Imperceptibly only."

In their off hours prisoners often talked with each other about their businesses or professional backgrounds. "When things were quiet and hunger wasn't too great, someone might talk about his specialty; he tried to educate others.[15] I don't know how much education one got, but at least you felt you were not a vegetable. Of course, having a relationship to somebody was one of the best ways to combat depression, so you dragged yourself out of your corner and tried to talk—about politics, about world affairs, about your hopes for the future." However, he didn't talk freely to everyone. "With some of the prison elite I was careful, and with others I was quite friendly. Many of them were communists or socialists and very intelligent and interesting." Bettelheim also said that in conversations he had to guard against megalomania and unrealistic hopes, because the backlash was too painful when his hopes evaporated.

Sometimes he got up early to steal a few free moments before the day started; then he'd trade rumors and gossip, inferring things from chance remarks elsewhere in the camp on the previous day. If the SS radio operator happened to step outside the radio shack, a prisoner working there could spin the dial and bring back word of the outside world. Scraps of news or total fantasies gave rise to wild rumors that swept from one barracks to the next. These early-morning rumor sessions had little grounding in reality, but Bettelheim took part avidly. He said that early one morning about a month after he came to Dachau, he suddenly caught sight of his frenzy in the midst of swapping rumors, and a thought flashed into his head: "This is driving me crazy."

It pulled him up short and warned him to get a grip on himself; he remained eager to hear rumors but modified his involvement by trying to see what he could understand about prisoners who repeated and embellished them—a defense in line with his effort to observe others and think about what was happening to them so that it wouldn't happen to him.

> Soon I realized I had found a solution to my main problem: by occupying myself whenever possible with problems that interested me, by talking with my fellow prisoners and comparing impressions, I was able to feel I was doing something constructive and on my own.[16]

He believed that using his mind in this way saved him, but when he began, it would have been "whistling in the dark on my part to view it so positively."[17] How long did it take for him to begin this kind of inquiry in a regular way? "Probably three months," he said, "before I had enough freedom in my own mind to study the situation and try to understand it, try to analyze it. You had to *resolve* to try to survive."

Bettelheim repeated his observations to himself, memorized his data, and rehearsed information while at work or on the assembly ground. Psychologically, the systematic research that helped him survive owed little to psychoanalysis. Freud had fascinated Bettelheim as long as he had a comfortable middle-class life, but in an extreme situation psychoanalysis was beside the point.

> Such realizations were not easy for me, but I had to arrive at them quickly if I wished to survive, and in ways I could approve of. . . . I had to accept that the environment could, as it were, turn personality upside down, and not just in the small child, but in the mature adult too. If I wanted to keep it from happening to me, I had to accept this potentiality of the environment, to decide where not to adjust, and how far. Psychoanalysis, as I understood it, was of no help in this all important decision.[18]

Prisoners faced sudden moments of crisis when an action or inaction could lead to disaster. For Bettelheim, what a person did in a crisis was more important than his motives, which were often ambivalent. Those who acted decently became better men, whereas those who did not became worse.

> As long as my own life was running its well ordered course, I could indulge myself by believing that the working of my unconscious

mind was, if not my "true" self, certainly my "deeper" self. But when at one moment my own life, at the next moment that of others, depended on my actions, then I concluded that my actions were much more my "true" self than my unconscious or preconscious motives.[19]

When Freud created psychoanalysis he saw society as a reasonably benign setting in which people could build satisfying lives, and as they understood themselves better, they could reassess their actions and hopes. Bettelheim in 1938 was thrown into an environment that demanded huge adjustments, where he felt the power of a hostile milieu to reshape men or destroy them altogether, and his psychoanalytic experience did prove helpful in one way.

It gave me a deeper understanding of what may have gone on in the unconscious of prisoners and guards, an understanding that on occasion may have saved my life and on other occasions let me be of help to some of my fellow prisoners.[20]

At the mercy of sworn enemies, Bettelheim came to realize that he had to keep himself from crossing a personal shadow line, an unmarked point of no return

to a life that had lost all its meaning. It would mean to survive as a man, not a walking corpse, as a debased and degraded but still human being, one had first and foremost to remain informed and aware of what made up one's personal point of no return, the point beyond which one would never, under any circumstances, give in to the oppressor, even if it meant risking and losing one's life. It meant being aware that if one survived at the price of overreaching this point one would be holding on to a life that had lost all its meaning. It would mean surviving—not with a lowered self respect, but without any.[21]

This point, he said, differed from one person to another and would even change with the passing of time. If a prisoner acted in obedience to a degrading order, as he often had to do to survive, he could not afford to give up his feelings—his indignation, his outrage, and his moral reservations about the act. This was crucial. A numbed response to debasement by the SS was understandable but subversive in that it suppressed feelings that made up the essence of the person's character. Bettelheim said that he learned to look at each undesirable act for its effect on survival and to decide whether the act was good, bad, or neutral in that regard. At the same time he kept a distance, small though it might be, from his own behavior, because the distance gave him the freedom to pass judgment on what he had done (or was about to do) and to adopt, with full awareness, the attitude most suitable at that moment.

> Those prisoners who blocked out neither heart nor reason, neither feelings nor perception, but kept informed on their inner attitudes even when they could hardly ever afford to act on them, those prisoners survived and came to understand the conditions they lived under. They also came to realize what they had not perceived before; that they still retained the last, if not the greatest of human freedoms: to choose their own attitude in any given circumstance.[22]

Personal integrity often clashed with survival, and so Bettelheim tried first to manage his internal conflicts. Mindful of his point of no return, he looked for a way consistent with his deepest values to resolve any survival dilemma. One of his friends had such a revulsion to food that he refused to eat and gave his ration to other prisoners. "The food was not very tasty, in fact it was disgusting, but you could get over it. Somehow my friend's autonomy, or whatever you would call it, would not let him eat the food. That was extremely self-destructive, but this is an example of how these things [personal integrity at odds with survival] might work against each other. His self-respect required him not to eat his food, and so he gave it away and it did him in."

BETTELHEIM quoted an old-timers' maxim that if a man survived three weeks, he'd survive a year; three months, and he'd live three years.[23] The saying was not literally true, but many deaths occurred soon after a new group of prisoners arrived, and the numbers declined in the weeks following. Bettelheim estimated the early death rate at about 30 percent when he was in Dachau.[24]

Old prisoners and the SS played a cruel joke on some new prisoners by telling them they had to report to an office for castration. In reality, the SS castrated only "race polluters" and some sex offenders, but many newcomers asked for directions to the castration office; their attitude of total obedience was, for Bettelheim, a sure path to self-destruction. He felt that he and some others had protected themselves by making a split between their inner and outer lives, a strategy that sounds schizophrenic but wasn't.

"It's a difficult thing to explain," he said. "You couldn't simply pretend to submit, because if you didn't to some degree mean it, the SS would recognize you were pretending, and they would kill you. I talk a great deal about the identification with the aggressor, the identification with the SS, or with their values. If you did this, you certainly increased your chances to survive, but on the other hand, you lost yourself. So actually, what you had to strive for was a viable balance between conforming to the degree that was necessary for your survival, and not conforming to the degree that you could get away with. If you did it right, you saved your self-respect. And you had to do this at all times, which wasn't easy—to recognize that, you know."

An extreme situation made emotional detachment a dangerous relief. Feelings had to be blocked lest they lead to punishment; but they also had to be inwardly acknowledged to avoid the loss of one's capacity for spontaneous response, because such loss deadened the self.

IN HIS introduction to *Unconscious Contributions to One's Undoing*, Bettelheim drew parallels between abused prisoners and abused children.[25] Such children feel that their protector has mistreated and rejected them, and since the parent rules the child's world, the betrayal is overwhelming. An abused child (and this includes psychological abuse) feels incompetent and worthless; his feelings flood his inner life and lead to self-destructive attitudes and acts. In the same way, the fact that a prisoner could not respond with open anger at SS brutality demeaned and demoralized him as much as the brutality itself. Bettelheim added that a therapist cannot overcome a child's history of abuse unless the child himself at some point works at it; similarly, a prisoner had to work consciously to avoid demoralization.

Bettelheim saw our inner and outer lives not merely as an intricate interplay or interweaving, but as two different expressions of (or perspectives on) the single phenomenon of consciousness. To repair the results of emotional damage, changing the outside is not enough; we have to deal constructively with our consciousness of what happened to us *inside*— how we saw, felt, and interpreted the experience—and we must take some action relating to it.[26]

The prisoner lived in a milieu in which he was powerless, so his feelings on that score were realistic, but they weakened him the more he yielded to them. If he could leave off dwelling on bad feelings and turn his attention to some positive aspect of himself, he felt a fleeting relief; and if he examined bad feelings rather than repeating or denying them, he had used the one freedom available to him. He might suffer the blows of a truncheon and go back to the barracks for nothing better than a loathsome bowl of soup; but if he could turn aside the inner blows to his self-esteem so that they did not fill his mind, he had a better chance. He did not control his outer world but could influence his inner world to make it slightly more livable. At any rate, such was Bettelheim's defense against the camp's demonic powers.

SOME PRISONERS found a defense in strong religious beliefs or convictions they didn't have before, and others relied on communist beliefs. "Some communists developed—you could call it a defense or a delusion, or whatever—the idea that the rise of Hitler and the camps was all a brilliant plan of Stalin to see to it that Germany and all of Europe became communist. I knew communists who held to this belief, and it supported them. It was not much of a defense in reality, but to a communist it was. They were convinced they were going to be the rulers of Germany, you know? In an extreme situation, which I called this, one develops certain defenses; they're necessary, or you die."

The Dukes of Hohenberg were in Dachau, and Bettelheim recalled that they were mistreated but stood up well when guards singled them out for abuse.[27] "Of course, this was the kind of distinction that confirmed their special identity, so in that way it would strengthen them for a moment. Being special helped them in this situation. You see, in their own minds, they were always surrounded by rebels anyhow. You might say that their self-esteem was based on a kind of snobbish illusion, though perhaps that's not exactly how I should put it.

"I think everybody feels special to himself—everybody. I felt this, and it helped me, as it helped anybody who could do it. It was a prop. Whatever you could do to feel special was a survival technique. I hope I don't pretend anything else about what I did, except that it was a survival technique for me. In fact, it turned out to be really different in that I could understand and could write a book. But I tried to say in the book that the way I did it in the camp was simply my survival technique. Other people did other things."

One psychological surprise Bettelheim mentioned in *The Informed Heart* was how well Jehovah's Witnesses dealt with camp stress. When I asked about this, he said that according to psychoanalytic theory they were thought relatively fragile, in that they had weak egos dominated by strong superegos, whereas in a well-adjusted person the ego stands up against the demands of the superego and the pressures of the id.

"After all," Bettelheim said, "the ego is invested with energy because of its services to the total personality, its main task being to preserve the life and well-being of the individual, and a person's ego just wasn't in a good position to do this in the camps. You see, egos didn't protect people in this situation, and so they distrusted themselves. This was one of the aims of the camp, to break down personality. But Jehovah's Witnesses stood up very well if their superego required them to stand up well. In one respect psychoanalysis was correct in that it said that the person has to approve of what he does, and it was valuable to me to understand that."

BETTELHEIM'S story of Dachau is long on analysis and short on brutality. However, his friend Ernst Federn, son of the psychoanalyst, Paul Federn, had no reluctance to talk about things that Bettelheim, for his own reasons, avoided. Ernst and Bruno had not known each other in Vienna and did not meet in Dachau, although they were there at the same time. Both were upper-middle-class assimilated Jews, but Ernst was eleven years younger than Bruno and much more of a political idealist. In 1934, at the age of twenty, he had joined wholeheartedly in the desperate leftish push to overthrow the oppressive Austrian government, and when the revolt had failed, he'd been arrested and held for four months. His name went on a list as a Trotskyite and Revolutionary Socialist, and four years later, when Austria joined Germany, the police took him into custody at once. They held him incommunicado for more than two months, then turned him over to the SS, who shipped him to Dachau shortly before the action that swept up Bettelheim and others.

The personal details in Federn's interview gave me a sense of Dachau that my various conversations with Bruno had not. For instance, they both spoke of favoritism in ladling out soup, but Bruno seemed to accept it as inevitable; Federn's story showed me how realistic Bruno had been, because when Federn protested the unfairness of not stirring the soup (so that everyone got a scrap of meat), his barracks foreman beat him into silence.

Federn also told of the frantic early-morning scramble in the barracks, where one day he squeezed his feet into someone else's shoes—shoes a size too small. By the time he realized his mistake he was pushing a wheelbarrow on the work site, and he stayed on his feet until they were raw and bleeding. At last he gave up and sat down, not caring what would happen. Guards seized him; in short order he was tried, convicted of the crime of refusing to work, and sentenced to hang on the "tree," a pole near Dachau's front gate. A rope bound his hands behind his back and was passed over the top of the pole, so that he could be hoisted up for everyone to see. He hung there for an hour with his arms twisted upward behind his back, a punishment the SS had copied from the Habsburg army.[28] He was hanged in this way at noon on Saturday, June 29; he remembered the exact date, he said pleasantly, because it was his father-in-law's birthday. The wrenching of his arm sockets could have crippled him and led to his death in the camp, but he quickly recovered the use of his arms. The damage from the shoes was permanent, and when I saw him he walked with a kind of pained hobble.

"Everybody worried about me because I was the first of the Viennese that this happened to, and when friends helped me into the street where our barracks was, people came up to me and said, 'How are you?' And I said—it just came out of my mouth—'Coming down is so *niiiiiice* that it overdoes [makes you forget or disregard] what happened.' It went through the whole camp, 'Ernst came down and made a joke.' Years later a man came up to me and said, 'I will never forget that you could *say* this.' It's my personality—whatever happens, I take it. As someone said, I always fall off the other side."

BETTELHEIM spoke little of what he actually did in the camps, in part, I believe, because he did not seek either sympathy or praise. He knew and said that many suffered more than he did, and no doubt he also knew some who were more heroic or stoic. However, to illustrate a point about how prisoners felt, he told of joining a work detail outside the camp, digging a ditch through the streets of Dachau to link the camp's sewer to the city's system. He had a vivid memory of a hot day when a guard ordered a prisoner to go into a nearby house for a bucket of water to be shared by prisoners and guards. Nothing else happened to make the event memorable, but the scene stayed with him, perhaps as a rare moment when he saw himself once more in the outside world. His point was that if prisoners could see civilians and be seen by them (especially by women and children), they did not feel so cut off from the rest of humanity.

At one point Bettelheim also dug trenches inside the camp, carted stone, and laid it flat to hold a drainpipe. As a rule he tried to avoid this work, although he said it was not as bad as the senseless labor. "You had to carry heavy stones from one end of the camp to the other, and then you had to carry them back. Or you had to run with them, and the guards chased you and hit you." For a time he joined the "Moor Express," a heavy open cart pulled by sixteen prisoners. "The advantage was that you were only one of the sixteen. If they hit, they hit randomly, any one of the sixteen."

One day Bettelheim's work detail came upon an SS officer beating a prisoner, and the *kapo* ordered his men to break into a run. They were not supposed to notice such things, and so they fled past with their faces turned away. They saw, but by pretending not to see, they showed

> clearly that they had accepted the command not to know what they were not supposed to know.[29]

As the men ran by, the SS officer called out, "Well done!" in a friendly voice but went on beating his prisoner. Bettelheim concluded that in curbing men's faculty to see and respond, the SS aimed to assault their self-determination. He argued that to see things, to have an inner response, and to draw a conclusion is "where independent existence begins."[30] Those who actually gave up seeing and responding within themselves had internalized the ethos of the camp. Prisoners who did this became childlike:

> To know only what those in authority allow one to know is, more or less, all the infant can do. . . . Deliberate non-use of one's power of observation, as opposed to temporary inattention, which is different, leads to a withering away of this power.[31]

Bettelheim also pointed out that the SS did not in fact expect total obedience; the unwritten rule that everyone knew and lived by was simply *Don't get caught.*[32]

HAVING no work assignment also incurred a risk, the danger of being noticed after roll call. Prisoners without assignments scurried across the parade ground to join one of the larger work groups and melt into the mass.

> This enforced anonymity was a successful defense against the real dangers of the camp. But it meant making deliberate efforts to give up individuality and initiative, qualities much needed for the constantly changing emergencies of the camp situation.[33]

Nevertheless, men were desperate to improve their chances by switching from one work group to another. "If you wanted to get out of a work detail," Bettelheim said, "the thing to do was to find a friend of the foreman and give him a few cigarettes, or a good talk, or make a case that you couldn't survive. Whatever seemed to work. You still risked your life if you did this."

What about the prisoner who had nothing to trade or bribe with? "Well, everybody had something. It might be thought that some hadn't, but, you see, some prisoners traded a part of their rations, their bread. That was also deadly, to try to trade your rations." Bettelheim could have traded some of his food, because he ate sparsely and reluctantly, but he didn't think it safe to trade. "I didn't trade anything, I never traded, because that was dangerous, to trade. My cigarettes I always gave away. I never traded, I never asked anything for it, because it was better for the person I gave it to if he didn't promise anything, and it was better for me if I didn't ask."

His sense of Dachau told him it was more prudent to build up casual friendships than to create obligations, so he bought cigarettes at the canteen and gave them away—cigarettes, because that was the best way to make friends. "I could always say, yes, I gave my cigarettes to a friend. That was accepted. You had to be friendly with everybody, because anybody could do you in. Very few could help you, but those who could were terribly important."

The *kapos* could help more than anyone else, and since Dachau had more than fifty labor commands, men tried to find the ones best for survival. Bettelheim guessed that in eleven months in two camps, he had worked in twenty different commands.

BETTELHEIM made a translation for me of one letter he wrote his mother from Dachau:

CONZENTRATIONCAMP DACHAU 3 K

The following orders are to be observed in the correspondence

1. Each prisoner in protective custody is permitted to receive and to send two letters or postcards during a month. The letters to the prisoner must be readily legible and written in ink and must not contain more than 15 lines on a page. Only letterpages of normal size are permitted. Envelopes must not be lined. In one letter not more than five 12-penny stamps may be included. Everything else is not permitted and will be confiscated. Post cards are to contain only ten lines. Photos are not permitted to be used as postcards.

2. Mailing of money is permitted.

3. Newspapers are permitted, but must be ordered through the postoffice of the concentration camp Dachau.

4. Packages are not permitted, since the prisoners can buy everything in the camp.

5. Petitions for discharge directed to the camp administration are purposeless.

6. Permission to speak with prisoners and visits to the camp are in principle not permitted.

All mail which does not conform to these rules will be destroyed.

—THE COMMANDER OF THE CAMP.

Name Bettelheim Bruno
Born on August 28, 1903
Block 22 room: 3.
Dachau 3 K the 28th of August 1938
My dearest! First a request: could you subscribe for me besides or instead of the Presse *the Frankfurter* Zeitung* *subscribe from September 1st on? I read only on Sundays, but then it helps pass the time to read the papers of the week and banishes a little the desolate thoughts—Rest assured about the ingrown hairs, they cause me only a little inconvenience.† Please give my condolences to Erika and her*

---

*The *Presse* was a Viennese paper, and Bettelheim ordered the *Allgemeine Zeitung,* a German newspaper, so he could give it to a German member of the prisoner elite who had done him a favor.

†His mother had asked about a minor problem that he mentioned in a previous letter, and her concern about a trivial complaint infuriated him, even though he realized she was only trying to show her sympathy.

family; as far as I am concerned I envy her husband. — * By now I have been already three months imprisoned and you can imagine my mood on this day,† the more so since I have no idea how long it will last. But please do not send me any encouragement unless it is fully justified, because otherwise it only makes for disappointment. Send me please each week RM 15–. Answer the following questions: Is the furniture in a warehouse?‡ How do you fare in regards to money? How much have you received in the meantime on your account? Take steps to get it through an attorney, also the advance of my balance. What do you hear from Norbert? How does it stand with the health of my cousin Richard, the husband of Hansi? Gina should travel in time to Cuba,§ before it gets too late; she is not to take any risks. Is she well? Edith should take care of her. All my love and all my longings are with her and all of you. How is Mina's health? I hope you all live well with each other and help each other in these hard times. If Grete has any chance for Colombia she should go there. On my account she need not and should not remain in Vienna; equally should Trude see to it that she gets away. I send her my most heartfelt greetings. Gina writes that only the hope for a better future maintains her, and that she works for it and she should not get tired of it. I embrace her and you all and send my best to all relatives and friends.

—Your Bruno

The censor's stamp appears at the bottom of this letter, along with the words "Control of the block leader."

A little less than a month later, Grete went to Munich because she got word that Bruno would be released from Dachau, and she wanted to meet him and go with him back to Vienna. However, on September 23 Bettel-

---

*Bettelheim's mother had told him that Erika's husband was dead.

†August 28 was Bettelheim's thirty-fifth birthday, and the thought of it agitated and depressed him. In years past, his birthday had become an occasion for a little teasing by friends like the Willigs, because it was the same date as Goethe's birthday. "We made jokes about it every year," Hans Willig said. "And he was pleased and very flattered," Wanda Willig added.

‡Bettelheim did not know it, but not long before he asked this question, the Viennese police had permitted some of the furnishings of his apartment to be shipped out of the country. His mother, his sister, and Trude had gone to the apartment to close it. The three women worked for several days packing furniture and putting various belongings in crates. Among other items, they packed the Egon Schiele painting that Bruno liked so much and shipped it off to Gina in America.

§Many refugees went to Cuba so they could reenter the States on a permanent visa.

heim left Dachau with a group of prisoners being shipped to another camp. Much later, a distant relative (also in Dachau) told Grete that Bruno's name had been called three times over the public-address system just after the prisoners left.

"If Bruno had still been in Dachau," she said, "he would have been home in a few days." She added that when Bruno did not answer, the SS clerk would have thrown out the order for his release rather than sending it on to the next camp.

CHAPTER 6

From Bad to Worse

IN THE summer of 1937, the SS began clearing land on the slopes of Ettersburg, a small mountain five miles north of Weimar. More than a century earlier, in the age of Goethe and Schiller, Weimar had gained worldwide fame as a center of German culture, a distinction renewed under the Weimar Republic, when Germany's capital moved there from the Prussian city of Berlin after the nation's defeat in the First World War.

An aristocratic Nazi landowner had left the Ettersburg property to the SS in his will, 370 acres of pine and hardwood forest on rocky and uneven ground, in a situation known for its harsh and unpredictable climate. Even in summer, drifting fog and low clouds often obscured the 1,568-foot peak of Ettersburg. With its rough and inhospitable character, the spot was a promising site for a new concentration camp, a camp planned and built to last so that when the barracks were no longer needed for prisoners, SS troops could live and train there. In July 1937 the SS brought the first group of prisoners to the mountainside to clear out trees, stumps, tangled roots, and underbrush, and this work proceeded throughout the fall.

The bequest also contained a famous tree, the huge and beautiful "Goethe oak," around which a legend, possibly true, had grown up. Several generations repeated the story that Goethe had often visited the mountainside when he wanted to get away from the turmoils of Weimar, and also when he met the married woman with whom he had an intense platonic relation for ten years. If he and Charlotte von Stein actually sat under this tree and exchanged ideas on art and culture, as they were said to have done, they had a lovely and serene view of the Thuringian countryside, with the Harz Mountains in the far distance. The SS spared the great oak for its cultural associations and also because it was covered by the Nature Protection Act. They even designated it as the "center" of the new camp, which soon became notorious for the violent abuse of prisoners. In eight years fifty-six thousand men would die there by starvation, disease, and murder.

At first the SS called the new camp Ettersburg, but a problem soon arose over its name. When word of the camp leaked out of Germany, news reports said that Ettersburg had been planned, at least in part, as a place to imprison Jews. Goebbels made a speech denying this and declared that no "Camp Ettersburg" existed, that the story was a lie spread by Germany's enemies. However, since the camp did exist, its name had to be changed, and toward the end of 1937 "Ettersburg" became Buchenwald.

LATE IN September 1938, an announcement suddenly came over the public-address system at Dachau ordering Jewish prisoners to pack their belongings after the last meal of the day and get ready for a trip. No one knew what this order meant except that Jews would be taken somewhere else. Where? They would find out when they got there. Everyone feared the train ride because of the beatings and blinding lights on the train from Vienna, but the trip went off without incident. "They gave us each a piece of bread," Bettelheim said, "and then they didn't bother us." Twelve hundred Jews were shipped from Dachau that evening, September 23, and another eleven hundred followed the next day.

The SS may have transported these prisoners without brutalizing them because they had already been "initiated" and there was no need to do it again. When the train reached Weimar and the jurisdiction changed from Dachau to Buchenwald, new guards fell on the prisoners in full fury. Bettelheim said that the Buchenwald guards "started to beat us because we were new to them, and they were afraid of us. They had to establish terror, their terror. We knew nothing about Buchenwald then. You learned about the other camps only when a prisoner was transferred, but at that time nobody had been transferred out of Buchenwald. The SS didn't have good quarters yet, and their life wasn't well regulated, so they had more to take out on the prisoners. We actually built the facilities at Buchenwald, and it was hard labor.

"It was a more cruel place, also. In Buchenwald a prisoner who broke down and went crazy was ridiculed and chased by the guards until he died. It was talked about quite openly, that somebody's going to be finished off, meaning killed." Here for the first time Bettelheim saw "moslems," the camp term for those who had become totally demoralized, showed little emotion, and were starving. They looked like scarecrows, spoke hardly at all, and shuffled when they walked; if given food unexpectedly, they took it with a brief but "grateful hangdog look." They scavenged for garbage, and barracks foremen and SS guards alike beat them. Bettelheim himself had lost considerable weight before he reached Buchenwald, but many of his fellow prisoners from Dachau were noticeably well fed, unlike those already in the new camp.

BUCHENWALD was at first a concentration camp for those in "protective custody" but soon became an important labor camp for armaments. SS Colonel Karl Otto Koch commanded the camp as a whole, and he put SS Major Arthur Rödl in charge of the prison section. Rödl had been at Hitler's side in Munich in 1923 when the Nazis tried to overthrow the Weimar government, and at Buchenwald he found ample reward for his loyalty.

Under Koch and Rödl the camp's brutality became legendary. Bettelheim avoided personal details in this regard, which led me to conclude that he had a lot to forget from his time in Buchenwald. My account of life there comes mostly from *The Theory and Practice of Hell* by Eugen Kogon, with some information from Ernst Federn. In one notorious incident in the spring of 1938 (before Bettelheim was there), a Gypsy prisoner escaped but was quickly caught. Koch ordered the man put into a cramped wooden box where he could not stand, sit, or lie down, but could only crouch. Chicken wire covered the front of the box so other prisoners could see him, and nails pierced the wooden sides to make him cut himself with the slightest movement. The man was displayed in the roll-call area for nearly three days, until his screams grew hoarse and animal-like. After the third night, Koch ordered him killed by an injection of poison.

The roll-call area also had a special flogging rack. Guards strapped the naked prisoner facedown on it, with his chest flat on the surface of the rack and his legs drawn forward underneath the rack. Bending the prisoner in a U-shape exposed his buttocks to maximum whipping.

SS regulations called for a medical examination of the prisoner before flogging, but doctors never found anyone unfit for the lash. Some took it without uttering a sound, and others didn't. "When the screaming began to irk the officers," Kogon reports, "they would order the band to strike up a march."[1]

One time SS Major Rödl had an opera singer stand next to the rack and sing arias while the flogging went on.

SS Sergeant Martin Sommer has earned a place in any brief sketch of Buchenwald, because he set the standards for the bunker near the gatehouse where prisoners were taken to be "questioned until they confessed." Sommer tortured chained prisoners and beat them to death with a pipe or strangled them with his bare hands. Also, he starved men to death in waterlogged cells swarming with vermin. Another routine: to pour boiling water over a man's testicles, then drench them with ice water; this was repeated until the skin of the scrotal sac came off in strips. Then he painted the prisoner's raw flesh with iodine to enhance the effect.[2]

Kogon lists trifling offenses that could bring down the wrath of the SS, such as unshined shoes, shoes too shiny, turning up a collar against wind or rain, straightening up while working in a stooped position, and many more. Prisoners at Dachau and Buchenwald lived in an atmosphere of threats, whether from random beatings or the practices of an enterprising sadist; but those who had the bad luck to experience both camps in 1938 reported that life was worse in Buchenwald and executions more frequent.

Kogon says Koch turned the grounds outside the walls into a showplace, with public gardens, a wild-game preserve, and a falconry court in "ancient Teutonic style" created as a tribute to Hermann Göring, one of whose many titles was Reich huntsman in chief. Prisoner-masons built huge fireplaces for the court; other prisoners carved oak paneling and massive oak furniture; and still others mounted graceful hunting trophies for its walls. Later, during the war, civilians came out from Weimar on Sundays to see the sights (admission, one reichsmark), although Göring never found time to visit the falconry court. As for Goethe's great oak, it stood inside the prison area and so had to be viewed from a respectful distance.

Ilse Koch, the commandant's wife, a woman remembered for her sadism, was a riding enthusiast and kept a stable of horses within the prison compound. Her husband ordered prisoners to erect an exercise building with walls sixty feet high; inside, a tanbark ring with ground-level mirrors allowed her to observe and correct her riding style while a band of prisoners played equestrian music. Kogon says thirty prisoners died in the rushed schedule to complete this structure, which Ilse Koch used on average three times a week.

Buchenwald also had a book bindery renowned for its exquisite leather bindings, and the camp's sculpture shop carved a handsome marble desk set as a Yule Festival present for Himmler in 1939. The same shop turned out models of Viking boats, much sought after and prized by SS officers all over Germany.

Harsher than Dachau, more arrogant, more depraved; such was the setting that Bettelheim was reluctant to describe in any memorable detail, but where he found himself in the autumn of 1938, with no end in sight.

At about the same time, SS Major Rödl, who kept a kennel of dogs, decided to prove that he could tame a wolf. One day the wolf attacked him, and Rödl shot it, then announced over the public-address system that the Jews had killed the wolf and would be punished. The Jewish prisoners understood what was expected of them and took up a collection to replace the wolf. They collected so much money that Koch added a small zoo to the camp's attractions, with monkeys, bears, and even a rhinoceros. When one of the zoo animals died, the Jews "voluntarily" replaced it; when food ran short at the zoo, the SS as a matter of priority dipped into supplies earmarked for prisoners. The bears sometimes did double duty, when Koch threw a prisoner into their cage to be mauled to death.

The horrid truth about concentration-camp life has been told and retold, but when Bettelheim wrote about the experience, he wanted to analyze what happened to a man's personality under extreme conditions. He believed that what had been done to him was less important than how he thought about it, how it threatened his sense of himself, and what it took to keep his integration intact. He made spare use of victimization details and instead examined the prisoner's inner dynamic, the demoralization that occurred if the prisoner did not seize rare opportunities to preserve the feeling that he could affect his own life. In applying this lesson to the larger world, Bettelheim held that the camps were an extreme example of the assaults a mass society makes on the individual and against which we all need to shield ourselves.

BETTELHEIM continued to hope that the efforts of his family and friends would finally free him. The Eichmann policy of terrorizing Austrian Jews to drive them out was succeeding in Vienna, with most eager to give up their property and emigrate, if they could find a place to go. Early in November 1938 in Paris a young Jewish man assassinated a minor German official named vom Rath. (The young man's family had just been deported from Germany to Poland, and he may have sought revenge.)

In reprisal, Nazi leaders ordered the Kristallnacht ("Night of Broken Glass") riots, two days of looting and violence by SA and SS troops. They arrested over twenty thousand Jewish men, of whom more than eight thousand were shipped to the already overcrowded Buchenwald, where the SS, as punishment for the assassination, had confined all Jews to their barracks and cut their rations. Kristallnacht had the effect, as it was probably intended to do, of raising the stakes for all Jews, in or out of the camps, and Bettelheim could only cling to his hopes.

BETTELHEIM believed it was a mistake for prisoners to identify themselves as having any special skill, because it meant that the prisoner could be singled out and punished if anything went wrong. Also, he might be passed over for release if he was too useful. "If somebody was needed, it was announced over the loudspeaker at roll call, anyone with these skills step out," he told me. At Dachau, for instance, many graphic artists had come forward to get relatively easy jobs. "Like idiots, they volunteered. It was quite clear to me that the ones who falsified papers would never get out. The SS would kill them to cover, you know, and that was all clear, but they did it anyhow. This is the problem of planning and rationality in that situation. For small advantages in the camp, many risked never getting out."

Koch appointed a half-Jewish prisoner named Berkmann to run the zoo, a man who had been an animal trainer in the circus and had written books under the pseudonym of Berko. Bettelheim had warned him not to admit that he was a trainer. "I said, 'Koch will never let you go. He needs you,' and of course that was what happened. The trainer died there, I don't know under what conditions, because that was after I left. But in the little free time I had, I learned a great deal about the training of animals and how one has to study their psychology, which I found extremely interesting. Where else in the world would I get together with a circus animal trainer?"

WE RETURNED several times to the topic of how Bettelheim survived and held on to his sanity by keeping a balance between compliance and noncompliance. The usual habits of defense didn't work, and their failure tilted the prisoner toward inner collapse. I asked about staying aware of one's point of no return, feelings about oneself that couldn't be tolerated. How could you decide?

"You couldn't decide it in a general way—you would look at the specifics of a situation. There was never enough time to make an elaborate decision, but I think one forms a basic attitude. It becomes habitual if you have to do it, you don't reason it out each time. That's not possible. It was really automatic. The SS couldn't know who was doing this, because the prisoners were to them an undifferentiated mass. If they thought about us as individuals, this would have been very dangerous for them. I understood this, and it helped me in many situations."

As an example of how the point of no return varied, he mentioned Ernst Federn. "At Buchenwald, we were on a chain of prisoners who threw bricks to each other, so that we brought them from a pile of bricks to a building that was being erected. Very heavy bricks. I think he threw them at me, and sometimes there was a moment when the attention of the guards was not directed at us and we could talk a little bit.

"I let some bricks fall and a few broke, so he made a critical remark like, 'Why are you so clumsy, why don't you pay attention?' I don't know exactly what he said, but I replied that it was never in my life's ambition to be a good catcher and thrower of bricks. And that startled him. My point is that when working for the SS he took it much more seriously than I did. And that's why he bawled me out. We talked some more after work and became very good friends. While his attitude helped him survive, in a way it made the values of the SS his own – the value that the prisoner should do labor that was good. Still, my remark, which distanced myself from this attitude, was, I believe, recognized by him as a more desirable attitude than his own."

I asked Federn about this incident, and he remembered it a bit differently. In fact, he said that Bruno had forgotten the episode until he'd reminded him of it when they'd met again years later, in America. "I was in charge of moving the bricks from a brick pile to the place where they would be used," Federn said, "and I was throwing the bricks to this man who kept dropping them. This seemed foolish to me. If the SS saw you, then you'd get in trouble, so after it happened three or four times I said something like, 'Who do you think you are? Here you are nobody!' And he stopped and said very forcefully, 'I'm Bettelheim! Who are you?' He was challenging me that he was somebody. And so I said, 'I'm Federn!' and this surprised him. He changed completely and said, 'Federn?' He was amazed, he couldn't believe it, because he knew my father. And when he found out who I was, that he knew me, so to speak, he was immediately very friendly." (I interviewed Ernst Federn after Bettelheim's death, and he remarked that in all their years of friendship, "Bruno never raised his voice to me.")

After Ernst's father, Paul Federn, emigrated to America, he asked many influential people to write letters pleading for Ernst's release. The king of Denmark, Governor Herbert Lehman, and other persons of influence who had been in analysis with Paul Federn sent letters, but to no avail. The Federn name was too well known, and Himmler refused. Ernst saw that he was a kind of hostage and so made plans to survive in Buchenwald. He joined the bricklayer's group, Jewish political prisoners (all communists or socialists) who realized that the war would bring a shortage of steel and concrete and decided to make themselves indispensable. Kogon says they were so valuable that the commandant of Buchenwald ignored direct orders from Berlin that would have sent the bricklayers to Auschwitz with other Jews. Bettelheim wrote about them, again from the point of view of their inner life.

> While nearly all other Jews were destroyed, most of this command was alive on the day of liberation. Had they served the SS poorly, they would have served themselves not at all. But had they taken professional pride in their bricklaying skill, without continuing to hate having to work for the SS, their inner resistance might have died, and they with it.[3]

Federn recalled that Bettelheim had also worked for a while in the carrier command of Gustav Herzog, a well-known Viennese journalist, whose price was two marks a week for the privilege of walking two abreast in orderly columns from one place to another. In *The Informed Heart* Bettelheim wrote of the advantages of such work and says that the greatest benefit of a carrier command was that the prisoner was inconspicuous.[4] Bettelheim said that some of the older German prisoners had money, and in the beginning so did most of the Jewish prisoners; after the expropriations began, "it became hard for even the Jewish prisoners to get money." He had been comfortably fixed in Vienna but "not a multimillionaire—by no means. Still, I could get a large sum of money together. That's why my sister finally went to Weimar to arrange for my release. If you had money, you bribed through a lawyer or some intermediary. My sister went to a Nazi lawyer in Weimar and paid him, but nothing happened. For instance, Marie Bonaparte paid a high ransom for Freud. I don't know to whom, you know I was never really interested, but some high official got a large sum of money, and then Freud could go.

"I don't remember exactly how much we had—the main value was in the business. We had lost a lot of money during the depression, and the money bought much more in Austria than here, but it was probably several hundred thousand dollars. The ten thousand dollars I sent to this country was a relatively small sum. Well, not small, but comparatively insignificant."

BETTELHEIM had come to Buchenwald at the end of the summer. In the fall, many mornings at roll call were so foggy that prisoners could not work outside the camp. In fog and darkness they might try to escape, and so the SS had to find ways to keep them busy after roll call. Someone came up with the idea of occupying the prisoners with "sport," a harmless name for a form of abuse that did not exist at Dachau.

> Sport might include push-ups, crawling on hands and feet through mud, rolling in the mud, snow or ice, and so on. At one time great heaps of gravel lay on the parade grounds of Buchenwald. Prisoners were forced to roll down them until their bodies were cut by the sharp edges of the stones. An hour of such sport usually did more damage than a whole day at hard labor.[5]

I asked Bettelheim if this had happened to him personally. He seemed to weigh whether he wanted to answer but finally said, "Occasionally I had to do the sport, whenever I wasn't on a command that worked inside."

LIFE AT Buchenwald was harsher than at Dachau in more than the brutality of the SS. For instance, the food was worse. "At Buchenwald the soup was much thinner," Bettelheim said. They still got a portion of bread every three days, but the work was harder, with less chance for extra food. Bettelheim guessed that he had come down to about half his weight in Dachau, and it stayed fixed at that level in Buchenwald.

I asked Federn about the food in Dachau and Buchenwald, and he said, "In Dachau we overate and gained weight. In spite of the work, and because there was a lot of food. In Buchenwald we had sometimes no food on Sundays; Jews didn't get food on Sundays. For no other reason than because they were Jews." Ordinarily Federn's weight stood at about 165 pounds, but in Buchenwald he went down to 100.

Another notable difference between the two camps dealt with defecation. "In Dachau," Bettelheim said, "they more readily let you go when you asked, 'Prisoner number so-and-so very humbly requests' and so on, then they permitted you to go. Usually right away, or after a short time. But in Buchenwald they forbade prisoners to defecate during the entire workday." He writes that when a guard at Buchenwald made an exception, he humiliated the prisoner by discussing his request so everyone could hear; and afterward, when the prisoner came back, the guard addressed him in ways that "shattered his self-respect."[6]

Among the small differences was that at Dachau most prisoners had individual bunks, whereas at Buchenwald several slept together. On the other hand, at Dachau the camp searchlights played through the windows at intervals during the night and often woke those whose closed eyes lay in the lights' path. However, according to Bettelheim, the greatest difference between the two camps

> was that at Buchenwald it was nearly always the group that suffered, not the individual. At Dachau, a prisoner who tried to carry a small stone instead of a heavy one would have suffered for it; at Buchenwald the whole group including the foreman would have been punished.[7]

Bettelheim said that a foreman in the quarry at Buchenwald had to judge whether or not a prisoner had a full load of stones in his wheelbarrow and to weigh the barrow under the eyes of an SS guard, who would notice if certain prisoners were being favored. I couldn't imagine Bettelheim working in the quarry and said so.

"The quarry was one of the worst places to work, and we tried to get out of it as fast as we could. I worked there several times, but each time never more than three days. I couldn't have managed, I had to get out, I wouldn't have survived. I'm not physically strong, you know, but in the quarry even when you were very strong they chased you up and down with these heavy stones. The broken stones, stones from somebody else, might fall on you."

When you got into such a command, he said, "you had to manipulate to get out of it as soon as you could if you wanted to survive." This meant finding a foreman of another detail who was a friend, or a friend of a friend, or one who would demand you because of your skills, or who could be bribed. Work assignments were made each morning, and it was assumed that the prisoner would report to the same detail the next day; however, he did not have to; he could take a chance and do something else.

"You could risk not to go and hope they won't look for you and find you. After all, there were about five to six thousand people lined up in early-morning fog or darkness.

"Particularly in the quarry, I remember that I felt if I went there I would die anyway, so I'd rather risk being caught from sending myself in a different way. Or you could go up to another foreman and say, 'For heaven's sake take me into your group today, otherwise I won't survive the day.' Sometimes he said, 'Get the hell out of here.' But sometimes he might say, 'Come along.' "

IN BUCHENWALD'S first year the SS did not segregate homosexuals, but in October 1938 their status changed for the worse. Until then, homosexuals were divided among the political barracks, and no one took any particular notice of them. However, the SS adopted a new policy and transferred all homosexuals to the "penal company," a special area where they were treated more harshly. Also, they had to work in the quarry every day. Bettelheim felt that they were among the prisoners most abused by the SS, "whether because of their own homosexual tendencies, I don't know."

Homosexuals who survived the quarry were later sent to extermination camps. Kogon writes, "Theirs was an insoluble predicament and virtually all of them perished." As might be expected, some men sent to the camps for homosexuality were not homosexual at all; someone had denounced them simply to get rid of them, for whatever reason. The disastrous result of a mere accusation was perhaps the Nazi state's most effective weapon to frighten and coerce its citizens.

WHEN BETTELHEIM and Federn came to Buchenwald, most of the prisoner latrines were open and unsheltered, with logs as seats on either side of a trench. "I built the latrines at Buchenwald," Federn remarked, referring to the fact that he was happy to have the job of erecting roofs over latrine trenches because it kept him out of the changeable weather. Later, after a typhoid outbreak, he and another man got the job of disinfecting the latrines. The two of them had the freedom of the camp for two months, carrying shovels and buckets of disinfectant from one latrine to another. One day they happened to notice the monkeys in the zoo eating marmalade; they stole the marmalade, a real delicacy at Buchenwald, and ate it themselves.

The SS ordered that only Jews should clean the latrines, but prisoners vied for the job. Federn remembered some of the well-known people who worked there, including Fred Praeger, who later founded a publishing house in America, and Benedict Kautsky, a prominent economist. Kautsky ran the "4711 detail" (named after the eau de cologne), which was popular because its members wore work clothes instead of prison uniforms and could take baths frequently after cleaning the latrine trenches.

Latrines could be dangerous: SS guards sometimes stormed in, caught prisoners sitting there, and beat them. If men using the latrines saw the guards coming, they scattered in all directions. Also, if the guards felt like it, they would throw a prisoner into the trench to drown in excrement and then report his death as an accident.

BUCHENWALD'S mountainside location exposed the prisoners to the worst of the winter weather, but even so, the day of December 14, 1938, seems to have been harsher than usual. The temperature dropped, and a snowstorm began to blow across the camp with gusting winds that cut through the scant clothing of those who had to work outdoors that day. Early in the afternoon the SS discovered that two prisoners had escaped, apparently hoping the snowstorm would reduce visibility and cover their tracks. Koch and Rödl called in the *kapo* of the escapees' command, their barracks foreman, and the top members of the camp's prisoner elite, all of whom speculated on where the two men might be hiding or what route they would have taken away from the camp.

It was decided to hold roll call in the snowstorm at the end of the workday. As long as the two men did not answer and could not be accounted for, the roll call would go on while the whole camp stood at attention in the bitter wind. Word of the escape soon filtered back through the prisoner elite to those working indoors, who understood that the SS would keep them out in the snowstorm past the hour of the evening meal.

> The main problem was to provide oneself and others with some protection against exposure, and to ready things for prisoners returning from work so that they could prepare themselves for the ordeal in a few minutes.[8]

Prisoners who worked indoors began to scavenge for food, paper, and rags to help their friends. It took great daring for them to slip away early from their jobs, collect whatever they could, then pool everything

> so that every prisoner in their group could have at least a bite to eat and some paper to stuff under his uniform before the night watch began.[9]

Men risked their lives to leave work without authorization, enter the barracks during forbidden hours, and break into supply rooms.

> It asked for frantic activity and great ingenuity. Doors into SS store rooms had to be broken open, bags of cement emptied (the heavy paper of these bags was the best insulation available), the cement disposed of so that the theft would not be noticed immediately, etc.[10]

Except for the elite, prisoners had nothing warmer to wear than a single sweater, and frequent inspections by the SS and the block foremen made sure that no one had any extra piece of clothing.

Group loyalties suddenly became crucial to survival. Jehovah's Witnesses and political prisoners, whose cohesion with their group was already strongest, fared best in the crisis. By contrast, prisoners in other categories (nonpoliticals and asocials, for instance) did not do as well, because members of those groups had less feeling for one another. Each person who risked his life to collect things for the emergency had to find enough for at least a dozen friends. Even these small but heroic measures could not have been taken without the active or passive help of the prisoner hierarchy, who at the very least had to look the other way.

At all other times, prisoners avoided the outside ranks or files of the roll-call formation, where prisoner-elite guards found it easier to hit anyone instead of reaching in to punish the actual offender. Bettelheim also hated the edge of the formation because he could see men being hit elsewhere on the parade ground. It was safer not to see, and it protected him from the helpless fury he felt when he saw a beating. However, this time he happened to stand in the forefront of the formation and so got the full force of wind and snow.

As the roll call began in the fading light of day, the windchill made the temperature feel like zero or below. Sunset came at about four-thirty, but even before then the assembly grounds had grown dark with the snowstorm, and the searchlights were turned on. Lights that usually swept the camp and its perimeter now played over the prisoners and pinned them down. No one could fade away from the back ranks on a lit-up parade ground and go off and hide.

Despite the searchlights the prisoners began to help one another by taking turns in the outside positions. Those in the front row slipped back, while others from the middle took their place. All except the weakest and oldest faced the worst exposure in the outer ranks, where a wall of prisoners gave a small but welcome shelter to those inside the formation.

The protective action was spontaneous, and at any other time it would have brought beatings from the prisoner elite and SS guards. The severity of the storm, however, seemed to make this moment different, even unique. Prisoner guards saw men changing places with each other, but they permitted it. They knew an extreme hardship had been imposed, and they also knew that they had to live with the prisoners later on. Many SS guards also permitted the breach of discipline as long as movements in the formation took place when their backs were turned.

Not all SS guards acted so leniently, but Bettelheim felt that those who did so may have been moved by the sight of this sudden esprit de corps.

> While they tried overtly to break such a spirit in the prisoners, covertly they had some grudging admiration for it, and utterly despised prisoners who did not act in accordance with it.[11]

Every time the roll call ended, it began again, and at last men started to drop and die. After twenty men or more had died, discipline broke down:

> A feeling of utter indifference swept the prisoners. They did not care whether the SS shot them; they were indifferent to the acts of torture committed by the guards. The SS no longer had any authority. . . . Unfortunate as the situation was, the prisoners felt free from fear and therefore were actually happier than at most other times during their camp experience.[12]

Bettelheim also notes:

> Once they had abandoned hope for their personal existence, it became easier for them to act heroically and help others.[13]

The prisoners stood in the wind and snow all night and through the next morning, answering a roll call that lasted until noon. Twenty-five men had frozen to death by morning and seventy by noon.[14]

In the snowstorm the prisoners had felt a kind of euphoria, but back in the barracks their elation vanished.

> They felt relieved that the torture was over, but at the same time they felt they were no longer free of fear and could no longer rely strongly on mutual help. Each prisoner as an individual was now compara- tively safe, but he had lost the safety that originates in belonging to a unified mass.[15]

NINETEEN hours in wind and snow left Bettelheim with a bad case of frostbite. "It was not really painful," he said. "I had no feelings because the flesh was dead, but I was worried about gangrene." If gangrene spread, he could not work, and prisoners unable to work did not last long in Buchen- wald. He needed medical attention, but after the vom Rath assassination and Kristallnacht the SS had forbidden any treatment for Jews unless the injury was work related, which Bettelheim's frostbite obviously was not; nevertheless, he decided to take a chance and go to the clinic. I asked how he prepared himself to approach the guard, and he said he thought it best simply to be spontaneous. "That's really not any different," he added, "from when you have to respond as a therapist to what goes on in your patient." With only guesswork to guide him, the therapist has to react quickly to things said and unsaid.

Men ahead of Bettelheim in the clinic line compared notes and rehearsed how they planned to persuade the guard to let them see the doctor. "I believe most prisoners were handicapped because they had a false picture of the SS as devils incarnate. Now, that's perfectly under- standable as a defense, but it's a mistake, a very destructive reaction, because the SS felt this in the prisoner's manner." The prisoner had to combat his own anxiety before he could deal with the SS in ways helpful to himself, but he was usually too wrapped up in his pain and anxiety, Bet- telheim said, to think realistically about the SS.

The other prisoners asked Bettelheim what he intended to do, and he told them he had no definite plan but would see how the guard behaved and try to respond accordingly. The men around him thought he had some plan he wouldn't share and became angry. No one ahead of him got into the clinic, but when his turn came, he answered the guard in a matter-of-fact way, with no air of pleading. He pointed out that he couldn't work unless his hands were treated and that since prisoners weren't allowed to have knives, he needed someone to cut the dead flesh away. The guard tried to pull off the festering skin but failed and waved Bettelheim into the clinic.

"I think the SS felt unconsciously that I approached them directly as human beings in a particular situation, no? And most prisoners approached them as if they were sadistic devils. So, they lived up to this expectation in many cases."

In talking about such matters, Bettelheim would frequently apply a camp insight to his work at the Orthogenic School. Here, he added, as a kind of footnote, "With beginners at the Orthogenic School, my most important work was to convince them and have them develop an attitude that these crazy kids are basically people just like us, not subhumans or whatever."

In writing about this episode in *The Informed Heart*, Bettelheim offers a long, complex, and fascinating analysis of the differences and similarities between persecutor and victim. This section of the book will reward a second or third reading, but I quote here only one short passage, in which Bettelheim shows how an appeal to compassion can have the opposite effect:

> When Jewish prisoners appealed to [the SS soldier's] compassion, the threat to his character structure was even greater. In order to conform to the SS ideal, he had to suppress all humanitarian feelings. Anyone who tried to arouse his compassion was threatening to destroy him as an SS soldier. . . . Only those who have seen the violent reaction of a person who is suddenly asked to yield to a suppressed desire can fully understand the anxiety such a demand would create in the SS who felt any compassion for his victims. . . . The violence, more than anything else, revealed that deep within him more humane feelings were aroused which he tried to repress and deny through overt cruelty.[16]

SOON AFTER the night of the snowstorm, the SS caught the escaped prisoners and sentenced them to hang after a roll call. "We all had to stand and watch," Bettelheim said, "but I didn't look in that direction. You were lined up and you were supposed to look, but with several thousand men they couldn't watch to see whether everybody looked. So I looked away. Later I saw the bodies dangling there dead. They kept them hanging there for a couple of days."

Bettelheim also said that committing brutalities made a guard's job easier. "Of course, when the SS put his cruelty into practice, he degraded the prisoner to a subhuman existence, and with a subhuman one doesn't have any empathy or sympathy. That way the SS could get rid of his anxiety. If he manages to make the victim subhuman in his own eyes, he relieves himself of any empathy. For example, during a war the enemy is often depicted horribly, as we did with the Japanese. This makes the war possible, or rather, I should say, palatable. This is something you find in less exaggerated form in normal life. I tried to say in some of my books about the work of the School that the same phenomenon occurs when we look at the insane. We can deal with our anxieties about them by declaring them entirely different from us, which they are not."

In our conversations Bettelheim never expressed a personal hatred toward the SS or the Nazis, and I was curious whether or not such hatred might have been helpful in the camps. "I hated the Nazis, I hated the Nazis, naturally," he said. "But—you see, I can't do it when I am confronted with the individual. So to say, my need to understand is greater than my need to hate. And why? Because understanding does something positive for me. The hate just doesn't."

I couldn't help wondering, if not from the power of hatred, where did he get his apparent will to resist?

"Well, I think the will to resist is very early, when the child says, 'I won't do that'—the 'no.' And some psychologists and psychoanalysts say that the 'no' is really the first great assertion of individuality, not the 'yes.' I feel this is true, because in the 'no' you set yourself against the environment."

BETTELHEIM also spoke of how and why the SS reacted to a prisoner's fear. The prisoner could not afford to collapse inside himself under threats, because "to be frightened was practically a death sentence." If an SS guard saw the prisoner's fear, no matter that he wished to evoke it, the sight nevertheless touched his own fears of death, ever in mind because the SS expected to be sent to the front lines in case of war. "The SS man had to continually combat his own death anxiety, and some of his violence was also to quiet this death anxiety. If you were frightened, they attacked you. And if they were frightened, it was the same thing. The SS man could never run away, as an animal might do. His only defense against fright was attack." In the pervasive atmosphere of threat, many prisoners resorted to fantasies of revenge against the SS, and while this offered relief of a sort, Bettelheim tried to avoid it because it took attention away from the immediate moment.

A prisoner's mixed feelings, especially about loved ones, weakened him and wore him down. Bettelheim believed that because prisoners felt so helpless, they raged against those they loved who remained free, and then felt guilty about their rage. This assaulted the integrity of their inner life, and to escape the pains of ambivalence many withdrew emotionally from those who meant most to them. Taking this path, they became weaker of heart and more fragile in spirit because they had detached themselves from their deepest source of emotional strength. Still, they looked forward to the two short letters they could receive from home each month.

"One purpose of the concentration camp," Bettelheim said, "was to make a hardship on the relatives. This was particularly true of the relatives of German gentile prisoners, who were in for political reasons. Their relatives were very cross with the prisoner because he inflicted such hardship on them. If they rejected him and separated themselves from him, the hardship was guilt for treating him in this way. If they didn't, the hardship was that they couldn't get jobs and were also in trouble with the Gestapo, so it was a no-win situation for them. It was a damn clever system."

One day Bettelheim received a letter from his mother about a psychoanalytic paper that a friend of his had presented in Switzerland. "I'm not sure, but I think it was Dr. Sterba. My mother meant to cheer me up, and she told me that he had presented some of my ideas in this paper and that they were very well received. Also, I had some small ailments. My mother was a very good person and she asked how I was coping with these small ailments. This annoyed me, because it was so ridiculous compared to what I was suffering just being in the camp."

The feeling aroused by the successful paper was not annoyance but rage.

> It sent me into a cold fury to think that my colleague was enjoying success with my ideas while I lived in such misery. . . . This was utterly

destructive to me in a situation where I could do nothing with my anger but internalize it.[17]

Bettelheim's mother also told him that Trude had left Austria, and this led to more unexpected feelings. "In a way, I was glad she got out, and in a way I was sorry, because there was always the hope I would see her again. So the feeling was always mixed."

Not long after Bettelheim had been sent to Dachau, the Gestapo summoned Trude to the Metropol Hotel, taken over as their headquarters in Vienna. She may have come to their attention because she taught in the Montessori school, but they may also have noticed her because she went to the SS office to ask about Bruno, a dangerous act for anyone not a relative. The Gestapo kept Trude most of the day in a bathroom at the Metropol and interrogated her several times. At the end of the day they released her but held her passport. The experience so terrified her that she decided to leave Austria by any means possible. Also, the connection with Bruno added to her fears. "She was afraid," Bettelheim explained, "she might say something damaging to me. She went because they interrogated her, and she didn't want to take the chance of hurting me if they called her again, as they might well have done."

A few days later the Gestapo returned Trude's passport, but she was no longer sleeping in her apartment, where she feared being found and arrested. On most nights she would seek out a friend at whose place she could sleep, because, she explained, "I was afraid that something might happen before I could really go."

Trude's affidavit supporting her emigration to America had come from the mother of the American girl, as a favor to Bruno, but even with her passport once again safe in hand, she saw no point in waiting for her quota number and visa from the uncooperative American consul's office in Vienna. "I only learned much later," she said, "that some of these [people] were not only anti-Semitic, they were also corrupt and expected money or other favors. In any case, it was obvious to me that I would have a long wait in Vienna, which I was not prepared to do after what happened to me."

Trude never expected to see Bruno again, and she wrote a letter saying good-bye. She gave the letter to the gentile museum curator who had allowed himself to be named head of the Montessori school, and he gave her some gold coins, which she hid in her sock.

Trude had made up her mind to walk across the Austrian border into Switzerland. Her friend Emmi from the Montessori school was now married and living in Spain, but members of her family would help once Trude got into Switzerland. She would need help, because the Swiss authorities did not want Austrian Jewish refugees. Border officials could turn her back without giving a reason; the Jewish-sounding name on her passport was reason enough.

Most of Trude's money went to pay a guide who knew the mountain passes across the Austrian-Swiss border. "Actually," Bettelheim said, "you didn't pay the guide directly, you paid somebody who paid him, and she found this person through my anti-Nazi political connections." Trude and the guide took a train from Vienna to the Tirol region in western Austria. The trek across the border would take two days and one night, and they carried knapsacks but no sleeping bags or heavy clothing, because they had to look as if they were only going on a day's hike. "If Trude had been caught," Bettelheim said, "she would have been sent to prison and then *really* interrogated. They would have thought she had something to hide, because she was trying to escape."

The strenuous climb and below-freezing temperatures at night made an illegal crossing an option only for the young. On the second day, Trude and the guide walked down the mountain slope through a forest and heard the Swiss border police calling to them. Trude spent a miserable night in the police station fighting off the advances of the guide, but the next day she persuaded the police to let her go to a nearby town, where one of Emmi's brothers lived, and he was very surprised but friendly and helpful.

Eventually she took a train to Zurich to apply for a visa at the American consulate, and she carried a precious letter of reference written by Anna Freud and Dorothy Burlingham. When she got in to see an official she handed the letter to him, and he read it, then tore it up and threw it in his wastebasket with no explanation. "From the way he acted," Trude said, "it was quite clear to me that nothing was going to happen in the foreseeable future."

Trude decided to emigrate to Australia, but first she went to see her parents in France, where they had gone from Switzerland. In the fall she took passage to Australia, and she arrived in December 1938.

As BETTELHEIM remarks in *The Informed Heart*, prisoners had mixed feelings about those at home, but they also hated the changes taking place at home because these implied a change in their own status within the family. I asked if he still thought this was true, and he said, "Well, I should elaborate here, beyond what I said in the book. What outraged prisoners was that people on the outside could change things, and they couldn't. You know, it rubbed it in—the helplessness—and I think that was part of the resentment. I don't think I brought it out in the book as I should have." As this anger and resentment grew, the value of the family in the prisoner's mind was damaged, which suited the purpose of his captors, since the SS in fact wanted the prisoner's family to abandon him and often tried to demoralize both prisoner and family by purposely misinforming them.[18]

The SS misinformed Bettelheim's mother several times about dates for his release. On one occasion she traveled to Weimar to meet him, only to be told that he had been released and was probably already back in Vienna, when in fact he was still in Buchenwald, five miles away. Another time the SS told her to come to Weimar, and she waited there for several days while the camp administration gave one excuse after another for not releasing him. At last his mother realized that her trip had been useless, and she returned to Vienna.

"I don't know whether they deliberately tricked her," Bettelheim said, "but I thought so at the time. Maybe it was *Schlamperei*—disorderliness, carelessness. It had the same effect. Once my sister was told to go to Weimar to receive me there, and she went to Weimar, and nothing happened. She managed to leave Vienna before I got out of the camp, which I had urged her to do. She converted, she became a Protestant, and the Gildemeester group got her out, to England. You had to convert to do that."[19]

It was the dead of winter in Buchenwald, and Bettelheim wanted to work on a command that would keep him indoors. For this he had to risk something he feared—a bribe. Prisoners with money could make life more bearable for themselves if they took care not to arouse the resentment of those who had no money with which to bribe, but it was still risky. It would have been safer not to use his money in this way, but at that moment the fear of days and weeks outside in the cold outweighed his fear of being caught in a bribe.

Bettelheim decided to get into the sock-mending detail, and of course he could not approach the foreman directly; the money had to pass through a third party, whose name and address he sought out discreetly. "I wrote my mother that I had an old friend who I understood was in distress and I would appreciate it if she sent money to such and such an address. The sum was seven hundred marks. I told her it would be very important to me for her to do that, and she knew what I meant. That was understood, you know. The SS might have suspected, but they didn't really care." After all, he said, he *might* have had a friend in trouble, and in fact the SS cared more that crimes like bribery should not be seen than that they should not happen.

Bettelheim had never sewed anything before, but now he learned to weave wool yarn and mend holes in socks. "That we learned pretty fast," he said. The foreman had over fifty prisoners in his command, most of whom had probably paid a bribe for the job. I asked how much work was done, and Bettelheim said that each prisoner might mend between a dozen and two dozen socks a day. "That depended to some degree on the hole you were mending, but everybody worked as slowly as they could get away with."

Mending socks indoors had allowed him to miss some of the worst winter weather, but something in the atmosphere of the sock-mending detail began to make him feel uneasy, though for reasons he could not quite pin down. His hands healed from frostbite, and he decided to leave, still without a reason he could put his finger on. He managed to transfer to another indoor assignment, this time to the "handicapped" detail, the easiest place in Buchenwald. While there he wore a yellow armband with a symbol indicating that he was handicapped, and the SS as a rule did not attack those wearing this armband.

"For a time because of my extreme nearsightedness, I was put in a detail that didn't have to work. There was no detail like this in Dachau, but in Buchenwald there was a group of the severely handicapped. A prison foreman had suggested that I could get in there, and at the time it seemed like a good idea. For the first few days it was interesting, because we talked, but then it became very boring to do nothing and just to contemplate your misery. It was worse than to be out and working.

"Also, it appeared to me to be dangerous. I got the idea pretty soon that the Nazis would kill those who were useless, and I was right. After my time, these were the first who were sent to the gas chambers. But after I had been there about ten days or two weeks, I realized it was a bad idea. There were no indications, I simply figured it out." Looking back, he realized also that the sock-mending detail had been a bad idea, because "everybody there was supposed to be handicapped. Somehow I knew it was not a safe place to be in the long run."

He left the severely handicapped detail by going out one morning and joining a labor group after roll call. "Work gangs were formed every morning. Either it was a permanent assignment that might last several weeks, or there might be different ones every day. If it was a dark and foggy morning you could slip yourself into a gang when you thought there was a very favorable foreman or easy work. You could offer the foreman something, but I don't remember doing this after the sock-mending detail. As I mentioned, bribing was dangerous."

For his next job Bettelheim chose hard labor. "It was a detail putting up a building—I don't know what the purpose of the building was—but I was working outside again. In a way, time passed quicker outdoors than indoors, but mostly I got on those other details to escape the cold."

ON JANUARY 31, 1939, an order came from SS headquarters in Berlin to remove all criminals from power in the prisoner elite. Federn, who mentioned this to me, never learned why. The SS suddenly ousted the criminals and asked for volunteers to take over the various positions of power. Many communist prisoners jumped at the chance to exercise power in the camp so they could help friends, strengthen their group, find advantages for themselves, and rise above rivals. On the next day, the "politicals" took over, and the criminal elite was out.

Bettelheim had a stroke of luck with this change. He happened to have become friendly with the prisoner who took over as his barracks foreman, a man named Alfred Fischer. "He was a few years older than I was, because he went to the university with my cousin who was about four or five years older. I really got to know him because of that friendship." Like Bettelheim, Fischer had been classified as a political prisoner and a Jew, but in his case his politics had assured him of a high profile: he belonged to the Communist Party and had also served as the doctor for the USSR's embassy in Vienna.

"He volunteered to be barracks foreman," Bettelheim said, "though I warned him not to. He would have done me many favors as foreman if I had let him, but I was afraid. Because again, you made enemies in the barracks among other prisoners, so I told him he should treat me like anybody else. I also told him he shouldn't accept the job of barracks foreman, because if he did it well they wouldn't let him out, and if he did a bad job he would suffer. But he did it because then he didn't have to go outdoors. It was very easy labor. Buchenwald was different from Dachau in that they let Jews be barracks foremen and have good jobs, and that was a real difference."

As it turned out, the best thing about Fischer was not that he could do favors but that he became the kind of friend Bettelheim could talk with and trust, a person who shared Bettelheim's interest in observations and speculations about men's psychological reactions to the extreme conditions of the camp.

BETTELHEIM spoke several times about the double-edged choices that prisoners had to make if they opted to hold power in the camps. "Every position of relative power was risky," he said, "because you were no longer one of the mass—you could be singled out." A prisoner working in the kitchen could eat more whenever the SS wasn't looking, but he was also expected to smuggle out food for his friends, which was more dangerous to do. Thus if he improved his chances of survival by getting a kitchen job, he soon faced other problems as a result. A prisoner foreman faced the same quandary: to please the SS he had to drive his fellow prisoners beyond all reason, but if he did that, he would also antagonize friends, because friends often expected to work for him. And no prisoner could get by without friends.

"The foremen might be too useful, or they might be flogged or killed if their commandos didn't perform. Most of all, the temptation to accept bribes was very great. So, you accept bribes, which practically all did, or most did, but if that were discovered, you would be immediately demoted and you might go into solitary confinement. And then you'd be dead."

Bettelheim did not, however, view the camps as static—they evolved. "In all prison situations," he said, "some way of life establishes itself." One example of this was the quick evolution of prisoner elites; another, the behavioral adaptations of prisoners as they sought to avoid punishment. But when the larger world outside the camp made itself felt, there were odd moments when prisoner and guard seemed almost on the same level.

Bettelheim recalled a moment like this in Buchenwald. Each barracks had an SS man as a special supervisor, and he visited the barracks every day to talk to the foreman, whose comments would become part of the man's report. He might sit down at ease, out of the sight of his superiors, and talk to the prisoners for a while. Bettelheim said that the SS man in charge of his barracks liked to discuss the news of the day, and that during the crisis when German troops entered Czechoslovakia, the man almost

went out of his mind with fear. He knew the prisoners were better educated than himself, and he asked whether there would be a war. And
when Roosevelt made a speech, the SS man would ask what it meant,
what America was going to do.

"As if we would know! So you see, in the same person the behavior was
between a tyrant who might kill you and somebody who's in the same boat
and chats with you. It was the closeness of living together that made this
kind of incongruity possible."

CHAPTER 7

The Worst Moment;
the Release

TOWARD THE end of our conversation about the camps, I asked Bettelheim about his worst moment, expecting him to speak of being beaten in Buchenwald; but he surprised me by talking about what happened in Dachau to his cousin Richard Schleyen.[1]

Schleyen was almost twenty years older than Bettelheim, but the two of them had become good friends, and as Bettelheim said, "We were fairly close for cousins." They were put in different barracks in Dachau and got together only a few times, in part because Bettelheim felt it would be an imposition to tell Schleyen his troubles or to look for emotional support.

His worst moment, he said, occurred on a hot summer afternoon on the parade grounds. He chanced to be standing in the front rank of the roll-call formation, the spot most exposed to SS eyes and cudgels, the place where a facial expression, a slight relaxation, an eye movement, or the shifting of weight from one foot to the other might provoke a beating.

The roll call dragged on in the heat; several thousand numbers had to be called out and answered while prisoners stood like statues except for the sweat that rolled down their faces. Most had been working all day in the hot sun, and one by one the weaker men began to drop. Bettelheim stood stiffly at attention and did not look around, although he could hear the little commotion whenever a prisoner slumped to the ground. When someone fainted in the roll-call formation, friends could not go to his aid. In fact, it was forbidden even to notice, and the person who tried to help could be shot on the spot.

Out of the corner of his eye, Bettelheim could catch a glimpse of his cousin. "I was about three or four rows away from him during one of those endless countings, and he collapsed. I couldn't step out and help him."

Bettelheim feared that Schleyen, in his mid-fifties and much frailer than himself, might die.

"Fortunately, they didn't kill him, which they sometimes did with prisoners who collapsed. They let him lie there, and then somebody carried him to the barracks at the end of the counting, and he recovered. I have many times dreamed about this. Of course, we talked afterwards, and he may have told me why he collapsed—after all, he was a doctor—but I don't remember. I think he was exhausted. Others had sunstroke and dehydration. But it was a horrible experience, to want to help him and to know that if I would do that, I would risk my life—and it wouldn't help him."

Schleyen survived, left the camp soon afterward, emigrated to Bolivia, and became a doctor on horseback, making the rounds of Indian villages, which he later told Bruno was the happiest time of his life. However, the event left Bettelheim with a psychic scar. His cousin's collapse forced him into the kind of dilemma that could demoralize a prisoner: if he acted, he might be shot; if he did not act and survived by suppressing natural feelings, then he reproached himself. He had to live with the memory of humiliation, degradation, and guilt for failing to uphold his deepest values and for having violated his sense of the kind of person he believed himself to be. Such incidents demeaned the prisoner and damaged his self-respect, despite the obvious commonsense view that any action might have led to death.

On one occasion in telling this story to a friend,[2] Bettelheim said, "I think I should have helped him anyhow." This startled his friend, and she said, "But look at everything you've done since then, look at all you've given to the world."

Bettelheim, at that point in the last year of his life, replied with a shrug that lifted his shoulders and both arms, with his hands open and palms up, and with one word called his whole career into question: "So?"

If his failure to act at that moment in Dachau still disturbed Bettelheim near the end of his life, then he had not stopped feeling the shame of not having acted well in a crisis. That was the standard by which he judged himself.

But why, I asked, was the Schleyen incident worse than having been stabbed and beaten or having his teeth broken? "You see," he said, "when you yourself were beaten, or whatever, firstly there was the pain, and secondly you were so busy trying to protect yourself, or to survive, that all your mind was taken up with the beating. So while it lasted, there was a complete concentration on what happened to you, and there was no

chance for reflection. Therefore, psychologically it was much more difficult when you were not directly involved."

IN THE days leading up to Hitler's fiftieth birthday, April 20, 1939, the
Nazis declared a period of amnesty and began to let prisoners go from
overcrowded camps. Bettelheim and his family had long since given up
their property as a precondition to his release and their emigration.
Friends in America had appealed on his behalf, and his mother and sister
had made their own appeals to the Gestapo. Word came at last in the second week of April, and Bettelheim was suddenly told to prepare to leave
Buchenwald.

I asked him how this worked, and he said that usually the commandant's office received, from Berlin, a list of the names of the prisoners to
be freed, but since this was not a matter of high priority to anyone except
prisoners and their families, the papers might sit on an SS desk for days or
weeks without being looked at. When someone finally picked up a set of
papers and acted on them, the commandant's office informed each prisoner's barracks foreman. "Usually on the morning you were to be
released," Bettelheim said, "they notified the foreman and he notified
you. Sometimes it would happen during the day, but that was rare. Usually in the morning."

Bettelheim did not report for work that day; instead, he sat in the barracks and argued with Fischer. Ordinarily, on the morning he was to be
released, a prisoner would go to the clothing barracks and pick up his bag
of civilian clothes (the same he had worn when he was arrested) and then
go for a body search. Stripped naked, he would stand while a guard
looked him over head to toe to make sure he was hiding nothing he could
take out of the camp—a scrap of paper with notes, a photograph, a letter
from another prisoner. Then he would dress in his civilian clothing,
which usually fit badly because of weight loss, and go to the main gate for
his travel money from the SS. If relatives had been told of his release, they
might be waiting for him just outside the gate.

On this day, Bettelheim was afraid to leave the barracks, because he
had already gone through the release procedure twice, only to be turned
back at the gate.

The first time, nearly all other prisoners called up with me were
released while I was sent back into the camp. The second time may
have been chance, because quite a few others besides myself were sent

back, and rumor had it that the SS had run out of money and could not pay the sums due the prisoners for the trip home.[3]

When I interviewed Bettelheim on this point, it was twenty-four years after he had written *The Informed Heart*, and he had reflected on his aborted releases countless times and had come to slightly different conclusions about them.

"I don't really know why it happened, that I was sent back to the barracks," he said. There might have been a personal element all along, or there might not; he couldn't be sure. However, when he put on his civilian clothes and came to the gate a second time and found that his name had been taken off the list, he went back to his barracks certain that he had been singled out by an SS officer he believed wanted to break him. He had once provoked this officer and had been severely beaten, and now he feared that the officer had recognized his name on the list. (I believe another reason he had not mentioned this possibility earlier was to minimize the personal element in *The Informed Heart* and in the details he was telling me; I got him to speak about this beating, still reluctantly, much later and only after I heard of it from Trude.)

The third time, Bettelheim believed it was a trick and refused to leave the barracks to go for the body search. His friend Fischer tried to reason with him, but Bruno told him flatly that he would not go, that he couldn't bear having his hopes shattered again at the gate.

"I felt at the time—now the thought comes back to me—if they turn me back again, I'm going to break down," he said. "I was really afraid that when I came to the entrance gate, they would send me back again, and I would have an outburst. That would give them the excuse to shoot me. My refusal here was spontaneous, and it was also self-protective, because I knew my limitations, and I thought that if this goes on I'm not going to be able to be the obedient prisoner. This was not an act of courage, it was in part an act of self-protection. It may be hard to understand, but that's why self-knowledge is so important. In fact, this is a typical example of how, out of self-knowledge, I tried to protect myself."

Luckily, Bettelheim had Fischer, who talked with him and calmed him down—a trusted friend whose words, presence, and manner perhaps lifted his spirits just enough for him to feel he could take the chance of going through the release procedure once more. In any event, the third time was real, and Bettelheim left Buchenwald for Vienna on April 14, 1939.

Six days later, the SS gave all the prisoners at Buchenwald a day off from work to celebrate Hitler's birthday; they also released about a tenth of the prisoners before that day's end. All day long, prisoners strolled around the camp and listened to the public-address system, because names were being called out—not numbers—and if a prisoner heard his name he went to the front gate and identified himself and was released.

Ernst Federn remained in Buchenwald until its liberation in 1945, almost seven years after he arrived there. I asked him about the Goethe oak, and he said that it stood in front of a "rather big building—it might have been the kitchen." He also recalled that in 1944 a bomb hit the camp during an air raid, and the oak caught fire and went up in flames, leaving only a stump.

I asked Federn if he had any particular feelings about the oak, and he said, "It was a big oak, like any other oak, and people said, 'That's the great oak,' and I said, 'So what?' "

CHAPTER 8

Freedom

DACHAU AND Buchenwald accounted for slightly less than eleven months in Bettelheim's life, but the cruelties he suffered there brought home an ugly truth. For him, the camps demonstrated a bedrock reality about *human* inhumanity (and vulnerability), a solid fact that any theory or description of our nature had to face squarely. He did not blink at the horrors he had seen and endured, but neither did he try to exorcise his experience by portraying it as a *personal* ordeal.

As for his release, he reflected upon it many times without ever reaching certainty in his own mind. Paula and Grete had written letters and paid Nazi lawyers; he had given up his property; Gina, in America, had appealed to the mother of the disturbed girl, and this woman had sought the help of New York Governor Herbert Lehman, who had perhaps persuaded Eleanor Roosevelt to intervene. Subsequently, the Department of State and the American Ambassador in Berlin had made inquiries, all with no clear effect. In fact, the entreaties may have slowed Bettelheim's release if an SS official in the chain of command happened to ask himself whether or not the prisoner might be more valuable than he at first seemed. In any event, Bettelheim could never settle upon an explanation that fully satisfied him.

ALONG with about a dozen others from Buchenwald, Bettelheim traveled by bus to Gestapo headquarters in Vienna. He had little more than a week to visit his mother, collect the necessary papers and permits, see a dentist for his teeth, and confirm his passage to the United States. He had his quota number, which meant that he should be able to get a visa quickly.

His clothes hung loose on him, but in any case he could take only what he wore—no suitcase, no hand luggage, no valuables or papers, nothing. Shock and deprivation had made him prematurely bald at thirty-five, and the beatings had left him with a dental condition that would trouble him for the rest of his life. On the other hand, all this fell away to nothing in the light of the huge fact that he had been imprisoned almost a year and now would be free.

His lumber business had been "sold" in proper legal fashion. A gentile competitor, Nikolaus Lackner, had taken over as owner a little more than a month after Bettelheim went to Dachau. The transaction took place with all the trappings of legality; the German purchaser agreed to "buy" the Jewish firm and all its assets for less than its worth, and shortly thereafter he made a "contribution" to the Nazi Party. The combined payments still made it a handsome bargain.

Bettelheim's partner, Schnitzer, went to jail (not a concentration camp) soon after Bettelheim was sent to Dachau. He was released a few months later and emigrated to the United States. Bettelheim refused to make any direct comments to me about Schnitzer, even off the record, and I wondered why. Later I heard that he had told others that Schnitzer, in the brief time he'd had, had managed to cheat Bettelheim's mother out of some money. As a way of closing the books on Schnitzer, Bettelheim finally said to me, "It was a bad time, and nobody should be blamed." In this remark, he referred to the behavior of Jews and other refugees; the blame for the Nazis and their sympathizers was too plain to need comment.

BETTELHEIM left Gestapo headquarters and went at once to see his mother. Her apartment had been seized, and she was living with a friend. She had her quota number for the United States, but it had not yet come up, so she simply waited. Grete had stayed with her mother as long as she could, even turning down an acting contract that would have taken her to America. But her mother had insisted, and by the time Bruno was set free, Grete had gone to England.

Bettelheim wondered whether he should press his mother to leave at once for Cuba, where she could wait safely, but he decided she should stay in Vienna, where at least she had a good place to live, some friends, and familiar surroundings. Being old, and apolitical, and a woman, she seemed in no danger.

His first impulse—to stay and take care of her—was that of a dutiful son but was also extremely foolish, as she pointed out. In any case, it would not help her; he would be rearrested if he didn't leave, and what good would that do her? Now that Grete was safe in England, it would be a relief to know he was out of danger as well. He should go to America, and she would soon join him there. She could not escape across the Swiss border like Trude, and she had no chance of bribing her way past border guards or being smuggled out of the country. She would wait, and he should get on with what he had to do and not worry about her.

BETTELHEIM had arrived in Vienna so exhausted that he spent the first few days either sleeping or arranging his departure. His mother tried to persuade him to eat, and he did so, though like many prisoners after near starvation, he could take food only in small amounts. Within a day or two, he went to the American consulate for his visa, where the first official he saw refused to issue it. The quota under which he had been accepted, the man said, was now used up, and his number was no longer valid. He listened, stunned, while the man offered him a visa to the Philippines. This was alarming, because the matter had been arranged as a precondition to his release; in fact, he had the letter and the quota number to show. However, the consulate officer said no, he could not get a visa for the United States. Would he like to go to Shanghai? Shanghai was an open city, no visa required.

Bettelheim left the consulate and hurried to Vienna's Central Post Office to telephone Gina and the wealthy American woman; however, he learned that telephone calls were no longer permitted, so he sent cables and then went back to his mother's apartment to wait. "I wired the mother of this girl, you know, and she obviously set the machinery in motion." On the next day he presented the same papers at the consulate. This time all was found to be in order, and he got his visa. "I saw a different official and went right through." Later he heard that the State Department had sent a special commissioner to look into reports of corruption at the consulate, stories of visas denied to one person and then sold to another. "The first official I saw read my number and correspondence and said no. The next day—no problem. Then all I had to do was get a physical exam and see the Gestapo."

IN GESTAPO headquarters for the second time in a week, Bettelheim came into a small office where an SS captain sat behind a desk, giving final approval to emigration documents. The captain was Adolf Eichmann.

"He was very polite," Bettelheim said. "After all, everything was already arranged. He asked me to take a seat, but by then I knew the SS very well, and I understood how he really felt, so I stayed standing." Eichmann asked a question or two, stamped the papers, and gestured that the interview was over.

Bettelheim had found a dentist to do emergency work on his teeth—not much, but enough to hold him until he got to America. In the rest of his time in Vienna he telephoned friends to warn them of what he had seen in the camps. " 'Leave Vienna, or you will perish,' I said."

His mother gave him Trude's address in Australia, and he sent her a cable to let her know he was free. A friend of his, also recently released from Buchenwald, had a visa for Australia, and Bettelheim gave him Trude's name and address so that she would hear from him in this way as well.

He did not like going out onto the streets of Vienna, but one person he had promised to see was the wife of Alfred Fischer, his friend and barracks foreman in Buchenwald. To his dismay, the meeting took place in a charged atmosphere because the contrast was too stark: Bettelheim had been set free, and her husband had not. Both of them knew that Fischer had less chance of getting out because he was a communist, and it made her bitter that his beliefs had left her stranded in this way. Bettelheim saw he could not help her and left her apartment uneasy and depressed.

WHEN BETTELHEIM arrived in New York, it was a bright sunny day in May. He had almost no money in his pocket, but how did he feel at that moment?

"It was wonderful to be out of the concentration camp—free. And I found it absolutely exhilarating—in New York, late spring, the air clear, beautiful. A beautiful feeling."

Gina had lived on the $10,000 the American journalist had deposited in an account in the States. "Fortunately for me," Bettelheim said, "he was an honorable man, and he did what he said he was going to do. He could have stolen the money, but he didn't. I'm sorry I can't remember his name now, it has been so long, but I believe he was a fairly well known American newspaperman, though I was barely acquainted with him. He was not Jewish, as I recall, just a nice man."

BETTELHEIM knew what he wanted to do with his life now that he was out of prison. Like many in the camps for less than a year, he had clung to the notion that nothing would have changed in his absence. Prisoners told each other they would take up their old lives, and this helped keep them balanced in a milieu that pushed them toward madness. It was a life-giving delusion, and Bettelheim had held it without reservation; doubts would have led to fears of a future more treacherous than he could bear. He expected to take up the threads of his previous life, not in the lumber business, which he hated anyhow, but in a setting where he and Gina would devote themselves to the American girl. When she had lived in the Bettelheim apartment and he could think and write about her, he had felt a fascination and a satisfaction not to be found in any other pursuit. Soon, with her family's support, he and Gina would help the girl as they had in Vienna.

This was the most promising new start he could imagine; the girl had given them common interests in their unhappy marriage, and now they would get another chance. Vienna's luxuries were gone, but caring for the girl meant a great deal, and perhaps as their marriage improved and the girl went back to her family, he and Gina would have children of their own. His English would also improve, and he imagined getting a university job teaching art history or aesthetics.

He might take a different path by putting aside his reservations about psychoanalysis as a profession and getting a training analysis. The American Psychoanalytic Association required members to hold a medical degree, obviously impossible for him now; but he had heard that the association sometimes waived the requirement for lay analysts from Europe who had come to the United States since 1933, and perhaps this might be done for him later on. In any event, he would talk things over with his cousin Edith Buxbaum, already established with a job and a growing practice. His future was still hazy, but at last he knew he had one; and on this bright day in May, exhilarated by the freedom he felt in his first hours in America, he could not have imagined anything better.

GINA SAID that she had sent a car to meet Bruno and bring him to her apartment in Yorkville. When she and Bruno sat down to talk, she quickly stunned him with the truth. "I had decided to get a divorce," Gina said, "but Bruno was very much attached to me, and he still thought to have children, start a new life together." Peter Weinmann had followed Gina from London to New York, and it no longer made sense for her to stay in a troubled marriage. The divorce would make sense for Bruno, too, when he was able to accept it. Compromises natural in Vienna became absurd in America, where divorce was more common. Besides, the stress of her problems had caused a stomach ulcer—her "immigration ulcer," Gina called it—and she was determined to get her life in proper order.

For Bruno Gina's decision was a disaster. "It was a great shock," he said, "when I came to New York to find that all I had counted on had collapsed." He had not the slightest idea how drastically Gina's feelings had changed during the past year; but in truth their whole world had changed, and with it her view of how she should live. He had fooled himself by imagining that this part of his old life would go on, an understandable hope but one that did not take Gina into account.

Perhaps most infuriating was the fact that the $10,000 nest egg had been all but spent. Gina, he said, "refusing to work with this child, as the plan had been, drew on the money to a very large degree, so when I came over only a couple of thousand dollars was left."

WHEN BRUNO stepped off the boat, it was as if time had stopped in the camps and would now start again. Gina saw, as he did not, that they had left behind the atmospheric pressures of their circle in Vienna: the well-meaning but guilt-making expectations of family and friends; the mixed blessing of a prosperous business; the intricate tetherings of social and family traditions, so pervasive in their set, that kept them on their path of life after religion no longer commanded personal loyalty. Above all, Gina did not want to live with him now that she had a chance at life with someone she loved more than Bruno.

His hopes were shattered, but they were hopes, not reality—hopes he had created as a defense against the chaos inside himself brought to the surface in the camps; they were simply the fictions, self-made, that he needed to survive that terrible time. Given his and Gina's losses, given the internal realities of their marriage and its history, and given Gina's feelings about Peter Weinmann, her decision to divorce him was clearly right, as sensible in its way as cutting dead skin from a frostbitten hand. But for him at that point it felt like a betrayal, coming so suddenly on the first day of his new life, and he was too angry to accept it.

At that disillusioning moment, Bettelheim was lucky that Gina had grown strong enough to hold her ground in the face of his shock, incredulity, and wrath. He had expected to stay that night, and the rest of his life, with her; but at the end of his first day in New York he walked a few blocks to the apartment of his cousin and aunt, who were waiting to welcome him.

WHEN GINA faced her feelings about the two men in her life and did the right thing for herself, it was also the best thing for Bruno, even though he could not at first believe it.

His aunt Jenny and cousin Edith had a small extra room in their apartment where he could sleep, and Edith had begun doing well enough to offer him a modest monthly allowance. She taught at the New School while building up her analytic clientele, and between the two jobs had even made enough to buy a car. Bettelheim had no way to earn a living just then, but he had at least started to recover his strength and health. In fact, Gina said he looked remarkably well when she first saw him. He was only a month out of Buchenwald, but perhaps the sea voyage and the regular meals aboard ship—and his high hopes—had done him good. He still needed to put on weight, and he had to pay several visits to a dentist to rehabilitate his damaged mouth, but while getting his feet under him he would buy new clothes, write letters, look for a job. In a way, that was the least of it, because he could bring his outer appearance back to normal much more easily than the way he saw himself from inside.

In truth, it was a struggle to regain the inner poise and the acceptance of life that he had enjoyed, to a degree, before the camps. He was out of love and out of work, and only through his stubborn self-awareness and the reassuring routines of everyday life could he begin to build up the kind of trust in life that would offer unconscious protection against the repressed terrors that turned into nightmares almost every night. Bad dreams showed how far he had to go before he could escape the inner consequences of the camps. But with the freedom to make his own way, and buoyed up just then by Jenny and Edith, he had a chance.

He let his mother and sister know that he had arrived safely, that he had moved in with his cousin and aunt, and that he and Gina would divorce. Grete was working to get their mother a visa for England, and he would try for an American visa. He began writing letters and going in person to the Jewish agencies that helped refugees, and he also contacted the government immigration offices. Sooner or later war would come, and he was anxious to bring his mother out of Nazi Germany.

Bruno also wrote to Trude in Australia. A month or so earlier he had sent a cable from Vienna, and it had found her despite being partly misaddressed. "It is hard to describe my joy," she said, "when I got that wire, and I told everybody about it. I somehow pretended that Bruno was my fiancé." In May they began to correspond, not quite a year after he had been arrested. "We wrote," Trude said, "and although the letters took forever, still, I knew a bit about what was going on, although not the whole story. However, it was quite obvious that he and Gina were not going to stay together, and so that gave me hope, and I began to try and get my papers together from the American consul so that I could finally get to the United States."

BETTELHEIM tried first for a college-level teaching post in New York City, but nothing came of his efforts. Through an organization that found places for refugee Jewish scholars, he began to write to colleges all over the country. The doctorate from the University of Vienna indeed proved to be a good credit, but with no teaching experience or scholarly publication, he would have to start at the bottom. However, others from Vienna had begun to make their way in America, and he hoped to do the same.

Among the first friends he sought out in New York were Hans and Wanda Willig, who had arrived in March, just two months earlier than himself. They had moved to Prague in 1932, a year after Wanda graduated from medical school at the University of Vienna, and Hans ran an import-export business while Wanda took a job in the hospital of the venerable Karljova (Charles) University. She got no salary but enrolled free in graduate courses and gained experience working at the prestigious hospital. She was drawn to a psychoanalytic study group headed by a fellow Austrian, Otto Fenichel, who soon became her analyst. After the Munich Conference she and Hans saw they had no future in Czechoslovakia, and at the end of 1938 they moved to Stockholm. The deep winter months in Sweden gave them second thoughts, prompting a move to New York in March 1939.

Less than five years earlier they and the Bettelheims had been on vacation together in Italy when the murder of Dollfuss had shaken everything up. Now their life had tumbled about again, and they struggled to start over, worlds away from Middle Europe.

Still not quite settled, Hans and Wanda invited Bruno to their apartment in New York. She eventually found work as a psychiatrist in the state prison in Bedford Hills and later enrolled at Karen Horney's institute for a training analysis. Bettelheim was one of a growing circle of friends who had fled Vienna and was now looking for a foothold in America. He seemed very quiet when he came to see them, Wanda said. "He just didn't feel like talking about his experiences in the concentration camp. But he was very concerned about his future here."

"He was a completely changed man," Hans Willig said. "He lost all his hair in the concentration camp. He had a shock of hair when we saw him the last time in Vienna—in February of thirty-eight we saw him, he had a shock of hair, and he came back and he was completely bald. Was incredible." Later he added, "We saw it from the outside, he got the whole brunt of it."

IN JULY 1939 Edith Buxbaum invited Bruno to join her for a trip across the country in her car, which he recalled as a "cabriolet" (a convertible). They would carry sleeping bags and sleep out most nights to make their money last. "I thought I might as well take the rest of the summer off, because I couldn't find a job," Bettelheim said. He was, however, still looking, and he scheduled two interviews in California; the trip would also give him a chance to see friends in the Midwest.

Every two or three nights he and Edith found a boardinghouse for bed and breakfast or a tourist court (as motels were then called), where they could bathe, wash out underwear, and make themselves presentable. America seemed astonishingly vast, and their adventure prompted memories of their Wandervogel days some twenty years earlier. Bruno did not rest well out doors on the ground in a sleeping bag, but between visits with friends (like Fritz Redl, in Chicago) and boardinghouses, he got a solid night's sleep now and then.

Fritz Redl had joined the faculty of the University of Michigan at Ann Arbor but had also taken an apartment in Chicago, and they stayed with him for a week or so. Through Redl, Bettelheim met George Sheviakov, a White Russian exile whose father had been the last czarist minister of education and who had himself made a career in education.

Sheviakov was an executive in a group with a project at the University of Chicago, a study financed by the Rockefeller Foundation through the Progressive Education Association (PEA). The Chicago group had been set up to evaluate the results of thirty public and private school systems across the country. Among other things, the study would compare the effectiveness of progressive methods with traditional or conservative teaching methods. Sheviakov and Bettelheim hit it off right away and talked for hours at a stretch.

"We really became friends, good friends, in a relatively short time," Bettelheim said. Sheviakov's work in the study group put him in touch with many people at the University of Chicago and elsewhere, and he promised to keep his eyes and ears open for Bettelheim.

FROM CHICAGO Bruno and Edith drove through midwest farm states, over the Rockies, and down across the southwestern desert country to southern California. Bettelheim's first interview was in Redlands, a town sixty-five miles east of Los Angeles, at the foot of the San Bernardino mountains. He had written to the University of Redlands, a small Baptist college, and been invited to apply in person.

To his surprise, they hired him on the spot. He would teach for two years ("probably German and psychology," he said, "I think so") at a modest salary paid from funds raised by the local Jewish community. Now only four months out of the camps, he had traveled to the far end of an enormous country and landed on his feet in a clean little town with a view of the mountains. The money was not much, but at least he could begin to make a living. Compared to his life a year earlier, Redlands was heaven.

Bettelheim had one other interview, with a professor from Reed College, in Oregon. This man was vacationing in Fresno and had asked Bettelheim to meet him to talk about an opening in the language department. At the end of the interview the professor asked if he would like to teach German at Reed. The terms were much better than the first job, so Bettelheim accepted and wrote Redlands a letter begging off. "I told them I would resign their job and they should offer it to somebody else. Which of course they were glad to do, nobody's feelings were hurt, because in this way two Jewish refugee scholars could be placed."

The first offer had eased some of Bettelheim's fears about his future, but his mother's precarious position made any relief tentative. On the other hand, with the second job offer, he felt a little better about life. He had always wanted to teach in a college, and he had heard that Reed was one of the best small liberal arts colleges in the country.

"The trip was wonderful," he said, "but we were both very tense. The aftereffects of the camps were still working in me." He worried about relatives and friends in Europe, and this colored everything he saw and felt.

Driving back east, they spent one night in Glacier National Park, Montana, outdoors in their sleeping bags. Toward dawn the sound of animals snuffling nearby woke them—bears prowling for food. "When I was a child my favorite fairy tale was Hansel and Gretel—you know, lost in the forest and finding your way. Thank god the bears were friendly. For Europeans like us, this was a *great* adventure."

Once again they stopped off at Redl's in Chicago, and there Bettelheim got another piece of wonderful news: his mother's visa had come through. She was leaving Vienna and would sail to New York. Her ship would dock a few days before he had to take up the job at Reed, and he could meet her.

WHEN GERMANY invaded Poland at the beginning of September and began the Second World War, Paula Bettelheim was luckily already on her way. Her boat docked at Liverpool briefly, and Grete went down to the pier hoping to see her; but under the new wartime conditions, no one could leave or board the vessel, and after a few hours it sailed for New York.

At about this time Bettelheim's fortunes took another sudden turn. Still in Chicago, he heard from Reed College. They were very sorry, but due to the war, few students would wish to take German; their offer was canceled.

"I was a greenhorn," he said, "because there was actually a verbal contract, and friends told me I could hold them to it. But it wouldn't have been a happy situation, and I didn't feel like fighting. So I had no job, and my mother was on the way here."

BETTELHEIM went down to the pier to meet his mother's ship, but its arrival was delayed several hours. As he waited, a letter came for him at the Buxbaum apartment, and Edith had it delivered to him at the pier. It was from his new friend George Sheviakov, who wrote that an empty desk had become available in the office of the Progressive Education Association's Eight-Year Research Study. Bettelheim could have the desk, a secretary, and a job—but no salary. Sheviakov urged him to come anyway: the staff members were first-rate, the kind of people he should get to know; he would learn about American research methods in education and about the education scene in general; and when a paying job came up, he'd be on the spot to get it. He could live in Redl's apartment, and he should come to Chicago right away.

Bettelheim turned the idea over in his mind as he waited for his mother, and he decided to do it. No pay, but a chance to prove himself by creating a research project. It was the narrowest of footholds, but until he had an income, his mother could stay with her sister and Edith, and perhaps things would work out as Sheviakov suggested.

IN THE previous year, Paula Bettelheim had had to vacate her apartment. She notified the Viennese police, and two officers came on her last day in the apartment to inspect everything and give her permission to leave. She was moving in with a friend while waiting for her visa to come through (which took a year, as it turned out). Her furniture and belongings had been disposed of, except for three packing boxes of Meissen and crystal, personal effects she could take with her when she emigrated. The boxes sat open for inspection on a table, and an officer happened to lay his hand on the box packed with Meissen plates and figurines. Paula said, "Please be careful!" and in answer the policeman lifted the wooden case and turned it upside down, smashing everything. Then he upended the other two boxes. When Paula reached New York a year later, she had few reminders of her life in Vienna, but by then it did not seem to matter.

AFTER seeing his mother settled with Jenny and Edith, Bettelheim went to Chicago. The research study already had experts in every category except one, the teaching of art, and nobody knew how to evaluate it. In getting his doctorate Bettelheim had ranged over art, philosophy, and psychology, and he thought he could develop a test that art teachers would find useful. "They wanted to know what students actually learned, and I had an idea of how that might be done. So far, all evaluation instruments in the field of art didn't measure anything."

In mid-September he set to work in the research-study offices, where he found himself more at ease with his colleagues than he had expected, and with plenty of time for coffee breaks. "We went every morning and every afternoon to a little coffee shop to 'shoot the bull' for a while, an hour or more. We were supposed to be talking about office affairs, but we talked about anything at all. I was happy to go along—it was all very friendly, and I was feeling a little more sociable. Anyhow, I was spending my own time, not being paid for the research I was doing, but hoping to get a job."

One day over coffee someone happened to mention the University of Chicago's Great Books program for undergraduates. Robert Hutchins, the president of the university, had more or less copied it from Columbia College's core curriculum, but Hutchins's flair for publicity made Chicago's program the best-known in the country.

A half dozen staffers sat around the table that day, including George Sheviakov and Joe Schwab (a biologist on the university faculty who also worked for the research study). Schwab began to praise the Great Books program in a way that annoyed Bettelheim, who argued that it was not a new idea; young people, even children, read those books in the *gymnasium*. Also, Chicago taught it all wrong, with no historical background; students needed a context in order to make sense of books from other eras.

Unfazed, Schwab redoubled his praise, until Bettelheim at last got fed up and said abruptly, "That's nonsense!" This shocked Schwab, and the dispute grew hotter. Sheviakov kicked Bettelheim under the table, but he went on finding fault with the program. Sheviakov kicked him again.

"I understood that George wanted me to shut up," Bettelheim said, "but I turned to him and said, 'Look, stop pushing me. I am going to say what I have to say whether Joe likes it or not. These are my convictions.' Joe got very excited, but he couldn't put any sense into me, so he gave up and went back to the office."

Afterward Sheviakov told Bettelheim that Schwab was one of Hutchins's closest friends, and Hutchins would soon hear that the upstart Bettelheim had belittled his pet program. Bettelheim had been undiplomatic, perhaps even foolish, but he couldn't unsay what he had just said. He could only hope they would let him go on developing the art test, which he would show in November to Ralph Tyler, who headed the Eight-Year Research Study.

CHAPTER 9

Trude; Bruno's First Job

I N AUSTRALIA that summer, Trude met the man who had known
Bruno in the concentration camp. "This young man appeared, telling
me a lot about Bruno and how he had managed to keep people interested in life—and alive—by telling them about his life. Bruno's analytic
training, his warmth and understanding apparently helped others to manage." Trude and the young man soon became, in her words, "more closely
acquainted."

They went on hikes in the bush—" 'Boiling the billy,' as they say,
which means that you took a kettle to make tea. I think it was almost
inevitable, with my longing for Bruno and our being such strangers in a
strange country, that we should become intimate. I don't think I really was
in love with him. Maybe him not with me either, but it was just a matter
of circumstances and loneliness."

One day Trude felt a severe pain in her abdomen; a doctor examined
her and told her she had an ectopic pregnancy. Conception outside the
uterus is life-threatening, and so she had an operation, followed by a difficult recovery. In the meantime Bruno had written to ask if she wanted to
join him in the States. He had been reluctant to do so before having a job,
but after Redlands and Reed he felt more hopeful.

While Trude was in the hospital the war broke out, and her Australian
status suddenly changed to "enemy alien." As soon as she could walk she
left the hospital to apply for a permit to leave the country, only to discover
that the military now controlled such permits. Feeling very unwell, she
took a taxi to a military base, but the officer in charge of travel papers
seemed uninterested. "I think I began to cry and beg him and told him
how my fiancé had just come out of the concentration camp, and I would
finally be able to join him. Whatever it was, it touched his heart, and he
gave me the permission I needed."

Trude borrowed money from a friend and booked passage to San Francisco. She arrived on Halloween and to her astonishment, the woman who had run the Montessori school in Vienna was waiting to meet her and take her home for the night. The woman also offered her a teaching job in San Francisco, but Trude said no. The next day she shipped her luggage from the dock to the railway station, and three days later she reached Chicago.

Bruno was not there; he had gone to Ohio for a job interview. However, friends met her train and brought her to a hotel in Hyde Park where she would await his return. Suddenly she got an even better job offer—would she like to start a psychoanalytically oriented school for younger children in Detroit? Again Trude said no. Bettelheim explained: "She said to me 'I didn't come all the way from Australia to go to Detroit, I came to be with you.' And that bothered some people—nice people, you understand—who had other plans for her and for me."

Bettelheim did not name the people but obviously meant the Sterbas, by that time well established in Detroit. Also, he did not attribute a motive, but Trude did. She had suspected that "there was something going on" when her former boss met her. "I got along fairly well with her," Trude said, "although I never quite trusted her." As for the first job offer in San Francisco, "I think she did not do that on her own steam. I think the idea came from the Sterbas, who did not really want me to be with Bruno, or eventually to get married to him." (The Sterbas, who had been analysts for Emmi, Bruno, Gina, Trude, the American mother, and the American girl, were also related to Peter Weinmann's wife and disapproved of a Weinmann divorce.) In fact, Trude cared little for what the Sterbas thought, but she worried what Bruno would think when she told him of her recent pregnancy.

ONE DAY toward the end of my visit with the Bettelheims, something suddenly prompted me to ask Bruno how he would characterize Trude in a few words. (At that moment I knew little of Trude's life; she did not wish to be interviewed and as yet had held back from telling her story on tape for her children.) Bruno looked startled by my question, but his first word, after the merest instant's pause, was "courage." I took this to mean the courage Trude had shown in her escape through the mountains, which he had mentioned, but later I came to feel that his deeper meaning included courage in personal relations, by being herself. He spoke also of

Trude's vitality and honesty, almost as if courage, honesty, and vitality made up three related strengths that reinforced one another in her character. We did not discuss these qualities, but I can believe that it takes courage to be honest about one's feelings, faults, or transgressions, and I can also see that such honesty may release energy that rekindles vitality, which perhaps brings a renewed source of courage.

In any event, Trude could easily have made up a story about the fresh scar on her abdomen, but with the courage to be honest, she chose to tell Bruno the truth. "That certainly was not an easy thing to do," she said, "and Bruno naturally was very upset indeed."

Bruno would never have mentioned so personal a matter to me, and I can only imagine how he came to terms with his feelings. Perhaps after the first shock passed, he noticed his own involvement, the fact that he had asked his friend to visit Trude, in effect putting two lonely people together. He also might have asked himself just *why* he had done this, and whether or not his own unconscious motives might have been implicated. Trude was attractive and alone in the world, so what should he have expected? Even so, after all the disasters in the past year and a half—his arrest, the brutal camps, the loss of his property and livelihood, his abandonment by Gina, losing the Reed job—Trude's words came as a shock he felt deeply because of the romantic hopes he now centered on her.

Trude's willingness to tell this particular truth about herself highlights her honesty, and in a calmer moment Bruno would have begun to recognize this. Instead of hiding something, she risked showing herself in an unfavorable light to the one person she loved and most wanted to love her. Perhaps she also meant to test his deepest intentions: did he really accept her and love her despite what she had done? And with a scar on her body to remind him?

Saying honestly that she did it, that she was responsible, lay directly in line with his own values: no excuses, no evasions, no attempt to defend. And she relied upon her own worth to speak for her. Honesty, even painful honesty, is surely the soundest basis for marriage, and Trude was honest.

Above all, by telling him of her aborted pregnancy and how it came about before he had made a commitment to her, she had given Bruno a choice. She had hidden nothing, and he could take her as she was or he could choose not to. Either way, she trusted the result; and, of course, in time they chose to bind their lives together for better or worse.[1]

WITH NO income between them, both Bruno and Trude had to find jobs soon, and both did. In early November, Ralph Tyler asked Bettelheim to show the group his test for measuring the growth of a student's sensitivity to art. Bruno had constructed the test out of art postcards pasted on large sheets of cardboard, and he offered it to his colleagues for review.

"Of all the scholars assembled there in the evaluation study, almost nobody understood what the test was about. It was a complicated exam in a field where testing had not been done before, and nobody knew what to make of it." Students had to match cards or groups of cards according to various kinds of similarity (or dissimilarity) they could see between works of art. By giving the test at the beginning of the course, and then a second version at the end of the term, the teacher could assess the student's growth in sensitivity to art.

Luckily for Bettelheim, the one person who needed to understand the test did so. Ralph Tyler liked it. "He looked at it and saw what I was trying to do and said, well, he thought it had possibilities and I should pursue it and try out my ideas. And then he did what I had hoped, he offered me a job."

In December 1939 Tyler took him on staff at a salary of $2,400 a year, paid out of funds newly provided by the Rockefeller Foundation. Bettelheim now became a Rockefeller fellow research associate, one rank higher than the research-assistant position he had been hoping for. He would have a year's waiting period before his divorce, but then he and Trude could marry. Also, he could now help support his mother, who was still in New York, living with her sister.

There may have been a hidden hand at work in Bettelheim's appointment, although Tyler certainly approved. "Some years later," Bettelheim said, "after I had already been at the Orthogenic School for several years, a writer named Milton Mayer was interviewing me for an article, and he asked, 'Do you know how you got your first appointment?'

"I said something like, I don't know, but I'm glad I got it, and so on, and Mayer said, 'I'll tell you how you got it—you had an argument with Joe Schwab, and after Joe thought about the conversation he became very impressed by the fact that you, an unemployed refugee who desperately needed a job, had the moral conviction to attack Hutchins. That you risked your livelihood and everything for your conviction impressed him so much that after he came back from the coffee break he called Hutchins and said that this man, this poor Jewish refugee from Austria, had the greatest moral courage he ever encountered—that he risked everything for his convictions. "This man we must hire," he said to Hutchins.'

"And so I got hired. At least, that is one version. Of course, there was no moral conviction involved at all—though I believed what I was saying. I didn't think about Hutchins, I didn't know Joe Schwab was a friend of his, I was simply, you know, shooting off my mouth. So you never can tell."

BETTELHEIM went on developing the art test, showing it to colleagues and teachers, perfecting it as a way to gauge the growth of a student's ability to interpret art. But something else happened that surprised him. "I discovered that it was also a personality test. That wasn't the intention, but on the other hand, I should have known, because everything can be revealing about the person. One only needs to know how to read the evidence."

The purpose of the Eight-Year Research Study was to establish whether or not progressive education was superior to traditional education methods. "What we did," Bettelheim told me, "was to evaluate school systems in the hope of finding which got better results. For this, tests were needed because you couldn't simply do it by impression. The program got bogged down when the war came, but an interesting point emerged when we followed the students to college."

What the Progressive Education Association found was that the choice of method made no difference. After two years in college, no perceptible superiority could be seen in students from either type of school. Bettelheim interpreted the result as meaning that the students became more mature and were also influenced by the values around them in college. "You must remember also, that in college they were away from home, and the home had, after all, something to do with the kind of high school they attended. It's hard to separate home influence from school influence, especially when the student is still at home.

"Actually, what the study showed, in my opinion, is that progressive versus conservative high school teaching had only very limited influence for later values. That's good to know in any event. And I was happy to be part of that study. It was the beginning of my life in America."

TRUDE got her first job with Woodlawn Hall, a Jewish orphanage in Chicago. She supervised the study hall, but she hated what she had to do, which was to "keep everybody quiet and at their work." She lived in the orphanage for nine months, and the room and board made up a large part of her pay, but she also received a small check at the end of each month.

Meanwhile, Bettelheim continued to share Redl's apartment. "We had a good time in this little apartment," Trude said, "with Fritz and other friends, [but] still I should mention that life with Bruno at that time was difficult indeed." Trude talked to an analyst about whether treatment would help, because Bruno was still feeling turmoil from the camps. But the analyst "would have none of it. Bruno probably wouldn't have had anything to do with it either . . . and I remember crying a lot."

Redl worked in Detroit but also came to Chicago for a few days at a time because he had a second job there. "I think it must have been that year at Christmas, or possibly the following year," Trude said, "that Fritz took us in his car on a trip to New York, and I was enchanted by the trees that were lighted with different-colored lights, a thing that I had never seen, because our Christmas trees were only indoors, and with candles."

After leaving Woodlawn Hall, Trude rented a room near the apartment, and later in 1940 she and Bruno took an apartment together. At about the same time, she borrowed money from a Jewish organization to take social-work courses at Loyola University. Her Austrian credits were not recognized here, and she had to go back to school to have the career she wanted.

Trude had last seen her parents in 1938, just before she went to Australia. She had visited with them in their small apartment in Tours, where they lived until June 1940, when the Germans invaded and the French government collapsed. They fled Tours on foot to escape the occupying forces and made their way more than a hundred miles south to Limoges, where they rented a single room with a small hot plate but no toilet. Trude's mother wrote that they knew no one in Limoges; they took lonely walks in the countryside and simply lived day to day, hoping to leave France.

Trude's anxiety about her parents could never lie quiet for long, and Bruno shared her fears. He also gave her whatever he could spare out of his salary, as well as raising money from friends to help her parents. On at least two occasions, he said, ship tickets were purchased and bribes paid to French officials; but both times permission was denied at the last minute. Trude's father fell ill, and after his death in April 1941, her mother moved to Puy l'Evêque, in the south of France, where she had a friend. Without her husband she was desperate, lonely, and depressed, the more so because Trude's letters sometimes took three months to arrive. Once more she went to Marseilles to take passage, but her visa was denied again, and she returned to Puy l'Evêque without hope. In the summer of 1942 her letters stopped. She had written earlier that she would commit suicide rather than go to a camp, and in the long silence that followed, Trude feared that this had happened.

In 1946 word came from a woman in Puy l'Evêque, enclosing the last letter from Trude's mother, written on August 25, 1942. Knowing she was about to be taken away, she had entrusted a neighbor with the letter and a few pieces of jewelry. The neighbor said the French police arrested her the next day in a roundup of Jews. For Trude this was the end of her mother's story, a lost parent whose fate could be imagined but never finally known.

Bettelheim wrote one essay about children of Holocaust victims, children whose parents vanished in circumstances that left the child without unequivocal knowledge of what happened and thus with no chance to mourn and grieve in the normal way. This unresolved state of mind, he says, complicates one's sense of loss, deepens it, extends it throughout life, and forces the person to remain silent about it. The event becomes an abandonment with no clear shape or limits and leaves the child no way to face his feeling of loss and get past it. When I read this essay in *Freud's Vienna* (after learning about Trude's story), I realized that Bruno was also writing about Trude's lifelong feelings of loss:

> The terrible silence of children who are forced to endure the unendurable! Their agony is mute; with all the strength available to them they need to bury in the depths of their souls a wound, an anguish which never leaves them, a sorrow so cruel that it defies all expression. . . . Such an injury hurts so much, and is so omnipresent, so vast, that it seems impossible to talk about it, even when a whole lifetime has passed since it was inflicted.[2]

When I interviewed Bettelheim in 1983, I also expected to interview Trude for a few hours, but she politely refused. She had gone out of her way to be gracious, to make sure I was comfortable, that I had meals and everything I needed during my stay, and this in spite of not feeling well herself from radiation therapy. She was so genuinely cordial that I thought perhaps by the end of the week she would relent, but she did not. Her past remained private. Bettelheim told me that one of the children had brought a tape recorder to her and that all three had asked Trude to tell them about her life, but to no avail. Why?

"It's too painful for her," Bettelheim said, adding how lucky he had been that his mother and sister got to safety. However, less than a year later, not long before she died, Trude changed her mind and made a tape for her children.

Most of her life she could not readily open the door on the past and let out her buried feelings about the fate of her parents; but her reservations did finally pass. I believe that Trude let go of this lifelong reluctance as her own last weeks approached; she could then talk a little about the most painful of her experiences, because she knew the day would soon come when her need for a terrible silence would also pass away.

TRUDE could only guess what happened to her mother after the arrest, but records now available show the rest of the story. The police ultimately sent Frieda Weinfeld to the French-administered internment center at Drancy, a suburb just northeast of Paris. Two weeks after her arrest she was put on Convoy 30, a train of boxcars, which left the Le Bourget and Drancy stations on September 9, 1942. The Jewish deportees did not know where they were being taken, but in two days the convoy reached its destination.

In the selection process on September 11 at Auschwitz, twenty-three men and sixty-eight women from Convoy 30 were judged suitable for labor and thus allowed to live. Frieda Weinfeld, five months short of fifty-eight, was not among those chosen and so was gassed immediately, along with about nine hundred others.[3]

CHAPTER 10

Getting a Foothold;
Starting a Family

Bettelheim's 1940 salary of $200 a month gave him and Trude
enough to live on, as well as to help his mother. On May 14, 1941, two
years and a month following his release from Buchenwald and
shortly after his divorce from Gina became final, he and Trude married.
They lived in Hyde Park, near Lake Michigan, where they took long walks
on the shore and went swimming on hot summer days. Sometimes on
free afternoons they visited the Chicago Art Institute, and they hiked into
the countryside on weekends. On rare occasions they spent two or three
dollars for tickets to a concert.

"We were so happy together," Bettelheim said, "we didn't go anywhere
that cost a lot of money. If we went out to dinner it was to the cafeteria at
the university. We felt very lucky to be alive. Of course in Europe it was a
terrible time. Almost every week we heard of somebody else who died—
old friends or relatives who couldn't get out." Later they bought a secondhand car and went for drives to places like the Morton Arboretum.

In England Grete waited for a visa and planned to come to New York
to meet her fiancé, a businessman named Otto Schindler who ran a mining company in Yugoslavia. His job gave him wide travel privileges, and
Paula Bettelheim had entrusted him with money and jewelry to take to a
bank in Switzerland. When Schindler arrived in America, Paula could
live on her own resources, and he and Grete would marry.

Grete at last came over from England and took an apartment with her
mother at Eightieth Street and Broadway in Manhattan. As for her fiancé,
"He got perhaps some of the jewelry into Switzerland," Bruno told
me, "and also some money for us, and he was to come and marry my

sister, that was the plan, as soon as he got his papers in order and enough money out. At the end of 1940 he was still running the mining company, and every day he was picked up by his chauffeur in a limousine to be driven to his office. One day when they opened the door of his limousine, he was dead. A coronary, I believe, though he had also been operated on for cancer. What he was doing for us was illegal, so there was no record of the money and jewelry he had brought out for my mother, and whatever was found was inherited by his sister. To whom he had not spoken for many years, incidentally. So that's how that came out."

BAD NEWS aside, Bettelheim enjoyed his quiet and scholarly job. He could not be sure where it would lead, but Trude knew what she wanted: a career and children; and Bruno fully agreed. As for himself, he hoped that by the time the research study came to an end, he would have found a position in the university's German-language faculty, or something in the humanities. Who could tell? He might even teach "great books" to undergraduates.

"I imagined I would have an easy and cultured life as a gentleman and a scholar. That would have suited me fine. I never liked the business world—in fact I hated it—and I always wanted to be a teacher. I was happy I had now a way of life a teacher could support."

RALPH TYLER, head of the Department of Education at the University of Chicago, was a very generous man. Whenever a friend in Europe asked Bruno about a visa, Bruno would go to Tyler for an affidavit, and Tyler would sign without question, making himself the immigrant's sponsor.

Bettelheim was still not firmly established; the research study was coming to an end, and he hoped Tyler would find something else for him. Earlier, Tyler had told Bruno that he couldn't get to know America if he saw nothing outside Chicago and nobody but fellow refugees. He should try teaching elsewhere, and in fact Tyler had a place in mind for the fall of 1941. "So he sent me to Rockford," Bettelheim said.

Rockford, about ninety miles from Chicago, near the Wisconsin state line, was a small women's college that hired teachers from the University of Chicago in certain subjects. Bruno taught art history at first, and later psychology, eventually spending most of the week in Rockford and one or two days working in Chicago, where Tyler appointed him an assistant examiner on the university's Board of Examinations. He wrote German-language exams and was delighted to have a growing foothold in his new surroundings.

He remained severely troubled, however; his future was hopeful, but his past kept coming back: he had left the camps, but they had not left him. In prison he had puzzled over the fact (also true of other prisoners) that his worst experiences never reappeared in dream form. His days were nightmarish, but even an uneasy sleep brought relief. Now free for three years, he found a reversal: he had good days and nightmare nights.

Near his eightieth birthday I asked him if he still had nightmares, and he replied, "Every month or two." What was the wish fulfillment in such nightmares? "I'm not sure, but obviously you are happy when you wake up and find it was only a dream, so I think maybe the waking is the wish fulfillment."

In speaking with me, Bettelheim used mild words—"aftereffects," for example—to refer to the anger, bitterness, and turmoil he had felt after he was free, but in the earlier years he was still too disturbed to speak in a mild way. Slowly he came to recognize that extreme environments had the power to disturb people long after they were "back to normal."

"I don't believe that extreme experiences are dealt with by the usual psychological mechanisms. The camps were meant to make the individual's normal character disintegrate, so that the person either perished or reshaped himself. Then he could be controlled as a part of a submissive mass. Not just his behavior was affected, but his inner self—who he thought he was. That was the most important thing."

In making a new life, Bettelheim wanted to close the books on the old one but could not. What had happened to his inmost self that had struggled to survive by dealing with the world? In Vienna he had been a successful businessman with Freudian answers to the questions of life; he was still a Freudian, but he was also something else, and writing seemed to be the best way to explore *what else.*

Of course, there were problems. Starvation often causes memory loss, and he feared he would forget specific observations made in the camps. This happened at the beginning, but as his health improved (in New York) forgotten material came back, and he made notes. In Chicago he tried to move beyond his notes, but a coherent piece of writing refused to take shape, perhaps in part because raw emotion rose up and overwhelmed him. At last in 1940, after he and Trude began living together, he started work on an essay he hoped would help him master his painful past. He did not wish to write an appeal to the reader's emotions — mastery did not lie in that direction — and so he tried for a detached manner, with a goal of analysis rather than reportage.

In his first months in America, Bettelheim found he could not speak freely about what had happened to him, and so he held back. "I met not just with resistance but with utter disbelief. This was before the U.S. entered the war, and many people simply could not accept that the Germans would do such things. I was told that I was full of hate and also that I was paranoid, and after I was working at the university for the evaluation study a friend actually came to my office and warned me to stop spreading these lies."

People in the Chicago area, and especially on the university campus, were frankly isolationist and "antiwar." Before Pearl Harbor, many students and faculty members followed the lead of Robert Hutchins, then a national figure with political ambitions, who gave open support to the America First movement. Talk of concentration camps angered isolationists, who dismissed the accounts as Jewish propaganda, but being disbelieved made Bettelheim determined to speak out, and to a wider audience than the people he met in Chicago. He decided to write an article for a psychoanalytic journal. He had seen no serious work on the topic, and he knew he was unmatched in his qualifications to formulate such a piece. Hutchins, who was publicly committed to independence of thought, could never object to a scientifically couched essay in a scholarly journal. Bettelheim would write a monograph with the kind of unarguable objectivity that bypasses questions of personal motive.

Of course, his motives *were* highly personal. How could they not be? For one thing, he wanted to speak and to be believed. The camps existed, they were a shameful blot on the Germans and the human race, and the world should hear the truth. At the same time he hoped to gain intellectual mastery over his experience by writing about it and perhaps to allay the unnerving rage that the memory aroused in him. Finally, he wanted to prove to himself that he had not changed in any essential way. Mere survival was not enough; he did not want to feel he had become a different person.

Working on the essay inevitably brought back images that shook him, and he tried to guard against this by raising the shield of rigorous detachment. But that led to a paradox: to write, he had to remember; but his reaction to memories interfered with coherent writing. Explanations not colored by emotions were hard to come by, and the process did not do all he had hoped. Too much had to be repressed rather than worked through, but he persisted.

His deepest dread (a death anxiety that flooded his mind and seemed to suffocate him) eventually faded into the background as he stubbornly worked out his ideas. Also, the daily pleasure of loving and being loved, combined with the satisfactions of a job he liked, gave him strength. If the writing brought back bad feelings too vividly, he could turn away to a home life relatively free from the angers of his first marriage; or he could occupy his mind with his other work.

Struggling with the essay helped him clarify, first and foremost for himself, the inner logic of the monstrous conduct of the Nazis. It solidified his grasp on his ideas and therefore on himself. More than once I heard Bettelheim characterize his attitude toward writing and its value to him with, "I never know what I think until I try to write it down." The essay in this light became a much needed thinking-out of events that obsessed him. Even before he went into the camps, understanding his feelings had come to be a habit and perhaps a therapy. He had long tried to do this, to question impulses without falling prey to easy answers.

From a psychoanalytic point of view, which Bettelheim continued to use almost as second nature, a person's character might be seen as the sum of his defenses. Every threat (inner or outer) calls forth a defense, and perhaps the worst threat is death. Most of us get used to the idea of death in a way that allows us to ignore it most of the time, but prisoners could not do this in the extreme conditions of the camps. With their defenses worn down by random abuse and the constant threat of death, they were unable to trust themselves; a survivor like Bettelheim who wanted to be the "same person" perhaps also wanted something more: he wanted not to fear death as the supreme master of life.

Bettelheim began the essay on the camps in 1940 and wrestled with it off and on through 1941. He finished it at last in early 1942, under the title "Individual and Mass Behavior in Extreme Situations." As the first systematic analysis of the concentration camps, it seemed to him exactly the kind of work that would be welcome in scholarly circles. The British government had published a report on the camps in 1939, but Bettelheim had taken the further step of analyzing behavior and intent. Also, American isolationists at the time had called the British report propaganda meant to influence American opinion, and Bettelheim hoped to minimize any such reading of his essay by making its tone cool even when dealing in disturbing facts.

Bettelheim returned to the themes of the essay at much greater length in *The Informed Heart* (1960), but as a first effort to outline the coercive methods, goals, and results at the harshest level of a totalitarian state, the essay is both awkward and remarkable for the pure seriousness that puts its ideas ahead of motive, ambition, or personal suffering. When he felt at last ready to show the piece, Bettelheim sent it to the *Psychoanalytic Quarterly*, a professional journal of prominence and distinction. However, within a few weeks the editors returned the manuscript. The rejection surprised and angered him, but he sent it out again, this time to *Psychiatry*—with the same result. It galled him to the point of fury to be dismissed out of hand by people he had respected as professionals in what might have been his own field, if life had dealt with him differently.

"I offered it to a number of magazines, and they all had a reason for not taking it. One said that I didn't take careful notes in the camp—I should have taken notes and brought them out—as if it was possible to take a scrap of paper out of a concentration camp, you know, which showed such an abysmal ignorance. Another said they could not believe my facts and conclusions and that I must be exaggerating. Others said that the data were not verifiable, that my findings could not be replicated, and so on. If I could have predicted the future I would have kept the letters I got from these magazines, but I didn't know the camps would become common knowledge. I thought they might be entirely disbanded and covered up."

After a rejection he sometimes put the manuscript in his desk drawer to avoid another turndown so close on the heels of the last. "I was angry and depressed, naturally, at not being believed on a subject that was so important to me and also to the rest of the world." In the end, the subject was too urgent to neglect, so he kept sending the essay out.

More than a year had passed when he offered it to the *Journal of Abnormal and Social Psychology*, edited by the Harvard psychologist Gordon Allport. Allport may have been drawn to the piece because of its clearly post-Freudian emphasis on the environment's powerful effect on behavior.

"I was convinced he would return it too, but I was astonished when he took it and said how important he thought it was. He told me he was going to stop and change the next issue, to put it in immediately." The essay ran as the lead article in the October 1943 issue of the *Journal*, while Bettelheim was still working at Rockford College.

In 1944 Dwight Macdonald reprinted it in the August issue of *Politics*, where it reached a different and wider audience. Macdonald's magazine had become a prestigious and influential forum for ideas, and Bettelheim's inclusion there marked him as an intellectual to keep one's eye on. "Macdonald and I became friends after this," Bettelheim said. "I visited with him, and we got to know each other, and he printed a few more book reviews and articles by me, which I've now forgotten."

Bettelheim had set out to describe the psychological impact of the camps upon the inmates (as well as on the guards and the population at large). He identifies stages that prisoners went through in their adaptation to camp life, as "new" prisoners became "old" prisoners, if they survived. He also describes his private adaptive behavior to defend against becoming demoralized, and he offers examples of behavior after individuals had been molded into a controllable mass. The piece made a striking debut, and Macdonald's follow-up put another stamp of approval on it, bringing Bettelheim the kind of attention a struggling would-be professor needed. However, by the time the essay appeared in *Politics* he had just taken over the Orthogenic School and had precious little time to capitalize on the opportunities suddenly at hand.

In 1945 the article came to the attention of General Eisenhower, who Gordon Allport said had ordered it to be reprinted and distributed to all military government officers in occupied Germany. This official acceptance gave Bettelheim small satisfaction: few in the outside world had listened before, and now most of the victims were gone. They had died in the camps before the world had noticed they were there.

ALSO AROUND this time, Gina and Peter Weinmann moved to Chicago. They had married, and he had found a job at the university. Bruno's friend George Sheviakov was just leaving Chicago, and so the Bettelheims helped the Weinmanns get Sheviakov's apartment, a very desirable place only a few blocks away from where the Bettelheims lived.

One friend Bettelheim had made soon after joining the research study was Benjamin Bloom, who also happened to be one of the first Jewish graduate students at the university's School of Education. Bloom had taken a job on the research study as an assistant to Ralph Tyler, and he went on to spend his entire career (which included the honor of an endowed chair) at the School of Education. I interviewed him at his office, where he was semiretired but still quite active, working on budgets the day we talked. He had published seventeen books, among them a study of peak learning experiences.

"When Bruno joined the faculty," he said, "we were almost the first Jews here. He had been through terrible experiences, and I think I became something of a confidant to him for a brief period in the early days. At least, he trusted me, and we talked at some length." Bettelheim found Bloom easy to be with, and they went for long walks on the Midway,[1] talking about their hopes for the future. It was 1939, and both men were looking to make their way in the academic world. Bettelheim also spoke of his interest in children and their psychology, of the American girl who had lived in his home, of the summer school for delinquents and the nursery school he had helped finance.

One day in 1942 Tyler told Bloom he was looking for someone to write a report on the Orthogenic School, which fell under his authority at the School of Education and was in a sadly run-down state. Bloom volunteered that Bettelheim had some knowledge and experience from Vienna that might be useful. Tyler called in Bettelheim and asked him to visit the School and submit a report. What should the university do with it?

The question started Bettelheim thinking: he liked the idea of a residential school for troubled children, because it seemed a better combination of the care and guidance that he and Gina in their home, and Trude at the Montessori school, had provided for the American girl. It was something definitely worth looking into; however, his first look shocked him. "They knew the place was a mess," he said, "but were wondering what to do. It was badly run, in part because my predecessor took in a mixture of brain-damaged, epileptic, feebleminded, and psychotic children. It was hopeless; it couldn't really operate as a school with that population—it was too chaotic."

The School had opened in 1912 as an experimental clinic but had evolved into a boarding school "for retarded and problem boys and girls one to sixteen years of age."[2] In its thirty-year history it seemed almost a stepchild of the university, although usually with several wealthy sponsors, some of whom had "problem children." *Orthogenic* was an out-of-date word, but donors accustomed to the name were still involved.[3]

"The director wasn't really interested. He did good research, but for him the School was a springboard, because he took the well-paying students into private practice and dumped the rest in the School. It was dirty, it was smelly—I couldn't stand the smell of urine and so on—and the children were not well taken care of. They were adequately fed, I will say that for him, but there was a lot of physical abuse of the children, partly against one another, partly by the staff. Well, I was so utterly disgusted by what I saw that I said to myself that if I told Ralph what I thought of it he would think this was the goddamn arrogance of a European who knows everything better and is critical of everything American. So I didn't write the report."

This was in 1942, when Bettelheim was dividing his time between Rockford and Hyde Park. Trude had become pregnant earlier that year, and she gave birth in November to their first child, Ruth. It was a happy moment for them, even though Bruno was away from home so much, and in spite of the continued aftereffects of the camps and the undercurrent of fear about Trude's mother, already dead in Auschwitz but her fate still unknown to Trude.

BETTELHEIM'S feelings about himself were helped in 1943 by Allport's acceptance of his essay, because it lifted some of the burden of an angry message that the world had seemed unwilling to hear. Betty Lou Pingree (later Rellahan), one of his students at Rockford, said that his easy manner gave a sense of intimacy in the classroom, where he chose not to stand at a lectern but sat facing the psychology class and taught by posing questions and asking for interpretations of behavior. After class Betty often saw "Dr. B." enjoying himself in the student coffeehouse with his table ringed by young people, one of the very few teachers who socialized in this way. In the college dining room he sat at the round faculty table with his fellow teachers, most of them women, and when Betty served as a waitress for that table she usually found her psychology teacher smiling, genial, and active in the conversation.

Bettelheim wanted to be a teacher who got to know his students as individuals, and so he asked them to write short autobiographies. Later he could catch responses at variance with what they had said about themselves—a method for moving subtly from formal acquaintance to insight. Had he become a professor of art history in Vienna, it is not likely that he would have socialized with students or asked for personal histories. These things, however, enlivened his work and seemed appropriate in his new American milieu.

In the spring of 1944, he taught a psychology course in which he decided to use the Thematic Apperception Test (TAT) but with significant changes. At that time the TAT was a fairly new test instrument and was also in some ways similar to the better-known Rorschach test.[4] Rorschach used abstract forms ("inkblots") to evoke a patient's responses for the therapist to interpret. The TAT used nineteen black-and-white pictures and one blank card. Instead of nonobjective forms, human faces and figures appear on most of the cards, but the scenes are composed in an ambiguous way to prompt a wide range of responses.

Bettelheim saw a possible pitfall in the TAT—that the therapist could easily project himself into the test taker's fantasy and give vent to his own unconscious drives while interpreting the results. He tried to avoid this with a surprising departure from the rules of the test. Also, he did not trust the test protocol that said test subjects should not be told they were taking a personality test. He refused to keep his students in the dark, both because he believed that many would guess it was a personality test and because he felt it was wrong to try to fool them.

The test called for making up stories about each scene, which took two class periods on successive days. Like Rorschach, the TAT creators aimed to stimulate answers so a therapist could interpret "regnant preoccupations and unconscious trends," as Bettelheim said in the paper he wrote.[5]

He also changed the test rules by telling his students not to enlarge upon their stories later. (The TAT required enlargement so that the therapist would have more material to explore, but Bettelheim had a different idea.) Over several classes he lectured about the purposes of the TAT and had each student give the test to another person and interpret the results. Finally, he gave the class a TAT taken by a thirteen-year-old boy, and he led a class discussion about the boy and his test.

A few weeks later he sprang his surprise: he brought back the students' TATs and asked them to interpret their own stories. In the intervening weeks he had prepared them with his lectures on TAT theory and practice. The critical point for him, however, was that he had given them time to forget their stories and come with a fresh eye. He saw no real purpose in leading the class through the TAT as its creators intended, and his adaptation of it had a meaning closer to home: he wanted to test a hypothesis about whether or not the TAT, as he used it, could help some students begin to interpret themselves without therapy.

These young women from the Midwest were not likely to become psychologists or go into therapy, and he hoped that his adaptation of the TAT would at least give them some inkling of their own psychic depths. Also, he wanted them to come to any insight on their own, rather than being told.

In the article he wrote later, he concluded that

most of the students acquired a greater understanding of dynamic processes than they possessed before interpreting their performance on the TAT. . . . Obviously it is difficult to ascertain such progress, since the students' psychological understanding before and after interpretation could not be measured.[6]

Earlier in the paper Bettelheim had noted that he believed that many of his students had begun a transference in their relationship with him.

Transference is the Freudian term for a process crucial to analysis, when the patient's feelings and wishes shift unconsciously from the parent or some other emotionally charged authority figure to the analyst; and this shift often brings the patient's unconscious neurotic impasses and defenses into his conscious mind so that they can be explored in collaboration with the analyst.[7]

The students thought they had made progress, and Bettelheim generally agreed, but with a pointed comment:

It is doubtful whether the method in itself would promote greater insight without the transference relationship.[8]

With this conclusion Bettelheim brought Freud squarely into the classroom through a teaching technique; he saw that his manner and personality had worked on the natural susceptibility of young people to become emotionally involved with their teacher, and he used this to turn them gently toward self-knowledge. Thus in his earliest formal teaching of psychology his grasp of Freud helped him promote the idea of knowing oneself. He did not expect clear results from his innovation with the TAT, a test already worlds away from behaviorist experiments where numbers quantify the action of rats; but what he did was personal and human in that it led to hints, for the students, about the unknown recesses of their own minds.

Bettelheim may have misjudged how far he could go in opening up the realm of psychology to the young women of Rockford; at any rate, for this or some other reason he was given notice that his contract would not be renewed in the fall. Betty Pingree at the time was not sure why, because he had quickly become one of the most popular teachers on campus. "I don't know if it was disturbing to the students or the faculty, but now I realize that he was probably let go," she said. She and other students circulated a petition and protested to the dean, a rare episode at a staid college like Rockford, but Bettelheim was already heading for another job at the end of term.

IN THE spring of 1944 Bettelheim heard from Ralph Tyler (who may have heard from Rockford that they were uncomfortable with Bettelheim). Tyler had long since asked for a report on the Orthogenic School, and now he wanted to know why Bettelheim hadn't written it.

"Now, that was typical of Tyler. If you didn't do something, he wouldn't push you. He would accept it. But by now we were on a first-name basis and very good friends, and I felt I could speak freely. So I said, 'Ralph, I tell you why. I needed a job desperately. I loved the job I was doing for you and I felt the only thing I could tell you was to ask whether the School was well insured. If so, burn it down. I didn't think anything could be done. Now since we know each other better, I feel I can tell you.' He laughed and said something like, 'Well, you can't shock me now, and this makes sense to me. But now that you've told me I really want the memorandum about what should be done with the School.'

"I began to smell a rat, so I said, 'All right, but I know what this work entails, and I don't want to run the School. I'm not interested; I did this kind of thing once in my life and that's enough.' 'Yes, yes.' he said. 'I understand. But please study the School and tell me what should be done to make it a good place for the children, a good place for treatment.'

"So, all right, with the understanding that I wasn't interested in running it, I wrote this memorandum, of which—of course—I've got no copy. I was helped in part writing it by Dr. Emmy Sylvester, who was then a prominent child analyst in Chicago, probably the best known after Margaret Gerard. She was from Vienna, though I don't think I knew her there, but in Chicago we all naturally got together. I knew about Redl's work, of course, and August Aichhorn, but mostly I drew on my own experience in providing a home and full-time care for the autistic child who lived with us in Vienna, and the summer school I financed at Schloss Schallerburg. Also, I knew of Trude's experience in the Montessori school, where they had some very difficult children and she was their teacher. She taught the girl who lived with Gina and myself.

"Anyhow, I wrote this memo and didn't hear anything for a couple of months, which was fine with me. I was still doing some research, and I was teaching at Rockford, and also I was making the German exams and helping out with other exams in the humanities. My plan at the time, or rather my hope, was for a job in the Art Department at the University of Chicago."

The head of the department, Professor Middeldorf, had recommended Bruno to Rockford, and Bettelheim spoke of him as a good friend who had promised an assistant professorship in the humanities, with emphasis on teaching art history, for which his degree qualified him. "That was," he said, "a very gentlemanlike job, and I wanted it very badly. It seemed ideal at the time, and I couldn't think about anything else. I hoped to get the kind of job here in America that would never have been open to me in Vienna, so I was very anxious.

"One day Ralph came to me unexpectedly and said, 'Are you free for lunch?' I said yes, of course. If the big boss asks, 'Are you free for lunch,' you're free for lunch. So we went to the faculty club, and he told stories. Ralph was a wonderful teller of tales. His store of tales is incredible, and most of them are very good. Some are very funny, some a little off-color and funny. But anyway he told stories one after another and entertained me gloriously throughout lunch. But when we were having dessert, I wondered what was going on, because he didn't ask me to lunch unless there was some business in his mind. Usually the business transaction began with the dessert, and he hadn't said anything. But then we had our coffee, and nothing was raised. Then he said, 'We're having such a jolly good time, why don't you walk me to my office?' Well, if your dean asks you to walk to his office, you do it. But he kept telling stories, and they were so good that I didn't realize we had passed his office. We went into another office, and I wasn't paying attention to what it was until the secretary said, 'Good afternoon, Dean Tyler. Please go right in. Mr. Hutchins expects you.'

"Then I knew something was going on. We went into Hutchins's office, and he was smiling and cordial. I saw he had my memorandum on his desk, and he said, 'Well, we have your memorandum and we think it's a very good statement. Your ideas for reshaping and reorganizing the School are very good, and we would like you to do that.'

"At this I became very angry, I couldn't help it, and I said, 'Look, Ralph'—I neglected the president, didn't answer him but turned to Ralph—'Look, Ralph, I told you I'm glad to write this memo for you but I

don't want the job.' Hutchins interrupted before Ralph could reply and
said, 'Yes, Dean Tyler told me that. We're well aware that you don't want
the job, but we want you to take it.' Now there I was in a terrible quandary
because, after all, my appointment as assistant professor in the humanities
was also dependent on Hutchins, and if I was difficult, if I turned him
down when he was so insistent, I wouldn't get the appointment I really
wanted.

"So after a lot more talk in which they both tried to convince me to do
it, they needed me, I'm the right man for it, they're going to give me all
the support, and so on, they said, what are my conditions? I was annoyed,
and I thought, all right, I'll set conditions they won't accept, so I said,
'Okay, a tripling of the budget and no questions asked and no questions
answered for five years.' I didn't think they would agree, and then I'd be off
the hook, but I knew it would take me at least five years to get the School
into shape.

"But then Mr. Hutchins turned to Ralph Tyler, and Ralph made some
remark, and Hutchins turned back to me and said, 'We think your conditions are eminently reasonable.' Then they both looked at me, and that
was it.

"When I got home to Trude that night, I said, 'I think I got myself into
a big mess today,' but it was a great challenge, too, and I obviously wanted
to do it in spite of my first reservations, which were mainly about the toll it
might take on my personal life. I could not have done it without Trude, of
course, but then we trusted each other so much because of all we had
been through. I think she said something like, 'Well, you can do it,'
because she understood what was required and also because by then we
understood each other so well that it didn't take many words."

IF BETTELHEIM was actually marking time in a psychosocial moratorium, he did not fully emerge until he was almost forty-one and found the
work that galvanized him totally. It took his whole persistent mind to
make the smelly School into a pleasant environment with the hidden
moral strength of a coherent therapeutic vision. And common sense.
Children would not simply be treated in a caring way; it was more than
that: the entire setting would give the troubled child a chance to settle
down, to become ready for the guidance he needed to learn and grow, to
feel better about himself, the world, his future.

Bettelheim and others have commented on some ways in which he
drew upon his concentration-camp experience and reversed it in the

School. Where the camp deprived prisoners, he offered abundance; where it blocked loving relationships, he encouraged their growth between counselor and child; instead of a harsh milieu whose extreme conditions pushed men toward inner collapse, he surrounded children with a benign environment that subtly promised a better life. The milieu was only the first step in the healing process, but it was the best possible setting (short of a happy home) for a child's growing integration of personality.

His idea was deceptively simple, but the School is not a simple model to copy. One can make a good case that it was uniquely obliged to Bettelheim for its happier results, a view he dismissed out of hand. Now that I've become familiar with the School over a period of time and through the eyes of many participants, I'm convinced that Bettelheim did develop a workable model. However, I also believe that to make the model succeed to the degree it did under him, it must be headed by a strong person with quick insights and instant reactions in a crisis; who is a shrewd judge of people; who is clear about his own motives and at ease with himself in his work; who has a rare and deep commitment; who puts the school and children first perhaps more often than he should; who does not keep normal hours; and who protects and hopes to teach *everyone* in the milieu. In short, someone like Bettelheim. This person must also be someone whose strong personality inspires and invites transference—someone who is, in a word, lovable.

By TURNING the demoralizing intent of the camps inside out, Bettelheim took a new approach to therapy, though at the time he did not realize it. At least a year passed before it dawned on him that he had unwittingly used the camps to structure the School. The core of total-milieu therapy owes much to his life experience but even more, I believe, to his dogged pursuit of the psychological meaning of that experience. Also, for many years, evolving a new approach to therapy was not just a professional ambition for him; it satisfied an angry need to work through and deal with his past. Learning how to help disturbed children grow gave him hope and, apparently, some measure of peace.

In his first book Bettelheim mentions his indebtedness to the ideas and efforts of Aichhorn and Redl on residential therapy, and he also credited Dr. Emmy Sylvester, who served as the School's psychiatrist for the first five and a half years he was there.[9] In the preface to *Love Is Not Enough* he said that she contributed to the development of the School's philosophy "and the shaping of its practice." About Redl, who came and observed many times, he added that their ongoing dialogue had

> now created a situation in which I no longer know exactly where his ideas end and my own begin.[10]

Bettelheim had no special training or academic expertise for writing a report on the School or for running it, but once he had accepted the job, he was more than ready to try. His angry reaction to Hutchins's offer and to Tyler's benign deception shows (to me, at least) how deep the idea had reached into his heart before he could acknowledge it to himself.

Tyler knew Bettelheim as a man of subtlety, force, and ingenuity in the research study and at Rockford, and Hutchins relied on Tyler, perhaps also recalling his friend Schwab's opinion of the Jewish refugee's character. So they took a chance; they ignored Bettelheim's lack of formal credentials (which they would surely have noticed and discussed) and reached outside the university faculties to name him. They bypassed good men in the Departments of Psychology and Psychiatry, the Laboratory Schools, Pediatrics, the School of Education, the School of Social Service Administration, and the Human Development Department. A dozen or more qualified academics could have been picked for the job, but Tyler and Hutchins singled him out, perhaps in part because nobody else wanted such a problem. If the Orthogenic School was not quite an orphan in 1944, it was surely an unwanted child.

However, once Bettelheim had made his report, Hutchins and Tyler saw a plausible plan and put the planner in charge. It is also plausible that if an outsider like Bettelheim, who did not have tenure, were to fail, it would be easy to terminate him and the university's connection with the School. On the other hand, he might work out; the memo's suggestions could turn the place into the kind of experimental center the university took as one of its reasons for being. Perhaps new educational models would come out of the School, or new ideas in child development and psychology. In any event, a few months later an "advisory committee" was named, made up of faculty from most of the departments that had been bypassed, but there is no indication that the committee ever gave any advice. Bettelheim was on his own.

IN TRUTH, he had no model for what he did. Formal study, an overwhelming event like the camps, the ideas of others—all these could go into Bettelheim's maturing views but do not account for the kind of sustained and original vision it took to develop the Orthogenic School. Intellectual influences and training count for little unless brought to fruition by a person's innate readiness to be engrossed in a particular kind of work, and to be satisfied with it. Broad insights about residential therapy from a nominal precursor like Aichhorn are available to everyone, but surely the touching and protective example of the doctor who saved the three-year-old Bruno's life had an unmatched power to inspire his vision; as did the *gymnasium* director who punished the teenaged Bruno strictly but with conviction and respect. I believe the first incident impressed Bettelheim with the closeness and caring intrinsic to the healing process, while the other showed him the firmness and distance needed in a good model for one's autonomy. However, even such feelings held in memory could become active only when they flowed into the ruling passions that gave meaning to Bettelheim's life.

The Orthogenic School, as he ran it, owed its conception not only to the camps and to psychologists who had tried and failed with a therapeutic milieu (or had had only a brief and limited success), but also, and more so, to Bettelheim's unique personality. We can see a direct line from his early and ongoing fascination with Freud to his deep, inquiring affection for the American girl. Despite a lapse of six years (1938 to 1944), this personal interest returned in full force when the chance came his way, and it became a professional interest that laid out a path for the rest of his life as he built up the School and perfected its therapeutic purpose. He had to do it, he wanted to do it, and doing it occupied him more fully than anything else he could have done. It occupied him so well that it even drew his thoughts away from the helpless wrath that smoldered at the back of his mind when he relived the inhumanity of the camps.

One evening toward the end of my stay with the Bettelheims, Bruno and Trude took me to a farewell party for their Stanford faculty friend Alvin Rosenfeld. Several couples had brought their children along, and at the party I ended up spending more time playing with the children than talking with the adults. This was unusual for me, but somehow the children caught my attention and held it, so much so that I stopped feeling a stab of bursitis in my shoulder.

We left the party early, because Trude had undergone a radiation treatment that afternoon and was feeling very tired. She held Bruno's arm as they walked slowly to the car in the growing dusk, and I followed a few steps back. A thought came to me about my reaction to the children at the party, and I said, "Bruno, I think I know your secret."

"So?" he said, walking with Trude and not turning around.

"When you're really interested in children, it takes your mind off your troubles."

"Dot's right," he said. I couldn't see his face, but the polite neutrality of his voice suggested that this probable truth held no interest for him at that moment. He was worried about Trude.

CHAPTER 11

The Orthogenic School: Taking Charge

W HEN BETTELHEIM had first seen the School, he'd turned his back on the chance to run it. The place needed too much, its demands would be all-consuming, and at that point the rejection of the essay was depressing him, enraging him, perhaps making him doubt himself. Unsure of his status with his superiors, he could not write a radical critique, the only kind that would have been honest. Now the picture had changed. The essay had been taken seriously by a journal of academic distinction, which made an enormous difference in how he felt about himself and his place in the world. When he visited the School a second time, in 1944, he did so with enhanced credibility and a boost in his self-confidence, an indispensable trait in anyone who would run such an institution.

He asked several of his psychology students at Rockford to come with him to the School, and three of them accepted. He had sized them up as good candidates for the work, and if things went well he would make them the core of the new staff while gradually replacing those already there. As it turned out, he did keep one staff member, a teacher named Anna Lukes (pronounced "Lucas"). He found Miss Lukes firm, forthright, and fiercely possessive of the children she taught, and they trusted her. His new plan called for the children to stay with their teachers throughout the day while counselors took time off, and a no-nonsense spinster was exactly the kind of strong teacher he needed.

"As the School developed, she became almost a legend to the children. They all loved her, when they got to that point in their development." Like everyone who mentioned her, he called her "Miss Lukes"; he spoke of her as a superb teacher, admired by other staff members for her strength, empathy, and common sense. "This made her good in a crisis, and in the early years there were times when I felt I could not have done it without her."

ONE OF the young women from Rockford, Betty Lou Pingree, arrived in early September. As she walked downstairs from the entry hall of the School, she noticed a black-curtained room in the basement, next to the dining room. It was the EEG laboratory (for the previous director's research), where the electric activity of a patient's brain was recorded and measured. The EEG machine disturbed her; in the darkened room it looked sinister, with its array of dials and needles, and she wondered what Bettelheim thought of it.

That afternoon Ping (as her friends called her) and another young woman from Rockford, Marj Jewell, took a group of seven- and eight-year-old boys out to the Midway to play football. Ping and Marj joined in the game themselves, as Ping had often done when she was a counselor in summer camp, but the boys went wild and turned on them. The over-wrought children attacked the counselors and tore the sleeve off Ping's blouse, screaming and out of control. Ping and Marj stopped the game and struggled to bring the frantic boys back to the School.

Bettelheim stood waiting in the doorway when his new counselors came across the street with the boys, and he ordered another counselor to take charge. Ping and Marj went back to their room and wept. Bettelheim asked them to come over to his apartment after dinner, and there the two young women poured out their feelings and confusion to him and Trude. He reassured them, telling them they could do the work of the School despite this first day's disaster, and he explained that their mistake was to put themselves on the same level as the children, to become "one of the boys"—just what a frightened child did not want. Troubled boys like this, he said, saw danger everywhere, and counselors had to protect them by giving them a feeling of order at all times. If counselors surrendered their adult control, who would protect whom?

NOT LONG afterward, Ping was happy to see Bettelheim get rid of the sinister EEG table and replace it with a Ping-Pong table. The somber black cambric that had darkened the room gave way to handsome linen drapes as he started to make the School's decor cheerier. Ping also recalled the stony-faced night nurse who posted a chart to keep track of the children's bowel movements. Counselors under the old regime were expected to hover near the bathroom, look into the toilet bowl, and take notes for the nurse, who then decided how much laxative to give the children. One day Bettelheim noticed the chart and asked, "Vot's dis?" When Ping told him, he snatched the chart off the wall, tore it up, and walked away. "That ended that," she said.

In *A Home for the Heart,* Bettelheim wrote about cleaning up the School and the subtleties that go into a good atmosphere. He was working with a three-story brick building that had been a pastor's residence, and he also had the church next door. Both were well built but hard to adapt to a residence where children could live and also go to classes. However, he would manage.

In the first week Bettelheim called a meeting of the whole School and promised the children they would no longer be hit or spanked by the staff. Several resignations appeared almost at once on his desk, and he was happy to accept them. His three students from Rockford brought his nickname, "Dr. B.," to the School, and of them he said, "Ronnie [Dryovage], Ping, and Marj all turned out to be wonderful with the children. Marj was at the School only for several years, but many years after she left, she committed suicide. She was a very beautiful and intelligent young woman, from a well-to-do background, successful parents and so on, but I'm afraid it was not apparent how troubled she was. When I heard the news I was shocked and depressed for a long time. I wished she had stayed longer with the children, and maybe she would have found out something else, something she needed, something important to her. But, of course, you never can tell."

Also in his first week Bettelheim clashed head-on with the staff over locks and keys. He ordered all exit doors to be kept unlocked so that a child could leave the building if he wanted to. Bettelheim did this by installing night latches on outside doors, which could be opened from the inside without a key, as in an ordinary home. Intruders, "robbers," parents, or other figures in a child's fearful fantasies were thus kept out without compromising anyone's freedom, and the children understood this as the purpose of the latch locks. Also, over staff protests, Bettelheim refused to lock children in a room "for their own good."

Both staff and children distrusted this sudden freedom at first, but no serious problems followed. "One thing I hoped to establish," Bettelheim said, "was that you can trust mental patients, especially children, if you are genuinely trying to make things better for them." He and Sylvester believed that in milieu therapy, a well-planned residence staffed by sympathetic adults could surround children with a seamless outward support that would help them develop inner strength and hope. "The basic message is that they, too, can learn to master their own lives. In my years there, we had many crises but no catastrophes, so I feel that my point was amply demonstrated. I've heard all the reasons against it, I've read the books, but we did it and it worked."

A few places in the School had to be locked, such as confidential files and counselors' rooms, but these locks all opened with a single key. Even after this system had proved practical, staff members kept asking for special keys, and this happened so often that Bettelheim concluded that multiple keys led to a complex hierarchy of status, which could be avoided only if most keys were done away with.[1]

Another form of status in the School was soon dropped: he closed the staff dining room, with its separate menu, and staff members and children thereafter ate the same food in the same place. This move did more than bring about a sense of equality; it also set the scene for unexpected therapeutic moments, especially for children with problems around food, like the boy who would eat food only off his counselor's arm. That was an opportunity to search for meaning in what the child did and observe with what feeling he did it.

BETTELHEIM also changed the School's regimen by cutting back the school day, ending it at three o'clock instead of five, so that children could go back to their dorms earlier, or out to play. He abolished homework, which eased pressures and made a clear boundary between schooltime and free time. The children spent from nine to three "in school," but lunch and recess periods reduced the actual classroom time to about four hours. Bettelheim expected youngsters to learn more in fewer hours as teachers gave individual attention, and with never more than eight in a class, he saw no reason why this shouldn't happen.

Counselors got the children up in the morning (often a difficult task) and shepherded them to breakfast in the dining room, then to various classrooms, where the teachers took over. At lunchtime the teachers went with them to the dining room. Off-duty counselors having lunch would see anything that took place during the lunch hour. To Bettelheim this continuity of presence and observation gave milieu therapy a huge advantage over usual institutional approaches, because it meant that a knowledgeable adult was always nearby in case of trouble; also, counselors would get a fuller picture of a child's behavior by being on hand at all times.

IN THE fall of 1944 a few children still came only during the day, but these were soon phased out. Children living in the School went home on weekends, but this too had to be changed. Bettelheim wanted to keep parents at a distance, in part because he was trying to take the children out of the nuclear-family setting, where they were in trouble, and put them in an environment that was in some ways like that of an extended family. Also, if a child was beginning to open up about unhappiness at home, it would be counterproductive for him to meet his visiting parents in the hallway or to see them every weekend.

From the start, Bettelheim ruled out epileptic, brain-damaged, and retarded children, none of whom he could hope to rehabilitate. Such children would be best cared for elsewhere, and for those already in the School he found places in other institutions, to make room for children he might help. In the milieu he aimed to create, each child could become close to a few persons without having to be intimate with others. In a nuclear family the daily pressure of close relations made life tense for disturbed children (and even for "normal" children at times), whereas an easier setting would give relief from unwanted nearness. A nuclear family had less breathing room, since the presence of major authority figures made it hard for the child to let down his guard. In a more relaxed environment like that of an extended family, a child could distance himself without feeling separation anxiety or abandonment, or risking disapproval and censure.

A PROBLEM Bettelheim would face with new staff at the School was keeping them motivated, and this is where the transference became crucial. He had seen that it played a part in the success of his experiment with the TAT at Rockford, and he had no doubt experienced it himself in his analysis with Sterba. In fact, at one point I asked if he had made a transference with Sterba, and he looked at me sharply for a moment, then said, "I suppose so," which startled me. My question had been spontaneous, with no conscious motive, at a time before I came to understand the importance of transference in holding the School together. It was a casual query with more meaning than I realized, and it set off Bettelheim's warning signals. His noncommittal reply was typical in that he did not tolerate anyone probing his unconscious, and my question was intrusive. This moment occurred during one of our sessions when I stayed with the Bettelheims; a day later I saw another example of how he guarded against me or anyone else seeking clues to his inner life. The second moment was also unplanned on my part and took place at the end of the week, when I happened to recall a simple "test" I had taken at a party many years earlier. It had given me insights into myself, not at a deep level but certainly into the unspoken trends of my personality at that time.

The test was abstract, consisting of six squares—one blank and five with lines or dots. I sketched it from memory and asked Bettelheim to fill in each square with anything that came to mind. Again, I felt no desire at that moment to look into his unconscious, although I now see that this was surely part of my motive. Bettelheim studied the piece of paper intently for at least a minute, then picked up a pencil and began to make marks. When he handed the "test" back I was quite disappointed, because he had carefully shadowed each square with sweeping horizontal lines that effectively drew a curtain over his inner life, showing me only that he did not wish to show anything by free association. His refusal was so clear that I did not bother to keep the paper.

BETTELHEIM maintained privacy over his thoughts and feelings (except for what he chose to show and how he chose to show it), but in the School his mentoring of the staff members on impasses in their work made some feel they were being intruded upon. Many soon left, some in anger hardly to be softened by the passage of time. Most new counselors started off with a conscious desire to help children, and this might on its face seem a good enough motive. However, Bettelheim knew very well that an unexamined altruism would not stay intact for long, and that a quid pro quo was essential for anyone to survive in the job. Nobody could care for disturbed and difficult children day after day merely out of good nature; staff members had to get something of value in return for all they gave, and the first thing they got was Bettelheim.

Those who made a transference and became attached to him got the benefit of his experience and insight, plus a close attention that to many felt loving. He had at first thought he might take some staffers into analysis, but this was not possible (as will be discussed later). He did, however, help his staff members with their work problems, which usually turned out to be psychic defenses. The other aspect of their reward, not always quick in coming, was a penetration into the seeming enigmas of personality: insight into the children, of course, but equally into themselves.[2]

Taking care of pathologic children inevitably aroused defenses, and a deep motive for working at the School flowed naturally from the worker's ongoing self-discovery. Without this glimpse of things defended against, the demands of the job would have been too much. The pay was nominal, but when staffers could find and face disconcerting truths within themselves, the reward was unique and added satisfaction to their work. Also, the children were often fun in spite of daily difficulties, and ideally counselors formed relationships with children that meant a great deal on both sides.

In the fall of 1944 Bettelheim found a new counselor, the first after the three from Rockford. Gayle Shulenberger (later Janowitz) was hired to substitute for the night nurse, a job she said was "just being there at night and being awake." (At that time, if a child felt ill or hungry late at night, he came to the night nurse.) In fact, Gayle did not fit Bettelheim's staff guidelines, since she had no college degree and she wasn't asked to write a short autobiography. In *A Home for the Heart* he is quite specific on these two points, so I asked him about Gayle's hiring.

"We were just beginning," he said, "and she walked in off the street, and my secretary hired her. By the time I asked her to be a counselor, we could see she was very good with the children. We were lucky—she turned out to be one of the best people I ever worked with at the School."

When the night nurse left for vacation, she told Gayle about a boy who would not eat because he feared being poisoned. Bettelheim had told the nurse to set out sandwiches and milk in the hall where the boy came at night. "She obviously disapproved of Bruno," Gayle said, "but I thought, 'That's interesting.'

"Bruno came up to me one night in the nurse's office and asked where I was from, and I said, 'South Dakota,' and he said, 'I never knew anybody from Souse Dakota.' " When he asked about her background, she said she grew up on a farm with lots of cousins and had a "wonderful life." She did not mention her unhappiness at losing her parents when she was young.

When the night nurse came back, Bettelheim happened to need a substitute counselor, so Gayle took the job. "I wasn't really a counselor yet, I was just filling in, and I thought the School was a crazy place." One counselor carried a stick and threatened children with it, "but she didn't last long." Gayle did not realize Bettelheim was building a new staff and setting the School on a different course, and she went on subbing without thinking beyond the moment. On her own, she wrote up notes about a retarded boy because she had decided that he wasn't actually retarded, but then he was suddenly transferred out of the School. Later, she told Bettelheim her opinion about the boy, and he surprised her by agreeing with her.

"He said the problem was the boy had been institutionalized too long, and he was too far gone to be rehabilitated. Earlier he might have been helped, but not now. I told Bruno about my notes, and he said, 'Why didn't you show them to me?' The truth is, I didn't know what was going on. After I found out you were *supposed* to write reports, I wrote about my kids. Bruno came up to me one day and said, 'I liked your reports, please give me some more.'"

When she went to her first staff meeting (she hadn't realized there *were* meetings), she heard Bettelheim give a speech outlining his plans. "He talked about how he had just come to the School, and he told us everything that was wrong with it, and what he was going to do to change it. That night I went home walking on clouds, because I was in on the ground floor of something new and exciting. I got so excited over the fact that he *knew*, that I could barely hold on to myself. Then he made me a counselor full-time, and that was it." Gayle, only twenty-one, stayed for the next seven years.

THOSE who worked at the School in Bettelheim's early years speak warmly of the "ice-cream sessions." It was not practical for him to invite the entire staff over to his apartment, as he had done with Ping and Marj on their first day, but later that fall, Gayle said, the staff began meeting informally at night. "After we got the kids to bed we went down to the kitchen and ate ice cream, talked over our day, sort of waited for Bruno. He would come down around eleven so we could ask questions and tell him things."

This friendly meeting over food seemed to help the counselors ease the tensions of the day. Everyone drank coffee and ate leftover desserts and bowls and bowls of the richest ice cream in Chicago. They laughed, cried, told stories, and got advice from an attentive and sympathetic Bruno and from one another. In the kitchen for a late-night snack, they felt an easiness not possible during the day, when the children's needs overrode all else.

This feature of the School's life was not planned; it came about spontaneously, and Bettelheim saw the value of it. He analyzes these night moments in *A Home for the Heart*, sketching an arc of discussion that

> begins with the "funny" events and moves on to "unusual" things as workers unconsciously test out how safe it will be to open up about the "exasperating" ones.[3]

The moral tone of the meetings was supportive and intimate, with friendly encouragement that allowed one "to search within oneself, as opposed to exploring only what has happened with the patient." The staff felt unsure of themselves, but at least the new methods had worked for one more day, and on that guardedly hopeful note they planned the next day.

> Knowing what we were going to do in broad outline helped us to sleep more easily.[4]

In these sessions we can see Bettelheim returning to his "Know thyself" imperative. For many staffers, however, the search within themselves soon bumped up against the blank wall of a defense, or fled to a pseudo insight (another defense) that bypassed the need to change and left the inner self perhaps ruffled but otherwise untouched. Those who stayed, stimulated by the work into deeper knowledge of themselves, went on to become collaborators in the building of the School. On average about two-thirds of the staff members quit or were fired within one year of hiring, but the one-third who could live with the clarifying shocks and tangled ambiguities inherent in self-discovery grew closer to the children, to Bettelheim, and to one another.

Late in the fall of 1944 Bettelheim announced that the staff would meet to vote on choosing a head counselor. He and Sylvester had anticipated that a new tone would be set in the School by getting rid of class and status, but commonsense exceptions soon cropped up. Dispensing with hierarchy was all very well, but the idea of a head counselor eventually led to "senior staff," who would be superior to newcomers and help them learn the School's ways. It was both apparent and desirable that counselors acquired status from their job performance, and those who worked well with children rose in authority. Bettelheim said that it took him about a year to see that his idea of staff equality had missed the point; it was a good principle, but it did not reflect on-the-job merit. He had sought social solidarity as the best way to get workers committed to the idea of a total therapeutic milieu, but

> it became clear that this idea of equality was an artificial way of achieving the goal.[5]

He could not get around the simple fact that people had unequal talents in caring for children.

"So we had an election," Gayle said, "and the staff voted for me, and I thought, 'Well, he liked my reports.' I believed he had told the other counselors to vote for me, because the idea that they would have picked me on their own was incredible." Years later, when she returned to the School for a visit, Bettelheim told her that her election had absolutely astonished him. He'd thought Ping would be picked, and when Gayle was chosen he decided he'd better find out who she was.

Betty Pingree and Gayle had become fast friends and told each other all about their childhoods. "One night a few days after the election," Gayle said, "Bruno came up to me with a slight smile on his face, but with those penetrating eyes, and he said, 'Zo! Your mother died when you were a year old! Your father was in a mental hospital! And you told me you had a happy childhood on a farm!' He was being funny. He's a great performer, and he had obviously talked to Ping and some of the other counselors. So I said, 'I did tell you that, and it's all true, and as the old song goes, *You can't take that away from me!*' He laughed and walked away."

CHAPTER 12

Writing

ETTELHEIM HAD no time for writing when he took over the School, but the stir caused by his essay had given him a taste for the renown of authorship. He wanted to be noticed for his ideas, and from the start he set his sights on a popular audience, as Freud had done.

> Freud's choice of words and his direct style serve the purpose of making the reader apply psychoanalytic insights to himself, because only from his inner experience can he fully understand what Freud was writing about.[1]

Writing in English, Bettelheim could not hope to emulate Freud's gift as a stylist; also, he already thought and spoke in the shorthand of psychoanalytic jargon. If he were to avoid professional language and give the reader an inner experience, he needed a good editor to help make his style more direct.

In late 1944 he met Ruth Soffer (later Marquis), a picture editor for the *Encyclopaedia Britannica*'s annual editions. Ruth, then twenty-six, had worked her way up from file clerk; she had no formal training as an editor, but her lively mind seems to have made a perfect fit with Bettelheim. At the time, Ruth (who had been divorced) was keeping company with a Viennese émigré who took her into the circle of his émigré friends. One evening around Christmas she went with him to a party in Hyde Park at the apartment of Gina and Peter Weinmann, where she fell into casual conversation with a bald-headed man in his early forties. She was stunned to find herself talking to the author of the article on the camps she had admired in *Politics*. "It blew my mind away, so I don't know much of what happened the rest of the night. Bruno and I must have talked until two in the morning."

Ruth also met Trude that evening, as well as Paula Bettelheim. "His mother was very elegant, and she had the carriage of a queen. Very gracious, but about as cozy as an icicle. Not terribly intellectual. She was a lady pure and simple—a lady of the late nineteenth century." Peter Weinmann happened to be away, but Ruth said that Gina dominated the room.

"She was filled with fire and vivacity, but at the same time tough as nails. Gina was Bruno's first love, I mean he was gaga. Of course, I'm sympathetic with that. There's an irrational part of yourself that belongs to your first love—this I know from experience." She recalled hearing Gina tell of life with Bruno—"saying that if she never saw another cathedral, it wouldn't be too soon. But mostly I talked to Bruno."

After the war ended, in 1945, the *Brittanica* began to plan a four-volume set that would cover 1936 through 1945, and Ruth suggested a piece on concentration camps. "I thought they were symptomatic of the whole decade and should be discussed. So I called Bruno, and that's how my work with him began."

She asked Bettelheim for sixteen hundred words about the camps. "Bruno said, in effect, 'You're welcome to the camp article, but I'm very busy. I don't have time to cut it. Would you be willing to cut it?' I said, 'Sure, if you trust me,' but actually the idea scared me. I was ready to pee in my pants because I had such a high regard for the essay and the author."

When the piece was finished, Bettelheim invited her for lunch. "He said, 'Are you interested in doing any editing for me?' I wasn't sure, so I said, 'For you? I don't know anything about psychiatry, I don't know Freud from a hole in the wall, I've never read anything.' Bruno said, 'Good!' because that was exactly what he had in mind. He wanted an editor who *didn't* know. He wanted me to read his pages and say, 'Bruno, I don't understand this.' That was the first thing he needed me to do, and that's what I gave him."

Bettelheim's job at the School was never more demanding than in the first two years, but for his writing he stole moments to speak with Ruth during the day and again when he worked late into the night. She became both a stimulus and a critical backup, so he could set down first-draft thoughts at top speed and not worry about consistency or polish. She blue-penciled his prose as her eye and ear tested his words, editing line by line to help him clarify his thoughts and pursue them into final form.

Soon she was immersing herself in the School, sitting in on staff meetings at night, spending most evenings either there or at home, making queries, corrections, and comments on Bettelheim's manuscripts. "I did two things for Bruno. I liberated him from the carefulness that any piece of writing requires—redundancy, contradiction, meaning; I did that. And I dollied up the English—I don't like long sentences or jargon. All that was the first thing. The second thing I gave him was a sounding board, which he absolutely had to have. That's how Bruno and I functioned. Everything he wrote, if he was terribly excited he would call me before he put it in the mail. And then I would get it, and read it, and either I loved it and was excited out of a year's growth, or I had misgivings, or whatever."

Ruth enjoyed her job at the *Britannica,* but her work for Bettelheim almost seemed to give her another life. "At the School I met people my own age, some a few years younger, and they were hopping with energy and curiosity and idealism. It was a fantastic world." After a time, she broke up with her émigré friend and moved across town to an apartment within walking distance of the School, so she would have more time for her new work.

In editing Bettelheim she never argued with him on a personal level. "But," she said, "I would fight like an alley cat over a passage in a book, or his reasons for something if I thought they were off base." One trait that troubled her, however, was that he was "totally unconscious of his autocratic behavior toward people." She once sat across from him at his desk in the office at night, going over something and talking about it. "He would sit there and peck away at the typewriter, making revisions, and then he would holler, 'Lucy!' to the girl who was just closing up shop. He would have something else for her to do. I'd say, 'Bruno, she's got to go home now!' And he would look at me startled and say, 'Oh, she wouldn't mind.' I thought he should at least ask her, but that's how it was from the beginning of his life. He had *never* been a 'servant.' Up to the moment he went into the camps, he always had an army of people to do his bidding. Not that he was a Simon Legree, but he didn't know what it was to stand in the shoes of an employee who's dependent upon you. That person's feelings never entered his head, which is astonishing for someone who could get inside the head of a crazy five-year-old."

Ruth's observation strikes me as accurate, but I would add that Bettelheim's urgency about whatever he was writing probably blocked out other considerations, such as what Lucy might want to do. He no doubt assumed that if she *needed* to go home, she would speak up and go. However, Lucy's attitude toward Bettelheim was perhaps not far from Ruth's. His strength of purpose, force of character, and emotional directness made him attractive to many around him, and he drew people in his wake in ways that served his ends and their motives.

Ruth edited Bettelheim for many years, and he paid her, but her dedication and independence of mind were beyond price. "He told me a thousand times, including in letters years later when he still couldn't believe that I wouldn't work with him anymore, 'Everybody is afraid of me. They won't talk back to me, they won't be critical, and I can't do without that.' That's what he valued, plus the incredible freedom to just pour and pour and pour and then go on to the next thing. Because he knew I would clean it up."

Until 1948, Bettelheim's writing was confined to articles (some with Emmy Sylvester), essays, and book reviews, and the diligent editing and candid questioning he got from Ruth Soffer set him on his path as a writer. Still, the welfare of the children and the running of the School remained his first order of business.

"I doubt if anyone with a family of his own would ever do what Bruno did," Gayle Janowitz said. "I remember Trude coming into the School crying a couple of times, and we heard enough to know she was saying, 'You spend all your time with these crazy kids, you don't have any time for your own.' They would go into the office and a little later she would come out and seem put together again, and go home. But Bruno was almost never home."

I asked Bettelheim if he remembered Trude in tears at the School, but he seemed genuinely at a loss. "There must have been some disagreements between us in the earlier years, but I can't recall them. Very few people really understood our relation, because Trude was a most independent person, and she gave me the courage and freedom to do what was at times quite difficult. And with the security in herself and in her relationship to me, she didn't need to have me around all the time."

I said that Gayle was probably recalling a moment late in 1944, and this prompted a memory about his daughter Ruth (two years old at the time). "She had pneumonia, she was in the hospital, and it was a battle of life and death for the little baby. We were most terribly upset. Well, it might have been that, it might have been something else, I have no recollection.

"But also at that time I had certain anxieties whether I'd be able to make the School work. It was a very ambitious project, but I couldn't really get full support from the university until they believed that I would succeed." In the first months he struggled to show progress, feeling, he said, that he "had to make a success before I really had the wherewithal to do it. But if Trude came crying, it was about Ruthie."

Bettelheim's anxiety was no doubt justified, but the formation of the advisory committee in November reassured him, because Tyler invited him to help select the members. Also, the university's support solidified: his predecessor spent $35,810 for the 1943–44 year, and he got $64,000 for 1944–45—not the "tripling of the budget" he had requested but a healthy increase of almost 80 percent. Bettelheim's first secretary, Mary Ellen Cowan, remarked on his close attention to detail. Every month the controller's office "sent out sheets that showed how much you'd spent and how much you had left in your budget, and he would go over these first and give them to me to detail out. He kept his finger on absolutely everything, whether it was administration or typing the reports on the kids that went into the files. Every detail. And he managed his time well, he was a well-organized man, and he took care of the business of the School very consistently."

When Bettelheim had to call the controller and argue about something, his voice would grow loud enough to be heard in the outer office, where Mary Ellen sat. "He always spoke quickly and firmly. But with all he had to do, he still didn't look harassed a bit. In fact, he looked charged. He moved quickly most of the time, he didn't stroll, going from one thing to another."

Mary Ellen left the School before *Love Is Not Enough* came out, but she read it, and I asked her why she thought Bettelheim's role is missing there. "I don't think that was his purpose," she said. "In fact, you won't get a clear picture of him and his role in the School in most of the books. His reason for writing was not to explain himself."

Bettelheim maintained a symbolic distance in his office but kept himself on display whenever possible. "His office had a split door, so the top would be open and you could see in, even if the bottom was closed. I remember one time a counselor brought in a child she couldn't handle, and Dr. B. ranted and raved at the child. Then they left, and Dr. B. turned around and had a smile on his face that was just beautiful. He had done what he had to do, but there was no real anger in him."

For Bettelheim's first year at the School, he was paid $3,600—$1,900 for the school and $1,700 for lectures. His title was principal of the Orthogenic School; he had no title in the Department of Education, but early in 1945 Tyler appointed him lecturer in education, and in October promoted him to assistant professor of education, with a salary of $4,000 (60 percent School and 40 percent lectures). The percentages did not reflect Bettelheim's overwhelming concern with the School, but the raise and the new title reflected Tyler's confidence in his protégé.

CHAPTER 13

Making the Milieu

A S BETTELHEIM said on many occasions, total-milieu therapy was not psychoanalysis, although it used psychoanalytic insights. He started from a conceptual framework that he and Sylvester had worked out, but the first two years kept him so busy that he could not stop to think about theory. "The realization of what the School should be came to me in the second year, and then it took five or six years to feel that I was where I wanted," he said.

The university predicated its funding on creating a "lab school" that would try out new methods of treatment. This was Bettelheim's earliest aim, and it remained a guideline as the School developed, but his attitude toward research later shifted. The change came about when he saw more deeply into his own motives for running the School, into the unsuspected responsibilities of his role (which became apparent as he lived the job), and most of all into what was best for the children. Treatment could be planned in the name of research, but the child's welfare had to remain the first and final criterion for everyone, including Bettelheim. Mistakes in treatment could be corrected; more significant were the conceptual errors that came to light as elements of the original plan proved counter-productive.

"I thought too much in terms of my own analytic experience and train-ing," he said. "I was much too anxious to uncover the unconscious. It took me a long time to realize how slow I had to go there, how destructive and overwhelming it can be, how chaotic. My first tendency was to lift all restrictions and to let the children do whatever they wanted, provided it wasn't self-destructive or hurtful to others." He had expected too much from the mere fact of freedom, a feeling that would have been natural to him even had he not been a prisoner five years earlier; but he saw children becoming terrified when this new freedom released their own destructive tendencies. "It took me some time to realize that this is much too scary, most of all because the children appear to *themselves* as monsters, which was contrary to what I wanted."

I mentioned Rabelais's famous motto for an imaginary academy, *"Fait que vous voulais,"* but Bettelheim shook his head. That could not be the School's starting point. And it had to combine, or integrate, several disciplines. "We had education first, learning so that the child could take a place in society. But we also had child development, social work, psychology, and psychiatry. And when we talk about creating a benign milieu, you must remember that there was not simply a single environment. Each child had his own therapeutic milieu," as established by the child's "envelope of care" with his counselor and by the specific course of treatment developed for him.

To Bettelheim the School's first task was to protect the child's symptoms—thus the friendly milieu and the casual approach of the counselors. "You can't study the symptom and understand it if you try to correct it right away. The only way you can change a symptom permanently is to learn why the child is doing it, not what it means in general but what it means to this particular child." Over the years he came to realize that the hardest thing for a new counselor to learn was to respect (*"really* respect," he said) the child's symbolic behavior. "But you have to do it, and you have to be genuine about it. Lip service won't work, the child will sense your ambivalence. Also, you have to understand that this behavior is the child's greatest achievement. To him, it is saving his life."

The counselor had to respect the child's private world for a long time before it opened up, by which time the youngster had become an individual about whom the counselor cared deeply. Her relationship to him was not the same as Bettelheim's, who could not work with children in the way counselors did. But caring deeply about individual children, Bettelheim said, was the point to which all counselors came if they found what they wanted in the School. "Anyone who couldn't do it at first would always see the senior staff doing it, so they could see it was possible, and think about it and hope to do it themselves."

ONE ELEMENT in the original plan that did not change was Bettelheim's determination not to accept children who needed only custodial care. In 1944 at least half were mentally retarded or had an irreversible

condition of the nervous system. The new program was for children diagnosed as hopeless but with nothing physically wrong. A survey taken just
prior to Bettelheim's arrival showed 63 percent tested as below average,
with IQs of 99 or lower, whereas three years later, in 1947, 88 percent had
IQs of 100 or higher—a reflection of the change in population.[1] "The
main point of selection was that the child had been tried in other forms of
therapy which had failed, or had been declared hopeless. We planned it
as the place of last resort." Some of the counselors (Gayle, for instance)
called the School "the Last-Chance Ranch."

Bettelheim's admission procedures also marked a departure from
usual practices. In most mental institutions, the staff examines the patient
when he enters the premises; Bettelheim turned this around and let the
patient[2] examine the institution. To some degree this was possible most of
the time, so that instead of finding himself viewed as an object to be
treated and cured, the child saw that adults in the School respected his
dignity.

Bettelheim empathized with the child's emotional isolation and
invited him to take a tiny step out of it by giving the message, "Form
your own opinion." He knew the newcomer would form an opinion anyhow, but by extending a genuine and courteous invitation, and by not
pushing, he could hint that the child's feelings mattered. A child did not
have to grasp this as a conscious message to be moved by it, if it was
genuine.

Once the child was living at the School, the counselors understood
not to pressure him with offers of help and sympathy. If they made a
friendly gesture, it was one that he could take or leave, without response.
A year might pass before a youngster showed warmth toward his counselor, even though she had been genuinely friendly and attentive all that
time.

Staffers also had to treat promises like an emotional minefield,
because many children instantly took a promise as a threat of disappointment. Bettelheim said that if a child's experience or feeling had been that
he could not trust promises from an adult, the counselor had to be careful
in making a promise because it was immediately disbelieved. "To earn a
child's trust so that he can believe a promise often took as long as two
years."

BETTELHEIM liked to cite a verse from Goethe to point up the School's
broadest goal. "In German it is very beautiful in the language and the

rhythm, but essentially Goethe describes himself by saying, 'From my father I have my outer appearance and my attitude to the serious matters of life. From my mother I have the enjoyment of life and the pleasure in fantasy.' This is how Goethe described the two sides of his personality. I often used this in teaching the staff, because, in a way, school for the child is the serious aspect of life. A child can accept school and deal with it if his home is devoted to the enjoyment of life and to his free-floating fantasies. In the dormitory they had much more emotional satisfaction, fantasy expression of inner problems. This is why they need both sides. Neither one side nor the other makes for the complete man, that's my point."

This broad-based and penetrating summary of the School's aims clearly echoes Freud's "love and work."[3] Bettelheim hoped to strengthen the children to grow up within a pattern that would later help them make a balanced and satisfying life for themselves.

As HAPPENED with many counselors, the work turned into a life of total dedication for Gayle, and she soon moved into the School. Delinquent boys in her group often ran away but came back after midnight—to find her waiting at the door. If they had stolen money (usually from a staff member), Gayle shut the door in their faces until they handed over what was left. Other counselors protested her making the boys wait outside, but she had to get the money or they would run away again. On many nights she took a flashlight to look for cash hidden under a bush or a pile of leaves, and when the boys showed her where to look, she took them inside, bathed them, fed them, and put them to bed.

One evening near bedtime Gayle took her group down to the kitchen, which at that time had a rack of knives hanging over the chopping block. "Somehow Harry* got up on the chopping block and before anybody knew it, he had a knife in his hand and threw it at me."

In a flash Gayle saw that it was her fault; she shouldn't have exposed him to temptation by bringing him where he could get a dangerous weapon. "He couldn't control himself and had to get his hands on it. So I just grabbed him and told him it was my fault." Harry's uncontrollable hostile impulses had brought him to the School, so it was Gayle's responsibility as a protective adult to keep a stimulus like the knife out of his reach. It also helped the other boys that she could recognize her mistake and say so. "I think I also had the feeling that it wasn't *me* he was throwing

*All names followed by an asterisk are pseudonyms.

the knife at, that it was something from his past. But I held on to him the whole time there in the kitchen, even while we were making fudge."

BETTELHEIM had a similar experience at about the same time. His predecessor had kept a candy closet locked, behind his desk, but Bettelheim left it open so the children could take what they wanted. He locked the office at night to safeguard confidential records, but he didn't like the office for himself and meant to move to another. However, with so much to do, he delayed.

"That was a mistake," he said, "as I realized one morning when I came into my office and found a meat cleaver on my desk with a note that said, 'This time it's on your desk, next time it'll be in your head.' " Two boys had entered by a skylight, unhinged the candy closet door, and set it in the middle of the floor.[4] "The boys were telling me that I wasn't doing my job, and I'm afraid they were right," Bettelheim said. "They were declaring that dangerous weapons like the cleaver should not be left where they could get their hands on them, but candy and cookies should. I relocated the closet the same day and spoke to the staff about how to handle a group of children in the kitchen, where the knives were kept. It was a good lesson for all of us."

GAYLE said that when Dr. Sylvester came to the School, Bettelheim would go to the door, throw it open, and escort her into his office as if she were "the queen of England. He was so deferential to her, so genuinely courteous, so very fond of her. They usually called down for tea or coffee, which we always had ready for her. They spent a few minutes in the office alone, and then she'd go and see a child and later come back and talk to us."

As the School's outside psychiatrist, Sylvester visited twice a week for most of an afternoon, usually to see an especially disturbed child and to offer insights in the staff meeting. Bettelheim had planned to take a few children into therapy himself, but when he tried to do this, the ones he didn't take became jealous. Their counselors resented it as well, and another solution had to be found. It came about almost by chance, through an unexpected bureaucratic demand from the university and by way of Trude.

After Naomi's birth in 1945, Trude had taken a job with the Child Care Agency in Hyde Park (so she would be closer to home than with the

Family Service Bureau in Chicago). Also in 1946, the university ordered Bettelheim to hire a social worker to see the children regularly. According to Margaret Carey, Trude's supervisor at Child Care and her best friend, "Bruno came home one night and said to Trude, 'The university says I have to hire a social worker. Do you know one who really and truly—oh dear!—cares about children?'" Trude recommended Florence White, Margaret's other close friend at Child Care, and Florence became the School's first social worker, a job that almost immediately turned into therapist.

Adding a social worker to the School's roster was likely an afterthought from an administrator who had little idea of what was going on there, but Bettelheim turned the irksome decree into a major improvement for the School. If it was disruptive for him to see children in therapy, he could move beyond the social-worker idea by asking teachers and counselors to give therapy sessions so that each child would get a chance for attention apart from his group. However, Bettelheim chose to call these sessions not "therapy" but simply "sessions," since he wanted to keep everyone focused on the idea that the milieu as a whole was meant to be therapeutic.

Bettelheim also began to notice that staff members needed therapy in addition to whatever insights they gained from the work, and Gayle said that he helped staffers get ready for the idea of therapy. "I remember the first time he mentioned to me that I might someday want to get help, I felt, 'Oh, sure, sure.' It was a hundred years from now, what are you talking about? But most of the staff did eventually get some psychotherapy. In working with the children, you had to learn where you came from; that was part of the excitement. Anybody who worked there for a period of years, that was where we grew up, that was our adolescence."

In Gayle's second year she began to work with Paul,* a boy whose mother had put him into a series of foster homes, day-care centers, and, finally, an orphanage. After Paul tried to kill himself at the age of ten, he was offered to the School under a court order, and Bettelheim persuaded Gayle to take him into her group. She had serious doubts: Paul's words came out garbled and no one could understand him; his raging tantrums were frightening, he was megalomaniacal; and he'd grown obese from constant eating. Gayle argued with Bettelheim that it was no use trying to help him.[5]

"I said he was too far gone, too old, he sat on my lap all the time, and he was enormous—ninety pounds. What did Dr. B. think I was, a miracle worker? But Bruno kept telling me I could do it, that I would see Paul improve if I just kept at it. He knew that was what I wanted to hear (I didn't know it at the time) and in a sense he may have been performing, but also he was dead serious. And he was right. Paul overate and got fatter, but in time things began to change. In arguing so much I really wanted Bruno to give me hope, which he very calmly did. With genuine assurance. And I believed him."

As shown here, Bettelheim had to instill confidence in the staff; if he were wishy-washy or even unconsciously ambivalent, everyone would sense it. Also, his self-belief had to be deep and genuine; bland hopes and a smile of good intentions would never carry the day. He had to perform, but he had to *mean* it if the staff were to believe his reassurances and the self-confidence he modeled for everybody.

I wanted to know how Paul felt about Bettelheim in later years, and I asked Gayle to find out if he would talk to me. He consented on the condition that I not identify him by name or any personal detail. A month later I came to his place of business half an hour early, and while waiting I noticed how well he spoke with his employees and to customers as they walked in the door, and how smoothly he managed his telephone work. He dressed well, handled himself with confidence, and was clearly in charge of a busy scene.

When we were alone, I said, "You seem to size up people the moment they come in." He smiled and said he learned that at the School, dealing with counselors—it was important to know what they were feeling. On the other hand, Bettelheim had stayed remote and had made him angry at first because he showed no reaction to Paul's temper tantrums. "At the same time, I got the feeling that he was interested in me and that I could talk to him, or get mad and carry on if I wanted to. I felt that no matter what happened, my rock and salvation always rested with Dr. B.—it was his authority. I never learned to 'love' Dr. B., but in my years at the School I learned to respect him."

Paul came to see his relation to Bettelheim as being like Heidi's with her grandfather, who at first seemed cold, hard, and opinionated. In time she saw he seemed to know what was right, that he was strong and respected in the community. "Many times," Paul said, "I've been able to persevere in traumatic situations by clinging to Dr. B.'s rock of strength. I think my ability to persevere comes from having seen him being strong in tough situations that I witnessed personally."

To Paul it was supremely important for the staff to understand a child's anxiety and his need to be *right* even when he had done something wrong. "That has been important in raising my own children. Also, the

success I've had with them has come from making demands very early—
not waiting until they were ten or twelve or fourteen and suddenly trying
to change them. From the start I wanted them to respect me, and to have
respect for property and for themselves."

Paul could not stay in the School past fourteen, and at that age he was
not ready for life outside. Bettelheim had visited several prep schools,
hoping to find good places for his "grads," but without success. He was
forced to recognize the sad fact that most of the children had not developed to a point where they could make the transition to such schools.

"Leaving the sanctuary of the School was shattering on my first day in
the outside world," Paul said. He could not stand his new foster family,
and some of his old behavior returned; however, he survived—and felt
sure enough of himself four years later to go back for the visit that Bettelheim described in *Truants from Life*.

Later I interviewed Paul again, hoping he could be more specific
about how he gained inner strength from Bettelheim's example, but he
said, "I don't know how this was instilled in me, but the biggest problem
in a traumatic situation is to calm yourself down so you can gather your
strength to see what the problem is." He mentioned Bettelheim's aloof-
ness and the calm atmosphere in his office. "He seemed a different person
when you talked with him alone. If he was in the dining room and somebody made a commotion, he could be stern. If some kid spilt his milk or
poured a pile of salt on the table and started throwing it around, and the
counselor didn't react fast enough, Bruno was there. He was like a lifeguard at the beach.

"Subconsciously, any one of those kids knew when he was doing
wrong and hurting himself. But Bruno blew the whistle on you, and his
reaction created the feeling of a time lapse. All of a sudden the spotlight
was on you, while everybody else stood still or faded like they were in a
total fog, and Dr. B. was there, saying, 'Don't do that!' And if you stopped
whatever it was—playing in the milk, throwing the salt, mashing the potatoes and flipping them, taking your shoe and throwing it across the room,
taking a bat and hitting the wall, taking yourself and pounding yourself
with a hammer or your head against the wall—then Dr. B. became a
bridge between you and your feelings, or your past. He was the parent you
felt didn't love you. But he could blow the whistle, and when you needed
him, he was there for you."

During Paul's visit to the School when he was eighteen, Bettelheim
noticed he was falling into an intense fantasy. "Dr. B. said, 'You shouldn't

have to use a mechanism of self-adulation. You really need to calm down, you get too wound up.' He's still right about that, even today. I was watching television the other night, and somebody in the movie was bluffing about something, and I felt a mounting attack of anxiety. I didn't want to see what was going to happen next. My throat tightened up, my heart started pounding. If I see something like this, the first time it's usually all right, but a second time and I can panic over it. So I turn off the TV or walk away. I can't diagnose it, but I deal with it."

Paul said that when Bettelheim put bars on the School's windows, all the children complained that he was making it into a prison.[6] "And Bruno said, 'The bars are there to protect you, not to contain you. Anybody who wants to leave—the front door, past my office, is always open.' But the way he said *past my office* stopped you. He was saying, 'If you can get past me, you can go!' And we all knew we couldn't get past him.

"Of course, we all forgot about the bars and accepted that they were to protect us from anybody coming in, rather than keeping us in the building or keeping us from jumping out the windows. He was a terrific salesman—after all, he convinced us that life was worth living."

THE SCHOOL'S milieu set the stage for a child's growth, but the events of growth were rarely dramatic. Bettelheim describes Paul's speech problems in *Truants from Life*, and I asked Paul whether he could recall any details of how he learned to speak. "It wasn't just one thing," he said, "not any kind of thunderbolt thing. I have a memory of being able to verbalize on a one-to-one basis, but I don't know if it was with Gayle or Mrs. White." The efforts of counselor and teacher, and the trust they engendered, helped Paul make progress in his use of language, but only as one aspect of a caring environment. Within all the steady pressures of the milieu, Paul grew in his ability to understand and speak as others do. However, he also recalled something that happened outside the milieu, and it was dramatic.

"I have the strangest feeling that one of the ways I learned to be vocal was in 1947, when I was twelve. I went to the movie *The Jolson Story* and fell absolutely in love with the voice of Al Jolson. The movie was playing at the Jackson Park at Sixty-seventh and Stony Island. I sat through three shows, and by the time I left I was singing all the songs all the way home. It had started snowing during the second show, and there was already four or five inches on the ground. I still imitate the voice of Al Jolson. Whenever that movie is on TV I watch it and go, 'Oh Mammy, buhbuhbuhbuh, I'd walk a million miles for one of your smiles'—though I don't consciously associate the song with the need for a smile from my mother."

Inside the soft framework of Bettelheim's milieu, the gradual growth of Paul's hope for the goodness of life was a response to the repeated attentions of caring adults. The goal of all their work was to help the child grow stronger in himself, and when Paul saw the film, he was at that moment ready for a surprising touch of something wonderful in the world outside. The benign experiences he felt on a daily basis had left almost no trace in his memory, but Paul rose eagerly out of himself when the human warmth of Jolson's singing opened the door for his own voice.

To get to this moment in the life of a troubled boy had taken years of effort by Florence White and Gayle Shulenberger—and they were not even on hand when the moment came; but, of course, their pleasure in Paul had primed him to enjoy himself, and as the loving adults in his life, they were inside him in the form of the values he had begun to absorb and the self-esteem he had begun to feel. If Paul did not consciously see that Jolson's yearning for a mother's smile echoed his own deepest needs, his unconscious mind knew it—and sent him singing through the snow, all the way back to the School, boosted by a new ability to answer warmth with warmth in a coherent voice.

"That reminds me," Paul said. "Patty used to sing us to sleep in the dorm. And I remember we all got bicycles for Easter in the spring of 1948, and Patty taught me to ride the bike in Jackson Park, in a big circle. The Orthogenic School was a very, very safe world. Dr. B. never said life outside it would be easy, and it hasn't been for me. Anyhow, adversity makes better mortar for building your life than having it all easy."

PATRICIA PICKETT (now McKnight) happened to know Betty Lou Pingree and heard about the School from her. Shortly after Patty arrived, in 1947, Ping was ready to leave, but the experience of the School would remain with her for a long time. Later she worked in another residential center for disturbed children and noted the difference Bettelheim's constant presence made, especially at bedtime. "He was always there after dinner, and he used to say that this was when it was hardest for children because the fearful fantasies came out at bedtime." Ping's heart sank when she saw the director of the other residence and his assistant put on their coats at five o'clock and walk out the front door. Staffers and children alike felt abandoned—and they were. Ping did not stay long in that job and heard later that many of the children had to be sent away to locked psychiatric wards. She believed that these same youngsters would have done much better under Bettelheim's care.

PATTY PICKETT had been intrigued by what Ping told her of the School, and when she graduated from the University of Chicago, she applied for a job and Bettelheim interviewed her. He surprised her by ignoring her studies; instead, he asked why she wanted to work at the School, and she told him of how she had mothered her two younger sisters after their mother died. "Probably he liked that I could just say what I felt, but also I didn't have a lot of preconceived ideas about how to deal with disturbed children. He said, 'When can you start?' and I started at the end of the week."

Patty came just in time to take a group of children to summer camp, a Bettelheim initiative reminiscent of the camp he had financed at Schallerburg only a decade earlier. However, these children were more disturbed than those Gina Bettelheim and Fritz Redl had cared for. "Our kids were terribly anxious and couldn't sleep at night," Patty said. "Also, the setup lacked the protection that the milieu offered, and above all, we missed the support of Dr. B., who was back in the city. These kids were just too frightened to enjoy the outdoors like normal kids would, so after another summer we dropped the camp idea."

Patty spoke of her problem with the end of the school day, when her boys rushed into the dorm at three o'clock, angry and tense, resentful of having been pent up in class. Also, one or two of them might get a package or a letter from home, when the rest didn't. Most had anticipated *not* hearing from home and were "all charged up, ready to be disappointed." She had a group of eight (and sometimes nine) boys, bursting with energy after school, eager to go outside and play ball. A few wanted to go to the library—"bookish types who were fearful of physical activity"—and getting an agreement on a group activity took all her ingenuity. Later it got easier as the boys developed special interests and hobbies, where she could "tune in" and work with them separately.

At Bettelheim's urging, Patty took a new boy into her group, a husky, thickset child who acted tough all the time. "He would come into the dorm and almost dare anyone to touch him, and if you happened to, he'd slug you." Her group was getting along smoothly, but the new boy disrupted everything; boys who had become friends began fighting with one another because of him, and Patty felt helpless and frantic. At her regular supervisory meeting with Bettelheim, she told him that things were falling apart. She was looking for encouragement, hoping he would say, *You're doing fine, keep on, it will get better.*

"I wanted sympathy, but instead Dr. B. sat back and looked at me and said, 'What have you done for him lately?' I can laugh at it now, but he really floored me. Luckily, I understood what he meant. I said, 'You're right. I thought I was doing a lot just keeping these kids from killing each other.' But Dr. B.'s question put me on notice." She saw she hadn't done enough for the child as an individual, so she started looking for what *he* might like, and eventually this worked.

Patty said that counselors learned from Bettelheim in different ways. "I provided grist for lots of staff meetings because of my mistakes. Dr. B. might really scold me, but I felt I was learning. Looking back I can see that others wouldn't have thrived if their mistakes were discussed in public, but I always felt he was trying to help me, not destroy me. Maybe I just needed to have someone really angry with me."

One night near bedtime Patty took her boys, bathed and in pajamas, down to the kitchen. "We were raiding the icebox, and I had one little fellow who always acted cool and never let his feelings show. That night he felt angry, but I didn't pick up on it." The boy took out a knife to cut some cheese and suddenly began giggling hysterically. Patty got the knife from his hand, but he jerked away and somehow chipped a tooth on the kitchen stove.

If a child was physically hurt, even in a small way, Bettelheim took it with the utmost seriousness. Called at home, he hurried back to the School, where he went into a fury with Patty and told her she should have sensed the boy's mood. His anger crushed her, the more so because she agreed with him.

On the same night, the Bettelheims were giving a party for a counselor who was leaving. Everyone off duty was expected to go, and after her boys were asleep, Patty went. She stayed awhile but all the time really felt like crying. Finally she excused herself and thanked Trude and started home. "I knew I wasn't good enough to work at the School, so when I got back to my room, I let it all go and cried my heart out."

Bettelheim had seen her leave and had asked one of the other counselors to follow her to make sure she was all right. Patty did not know this and went to his office the next morning and said she wanted to resign. "I

thought he'd be glad to get rid of me, but he said, 'That's ridiculous!'"—
with an air of confidence that buoyed her up and convinced her to stay.
"It was a tremendous turning point for me, because I knew if he could be
furious and then tell me to stay, I must be doing something right."

Patty worked at the School for almost six years, but after she married
and left, Bettelheim stayed fresh in her mind for a very long time.[7] "Honestly, I just loved the man. I always wanted to tell him that, whenever I saw
him, to go up and say, 'Thank you.'"

"What were you thanking him for?" I said.

"That's what he asked me when I finally did it. But I had this feeling of
gratitude, though I'm not sure what it's about. Mainly, he helped me face
my own emotions, and that was hard, given my family background, where
nobody showed much. But it made my life immeasurably happier. I savor
things in a way I never could have before, and my relations with my husband and my daughters reflect what I feel Dr. B. did for me. He helped
me know myself better in a way that gave me more control of my emotions—as much in control as I want to be. Everything's more satisfying.

"My other feeling is one of awe. I never had an easy relation with
Dr. B., like some of the counselors, perhaps because I also went to him for
therapy. But I never saw anyone who could be so dedicated twenty-four
hours a day to the idea that human beings in trouble can be helped. He
had to be tough because of the responsibility he assumed with those kids.
That was his job, and he didn't hesitate."

AT THE OUTSET, among all the other jobs he faced, Bettelheim had to
calm the School's atmosphere. The range and level of disturbance he
had found there—children attacking staff members and one another;
children being spanked, hit, and physically restrained by the staff—could
easily have turned into bedlam. However, he took charge firmly and to
such good effect that several counselors who joined the School in the
early years (before it was talked about on campus) told me they visited
the place and did not realize they had applied to a school for disturbed
children. The youngsters may have had bedlam in their souls—that was
the ultimate challenge—but Bettelheim made the benign milieu start
working at once. As Patty said, he didn't hesitate.

CHAPTER 14

Transference; Therapy; Staff Meetings

MANY COUNSELORS started with Bettelheim by quickly making a strong transference, which is also crucial to psychoanalysis. In taking a close associate and subordinate like Patty Pickett into treatment, Bettelheim opened himself, as he knew he would, to serious criticism from others in the profession. In fact, when I asked Gina Weinmann what she thought of the Orthogenic School, her first remark was that Bruno should not have given therapy to counselors.

It's a strict rule in psychoanalysis not to analyze someone close to you, but it's also a rule that has been broken many times. Freud analyzed his daughter Anna for three years.[1] Jung tried to analyze his wife, Emma, and even had an affair with his first analysand, Sabina Spielrein; one of Freud's early adherents treated his own five-year-old son, with Freud's help.[2] Finally, Bruno himself had gone to Gina's analyst, which almost certainly was a mistake for him, as it may also have been for her.[3] The drawbacks were obvious, but he did it and lived with the results.

Bettelheim offered therapy to many associates at the School, in part to keep experienced staff members and to make them better workers. Often a transference had begun in the very first interview, and I'm sure he knew it, looked for it, and counted on it.[4] The involuntary redirection of largely unconscious feelings of love, hate, dependency, fear, authority, and the like gave the new counselor a quick investment in working with Bettelheim. As the transference deepened, it became a kind of unseen animating force that held the School together; it bound people to him, to their jobs, and to the milieu. The transference also prompted the counselors' desire to learn from the person who had suddenly become big and present in their thoughts. I believe many staff members loved Bettelheim — ambivalently, of course — but also that anyone who came to suspect that the director had taken unfair advantage would ultimately depart with bitter feelings.

WHEN A staff member showed signs of needing therapy, Bettelheim faced complex choices. He thought first of the children, but in caring for the staff he could not neglect a counselor's needs. If he offered therapy when he wanted to hold someone for the sake of the children, how objectively could he examine the question of whether or not the counselor might be better off leaving the School? To keep good people, or even some who were barely passable, Bettelheim had to test the limits of his authority and integrity. Some ex-staffers believe he overstepped his bounds at this juncture, and the urgency he felt about the children no doubt at times colored his advice in dealing with a staff member's problems. Inevitably, the milieu stirred yearnings and unconscious needs in one and all, and Bettelheim meant for the School to benefit everybody, including himself. However, keeping a staff member for the wrong reasons could easily become disruptive, and I doubt that a week passed without Bettelheim trying to balance the therapeutic interests that might come into conflict.

GAYLE SHULENBERGER JANOWITZ had mentioned that Bettelheim took some counselors into therapy and said this couldn't be done now because it would be "too controversial." (Patty Pickett McKnight said this as well.) I quoted Gayle to Bettelheim, and he reacted with a little shrug, then briskly added, "Well, I did it all the time."

I asked if he meant psychoanalysis. "No. Analysis I couldn't do. Not in this situation, because I was too much of a real person in the lives of the staff. It was not analysis of the unconscious. In modern terms it was ego supportive, rather than a deep uncovering."

This seemed plausible to me at the time, and I didn't pursue the subject. Later, I talked with Karen Zelan, who came to the School at a point when Bettelheim had already done staff therapy for over a decade. Karen said that even if a counselor had gone to Bettelheim only for a supervisory session, insights of a very personal nature might come out.

"I didn't call it therapy when I saw Bruno, because it seemed unorthodox to me for him to wear two hats—therapist and boss. Trying to give therapy to the staff and teaching them was a flawed model. I remember a staff meeting in which he talked about the fact that he was the director and our teacher; and yet he often tried to help us personally. I think he meant to liberate our conflicting feelings when he spoke about these two aspects in staff meetings. Then it was up to us to choose whether we, personally, were being helped sufficiently *and* being successful enough at the School to continue working there.

"I believe it's also accurate to say that he didn't try analysis in that situation. Many of the conversations I had were about the difficulties of the work, especially the countertransference issues.[5] Bruno couldn't help evaluating us as workers when he was also trying to help us with problems of transference, and sometimes those two things were in conflict. So his ultimate loyalty was to the School's therapeutic functioning, which included loyalties to both staff and children, sentiments that were sometimes combined into one dramatic intervention."

Karen also sees transference in most relationships—"never mind therapy. People tend to see either themselves or other people in acquaintances, and I think this is almost automatic.[6] But countertransference had to be dealt with at the School, because the children were so disturbed that they inevitably disturbed the staff."

At one point Bettelheim tried to deal with his conflicting roles by hiring a therapist, Itamar Yahalom, to take over with some of the staff. However, this didn't quite work out either. "The counselors who worked with Itamar," Karen said, "may have wanted to see Bettelheim; if it had been me, I would have worried that I wasn't important enough to Bettelheim if he'd refused to listen to my problems. At the time I thought there was no real solution to the problem."

I asked about offering analysis outside the School, and Karen said that this would have raised questions about the staff's commitment to the children. "If you joined the School knowing that you would get psychoanalysis as a perk for working there, then people would start with that consideration as a goal, conscious or otherwise."

Bettelheim had no way to care for the children except through the daily good efforts of those whose caring built up a child's trust; but when a counselor's impasses began to interfere, Bettelheim offered therapy so that the person could struggle on. Self-analysis and on-the-job insights were simply not enough to keep people from leaving; and when a beloved counselor departed, her group suffered. The School lost not only years of experience but also the counselor's intense and therapeutic personal ties to her youngsters, some of whom felt abandoned for many months afterward.

Of course, staffers might leave, but Bettelheim did not; he held his place above the staff as the active symbol of the School's permanence, the resolute authority who fostered and exemplified the School's healing powers. He made hope systemic, beginning with himself, a system resting on the rock of his conviction that all would be well, that the School would survive, that the children would get better. Further, had he not been forceful, genuine, and transparent in his hopes, his little world would have slipped into mediocrity.

In private therapy, in supervision, in casual encounters, and in staff meetings, he gave counselors and teachers intellectual stimulation, emotional support—and harsh reality, as he saw the need for it. His harshness, real and perceived, often dominated the staff meetings, which were exciting to see because they stirred guilt, provoked fear, aroused anger, pointed the finger of responsibility, offered revelations—and solidarity. They brought teaching to therapy and therapy to teaching, and in my view were more important than the individual sessions. Discussion, insight, confession, recognition—all these took place in a setting in some ways approaching group therapy. The staff coalesced into a coherent group through loyalty to the milieu, to the children, to Bettelheim, to a desire for the light of understanding. And the meetings sometimes rose to the catharsis of high drama.

Ruth Soffer sat in on scores of staff meetings, which she called intense but indispensable learning experiences for everyone at the School. (On occasion members of the kitchen and housekeeping staffs also attended.) Many years later, as head of intake training at Children's Psychiatric Hospital in Ann Arbor, Michigan, Ruth helped train medical and psychiatric personnel in what to look for when admitting children for treatment. The contrast between the Orthogenic School and Children's Psychiatric shocked her. "For a long time I was just aghast. I didn't know where to turn. I'd seen how things worked with Bruno, how he helped the staff, and so it was a nightmare to come into this new situation when I was still saturated with the Orthogenic School. The training just couldn't be compared, and I felt like everyone was being cheated.

"Don't misunderstand me—Children's Psychiatric was, and is, a good place. But nobody could give what Bettelheim gave his staff. He had passion, he had insight, he saw everything, he cared about everything." She said he could not ask his staff to keep giving endlessly to very sick children on a level of care and attention they had never experienced for themselves, and so he gave them his care.

"It was not analysis in the sense of working intensively on their intrapsychic problems, but it made a difference in their psyches when they went back to the kids. In a funny way, he created a setting in which the counselors could 'grow up.' It was like raising children—all the time, you and your husband model life for your children. You can tell them so-and-so, but the behavior they pick up is what you're doing every day. Bruno set an example for the counselors—an example of caring for sick children, of always thinking about why they were the way they were, of being fascinated by the workings of the mind."

BETTELHEIM could be pointed, scornful, harsh, and (some felt) demeaning in staff meetings; yet everyone came, eager to be on hand. Fae Lohn (later Tyroler) said that Bettelheim never "yelled" at her, perhaps because he knew it would devastate her.

"He yelled at the ones who could stand it. If a counselor tried to show off in a meeting, he got shot down, and some quit, very angry, but others went on more strongly." She also thought Bettelheim was at times too easy, especially in the night meetings in the kitchen. "I remember gallons of wonderful ice cream, people laughing and crying—of course in that setting Dr. B. mainly helped us put ourselves together for the next day."

Bettelheim often read a counselor's report aloud at staff meetings. (Counselors spoke their reports into a dictation machine, and they were transcribed by the office staff.) "And then someone would really get it. He'd say, 'Why did you do that? Are you trying to make these kids crazier?' Then he'd show how the counselor had been hostile or provocative." He'd blast the person who had promised a youngster a book, or a haircut, or a treat but hadn't followed through, which could lead to the child taking out his anger on another child. "When Dr. B. saw this," Fae said, "he'd just go off the scale. His point was that the counselor first bought off the child with a promise and then punished him by not doing it."

Fae also believed that Bettelheim took a lot of "craziness" in staffers if he felt they had promise. "In fact, his tolerance for people's foibles came because he thought they were going to pan out for the kids. But he made serious errors in hiring staff members who were probably too disturbed themselves. They were fired, or they just left, but I don't recall much of that."

Once Fae had a dispute about a child with her co-counselor, who told Bettelheim he couldn't work with her. This was not material for a staff meeting; instead, Bettelheim called her in and spoke quietly, appealing to the best in her but making her aware of her unconscious needs, which at that moment were leading her into behavior disturbing to the child. "He said I didn't *mean* to be that way, that I was isolating myself. First *understand* what you're doing, then decide what *you* want to do—that was his attitude." He shamed and embarrassed her but also relieved her. "He shook up my image of how wonderful I was, and I began to look at myself for the first time. It was Bruno at his best—gentle, appropriate, everything on a manageable scale."

Louis Harper got the full treatment one day when Bettelheim caught him ignoring a child's efforts to talk about his mother. The boy was indirect, but Bruno saw the connection and put Lou on the spot. "He read my dictation aloud and said, 'What does this child have to do to make it obvious to you?' And of course I felt humiliated. It was just so true. I wasn't able to help the kid right away—I was still too hurt the next day—but in a few days I did. I can look back now and say, 'Why on earth did that bother me so much?' But it still sticks with me, and I think Bruno dramatized things just so they *would* stick."

Lou, a navy veteran, had started as a substitute counselor and then began going to staff meetings. When another staffer quit, Bettelheim hired him full-time. In the first year, Lou had troubling dreams in which he abused the children. He told nobody about them, and they finally went away in his second year, perhaps because his self-confidence had grown. Ugly dreams were not necessarily ominous signs in a new counselor, and he also thought about them a lot, which helped him master his feelings. Lou had not admitted to himself how deeply the children frightened and angered him, and the dreams may have let him go on by venting angers and fears during sleep. Lou's stubborn self-examination was just what staff members were expected to do.

Margaret Carey was another who had trouble in staff meetings. She said, "Dr. B.'s real teaching was not a matter of helping you recognize something in the child's behavior, but doing it with yourself. You and he didn't really talk about the child so much. His attitude was, 'You're a decent person, why are you having all this trouble with the child? You don't mean to hurt him, so what's going on in you?' At times I've had to go round Robin Hood's barn to see something, and he'd really get after me.

"I understood very early that I should never tell him anything that would hurt me if he said it in public. So I never did, and we got on pretty well. But he could use things against you, or make you anxious, put you in your place, make fun of you. I couldn't take it, so I didn't tell him anything he might use in public. Of course, if he made you anxious, some new thinking might come out of it, some new way of looking at a situation or at yourself."

Margaret's fear of being ridiculed in public was well justified, and her reticence was self-preserving. Bettelheim's verbal shock therapy (meant to pierce a person's defenses) felt rude and hateful to many, but he was driven by principle to say almost anything to get results for the good of the children; and no doubt he saw it as good for the staff member as well.

I suspect he calibrated such shots even as he made them, because if he overdid it, he risked losing the person. He gambled on his own importance and on the person's strength of ego in facing himself. It took grit to survive episodes that left one with less self-esteem and a self-image needing damage control. Shelton Key, a counselor and teacher, made the telling point that you could see when Bettelheim had lost hope for a counselor because he no longer gave the person a hard time in meetings. An attack usually meant he still wanted his "victim" as an ally, and he embarrassed people to expose weaknesses they would be better off without, at least when caring for troubled children.

Ruth Soffer Marquis had told me the meetings were major learning experiences for the staff but that Bettelheim's conduct bothered her for years. "On one level you could say he was horribly cruel in every single staff meeting," she said. Once, years later, when she came back to Chicago to work with him editing a book, she asked him to explain how the staff members could take it. "I mean, I couldn't take the kind of treatment he gave them; I think I would fall apart. I told him I wanted to ask them how they could stand it. And he said, 'Well, why don't you?'—just like that. His fearlessness in telling me to go ahead suddenly reassured me. It told me that I was cockeyed about something.

"In any case, I went to them and asked them, and you know what? They couldn't understand what I was asking. I talked to several counselors apart from each other, and when they finally got the gist of it each of them would say, 'My God! If it weren't for the staff meetings I wouldn't even be here—that's where I learn! Of course, it's painful, but not like you imagine.' "

Margaret Carey said that at times Bettelheim seemed to single her out, along with Steve Herczeg, a counselor—so much so that she would say to Steve, "What's going on with us?" I asked Steve about this, and he recalled that his worst moment with Bettelheim came in a staff meeting when Bruno took him to task for neglecting a responsibility.

"One of my kids had to be taken to the draft board and registered," he said. "I had to get a letter from George Perkins, the School's psychiatrist, so the draft board would know what to do. But Perkins didn't write the letter, and I didn't pursue it or ask for it again. When Dr. B. found out I had let the matter slide, he really raked me over the coals. He'd done it before, but this time I felt like he was nailing me to the wall, and I thought if he ever attacked me that way again, I'd leave the School. He didn't, maybe because I learned something in that exchange with him. But he made me feel stupid."

Steve had hesitated to ask for the letter because Perkins's authority as a doctor overawed him, and when Perkins did nothing, Steve took it as an excuse to do nothing himself. Steve said Bettelheim saw the inhibiting effect of Perkins's authority and attacked him as a counselor for not asserting his *own* authority and living up to his responsibility toward the boy.

When I spoke with Bettelheim about the incident he did not remember it but told me what his concerns would have been.

"In general I felt that we have to obey the laws of the country, and if the law was that you have to be registered for the draft, you had to do it. Also, if he was letting someone else's authority dominate, I was trying to protect him from that. He was staff, and he was responsible, and he couldn't blame somebody else. With this child he was in the paternal role, and he had to accept that responsibility. He might have felt I was 'nailing him to the wall,' but that wasn't my purpose."

Steve had added that in fact he did not feel Bettelheim's attack was angry. "Dr. B. was very forceful, and when I felt 'nailed,' it had to do with my own level of repression. Bettelheim insisted that all behavior was meaningful, so you looked for the meaning. And he never let anything pass. If I walked into the staff meeting late and said, 'I'm sorry I'm late,' he'd say, 'You're not sorry,' and go on without missing a beat. Later I figured out that my lateness had to do with my grandfather beating me after school."[7]

THE SCHOOL'S staff meetings were not simply a matter of a counselor being grilled while others listened and watched; Bettelheim wanted to engage the feelings of everybody else and bring them to the struggle for understanding, as I learned during my 1983 visit. I had told Bruno I was especially interested in writing about him as a teacher, and he said one afternoon, "Well, you should see what I do." He invited me to a seminar two days later, one of a series at Stanford organized by Alvin Rosenfeld who headed the child psychiatry training program there. Material from these seminars was used (in heavily disguised form) as a basis for *The Art of the Obvious,* cowritten by Bettelheim and Rosenfeld and published after Bettelheim's death.

I interviewed Rosenfeld on the day before the seminar, and he mentioned that Stanford did not pay Bettelheim: the seminar was an elective course with no credit toward a degree or a license, but the students came because Bettelheim was unique in how he helped them learn.

"Nobody else *teaches* the way he does. A therapist who presents a case to him leaves the session feeling altered in some way, led to a new point of view that's more common sense than theory. And it all happens inside his head. Bruno's questions are often so simple that you know you should be able to answer, but something blocks you."

Rosenfeld said that Bettelheim used the therapist's blind spots to teach everybody in the room. "Those watching the presentation identify with the one who can't answer the question and start trying to answer it in their own minds. It's like solving a mystery. You're baffled, and you sense something obvious staring you in the face; it reflects something in *you* that is blocking therapy's progress, something in you resisting what the patient is trying to communicate. Then, if you're serious, you struggle with the dilemma—the countertransference in technical parlance—and begin to learn. If you find a way out of your own blindness, you change. Bruno gives you a chance to grow, to discover the unconscious at work in yourself, and the rest is up to you."

"I guess he's rough if you're unsure and trying to hide it," I said.

"Right, and we're all unsure a lot of the time. It's in the nature of therapy to wrestle with uncertainty, glimpse the truth only fleetingly, and struggle with feelings and dilemmas we need to understand emotionally but that we may also need to hide from. Confusion and 'not knowing' may be our only defenses against frightening feelings and overwhelming experiences."

Bettelheim, he said, did a good job of accepting the doubts inherent in psychotherapy and in struggling to comprehend the deep messages and often irrational feelings buried in what the patient says and does. "He tolerates uncertainty and listens patiently until the truth becomes clear to him. Also, he happens to be the smartest man I've met in the profession."

When Rosenfeld first realized this, he found himself both admiring and being jealous of Bettelheim—and wanting to be like him. "Some of the people around Stanford feel he's malevolent—I don't. He has a social style and a teaching style. Socially, he's gracious to a fault. When you visit his home, you feel like an honored guest. When he's teaching, his honesty and unflinching straightforwardness often make you uncomfortable, because his questions are directed at defenses that interfere with your doing therapy. That's very personal. Think about what he writes in *Freud and Man's Soul*; he interprets defenses as the subtle means by which I deceive myself about my true nature. And he makes you look at your true nature. Not always comfortable!" To Rosenfeld, a person's level of annoyance with Bettelheim in the teaching context seemed to reflect the depths to which Bettelheim had agitated the therapist's defensive self-deceptions, the ones that interfered with therapy's progress.

Rosenfeld also spoke of Bettelheim's respect for the therapist, adding, "But it doesn't always feel that way if you're the one in the spotlight. It's not because your peers are there; I've felt the same way presenting to him in private. You're uneasy because you can't suppress what you're seeing in yourself. He won't let you weasel out and rationalize—that will stop you from learning and from treating your patient effectively. But, and this is important, he also helps you see at the concrete here-and-now level you're at, not at some abstract or theoretical level. He's like Semrad [a psychology professor at Harvard] in that he feels that reading too much in training impedes your growth as a therapist, because it puts a distance between you and your patient. Semrad always used to say that the patient is your textbook. Bruno, too, looks for a person's uniqueness, not how he fits into this theory or that."

Bettelheim once told Rosenfeld he didn't mind letting people get angry at him, because in that way he gave those who couldn't learn from him an easy out. "People who can't stand his methods get anxious and upset, call him a son of a bitch, and don't come back. They think they're okay and he's no good. Also, his clarity about his beliefs can be upsetting. He knows exactly where he stands, he takes where he stands as a firm point of view, and it's unswerving. Knowing where he stands and standing by his convictions gives him great power to see clearly."

"And that shakes other people's points of view?"

"Yes. For one thing, it's impressive, maybe a little scary, to see a man who knows his mind so well. And he's usually right. I've been running these seminars for six years, and what he does still astonishes me. Sometimes I think for days about what he has said and talk about this new insight with colleagues and friends. He makes me reconsider what I think I know, and all he says is, *I know what I think, and here's how I see it.* And he's always clear. He's not worried about getting along with everybody: he's worried about teaching and making you into a more effective therapist. The more I think about him, the more I realize that his greatness is as a teacher, an ultimate teacher. He's great in his books, but as a teacher he's a genius."

THE NEXT afternoon as Bruno and I drove over to the place where the seminar would be held, he said, "This is what I do best." Then, with just a hint of a shrug he added, "Well, I should hope so—it's been my whole life."

A YOUNG doctor and analyst in training, whom I will call Frank, presented a case with which he was having difficulty, and despite Rosenfeld's comment that Bruno meant to bring *everyone* into the teaching process, I was not at all prepared for what would happen to my sense of myself when he began questioning Frank. The presentation, as Rosenfeld also suggested, unfolded like a detective story, with Bettelheim teasing his way through Frank's blind spots and hesitations, raising questions about the patient and his feelings.

Bettelheim did not offer direct interpretations; instead, he seemed like a shaman weaving a kind of spirit dance around the young doctor, drawing him along to insights on his own. Later I made a note of my impression of this aspect of Bettelheim's method: "Sometimes he leads, sometimes he follows; his mind darts in circles like Robin Goodfellow, but he is not playing tricks. He is teaching by courting the intelligence of the young person who has come to learn from him." He found ways to prompt new thoughts in a student who needed a deeper grasp of the patient's point of view, which Bettelheim seemed to have intuited almost at the start of the presentation.

When the teaching session was in progress, my emotions were not calm: I felt certain that Bettelheim was angry with Frank and that Frank was feeling his wrath. The questions seemed relentless, and since I could not answer them any better than Frank, I began to find myself ill at ease, then troubled in ways I did not understand. An image came to mind, of a rabbit in the middle of an open field, frozen with panic while a predatory bird hovered overhead. I felt paralyzed, demoralized, helpless, and ashamed of my ignorance and confusion; I even feared that Bruno might suddenly turn to *me* with a question that would expose my inner chaos.

Nevertheless, during the seminar Frank remained the "rabbit" in my mind; some of my fears had surfaced, but I didn't realize that I had also projected deeper fears onto Frank—such a reaction being exactly what Bruno sought as a means of involving everyone in the learning process. I had worked with him for years, I had read his books and discussed his ideas, and when I came into the seminar I took it for granted that I knew enough to hold my own; yet now I saw that I knew nothing. For long moments that afternoon it was as if disparate voices babbled frantically in my head.

Late in the seminar Frank mentioned a detail that made Bettelheim perk up. His questions turned sharp as he focused on one bit of the patient's symbolic behavior, which he asked Frank (and finally anyone else) to explain. No one could, and he kept asking questions in a demanding voice. It seemed to me that tensions mounted in the room, and I know that we all became subdued and silent. The only sound was Bettelheim's voice picking away at our nerves. A bedlam.

Suddenly a man a little older than Frank looked up from his clipboard and called out the answer. A shout of laughter rose up, and a wave of relief washed over all of us as we felt the truth just spoken, an image that broke the tension and lit up our darkness like a flash. The session was now a short story with a surprise ending; the truth had been there all along, "staring us in the face." Instantly and in the midst of our laughter, Bettelheim, still seated, made a little bow toward the man and said, "Sank you very much."

Months afterward, when I showed Bettelheim my pages about the seminar, he objected to the phrase "hearing the session," because the important factor was a "participation in it at various degrees of personal involvement." That I "heard" or "saw" the presentation carried less weight than what I felt; my emotional involvement in the puzzle of the patient's behavior served to stimulate my thoughts. Later I realized that the same dynamic held true in the daily staff meetings at the School, where Bettelheim had taught in this way for decades.

Both Bettelheim and Rosenfeld said that Frank did not feel the panic I imagined during the seminar, but they kindly refrained from telling me I had been projecting. Frank confirmed later that he saw Bettelheim's questioning not as an attack but as helping him "up the mountain."

As a result of the seminar another insight took shape for me, into Bettelheim's approach to therapy with children, which I began to grasp that afternoon and confirmed in conversation with him later. The first step in therapy is usually characterized as observation of the patient. However, Bettelheim insisted that even *before* meeting the patient, the therapist should review what he "knows," then follow this by considering the child's experience and life situation and asking himself what he would feel if he were in the same predicament. Only then should he start to "observe." The order in Bettelheim's procedure, if there is an order, would be: 1) information, 2) introspection, 3) observation. Or, to put it less abstractly:

1. What do you think you know?
2. What do you feel for the child? (That is, what do you feel of how his world feels to him?)
3. What do you see in his behavior?

However, that's not quite right, either. All three "steps" must remain constantly in play in the therapist's mind. It is not a one-two-three process, because each step sheds light on and is illuminated by the other two. The therapist may be misled by inaccurate, inadequate, or biased "information," which, if it comes from the parents, would most likely leave out their possible contribution to the child's condition.

After the seminar Bruno asked if I had learned anything.

"I'm not sure," I said, and I truly wasn't.

"That's maybe an honest answer," he said, "because maybe you learn something tomorrow that changes what you learned today." His voice was teasing but serious. I knew I'd been shaken to the roots but didn't yet know why. I hadn't been able to reflect on what I'd felt, didn't see how I'd taken part in Bruno's learning process, glimpsed no perspective on the fact that my emotions had betrayed me, and didn't grasp that my terrible feelings were crucial to his method. Despite moments of virtual chaos an hour earlier, I was now calm enough to think about dinner—and intrigued enough to wish for another seminar. Yes, I feared Teacher's wrath, but the climax when the room burst into laughter was so glorious that I wanted more of the strange turmoil Bruno stirred up.

However, one thing still bothered me: I was sure Bruno had handled Frank in a hostile way. (As mentioned above, Frank told me later he did not think so, and I had agreed with him for a long time, especially after I saw into my projection of fears.) Now, many years later, I have again come round to the view that Bettelheim *did* attack Frank, even if Frank didn't realize it. The attack did not rouse feelings in him like my own, and in a way Frank and I were both right but both wrong. He was learning from Bettelheim, and his genuine commitment to his patient may have shielded him from the sting of some remarks, as well as from the edgy, angry, impatient tone I still remember in Bettelheim's voice.

The idea of Bettelheim's hostility disturbed me, and I thought it showed an inconsistency in his attitude. This had led me to ask, "If you're so concerned with the patient's self-esteem, how about the therapist's? Why did you attack his dignity?" Oddly, even as I framed the question, another question came into my mind: *Did he really do that?* It seemed obvious that he had attacked Frank, but some hidden voice prompted me to question myself. My unspoken doubt was perhaps a hint from my unconscious of the degree to which my loss of inner balance had colored the scene I was part of. However, Bruno answered firmly that he had indeed attacked Frank's dignity, and he told me why.

"Because," he said, "it is a false dignity—dignity of position, not truth or life. With false dignity, he can never help the patient. He must learn better, or he cannot teach. Also, one is a patient and one is a doctor, and we know which one has to be able to take punishment. Better Frank should fail talking to me than talking to the patient. At least I can help him—if he wants it."

"He seems to want it."

"Yes, that's the hopeful thing."

"How do you think he'll do now?"

"Who knows? Probably okay, I tell you why. First, he cares enough to put up with what I do to him in public. Second, it's not a hard case, so he'll find how to help."

"Why isn't it a hard case?" It had seemed very hard to me.

Bruno explained that the child's parent had done a lot of things right, had been good enough in many ways, and so the therapist could be reasonably hopeful about helping the youngster sort out his troubles.

AFTER thinking about the seminar over the months and years, and writing about it several times, I came to the conclusion that Bruno was also attacking the false dignity of everyone in the room—all who might identify with Frank, who perhaps thought they were feeling *for* or *about* Frank when they were only deflecting fears of their own inadequacy. It was certainly true for myself, at that time just setting off on a long inquiry into Bettelheim, far longer than I could have imagined. In drawing this portrait of him, I think it fair and useful to have added this small touch of myself, to sketch a scene where Bettelheim affected me in a deeply personal way. His seminar led me to look into myself and eventually see and set to rights (I hope) feelings of false dignity that had no decent place in my heart.

I knew that Bruno held himself back by not "giving the answer," that he probed and questioned so students could find answers for themselves. However, in a letter written after I had sent him a version of the seminar, he added a point about his method that I had missed, saying that the skill of the teacher is to keep much of what he knows to himself,

> because to teach it at this moment would serve no useful purpose but to show off how much he knows and sees. As a matter of fact, the teacher must give the students the chance that they feel better than he is, otherwise they can't take his superiority in so many[8] respects. Every good teacher knows that and acts on it, whether or not he consciously knows it. If the students cannot feel at times superior to him, they could be destroyed by his superiority. But this is an endless topic that is involved in good teaching, and one of the things is that one must at times be a bad teacher, so that the students can keep their balance and self-respect.[9]

Bettelheim understood that no teaching method works better than inducing an idea or insight to occur in the student's mind through his own powers; conviction is irresistible if we *see* rather than being *told*. So, for Bettelheim, teaching usually required him to hold back. But there was more to it than that, as he shows in this letter; he was wary about overwhelming students—and with good reason. If he felt he could teach and influence a student, he questioned but held back; but if he wanted students to give up on him as a teacher, he could beat them down and send them off angry enough to reject "Brutalheim" and retain some measure of self-acceptance.

CHAPTER 15

The First Book

MASTERING HIS own way of teaching had taken long years of practice, and as he was doing it, Bettelheim the teacher was also Bruno, husband and father. His preoccupation with the School left less time for family life, although Trude once assured me he was "religious" about being home for dinner and the early part of the evening. In the late 1940s Ruth Soffer became a frequent visitor in their home when she began to work closely with Bruno on his writing, and as many have done, she marveled at his sheer vitality.

"His day was incredible, it went on and on, and he did everything. I mean, he wrote books, he wrote articles, he gave speeches, he ran the School, he taught classes, he gave seminars all over the place and to all kinds of professions. *And* he had a family."

She felt he was a good father—up to a point. "One time when the girls were very little, and I came to baby-sit," she said, "I remember seeing Bruno paint a crib for Naomi. It was secondhand, bought in a thrift shop, or something, and he painted it a beautiful blue. The crib was just darling when he got through with it, and he was terrifically proud of himself. It was charming, but I couldn't help thinking, this is how men see being a partner in a relationship with children. That it's fun to do, but essentially it's a one-shot deal."

The Bettelheims usually invited Ruth to spend Christmas with them. In the early years they also invited Fritz Redl, and he always drove Ruth home. "Nobody said anything, but I think they were hoping to fix us up."

I asked Ruth how she remembered Trude from that time. "The most remarkable thing about Trude was how realistic she could be. More than anybody I ever knew, she never fooled herself, either about herself or about anyone else. She was as free of illusion as a person can be, and that's a rare quality. On the other hand, Bruno was filled with illusions—his misreading of Gina, for instance. He really told himself that when he got to America they would resume their relations. He fantasized it, and he *believed* it."

After Ruth Bettelheim's birth, Trude had hired a housekeeper, Lillian Brown, a black woman who would arrive just after breakfast and stay until late afternoon. She washed dishes, shopped, did the laundry, and cleaned the house; she also took care of Ruth, and later of Naomi. When the two girls started school, she made lunch for them and welcomed them home with a snack at three o'clock. Trude came home from her job around four, Lillian left for the day, and Trude made dinner for the family.

Ruth Soffer said of Lillian, "She was wonderful, but I thought they had delusions about her like southerners used to have about their trusted house help—if you know what I mean. They saw her as almost a member of the family, and there's no question she was close to them, but she knew she was an employee."

Naomi did not agree that her parents saw Lillian in this way—they were clear on the fact that she was an employee, although she may have had feelings that went beyond this. Lillian's only child had been stillborn, and Naomi told me that Trude's second pregnancy was said to have excited Lillian because she looked forward to taking care of the baby.

"The story goes," Naomi said, "that my mother came home from the hospital and handed me over to Lillian and said, 'Here's your baby.' Lillian had a very strong personality, but I think she enjoyed being there, so she was easy to get along with. Of course, she was a black woman needing work, so she was obviously a subordinate in the family. However, she was there throughout my childhood and even after I left home, and she took good care of me, and I loved her. She was my second mother."

One winter day when Naomi was still very young, a heavy snowstorm hit Chicago and disrupted public transport. Lillian's long trolley ride from her neighborhood to Hyde Park was delayed. Trude had left for work, and Bruno waited for Lillian, growing edgier by the minute because he was anxious to get to the School. Lillian told Naomi long afterward that Bruno reprimanded her for being late that day and not having called. "She said to him, 'What was I supposed to do? Find a telephone and miss the next trolley and wait another hour?' According to Lillian, that was the last time he ever reprimanded her."

In this sudden clash of School and family needs, Bettelheim could have called someone from the School to baby-sit for an hour or two, but he chose to stay home himself. In due course he saw that he was in the wrong and that he had been blind to the hardships in the life of someone very close to him—someone who made it possible for Trude to go to her job, someone who could be trusted with the children; no wonder he never again spoke sharply to her.

ONCE ON a visit in the late 1940s Ruth Soffer saw a Bettelheim unlike the man she knew as absolute master of School and classroom. One afternoon she and Bruno left the School and went to his home, and when they walked in, "It was the kind of thing you've seen or done a thousand times—Bruno called out, 'Hello, I'm home.' Trude was cooking dinner in the kitchen, and she came into the living room and said something in a quiet voice. I don't remember what it was, and it was nothing really serious, but her tone came across as a kind of scolding. Not in fact nasty, but she was annoyed, and you could feel her irritation. I'm not sure what I expected from him, but his reaction amazed me. Suddenly I had the mental image that he had shrunk from top to bottom and wanted to curl up and hide somewhere. I'd never seen anything like that with him before."

Ruth saw another instance of Bruno's emotional dependence when she was riding with him and Trude in the car one night, driving along the Midway in the dead of winter, with snow and ice everywhere. "They were taking me somewhere in Chicago. We all sat in the front seat, with Trude driving, me on the outside, and Bruno in the middle. Something in the car wasn't working right, and Trude spoke in the same way—not really nagging, but irritated and impatient and scornful, as if he were inept or not doing something he should, about the car. I was shocked at Bruno's tone of voice when he replied, and his manner toward her. He was like a nine-year-old being scolded. An image flashed through my head, an image of all the thousands of people in the world who were so terrified of him, and I thought, if they could only see him now! The difference at that moment between the public and private Bruno was just enormous."

RUTH HELPED Bettelheim significantly with his first book, *Love Is Not Enough*. From time to time he had spoken in public about the School, and at some point in the late 1940s he agreed to do a presentation to a psychiatric organization in Chicago. "We decided to show a day at the School," he said, "that one staff member would describe the getting up in the morning, another the afternoon activities, and so on. I'm not sure, but I think this was my idea, and I believe I gave an introduction."

The program was limited to an hour and a half, time only to sketch the day in broad outline, but the presentation was so well received by the group of professionals that Bettelheim decided to write a book along the same lines. He and Emmy Sylvester had cowritten at least six papers, mostly on the School, and he had also published other papers, reviews, and articles on his own. He and she talked of writing the book together but disagreed at once on the kind of writing they should do. Bettelheim was all for a popular audience, whereas Sylvester did not wish to address anyone except professionals. As a compromise they agreed to write separate chapters and then compare results. Even this proved unhappy, because Bettelheim worked very fast, while Sylvester produced almost nothing as the weeks passed. It became obvious that the collaboration was going nowhere, and this led to a break.

"Dr. Sylvester was my psychoanalytic consultant from the first years," Bettelheim said in answer to my question about the matter, "and I must say she was very helpful to me, but then we had a falling out." He said that she wanted to coauthor the books he wrote about the School—"a reasonable demand in a way, since we worked closely together, but she was so finicky in her writing and so orthodox psychoanalytically, that I couldn't do it. And thus our friendship broke over the issue. She was very miffed about it."

Sylvester resigned at the end of 1949, but she and Bruno kept their quarrel to themselves to protect the children and staff, to whom the break would have felt like a divorce, or worse.

Bettelheim told Ruth Soffer nothing about why Sylvester resigned, but Ruth naturally took his side on the question of style. "I believe I edited two articles they wrote together, and what she gave me was terribly stiff and pedantic. I think trying to write with her held him back, but with *Love Is Not Enough* he came into his stride and went full steam ahead, just turning out more writing per minute, with more originality and variety of focus than I had ever experienced. I would get twenty-five pages of typescript in the mail, and while I was working like a maniac on that, he was already writing the next twenty-five. So when I brought the first batch to him, he was ready with more.

"I remember sort of unconsciously linking it with having thrown off Emmy Sylvester. Until then it was like he had a monkey on his back, or shackles, and when he threw her over, he just went, 'Wow—I'm home free,' and he went ahead like a steam engine. The sense of freedom, I smelled in his excitement about writing. He couldn't seem to get it down on paper fast enough."

Ruth thought perhaps Emmy was angry also because she believed that Bettelheim borrowed her ideas. "It's true that she was at the School twice a week, and they talked about everything, so any of his ideas were hers and any of hers were his. It was an active relation—she worked there, though it wasn't her main work. They were doing it together, but it would be silly to use the word 'partner.' He was running the School with her input, which was very important, but remember, he was there not two but seven days a week, so it wasn't an equal kind of thing. But she was incapable of writing except pedantically, and he just hated that. I can understand Emmy Sylvester's annoyance—when she and Bruno met, she already had a practice and he was nowhere.

"Then he became like a meteor, and whoever the hell heard of Emmy Sylvester? But long before that happened, I got to know her in the staff meetings, and she struck me as a sourpuss, if there ever was one."

Sylvester left Chicago and relocated on the West Coast, where Bettelheim later reestablished contact with her and referred patients in the San Francisco area to her. Naomi recalled a family vacation in the late 1950s when they spent a day at Sylvester's home in Marin County. By that time relations between Bruno and Emmy had grown cordial again, at least on the surface.[1]

JEREMIAH KAPLAN, who had founded the Free Press when he was twenty-one, had been in business only about a year when he heard from Morris Janowitz, probably sometime in 1948, that Bettelheim might write a monograph on the Orthogenic School. Janowitz was a sociologist who taught at the University of Chicago. He had become friends with Bettelheim, and they were working together on a study of prejudice. "Bruno had a reputation of being brilliant and difficult, and Morris thought I should talk to him," Kaplan said. He signed Bruno to a contract for a 128-page monograph, and he and Bruno soon became friends. Bettelheim liked the enthusiasm and self-assurance of the younger man, just then beginning to make his way in the publishing business, and they had dinner at each other's apartments, met at other dinner parties in Hyde Park, and generally kept in touch. They seemed to meet at least every two weeks, Kaplan said, and he noticed that Bruno never stayed to the end of a dinner party, even at his own apartment, but excused himself and went back to the School.

"Clearly, Bruno was the School, and the School was Bruno. It was idiosyncratic for the university to let him run the School in that manner, but it was really Bruno's moral suasion—or rather, his sheer moral force—that carried things along." Instead of 128 pages, Bettelheim turned in a full-sized book. "It was unlike anything we had ever talked about, but wonderfully written, so we tore up the contract and started over. The manuscript didn't have to go through an editing process—it was ready for the printer when it came in."

The weekend before I interviewed him, Kaplan had reread *Love Is Not Enough.* "It's a wonderful book, a really wonderful book," he volunteered. "For its time an extraordinary book, which is why I think it was so eagerly and well received. I believe that as long as we need to care for sick children, people will read Bruno's work."

DURING the late 1940s, even before *Love Is Not Enough* was published, Bettelheim's reputation was growing both at the university and within his profession. Word of mouth about the School soon brought patient referrals from therapists and clinicians, first from the Chicago area and then from around the country.

Bettelheim had become someone much talked about, which helped with the periodic problem of finding new staff members. Bright students were drawn to his lectures, and when he announced in class that the School had openings, good people applied. In hiring, he usually made up his mind quickly: he looked the person over and asked questions to explore whatever caught his attention; however, he either *liked* the applicant or he didn't, and he usually took his instincts seriously. He told me that he looked first for "ego strength" (a college degree might be an indication of this), and that of course the person's genuineness and feelings for children also counted. He made mistakes, but he never found a better way of hiring than by letting his whole self respond.

Many former counselors remember their first meeting with him quite vividly. Fae Lohn, who came to the School in 1948, brought along a letter of introduction to the interview. Bettelheim mentioned that she would have to work on weekends as a part-time substitute, but Fae was enjoying her personal life so much (at Roosevelt University in Chicago) that she said she didn't want to work weekends. Bettelheim picked up the letter and sailed it back across his desk. She caught it and said, "I've changed my mind, I'll take the job."

Bettelheim had surprised her, but her own response surprised her even more, and she has thought about the moment many times. "Dr. B. took me totally at my word. He was dismissing me, no questions asked, and this enabled me to change my mind suddenly. I hadn't had many choices in my life up to that point, and I think in that split second I realized I had a choice. That was gratifying and intriguing. I had no idea what the School was about, but I saw Dr. B. as a person who was *clear*, and that was very important."

Benjamin Wright came to the School two years later, a student with an Atomic Energy Fellowship in nuclear physics who had found himself losing interest in the idea of becoming a physicist. He had studied with Lloyd Warner, the most eminent American sociologist of the day, and later with Carl Rogers, the "client-oriented" counselor who headed the university's Department of Human Development. Then Wright heard Bettelheim lecture, and he was hooked.

"For about a year I was trying to decide between these three men. So what was it about Bruno? Well, he was brilliant, but it wasn't just that. And it wasn't fame, because at the time he wasn't as famous as Warner or Rogers. I think it was his sincerity and genuineness. When I talked to Bruno I felt I was really talking to Bruno, and with the others it might be a little bit of a game, you know? Bruno captured my imagination—he represented the strength and seriousness I needed."[2] Either Rogers or Warner would have mentored Wright and helped his career in their fields, but Bettelheim seemed to offer something more: a way into his inner life. At a lecture in May 1950, when Bettelheim said he was hiring at the School, Ben suddenly made up his mind.

"Not that I was particularly interested in schizophrenic kids, but after class I went up to him and said I wanted to apply. 'Are you crazy?' he said. I knew the right answer was *yes*, so I said, 'Yes.' I'd been studying him, so I knew what he expected. He said, 'All right, come over at three o'clock.' "

Later I asked Bettelheim why he said, "Are you crazy?" It turned out that he knew of Ben's Atomic Energy Fellowship, "which was very prestigious at the time, and I wondered why he wanted to give that up to work as a counselor—a crazy idea, no? He had his reasons, and I don't think he ever regretted it, but I was trying to show him that this was a major decision."

In the interview that afternoon, when Bettelheim heard that Ben had been analyzed as a child by a woman who had trained with Anna Freud, he called Ben a "father murderer" and asked why he should have somebody like Ben around the School, trying to murder him all the time. "That was a pretty safe shot," Ben said. "Almost every boy is, but it was certainly an interesting opening. My father had died when I was nine and living with my mother in New York, so Bruno's remark aroused my emotional involvement with all that."

Bettelheim told Ben he'd give him a trial and turned him over to Gayle Shulenberger to learn about the School's methods and to observe the children.

"I remember him walking into the School," Gayle said, "looking like a hippie kid himself, with long hair and sandals—but he came along very fast."

ALSO IN 1950, Mary Jean Riley, a young woman of conventional Catholic upbringing, found herself feeling oddly uncomfortable with her life, wishing she had a job she could really put herself into. A friend mentioned the Orthogenic School, and she applied, not understanding that the children were emotionally disturbed. Her interview with Bettelheim lasted more than an hour, and he spent most of the time trying to convince her not to take the job.

"He made a striking point about my religion," she said. "He talked about the possibility that I might lose my faith if I worked at the School." She felt he was being fair in warning her, but it made her even more eager for the job—"which I suppose was something he wanted to find out."

THE FIRST step in a counselor's orientation was to follow a seasoned staff member and observe. Bettelheim picked Joan Little and Gayle Shulenberger to show Fae Lohn the School's ways. "I barely saw Dr. B.," she said, "but the essence of the School came through clearly—that the children came first." The careful planning, thoughtfulness, and respect for the children astonished her.

Fae's first inkling that she had a lot to learn came as she observed Joan Little and her group. One girl was reading a Louisa May Alcott novel, and Fae volunteered that she liked it. "I started to talk about the book, but Joan immediately let me know to back off, that I shouldn't impose my interest on the girl, even in a mild way. She pointed out that nobody had asked me anything and said I should just watch and see how things were done. That really took me aback." It also helped that Joan corrected Fae

without a chastising attitude and simply called attention to the fact that
Fae didn't need to ingratiate herself. "You had to take the kids as they
were, give them what *they* needed. Don't impose, just sort of hover and
follow and try to understand."[3]

Mary Jean Riley's orientation came with Patty Pickett and her group of
boys. "Patty had a marvelous way with them, so I didn't get the impression
of crazy kids as much as I would have if I had started with one of the
younger and less well-organized groups. We went shopping that day, and I
watched the boys play chess, and I thought, 'What's so difficult about this
job?' " Not knowing she was caring for disturbed children may even have
helped Mary Jean in her first days, but in any event, after two weeks she
had done well enough for Bettelheim to start her as the second counselor
in the girls' group. The School had about forty children, divided into five
dormitory groups: four for boys, one for girls. Mary Jean asked Bettelheim
why he had only one group for girls, and he told her that the School got
far fewer referrals of girls. He thought many parents felt it was easier to
keep disturbed girls at home than to keep boys, but in time he hoped the
School would have more girls.

On her first day alone as a co-counselor, Mary Jean got into trouble
with her group and had to send for a senior counselor to calm things
down. But she learned quickly, she had good instincts, and she found the
work hard but fascinating. Within three years she had become the kind of
counselor others sent for when things got out of hand and had to be
calmed down.

THE SUCCESS of *Love Is Not Enough* in 1950 raised Bettelheim's profile
even higher and led to a host of invitations for him to address groups in
Chicago and elsewhere.[4] "Actually," Ruth Marquis said, "I don't remember the reviews of *Love Is Not Enough*, though I'm sure Bruno looked at
them. We didn't think in terms of the success of the book; we were just
glad that it was done and out." She continued to edit his writing but also
helped redraft some of his speeches.

Bettelheim often preferred to speak without a text, as he chose to do in
a series sponsored by the Menninger Clinic in 1951 in Chicago.[5] Karl
Menninger had become interested in Bettelheim in the late 1940s and
wrote him a thoughtful letter praising his February 1948 *Commentary*
article on the victim's image of the anti-Semite. Later in 1948, the *Bulletin
of the Menninger Clinic* published Bettelheim's paper "Closed Institu-

tions for Children?" When the clinic organized the series on the "normal child," Bettelheim, a new and lively voice in the field of child development, was an obvious choice for one of the lectures. In fact, he had already taken one youngster the Menninger Clinic had diagnosed as hopeless and helped him significantly in the School.

The audience expected Bettelheim to deliver a paper on the "school period" in the life of a normal child; instead, he spoke impromptu, threatening at times to read the twenty-two-page paper he had brought along. He also switched to the Freudian term *latency period,* so as to smash the icon of "latency" he knew many in the room respected. He believed people should take a critical look at Freud's concepts rather than repeating them as dogma, and he made his case by being outrageous, lighthearted, and funny while attacking the biases of his hearers.

"You know," he said to a roomful of parents, doctors, and psychology professionals,

> in the latency period nothing happens. So I really am supposed to talk about nothing. But I have these children in the Orthogenic School in the latency period, when nothing happens; and in desperation, thinking what I could tell you tonight, it occurred to me that one of these children in the latency period where nothing happens came to me and, after he had set several fires, after he had been in institutions, after he had been exposed to psychiatry, after he had raped his baby sister and badly hurt his mother and sister and a few other people, not to speak of stealing and so on . . . he came to me, and one night after he had been there a few days, he said, "I don't know why I'm here; I have no problems." He might as well have said, "I'm in the latency period, and nothing happens there, and that's why I'm here."
>
> Why is it such a difficult period? Because . . . there is really no fun in the latency period; at least, I cannot see it. . . . The child in the latency period, the normal child, is not permitted any of [the] satisfactions [of fantasy and masturbation]. All he is supposed to do is learn; and how great fun that is, you know. . . . They of course are very much interested to learn about sex; all children are. But . . . they are supposed not to be interested at this time, because that's how Freud has written in his statements on the latency period.
>
> They collect nonsensical things . . . stones, stamps, trading cards, one card is as ugly as the other. The most neurotic compulsive defenses, but if it's a kid in the latency period, it's a good hobby for him. This [attitude] of course prevents us from asking why children in

the latency period need these defenses; but they're not supposed to need them, because nothing happens in the latency period.

The children are terrified; so what to do with an anxiety-ridden personality? The best treatment obviously is to create further anxiety. So they just love to ride horseback, they just love to jump into the pool, they just love to sled or ski. I think the only equipment I really have to run this Orthogenic School is that I consistently all my life have been a sissy. . . . I don't believe that to do dangerous things is the best method to combat anxiety.

He commented on how we impose upon children in the latency period and on how their value to us has changed:

As I have told you, it really takes twelve years of schooling to break an honest-to-goodness human being so that he becomes a useful member of society. . . . One of my schizophrenic boys summed it up—I think I said that in my book, although I didn't put it as vividly as he said it— after he again made some progress in school, he pounded the table and screamed at me, "Progress! Progress! All I get is progress, god-damned progress! To hell with your progress!" All they get is progress; they don't get achievement, they don't get independence, they don't get instinctual satisfaction. . . . The latency child in our society has no status whatsoever in the family beside being pushed around and given the goal of the bone which we throw to our dog. . . . From chickens to the tending of sheep, in a society where the child learns the trade from the father . . . the child—the latency child—had a stake; is re-spected and contributes. . . .

That was, of course, before the technological age, when the child was degraded not to somebody who contributes to the family, but somebody who is a burden to the family. We must face up to the fact that nowadays the children are economic burdens to their families; if you are very well-to-do, the burden is not heavy—but they contribute nothing but headaches. Therefore, we now base our family life on love. Now love, it seems to me, should be the result of services ren-dered. . . . Love grows on you as you live together, share difficulties together. Could I possibly tell you what these children share with you that they should love you for, or what you share with them so that they could grow on you?

In the question period that followed, someone objected that Bettel-heim had simply destroyed prejudices and had not told the audience anything positive, any ideas to take away with them. He did not dispute this point but declared himself very satisfied with his performance—perhaps because his listeners had laughed so much at his relentless analysis of the contradictions in how we treat children in the latency period. He got a first flurry of questions from parents, but the professionals in the audience held back. He noticed this and teased them:

> What about some of the psychiatrists and the physicians—don't they have any questions? I scared them good!

Of course, this brought another laugh.

Many questions from the audience implied the larger question of how we can help children learn and grow so that later in life they can become "useful members of society." Bettelheim relented in his no-advice stance and offered a piece of common sense:

> So why are you so afraid that the child won't learn to fulfill the tasks of society? The most difficult tasks, interestingly enough, are so difficult that you can't impose them. . . . The really important things you never can teach. All you can do is set an example, which the child will copy or not copy.

And then he asked a question always meaningful to him:

> Do you really think that this is such a society that you want your child perfectly adjusted to it?

A little later someone in the audience said, "By your question, I figured out that you do not want your children to be adjusted to this society."

> BB: Exactly. I am discovered; I am sorry.

> Q: Do I take that correctly to mean to rule out their ability to take what comes to them in this society?

> BB: How did I get up this tree in the first place?

A moment later he explained what he hoped for his own children (he had two at the time):

> To endure what they cannot change, and to change what they can change without paying too high a price. I don't want them to be

revolutionary; I have no use for revolutionaries. I don't think revolution really ever changes anything. I think the changes are the slow
drops which make a dent in the stone. You know, every one of us can
change in his own life things a little bit for the better. And let's forget
about the huge changes. Once I was young and foolish, too, but by
hard experience I learned that those who want to change the whole
world are those who are usually utterly unable to change themselves;
they want the whole world to get in line with them or their ideas.

Earlier in the speech he had offered one of his deepest values:

You know very well that the most important thing to teach children is
the value of human emotions, the genuineness of human emotions;
because that is really the essence of life.

About how and why he imposed certain values on his children, there was
this exchange:

BB: By and large I never ask my children to do anything because
it's good for them, or good learning for them; I ask them to do only
those things I want them to do. I want them to behave fairly
decently at the table—fairly; my standards are very low. But I want
these minimal standards adhered to, and by golly they're going
to adhere to these standards and that's all there is to it; but
not because otherwise they won't be socialites, they won't be
accepted in society—just because I want them; that's the kind of
tyrant I am.

Q: But what makes you think that you're right in that?

BB: I don't care. Now why do I say that, and why do I stress it? For
a very simple reason, that an honest-to-goodness human relationship is a two-way relationship, in which I have certain rights, too;
rights which I have earned because of the services I have ren-
dered. . . . I want my child to understand that if this child wants to
have a good relationship to me, there are certain minimal things
the child has to do to maintain it.

ALTHOUGH wholly serious, Bettelheim had great fun with this group,
most of all during the question period. The moderator who introduced

him had told the audience that the speaker would like "as many questions as you can possibly ask." In the same way, he valued young mothers' questions in the Saturday-morning meetings (1948–52) later condensed in *Dialogues with Mothers*. During my 1983 interview in California, he happened to mention making grand rounds in a hospital in Massachusetts, and I wondered why he would travel across the continent at the age of eighty to spend a day walking through a psychiatric hospital. He said he needed the direct response—it stimulated his mind.

In what way? I asked.

"Because firstly, many of my ideas take on a more definite form as I try to explain them to others; in other words, to teach. In one's mind things can be pretty vague, and yet you believe you understand better than is actually the case. I couldn't have written the books about the School if I didn't have to explain things to the staff in ways they could follow. You see, there's a great danger you don't really understand something you feel you know. But if you can't explain it to others, then you don't understand it fully. Freud would never have discovered psychoanalysis if he hadn't written down the dreams and his interpretations of them for others to read.

"Also, when I teach, what interests me is not my lecture, which usually bores me. I know what I say already, so it's not new. But the question period, the challenges, they are valuable for me. They force me to come to grips in much more complete terms, so that other people can grasp the idea."

Did he change his mind in the process? "Not really. I modify my conclusions, but I rarely change. It's just that the same thing can be viewed under many different perspectives, *ja*? It's the same thing, but it looks different, and maybe the changed perspective makes your idea clearer to somebody."

CHAPTER 1 6

A Growing Reputation;
the Next Stage
for the School

A s THE 1950s opened, Bettelheim was getting more patient referrals
than he could handle. Each child took years of therapy, and the
turnover in the milieu was so infrequent that the School kept no
waiting list. When Bettelheim saw that a child would probably leave in a
few months, which usually happened no more than three or four times a
year, he looked at his current correspondence to find a new child. At the
same time, he continued to hire new staff members, as people were fired
or left for their own reasons.

The next stage for the School was to enlarge it with new dorms, which
were finished in 1952. His growing reputation, as well as his ability to persuade possible donors, had enabled him to raise money for the School.
The new dorms let him take in a few more children, and at the same time
he lifted the age limit that forced youngsters to leave at fourteen. After
1952 no child need be sent out into the world prematurely, as Paul had
been. Bettelheim also upgraded the milieu by getting rid of the double
bunks[1] and giving each child his own bed and exclusive space, thus aiming toward the *individual* milieu he regarded as essential.

BETTELHEIM rarely hired anyone without an interview, but in 1952
Jacquelyn Seevak (later Sanders) got her job through the mail. By chance
she had seen a notice on a bulletin board at Harvard about openings at the

Orthogenic School. One professor told her Bettelheim was impossible (someone he knew had left after two weeks), but a second said Bruno was an interesting man. She sent off letters of recommendation, a transcript, a short autobiography, and a snapshot; Bettelheim hired her by return mail, and she packed her bags and went to Chicago.

When she arrived at the School, she felt as if she was walking into a construction site, because although the new dorms were completed, older quarters were still being remodeled, which gave her a sense of constant upgrading. She entered cautiously, her long hair pulled back in a braid, wearing her best neat gray suit, and was startled when Bruno met her in his shirtsleeves. "I was rather shy, really, and I didn't expect him to be so homely." His book had been published without an author photo, and she had imagined him as a handsome, distinguished-looking doctor.

This first meeting did not seem to go well. "He was really terrible—he said my voice was too soft, that I should leave off my Radcliffe manners, and that I didn't look like my picture." He did remark that he was glad she didn't wear red nail polish because it scared adolescent boys; then he called in a counselor to show her around the School—an unkempt, chain-smoking young woman in sandals and blue jeans. "I'm sure he brought her in because she would contrast with the way I had dressed. I was stunned. If the job had been in Boston, I'd have thought, 'This guy's a nut!' and not have come back."

Later she heard that Bruno told the staff he thought she was wonderful and mentioned her Radcliffe degree, no doubt feeling pleased to be getting an applicant from one of the best colleges in the country, one that was definitely a part of the "Establishment." Jacqui saw him in the dining room a few hours afterward, and he apologized for having been so harsh, saying that she now looked more like her picture (she had changed her clothes). He added that her soft voice, after all, was a reaction to her mother. Jacqui's mother had a shrill voice, and Bettelheim's insight seemed like sheer magic. Years later Jacqui reread her autobiography and saw how revealing it had been. The insight was easy—"but he made the connection, and that was fascinating to me."

Bettelheim assigned her to follow and observe with Fae Lohn, by that time a senior staffer and four-year veteran. "I came into the dorm with Fae, and a tubby kid offered me his chair, and Fae said no. She told him she'd be happy to take him on her lap if he wanted, but he didn't have to offer me his chair, because this was a school for children. If anybody in the room had to stand, it would be a grown-up, not a child. That was memorable."

Fae left Jacqui alone with the group for a few minutes, and one of the boys climbed onto a bed and began jumping around. The group had been well behaved with Fae, but now this boy suddenly talked about killing. It frightened Jacqui, but when Fae came back he settled down again.

Coincidentally with Jacqui's arrival, Bettelheim started to focus on autism, a condition formally described by Leo Kanner only eight years earlier. "One of the first kids I worked with," Jacqui said, "was autistic. It was a very new thing; it was so new that I don't really fault him as much as the autistic people want to. What he said was not so very different from what people were saying at the time. Autism was Bruno's intellectual challenge for a while, and then in the sixties the next thing he focused on was the adolescents. The new adolescent unit was built after I left, in sixty-five, and I feel it made the School too big."[2]

SPEAKING of Bettelheim's teaching methods, Jacqui thought that the value of dictation by staff members was to create a situation in which they might end up teaching themselves by reviewing exactly what happened with the child.

"It was a very good way for the counselor to develop the analytic skill that Bruno was committed to. It was like what Freud did; he brought you to examine what exactly had transpired in your head. And your feelings. Or what had transpired around you. Bruno also had a way of helping you to grasp how somebody else feels, how to put yourself into their shoes. He would use wonderful analogies and hypothetical situations that you could visualize to be able to understand what was going on with a child."

One aspect of Bettelheim she did not like, Jacqui said, was his use of guilt. "We always felt like everything was our fault, and he encouraged this, made you feel that if you did something wrong, you could have known to do it right. He would carry on and act like you were terrible because you didn't do something right. That would sometimes immobilize me when I was younger, but later, as we had some success together, that didn't happen because I knew how to deal with him." She added that guilt was a strong motivator because it gives a feeling of power, that responsibility for failure and responsibility for success go hand in hand.

"Sometimes he would sit in a staff meeting, and if nobody brought up anything he would have a fit, and he'd walk out of the room and say that 'these people' were terrible because they had nothing to discuss. 'All these problems, and there's nothing to discuss.' People would hesitate to bring up anything because they were afraid he'd yell at them. At times he would embarrass people, but there were also times when he could be quite poetic."

As for his writing, Jacqui said, "He wrote reams and reams and reams, then he would cut and paste, cut and paste. And then he would go over everything again, and over and over. I've never seen anybody like that. He'd take what he'd written and go over it umpteen times, and then he'd have it edited, and then go over it again and again and again."

Among his books, she singled out *Love Is Not Enough.* "It shows the best of what people were trying to do in residential treatment at the time. Bruno really articulated it so well that for some it was like a beacon about how residential treatment should be. The most important part of the treatment is that it happens every day, and he was certainly involved in the daily life of the kids. He made a school and developed its traditions, but he had to go beyond it—he always wanted another challenge."

Louis Harper offered an interesting sidelight on the effect of construction work such as Jacqui Seevak had walked into the midst of. He said that the School would invariably lose staff when any construction took place. "People took the opportunity to drop out." He wasn't sure why but added, "Either they couldn't adjust to the change, or it sparked doubts in them."

He also mentioned one small but useful development that dealt with daily transitions within the School, the "in-between times" when children went from one activity to another. Bettelheim wrote about this in *Love Is Not Enough,* before the School had found a smooth way to make sure children got from dorm to class and back again. Every morning counselors took their dorm groups to several different classrooms; at three o'clock, teachers had to take students back to their various dorms, which meant making several stops. This came at a moment when the whole School was in motion, and sometimes a child straggled. Mixing ages, dorms, and classes gave children a wider field of social relationships, which Bettelheim wanted, but in the bustle and distraction of in-between times, a child might wander off and get lost for a few minutes.

A simple answer to this problem became routine so quickly that nobody could remember who thought of it.[3] Someone suggested that counselors should take their groups to a central location in the morning—the auditorium (in the church building next door to the residence).

There teachers could assemble their students and shepherd them to their classrooms. At the end of class, teachers took their students back to the auditorium, where the children regrouped themselves with their dorm mates and counselors.

"That pretty well eliminated the in-between problems," Lou said. Also, bringing the whole School together led spontaneously to one of the most popular features of the school day, the three o'clock meeting. A teacher might teach a new song, Lou said, "or someone would speak on a topic of the day. Dr. B. often had things on his mind, or he'd just ask if anyone had a question, and someone always did. We all looked forward to it. The kids did things too, and it added to the feeling of solidarity at the School."

ANOTHER way Bettelheim created solidarity (and at the same time made each child feel special) was the celebration of holidays, especially Christmas. At a big Christmas party on the last day of classes, each child got a stocking full of presents. (Any child who did not go home for the holidays got another stocking on Christmas morning.)

One Christmas Lou became very angry with Bettelheim, the year he had eye surgery—"back in the sixties when you had to lie sandbagged to keep your head from moving while you were recuperating." Bettelheim had told the staff he would return after Christmas, but he could not resist the temptation to leave his bed (probably against doctor's orders) and come in to check on things. "We'd all worked twice as hard in his absence, put in longer hours, planned all the activities. He wasn't even supposed to be there but came in at the last minute and started to criticize. This was wrong, that was wrong, we didn't buy enough presents for the kids, and on and on. I thought, 'Not enough presents? That's crazy.' I doubt anybody told him he was overdoing it, but we were terribly hurt. I think he needed to feel a part of things.

"However, I must say that at the big holidays he created lots of excitement for the kids. The enthusiasm was contagious, and every year we tried to make Christmas bigger and better than the year before."

The party always had a Santa, played by Lou or one of the other men in the School. "Bruno would never get into a Santa suit. He insisted the kids should have Santa Claus, but he didn't want them to see him in that role. Also, he liked to dramatize the occasion by reading telegrams. He'd come into the party with a yellow envelope in his hand, and he'd open and read this telegram from Santa Claus and say, 'He's on his way!' Bruno was a bit of an actor, you know—he'd say things like, 'We're waiting for him!' to raise the excitement, and we all got into it."

JOSETTE WINGO, who had been a navy antiaircraft gunnery instructor in World War II, worked at the School between 1947 and 1950. She, too, was impressed by the attention Bettelheim gave to holidays for the children, and she offers a glimpse of him at an Easter party.[4]

"Dr. B.," a child asked, "how does the Easter bunny carry all the eggs for all the children in the world?"

"He has a little wagon," Bettelheim said.

I'm sure he understood that drab factuality would have been the wrong note for the child at this moment; the party was not a scene where Bettelheim needed to invoke the reality principle. The child was enjoying a fantasy he had perhaps almost outgrown, but no doubt Bruno believed he could benefit from many more such moments before he was ready to absorb the sterner lessons of life.

LOU HARPER worked at the School for twenty-one years, which prompted me to ask him about changes in the School that he had seen in his long tenure. However, he chose to make a general and larger point, that change was continuous. "That was Bruno's attitude and intent, that the School had to grow and develop, that it was dedicated to change— to the personal and physical growth of the children and to the professional and emotional maturing of the staff. And real change is a slow, progressive thing, not something dramatic."

ONE CHANGE that could not be avoided was staff replacements, as workers were fired or left for their own reasons. From a statistical point of view, most of Bettelheim's hiring decisions were mistakes—obviously, since most hirees left before the end of a year. But he could live with this kind of failure because the method was actually trial and error, with enough trial and success to make it worthwhile. He usually hired graduates looking for a first job and still young enough to be influenced by a strong director.

Shelton Key, who came to the School in 1953, was at least ten years older than most new staffers. He had a religious background and was working part-time as the chaplain in a school for handicapped children while studying for a master's degree in the university's Divinity School. Having grown up in Mississippi with what he later felt was an overproper, emotionally restricted family life, he went into psychoanalysis for several years and found it helpful.

Residential work with children interested him, so he took one of Bettelheim's lecture courses, and after class one day he went up to ask about a job at the School. Bettelheim invited him to come to his home that evening for an interview. "I found him baby-sitting his three youngsters," Shelton said, "and he talked about my career plans in a very respectful way—not a typical first interview."

Shelton was planning to write his master's thesis during the summer and so offered to start in the fall. Bettelheim said no, he had to start July 1. That was when the school year began, and that was when they would need a new counselor. Other counselors were doing academic work outside the School, and he could too. "It's true that most people didn't," Shelton said, "because their involvement with the School was so great, but it could be done." He started on July 1 and eventually wrote his thesis in his spare time.

IN THEIR first year, inexperienced counselors like Shelton could easily lose control of a group. Alone one evening, filling in for a counselor who was away on vacation, he had a disaster.

"It feels like the first day or the first week," he said, "but it couldn't have been so soon." (It was in fact near the end of his first year.) "I was new to the boys, but I thought I was handling things pretty well. It was getting toward bedtime, and the kids were taking showers. Suddenly one fat little boy came out of the shower and began prancing around the room naked, dripping water."

Shelton hesitated, and the boy ran back into the bathroom and got a mouthful of water. He ran straight for Shelton, punched him in the stomach and spewed water on him, then ran away laughing. Shelton tried to grab him, but he was wet and slippery. The others egged the boy on, and he ran around the dorm just out of Shelton's reach, laughing hysterically.

"Finally, as he ran past me I reached out and gave him a good whack on his bottom. I slapped him so hard that it left a bright red handprint. That stopped everything, and one of the older kids said, 'Now you've done it! You're gonna be fired!' " The older boy went downstairs to find a senior counselor, and the dorm fell silent as everyone waited to see what would happen.

"I was still in a turmoil," Shelton said, "when an attractive young girl walked into the room, a senior counselor I had never met. She asked the boy I'd hit what the trouble was, and he told her he was scared because he didn't know me and didn't know if I could take care of him. This young girl sat down and talked with him awhile, and that calmed him."

When the boys were in bed, the senior counselor suggested that Shelton read the nighttime story. He began reading, and a few minutes later she tiptoed out. The boys soon fell asleep, and he sat in the dorm thinking about his disaster. He didn't understand how this could happen to a person like himself, who had completed a successful analysis, who was mature and had some knowledge of the world. "This young woman had rescued me and put me in charge of the group again, which felt good, but at the same time I resented it horribly. And that was my first experience with Mary Jean."[5]

At last Shelton pulled himself together, left the sleeping boys, and went downstairs to talk to Fae Lohn, who was in charge of the School during Bettelheim's first extended absence in 1954. He was ready to tell Fae he would resign because he had let his group go utterly out of control and had violated a cardinal rule — he had hit a child. He could talk easily with Fae, whom he knew personally because her fiancé, Bob Tyroler, was one of his best friends. Fae told Shelton he shouldn't have hit the boy but that his action was a lot more straightforward than the way some people treated the kids. He knew who she meant, and they continued to talk.

"Fae and I relived the incident in detail, and she showed me I had made four or five mistakes before I slapped the boy. She took the tack that permitting him to come out of the bathroom naked and walk around was probably my first mistake, that right away he had overstimulated himself. I shouldn't have let him act out." After talking with Fae, Shelton decided to wait until Bruno came back; then he would offer his resignation.

In the following weeks, one person gave him a very hard time. "She was senior staff, and she kept asking what were the motives of someone who says he wants to work with kids but really wants to beat them up? It was unfair needling, but I took it." He suspected her of projecting her own hostilities onto him — a typical questioning of motives that went on all the time at the School as staff members tried to understand behavior. In any event, the other counselor's needling made Shelton want to stay and prove her wrong.

Mary Jean commented that the boy's acting-out behavior had added to his fear. Coming naked from the bathroom was probably a way of saying, "I am unprotected," as well as a gambit to seek protection from a strong adult who could sense his anxiety and relieve it. The fact that Shelton did not immediately stop him roused greater fear and sent the boy into hysteria.

"That's the kind of mistake you make," Shelton said. "Bettelheim fired some people for hitting kids, but I believe he looked at it in context, such as what it told about the counselors. Anyhow, I spent the next two weeks expecting to be fired, but he came back, and I stayed."

I asked Fae to retell the incident from her point of view, but she had forgotten it entirely. I described it, and she said she probably saw it only as "an honest human experience. Shelton didn't try to kill this child, or turn him over and spank him, or really beat him up. It wasn't a vicious attack but quite understandable, given Shelton's lack of training at that point."

For Shelton, his mistake led to a peak learning experience that left a vivid memory. Fae's lack of recall suggests that for her it was a passing matter, which she dealt with on the spot in the midst of more serious concerns. I asked Bettelheim, but he had no memory of it at all. For him, if he actually had heard of it, summoning it up would have been like trying to remember a little wave he had seen in the middle of a long sea voyage.

FAE RECALLED another kind of mistake she had made in her early years, one apparently easy for counselors to make. "I had a battle of wills with a boy about something. This kid was very angry and I said, 'I'm angrier than you are.' I'd heard another staff member say this, so I thought it was okay. But when Dr. B. read my dictation, he really lit into me, saying what an infantile response this was. I became terribly upset, and that's often a sign that you're learning something important. Bruno said, 'What did you mean that you're angrier than he is? You're here to help him with his anger, not show him yours is worse.' "

Later, Fae reflected on Bettelheim's tone of voice and came to feel that his response to her was less anger than puzzlement. "He was trying to understand what was going on with *me*, but he saw too clearly that I had done something stupid, so he was frustrated." Fae said she had made two mistakes: one was her effort to overwhelm the boy with her emotions; the other, to copy someone rather than to respond with her own feelings.

"That was the real mistake. Dr. B. always urged us to be ourselves, not go around borrowing, because the child would sense the falseness and respond worse because of it. Dr. B. usually didn't suggest what we should have said. The way he asked questions, it became self-evident."

Counselors unraveled their mistakes, and often themselves, as they replayed an incident under Bettelheim's probing. In this instance his questioning helped Fae see that she had had more options than she realized at the time—always a valuable lesson in the milieu.

COUNSELORS who survived their mistakes (and coped with the inner turmoil mistakes aroused) could go on to do things that were astonishing. One such moment for Fae came with Joey,* an episode Bettelheim highlighted years later in *The Empty Fortress*, in part because it modeled the way empathy worked. Joey, who felt he was run by machines that he created but could not control, laid imaginary wires in the dining room between himself and an imaginary socket in the wall—to digest his food. He also turned his bed into an automobile with attachments taped to it: a speaker (so he could speak and hear), a steering wheel, a battery, and so on. He kept a carburetor nearby for breathing, and whenever he left the dorm he carried a little motor. An unexpected incident with the motor proved for Bettelheim that a caring counselor could act spontaneously, ingeniously, and with empathy in a crisis. I asked Fae to retell the story.[6]

A new child, she said, would not be taken outside the School in his first six weeks, the time he needed to begin trusting the counselor enough to stay near her. "After all, we had suicidal and homicidal kids there, and we had to be careful." Just after Joey's six-week period, Fae took her group for a walk on the Midway. Joey gave her his motor to carry, but after they crossed the street he suddenly went wild and darted back into the traffic. Fae stood still, fearing that if she ran after him it would spur him on.

"I panicked. It must have been only a matter of seconds, but I was terrified, and then without thinking I held up the little motor, desperate for him to see it. He had given it to me for safekeeping, and I wanted to remind him I had it. This isn't the kind of thing you think through and then do, but it worked; he came back. But then he fell apart."

Joey scratched and clawed Fae, and she had to fight to get him across the street and back into the School. "I can't remember if he bit me, but he did everything else." Upstairs in the dorm, he was still struggling and screaming at the top of his lungs. Fae was a seasoned counselor at that point, but she could barely hang on to him and make sure he was safe. Then the realization that Joey could have killed himself overwhelmed her. Another counselor took charge, and Fae went back to her room trembling and weeping.

Bettelheim wrote the story as if it were only about Fae and Joey, and as usual he did not show himself defusing Fae's crisis. "It left me almost shattered, but he had a point of view I didn't expect. He listened, he calmed things down, but he showed me he was not going to get upset by the incident. His stance was, 'This is what we have to deal with, you'll get over it, you'll go on.'"

At first Bettelheim's attitude annoyed Fae. She felt she deserved his sympathy and understanding, but he kept a cool distance. "Appropriately, I now think, because it calmed me, and that was essential. He was as soothing and gentle as one could want, but the reality was that I had to go back and work with Joey." She also said the incident improved relations between Joey and the other children: they saw what he needed, and if they could allow for him, they could allow for themselves; and if she could help him, maybe she could help them.

"At the School you didn't function out of any abstract altruism or even a *wish* to understand. That was crystal clear, and I see it holding a hundred percent today in my practice. You do things for your own reasons, and the better you understand that, the better it is for you and others. You always focus on the patient, but there's a parallel process within yourself."

FAE HAS often used a Bettelheim teaching method when she talks with nursery and grade school teachers. "He would say, 'Why do you suppose this child did so and so?' I'd say, 'I don't know,' because I didn't. He'd say, 'Well, how do you suppose this child was feeling doing that thing?' Still I didn't know. Then he'd say, 'Well, what would make *you* behave that way?' Always searching for motive, those were his beginning questions, and if I was still stumped, he would say, 'Well, what would make *any* person behave this way?' Often, that did the trick—it took me off the hook. I wasn't talking then about myself, or the child. If you only got the barest glimmer of it, you were in business.

"He usually had a pretty good idea himself, but he wanted *you* to understand. It's not the same if he tells you; many psychologists are too much in a hurry, or whatever, but it has to happen with the workings of your own mind."

Bettelheim often gave her an observation or a psychoanalytic principle afterward—"an abstract idea for you to build on. He was unflagging in his search for understanding, and he'd work with you if you made the effort. And if you didn't make the effort, he'd try to understand why not. That was Bruno."

IT WAS also Bruno's way, as Jacqui Sanders noted, to look for new challenges. One such challenge was to take in ever more difficult children, with whom he could test the limits of the milieu and staff, hoping to demonstrate a wider range of therapeutic success. The further he pushed, the better model the School would establish to help disturbed children.

Sometimes he unexpectedly found the limits, even with the best of his workers. Toward the end of Fae Lohn's time at the School, she switched from counselor to teacher so she could have more of a personal life; in the demanding job of counselor she found herself torn by conflicting loyalties between her dorm group and her new family life with Bob Tyroler. Around this time Bettelheim took in an extremely difficult teenaged girl and put her in Fae's class. She was like a feral child, Fae said, because during the war her parents had hidden in a basement and had stifled her infant cries to avoid discovery by the Nazis.

One day the girl bit Fae's arm severely, and Fae went to Bettelheim to protest. (The same girl had attacked him earlier.) "I told Dr. B. that I made mistakes but would not tolerate being bitten for them. Dr. B. agreed with me about this girl, but it was tragic, because she had to be sent away to an institution. Dr. B. just couldn't turn her down—he wanted to try, but it was a mistake." In retrospect Fae felt that both Bettelheim and the staff had simply overreached in accepting the girl, but she understood his need to do so.

FAE COMMENTED that Bettelheim perhaps also overreached in trying to get some staffers to stay. "The guilt could be enormous, and I was very susceptible. Dr. B. used guilt—'You owe it,' he'd say. Those of us who worked five or ten years had a capacity for guilt, and he played on it, he embellished it. Not directly, but the aura he created was, 'How can you leave these children, with all they've suffered?' Some paid a high price in their personal lives for their feelings of guilt, and I get unhappy when I think about that. He evoked your sense of commitment and responsibility without exactly touching the guilt button, but it was close and maybe had that effect."

Bettelheim's constant need for committed staffers no doubt led him to press unduly in some instances; and if he held back from imposing guilt directly, it was perhaps because he realized he might go too far. But he went as far as he could because there was one thing he could not do in the School—duplicate a counselor's warm and intimate relation with a child. Able counselors like Fae created the necessary connections with children; then, by virtue of a child's trust in his counselor, he could also begin to build up, in the best possible way,[7] a reservoir of hope about himself and the world, hope to be drawn upon and held with the strength of intuition. A counselor's semiparental closeness with a child was essential for that child to grow, but as the ultimate authority in the life of the School Bettelheim remained distant. However, Ben Wright pointed out, Bettelheim was also immediate and intense.

"His relations with children were a thousand times more close than any psychiatrist or director of any school I've ever seen. He knew each of those kids personally and visited with them almost daily. He didn't dress them or undress them, and he didn't stand in the bathroom while they sat on the toilet, but they saw him in the dining room and around the School. If they were afraid of him, then that's a useful way for a child to organize his inner life, to cope with the fear of being overwhelmed by chaotic impulses. You need somebody you are afraid of who is stronger than you but whom you nevertheless trust not to hurt you. Then the fear has a positive aspect to it."

Ben also made the point that the counselors' reports were a brilliant teaching device. Bettelheim read them all, thousands of pages a year, and where he saw something crucial happening, he marked the margin to guide or jolt the staffer. "The counselors had to think about what they did," Ben said, "and then Bruno thought about what they *thought* they did, and then they thought about what *he* thought."

By inducing reflection in this way Bettelheim led counselors to dig for deeper meanings and to remind themselves of their goals as their understanding grew. Ben believed that the School would have been far less effective without the dictated reports enlivened by Bruno's comments that prompted the child's caretaker to respond afresh.

"If you just go on," he said, "and don't think about what you're doing, you bounce from one impulse to the next, you keep paddling so you don't sink, but you don't know where you're going. Bruno forced them to think, which gave them a second voice. That's where culture comes from. That's what intellect is about. In most places like the Orthogenic School, the stresses of the occasion are so great that there's no chance to think. You fall into bed at night exhausted. The only time you 'think' is once a week, when the psychiatrist comes, and he spends maybe fifteen minutes with the child and never sees whether you followed through or what happened until a week later.

"Bruno was there seven days a week, year after year. Just take bedtime—kids raise hell, they start breaking things, they go crazy. Bruno wasn't in Winnetka, he was there."

WHILE pushing the School to new heights, Bettelheim also demanded more of himself in the rest of his life, and in a way that was no doubt hard on Trude. For him to dominate the School, the School had to dominate his day; but he also wanted time to write. He craved the huge demands and rewards of the School; he pursued the writing that it partially inspired; but he was also determined to have a family, with all the time, attention, protectiveness, moral presence, and emotional intimacy it takes to be an even halfway decent father and husband. He remarked to me several times that he "couldn't have done it without Trude," which I at first took to mean running the School while having a family. Now I believe the "it" was not just the School but his whole life. Nonetheless, I am positive their relation had serious problems for many years. Bettelheim generally did not talk to me about his home life, and I rarely wanted to ask. However, in a friendship of twenty years, impressions are bound to occur and persist; and whether I call it intuition or imagination, I have formed a clear impression that I cannot dismiss, an opinion that rings true for me in light of all I know and feel, that Bruno and Trude lived through an unhappy time with each other, most probably in the years between the birth of Naomi in 1945 and the conception of Eric in 1952.

If I were to portray Bruno on canvas as he looked in his mid-forties, I would sketch hectic activity above his head and on all sides, under a sky suffused with the kind of surreal light that sometimes brightens the air just before a storm. At the edge of the canvas a patch of sullen cloud would hint at a threat of weather barely off scene that might rush into the world of the portrait.[8]

However, in Trude's and Bruno's life together, the storm never came into the picture where anyone beside the two of them could see it. Yet I can imagine it, because I cannot doubt that Trude long resented the depth and scope of Bruno's preoccupation with the School; nor can I doubt that she felt lonely and bitterly neglected night after night, with no end in sight.

These were the years in which Bettelheim created new ways in child therapy; years when he also turned to writing books; years in which he launched *Love Is Not Enough* and put together a good portion of *Symbolic Wounds*; years when his work life consistently overbalanced his family life, when most of his time, most of his inner force, most of his mind's power and his heart's desire centered on the School, on the children, on the staff. And these were also the years in which Ruth Soffer glimpsed a Bruno the world never guessed at, a man abruptly demoralized by a quiet scolding from his wife, whose words he must have felt as utter scorn—as they may have been.

Whatever troubled Bruno and Trude, it was, I believe, resolved mainly through Trude's independence of spirit and her clear eyes in judging Bruno's need for the School and all else he had to have; by her common sense in making peace with her entrenched resentment at his nightly absence; by her acceptance of the weighty role of his books in his drive for self-definition; and at last by her decision, for it was surely hers, to have a third child. She said to Hans Willig, "Well, I'm going to try once more," a decision that set herself and Bruno on the path they followed from that point onward. I seriously doubt he could have continued to dedicate himself to his work in the way he did without her steady hand at home, and her love.

BRUNO created the books, but the books created a Bruno with whom Trude wished to renew her life. She knew a great deal about troubled children because of her experiences in the Montessori school in Vienna and from supervising adoptions and doing play therapy in Chicago. As a social-work professional, she would have recognized how fresh and vital Bruno's ideas were in *Love Is Not Enough*, which summed up one phase of his life's effort, and she ultimately accepted his motives for work hours that verged on obsession.

The books, and his unforgettable presence, brought Bruno a prominence no one could have predicted, but I doubt that the glitter of his growing celebrity impressed Trude. I believe it was her empathy for his work and his writing that led her to accept the time, energy, and attention he gave to the School and the gap it left in her life. And as he met with her acceptance, he came to be the Bruno who was indeed "religious" in his observance of family time, the Bruno who no longer shrank from her quiet anger. At any rate, such is my intuition about those years and about the meaning of "love is not enough" in the complex lives of Bruno and Trude. It could never have been enough that they merely loved each other; out of love and need, each had to understand the other and truly accept whatever could not be changed.

CHAPTER 17

The Next Books;
a Knack for Controversy

WHAT HAPPENED at the School was an ongoing stimulus for Bettelheim and thus also for his writing. However, he tended to explore ideas and evolve an approach before committing himself to a major undertaking like a book. He often asked friends and acquaintances what they thought he should write next, not as a kind of informal poll, or to test the publishing waters before diving in, but mainly, I believe, to sample his own thinking. He had to test his inner waters to be sure that heart and mind agreed. If he took time to reflect on his responses to a subject, he could gauge the depths of his interest and so set himself the task of writing a book with little danger of becoming bored. He told me that at one point he had signed a contract to collaborate with Edward Shils on a book about education but soon saw he did not want to do it and returned the advance to the publisher.

As a rule, Ruth Soffer expected a book to take three years to complete, with Bettelheim's writing and her editing. "He didn't plan what he was going to write by saying, 'I'm now going to write a book about so-and-so.' More often than not, he would write thirty pages of something and send it to me. I'd say, 'What I'd really like is—,' and maybe I'd suggest going back to some point *before* his starting point in the piece. After that, the book would develop. Jerry Kaplan was always after him to write something or do a collection of pieces, but I don't really remember how the next book, *Symbolic Wounds*, got started."

In fact, Bettelheim began thinking about symbolic wounds when he became fascinated (probably in the late 1940s) by the behavior of two boys and two girls at the School who formed a secret society. Among other things, the boys agreed to cut themselves once a month and mix their blood with the menstrual blood of the girls. All four swore to help one another get ahead in the world of entertainment when they were ready to make careers. However, as Bettelheim writes in *Symbolic Wounds*, the youngsters were also trying to master some of the anxieties brought on by puberty. Counselors knew the secret, but in accord with the ethos of the School, they allowed the children relatively free rein and intervened only at the last moment. Details of the secret society reminded Bettelheim of primitive initiation rites, and he began to read up on anthropology to write a paper for a psychoanalytic meeting.

> What began as a short paper grew into a monograph as I found myself confronted with an issue that seemed to pose a central theoretical problem of human psychology. . . . Under which frame of reference can human behavior best be understood, that of inner freedom and human autonomy, or that of coercion by blind instinctual forces or the insensible powers of tradition?[1]

Bettelheim came down, as might be expected, on the side of autonomy and choice. He did not dismiss environmental factors or the pressures of instinct, but to grasp a child's problem he always looked for the child's own interpretation of his experiences and feelings.

Bettelheim's research and thinking led him to question the well-known Freudian idea that male circumcision symbolized castration. Freud had speculated that the practice originated long ago in the "primal horde," where the cruel chieftain-father castrated his sons and took all the women for himself. Bettelheim doubted this scenario, and by scrupulously using Freud's own scholarly sources to reach a different conclusion, he hoped to open a dialogue to correct Freudian thinking on circumcision. Correcting ideas that had become dogma was risky enough, but Bettelheim also thought Freud's theory of penis envy was incomplete.

"I never doubted penis envy," he said. "It's obvious to anyone who has done analyses of women." However, he had come to see that men have comparable feelings toward women, especially envy of their power to create life. I asked why he thought Freud wrote about penis envy but not vagina envy. As I saw it, Bettelheim's concept seemed only a logical extension of Freud's original insight.

"Freud grew up in a much more patriarchal society, over a generation earlier than myself. Oh, he says occasionally that women are 'superior,' but he wouldn't admit that men are envious of women. In his love letters to his fiancée, he speaks of her weakness and the need to protect her, et cetera. Even a genius bows to the prejudice of his age."

Bettelheim said that when he finished reading his paper at a conference chaired by Karl Menninger, Menninger brought him up short with a quiet but indignant aside: "Who are you, that you think the mantle of Freud has descended upon you, that you can make such radical deviations from theory?"

Later, Bettelheim's friends (or those he thought of as friends) turned away when he walked up to them. They would not discuss the paper with an upstart who imagined he could correct Freud. The rebuff showed him once and for all that he had no welcome in the world of conventional analysis, and he told me this was the last professional paper he presented at a psychoanalytic conference. In my opinion, he had been unrealistic about the extent to which analysis could free the mind; one thing it did not seem to do was to free a person's mind *about* analysis, especially if he was an analyst who feared losing group acceptance. Out of his naïveté, this was the reality Bettelheim had overlooked.

In 1983, I asked how orthodox Freudians felt about him now. "Very ambivalent," he said. I suggested that perhaps they were jealous of his success with his books, or envious of his public prominence. He, however, refused to ascribe jealousy to anyone and said he thought analysts had a grudging interest in him.

"They see I've done a few unusual things, but I'm not a good union man. Ultimately, I knew there would be no pleasing them, so I didn't try. I went my own way and did not want to become a part of the hierarchy. You see, most analysts gravitate to a very narrow group. None of them really achieves anything—any preeminence, for instance—not on their own. Though they talk well, they don't write well; the product is too erudite, too much in the private language of analysts. It's like a secret society, like the Freemasons, where there is an inner circle, but you rise through the ranks, degree by degree. I wouldn't do that, so I would have been an inconvenient member in any case.

"Also, I'm skeptical about sacred cows, which is what Freud has become, unfortunately. Most of those prominent in the organization would like to do original work, but if they do, they can't rise through the hierarchy." He added that he had tried to avoid holding office in any organization, because the price was too high: you had to speak in the voice of consensus.

Despite, or perhaps because of, the chilly reception for his ideas, he went ahead with the book on symbolic wounds, setting vagina envy along-side penis envy as a matter of psychology. He may have felt that once the evidence was laid out fully, analysts might modify their opinions privately and drop a few dogmas. In any event, everyone would know where he stood. He also had in mind a larger issue he had discussed with Ruth Soffer:

> I hope that this study may lessen the male-centering propensity and shed new light on the psycho-sociological role of woman; that it may indicate how much more that is feminine exists in men than is gener-ally believed, and how greatly woman's influence and strivings have affected social institutions which we still explain on a purely mascu-line basis.[2]

FOR SEVERAL years Bettelheim had urged Ruth to go into analysis, and she did so in 1950. "Bruno bugged me until I gave in, you might say. Any-how, I went five days a week to his friend Dr. Kamm—well, they weren't exactly friends, but they'd known each other a long time. Bruno thought he'd be good for me, and in fact he turned out to be a marvelous analyst. But after the first three months he gave me an ultimatum. He said, 'Madam, if you want to worship on the altar of your defenses, that's fine, but you're wasting your money and my time.' So I settled down to business and went two more years and was finished."

Ruth worked on *Symbolic Wounds* in its early stages, first as a reader and note gatherer. She read anthropology for six months and typed out passages "on a dinky little typewriter at home. Bruno did lots more on his own, but I gave him voluminous excerpts, especially of Spencer and Gillen, who were the sources Freud had used. As he says in the book, he wanted to do justice to Freud by relying on the same literature."

Ruth also edited the first two chapters of the manuscript but then told Bruno he had to get another editor, and she suggested someone. "It was really time for me to do something different." She had eighteen hundred dollars left over from money allotted to her analysis, so she took it and went to Europe.

The analysis with Dr. Kamm had given Ruth the inner freedom to make a new beginning, and at that point she knew she wanted to have a family. Breaking her Chicago routines seemed a good move, and a leave from the *Britannica* and a long vacation felt like the start of a new path in life. As it turned out, she met Stewart Marquis in Europe, and they married when they returned to the States.

"In 1954 Bruno went to Europe with Trude and the Janowitzes," Ruth said. "This was just before the final page proofs for *Symbolic Wounds* came in, and he asked me to take care of them for him. I was still doing a little work for him after I came back from Europe, while I also worked for the *Britannica* and before we moved to Tennessee."

Almost at the last minute Ruth found a serious mistake in the proofs. Someone had changed a word or two in a sentence toward the end of the book in a way that reversed Bettelheim's meaning, and the mistake had not been caught in the previous set of galleys. The publisher insisted the correction could not be made in the way Ruth knew it should be unless Bettelheim ordered it.

"I really panicked, but then the School managed to track him down by cable, and he got the mistake fixed."

Ruth could not remember the exact word change but otherwise recalled the incident vividly. The reversal may have occurred because a printer unconsciously rejected Bettelheim's point of view, which was daring in 1954. For instance, he speaks of a puberty rite among the Omaha Indians in which young people could choose their sexual identity on the basis of a dream, and he says this might have been an "admirable solution" if such sexual choices were not final and absolute

> but could be temporary or tentative and of varying intensity or commitment to the ways of the other sex.
> What needs to be satisfied is the desire of both men and women to play a significant part in the duties, obligations and prerogatives, the activities and enjoyments that in our society happen to be thought of as belonging to the other sex.[3]

Bettelheim agreed with Freud on bisexuality and thought bisexual feelings should not be denied or experienced with guilt. Some unknown hand had altered a word or two in a long passage where he implies the need for more leeway for men to become aware of their feminine component and women their masculinity. He also suggests that these feelings can best be explored behind closed doors within a satisfying relation between a man and a woman, who may alternate roles occasionally. A return to puberty rituals could never offer emotional guidance or relief, but he says that solutions might be sought that are more personal, more socially effective, and more satisfying in private.[4]

"He was trying to suggest gently," Ruth Marquis said, "that we should have a little more tolerance of who we are, that we live with mixed feelings and can make different choices. It horrified me that somebody reversed this. Maybe they couldn't believe he meant what he said, but thank goodness we got it back the way he wrote it."

IN 1954 Ruth Marquis became pregnant; not long afterward, she and Stewart moved to Tennessee, where he had found a teaching job. Her pregnancy was dangerous because she had had lupus a few years earlier, but things went well, and she gave birth to a daughter. She had less time now, but Bettelheim continued to rely on her for smaller editing jobs—book reviews, for instance. She still could not make the kind of heavy commitment that editing a book-length manuscript would require, although she had worked a little on *Truants from Life* in its early stages, with the understanding that Bruno would turn to others for the bulk of the editing. He did so successfully, although not totally to his satisfaction. He missed her questions of every kind, which challenged him to clarify his ideas and thereby strengthen them.

Ruth said that for years Bettelheim called her almost every day when he got to the office, to talk about his writing and anything else that came to mind. It was easy for him to elaborate his thoughts with her, to discuss anything, and their ongoing dialogue extended to letters from him that are often blunt and unguarded. For instance, he published a politely unfavorable critique of the Ernest Jones biography of Freud, but his remarks to Ruth in the editing process reveal the passion behind his cool and precise words. When he sent her the review to edit, he wrote:

> I have the uneasy feeling that I've repeated the same criticism several times. While I feel that Jones' biography, contrary to its universal acclaim, is an incredibly lousy job, I do not wish to sound emotional in my criticism. I wish that my negative opinion should come through as far as I support it by what I say in the review. Otherwise I leave this difficult task in your experienced hands.[5]

"This was typical of how we worked," Ruth said. "Bruno's writing was like a safety valve for him, but then I toned down the anger, as he wanted me to do. I think the editing made a review like this more credible as a piece of public discourse."

A week later (September 28, 1956) Bettelheim wrote to Ruth about the review he *wished* he had written:

> The biography stinks much more than I suggest, but what's the use. The real thing to write would have been to show how the good things [in] psychoanalysis came from that part of Freud which official psychoanalysis, and with it his biographer, totally neglect, and how they copy and enlarge on all the bad things Freud was. But lo and behold, finally somebody wrote the article I always wanted to write[6] and never got around to, namely showing why only very sick people become analysts (this was true for Freud and Jones and what not, but this is what to hide once and for all this biography was written, and that is why it was so universally accepted) and how the practice of psychoanalysis makes them only become sicker and sicker, though they continue to help people. Now this was true for Freud, too. The Freud of his own analysis was a much healthier person than he was after practicing for some ten years and more what he had discovered.
>
> In short this guy had the courage to say what everybody knows: having to suppress his own reactions to the patient's love and hate drains the therapist so much of all feelings that finally he becomes unable to have any relation to anybody. Then he is a good analyst, but a total failure as a person. The Freud who could say that analysis is a cure through love (which he vehemently rejected some ten years later, and ever thereafter) was the Freud who had just discovered it, but hardly begun to practice.

Some weeks later (in a letter dated "Thursday — 56") Bettelheim wrote in a fury about a conference he had just attended on the psychiatric in-patient treatment of children:

> An exhausting week during which I had to listen to all the great experts on psychiatry and child analysis holding forth that either psychotic children ought to be shocked, or tranquilized, or kept in cold storage for the one or three weekly analytic hours, the residential staff's main task being not to interfere with what happens in this hour, not to alleviate the child's night terror when it occurs, but to make sure that as much as possible of this terror is preserved and haunting the child during the days til he sees his mighty psychiatrist, that all res-

idential workers with the exception of the psychiatrist must be full time, the psychiatrist of course only part time, that all but the psychiatrist must attend church regularly, and what not and being by all this in such shock that I did not even explode all over.

RUTH'S second pregnancy ended in a miscarriage, and with her third, the doctor ordered her to stay in bed until she came full term. She and Stewart had no savings; they were barely getting by on his $5,000 a year from the University of Tennessee, and now she had to hire someone to take care of her young daughter and do the housework. Ruth had supported herself for years, and now being immobilized and needing money left her panic-stricken. In desperation she wrote to Bettelheim: did he have any more editing she might do?

"Back like a shot came a big package of transcripts from the seminars with campus mothers." She had sat in on the Saturday-morning sessions in the late 1940s and early '50s, and she'd loved them. "You can't imagine how much fun they were, and he was at his darlingest then."

When Ruth received the raw manuscript, some of the dialogues had already been turned into magazine articles. She had to make sense of a huge mass of material, structure it, edit it, and shape it into a book with Bruno's voice and stamp. She was surprised in reading the later transcripts to see that he seemed to have lost interest after she left Chicago; he was irritable and sharp with the mothers, who could be blank about their defenses and clueless about their own motives. Their defects of common sense about themselves and their children no doubt made him more than impatient, so that he finally gave up the seminars. Ruth asked him about his change in temper, and he replied, "Because you weren't there," an answer perhaps intended in part to make her feel guilty for going off to have a life of her own after having become almost indispensable to him.

Ruth seems to have been a kind of catalyst for Bettelheim; he needed to sound out his ideas with a person who accepted him *before* she understood him, who would ask good questions in good time. She did not have to say anything in the seminar, but with her in the room, he was reassured of his audience. At this point in his life he must have benefited from the simple presence of a friendly ear, someone who always questioned him with no intent of personal challenge; then he could be at his best, avoiding the distraction of his own anger at his listener's resistance. When Ruth challenged the wording of ideas he had put on paper, it was a different matter; he trusted her to tell him what she had not understood, and so it was *his* resistance that had to be overcome in solidifying a sentence or a concept.

Perhaps of equal importance, Ruth (at the time of the seminar) was not directly responsible for children, as the mothers were and as were his counselors. His feelings when he talked with her would not be the same as for campus mothers, whom he felt he could never teach enough, or quickly enough, to make a difference in the lives of their children. In the seminars she attended I believe he was engaging at least as much in his endless conversation with Ruth as with the mothers who appeared briefly and then went back to their own environments.

As a book, *Dialogues with Mothers* seems to have held no more than a passing interest for Bettelheim, who in the meantime had again turned his attention, with some reluctance, to his concentration-camp experiences in order to write *The Informed Heart*. Ruth had long urged him to do this, and she worked on that book also and gave it its memorable title.

The Informed Heart came out in 1960, and *Dialogues* followed in 1962, the same year as the new edition of *Symbolic Wounds*. "Bruno wanted to revise it," Ruth said, "because some of the anthropological criticism was justified, but more than that he wanted to strengthen his thesis and make the book more readable. The second edition became the version he was really pleased with." This time around she edited the whole book, making it less academic in tone than the first had been.

As a rule, Bettelheim never answered critics, but several reviewers had so thoroughly misunderstood *Symbolic Wounds* that he wanted to reject their misconceptions as firmly as possible and in this way reaffirm his positions. In the preface to the 1962 edition he wrote:

> I was accused (and rightly so if such be wrong) of "lumping all primitive peoples together"; and of "equating child, psychotic, and primitive man." And it is true: I am convinced that all men share certain feelings, desires, and anxieties, that these are common not only to various preliterate tribes — as well as to children, psychotic adults, and primitive man — to all of us. . . .

... Thus, far from wishing to draw parallels between primitive man (preliterate or otherwise) and schizophrenic youngsters, I tried to show how parallel are the primitive wishes of all men. ...

... My book does not deal with primitive man (a concept I have no use for) but with the primitive in all men (which interests me greatly). ... I believe puberty rites to refer to something so primitive that we all share in it.[7]

Misconceptions are not easily dispelled; the French translation of *Symbolic Wounds* (1971) contains a note added at the publisher's request by an anthropologist who continued to repeat a misunderstanding of Bettelheim's position.[8] Where Bettelheim asserted a common humanity by showing parallel wishes, some persons persist in seeing a specific equivalence.

From my point of view, such persons are probably denying their own hostilities and primitive wishes; of course, Bettelheim knew better than to characterize critics in this way, and so he simply offered his position in the words quoted above.

BESIDES keeping in touch with Ruth by phone, Bettelheim often sent her things to read and carbon copies of his correspondence. In 1960 he sent her a monograph by Jules Henry and asked her to set down her reactions to it. He respected Henry because of Henry's sociological study of the School's work structure as contrasted with that of a conventional psychiatric hospital.[9] The monograph Bettelheim sent to Ruth was an early draft of part of Henry's final book, *Pathways to Madness*, in which he described four American families where psychosis had occurred.

Ruth had liked the monograph, but before she could reply she received Bettelheim's letter to Henry discussing it, a letter that she read with growing excitement. Bettelheim did not think Henry gave a proper account of the plight of mothers home alone with children, and when Ruth saw his empathy, which she had not guessed, it nearly overwhelmed her. She said, "I exploded on paper to him with all the stuff I'd been struggling with for several years."

As a working woman with an interesting and highly responsible job for more than ten years, she had found the sudden isolation of motherhood in a small southern town almost too much to bear—and she had also felt guilty about feeling this way. She fired off a long letter to Bruno with her ideas and observations, many of which he used in his next letter to Jules Henry. When Ruth received the second letter, "I wrote to Bruno my higher-than-a-kite response to *that* letter." She told him she wished that just once a month she could have a whole day

> to wake up belonging to myself, take a bath in the daytime when I'm not tired, have a B.M. when I need to, and sit on the toilet without listening anxiously for sounds of calamity below. . . . The truth is that the unnatural isolation of the mother with her children—particularly the first child—is as insane for the child as for the mother. . . . You cannot imagine what it means to me to read in your letter that all this, and much more, is not something I alone imagine and distort. . . . I know that I would choose and value Stew for a friend if we weren't married already. But I also love myself infinitely, and I love life even more— and I want all of it! ("Friday—10/60")

Ruth was so stirred up by Bettelheim's recognition of feelings like hers that she decided to write something about the conflicts in many mothers who had gone from workplace to home. She called it "The Private Revolution," and her first sentence was, "For 22 million women holding jobs in America, woman's place is no longer in the home." She finished the essay in December and sent it to Bettelheim, who liked it and suggested revisions, saying,

> Since you want me not only to praise but also to discuss, I shall try to do for once for you, poorly, what you always do so well for me.

He first discussed the concept of "self-fulfillment" and suggested how to make it less vague. Then he wrote:

> On page 4 you say that the non-fulfillment of these cravings plagues women more and more. You will be interested to know that it also plagues men more and more. At the last psychoanalytic meeting Helene Deutsch said, in a paper on frigidity in women, that this has recently become even more of a problem of men who worry intensely about themselves and their masculinity because the women are frigid. Actually Helene Deutsch saw it wrong and you see it right. The women are dissatisfied for the reasons you state and the men feel defeated as men because whatever they do and try they cannot satisfy the women because sex alone cannot make up for all the other things they are missing in life.

I have absolutely no hesitation if you want to quote me, but I really see no reason why you should. Your ideas on this and other matters are shared ideas, and if they see the light of print under your name I shall be delighted, particularly since I would be hard-pressed to know which of these ideas originated with me or which with you. So just skip my name in footnote 2 on page 9 and write the rest without quotation marks as your own ideas. Why shouldn't I secretly godfather some of your ideas when you have godfathered so many of mine? Remember, after all, all we think is the result of some social interchange with somebody.

In addition, Bettelheim encouraged Ruth to try to place her essay, and she sent it also to an old friend, the editor and writer Daniel Bell, whom she had known in Boston. He suggested several magazines, but Ruth made only a casual effort, trying a couple of them. She felt no urge to publish; at that moment, knowing how Bettelheim felt about the loneliness and difficulties of women like herself was enough.

Ruth believed, and I agree, that she had a small but significant role in Bettelheim's career as an essayist because of her contribution to his views on women. "When he first started feeding me Freud, I remember coming back to him just speechless with wonder." But she had a reservation. "I said it sounds as if there's really only one sex in the world, and that's boys. And he laughed and said—now remember, this is in the mid-forties—he said, 'Well, you're very bright,' and we both laughed. And forgot about it."

In "The Problem of Generations," published in *Daedalus* in 1961, Bettelheim remarked on Freud's orientation toward males, and Ruth reminded him of their mid-1940s conversation, which she later saw as the start of a long dialogue between them about men and women. The *Daedalus* piece caught the eye of Robert Silvers, an editor at *Harper's Magazine*, who suggested that Bettelheim write an article to be called "Growing Up Female." Silvers wanted the title to echo "Growing Up Absurd," Paul Goodman's book that made the conventional argument that young women have an easier time growing up in American society because they can, as Silvers summarized it,

find fulfillment in marriage, and in child-bearing and rearing. You show that the problem is not so simple, and it seems to us that one point of departure might well be that under present conditions the fate of the girl "can even be harder than the boy," although this is little realized.

Bettelheim sent Silvers's letter to Ruth and asked for any notes on the topic. She replied with her thoughts and soon thereafter was editing the piece, parts of which followed some of the material in her unpublished article. She agreed with Bettelheim that ideas discussed between two people become something needing no attribution, and in talking to me about the genesis of "Growing Up Female" she made clear that she was not trying to claim credit; her point was that people in the academic world should be freer with their ideas. She admired the generosity of spirit in the letters that went back and forth between Bettelheim and Henry, as well as Bruno's correspondence with David Rapaport and with Peter Wolff, where they helped each other by testing out and clarifying their ideas.

"In Bruno's letters to Jules Henry he was, in effect, offering Henry these ideas and the chance to publish them first, because the ideas were a good commentary on what Henry was trying to do." By contrast, she thought that academic competitiveness had become so aggressive that "people won't even burp in public because they're saving it for their own manuscript."

The *Harper's* publication of "Growing Up Female" in 1962 put Bettelheim momentarily and inadvertently in the forefront of the "women's lib" movement. Betty Friedan's *The Feminine Mystique* was still in galleys when Bettelheim received a letter from the book's editor, George Brockway of Norton, seeking an endorsement. Brockway noted that the Friedan book "deals with many of the ideas expressed in your recent article in *Harper's*." Bettelheim, however, sent the galleys to Ruth with a handwritten note: "I have no time to read this—maybe you are interested?"

Bettelheim's status as a public thinker had now taken a quantum leap. "He got invitations from all over to talk about 'women today,' and we recycled 'Growing Up Female' over and over in speeches and women's magazine articles," Ruth said; and she called the public response a "firestorm."

As RUTH's children grew, they wanted to help her do her work. When they learned the alphabet and numbers, they sorted index cards and transferred pagination. Later on, the whole Marquis family visited with the Bettelheim family in Hyde Park and had dinner at their house, and in the course of his travels Bettelheim came to see the Marquises at Michigan State University, where Stewart had found a new position.

"Bruno took us to dinner at Kellogg Center," Ruth said. "The kids knew all about my work with him, and they were so excited at going out to dinner with him they could hardly breathe. Kellogg Center has a very elegant dining room, so they were all dressed up and on their best behavior. Bruno handed them the menu and said, 'What would you like?' And they just looked at him, absolutely mute. So he said, 'You can have anything you want,' and that blew their minds. For weeks afterward they kept saying to each other, 'He told us we could have anything we wanted!' I think he was trying to put them at their ease because they looked so polite.

"Later, when he and I were talking and they weren't around, he said something like, 'They're darling but too restrained.' I was shocked and horrified, and I said, 'My God, we don't pressure them.' And Bruno said, 'You fool—of course you don't pressure them. You pressure yourself, and they're *your* kids.' "

"GROWING Up Female" caused a stir not because it was controversial; it was simply ahead of the curve in social commentary, a fact of timing for which Bettelheim could thank a sharp-eyed editor. However, he published two other notable essays in the early 1960s that raised his profile because of their disturbing content: "The Ignored Lesson of Anne Frank" in 1960, and "Freedom from Ghetto Thinking" in 1962. Both provoked torrents of protest, even abusive letters from those who said that Bettelheim was "blaming the victim." The Anne Frank essay might now come under the scholarly heading of "reception studies," because its chief aim was to criticize the public's reaction to Anne Frank's story. In fact, Bettelheim did not blame her; he blamed an unthinking audience for bowing to the premise of the play based on the diary that keeping the family together was the highest value under the extreme circumstances they faced. Bettelheim saw this as precisely the wrong thing to have done. However, he wrote,

> my point is not to criticize what the Franks did, but only the universal admiration of their way of coping, or rather of not coping.[10]

The Franks had hidden in a concealed space, trying to maintain their life together as best they could. After two years they were betrayed, and all died except the father. Audiences swept away by the pathos of Anne's story (or who found an icon in this poor girl) conveniently averted their eyes from the realities of her time and place.

In the essay Bettelheim also made the unsettling point that the first step of nonresistance to degradation sets up the next step, until

> in the deepest sense the walk to the gas chamber was only the last consequence of these Jews' inability to comprehend what was in store; it was the final step of surrender to the death instinct.[11]

Most of all, however, he objected to the audience's love for the "moral" of the story as dramatized: "I still believe, in spite of everything, that people are truly good at heart." We can feel the need of a sensitive, thoughtful teenager for that illusion, and it does her no discredit; but for an adult to mention this "moral" in the same breath with the murder of millions is pernicious folly. Further, to feel forgiveness after laughing over scenes in a play about a young girl who is about to die embodies an attitude that, for Bettelheim, was softheaded to the point of lunacy. He wanted to warn his readers that the human heart can be malevolent, murderous, cruel, violent, and bloody beyond belief. People are *not* good despite everything, and *you're* a fool if you think so. A trapped teenager could say it, but not a free adult who knew the consequences of the Frank family's choice.

Bettelheim looked beyond his sympathy for Anne Frank and was alarmed and dismayed by what he saw:

> . . . the universal and uncritical response to her diary and to the play and movie based on it. . . . I believe that the world-wide acclaim given her story cannot be explained unless we recognize in it our wish to forget the gas chambers.[12]

He knew that the camps, including the death camps, had been easy to create as institutions of a totalitarian state and that the Final Solution bears witness to an invisible inferno within the human spirit. He wanted people to understand this; he had no patience for the blindness of those whose feelings about a monstrous event ran no deeper than comfortable tears and a nice dinner after the show; people who felt but did not think, whose passing sadness did not honor the truth about the enormity perpetrated by the Nazis and their enablers.

Bettelheim directed his blame at anyone who reacted with mere sentiment to the horrors of the Holocaust, but by pointing out options the Frank family might have had, he bruised the feelings of many who had wept over the play. Some turned on him with outrage and open hatred, and to them he was a pariah for the rest of his life. However, after more than forty years, the stream of informed opinion seems to have flowed in the direction he first mapped out, as others have written of the dishonesty of the play and the self-deception of audiences everywhere.[13]

The child in her hiding place who could for a moment believe that people are "good at heart" could also say, with mature and desperate honesty, "Let the end come, however cruel." The reality we should contemplate in Anne Frank's story is that she was arrested on information for which the informant received about one dollar; that she was transported, with the usual brutality, to Auschwitz, where she was chosen for work rather than being gassed; that she was given a tattoo to replace her name, as one detail in a highly efficient system for the destruction of Jews; that she was transported again, in a cattle car, from Auschwitz to Bergen-Belsen, where she shivered in a flimsy tent that was her only shelter against the winter's wet cold; that her clothes in her last months of life were a few thin rags which barely covered her nakedness; that she was starved, that she was covered with lice, that she contracted typhus, that she cried out helpless and alone in her last days; that her end did not come quickly, as she had hoped, but was protracted, and that she suffered and suffered until her last spark of life was snuffed out.

ONE MAY doubt that in the months between Anne's arrest and her death any hope about the goodness of people passed through her mind. The fake warmth of the play's famous "moral" can now be seen as a sad and sickening instance of the seductive folly of conventional wisdom and of the age-old madness of crowds.

Bettelheim, in swimming against the stream of opinion in his time, has been vindicated by others who came after him with comments that were surprisingly close in spirit, and it matters little whether or not such writers had read what he wrote in 1960. The fact that some people came to this opinion in their own way and voiced it out of their own spirit is the kind of satisfying reality that would have given him a moment of hope about the human race, whose salvation, at many other moments, he despaired of.

BETTELHEIM'S other brief foray into controversy in the early 1960s came with "Freedom from Ghetto Thinking" in 1962. He knew that he would be taken to task for his arguments, but the urgency of his message overrode any concern for what people would think of him. Public opinion carried great weight—how could it not? But in his view, a person's opinion of himself had to be the voice heard above all others. Reputation could burst like a bubble, for reasons beyond one's control, and it was not worth a serious man's efforts. Bettelheim always felt safe standing on the ground of his own convictions, which he thought through to his own satisfaction before offering them to the public.

When he revised "Ghetto Thinking" for his 1990 book of essays, *Freud's Vienna*, he placed it last in the table of contents, as his final word on the subject. He stressed again that he had no quarrel with the Franks,

> least of all with poor Anne. But I am highly critical of the ghetto philosophy that seems to have pervaded not only the Jewish intelligentsia but large segments of the free world. We seem to find human grandeur in submitting passively to the sword, in bending the neck.[14]

In his usual way, he wrote to teach, to warn his readers once more that carrying on a normal life "can be fatal in extreme circumstances." In the world he knew, those who glorified a passive response to oppression were dangerously out of touch with reality; he also believed that cultural attitudes, in part, led to the inertia that kept ghetto Jews from trying to defend themselves against the Nazis,

> in their inner feelings of resignation, in the careful eradication, over centuries, of tendencies to rebel, in the ingrained habit of believing that those who bend do not break.[15]

Bettelheim's critics tend to look mainly to external factors to explain the fate of ghetto Jews, whereas he tried first to imagine their state of mind. His approach has limits, but the fact remains that by treating Jews as a coherent and stable group, the Nazis were able to commit mass murder with abhorrent efficiency. The more strongly the victims held to group solidarity without resistance, in whatever form, the closer the Nazis came to their Final Solution. It put a powerful logistical lever in their hands. Because Bettelheim understood others by looking also into himself, and because he had faced some of the extreme conditions that lay in wait for ghetto Jews, it should be clear (although he does not say this) that when he argued that the victim's inner life made him vulnerable, he spoke of himself.

In like manner, at the heart of Bettelheim's approach to a disturbed child was the psychological effort to uncover the child's interpretation of himself and his experience. How the child had been hurt, and by whom or by what, was important, yes; but more significant for his recovery was his inner response: the faulty defense that came unbidden to his mind. Both in ghetto thinking and psychosis, Bettelheim sought insight into the ideas, feelings, and attitudes that made up a person's point of view, the purely internal and self-created vision out of which one acts. Or does not act.

NOW THAT more than half a century has passed, with massive and detailed studies of the Final Solution, it is nevertheless troubling to try to look objectively at such a horrid event. Leaving numbers aside, it remains the most grotesque, malicious, and blameworthy human action of the twentieth century, and those who do not recognize this are themselves in my view worthy of blame. But in this discussion we need to name its purpose and method.

My own thinking, which I believe parallels that of Bettelheim, is as follows: if group solidarity (loyalty to family, to neighbors, to a religious or ethnic group and community) is a value that trumps all others; if those separated from the group feel weak and fearful, so that they are motivated to stay with the group at all costs; if the group has provided safety much of the time, even though it has no ready means to resist attack; if a person learns from his earliest impressions that resistance to aggression is more dangerous than nonresistance; if the weaker group has long lived surrounded by some stronger group; if the strong group honors a dishonorable tradition of abusing and oppressing the weak group; and if the drag and pull of all these influences, or some combination of them, finally converge—then the stage has been set for the kind of disaster that befell European Jews.

Nazi cruelty involved an express purpose toward the Jews: to clean out an imagined source of filth and evil. Men who would murder for the sake of purity take revenge for their own sick fears, and when the Nazis and others dared at last to act upon the logic of their hatred, ghetto solidarity helped the killers. Moreover, those who had wished in their heart of hearts to destroy the Jewish people were not uncertain or slow to act. The oppression was real, as Bettelheim knew from personal experience, and its aim was understood by the oppressors with the minimum of discussion.

Their emotionally sanitized phrase, *Final Solution*, expressed and masked their intent in a cool and satisfying way. Destruction was its purpose, and securing the victims' mass cooperation was its prime method.

The victimization was real, which Bettelheim did not deny or play down; but he held to the principle, drawn from his repeated reflections upon himself and his experiences in extreme conditions, that we govern ourselves, to some degree, even when we are most governed by others; that instead of giving in, we can run away; or if we can't run away, we can resist; or if we can't resist, we can end things by our own hand. If we take none of these paths, all ugly and frightening, then we believe and fear that the result would be worse than giving in.

Self-government, or autonomy, was Bettelheim's starting point to inquire into anyone's attitude, behavior, or responsibility. Toward the end of "Ghetto Thinking" he writes,

> It was not my intention here to judge either Anne Frank or the six million other Jews who perished. I do not wish to criticize nor to whitewash, but to understand and to learn. What I plead for is that we do not despise the lesson the six million victims unwillingly taught us at the cost of their lives. Ghetto thinking is not a crime; it is a fatal mistake.[16]

In revising this essay he chose his words with great care, because he had been accused of blaming those who had suffered most. In fact he did not blame the dead; he was anxious to remind the living of the autonomy that is our common birthright and the dignity that we must preserve; and he did so by insisting on responsibility for one's actions, mistakes and all. At the same time, he wanted to caution his readers that ordinary men may harbor deadly desires that can drive them, in given circumstances, to become mass murderers. Often this fact is paid lip service, but the reality is hard to integrate into one's view of the human race, since it requires grasping an insight that repels us.

In writing about Anne Frank, Bettelheim tried to raise doubts in those who idolized a fatal mistake, a ghetto-thinking mistake—and I would like to spell out here what I think he meant by "mistake." Throughout his life at the Orthogenic School, he kept a good dictionary close at hand to use in the work of the School, a resource for analogies and metaphors and to dig out precise shades of meaning that sometimes illuminated a problem. In this spirit I take the liberty of quoting on his behalf a dictionary usage note that I believe he would endorse:

Mistake often implies misunderstanding, misinterpretation, and re-
sultant poor judgment, and is usually weaker than *error* in imputing
blame or censure.[17]

The ghetto-thinking mistake, easy to understand in the light of the
culture, history, and traditions of the ghetto, taught attitudes that were
implicated in the destruction of millions. Even so, I believe that Bettelheim intended less "blame" than is suggested in the mild distinction the
dictionary draws. He had seen enough of life in all its aspects to realize the
absurdity of blaming anyone whose mistake proved fatal to himself.

Also, underlying this essay was a personal matter that Bettelheim did
not reveal in the text and did not often discuss with those around him. As
an assimilated Jew whose family had prospered in Vienna for three generations, his own thinking had unmistakable traces of the ghetto heritage he
thought he had abandoned. The impulse to "keep the family together"
was almost as natural to him as to a ghetto Jew, and so at the time of the
Anschluss, after talking with his sister, he felt morally bound as the head of
the family to make the right decision. However, he made a mistake that
might have proved fatal when feelings of guilt clouded his judgment at
the thought of leaving his mother and sister.

He took full responsibility for staying in Vienna, and until the last year
of Trude's life he did not tell her that Grete had become hysterical when
he had said he was going to America. Obviously, a ghetto-thinking mistake took him to Dachau and Buchenwald, and that and his guilt at his
sister's hysteria were his personal responsibility.

Bettelheim sometimes liked to say, "Good judgment comes from
experience, and experience comes from bad judgment." He had reason to
upbraid himself for bad judgment, but afterward he blamed no one else
for his experience. He had made the mistake.

BETTELHEIM had one other bone to pick with the Anne Frank audience—the use, or misuse, as he saw it, of the word *innocent* to describe
Jewish victims of the Nazis. He knew he would provoke, that he would be
attacked, ignored, or misunderstood, but he went ahead to discuss various
nuances of meaning in the word *innocent* to show that it does not fit. He
concluded,

I think that what we are trying to assert, by implication, is that those
outside Germany who did not stand up and fight are innocent of guilt,

though at bottom we know we are guilty of nonparticipation, guilty of not having done all we could have done, and the more we should have done. That is why Jews do not speak of innocent Gypsies or Poles; we do not have the same feeling of obligation to them—we do not feel we should have fought to save them from destruction. The tacit, and I believe unconscious, argument seems to run: if those Jews who lived directly under the Nazis could be so innocent of what the Nazis were up to, if they could have overlooked what Hitler said he was going to do (and did), then we who were so much farther away are blameless for having kept ourselves in similarly "innocent" ignorance.[18]

In short, Bettelheim thought that raising a frequent cry of "innocent" was a clue to unexpressed, probably unrecognized guilt feelings on the part of persons who suspected they were not as innocent as they wished they were. Between perpetrator and victim, it was obvious who was the sinner and who was the sinned against, but in psychology that was not his stopping place. He did not like rhetoric that seemed able to speak of little else besides guilt and innocence, because such rhetoric failed to suggest how people got where they were and what could be done about it.

MUCH GHETTO thinking can be accounted for, if one wishes to do so, by history and firmly internalized cultural values, but Bettelheim also added a touch of Freud to his analysis by arguing that traditional restraints on the death drive have been lost in our time:

The twentieth century did away with ancient barriers that once prevented our destructive tendencies from running rampant, both in ourselves and in society. State, family, church, society—all were put to question, and found wanting. So their power to restrain or channel our destructive tendencies was weakened. . . . [Now] only man's personal ability to control his own death drive can protect him when the destructive forces of others, as in the Hitler state, are running rampant.[19]

Like Freud, Bettelheim believed we have death tendencies—the death drive that Freud called Thanatos. Bettelheim wrote that those who went passively to the gas chambers were irresistibly flooded by such feelings—the *drive* toward death and the *need* for death, which he understood as aspects of Thanatos. He had been almost overwhelmed by such feelings on the train to Dachau, until his defenses took over and protected him with an illusion of amused superiority to his captors.

For those in the power of the Nazis, as he had been, the death drive arose spontaneously and could be fatal if it overwhelmed a spirit too demoralized to hope for survival, as he felt was the case with ghetto Jews in their last hours and moments. Struggle was useless, hope was useless, life was useless. Even breathing was useless, except to breathe in the gas and let life go.

Bettelheim also saw the aggressor's hostility as another aspect of Thanatos. A guard, by acting on his hostility, could suspend his own feelings of vulnerability to the death drive when abusing or killing someone else; but a victim, flooded to the limit of his heart and mind, seeing no way out, surrendered to his death drive as willingly as we surrender to the other great and innate human drive, which Freud conceptualized as Eros, or life.

During her two years in hiding, Anne Frank's diary became her life; but I believe she had a mordant foretaste of Thanatos at the moment she was moved to write, in a flash of prescient genius, "Let the end come."

CHAPTER 18

The Indispensable Other

ETTELHEIM KEPT his eye on everything, but to build a sheltering milieu for a child, the child had to form a bond, and for this the counselor was indispensable. Between Bettelheim and staff members, a deep relationship often sprang up in the first odd rush of transference, whereas a counselor had to invest months or years of genuine care just to *begin* to earn a child's trust. Some did the job well, others less well; at times a "natural" like Gayle Shulenberger came along, and counselors of her caliber usually stayed for many years.

Karen Carlson (later Zelan), who came to the School in 1956, had started to major in music at Oberlin College, then began to consider a clinical career working with children. In her junior year she switched to psychology, only to be bored by the experimental psychology she had to study. However, she had read *Love Is Not Enough*, and after graduation she moved to Chicago. She shared an apartment and bought her first piano, intending to keep up with her music; but somehow psychology was on her mind. Still feeling tentative, she applied for an office job at the Orthogenic School, expecting to look the place over. As she sat in the waiting room, Bettelheim suddenly walked in. To her surprise, he invited her into his office and began to interview her. After a few minutes he abruptly asked, "Well, do you want to be a secretary or a counselor?"

The question stunned her, and when she didn't reply, he went on with other questions. After some moments she realized she wanted to be a counselor, and she told him. He promptly asked her to move into the School, but the idea intimidated her, because she did not yet feel a deep enough commitment. Instead, she moved in with friends in Hyde Park.

Bettelheim assigned her to observe with Inge Fleischmann (later Fowlie), who had a group of girls—two autistic children and several "borderline schizophrenic" adolescents (a term Bettelheim hated). On her first day, Karen kept her coat on the whole time. Inge saw her uncertainty and pointed it out, saying, "When you don't take off your coat, the kids know."[1] Counselors made remarks like this to each other almost every day, Karen said. "Once I left some candy in the dorm, and Inge said, 'If you want to give the children something, give it, but don't just leave it there.' She said it in a nice way, but we were being taught, analyzed, and observed at the School *all* the time."

Karen soon showed a natural gift for working with the autistic children Bettelheim was then bringing into the School. She believes that her empathy for extremely withdrawn youngsters may have come in part from her early family life. Born on an army post, she had grown up moving on average once a year when her father, a professional soldier, was transferred.

Some counselors were uneasy or frightened around autistic children, but Karen saw their withdrawal as a kind of peace, or at least a truce, and she enjoyed getting them to open up. "I remember sitting there with them for long periods of time, saying nothing. I felt totally comfortable with them, and that continues today."

She learned so quickly that when Bettelheim decided to give Inge a new group of girls, he made Karen the junior counselor. Some of the girls were only six years younger than Karen, and on her first afternoon alone and in charge, they tested her. She was barely keeping on top of things when a young man walked in. He was slightly older than the girls but still in his teens. "I thought, 'Oh, no, I have to deal with another kid.' " However, he turned out to be a former student of the School whom the girls knew and liked. He was Sandy Lewis, already "making it" in the outside world, and the girls were excited to see him and talk with him. After half an hour Sandy said to one of the girls, "How's she doing?"—meaning Karen.

"Of course, they all said I didn't know *anything*, and why hadn't Dr. B. hired someone better, and why couldn't they go back to their favorite counselors, the ones they'd had before the groups had been reshuffled. At which Sandy turned to me and said, 'Do you want to know how to do this job?' I said, 'Sure,' and he started listing what a counselor should do for the kids. I could see his ideas were right on target. My point is that you could learn from anybody at the School, and I learned a lot, unexpectedly, from a very bright former student."

After nine months, Karen told Bettelheim she was ready to move into the School. "I went into Bruno's office and said, 'I'd like to move in now, I think this is working out, but you know I have a piano. Where will I put it?' And Bruno said, 'Oh, you can move your piano in.' "

That evening the movers couldn't get the piano up the stairs to Karen's room on the third floor. She called Bettelheim at home, and he told her to put it in Miss Lukes's classroom, where it stayed for Karen's eight years at the School.

"Bruno's attitude was typical—he knew how important the piano was to me and was saying, in effect, 'We love you, so we love your piano.' He and the School accepted me as I was, and that included practicing at night and waking everybody up, if I chose to." His response exceeded her expectations—it surprised her to find her *piano* welcomed. "He attracted people by the way he understood them, and he would wind you into his life."

Karen also said that exceeding someone's expectations was a Bettelheim technique for teaching the staff. "I think he felt we could only exceed a child's expectations, which he wanted, if we experienced that feeling ourselves. But he couldn't do it for everybody, and this made some people unhappy."

Karen had bought an old player piano, but the playing mechanism didn't work, and Bettelheim ordered it repaired. Soon youngsters were inserting perforated paper rolls of music and pumping away furiously on "Flight of the Bumble Bee" or "Swanee." Years later Karen left the piano behind, and when she came back on a visit she saw it had been brightened up.

"A friend, Kathy Lubin, painted it, a kind of Cape Cod folksy job, and it was beautiful. She gave the piano her own personal identity, which you had to do, because that was Bettelheim's intent." He also encouraged staff members to learn from each other, because the broadest and deepest range of lessons came through personal friendships, like that between Karen and Kathy. "I've rarely seen it in other treatment situations," Karen said, "but this kind of relation emerged from the atmosphere Bruno created."

BETTELHEIM did not rearrange groups unless he had a specific object in view. He might see a better mix of children, especially if newcomers were on hand. In any case, the older students had to be able to stand the new arrangement. When a child had the strength to adjust to the change, his bonding might be transferred from one adult to another. After all, one of the purposes of the school was for the children to grow and become more adept at coping with unexpected turns in life.

After Inge's and Karen's new group settled down, Bettelheim gave Karen her first therapy case, a twelve-year-old autistic girl who had just come to the school. Because of her age she was considered hopeless for any meaningful rehabilitation—an opinion he hoped to disprove. Elsie* screamed obscenities at counselors and students alike; she provoked and disturbed the children around her, and they sometimes retaliated.

One day in a staff meeting Bettelheim discussed the need to anticipate acting-out behavior, with the obvious point that it would be easier to prevent it than to catch it in midflight. "One thing you grasp right away if you're working with autistic kids," Karen said, "is to read their intentions. Nobody can tell you how to do it, but you have to do it anyhow. Most staff became very adept at reading behavior, or they didn't make it at the School."

A few hours after the staff meeting, in the dining room at suppertime, a girl from another group suddenly approached Elsie from behind, hovering over her intently. With no warning she fixed her hands over Elsie's wrists and held them in an incredibly strong grip. The thought ran through Karen's mind, "I really shouldn't stop this girl—but I couldn't *not* help Elsie, because she was being 'attacked,' and so I had to go against what I had just heard from Bruno."

The other girl's counselor sat at the staff table off duty and made no move to intervene, so Karen knew she had to do something. "Spontaneously, I fixed my hands over the girl's wrists in the same way she was gripping Elsie, and I held her. It worked like a charm, though I don't exactly know why. I liked her, so maybe she felt some kind of caring in my body when I took her wrists, or perhaps she stopped because she understood that at least I saw what she was doing. Nonverbal communication like this went on a lot—you had to understand it and act spontaneously in order to survive."

When Karen came off duty that evening, three counselors who had been in the dining room asked her why she behaved as she did when they had just had a staff meeting on being attentive to a child's acting out. Their questioning overwhelmed her because she was a beginner and prone to thinking she had done something wrong. "I wasn't strong enough at that point to feel maybe they were wrong, and so I felt *I* was wrong."

At midnight Karen left the School; she walked the streets of Hyde Park for hours. "This was a suicidal act on my part, because Hyde Park is bounded on three sides by very bad neighborhoods, but I felt I had to leave—I couldn't defend myself against my colleagues. To be true to myself, I had to get out of there."

The next morning Karen went into Bettelheim's office and told him what had happened: she had wanted to protect her patient, so what was she supposed to do? Bettelheim came to her defense, and if he hadn't, she would probably have resigned.

"He said first of all that it wasn't fair to be 'jumped on' by three people—the discussion should have been between the girl's counselor and me, and the other two should have stayed out of it. Period. He said I was right to protect my patient but that the girl's counselor who had watched the whole thing was also right to complain about what I did to *her* patient. He recognized that staff members come into conflict when their kids go at each other like that, and he drew some general conclusions about milieu therapy.

"This was a teaching situation for him, because two complex things were happening at the same time. First was a staff-child problem—knowing how to handle a tricky moment between two highly symptomatic teenaged girls, which I had done. The second problem was staff-staff, and both things got mixed up together, badly. To make matters worse, I got a paranoid notion afterward that the three counselors had wanted me to mess up. They'd been there four or five years, and here I was, after only a few months, doing well with Elsie, who was, for me, very difficult."

In fact, Bettelheim expected staff jealousies to occur in milieu therapy. He tried to help workers recognize and integrate such feelings, which he thought could serve to strengthen them as their understanding grew. That happened in this particular situation; one of the counselors present in the staff room was Inge, who had already befriended Karen. It was hard for Karen to feel criticized by someone she admired, but soon their friendship deepened, so much so that they still keep in touch and feel close, although they live two thousand miles apart and more than forty years have passed.

As for the girl who seized Elsie's wrists, she had improved markedly at the School but at that moment faced a severe impasse. Her development had reached a point beyond which nothing seemed to budge her, and a year later Bettelheim unhappily sent her to an institution. When such a moment came, the choice was harsh, but it had to be done. For a counselor who cared deeply about a youngster, the loss was the worst of all nightmares. In one instance with another child, the bonding between counselor and child was so intense that Bettelheim waited until the counselor had gone on vacation before sending the child away. It would have been too much to ask the counselor, Mary Jean Riley, to join in a tragic decision, and he took it upon himself.

ONE DAY Elsie had been hostile toward Karen for hours, and Karen was at her wit's end. With no friends among the other children, and only Karen among the adults, Elsie at that moment had little chance to ease her bitterness, come out of her isolation, or soften her total defiance. Then Bettelheim suddenly intervened.

"Elsie was acting up so badly that probably someone told Bruno I was in trouble. He roared into the dorm and started yelling, 'BE NICE TO KAREN!' and Elsie calmed down like magic. I think he was telling her two things: first, that she was capable of being nice. Kids who act out a lot often believe they're horrible and that everybody else is horrible. So he was telling her she *could* be nice. The second thing was, 'I care about Karen.' The children admired him, and if Dr. B. valued a person, they felt they should do the same." I asked whether or not it would have worked if Inge or anyone else had yelled, "Be nice to Karen!" She thought not; only Bettelheim had the aura of supreme authority.

Counselors created the personal warmth that surrounded the child, but Bettelheim moved in a more distant realm. He was a force protecting (or threatening) everyone in the School, like Jehovah brooding upon the face of the earth; and in this guise he could appear on a scene with a thunderclap of authority that sometimes worked wonders.

"If the counselor changed her perspective slightly on the basis of Bruno's insight," Karen said, "she could settle the kids down. But if she was too much of a novice to understand, senior staff had to pick up the pieces Bruno left." For the children, he was the law, the ultimate "do" and "don't," and that role wasn't possible for counselors. With them, it was more like the child fearing the loss of a mother's love, but when Bruno corrected a child, Karen said, "it was a bolt of lightning."

Also, Bettelheim nurtured the staff but not the children. "He said something interesting about why he didn't try to nurture the children directly and build up a close relation—that he couldn't reach everybody, couldn't have it with forty or fifty kids. But he did want to have an impact, which he could do by shaking them up from time to time, and he fell on them like the wrath of God. He shook up a child when his judgment or instinct told him to. He wasn't always right, but it was a good division of labor between the counselors and the director, and it worked well most of the time."

BESIDES being so self-isolated, Elsie was memorable because in all of Karen's eight years, she was the only one of Karen's girls to take up the challenge of the School's open door. One day she was giving Karen a very hard time and threatening to leave. She pushed and goaded Karen until Karen finally snapped and said, "So *leave!*" This shocked Elsie, who both feared and wanted to leave, and she ran out of the School and down the street.

"I got scared," Karen said, "so I put Betsy [an older girl] in charge of my kids and followed Elsie. From the School's front entrance you can see long distances, and I saw her. She was more frightened than I was, and when she saw me behind her, she almost wept. This was a kid who never cried at all—her life was too awful for crying—but this time I saw tears. She was glad I followed her, and maybe this was part of what she was trying to find out."

After Karen had been at the School for a year or so, Bettelheim held a staff meeting in which he talked about the children's progress. He said the dorm group that had done best in the year just past was Inge and Karen's. "I was shocked—flabbergasted and happy. I still remember to this day, Inge beaming! And she was quite beautiful when she beamed that way.

"But Bruno also had a point to make, because he couldn't single out anyone for praise without unsettling everybody else. He said our kids did well because Inge and I really *shared* them, and they could evaluate the differences between us at the same time they felt loved and cared for. He explained that when two adults at the School shared children in this way, it was like having two competent and loving parents. It fosters mental health because children, even seriously disturbed children, can then move normally through the oedipal crisis. If two counselors welcome the child's different reactions to them as dissimilar 'parents,' the child has psychological possibilities that help build up personality as the child makes choices, forms opinions, and identifies differently with each 'parent.' "

AT THE time Bettelheim hired Karen, he was planning to raise the School's enrollment by accepting more girls, and he soon had enough to justify forming the new group with Inge and Karen. A year later an older counselor (the one whose patient had attacked Elsie) left the School. Bettelheim asked Karen to take over this counselor's group and said she could bring Elsie with her.

When a pair of counselors did as well as Inge and Karen had, the junior counselor would be promoted to have her own group. However, an autistic girl, Marcia, had recently joined Inge and Karen's group, and Bettelheim said Karen would have to let Marcia stay with Inge. Both counselors had grown attached to Marcia, and Bettelheim credits both prominently in his account of Marcia in *The Empty Fortress*.

"I think Bruno anticipated a fight between Inge and me over Marcia," Karen said, "which is exactly what happened." For several days she talked with Bettelheim about the change, all the time refusing to give up Marcia. Her old group was named Tiger Lilies, and one day she walked into Bettelheim's office wearing a striped headband suggestive of a tiger's markings, indicating that she wanted to stay with the old group (and Marcia) rather than taking over the new group.

"I'll admit now, at this late date, that I was being a little bit mischievous, that I had guessed how he would react, and I wanted that reaction. He noticed the headband instantly, and I believe it convinced him to let me stay in the old group. This shows how much importance Bruno put on people's behavior, not just what they said, and I had learned that very well."

Then another counselor told Karen that Inge had said she would get Marcia because of seniority, that this was how Bettelheim worked.

"When I heard this I blew up and protested to him. So Bruno called both of us into his office and began by saying how skillful Inge had been in working with Marcia. Instantly I knew he was leaning toward me as Marcia's therapist. Why else start by praising Inge so conspicuously? He kept stressing it, and I stayed quiet, waiting for him to get to the point—his decision."

Bettelheim went on to say that he believed Karen and Inge were not merely fighting over Marcia but also over him. He said he was very attached to both of them, that they worked intensively with him, and that he relied on both.

"This was all true, so I just kept waiting, not saying anything. Finally he said he couldn't make the decision, because we were both too important to him. We would have to work it out in our own way. He didn't suggest how; that was up to us."

Bettelheim had spoken mostly of Inge and Marcia in the meeting, but Karen recalled one point he made about her: that she was unusually sensitive to Marcia's pathology, as indicated by the reams of anecdotal accounts she had already produced. He had spoken warmly of both but left them with an implied question—"What will be best for Marcia?"— and with an impression that they were capable of deciding the issue without him.

Bettelheim had brought the two counselors down to earth and also faced them toward each other while implicitly encouraging them to turn inward.

Inge and Karen left the School (and the milieu) and went for a long walk, first along the Midway, and then onward down Sixtieth Street until they came near Cottage Grove, far beyond the neighborhood of the university and Hyde Park.

"Inge wasn't angry or unfriendly, and I wasn't either," Karen said. "She was usually very cheerful and outgoing, but as we walked that day, she was quiet." The idea of a walk had been spontaneous, and it was almost as if they had embarked on a kind of journey. Somehow they did not want to come to grips with the problem in familiar surroundings, and as they walked they also put the university behind them. Walking took energies that otherwise might have raised the stakes and fueled an argument if they had sat down in a room to face off for a negotiation. But rather than looking at each other in confrontation, they chose to walk together, facing the same direction.

"Inge was quiet at first," Karen said, "but then became chatty and full of thought. I didn't know where she stood, but for myself I kept wondering how I could possibly give up Marcia. Finally Inge sighed and said, 'Okay, she's yours. I'll be the baby-sitter.' I almost cried with relief but protested she wouldn't be a baby-sitter, that wasn't it. And as a matter of fact, Inge remained extremely important to Marcia in the way Bruno had pointed out earlier about our group. My style and Inge's were very different, as our personalities were different, and Marcia eventually began to think about and use the differences between us. Like Bruno said about parents."[2]

BETTELHEIM considered Karen one of the best clinicians at the School, especially with autistic children. "Unusually sensitive" was how he put it to me, not as if to praise her but simply as a statement of fact.

One day Karen took Marcia for a swim at the university pool a few blocks from the School. They had to cross the Midway, bustling with traffic, and then make their way through a busy campus. Marcia began taking tiny steps to show her reluctance and discomfort in the midst of all the sudden motion. Without thinking about it, Karen matched Marcia's pace step for step. Bettelheim had been lecturing on campus and was driving back to the School when he caught sight of the pair. He stopped his car for a traffic light, just in time to see Karen's handling of Marcia, including the tiny steps.

Karen had not noticed him, but when she came into the staff room that evening, he began to praise her to the skies. "I didn't even know what he was talking about. I had forgotten the little steps, but he said they showed I had entered into Marcia's world, that she saw I understood her feelings about the traffic. I did understand, but most counselors learned to do this sort of thing routinely."

FOR MANY years now, Karen has practiced as a therapist, mostly with children and adolescents. From time to time she takes autistic children as outpatients, with good results. Like Bettelheim, she considers herself a clinician operating from an empirical base, relying on experience and insight rather than following a theoretical deduction.

"Bruno wouldn't let you look at a child and say something that came from a textbook. As a clinician he threw the book away until he understood the patient from the patient's own point of view. It wasn't just a cranky dislike of theory, because Bruno could hold his own with anybody on theories in psychiatry and psychoanalysis, and *The Empty Fortress* is full of theory.

"Actually, I like dealing with theory, but when I'm doing clinical work, I believe Bruno's approach is best. The value of doing clinical work inductively is that you don't prematurely label patients. Bruno taught us to listen to the patient's version of things. If you start from the book, deductively, you only resonate with 'book knowledge' and maybe neglect what's going on in the patient. Working inductively, you get to know the patient through your own observations and ideas and feelings, and this has remained a very important point for me."

WHY, I wondered, do American psychiatrists now almost universally tend to see neurological causes for autism? "Actually, there are two reasons," Karen said. "First, it's easier to live with a neurological cause; nobody's to blame, there's no guilt. If you assume an emotionally clean defect, the therapist doesn't have to do much besides offer a diagnosis. Nobody expects him to have a cure. He may direct the patient to an 'experimental' program, or he may try to ameliorate a bad situation somehow, but basically he's off the hook.

"It's very clear that the field as a whole wants to believe that parent-child relations have nothing to do with autism. That's possible, but remember, even if you put aside the 'initial cause' of autism, parents with this kind of child are *bound* to react to the disturbance, and their *inner* reaction affects everything else they do with the child. It's too horrible a thought to believe that maybe you 'caused' the child's autism, but Bettelheim's attitude about autism was that it's helpful to find out whether there is or has been a psychological component while the child was developing. People shy away from psychogenic causes, because this means that good parents may have done something wrong. We simply don't want to think this."

Bettelheim faulted parents of autistic children, Karen said, for defending themselves rather than attending to the child's needs. It upset him also that parents failed to see the intelligence of the autistic child and his reasons for behavior. "He said this about the staff as well, so you can see it's a fairly common reaction, one that protects our image of ourselves."

To Karen, the parent of an autistic child is trapped: "If you accept the psychogenic premise, you feel guilty and condemn yourself, which makes things even worse for the child, because we resent those toward whom we feel guilty." The other aspect of the parent's trap is that if it's all genetics, the parent faces endless suffering, burdened by the child for whom little can be done.

Karen sees another reason for an adult's defense of himself: it's hard to imagine an infant experiencing its home life as being so awful that the only response is to turn away totally.

"If we try to visualize this in an otherwise normal family, we usually draw a blank. It challenges us: Who do we think we are? Am I who I say and think I am, or am I also somebody else? Even a good clinician avoids this idea and looks for a cause that doesn't suggest parents can be destructive to a baby without knowing it. If we grant that the unconscious can be so deceptive and powerful, then we open the door to an unpredictable chaos. Or so it seems."

Another reason the neurological explanation is tempting, she believes, is that it holds out hope for a medical cure — "a pill, or some combination of chemicals. That's fine, and maybe the researchers will do it someday, but what about all the kids who are autistic *now*? And what about the ones who have grown old in the last thirty years while waiting for a medical cure to be discovered? Officially there's no hope, so the therapist doesn't have to try. His peers won't think less of him, and he won't think less of himself. Not consciously, anyhow. Every therapist gives up on some cases; you can't help it. Even Bruno gave up sometimes, but he fought harder than anyone I've ever seen *not* to give up on a kid.

"But what angers and disturbs me is that most professionals can't even *imagine* a psychological cure. They pooh-pooh Bettelheim and attack *The Empty Fortress*, or ignore it because they can't afford to look at what he says *could* be done. Teachers don't recommend the book to would-be clinicians even if they liked it years ago when they read it in college, because this would require exposing themselves, going against the climate of opinion in their whole field. Maybe I'd be the same way if my living depended upon that kind of peer acceptance, but since it doesn't, I can say what I think.

"Another thing: if therapists could imagine the possiblity of a psychological cure, even some approach that made just a little difference, then they would have the responsibility of figuring out a way to do it. But you can't imagine approaching autism if in your heart you believe you'll fail. I used to think that the child's upbringing had something to do with autism. That was the prevailing view when I worked at the School. But now I know from direct work with parents that not only can autistic babies appear 'normal,' then develop autism later, but also that the parents resonate appropriately both to the healthy and to the autistic in their child.

"Of course, the work at the School was very hard, and we failed a lot, and even when we failed it took extraordinary amounts of time and energy and commitment. Years, really. But with many of the children who came to us with a diagnosis of autism, which we later confirmed, we made a difference. It wasn't all cures, as Bettelheim freely admits, but some of the kids made it, and the lives of many others were definitely improved. Bruno's attitude was, just make it better however you can, and it's a vast difference for the child.

"I know there's been an effort to discredit Bettelheim on autism and what was done at the School, and this comes partly from some who left the School with a grudge against him, but in the long run it won't work. By the way, one fact that many who try to dismiss Bettelheim's approach don't realize is that children came to us with a diagnosis of autism from highly respected psychiatric clinics, psychiatrists, and analysts. The admitting symptoms were all there in Kanner, they were not something we made up. But sometimes the School did not agree with an admitting diagnosis, and lucky for the kids, too, because they could come in with papers that said 'brain damaged' or 'feebleminded' and then turn out to be neurologically sound. Five or ten years later they might be very close to normal despite having been classified as hopeless by everyone who saw them before they came to the School.

"Things are worse in psychology today because everybody is so quick to give up, cry 'disability,' and label the child for life—label him in his own eyes, make him believe something bad about himself. That's one of the first things I look for in my practice, the mislabeling, and lots of times I find it. If you call a child 'disabled,' the questions stop right there. At the same time, you're letting adults off the hook, which is certainly reassuring. But if a child first develops for a time within normal limits and then later becomes autistic or psychotic or disabled—severely disturbed, by whichever name you call it—then you should look into the possibility of forces that have to be dealt with in a special way."

BY THE time Karen had worked several years at the School, it had become world famous, with its methods developed, written about, and discussed widely. Bettelheim had built up a staff with depths of experience, and money was no longer a problem. The School was attracting more referrals all the time, but in spite of the demand Bettelheim tried to keep tuition rates low and to make several scholarships available on the basis of need.

The idea of residential treatment for children in a setting influenced by psychoanalysis had been tried by others, but Bettelheim had proven uniquely able to put his methods into practice, impressively and over a notable stretch of time. The difficulty of his cases, the radical common sense of his approach, and the striking improvement in many children who had been given up by other authorities as hopeless—all these factors justified the School's reputation within its own field. I mentioned to him that I had heard veiled references to some analysts having sent their own disturbed children to the School; however, he chose not to reply and simply shrugged.

AFTER the School had expanded to let children stay until age eighteen or in special cases even older, a new and disconcerting problem arose. With no threat of "graduating" at fourteen, some students tended to take the School as their whole world, as if they would never have to reenter society. This overadaptation to the milieu tended to put therapy on hold; if the child wanted to stay forever in this pleasant place, why should he change? To a ten-year-old, the age of eighteen was a lifetime away, and much of the motive for learning seemed to evaporate. Karen said that in 1959, her third year, Bettelheim held a series of staff meetings to solicit ideas to counteract this trend. If a student showed a tendency to overadapt and the staffers felt he could do better, they had to figure out an intervention to push him along.

At this time, Marcia had been in the School for almost three years and had begun to talk and to interact with Karen and others. A developmental idea in Piaget inspired Karen to get Marcia into playing with water. The girl never tired of it, and Karen played alongside her for months on end. However, she showed no inclination to learn to read or write.

"Shelton Key was Marcia's teacher, but she wasn't learning much, and he got the idea of adapting a Montessori method to help her learn. His approach was tactile stimulation—first he had her roll up strands of clay, which she played with for hours." Shelton then taught Marcia how to make letters out of the strands and eventually helped her spell her name in clay.

"She got very excited, because this was a tremendous advance for her. She learned to spell words, and Shelton slowly led her to reading. When she became able to read a simple text, it was just marvelous." Karen believes that this kind of advance was the Orthogenic School at its best, because the child had a constructive relation with *other* staffers, not just the closest counselor.

One counselor called the new policy of intervention "pressure with a clear purpose," the purpose being to get a child to think about his future after leaving the School. "You could reduce symptomatic behavior with our empathy and the rest of the milieu," Karen said, "but that was only the beginning. The hardest part was getting kids to give up the School. The ones who could do it made the transition, but that wasn't everybody. There's no question, though, that a great percentage were able—after being socially dysfunctional for years—to take a place somewhere in society and have a life. In Marcia's case it was a sheltered home environment, but we brought her a long way just to get to that."

BETTELHEIM had one signal strength that he used on to energize the School's counselor system: his ability to help others find within themselves feelings like the child's feelings. Over and over he prompted staffers to pick up resonances from their past, insights that opened doors of empathy into an unhappy child's world. This was crucial for the ongoing work of the School and its promise of total care. The counselor who caught even a distant echo in her own feelings became a better caretaker and friend for the child.

In applying this particular talent, Bettelheim followed his natural bent for seeing into what children were feeling (insight based inevitably upon his own feelings). Ruth Marquis saw it many times and said, "Bruno had an almost spooky sense of the child's unconscious. More than anyone, he often knew at once what a child was thinking—sometimes before the child himself knew."

If Bettelheim saw why a child had suddenly gone out of control and the counselor was baffled, he held back his insight and stubbornly persisted with question after question until the counselor found an emotion that bridged the gap with the child. Also, when he was called on to deal with a child in crisis, Bettelheim first tried to see how the episode worked as the counselor's crisis. Whatever the severity of the child's behavior, he usually dealt with the counselor first and then the child, on the assumption that the counselor had contributed to the child's loss of control.

On the other hand, if Bettelheim could not read the child quickly, as often happened, he and the counselor might list as many possibilities as came to mind and then try one or two. Margaret Carey, who worked as a therapist at the School from 1960 until well into the 1980s, said, "He was awfully good at coming up with alternatives, and if they didn't work, he didn't stop there—he'd think of something else."

No doubt other psychologists have gifts of insight equal to Bettelheim's, but he established and developed a setting he believed would nurture disturbed children, and it worked. However, in spite of building a unique and groundbreaking school, he did not finally think of it as a model for others. He usually argued that schools would differ from one another, because any school would evolve in line with the character of its principal. He may have felt otherwise at times, but that was his last and fully considered position. And as he said to me on several occasions, "I just wanted to show it could be done."

"I believe the true genius in Bruno's work with disturbed youngsters," Karen said, "was to discover what was *sane* in their behavior instead of just focusing on what was insane. That's what he tried to get us to do, and *that* would be a good model for people in our profession."

"BRUNO took psychoanalysis," Karen said, "and shook it down and applied some of its tenets to the milieu. Once he became successful at this, he then expanded and reapplied these tenets to other realms, such as normal mothers rearing normal children. First, a distilling; then an expanding." The School's chief purpose was to help particular children, but Bettelheim saw it also as a source of ideas for teachers and therapists — and, later, mothers.

Toward the end of his life Bettelheim thought once again of meetings on the *Dialogues with Mothers* model but mainly as an exercise of his powers to give him an afternoon's reprieve from the feelings of uselessness that depressed him in his last years. By then he had already published *A Good Enough Parent*, which contained the best parenting advice he was likely to put into a book — that parents may be able to imagine their child's point of view by searching out similar feelings in themselves. In other words, empathy.

WE CAN see an example of Bettelheim's teaching method as well as the uses of empathy in a brief episode between Karen and a teenaged girl, Julia.* Karen worked with Julia's group but was secondary in her life; Inge had become her "special person," and Karen usually got along with Julia more easily than Inge did, because Inge and Julia had an intense, ambivalent relationship that had started long before Karen knew Julia. Karen was thus more free to simply enjoy Julia's company. Julia was extremely depressed, and Inge and Karen looked for ways to get her out of bed on weekends. At last they hit upon the idea of asking her to serve coffee at breakfast in the dining room.

"One morning she was so depressed that she was teetering with very hot cups of coffee," Karen said, "and I suddenly became afraid she would spill it on the other children. I said or did something to protect them, and Julia saw that I was being critical and not protective of her. Actually, I don't think I said anything to her, but she saw what I felt. She ran out of the dining room and hid in the bathroom next door, crying."

Karen was frantic because she knew she had somehow set it off, though at that moment she didn't see how. She couldn't get Julia out of the bathroom, and Bettelheim was at home on weekend mornings, not to be called.

"I only called him at home twice in eight years, and this was the second time. He got on the phone and I told him what was going on. He listened, and then he said, 'How would you have felt if your parents accused you of spilling coffee on your sisters when you hadn't done it?'

"I spluttered and said I thought Julia was going to spill the coffee, and I didn't want to take that risk. All Bruno did was to repeat the original question. He put the burden of discovery on me."

Karen tried to remember how she would have reacted, but the moment was too pressured, and she couldn't.

"Bruno finally said, 'You would have *hated* it!' That was all, he was very economical, but suddenly everything fell into place. I tuned in to my childhood imagination. He didn't have to say any more."

Julia still hid in the bathroom, crying angrily, but Karen felt it was a good sign that Julia hadn't insulted her, as she often did when she was angry with a counselor. Karen spoke to her through the closed door and told Julia that she was right, that she had been trying her best and had actually done well in spite of feeling terrible.

"I didn't say very much through the door, but it was enough. I hate to keep using the word, but once again things worked like magic."

Julia stopped crying and came out of the bathroom and went back to the dorm. She was in a good mood the rest of the day, even making jokes.

"Believe it or not, this kind of thing happened all the time. That was the life of the School as everybody lived it, because Bruno was always there to ask the right question."

WHEN KAREN CARLSON and Joe Zelan decided to get married, they talked about her future at the Orthogenic School, where the demands on her time at first seemed unworkable, very much at odds with being married and taking care of a household. When she broke the news to Bettelheim that she might have to leave the School, he refused to be drawn into a discussion of what she should do. She had become one of his mainstays, but he would not advise or persuade her. "Bruno's words still ring in my ears—*He wants a wife! He wants a wife!*"

After Karen made up her mind, she told the girls in her group. They loved her and so felt her impending loss as betrayal and abandonment— all except Marcia, whose autistic withdrawal remained despite the closeness she had begun to feel with Karen. However, her lack of concern puzzled Karen. Then a few days later Karen realized that her resolve was wavering and that her mind wasn't made up after all. Her doubts kept growing until at last she knew she could not leave.

"I decided that it made sense for me to finish up my work at the School in the same way my husband was completing his doctorate, and that's how I resolved continuing to work at the School."

Joe told me he saw that he had to let Karen take her time, and in due course they married, and Karen stayed. All her girls welcomed her change of heart except Marcia, who still didn't react. In fact, Marcia behaved as if she had known all along that Karen would not leave her. The less symptomatic girls, the ones relatively closer to reality, had all been surprised, whereas Marcia hadn't.

"On that question she knew me better than I knew myself, and this made me even more interested in her problem. We think these autistic kids are out of touch with reality, and of course they are in some respects, but somehow Marcia knew I wasn't going to leave her."

Karen had been part of another strange event with Marcia a year earlier. Before Karen met Joe, she had been going with another young man, but she had broken off with him and thrown out all his letters. She had never mentioned his name in front of Marcia or anyone else at the School. However, when she severed the relationship, Marcia, who almost never used language at that point, began to whisper the young man's name. Karen was stunned, then baffled. How could Marcia know the name? And why keep repeating it?

I asked if Marcia had perhaps seen the letters Karen threw out. But this was impossible; she had dropped the letters into a wastebasket on the third floor at a time when Marcia spent most of the day and night lying motionless in bed on the first floor. At rare moments she would go to the table in the dorm, but hardly ever out into the hall for a drink of water. Also, she had not yet learned to read.

"She was nearly immobile," Karen said, "but despite her passivity, or maybe because of it, she was incredibly attuned on a single level of experience—attuned to me because, at times, I was her means of survival. In a way she was 'reading my mind' but taking no active part in her own life or the life around her."

Nobody believes that autistic children are telepathic, so Karen could only puzzle over the mystery. Finally, she recalled that a few years earlier a boy of that name had lived at the School. He left before Marcia arrived but had been a friend of Betsy's, who was still there. Probably Betsy had mentioned the boy's name to Karen in Marcia's presence, and Karen might have reacted with body tension, a flicker of expression, or a half second's silence. If Marcia had picked up Karen's fleeting reaction, then perhaps she repeated the name to elicit the reaction again and get Karen's attention.

Karen agreed with Bettelheim's conviction that there is an inner logic for any behavior. Although she could not finally explain Marcia's eerie whisper, she guessed that saying the name was the girl's way of taking a tentative step to reenter the environment from which she had otherwise withdrawn. The whispered name could also be seen as a hopeful sign that Marcia wanted to make deeper contact with Karen. As Karen felt this and responded with more hope about working with Marcia, Marcia would sense the hopefulness and perhaps feel better about herself. Such reciprocal effects between counselor and child lay at the heart of Bettelheim's methods; without this dynamic, the School would have been just another hit-or-miss residence for troubled children. When Marcia read Karen's unconscious intention not to leave the School, she was demonstrating the reality of her bonding with Karen and the acuteness of perception that Bettelheim and others have noted in many autistic children.

KAREN said, as did other counselors, that Bettelheim's presence had a steadying effect, especially during his rounds in the afternoon and evening. He made a point of being there at bedtime, when the planned activities of the day gave way to children's fears and the isolation of the night.

In Karen's fourth or fifth year, she took a new child, Edie,* into her group. Edie suffered from extreme depression, and on her first night a crisis suddenly came up. Next door, men were demolishing a building, and they went on after dark under lights rigged to let them work all night. The glare, the grind of heavy machinery, the crash of brick and timber were too much for the child. She began to sob uncontrollably, and Karen became frantic.

"I went for Bruno and he came and sat on Edie's bed. He spoke very gently to her and ran his hand over her hair. It was nothing unusual, but it worked, maybe because he was so calm himself and so genuine about wanting her to feel better. He said the noise was terrible and how frightened she must be on her first night in a strange new place. He validated her by saying she had reasons to be scared. This let her feel her reasons were good, not irrational, and she went to sleep even though the noise continued."

Karen rarely called on Bettelheim for help, although she once had to do so with Vivienne,* a five-year-old who was disturbed by other children's blue eyes and often tried to scratch them out. In infancy Vivienne had been left in her crib, where she was passive and uncared for most of the time. At eighteen months she turned violent and dangerous to any child who came near her and so was not allowed to play with other children. In the School, Karen had to watch her constantly.

"Vivienne is not written up in any of Bruno's books, but she had an amazing intellect. She's the only child of whom I can remember him saying, 'I wouldn't mind exchanging my brain for hers.' At seven she asked questions so sophisticated that you were astonished they would occur to a child that age. And it was surprising how much damage a tiny child could do to an adult. Once Bruno had to grab her in the dining room because she was kicking him. Afterward he said, 'Why do you buy her such heavy shoes?' and so we bought her sneakers."

At the School Vivienne began to develop illnesses. She had not been exposed to the usual childhood diseases because she could not associate with children her own age without attacking them. Having built up no resistance, she caught everything that was going around. One time she came down with a gastrointestinal infection that dragged on for days, until she was on the verge of dehydration. Karen tended her day and night.

"Bruno came in and said, 'Don't give her any water,' but she wouldn't drink anything else, and I was frightened. So I gave her a few teaspoons of water, which she promptly threw up. I went to Bruno's office and told him, and he got really distraught. He said, 'I told you not to give her any water! Make her some chamomile tea!' I said, 'What's that?' and he got disgusted and said, 'My god, where do you kids come from?' He went off and came back from the kitchen with some chamomile tea and sat on Vivienne's bed and spoon-fed her.

"Of course, I had been living with her for days, worrying whether she would survive. Bruno didn't have to do this and could step in at a moment's notice and be warm and nurturing and cuddly, whereas I was nearly out of my mind.

"But, by golly, he reversed the dehydration. Later on, when I stopped being frantic and could think about things, it impressed me that a famous and important man with huge demands on his time thought it worth his while to sit and spoon-feed a very sick little girl."

VIVIENNE also turned out to be crucial in Karen's development as a clinician. One day she took Vivienne outside to the School's play area. It was
raining lightly, and the girl, now seven, began to scream that she wanted
to go back inside. Once inside, she started to scream again to go out. In
the midst of all this, she screamed that she was afraid of the rain.

Bettelheim had recently discussed Piaget in a staff meeting, and Karen
was reading one of his books in her spare time. "Piaget's work on cogni-
tion shows how a child begins to think. He's hard to read because he
leaves out all the emotional side of psychology, but that's also his
strength—focusing on a single element so you can really see it. I was
intrigued and wondering how to apply his ideas, and suddenly something
struck me about Vivienne.

"So I said to her, 'Since we come inside when it's raining, do you think
if we go outside that the rain will stop?' She said, 'Yes!' and I knew I was
on to something—how she thought. She calmed down at once, because I
had showed her that I understood her reasoning. That was the end of the
screaming on that issue—though not the end of her fear of rain. Later on
she tried to control the rain in a different way. She yelled like a cheer-
leader, 'Come on, rain, rain real hard! Come on, thunder, thunder real
hard!' "

In the next staff meeting Karen told how Piaget's ideas had helped her
understand Vivienne's thought processes and the difference this made. "It
was important theoretically, because in those days we tended to believe
that if you permitted the venting of emotions, this in and of itself would
help the child. But it's more than that, and different." In this instance,
Karen had pursued an intellectual understanding that proved a direct
channel to empathy. Vivienne, like Edie, was helped because she felt herself understood.

"She finally felt a communication with someone directly, because of
the way I spelled out her belief that if we came inside when it rained, we
simply had to go out again to stop the rain. A reversal. Since then, I've
found this kind of thinking in a great many children, but the insight with
Vivienne was my central experience as a clinician in seeing how Piaget's
ideas apply. Bruno seemed to do it instinctively, but I believe it can be
learned, maybe by starting with the premise that we all thought like this in
our early years, although we can't remember it."

Bettelheim rescued counselors now and then, but the School succeeded clinically because he delegated wide powers. "As senior staff,"

Karen said, "it was our job to 'cure' the kids. He insisted on this—that he wasn't doing it, we did it, and he didn't let us forget it. Yet he was always monitoring, evaluating, thinking, and feeling with us. He delegated on two levels: responsibility for the children, and responsibility for day-to-day staff training. He ran the staff meetings, focused on what seemed relevant or immediate, and he also saw senior staff in his office. That was it."

Bettelheim distanced himself from daily care except when his clinical judgment was called for. "He was usually right on clinical matters, but one time I really disagreed with him. Elsie had lived at the School several years without a visit home, and I thought it was time, but Bruno said no. I knew he was wrong, so I walked into his office and said, 'She's ready, she's going,' and he backed down. He knew I knew Elsie better than he did. So she went home for a visit and came back pleased with herself."

Many who worked at the School spoke of Bettelheim's presence as having a reassuring effect on both children and staff. One of Bettelheim's successors, Jacquelyn Sanders, confirms that after a chaotic episode her presence often helped students settle down. She attributes this to their sense of her power over their lives and a trust that she would act in their best interests.

No doubt this was true, but when I asked Bettelheim about what made the School work, he reversed the order of the concepts of power and trust, speaking first of the atmosphere of trust he had tried to create for everybody. Even the power he exercised when he slapped or hit a child protected, in his view, as I discuss later, the milieu as a whole and also the child from his own worst impulses. The first person the child learned to trust was the adult closest to him, not Bettelheim; then he learned to trust the little world of the School, and finally, to some degree, to trust himself in dealing with life. The staff trusted the director to protect them and help them grow, as he also protected the students by providing a benign milieu.

WITHIN the milieu, the resistances Bettelheim faced in staff members took top priority in his never-ending training process. Karen spoke of his readiness at all times to help anyone think through a problem. He tried not to ask defensive questions himself or to give defensive answers, and defensive replies from a staff member could make him lose his temper.

His mental stance, which I have come to esteem in the course of writing this book, reminds me of classical Greek sculpture, where gods and mythic heroes stand before us naked and natural, unselfconsciously revealing the intrinsic beauty and power of the human body. Their lack of armor suggests that authentic power accrues to one willing to risk himself and engage life without defenses. The naked warrior-hero, taken as metaphor, implies that one's own self is the best defense, that character shapes fate in the struggles of life. Such a figure has no shame, nothing hidden except his ingenuity of mind, and you see him as he is. A whole being confronts you, one whose action is likely to be immediate, direct, vigorous, and personal.

Bettelheim trusted his mind as his best self, very much including its unconscious promptings. He tended to respond sharply, and perhaps this quick parry that aroused anger was his own defense; but typically he engaged at close quarters, mentally, in a kind of play that was also utterly serious. This took energy, but not as much as if he had hidden behind rigid psychic defenses that demand deep resources to maintain or dismantle. Bettelheim seems to have freed himself from defensive attitudes when he took on the role of authority in the School—or perhaps before. Using so little psychic energy to maintain his image of himself left him focused on the multitude of tasks he set himself each day, and his exchanges with others unleashed new energies as he uncovered what he felt and why he felt it.

When a counselor held tight to masks raised by the unconscious, Bettelheim could not tolerate it, and most such staffers left sooner or later, either on their own or when he rectified his mistake of having hired them in the first place. He did not always correct his mistakes quickly, in part because the children needed caretakers, but also because he was not invariably right in his judgment of those whose work he valued even a little. His job did not allow time for fighting with staffers; it might have helped some of them if he had done so, but the School was for children whose defenses had disabled them and made them outcasts, not for green college grads who were also inflexible.

"One day I remember Bruno being exasperated at several counselors," Karen said, "who were very needy and quite dependent on him and balked every step of the way. He came into the dining room to the off-duty staff table and said loudly—I could hear him from across the room— 'This *is not* a school for counselors; it's a school for children!' "

Unlike the School, the university classroom was an arena for combat where he might argue coldly and ferociously with a student in a battle that would excite and teach others. And he probably enjoyed it. But in the School he wanted counselors for the children's sake and so could take some opposition from those who had demonstrated commitment. However, he taught the willing, not the half willing who tried to shift his attention from the children to themselves.

Karen understood very quickly that she had to do things his way but in her own style and out of her own feelings. "I saw I could learn from him — he knew a lot about sick kids that I wanted to know, so I didn't resist." Doing things his way did not mean copying or working by rote, because this would make the counselors his puppets. Perhaps some were, but such workers could not enter into authentic relationships with the children. A relation had to be real in order to promote healing, and a counselor who stifled her feelings of insecurity or confusion could never give the child a better emotional milieu than he'd had at home. Once the child began to get the idea that he might make friends beyond the counselor, he could perhaps make compromises in the hope of a wider range of reciprocity.

Bettelheim's own obvious sincerity in helping the children set a tone and offered a model for everyone else. However, the children did not become deeply entwined in his life in the way staffers did. The child's first loyalty, first trust, first hopes, all flowed from and returned to the counselor. And these feelings had to be well grounded before he could progress toward a more sophisticated and mixed feeling like respect.

One of the children summed up Bettelheim as the School's "janitor and policeman," a job description apt enough for him to repeat on many occasions. The janitor keeps things clean and orderly, while a good policeman upholds the moral order that protects one and all. A strong protector also threatens the unruly and destructive forces that unhappy children often fear as their essential selves, and I believe that Bettelheim's most ominous demand was not for good behavior but that students look into themselves. Their respect for his authority, when they felt it, mixed love with fear, in the sense that we love or depend upon the one who protects us and fear his or her strength and its possible loss.

When Bettelheim left for a lecture or a vacation, his absence strained staff members to their limits as the level of emotional disturbance rose and the children's symptoms burgeoned—"because," Karen said, "his presence had become a part of the security the kids found there." Bettelheim knew this and honored it by giving them twelve or thirteen hours a day, and only a few hours less on weekends.

KAREN continued to work with the obstreperous, angry, and brilliant Vivienne; much of what the girl said was meant to protect her unique vision of reality. It was almost like a personal religion: she had built up an elaborate system of magic to shield herself from anything said in her presence that she feared might be true but at odds with her beliefs. If a remark appealed to her, she canceled it with magic words and gestures to keep her inner world intact. She censored facts and opinions from others with magic rituals that frightened some of the children. For one spell she chanted, "Criss-cross, criss-cross," and traced a cross in the air near the person whose words she wanted to negate; for her, this erased any meaning that threatened the integrity of her system for coping with a situation. The staff understood that if these intrusions were not tempting, she would not have tried to obliterate them, and everyone took her spells and gestures as a hopeful sign. However, Vivienne's magic had to be unraveled, or nothing would ever touch the despair of an inner world defended by magic.

Karen began to explore the meaning of anything Vivienne wished to crisscross out of existence, taking care not to impose her own meaning on the girl. Karen realized that only when Vivienne's language became a part of her own adult vocabulary would the girl even listen to her or hear the outside world.

One day at noon Bettelheim came into the dining room as he always did, and Vivienne looked at him. He noticed her interest and came over to chat with her briefly. After he turned away Vivienne became excited and told her teacher that Dr. B. liked children because he had come over to talk to her. Karen, off duty at the staff table across the room, could see Vivienne's excitement about Bettelheim, which was unusual behavior for her. Bettelheim joined the off-duty counselors for lunch, and a few minutes later when the teacher got up to take her class back to the classroom, Vivienne slipped away from the class group unnoticed and walked over to Bettelheim.

"She approached him very solemnly," Karen said, "and stood in front of him. She said, 'Criss-cross,' in a quiet voice and made a cross in front of his face."

Bettelheim looked intently at Vivienne but did not reply, and the staff table fell silent as the counselors waited to see what he would do. Karen glanced at her watch; she knew Bettelheim would answer the girl, and the fact that he did not do so instantly meant that he was thinking. In a few seconds everyone in the room had turned to see how he would deal with Vivienne, and time passed with the whole room sitting silent as he continued to gaze at her. She stood motionless, looking into his face as he looked into hers.

"Most of the time this kid never stood still," Karen said, "so her immobility was extraordinary." Some of the counselors had to suppress nervous giggles, and Karen felt like laughing but stifled it. Vivienne's teacher suddenly missed her and came back at the moment Bettelheim was about to reply. After a full minute facing Vivienne silently, he spoke in a tone the same as hers, quiet and utterly serious.

He said, "Cross-criss."

Nothing more besides reversing the words of her spell.

"Vivienne stood there totally nonplussed," Karen said, "until the teacher led her away. Bruno's manner reflected the fact that Vivienne took 'Criss-cross' seriously and that he took it just as seriously. Otherwise he couldn't have reached her. The teacher told me later that Vivienne had an amazingly good day after that."

Bettelheim's reply proved to be the first step in unwinding Vivienne's cocoon of magic. Before long she began to talk directly about her magical thinking, and eventually she gave it up. By working on the child's level and in her language, he had forced her to reconsider her magic because he had reversed it. He respected her view of it, but he also challenged its usefulness. At the instant she had asserted power over him, he had treated her intention as real; but a minute later he had asserted his own power, not over her but over himself, saying, in effect, "I can be who I am."

Karen said it relieved Vivienne to see that Bettelheim could reverse her magic and return himself to his original state. She had liked the "uncrossed" Bettelheim, so when he unwound her spell he made himself available to her again. Not in a pushy way, just available. And if he could do this, he was also strong enough to protect her.

Further, in showing Vivienne's magic to be weaker than she supposed, he had reduced it to the level of ordinary efforts to manipulate things, where the outcome is not always predictable. As a model for action, using magic is not so different from dealing with reality; in both cases, the conscious intent is, *I do this in order to get that.* Once Vivienne learned more about cause and effect in the milieu, she could begin to test the uses of reality and gradually replace her magic rituals with more rational behavior.

Finally, Bettelheim did not threaten Vivienne directly with "Cross-criss," since it also implied control of one's environment by first controlling oneself.

Bettelheim's reply had probably come to him at once, but then it took a full minute, timed on Karen's watch, for him to imagine how Vivienne might react. Or, he may simply have wanted to hold the restless child's attention and keep her focused intensely on him to make a more lasting impression by creating suspense in her mind as she waited for his response.

I asked Bruno about this moment with Vivienne, but he had forgotten it completely. As with so many of his interventions, he did it and let it pass. He did not need to reflect on it because it was not a puzzle.

"Bruno seemed to have all the pieces in place when he intervened in a crisis," Karen said. "Maybe that was just my wish, but I believe he knew exactly what he was doing, that he grasped the psychology of the particular child, and I think the secret of his effectiveness depended in part on the anecdotals we dictated at such length. They kept him in touch with the kids."

BETTELHEIM urged the staff to shoulder responsibility for setting things right if a child suddenly went into crisis. Once when he was in Israel, Karen supervised the girls' floor, and she tended to avoid the worst acting-out children, just hoping to struggle through. When Bettelheim returned, she noticed that he actively sought out such children. "He made it a point to focus on these crisis-ridden kids, and that was just the reassurance they needed to ease their crises. This was a lesson to me, and the next time I was left in charge I tested it. Sure enough, when I initiated the approach, they calmed down."

Of course, the approach had to come in the right spirit and with genuine interest in order to work. "Maybe Bruno had a natural affinity for these acting-out children more than I did and so approached them simply because he liked them—I don't know. Anyhow, I proved to myself that it was wise *not* to avoid the kid who waved the red flag, and I learned that from Bruno."

AS KAREN'S years drew to a close, Bettelheim planned to move the school in a new direction by starting an adolescent unit that operated with a new treatment plan specific to adolescents. As a former staff put it to me, "The basic idea was that they would have more of a say in what they did and would be less supervised by the staff. He wanted them to have increased freedom and responsibility, still within the framework of the school. The adolescent dorms were farther away from the main building, where the office was, but that should not have mattered if it was working right. However, the unit was closed some years after Bruno left."

KAREN has now come to believe that she underestimated one crucial question that haunted the children: *Why were they sent to the School?* The separation from their parents shocked and hurt them far more than they were encouraged to recognize and express. Bettelheim spared no effort to give each new child a warm, genuine, complete, and carefully focused welcome, but the insidious fact remained that the child felt his parents had abandoned him. Children could not help fearing they were outcasts because their parents had sent them away and no longer took care of them.

The School was a school and not a home, but it was enough of a home to make a child doubt his parents' love. He could deal with his anxiety by denial, evasion, displacement of anger, rationalization, or any combination of defenses, but his parents' action still threatened him deeply. Until he came to grips with that and began to understand why his parents did it, he might make a truce of sorts with his feelings but could have no real peace.

"As a counselor, I thought that being at the School was wonderful," Karen said, "and I just didn't pick up on the child's feeling that he had been abandoned. Some of us might have been happy to be away from home, and if so, we failed to notice any attachment the child had for his parents, misguided though it might have been. Let's say a kid came to us twiddling all day long—naturally I thought the parents must be awful. But the child could still have an attachment to them. I should have paid more attention to that, and to the child's suffering at being thought so sick he couldn't live at home anymore. Later he goes back home without ever facing the fact that his parents gave him up to the School because they couldn't handle him. Then he's going to turn his anger against the School, or toward Bruno or the counselors. *Not* his parents.

"I should have been more sensitive to the separation-anxiety issues, but the way I felt about my own parents blocked me. I'm sure Bruno was aware of the implications for the child, but being postadolescent, I wasn't."

But didn't the School look for a child's willingness to come?

"Yes, Bruno usually said, 'Do you want to come to the School?' and got some kind of assent, so that in a narrow sense the child was self-selected. But by that point everyone knew what the answer would be. We'd had at least three meetings with the child, during which he'd also looked us over. And still he might say yes mostly because he felt he was supposed to."

In fact, self-selection for a child could never be the same as for an adult. A child who saw himself at the center of a family crisis (a crisis the School supposedly would resolve) would feel pressured to do what was expected of him. Children do not have the same options as grown-ups, and so their self-selection could never be more than partial. Nonetheless, Bettelheim's nod toward the child's autonomy opened up far-reaching possibilities, with major implications. By showing that the child's own wishes would be taken into account at the School, he treated all young-sters as unique individuals and also dramatized the idea that they could become autonomous at the School. In the final analysis, autonomy took precedence for Bettelheim over any other concept as the School's goal.

As for encouraging a child to explore feelings of abandonment, this might have had unhappy, even dangerous, consequences, depending upon what else the child was feeling. In a very deep sense, the child *was* abandoned by his parents (for very good reasons, of course), and his sense of abandonment, conscious or unconscious, was one realistic ele-ment in his skewed view of the world. Bettelheim was too acute not to have been aware of this fear. Abandonment, real or imaginary, is a solid basis and a good reason for anyone to become the Robinson Crusoe in his own life's voyage and to rescue himself. Also, it is unreasonable to think that everything in life has to be explained; the best that can happen to someone seeking self-understanding is for him to go far enough to become self-acting and self-determined in how he lives. In other words, autonomous.

However, in the design of a total therapeutic milieu, autonomy had to be more than a promise or a far-off goal; its possibility had to attend the child from his very first moments in the School. Even though he could do little to avail himself of the broader freedoms of autonomy, the milieu offered many chances to make personal decisions within a structured life. Bettelheim encouraged the careful exercise of a child's decision making, his powers of choice, as a way to nourish the growth of a firmer inner self.

"I don't believe you can prepare people," he said on more than one occasion about how he hoped his methods would serve the students, "but you can strengthen them." In his lexicon, the slow building of inner strengths, brought about by the child's learning to balance the demands of the pleasure principle with the restrictions of the reality principle, defined what Bettelheim meant by growth.

IN 1964, after eight years at the school, Karen left to pursue her goal of becoming a clinician in private practice. She and Joe wanted to start a family, and new career opportunities took them to Berkeley.

"What we learned with the so-called 'crazy' kids was not about something called 'craziness,' which is a broad label. Bruno wasn't teaching labels but the depths of human nature, leading you to see them in yourself, showing how we all share behavior in some way. When I finally understood something about a 'crazy' child, I understood something inside myself. All the time, Bruno said, 'Don't use different yardsticks for the crazy and the sane. It's human nature, and common to us all.'"

I THOUGHT Karen would be a good person to ask for an overall impression of the School, and she said that when she looks back, the first thing that usually comes to mind is how exhausting the work was, so tiring that it could have been done only by young people. Once she walked into another counselor's dorm and found her fast asleep on the floor.

"Two autistic children with the flu were sitting on her back and playing quietly. She'd been up all night taking care of them, and they were content just to be there with her and let her sleep."

Even in sleep, the young counselor remained the indispensable other for the children she cared for, which was, of course, exactly in line with Bettelheim's intent.

CHAPTER 19

The School
in Its Maturity

BY 1960, when Bettelheim hired Margaret Carey, the School had come into its institutional maturity. He might expand it or modify it, but the invention of total-milieu therapy had been accomplished. Margaret could claim a tangential connection with one Bettelheim innovation—therapy sessions for the children—because of her recommendation of Florence White, whose job evolved into therapy, as the first social worker at the School.

Margaret was also Trude's best friend and had been her supervisor at the Child Care Agency in Hyde Park. After Margaret left the agency in the 1950s, she and Trude remained very close. She often visited the Bettelheim apartment to play with the children and to have dinner.

"I remember being there for a Christmas Eve party," she said, "and thinking that Bruno was the most generous man I'd ever encountered—they were just so generous about gifts to the children."

After leaving Child Care, Margaret started an analysis and also went into psychiatric social work. When Bettelheim heard about the analysis and her need for extra money, he hired her as a substitute for Sundays, when the kitchen staff was off, and her group always made their own Sunday-night supper.

"I knew to keep them away from matches and knives, and as for food, we fixed something simple—hot dogs, or eggs. And Bruno said, 'You're not a very good cook, but you're good with the kids.'"

In 1960 he offered Margaret a full-time job as a therapist. The two of them had known each other for fourteen years, but, she said, "I didn't really know Bruno better than anybody else, because he kept people at a distance. He could be utterly charming when he wanted to, but you just didn't know him. When I went in for the interview, he said, 'There's no sense us interviewing, we're both much too nervous for that. You can turn up on Monday morning.'

"When Bruno hired me, he told Trude he could have had a psychiatrist from Sweden, but he didn't because she'd always be opposing him and challenging him, and Margaret wouldn't. Margaret would be much more compliant. And of course he was right."

As mentioned earlier, Bettelheim wanted to keep everyone focused on the idea of the whole School as a therapeutic milieu and so refused to single out a particular hour's activity and call it therapy. For that reason, the forty-minute periods were simply "sessions," a term he used even after he came to see the milieu as merely the beginning of therapy.

Margaret said that Bettelheim would not start a child in sessions until he "could talk about at least some of his difficulties in front of the group. He didn't want the kids to feel they were so bad that everything had to be said to a therapist in private. It was up to the child to say he wanted to see you, but mostly they didn't say no."

The sessions had a different purpose from a child's meetings with Emmy Sylvester or her successors, who used their infrequent contact to look into specific problems and to evaluate progress. The unique value of the sessions lay in their many private opportunities for a child to say or show what was on his mind.

Patty Pickett McKnight said, "After Dr. B. was sure of your commitment, then he would ask you to be a therapist." Toward the end of her first year, he assigned two children to her. "He did this when he felt a child needed one person all to himself, because not everything could be said in front of the group. The kid had to be ready for it, and when you saw him you then reported everything from the session in the dictation and talked it over with Dr. B. later."

Ruth Marquis, who visited the School in the early years, often several times a week, commented on Bettelheim's attitude toward the sessions. "Bruno would become absolutely furious," she said, "if he caught a therapist acting like a professional psychiatrist and putting the child off—saying, 'We'll talk about that at your next session, come back and see me Tuesday.' He insisted that the therapist talk about whatever the child wanted to talk about, and do it *immediately*. He thought the child should not be asked to hold his rage, or his feelings, especially in a therapy session.

"However, the sessions, at least in the early years, were really an adjunct to the work of the School, a kind of concession he made to conventional psychiatry. Bruno was much more interested in the marginal interview with the child. He and Redl worked that out, and Redl wrote about it, but Bruno described it briefly in *Love Is Not Enough*. A marginal interview is a conversation that takes place on the edges of some other activity—with people around and while everybody is focusing on something else. It's also the ideal way to pick up on the child's feelings.

"When I worked at Children's Psychiatric Hospital in Ann Arbor, the residents who got the best results were the ones who could walk about the wards and speak casually with the patients. It's the same thing. Besides, kids like those at the School at first might not be able to bear the intensity of being one of two people isolated in a room. The scene of the marginal interview was much more diffuse, with less pressure on the child."

INSTEAD of reasoning through the "social worker–therapist" change in his controlled environment, Bettelheim may have simply trusted his first principle, caring about children, and developed the staff position in line with the logic of the School. In sessions, a child could play with toys and so reveal insights into his feelings and concerns, which would help the staff plan activities and shape the course of his treatment. Also, having toys in the therapy room, usual in child analysis, tended to make the interview marginal and to take the pressure off the child in a situation where the adult embodied the goodwill of the milieu and its optimism about the child.

"When I was still new there," Margaret Carey said, "I felt I shouldn't be touching the children, so I held back from being physically affectionate. I remember a very needy child who I should have been warm and friendly toward, and I wasn't. Dr. B. got very angry at me, because he saw the child's need and thought I should have filled it."

Margaret mentioned what several of the other counselors also did, that in the design of the School Bettelheim let most feelings of closeness come from the staff, while he kept a considered distance. She, too, noticed that he read moods. "Sometimes at lunch he would come over to a table and feed a child himself," Margaret said. "He wanted to make the child sure he was liked; at the same time he was trying to meet primitive needs, like our need around food. He didn't do this often, but he would suddenly feel a child's need and come over and feed him. He was just somewhat of a genius at sensing what a child was about."

After a year at the School, Margaret thought of going elsewhere but decided against it. She knew most places never got below the surface of a child's problems, and at the School they were really doing things. She stayed for twenty-eight years, living nearby so that she could walk over for sessions and staff meetings. Many of her successful students came back to visit, because her seeing them in sessions did not automatically end when they left. They trusted her, they had become attached to her, and the "child" could always return for a session (or a number of sessions, but not in school hours) after going to college or getting a job.

Margaret said that Bettelheim was extraordinary as a therapist in his ability to come up with an endless flow of ideas about a child's problem. "We were dealing with the unknown at all times, but he had a freedom of mind I hadn't experienced before on other jobs. He was inventive. He'd go over the various possibilities, and at the end you'd commit yourself to something. Then, if it didn't work, he was always ready with another approach."

Toward the end of our conversation, she said, "Looking back, I wish I'd asserted myself more, and challenged him and questioned more. Then maybe I'd have learned more, but I don't have one minute of regret for having been at the School. I've seen many institutions, and I was terribly impressed with the Orthogenic School, because there it was the child who counted."

AS THE School developed into its maturity, Bettelheim was getting staff applicants who knew something of his work and were perhaps slightly more mature themselves. In the early years counselors had come mostly from the Chicago area and did not always know what the School was about; but by the 1960s the process of self-selection brought would-be staffers from around the country and even from overseas, usually with at least one degree and a strong impression of Bettelheim and the School. However, for working with the children (and especially for the forming of a warm relationship) he continued to prefer young people who had not yet tried to make a place in the world; as mentioned earlier, he also hired those for whom he felt an instinctive liking and who he could see liked him.

Kathy Carson (later Lubin) came to the School in 1961, but she had known about Bettelheim for years. She grew up in St. Louis, and one summer when she was still thirteen, she fell in love with the boy next door. In fact, he was a nineteen-year-old college student home for summer vacation, and in one of their long conversations he told her about the unusual school at the University of Chicago where he had worked as a substitute counselor. He gave her a copy of *Love Is Not Enough*, which she began to read dutifully, hoping to impress him. To her surprise, the book impressed her, with an appeal so deep that she remembered it for years, long after the boy next door had moved away.

She attended college at Washington University in St. Louis, where one of her professors, the sociologist Jules Henry, spoke about the Orthogenic School, and she recalled how much she had liked *Love Is Not Enough*. Henry had observed and written about the School and knew it quite well.

Kathy, now a college junior, was going with a young man who had been accepted by the University of Chicago Law School, and she began to think of transferring to Chicago to finish her B.A. If she did, she would need a part-time job, and the Orthogenic School came to mind. Over the Christmas holidays she visited her boyfriend in Chicago and made a point of calling the School to ask about jobs. To her amazement, Bettelheim answered the phone.

She could not put her finger on the reason, but the mere fact of speaking with him made her nervous, and yet her curiosity kept her on the line. She had just reread *Love Is Not Enough*, and in it Bettelheim came through as a man uncommonly sensitive to disturbed children, which attracted her. However, her first conversation with him was almost her last; when she said she had to finish her degree, he said sorry, but he only hired college graduates. For some reason she resisted being put off, and he finally agreed to see her the next day.

"It was a bitterly cold day in January, and I was terrified, perspiring heavily underneath my coat. When I got inside I was afraid to take it off, because I was literally drenched and shivering." Bettelheim came into the waiting room and asked if she would like to take off her coat, and she said no. He looked surprised but invited her into his office just across the hall.

In thinking about the interview much later, Kathy concluded that it had frightened her because she believed Bettelheim was so insightful he could easily see into her—"see things about me that I was ashamed of." They sat down in his office, and her guard went up instantly when he chose not to sit behind his desk. Instead, he drew up a chair uncomfortably close to hers and began to ask questions about her and her interest in the School. After a few minutes of conversation, as she sat there in her heavy coat, he suddenly said, "How does it feel to be so pretty?"—which stunned her.

"The question didn't feel like an indirect compliment but as if he was truly inquiring, that this was a fact to be interested in, that being pretty had an influence on a person, and so what influence does it have on you?"

To her consternation and horror, Kathy felt an irresistible welling up of emotions; tears came to her eyes, and she didn't know why.

"His question had suddenly touched me, but I couldn't think of anything to say except, 'Well, I suppose that it has negative effects and positive effects,' and when the words came out, I thought, 'God, that's a stupid answer.' But Bruno just looked at me intently for a moment—I hoped he wouldn't notice how affected I'd been by his question—and then he said, 'You're hired.' "

Kathy arranged the transfer of her credits and moved from St. Louis to Chicago. She had already made the emotional transference to Bettelheim that he needed, and he was no doubt struck by the common sense of her reply and the depth of her feelings. In his eyes, a quick transference and an unencumbered intelligence made Kathy, at age twenty, a good prospect for the School.

ON HER first day a month later, Kathy became upset and depressed by a boy in a class she observed. He played with his saliva endlessly and made spit connections from his mouth to his knee, to other parts of his body, and to the furniture. "As I watched him I knew I couldn't work with someone like that—what would I do? I thought, 'This is a mistake—why did I ever come here?' "

The boy's teacher, however, impressed Kathy with her patience and with her interest in the children. "Her attitude—she was a wonderful teacher named Hazel Osbourne—began to draw out my own interest, which helped me a lot."

Later that day Kathy spoke to a senior counselor about the boy and her feeling that he was repulsive. "This person had encouraged me to ask questions, and so I asked how long she had been at the School, and she said for eight years. I said, 'Do you like it?' and she became very huffy. She said, 'Of course I like it. Do you think I'd stay here for eight years if I didn't?' Then I felt terrible, that it was a stupid question."

Bettelheim came by at that moment and asked what they were talking about. The senior counselor toned herself down, but Kathy still heard the irritation in her voice. "When we told Bruno, he turned to her and said something like, 'Well, you've got to have patience. She is barely able to keep her head above water, much less swim.' I thought perhaps he was

saying this to remind her what it was like to be new at the School, how difficult it was.

"There may have been other reasons also, but for me the surprising
effect of Dr. B.'s comment was that I suddenly understood why I had
asked the question. His words relaxed something in me so I could think
and feel, and I realized the question came into my mind at that moment
because I couldn't imagine staying longer than two more minutes. But
here she'd worked eight years! That gave me some perspective, but the
really helpful thing was being able to understand myself—why I'd asked
the question."

Kathy could not remember who the counselor was but said that she
left the School a few months later. Her anger at a novice's question suggests a doubt or ambivalence about her own commitment at that point; as
for the boy, unfortunately, within a year he had to be sent away to a state
institution.

KATHY'S fear of Bettelheim included staff meetings, which she
approached in a state of near panic. She would start off terrified—"butter-
flies in my stomach"—but as soon as Bettelheim engaged with someone
else, she would relax. For six months he did not single her out; then one
day in the middle of a meeting, he did.

"He had looked at me, and suddenly he turned to me and said, 'Zhe
hinches are ghrowing.' I didn't understand, so I said, 'What did you say?'

" 'I *said*, Zhe hinches are ghrrrowing!'

"So I said to myself, it sounds like he's saying, 'The hinges are growing,' but that didn't make any sense. It was either his accent or I was going
crazy. He saw I didn't understand, so he stood up in the middle of the staff
meeting and gestured for me to follow him. I did, and we went to the
dorm where I was a counselor, and he pointed to fluffs of dust on the door
hinges. Then he took out his pocket handkerchief and dusted off each
hinge. I thought, 'This great man, he's noticed these hinges, and he's
actually cleaning them. Okay, that's impressive'—but I didn't get his
point. I was afraid to say anything, so I just followed him back to the staff
meeting, where everybody sat waiting for us to return. That's all he said,
but I still didn't get it."

A few days later an incident with an autistic girl illuminated Bettelheim's point for Kathy. The girl turned out to be the only one in Kathy's
group who didn't eventually "make it," but at the time she was simply the

most difficult to care for. One of the other girls came running to Kathy and said that the autistic girl was trying to hurt herself. Kathy ran back to the dorm and found her with her hand in the crack of the door, touching the hinges. If the door closed it would crush her fingers, but Kathy saw that she was merely fingering the hinges cautiously.

Later, Kathy reflected that she could not understand anything the girl tried to say and could think of nothing to help her—but at least somebody could keep the hinges dusted. The housekeepers had missed the dust, as had both counselors, but Bettelheim saw it and the girl saw it. The point was, Kathy had to pay more attention to the girl's physical environment.

"Obviously, *she* was paying attention to it. This incredibly withdrawn girl was suddenly responding to a hinge, and somehow Bruno had guessed that she might. But that was typical of what made the Orthogenic School unique, the close attention to little details that most people think make no difference."

Typically, Bettelheim had made his point to Kathy but left the lesson unglossed, trusting that she would get it in her own good time.

IN KATHY'S first year, a girl in her group dreaded rainstorms and became agitated whenever one started. "It's hard to describe how unpleasant this was, how intense, and how helpless we felt. She was distressed because she believed she caused the storm, and it did no good to say, 'No, you don't cause it.' She just went on wailing. None of us knew how to help her."

One day a storm blew up, and the girl went into near hysterics at the thunder and lightning. The rain began coming down in torrents, and she grew even more frantic; Kathy could do nothing but stay with her until the storm passed.

Suddenly Bettelheim appeared in the doorway to the dorm, soaking wet.

"He had just come in from the outside, his hat dripped water, he was drenched all over. He stood in the doorway with a handful of papers, and they were a soggy mess. He was making puddles on the floor, his clothes were so wet. He came into the room and charged over to the girl and started to shout, 'WHAT HAVE YOU DONE? LOOK WHAT YOU'VE DONE! YOU'VE RUINED MY PAPERS! I WAS GOING TO CLASS, NOW YOU'VE WRECKED MY LECTURE! AAAAAAAGHHH!' He carried on wildly, like he was furious, much more agitated than the girl was.

"She gasped and her eyes grew wide and she started to beat her breast, and she said, 'No, no, Dr. B., *I* didn't do it! I don't cause the weather—no, *I DON'T CAUSE THE BAD WEATHER, IT'S IN HERE!*' And she gestured toward her heart with both hands. And Bruno said, 'Zot's right! Zot's where it is!' And he walked out of the dorm, leaving a trail of water.

"I don't think the girl had been putting us on or knew this before she said it—it was just that Bruno suddenly got to her, it was such a shock to see him there, drenched and furious. Of course, this kind of intervention is only a beginning, an opening of the door. There was endless work bringing out everything else."

A YEAR after my interview with Kathy Lubin I asked Bettelheim about this intervention, but he could not recall it. "It's too long ago," he said. "Somebody else has to remember these things. It might come back to me in my dreams sometime." However, I persisted and eventually asked why he had dramatized the girl's fantastic illusion in that way. By this time he had begun to recall.

"Well," he said, "I was curious about what she would do if I did this. I hoped—I only hoped—she would wonder whether she really controlled the weather. I didn't say, 'This is an illusion'—I *never* said that. I said, rather, 'Look what you did to me, you made rain on me.' I put it in real terms, with myself as the subject. You see, I was saying I was the fool to believe her, not she was the fool to believe that she controlled the weather. If I was the fool, it was easier for her to accept."

I realized later that Bettelheim had dispelled an illusion by cooperating with it. At a casual glance, one might imagine that he had opened the girl's defenses from the outside with a clever bit of playacting. However, as he well knew, defenses are breached only from within, out of the person's own desire. Here he could count on the girl's wish that no harm would come to him and her wish not to be responsible for such harm. A week or a month earlier, the intervention might not have worked, but by the time he thought of it, the girl apparently had developed enough of a relationship with him and trust in the milieu to be ready for the self-insight that became the first chink in her psychological armor.

CHAPTER 20

A Boy's Conscience

IN 1963 an eight-year-old boy whom I will call Wyatt* came to the School, then at the height of its fame and perhaps as effective a milieu as Bettelheim could build. I have now known the adult Wyatt for about ten years, and I chose to interview him for two reasons. The first is that after Bettelheim's death Wyatt introduced himself to me with a piece of writing that surprised me. It was not salable to any magazine I could think of, but I valued its detailed analysis of a single sentence Bettelheim had uttered in a brief crisis to teach Wyatt something. The sentence riveted my attention as a model of how Bettelheim taught, and Wyatt's analysis showed me that he had learned.

My other reason for asking him to talk to me was that Bettelheim had hit or slapped him a number of times, and I wanted to hear how the experience looked to a former student who as an adult did not seem to hate Bettelheim.

Wyatt has given me only a skimpy version of what brought him to the School; he has told me that he began to read and write before he was three and that he felt impatient to show himself superior to everyone around him, especially adults. He did not like being a child, for what seemed to him a good reason: adults have power over children.

Being bright can sometimes make things worse instead of better for a child with a prickly personality, and when Wyatt provoked trouble in the schools he was sent to, his parents took him to a series of psychiatrists. Wyatt made no friends and kept finding himself at the center of sudden turmoil without knowing what he had done to stir it up. One school after another refused to tolerate his imperious manner, his know-it-all remarks, and his infuriating presence. At last, in 1963, a psychiatrist recommended the Orthogenic School.

Entering Bettelheim's well-developed and benign milieu meant little to Wyatt; he was a child with a sharp tongue, a nimble intellect, and a penchant for angering everyone with his overbearing identity. He told staff members that everything they thought, said, and did was stupid, and he made some of them cry. He had high expectations for everything *he* did, though perhaps he was best at insults that stung. He also hated getting out of bed in the morning and raged at anyone who tried to rouse him. It seemed to him only reasonable to stay in bed, because he distrusted what the day would bring.

Despite all this, the counselor who agreed to work with Wyatt, Diana Grossman (now Kahn), took an immediate liking to him. He remained at the School almost thirteen years, after which he went on to earn degrees from Yale and Columbia. He freely credits Diana, Margaret Carey, George Perkins,[1] and Bettelheim with having saved his life.

WHEN I met Wyatt he was making his living on Wall Street, writing financial analyses in investment banking. He had lost a number of good jobs (personal relations in offices turned rocky), but he usually landed on at least one of his feet, in part because he never stopped trying.

Now that I have gotten to know Wyatt, who still hates to get up in the morning, I can sense a tension beneath his surface demeanor, like that of a circus performer whose ordinary day's work is to walk a tightrope with no net below. On social occasions Wyatt's manner is open, engaging, and talkative; in more private and personal moments, he seems even more open, often carried along by a conscious optimism. He has not quite lost the need to show himself as a superior person, and suppressed anger sometimes flickers over his face; but he does have an acuteness of mind that makes him interesting to be with.

Wyatt's early reading seemed unusual, and I asked if it might have had anything to do with his problems. "In actuality, I had an advantage at the School," he said, "because I didn't have to worry about freeing up my intellect, as so many of the kids did."

One aspect of his problems was feeling isolated: "Not so much from others but first of all from myself. I felt as if I were looking at my life through a wall of glass bricks. If you have your emotional life walled off from yourself and you're not even feeling, then that affects the way you deal with other people."

Later I pointed out that Wyatt's lack of feeling resembled the schizophrenic reaction that Bettelheim noted in himself on the train to Dachau, the sense that events were happening to someone else. However, when I used the word *schizophrenic*, Wyatt objected: "I don't think I was schizophrenic—just unhappy."

He has a good point, in that the medical term labels the person in a way that makes him alien to the rest of us, whereas *unhappy* is a common-sense word everyone has used about himself. *Unhappy* is a suitable starting point, and Bettelheim repeated this theme obstinately: *don't* begin with a disturbed child by thinking of an abstract diagnostic term. For him, the term *schizophrenia* was a dot of passionless shorthand that did not do justice to a complex set of emotions in a failed adaption to life.[2] When he and the staff grasped the particulars of a child's disturbance, they could empathize their way into the content of his symbolic defense; then they could begin the long and many-sided conversation that would draw him out of himself and into the world of the School.

Wyatt's habit of self-estrangement disrupted his emotional growth and reinforced the isolation he feared. The milieu served first as a soft nest, an outer world that would allow his inner world to let down its guard as he began to feel cared for and dared hope for more. But as Diana Kahn said, "It wasn't easy to make the children feel *cared* for."

DIANA was Wyatt's counselor for his first six years at the School, and from the way he spoke of her she seemed reliable and friendly, so that at last when he believed in her attachment to him, he felt safe in attaching himself to her. However, he does not see her in my words.

"The main thing was that Diana was Diana—her own person, doing what she felt like, behaving instinctively," Wyatt said. "She didn't go around being sweet and lovable, she was not Pollyannaish at all. No question that she tried to take care of me, but she was tough."

Diana fought with Wyatt every day, and this reassured him. "She wasn't distant from what I was feeling, or trying to be the nice person in spite of the crap I dished out; she was in the trenches with me, and that made a huge difference. It wasn't somebody 'making nice'—I could have seen through that. But she reacted angrily, maybe because she understood that fighting was the only way I could show any love at all, or anything, any kind of relation at the time. Also, she didn't just accept the fights, she got angry and fought back, and that was right for me. I'm not sure what Dr. B. thought about all this, but he didn't stop us. More important, no matter how much we fought one day, she'd be there for me again the next."

With Wyatt's permission, Diana told me her side. "I didn't understand that fighting was his way of showing a relation. I just liked him a lot and was tremendously interested in him." As for her anger and the fights, she said that nothing could be understood without looking at the issues they fought about. "How did I fight back and what were the fights about? There were essential themes; the main thing was whether he was a grown-up or a kid. His whole defensive system was that he would evade the evil-oppressive power of grown-ups by being superior to them, smarter than them, and in charge."

What was wrong with independence for Wyatt? "If the fight had been a drive for autonomy, I would have respected it and given Wyatt space and validation for his initiative and credit for wanting to be in charge of his life. The fatal flaw in his assertiveness was that if I let him win, he would lose, because his world would remain intact. He would continue to hide his terror of adults by pretending he was more powerful than they were, pretending he needed nothing, that he was not a child, not vulnerable, and would remain as I sometimes saw him, as lonely as a lost puppy."

At eight Wyatt trusted no adult and had almost nothing in common with children his own age. He had grown alienated from everyone, including himself; he had a conscience with some sense of right and wrong but could take no one's feelings into account except his own. Diana fought with him because she had quickly become involved with him, and it was natural to fight rather than to submit to his anger.

"But what I fought for and how I did so was fully censored and disciplined by myself. Those parts of my true emotions which I selected for expression were useful for him and *his* issues. Most of the time the struggle was about trusting me or letting me be the parent and him the child."

Wyatt often declared he was a better caretaker than she was, better at everything she did as a counselor, better, *better*, BETTER!

"Diana once told me," he said, "she'd rather stick her head in an oven than get me up in the morning, because I was such a holy terror. I'd yell at her—'Close the curtains and GO AWAY! I'm not getting UP! I don't want to see ANYBODY! I'm not getting DRESSED! I'm not going to SCHOOL! Leave me ALONE!' This was in my first few years, but I was never a morning person, to put it mildly."

Diana could not let him know the extent of her occasional hurt feelings. In fact, she often felt cheerful despite their daily warfare, but it was hard to hide her less cheerful reactions from him. Keeping the wrong message out of her face demanded strict self-discipline. He was a tough nut to crack, a brat with a big mouth, but she enjoyed him and sensed beneath the surface of his frantic self-assurance an unhappy child in constant need. So she kept at it.

At first it was not clear that her approach (based on a hypothesis that had been developed by herself, the staff, and Bettelheim) was working. But then Wyatt began to let her take care of him and to let himself be a child.

"Those times were very touching and we both felt close," she said. Their relationship was starting to grow, but the confirmation of the hypothesis about Wyatt meant more to Diana than her personal enjoyment.

"Dr. B. inspired us not to look for affection or closeness from the children but to feel good about our performance as counselors if we saw that our hypothesis about what the child needed was correct. The gratification for counselors was not to receive love from the children, but to make possible those moments when the child let himself get what he needed."

One mistake some children made was to reach out to counselors with insincere affection, but an alert counselor did not accept it. "A new child soon learned that he was not expected to take care of the grown-ups, and he would be respected for expressing the truth of his own emotions."

Wyatt's faulty defense against his weakness and fear had to be met every day by a strong and sincere adult who would not give up, so that in time he might work through his need to pretend he was self-sufficient. Diana said that in repeating his theme, Wyatt did not show inchoate aggression, as some children did. "It was more like ill temper. He was a worthy opponent, and while my performance was wholehearted and authentic, I also had to make sure that it was carefully disciplined."

JUST OUTSIDE the counselor's chrysalis of care, Bettelheim stood as the School's leader and prime mover. With sixty children, Wyatt said, "It wouldn't have worked if he tried to be like another counselor. He might have run the School without being so fierce and authoritarian, but that was his personality."

BY THE age of nine Wyatt had lived through a year of daily fights. He felt Diana's personal commitment, that she was not a "professional" caring for children but a genuinely warm person whose kids were her family at that moment. She was there to make his life better, but he could also tell that her work with him sometimes made her happy, and when he saw this, he liked it. She did not press to get close to him but waited for the closeness to come naturally whenever he opened up to it. She became his bedrock, and in that first year, he was doing what Bettelheim hoped he would: forming an unseen bond with his counselor, a bond containing elements of conscience.

IT MAY be helpful to think of conscience as our hidden link to one another, a relationship within ourselves that stabilizes other relations, one that starts in the home and extends outward. Conscience can be stronger (or weaker) than the laws of society and more exacting in its rule than the rules of tradition. The forceful convictions radiating out of Bettelheim's moral presence carried some of his standards into the attuned unconscious of children, much as a father's moral presence (or absence) does; and being master of the School, Bettelheim charged its atmosphere with an inescapable reality that showed the limits the child's conscious mind needed to know.

Wyatt's comment that Bettelheim did not have to be fierce and autocratic is one with which I disagree. He could not have risen to his conscious and unconscious standing in the School except as an autocrat who was feared. Adding symbolic *father* to real *schoolmaster*, he redoubled his moral authority to reach that part of the unconscious that is the superego, as well as to tighten his influence over the conscious part of the personality that tries to grasp reality and use it.

Bettelheim made no special effort to be liked by the children, except in rare instances. He had to resist doing so for their own good, holding back from being an impulsively loving father to them, because that would have been false to his position and to theirs. Instead, he made himself felt as the real-world force and guide above them, one to be feared for the slaps and shame he dealt out, but still trusted as ultimate protector. He gave blame more often than praise—"That was also his personality," Wyatt said.

Once again, I see something else, something more. Bettelheim made a point of blaming children at moments when they showed the destructive impulses and habits that had made their parents send them to the School. Only someone focused on a child's future, and on his own duty as a governing principle in the child's life, could have routinely given up the easy popularity he might have had from those who depended upon him for sanity and life. The look of love in the eyes of flawed and fearful children could have been a subtly corrupting pleasure, but he did not waver from his aim of making them strong.

As mentioned earlier, Bettelheim encouraged transference in counselors but did not want the children to be attached to him in that way. For them he became an influential model of self-rule (autonomy) and an example of the personal power of autocracy. He ruled the little world of the School, but in the larger world his power would vanish, except in imagination. Children knew they could leave the School and expected to do so, at which point Dr. B. would no longer wield power over them. But imagination can be powerful, and habits of autonomy, strengthened by a more balanced superego—one with its own autocracy and limits—could lead to a better life. Many children came to him either lacking in superego or having it in some overwrought form and so needed the balance they could achieve in the milieu.

PSYCHOANALYTIC terms raise a problem here. Bettelheim wrote in *Freud and Man's Soul* that the word *superego*, invented by Freud's English translator, creates an emotional distance in the reader: we simply do not think of "superego" as *us*. On the other hand, *Über-ich*, a word Freud coined, has a warm ring for readers who come to psychoanalysis in German, and French readers benefit from a close translation, *surmoi*. Bettelheim argued that the warmer terms draw readers into the personal commitment of saying "I" when applying psychoanalytic concepts to themselves, whereas *ego* and *superego* fail to inspire a warm private feeling. However, the above-I and upper-I that he suggested to bring us closer to Freud do not do so; the two terms are not idiomatic and never will be and so cannot replace *superego* in English. We have no useful English equivalent to Freud's word in German, but by writing both of superego and conscience, perhaps I can clarify my point about Bettelheim's presence in the School.

In no sense did he create or become the children's conscience or superego. In *Freud and Man's Soul* he wrote of how it is formed,

> that it is the person himself who created this controlling institution of his mind, that the above-I is the result of his own experiences, desires,

needs, and anxieties, *as they have been interpreted by him,* and that this institution attained its role of power because he, the person, *internalized in its contents the demands he made—and continues to make—of himself.* (Emphasis added.)[3]

Within the comforting milieu and by means of experiences with the staff and himself, Bettelheim aimed to modify a child's damaging interpretations and impractical self-demands. Having made children anxious and angry, he could hardly doubt that some would hate him as the focus of their fears; but they might also internalize the protective premise of his attitude toward them. If many never got over the rage aroused when he slapped them—a clear possibility—he had helped by acting as a lightning rod for feelings they could not direct toward the parents who had delivered them into his hands.

So what is conscience or superego? Usually (and like most people?) I act as if my conscience is nobody's business but my own, and if I have to get around it I can do so discreetly. I have also noticed that people who don't have it don't seem to miss it, and I recall Mark Twain's remark that if he had a "yaller dog" that gave him so much trouble, he'd shoot it. Without fully understanding it, we have a speculative grasp of how it is formed, and yet we know instantly what we mean by the word *conscience*—which I will use in tandem with *superego.*

Shakespeare's 151st sonnet opens with a surprising piece of common sense about conscience and parental care:

> *Love is too young to know what conscience is,*
> *Yet who knows not conscience is born of love?*

"Love" in this sonnet is the baby Eros, whose sudden and capricious darts symbolize a passion that ignores conscience, but the first two lines also say that babies are born with no moral sense and that the love of a parent helps form it. We can extend this insight by noting that after infancy and while still dependent upon a parent's good care, the child develops the spontaneous inner guide[4] to right and wrong that we call conscience. Love and fear make up its opaque core, not necessarily a fear of physical punishment but certainly a fear of the loss of parental love and care. In this way the parent's love gives rise to conscience, an order or institution the child himself creates out of instinct, self-interest, and his innate drive to survive.

With luck, we can at first take parental love for granted and feel our parents' protection and strength almost as an extension of ourselves; but later we discover that their power is not our power and also that we are at the mercy of their good opinion—and their flaws. When we see we are only one of their many concerns, we may bristle at the control implied in our weakness and their strength. But, as a rule, we adapt; within limits, their limits become ours. If they think us worthy, we internalize this feeling, and their acceptance of us turns into unconscious self-acceptance even as we loosely conform our behavior to their expectations, some of which become our expectations of ourselves.

At some unpredictable point a child will begin to respond to his inner promptings without thinking of his parents. Feelings of fear and guilt will rise up to nudge him along without overwhelming his self-esteem; easing guilt with a self-correction may even add to his self-esteem, and a child strong enough to continue to build on his sense of self-worth has a good chance to enjoy the satisfactions we find in love, work, and life.

Perhaps as much as anything else, the way a child's parents feel about themselves (and behave toward him and with each other) will affect the course of his moral growth. Hints of autonomy and habits of self-regulation seem to be best absorbed by a kind of steady osmosis within the reliable world of the family. Over time, children who managed to stay at the School no doubt took on some of the attitudes, standards, and demands of a director who felt good about himself and spoke his convictions boldly. However, the counselor's investment of feeling, the love that could be lost, remained the singular and enchanting token of life that beckoned the child out of his isolation.

Bettelheim, forthright and upstanding as the School's superego figure, modeled autonomy, judged behavior, and made reality-demands the counselors could not. The children (and Wyatt is a good example) feared him in a way they would never fear a counselor, but the risk of being abruptly taken out of the School was a fate they feared more than the menace of Dr. B. Value judgments, superego standards, can come from any source and do not require love, but conscience needs to know love to find its voice. Love alone was never enough at the School—merely indispensable, like the counselors.

FOR A YEAR Diana got Wyatt up in the morning and put him to bed at night; made sure he ate meals; tended him when he was not feeling well; played with him when he wanted company; found him interesting things to do and books to read; took him on outings with the group. This was all to the good, but the most important thing for Wyatt remained the same: to believe in Diana, he had to fight with her every day, and she had to fight back. Then he had to see her at his bedside the next morning.

Meeting endless needs was Diana's daily routine as she tried to antici-pate Wyatt's wishes so that his day would go smoothly. She also had to think of her own needs, which she showed Wyatt both directly and indi-rectly, so that he never had to cope with a hidden agenda. Even on her day off, Diana stopped by and said hello to the group, not out of duty but simply to see what was going on. Wyatt felt that Diana's co-counselor dis-liked these visits and tolerated them only because Diana was the senior counselor.

But *he* liked them.

One evening near bedtime when Wyatt had been at the School for about a year, he was sitting on the dorm floor with his building set, putting together a skyscraper. Fascinated, he lost track of time as he fit what seemed like thousands of plastic pieces neatly into place on a large board.

Diana went out to get the bedtime snacks, and when she reappeared in the doorway carrying a tray of drinks and cookies, she told Wyatt to pick up the board and put the set away, as it was almost time for bed. Her man-ner was easy and casual, but her mild words angered him. She was being unfair; he *had* to finish. If he put the board away, he couldn't save what he'd already created—it would be ruined. He had to do it *now*. Couldn't she see that? In a flash he knew she'd done this for her convenience, because she was an adult, and his rage blazed up. He had to *smash* some-thing.

"I picked up the board," he said, "and dumped everything right in the doorway and said, 'Now *you* pick it up!' "

Plastic pieces rattled across the floor, and Diana fled in shock. "She ran to the kitchenette," he said, "and I found her there crying. Suddenly I felt terrible, because I realized how much I loved her, and here I had hurt her. I had never thought I was important enough to make her cry. I felt sorry, ashamed I had hurt her and didn't know what to do. The only thing I could think of was to go back and pick up the pieces, so I did. Just then

Jacqui came into the dorm—she must have seen Diana crying—and saw the mess. Maybe Dr. B. was away and she was in charge, I'm not sure. She didn't ask questions, just gave me a good slap.[5] Oddly enough, slapping me wasn't necessary at that point, because of how badly I felt. It was meaningless, and I more or less ignored it. I had a lot more on my mind than a slap.

"Finally, I decided to go back to Diana in the kitchenette, to be with her. I don't remember how we made up, although I think I told her I was sorry. But what I felt when I saw Diana cry will stay with me the rest of my life."

WHEN THIS happened, little had changed in Wyatt's personality that one might have noticed. However, he had developed a soft spot—he cared about Diana's feelings, and his growing trust in her had become an unconscious force within him. Up to this point his sense of right and wrong had told him he was never wrong. Now he was wrong, and he knew it. He needed no bossy adult to say so. Freud's "autocracy of conscience which rules the anarchy of id" suddenly handed down its first verdict on Wyatt: *Guilty!*

He was still a severely disturbed youngster, but for a moment he had let down his defense of total hostility to adults. Now Diana was different. His feeling about her *and* about himself was a tentative step in the reintegration of his personality as he inched closer to her. Unnoticed, she had taken an honored place among the values in his superego, possibly because he felt his value in her eyes.

When I asked Wyatt just why the skyscraper incident felt so crucial to him, he said that it showed him how much he mattered to Diana. He skirted any criticism of his parents, with whom he has long been on good terms, but for whatever reason, in his early years he had apparently interpreted his life at home in a way that made him feel he did not matter to anyone.

An interesting side note here is that Diana got a happy result in the convergence of two failures. She failed as a caretaker when she did not pick up the intensity of Wyatt's feeling about the skyscraper, and she failed at self-discipline when she showed him how deeply he had hurt her. In this case two wrongs made a right but only because she had already begun to win his heart. Like magic, the tug of love and his insight into the meaning of her pain swept away his anger, and he was morally mature enough at age nine to take blame.

"Despite all our battles—and we were famous for them in the School—she cared enough about me to be hurt. This astonished me. And I felt responsible for what I had done. I realized then that I had to find another way."

THE BENEVOLENT pang that stung Wyatt was so electrifying in comparison to Jacqui's slap that the slap went unfelt. His growing conscience, with its means of self-correction through guilt, had delivered its own blow from the inside. Getting to this point had been a year's work, a long time in most types of therapy, but Wyatt's journey to a viable self had only just begun. He and Diana had five more years together before she left the School, and in fact some of their worst moments lay ahead.

Ideally, a growing conscience will gradually render corrections by adults unnecessary as the child's inner controls take hold. However, there was no easy path to this in the School, because in many children a faulty superego was their major problem. The reality of the mind's autonomy and the roadblocks of a child's defenses created moments of crisis, but Bettelheim was there to step in. He slapped or hit Wyatt many times, with perhaps mixed results. Wyatt remembered one slap (a year later, age ten) that he felt had some justification, though he questioned it eventually.

"I had been yelling at the staff and calling them stupid," he said. "Someone told Dr. B. about my tirade, and he came and called me out of the dining room into the hallway. He took off my glasses and slapped me several times and said, 'You should behave yourself so I don't have to take you out here and slap you.' But my feeling about him at that moment was, 'Gee, this is quite unexpected.' What surprised me was his manner, because he was so sensitive about punishing me." Afterward, Wyatt thought, "He isn't such a monster after all—he didn't really *want* to have to do this."

One time Bettelheim hit Wyatt just below the eye and made a bruise that hurt for a day or two. Wyatt felt he did not mean to do that, although the pain was less important than the humiliation.

"After all, he wasn't dealing with a child who had an undeveloped intellect, like some of them. And yet, maybe he didn't care about my ability to reason, that when he hit he was trying to reach the primitive instinctual hidden side, the angry will. I don't know."

When Wyatt looked back at himself at about age fourteen, he rejected his idea of kindness-while-slapping. He thought perhaps he'd been taken in by charisma, or that he was identifying with the aggressor.

"Maybe by looking at him as good and decent while I was hit, I was making an unbearable situation bearable by ascribing positive motives to my attacker. On the other hand, maybe he was being kind in the sense of giving me what I needed to *get* to fourteen, so if he hadn't attacked whatever attitude he was attacking, the attitude might have continued to grow and develop in a self-destructive way."

I asked Diana how she saw Wyatt's spontaneous liking of Bettelheim, and she said, "I think he had that feeling at the time because Bettelheim's paternal manner even when hitting kids did communicate love and caring about the child."

BETTELHEIM could not always make the School a trouble-free milieu for the children, because they sometimes disturbed one another. The total therapeutic milieu also varied in its consistency with the behavior of the staff, and Wyatt commented on both children and staff:

"If you were up three nights in a row because a kid in your dorm was acting crazy, that was hard to take. The quality of your life depended on the other children around you and also on whether the staff was good, bad, or mediocre. Dr. B. couldn't get ideal counselors all the time and had to make do with some who were really half-assed, but it couldn't be helped. And he had to train new staff year after year, and watch new people making the same old mistakes.

"On the other hand, his own contributions were above and beyond the call of duty. He gave himself, he didn't hold back, because he really cared about the kids, but some of the work must have driven him crazy. He had a sophisticated intellect, yet there he was, mired down in housekeeping duties. He'd come into the dorms and say, 'Put your toys away, it looks like a pigsty in here.' "

Diana commented, "Yes, he was sometimes mired down, but Bruno felt no detail was too small for his attention, because it affected the quality of the therapeutic milieu." Of course, the quality of the milieu also reflected the intent of the director and his commitment to the children.

WYATT felt that the negative reports after Bettelheim's death had left an exaggerated impression of how much he hit the children.

"Diana called up after she read one of the articles and laughed and said, 'Wyatt, you didn't get hit more than once a week!' Actually, it wasn't nearly that often during my first three years. After my fourth year I don't think Dr. B. ever slapped me again. But some of his yellings felt just as humiliating to me. He did slap some of the older kids publically, and the terror of this was not just humiliation but finding the appropriate response to protect your dignity."

Wyatt pinpoints a fateful need here, one that Bettelheim knew in the camps: restoring one's dignity after humiliation. In part, he slapped a child like Wyatt to keep him from getting false dignity from a hostile act, and the counselor was expected to come forward at once with personal comfort and love to help restore the child's feeling of self-worth. Bettelheim often had to make a snap judgment about hitting to protect the milieu and all in it, including the child himself; and as Wyatt noted, this was his job alone: counselors couldn't hit. "You can't play policeman and develop trust at the same time," Wyatt said, "especially with kids who have learned not to trust adults from year one. You can't punish and nurture all in one breath. No kid can accept that."

Wyatt said that a child who broke windows repeatedly would not get hit unless Bettelheim believed he was showing defiance or could have done better. As for destructive acts with symbolic meaning, Wyatt offered an example. "Let's say a kid was too quiet, he's had trouble expressing himself, and then he suddenly takes the pitcher with our afternoon snack drink and pours it out in the middle of the floor—would he get hit? Of course not. We'd all sit up in awe and watch him, because this was wonderful, and if he was getting what he needed with the pitcher, then maybe we would too, in our own way."

Wyatt could not list all Bettelheim's reasons for hitting, but one sure-fire way to get him angry was to compare yourself to someone else, saying you were better. "Competition wasn't bad per se, but it was the wrong motive at the School. If you put somebody down and said or implied that you were better than that person, Dr. B. became furious. When he saw you doing this, he smacked you or yelled at you in public. He always said that you were in the School for two reasons—to know yourself, and to compare where you started with where you were now. He said this over and over."

Wyatt admitted he was too competitive (and perhaps still is), and for the kind of growth he needed, competition was irrelevant; also, it showed a trait Bettelheim saw as self-destructive in the context of the milieu.

"He wanted you to create standards for yourself and live up to them without comparing yourself to anybody else. He was always totally serious about this. Of course, it didn't stop people from being competitive after they left the School."

Diana commented that competitiveness also took the child away from facing how bad he felt about himself, that a child "had to find better ways to develop himself so he could like himself more, without the empty reassurance of fantasy, or of bragging and competing over stupid things."

Despite many positive feelings about Bettelheim, Wyatt said, "He could put people down like swatting a fly, both staff and kids. This is what gave him a large part of his power. He really knew how to get under someone's skin, and when he did it maliciously, he created long-lasting ill will. I know you're going to ask me if I'm sure it was malice, but it certainly felt like that."

DIANA disagreed with Wyatt on the question of malice. "I was seeing things from another vantage point, of course," she said, "and I had my own differences with Dr. B., but in my opinion he wasn't malicious. He always had a positive, thoughtful point in what he did and said. And I never saw him indulging in whims. That wasn't his way; he was much too conscious of his goals.

"As for goading people, yes, he did act in provocative ways, and deliberately so, but often it turned out to be constructive. And yes, he jumped to conclusions, but most of the time he was right. Very often the point he was trying to teach just wasn't immediately apparent to onlookers, and so people felt hurt and resentful, or confused. If they identified with the person he was giving a hard time, they thought he was cruel. I'm sure they really believed it because it looked that way to them, but I can only say that I saw something else that usually made a lot of sense in the situation. The thing was, you could never get away without having *some* reaction to Bruno."

WYATT liked the School's consulting psychiatrist, George Perkins, far better than he liked Bettelheim, perhaps because he saw Perkins only for an hour or two every six months, which made it easy for children to get along with him, especially since he looked and listened and did not correct. One thing he looked for in the child was a little change that someone living with him might miss. If Bettelheim was the Eye of God or the cop on the beat, Perkins was the visiting grandfather. Bettelheim's presence was a constant reminder, but Perkins exerted little pressure.

"He was very wise and very gentle," Wyatt said. "He was tough but just not as aggressive as Dr. B., who could be brutal. However, both of them understood kids intuitively and quickly, and it was easier for me to talk to Dr. Perkins. Also, Dr. B. had a short attention span. His mind worked so quickly that he would figure out what was important in a situation and reach a solution while everybody else was still struggling to catch up. By that time he was racing on to the next thing."

IN THE first few years Wyatt often felt like walking out the door and going home. His family lived in Chicago, and even at age eight he could have found his father's office by train, so the thought of running away was tempting. But he didn't—"in part because I would have had to deal with Dr. B. later, and it just wasn't worth it. That's what I felt at first, but later on I didn't want to run away, because as difficult as the School was, I knew I needed to take control of my life."

CHAPTER 21

Keeping It Going

IN ITS maturity the School reached a smoothly running state, an operational plateau, that allowed Bettelheim to absent himself from Chicago more often, as he took days off to travel and give lectures. However, one chronic headache in an establishment that had taken on a life of its own was, of all things, marriage. Many of his young women were eminently marriageable, both in age and personality, and if a female counselor seemed headed for marriage, Bettelheim sometimes found ways to make himself agreeable to the lucky young man.

This eventually happened with Marc Lubin, who married Kathy Carson while she was still at the School, and I interviewed them together. At college, Marc had decided to become a psychologist, and *The Informed Heart* was one of the books he read. Like so many people drawn to Bettelheim through his writing, Marc felt a subtle force in the book that seemed to make it a part of his permanent mental library. He entered the University of Chicago for graduate work, and one day a friend asked him to come along to a Bettelheim lecture. He would not be noticed, because students always crowded the classroom.

"I hadn't registered for the course," Marc said, "but we walked in just a few minutes after class had begun, with maybe seventy people already there. To my horror, Bettelheim looked at me as we came in and said, 'Are you signed up for this class?' I said no, and he said, 'Then get out!' "

Marc left the classroom hot-faced and humiliated, but despite his embarrassment he recognized that he had tremendous respect for this professor. "He was saying, 'If you're not paying for this, *out!* Others are.'"

Naturally, Marc went on to take every course Bettelheim offered, four in all. "He singled me out for the famous treatment a few times, but it was no big deal so far as I was concerned."

Marc once raised his hand to answer a question, and he gave an elabo-rate and correct answer. "Bettelheim dismissed it with, 'Yeah, well, every-body knows that.' If you tried to show off as a bright graduate student, that was absolutely the wrong way to go with him. He wanted a simple, direct response that involved real feelings—your own. This was unheard of else-where at the university, and it was terrifying for lots of students."

Marc did not expect Bettelheim to have any abiding interest in him or the other students, because Bettelheim walked into the classroom as the *teacher*, with everyone else there to listen and learn. "That was the rule," Marc said. He also understood that Bettelheim did not seek relationships of any depth with students because he was preoccupied with the School.

"It's true, the classroom teaching was done with his left hand, but also with high drama and lasting impact. There were all these stories that he was a horrible man, but you couldn't get into his classes. They were packed, all of them. A lot of people hated him, but there are many like myself who think he was the most meaningful teacher we ever met.

"Some of those with loyalties to the client-centered psychotherapy group at the university thought Bettelheim was assaultive, authoritarian, a real Nazi, and so on. But I think their problem was, they couldn't stand that he was strong and clear and forceful, raising their doubts around some of the basic truths about human beings. Also, certain people are afraid of being dominated and controlled by a strong male figure. For some reason, it's just too much of a threat.

"Maybe those who were appalled wanted softer teachers who would validate them as they already were—or thought they were. Bettelheim didn't do that, at least in class."

Marc now believes that Bettelheim narrowed his audience needlessly by his manner, that he could have had a much wider following if he had been a shade more tolerant. "But in the classroom he refused to compro-mise. When I started teaching I had an abrasive edge but then found I didn't want to be that way, that I'd rather enlarge the circle than narrow it. Still, he absolutely created my career as a teacher."

Marc also attended a weekly seminar on psychoanalysis Bettelheim gave at the School. "People could bring up any problem they wanted. That was one of the ways he taught—through problems." Marc was work-ing in a residential treatment center on the North Side of Chicago, and in his first week he had to take a schizophrenic boy downtown for his psy-chotherapy hour. The other counselors warned him about the boy, saying that he would ask for an ice-cream bar but shouldn't get it, "because he's always too demanding."

Marc talked about the boy in the seminar, intending to ask a question. "I don't remember what my point was, but Bruno derailed me before I got there. This was characteristic of his teaching—you'd never get to where you thought you wanted to go. I came to the point where the boy asked for the ice-cream bar and I said no. Dr. B. interrupted and said, 'Why did you say no?'

"That stopped me. I mean, *dead*. I can still remember the sudden shame, the humiliation, the sense of being pinned by his question. He had touched something, and I knew it. Instead of thinking about the boy, I was responding to the anxieties of my colleagues. It's horribly embarrassing to be caught like that, but I was glad Dr. B. asked, and I said truthfully, 'I probably said no because I was told not to give him the ice cream.' The truth never got you into trouble with Bettelheim, but resistance to the truth did.

"Bruno simply said, 'How can you expect to make a connection with this boy if you say no to him based on someone else's opinion and not through your own relationship with him? He'll understand that, and you'll never make contact with him.' I still tell this story in my own classes, because it's so basic—you've got to have your own convictions in working with disturbed people, not somebody else's. The important thing is that no one had ever stopped me and said, 'Why did you do that?' But Bruno did."

At another meeting the seminar discussed working with disturbed children and what to do if a child asks, "Did you have sex with your wife last night?" Bettelheim suggested role-playing to act out the possibilities, because he did not like the formulations in the book the seminar students had just read. He played the child, and Marc played the therapist, taking a properly cool and distant approach with *Why do you ask?*

Bettelheim said, "Aaaachh!" in disgust and waved his hand like he was swatting Marc down. Then Bettelheim played the therapist and another student played the child and asked, "Did you have sex with your wife last night?" Bettelheim said, "Yes! And what do you think of that?"

"I'm not even sure that's the right thing to say, but it jolted me, and I felt it was marvelous for a couple of reasons. First, he was giving the kid credit for asking a legitimate question, and he was responding directly and being discreet at the same time. 'Why do you ask?' implies that you may not have a good reason; it puts the questioner down. It's an evasion, whereas Bruno's reply brought him forward to the kid and was totally engaging. Not that I've ever tried his approach, but it might bring interesting results."

Of course, Bettelheim was not laying out a formula by which a child should be interviewed; he was demonstrating that the psychoanalytically correct reply, "Why do you ask?," is actually loaded with implications that the child will feel. However, if Bettelheim was actually interviewing a child, we could be sure that his response would emerge from what he could read in the child's face or hear in his voice.

Marc said that Bettelheim would sometimes go through a classroom asking a question like, What is an ego? "And of course all the brilliant grad students were saying, 'An-ego-is-that-part-of-the-psyche-that-demands-a-superego-and-responds-to-reality-pressures,' et cetera. And Bruno would say, 'Nope,' and move on to somebody else. It was nope-nope-nope-nope all around the room. Then finally somebody said, 'An ego is a concept,' and he'd say, 'That's right!' and get all excited and turn to the rest of the class and say, 'That's all you know, you people!' It was fun, it was dramatic, it was apocalyptic, it was full of revelations. I never saw another teacher make such a display of his feelings, and he was so involved in his subject matter that he brought you into it too."

Even though Marc took four classroom courses, Bettelheim did not seem to know him until it became clear that he and Kathy were going to get married. "Then he treated me very politely, because she was a part of the School and very valuable to him. In his mind, everything centered around the School."

Ordinarily, the Wednesday-night staff meetings that Kathy had to attend would have been closed to Marc, but as a courtesy Bettelheim let him sit in. He also suggested that Marc read transcripts of years of past staff meetings.

"It was quite a learning experience. This way, I not only knew him through his classroom performances, but I learned how he taught just from reading the transcripts. He knew I wanted to learn from him, and that was one of the reasons he did it, but I doubt he would have done it except for Kathy. When he wrote A Home for the Heart, he asked me to select some of the staff meetings that would be good for the book, and I did."

AROUND this time, Bettelheim heard of a young girl in the university's Medical Center hospital who had terminal anorexia. The doctors had tried intravenous feeding, but the girl wanted to die, and they didn't believe they could save her. Bettelheim visited her in the hospital, then had her brought over to the School so Kathy could interview her. She was painfully emaciated—"like a concentration-camp victim"—but Kathy, who had never heard of anorexia, liked her and told Bettelheim all the reasons she should be admitted.

Kathy said that at the next staff meeting Bettelheim gave an electrifying lecture. "He said the girl was dying and it would be a risk to take her but he felt we should. In the early years the School had been a pioneering venture, and nobody knew if it would work. However, it had gradually become successful, slowly improving its methods over the years, and now it ran so well that he thought we were becoming complacent. We did the work, but we no longer recognized that it was a matter of life and death for the children. That shocked us!"

Bettelheim told them that if they took the girl, her case would demonstrate a truth they seemed to be forgetting, that *their* decisions meant the difference between life and death; it was a gamble, but it would dramatize the deepest meaning of their work. Whether or not they could convince her that life was worth living, they would see the results directly and perhaps soon.

"He wanted to reinfuse the School with a sense of mission," Kathy said, "and he was so impassioned that everybody got excited and wanted to do it. So we took her in, and she joined my group. And it was a nightmare."

At that point Kathy was a six-year veteran, but the girl reacted to her with such hostility that it felt as if she were starting all over again.

As for Marc, he had imagined that Kathy would begin to draw away from the School when the two of them married—but now they were married, and suddenly the opposite was happening. The School and Bettelheim had recaptured Kathy and redoubled her duties. He became furious, and at this point Bettelheim, no doubt seeing Marc's anger and hoping to soften him, sought to bring him closer to the School—hence the idea that he immerse himself in staff-meeting transcripts, which Bettelheim knew he would find fascinating.

If Marc remained resentful, Kathy would have too great a conflict in loyalties and could not work properly with the girl. Since Kathy loved Marc and wanted to live with him, Bettelheim had to find a place for him in the orbit of the School. He could not hire Marc, because Marc had other priorities, and so he persuaded him to take on a task related to the School, one that appealed to his intellectual curiosity as a psychologist and his personal desire to learn.

"It was a tough time in more ways than one," Marc said. "This teen-aged girl was so vindictive and bitter that she intimidated Kathy's co-counselors. Five of them left the School in five months, and the School took so much more out of Kathy that we were together less then than before we got married."

Kathy, too, became angry at the demands on her. It was hard enough dealing with the girl's hostility all day long, but to make matters worse, it took her away from the rest of her group; and not having a strong co-counselor made the hours longer. (Later she decided that the five new counselors would not have worked out in any event and that the girl's hostile attitude had simply sped up the winnowing process.) Kathy also felt the burden of the girl's life: if she didn't eat, she would die. And every mouthful turned into a battle. Breakfast, lunch, dinner—Kathy sat through each meal, pushing the girl to eat. Eventually she found a tactic: *create an ugly scene.*

"She absolutely hated scenes and always spoke in a low tone of voice, but that gave me leverage. I could raise my voice and embarrass her. I said, '*EAT* your mashed potatoes *AND* your gravy *AND* drink your milk. Then I'll stop yelling and making a scene.' As she got more resistant, I got louder. She was always saying, 'I won't eat, I won't eat,' so low that only I could hear her, but I just kept raising my voice."

The girl could still walk when she came to the School, but she moved painfully and deliberately, as if her body were fragile, all the while looking at Kathy and others with vague disdain. She gained weight slowly under Kathy's pressure and after some months was no longer in danger of dying. Kathy saw enormous strength in the girl, who fought every inch of the way, keeping up both her hostility and her resolve in the face of all of Kathy's efforts, excoriating everyone around her as *horrible* people who were making her *fat.*

"I thought," Kathy said, "if she could only hook up that stubbornness to something positive, she could do anything. She seemed passive, but inside it was another story. There was a sparkle about her, a sense of the struggle going on within. I always believed she would make it, and she did, but the hardest thing for me was neglecting my other girls. She forced me to attend almost exclusively to her needs, and meanwhile this other one over there is hanging from the chandelier. It was impossible. She drained me dry."

"That's a genuine issue," Marc said, "when you neglect others in the group in order to help one. For the girls Kathy didn't have time to help, it was an irrevocable loss. They were right to be resentful. I once discussed this point with Bettelheim in relation to my own work, and his attitude was very practical. He felt that you save the one really desperate kid, and the others will manage. We talked about it in one of his seminars when I asked for help with a boy I was very attached to in the residence where I worked. One day the kid became upset and stormed out of the living room area, and I said to Dr. B. later, 'I didn't go with him, because I was with the other kids.' And Bruno said, 'Don't you think this boy needed you at that moment?'

"He was right, of course. His message was that if someone is on the edge, you go to the person on the edge. The rest of them will make do. After that, I gave the boy more of myself because I felt permission to do so—also permission to tolerate the rage of the kids I left behind, which I didn't want to face. You feel guilty when you do this, but you can get rid of the guilt if you feel you have permission from the 'superego in attendance' to care for the desperate child. You can't worry about everybody's reaction; you have to go where you think the cause is greatest. Bruno felt the danger was worrying more about your self-image than about the child, and once I understood that point and made it my own, it cut through about eighty percent of the staff-child interactions. 'Don't bother preserving your self-image.' He put it just that way."

CHAPTER 22

The Three Things — and Empathy

IN THE eight and a half years Kathy worked at the School, she never sent for Bettelheim in a crisis.

"He didn't like to be viewed as a troubleshooter, or as a putter-outer of fires. Sometimes he had to, but he encouraged us to handle everything short of violence that we couldn't control. We were the ones expected to be on the front lines, and with my girls, it just never happened that he had to intervene."

I asked about violence at the School, and Kathy recalled the time when a boy attacked Bettelheim and kicked him in the testicles. She did not see the incident but soon heard about it and knew the aftermath. Staff members were so shocked that they froze and didn't help Bettelheim (as had also happened earlier when a girl attacked him).

"It occurred in front of other children, and so Bruno thought he should discuss it in a meeting with the kids. He talked about the meaning of what the boy had done and why he would kick him in that particular place. Ask him about it. I think he'll remember."

WAS BETTELHEIM a model for the staff? Kathy said yes and no. The long hours and his single-minded devotion to the children embodied values that successful staffers took as their own, and in that sense he was a model; however, he disavowed himself as a model for the counselors' *behavior* with the children.

"He didn't want people to think they could get it right by copying or by echoing him," Kathy said. "That wouldn't work at all. You had to do it your own way. But over the years, any time Dr. B. heard a complicated formulation of an emotional issue, he would interrupt the person and say,

'Aaaach, you young people! You all know so much! Me, I'm simple-minded,' and then he would go into the 'three things' he knew. Actually, I've used them over and over. They seem to be simple pieces of wisdom, but they're more complex than you realize at first, and very hard to integrate into your own perspective.

"Making them a part of yourself is not a simple matter. A couple of times I've stood up in front of a group, intending to say the three things, and then I forget one and have to grope for it. The reason I forgot was that the three points were not yet fully integrated into my thinking. In supervision Dr. B. repeated them many times, and eventually you learned to use them."

EVERYONE who worked with Bettelheim for any length of time seems to have heard his claim of being simpleminded and knowing only Three Things. Sometimes the order of the things would change, and at other times it was Four Things instead of three. Karen Zelan said she kept notes and once showed Bettelheim that he had raised the count to Six Things, though he didn't name them all at the same time. However, it is generally agreed that in his later years at the School, Bettelheim's Three Things (all clinical reminders) were:

1. The end is in the beginning.
2. The patient is always right.
3. When a child's behavior baffles you, ask yourself, "Under what circumstances would I behave this way?"

The first point refers implicitly to the patient's distant past but more specifically to his recent past. "Bruno also told us," Karen Zelan said, "*When the patient talks of the past, talk to him of the present; when the patient talks of the present, talk to him of the past.* This was a brilliant way of capturing the basics of the transference concept, and I have remembered it all my professional years and used it regularly. Bruno never said to get as near to the submerged memory of the original trauma as you can. You can't get very near to it, as Sigmund Freud himself said many times over, and therapists who think they can run into trouble. His daughter Anna elaborated on some of these ideas in her book on the mechanisms of defense, which shows how useful it can be to explore the defenses as behaviors in their own right, with their own legitimacies. When you are able to turn the patient's passive experience (whether traumatic or not) into something active, you are helping the patient gain control of his life. This doesn't necessarily lead to a 'cure' but it often leads to a better life adjustment. This is what I've found to be true in my practice."

Also speaking of the recent past, Kathy said, "It's important to be able to retrace your steps, even about an episode that happened several hours ago and only took a few minutes. If we got into trouble with a child, the tendency was to start explaining why we *imagined* the child exploded about something, but Dr. B. didn't buy that. He always pushed us to retrace our steps to the *beginning* of the interaction, because that's where we'd find the seeds of whatever had gone wrong. He showed how predictable it was for things to end badly, that the end came from the way you handled the beginning."

As for "The patient is always right," common sense tells us the disturbed child is obviously wrong, but Bettelheim wanted counselors to grasp the fact that the child *believes* he is right. Then the therapist has to face the emotional reality that the child *is* right, given his version of his own history.

"Bruno insisted that if a person does something, he had a *need* to do it, a need that we had to understand," Karen said. "He insisted that the therapist should start where the patient starts and not begin by making assumptions. That's why he liked hiring young people who hadn't been trained before. He wanted to teach approaching the patient not with what you know from the book but informed by your own instincts."

The second of the three things also reminds the therapist to *persist* in seeing that the child is "right," no matter how bizarre his actions may continue to be. Bettelheim expected meticulous attention to behavior, and as the therapist learned to speak with the disturbed child on his own terms, the child could begin to see what was "wrong" or self-defeating about attitudes and actions.

Bettelheim's first two points seem easy, but his third—"Under what circumstances would I behave this way?"—challenges the therapist to empathize with the child and to approach him *first* through feelings. The counselor had to find something within herself that resonated with the child's symptoms. Of course, summoning up empathy is not like ordering a ham sandwich; it doesn't appear on demand. Not quite. But those counselors who found more depths of empathy in themselves as they became more absorbed in a child also had more success at the School. Bettelheim always held that the empathic ability would grow with practice, and so he made it a goal for counselors.

Bettelheim did not agree with the dictionary definitions of *empathy*, a relatively new word in English that is hard to pin down. It refers to feeling what another person feels, which we can't actually do, because we only *feel* what *we* feel. So how can we feel the feelings of another, or empathize? Bettelheim has a kind of answer in *A Home for the Heart*, where he distinguishes between compassion, sympathy, and empathy. Compassion, he says, is feeling *for* the other person, and sympathy is feeling *with* the person; but in empathy, we experience for brief periods the feelings *of* the other — that is, we feel *the same way* he does. There can be no empathy without compassion and sympathy, but for empathy to occur, another experience must implement them: an introspection, which, on the basis of our experience, permits us to feel as the other person does.[1]

Empathy does not appear in the *Oxford English Dictionary*; however, it was accepted into American English as a translation of a German word meaning "a feeling in." One French dictionary translates *empathy* as "*pénétration par sympathie*," words that suggest acute insight through sympathetic feelings, and also that we can go *into* another person's feelings, which is not quite what Bettelheim meant. He saw empathy as an *observable event in ourselves* that we can look into and describe. *Webster's* calls it "projection," but Bettelheim disagreed:

> Projection is entirely different. . . . Projection is essentially self-centered, while empathy, though drawing on one's inner experiences, is centered on the other. In projection, one sees oneself in the other; in empathy, one feels the other in oneself, not as a totality as in introjection, but only as the other is feeling at this very moment, and without going beyond the boundaries of the self, which remain intact.[2]
>
> It is impossible to teach this kind of empathetic sensitivity. Staff members learn it only through experiencing their own attitudes.[3]

This last remark needs to be expanded upon. Obviously, we all know our attitudes: they occur vividly in our stream of consciousness. However, few of us undergo the kind of scrutiny (and self-scrutiny) of motive and attitude that was routine at the School. A counselor who asked herself, Why did I think or feel that? might gain insight into an unconscious reaction that had hurt the child but defended the counselor's self-image. A defensive attitude, energized by the unconscious and thrust forward under the hidden sponsorship of the superego, might be breached by persistent inquiry when a counselor learned to find the fault lines in an attitude that had at first appeared seamless and self-evident.

Attitudes caught and delved into are self-centered, but since a counselor's self-questioning also had a conscious motive about the child (to understand him), the child became the center of inquiry.

Bettelheim writes about a comment by Freud that he saw as relevant to the idea of empathy:

> Freud does not specifically discuss empathy but relies instead on his explanation of what is going on when it occurs. He speaks of what he calls "the sympathy of one unconscious to another," thus making it clear that this can never be a rational process. On the contrary, he warns that conscious rationality interferes with it.[4]

If empathy is not a matter of rational understanding, how can a person achieve and enhance it? The little tug of empathy can't be goal-directed, although we can question attitudes that seem to interfere with it.

A counselor had to begin by liking—probably for unconscious reasons—the child she volunteered to work with; so, in a sense, empathy begins with empathy. And it was looked for, because senior staffers always kept an eye on a new counselor to see whether or not she still genuinely liked the children in the midst of her struggle to survive. They picked up signs of spontaneous sympathy in their colleague's voice, face, or gestures. Inevitably, her feelings were tested when a child acted out a severe disturbance; then the question became, If a child flustered or frightened her, how did she handle her anxieties? A frozen smile, a blank face, denial, withdrawal, emotional distance, a change of subject? And did at least some tone of sympathy reappear after the dust had settled? The staff noticed, monitored, and evaluated, all in a day's work.

To reach deeper empathy, a counselor had to understand her own reactions to a child, and just as "the patient is always right," a counselor was always right, because every response was relevant. Her reactions came into her mind for real reasons, and self-questioning could make reasons accessible.

Counselors who held too stubbornly to their defenses were wrong for the job, and naturally this was true of most workers Bettelheim hired. But when a counselor found feelings in herself that paralleled the child's feeling, she could extend the empathy that would help her see him better and thus experience the "sympathy of one unconscious to another" of which Freud wrote.

Bettelheim also made the point that unresolved remnants of a staff member's past could be either the worst barrier or the best asset when working with patients. Such emotional blocks

> are impediments when they are acted out; assets when they are judiciously *acted upon.*[5]

He noted that most psychiatric hospitals expect workers to hold back from acting upon their own emotional preoccupations. However:

> Since we all have emotional problems, this is impossible. They are the main incentive for [the therapist] to help psychiatric patients on their incredibly difficult road to recovery. *Without this source for empathy with the patient,* psychotherapeutic work could never succeed.[6]

Bettelheim offered his three things as reminders to put the spotlight on the patient and to explore emotions in ways that could lead to the kind of insight that led to further work.

In *The Empty Fortress* Bettelheim wrote that the child often cannot say what preys on his mind and so asks and answers questions in silent, indirect, or symbolic ways, to which the therapist must be sensitive. But the School's work was not simply a matter of empathy and intellect, heart and mind. In the end, wherever possible, the child had to *work through* in the psychoanalytic sense and reexperience painful feelings in appropriate ways with a trusted person. This was perhaps the child's most difficult task, once a close relationship had been formed, and each child worked through in an individual way and to a degree different from all others. In total, the benign therapeutic milieu — "common sense organized"[7] — surrounded the students and staff with encouragement and support, quietly suggesting that their efforts to grow were worthwhile, as was life itself.

CHAPTER 23

Helping Someone Else,
Helping Yourself

As NOTED earlier, a strong motive for staffers to put up with their long hours, low salary, and work that was often disturbing was to learn about themselves while caring for the children. In later years, some students also learned in this way when they were able to stay in the School past age fourteen and help younger students. A few came back as adults: Sandy Lewis, for a short time, as a counselor; Betsy, to teach (chapter 25) and Bertram Cohler, who served as director twice. However, the milieu also gave many adolescents a chance to learn by caring for younger children. Bettelheim never saw this as part of his plan or method; a student had to come to it out of his own desire, through his own impulses, by his own choice, and as a form of autonomy.

At seventeen, Wyatt reached this point. Diana had left when he was fourteen, and for months on end he'd swung between mourning and fury. On the days he saw Margaret Carey in sessions, her love and counsel softened him, but he missed Diana bitterly. Feelings of loss and abandonment filled his mind. She had made life bearable, and nobody Bettelheim hired could take her place. Despite the best efforts of the other counselors, his everyday existence dragged on aching and empty, a vast boredom punctuated by bursts of anger.

Deliverance came, but not as a sudden revelation; rather, it followed from the milieu's founding principle as a good place to grow. Having lost the beloved adult who nurtured his inner growth, Wyatt resolved at last to become more grown-up on his own. In the model of the milieu, this meant that he could help himself by helping someone else, as counselors did, within the immediate but gradual process of protecting a child and fostering commonsense attitudes.

After Diana left, Wyatt had been moved to a group of older boys, a group that changed over the years. At seventeen, he was the oldest in it, and he became aware of two subtle but striking differences in his personal milieu: first, that the younger boys naturally looked to him for guidance; and second, that he wanted to help them. He knew that no matter how experienced in the ways of the School an older student was, he could not take the place of a counselor, because he did not have the authority of an adult, nor did he know the outside world as an adult did. However, Wyatt felt he could be useful.

"Because the School was really set up for younger children, helping the younger ones showed that you could change what had happened, that there could be a more hopeful future, and this makes you feel worthwhile."

At seventeen Wyatt grew fond of a new boy in the group, nine-year-old Timothy.* It took real effort for Wyatt to be with him, because Timothy lived in constant terror. He imagined committing hostile acts, and since he could not tell his actions from his fantasies, he feared revenge at all times and from any quarter. To defend himself, he attacked others without warning and for no apparent reason. Wyatt tried to reassure him, but the boy still saw danger on all sides.

Despite his unpredictable hostility, Timothy endeared himself by declaring all his feelings so openly that it was sometimes funny. For instance, if he walked into the dining room and saw frankfurters on the menu, he screamed at the top of his lungs, "Fried dicks for lunch today!"

After some months during which Wyatt rarely let his guard down, he began to succeed in calming Timothy. One day they had just left the dining room when Timothy suddenly grabbed Wyatt's arm and jammed his elbow against a brick wall. A sharp pain ran up Wyatt's arm, and he yelled, "Cut it out!"

He looked up to see Bettelheim bearing down on them, eyes blazing, a furious expression on his face. Bettelheim may have smelled trouble before the boys left the dining room, but probably he heard the commotion in the hall and rushed out. He said in a sharp voice, "What do you expect Timothy to cut out and with what do you expect him to cut it?" Then he turned abruptly and went back into the dining room, leaving Wyatt to make sense of his words.

Bettelheim was teaching Wyatt, and he did so in his preferred mode, with a pointed and provocative question that explained nothing, contained everything, and cast a dazzling light on a motive or moment. He knew what "Cut it out!" would mean to Timothy, and he had intervened, doing so as much for Wyatt as for Timothy. In a flash, Wyatt saw the mistake he had just made. "I thought, 'Damn! He's right again! How could I have been so stupid?' "

Wyatt understood that Bettelheim did not object to his cry of protest, which was justified, but to his terrible choice of words. Everyone knew that Timothy's mother had lost her finger in an accident and that Timothy somehow took it as his fault. He expected retribution and dreaded that someone would cut off his penis. This was always on his mind. Wyatt's "Cut it out!" was the worst possible choice of words and sent Timothy into a screaming panic.

In fact, Wyatt did not discuss the episode with Bettelheim later, because he felt he understood the question and needed no further guidance. Bettelheim had intervened to defuse a problem and to protect both Timothy and Wyatt, as well as to give Wyatt a five-second "lesson," which he did irritably and with the utmost economy. His words scored with Wyatt, and his success in this little moment coincided with his enduring object, a good atmosphere in the School, which he never stopped monitoring.

Getting insight to blossom inside a student's mind was the heart of Bettelheim's teaching method. When Wyatt saw what was wrong with his words he was doing exactly what Bettelheim wanted; he had been prompted to think for himself, the commonsense goal of all teaching. Imparting knowledge in a formal way, though sometimes unavoidable, brought shallow results in a clinical situation. Bettelheim wanted those learning from him to reach answers through the working of their own minds and not because they were *told* by an authority. Only in this way could an insight have the force of revelation. In the unforeseeable crises of life, authority lies within our head and heart, where much is decided on the spur of the moment, with scant information and little chance to weigh alternatives. On the other hand, if Wyatt had not understood, he could have asked Bettelheim what he meant. Bettelheim could assume Wyatt would speak up if need be, because Bettelheim's teaching style was to explore the many possible meanings of a single act and to draw a detailed picture of the defensive environment the child had woven around himself. But this was not necessary here. The sharpness and severity of Bettelheim's voice clinched the lesson and left Wyatt with an impression of that moment so clear-cut that he was able to analyze the various levels of Bettelheim's one-sentence intervention decades later in the article he sent me.

WYATT spoke of another instance of Bettelheim making a lesson out of a situation with some older children and a younger one. "I remember seeing Dr. B. with a girls' group one day. These were older girls, and a smaller girl of five or so who was very noisy and really crazy had been placed in the dorm. One afternoon she came over and climbed into the lap of an older girl, which was really unheard-of, because the first rule you learned was that kids couldn't touch each other. You had to respect everybody and their privacy and space. But this little girl started climbing all over the older girls. So one of them complained to Bruno that she didn't want to take care of this five-year-old, that it wasn't fair. Obviously, she expected Bruno to agree with her—but he didn't!

"He turned to the group and said, 'How in the world are you girls ever going to learn to be mothers unless you have some experience in taking care of somebody who needs you?' It was a real lesson. Implicitly, he was telling them that motherhood isn't some magical ideal, that it may stir up angry feelings, that a mother can resent taking care of her own kids. This helped the little girl, but Dr. B. was making the point for the older girls even more. He could usually find an exception to a rule when he saw that somebody needed it. The School as a whole was dedicated to the individual, and if a person needed something, Bruno would bend every rule he knew to make it happen."

Everyone in the School understood the rule about not touching, which the youngest girl had broken. "We all welcomed the rule, and only the sickest and craziest kids would actually hit somebody. And if they did, even they would feel bad about it afterward. Of course, if one kid punched another—and this almost never happened—he'd usually get slapped by Dr. B. Not always, but he didn't shrink from taking that role, keeping order."

WYATT said (as did several counselors) that Bettelheim seemed to see his role as shaking up children unexpectedly.

"He wanted to shock kids into looking to the consequences of their actions. One time when I was about eleven he punished me for something, and in that instance I just knew he was totally wrong. The punishment wasn't so much for what I'd done—it was my arrogance, my nastiness, my extreme isolation that made him angry. I had been at the

School maybe three years, and he suddenly made a big to-do about something and slapped me. I was convinced that I was right and he was wrong, that he was being unfair. On the facts of the case I was probably right, but looking back now, twenty-five years later, I'm not so sure. He used his intuition about me and just went ahead.

"Sometimes he said, 'Do you need a beating?' in a perfunctory way, as if he didn't think what you'd done was so terrible but that he had to say something to keep the staff happy. Once we were laughing about a scene in a movie, and I used the word 'titties,' which all the other kids thought was funny. But the counselor must have complained because Dr. B. came up to me and said, 'Vell, do you need a beating?' And I said, 'No,' and he said, 'Fine! Then behave yourself!' and walked out. The staff used him as the 'Big Bad Wolf,' and he knew it."

Wyatt and others liked to imitate Bettelheim making rounds, and they would walk with their hands behind their backs, leaning forward to make their shoes squeak on the floor like Bettelheim's rubber soles. "We'd come pacing into the dorm and turn in a circle in the middle of the room, then walk up to one kid and say, 'Vell, how iss everybody? Iss everybody all rrright? Okay, good night,' and walk out. 'Vell, do you need a beating?' became a joke phrase, but getting slapped was no joke."

It puzzled Wyatt at times when Bettelheim did not get angry about misbehavior. "One day I found some empty ice-cream cartons, and we started to play with them. The School served tons of ice cream for the holidays, and it came in big ten-gallon cardboard cartons. So we began to pretend we were building a chemical-waste factory. After a while, I had this huge container brimming over with a weird liquid mixture, and I picked it up to carry it to the bathroom and dump it down the drain, when suddenly the cardboard bottom fell out, *splat!* Paint and glue and god knows what went pouring out over the dorm floor and rug. It was a catastrophe, and it took forever to clean up the mess. I was utterly terrified that Dr. B. would walk in and explode at me when he saw an inch-deep layer of muck. But he didn't. Later, at the dinner table, when someone told him, he actually laughed and thought it was all very funny. So you see, I put somebody down, and he smacks me; but I spill ten gallons of gunk, and he laughs. It didn't quite make sense back then, but it does now."

WYATT also talked about the therapy sessions, and he said that Margaret Carey grew to be as important to him as Diana. Margaret was totally on his side, so much so that some matters she heard in a session she held in confidence rather than telling everything to Bettelheim in dictation. (Bettelheim doubtless realized this but made allowances in order to keep her—another example of bending rules for individuals.)

In sessions the child played with a dollhouse, with dolls and other toys, and what he felt about a parent but couldn't say often came out as a feeling about a doll or a stuffed animal. "The emotion's source would be disguised," Wyatt said, "or otherwise the child couldn't express it. That kind of play made everything safe, but the therapist needed the sensitivity to understand what was going on inside you and to encourage letting things out that were hard for you to cope with."

WYATT had serious doubts about telling one incident he recalled, because so much has been made of Bettelheim slapping or hitting some children at the School. "I was only a little kid when it happened and naturally interpreted it in the worst way. Personally, it shows me once again that I can understand something later in life that I probably misinterpreted completely at the time. Of course, I still have doubts."

When Wyatt was about eleven, there was an extremely disturbed teenaged boy at the School. "Dr. B. really had battles with this kid, hitting and screaming at him, and it terrified me. We would hear the boy yelling out in the hall at night, and this went on for several weeks. I don't know the circumstances, but this child could put himself into a kind of epileptic trance. He would turn his face up to the ceiling, and he'd be out of it. One night I happened to catch a glimpse of them together—the kid had dropped to the floor, he was curled up, shielding himself, and Dr. B. kicked him. The violence was terrifying, but not because of the kick. Dr. B.'s force of personality, the emotional violence, was overwhelming. Even now I'm not sure I've got the incident in perspective. Maybe he was acting out his frustration that the School was failing, or maybe he was trying to knock some sense into this kid—fighting *for* the kid by kicking him, desperate to keep him out of an institution. But he lost. A few weeks later this child had to be sent away."

I SHOWED my account of this incident to someone not connected with the Orthogenic School but whose instincts about children I have come to trust. This person made two comments: first, that a child can scream bloody murder when almost nothing is actually happening and that if the boy had anticipated a fight with Bettelheim, he might have begun screaming simply out of panic. The second point was that if an adult—a counselor—had witnessed the scene, she might have seen something that the eleven-year-old Wyatt would not have noticed or understood because of his own fears.

Perhaps the most deeply disturbing thought to any child in the School would have been that Bettelheim could not control himself. This was more than a physical threat: it would have been a threat to the children's integration. If their ultimate authority could not control himself, how could they learn self-control? Since Bettelheim surely recognized this, I doubt he reacted solely out of frustration or let his feelings run away with him. His feelings were genuine and spontaneous, but they ran in the direction he wanted them to go.

I ASKED Wyatt to tell me a little more of how hitting might help a disturbed child, and he gave me an example from his own experience. "When I was about eighteen, I was still very involved in caring for Timothy. One day he threw a tantrum and kicked me in the testicles, and I knew instantly that I had to smack him.

"It took no brains at all to realize, 'Okay, he's got to get punished for this *right now*, because if he isn't, he's going to keep on until he really hurts himself or somebody else.' He would act out until somebody stopped him, and he'd feel worse about himself each time he did it successfully. More of a monster. Somebody had to retaliate for his own good."

Bettelheim had left the School by the time of this incident, or he would have been called in to deal with Timothy. The counselor tried to block Wyatt from hitting the boy, but he darted around her and slapped Timothy. "In this case, she couldn't understand intuitively what had to be done. I did, and I acted on it. I didn't have time to sit down and explain it to her; it had to be dealt with at once. Maybe Dr. B. felt the same way about the child he kicked: if he didn't try to change the kid's course, nobody would. Dr. B. could live with failure, but he couldn't live with not trying."

Wyatt called Timothy's problems "monumental." Once, in the middle of the night, the boy urinated on another boy's head, and Wyatt hit Timothy immediately because he didn't want to go to bed every night worrying it might happen again.

"Another thing: we had black cooks and maids who looked after us with real devotion, and if you were rude to one of them, you could get into serious trouble, because Dr. B. wouldn't tolerate it. Some of the craziest kids might do this, like Timothy, who was from the South. When he started talking about 'niggers,' the rest of us just wanted to fade into the wallpaper. The maids didn't like it but didn't actually seem bothered, because they understood who the slur was coming from. And Timothy was so likable in his own way that I guess they were prepared to accept it as part of his acting out.

"Demeaning the cooks and maids almost never happened—the consequences were too clear. Besides, we really liked them, and they knew it. They knew they were making a contribution, especially the cooks. Dr. B. always said that the successful kids who left the School invariably asked to see the cooks when they came back for a visit. The place wouldn't have worked without good food and plenty of it. Nobody was ever denied food as a punishment, that was another major rule."

WYATT thought most children at the School were both sensitive and highly intelligent, with a streak of sanity that could be built on, and with special talents. "Once, my group had the youngest child in the School at that time, and I liked him, though he was a fusser. He complained constantly, nothing was right. But at six this kid was a perfect speller. Somebody would say, 'Hey, how do you spell such-and-such?' and he'd look up from across the room and spell it. Or if you'd hit a note on your xylophone and say, 'What note is this?' he'd call back the note, because he had perfect pitch. He was a brilliant and sensitive kid, and there were many nights I got up to help him find his cuddle blanket or some such. But I get very angry when I think about what happened to him after Dr. B. left, which was both the fault of the School and his parents. He's doing all right now, but he had to suffer a lot because mistakes were made, and that makes me sad and angry when I think about it.

"A brand-new counselor couldn't possibly know what I knew after ten years. Older and more experienced children, those who were making it, really helped keep the roof on. Dr. B. didn't just permit this, he encouraged it. He always looked for the strengths people had, encouraging them to try things. He wasn't infallible, but he didn't agonize when he was wrong. If he made a mistake, he made a mistake, and his attitude was, 'Let's get on with it.' "

As for acknowledging mistakes, Wyatt said that Bettelheim would do this in a general way but that it was difficult to get him to acknowledge a specific mistake. "If staffers thought that Dr. B. had clearly overstepped the mark, and if they really argued their case, then he'd usually back off. Not necessarily because he thought he was wrong, but because he knew that if someone felt so strongly about an issue as to fight with him, then that feeling was coming from a very deep source, and he wouldn't trample on it."

Diana noted that as a staff member she could see some things that Wyatt didn't. "Once Dr. B. felt you were committed and proven, he would ask your opinion and simply follow it in regard to the children, because you knew them more closely than he did. He wanted things to work through mutual respect and partnership, not just through his authority."

Nevertheless, to Wyatt the manner in which Bettelheim ran the School owed more to the Old Testament than the New. "He was stern and unrelenting, like the God of Moses, and while he made sure there was justice and fairness in the School, he definitely didn't take the New Testament line of *We'll forgive you and love you*, and all that. I guess he felt we would be better off if we learned to live by certain rules and made them our own, than if we had to go around looking for someone to let us off the hook."

As a child, Wyatt did not tell his parents about being hit, for reasons that still seem sound to him. He knew they had made sacrifices to put him in the School, and he didn't want to upset or disappoint them. Also, he feared they would take him out, and despite his unhappiness at the School he didn't want to leave. "Yes, the School controlled you, but I felt that *I* was gradually getting control over my life, and I didn't want to give that up."

IN HIS early teens, Wyatt sometimes tended the Japanese goldfish in the pool in the Orthogenic School's courtyard. "They were the big ones, the koi bred for the Japanese imperial ponds to be especially beautiful when you look down at them. I enjoyed them a lot, feeding them and so on. One day I noticed a teenager, an older kid not from the School, standing beside the pool doing something, so I went over to see what was going on."

Wyatt introduced himself and found he was talking to Bettelheim's son, Eric. "This was very surprising," he said. Bettelheim's strict rule that his family life was off-limits to the children at the School had a purpose.

Counselors and teachers met Trude and the Bettelheim children at the Christmas Eve party in their home a few blocks away, but Bruno saw serious negative possibilities if he let the students come into his private life: among other things, it would provide them with material for fantasies about him as a real father.

"Eric had come to treat the fish for ich [a disease]. He started explaining to me how to take care of fish like these. Since he was a few years older and knew a lot about them, the conversation fascinated me."

The medicine for ich usually takes one dose a day for at least a week, and so Wyatt saw Eric several times that week and occasionally in the weeks that followed, as he came back to tend the fish. However, Wyatt's clearest memory was of the first day, when Bettelheim came out of his office and looked at them while they were talking beside the pool.

"I thought he was going to come over to us, but he just looked for a moment and then went back inside."

WHEN WYATT (and the School) decided he was ready to go to a high school, the University of Chicago Laboratory School was the obvious choice.[1] He could walk to the building, and it was known as one of the best high schools in the country. Wyatt agonized over this first venture into the outside world; he was sure he could handle the studies but worried about handling himself when his classmates learned he was from the Orthogenic School. Nevertheless, he went, and it worked: he lived in the School, walked to classes every day, kept a high grade average for two years, and even audited some of Bettelheim's lectures. Wyatt's separation from the School took place over a period of several years, advancing cautiously with Margaret Carey's continued support. As he grew within himself, the milieu became a "warm bed," not an analogue or a model for the real world. Like all students, he had to leave in order to face the risks of ordinary life and its new levels of accountability.

"The truth was, you left the School and joined the human condition. That was *it*. And Dr. B.'s method always pointed toward accepting the human condition. When students didn't accept themselves and like themselves for what they were, then there was no arguing with him. He was totally unyielding. To him that point outweighed everything else, and he never wavered on it. You had to accept yourself. But he took it to unbelievable lengths, like when I battled him over deodorant. I was an adolescent, and adolescents worry about how they smell, so one day I brought some deodorant back to my room. However, Dr. B. saw it and didn't want me to use it. He simply said, 'I don't think you smell,' and he insisted on taking it away. I resented this and I just got some and hid it.

"I remember, too, he blew up when I asked him about going to Harvard or Yale. He yelled at me—probably he didn't want me getting self-validation from the outside; it had to come from within. Of course, after I went to Yale, he delighted in talking about one of the School's successes at Yale."

On the idea of external self-validation, Diana said, "This wasn't just Dr. B.'s preoccupation—this theme was especially relevant to Wyatt. So Bettelheim was responding to his sense of the child's values that he thought were off-balance and might not add to his inner strength."

ONE SATURDAY toward the end of his first year in the Lab School, Wyatt was walking across the campus, on his way back to the Orthogenic School. When he reached the Midway, Bettelheim happened to be standing there waiting to cross. Bettelheim had started his retirement but was coming back for lectures and to consult at the School. The traffic light changed, and as the two walked together, Bettelheim asked casually, "So, how are things?"

Wyatt had been upset all day for no particular reason and began telling Bettelheim that he was depressed. "I had started to emerge into the world after spending eleven years in the Orthogenic School, and I was frightened. When we reached the front of the School, Dr. B. unlocked the door, and as we walked into the foyer together and stood outside his office, he said, 'Tell me, how are your grades?' 'Oh, they're pretty good,' I said. And he asked, 'What's pretty good?' He always wanted to know everything exactly. So I said, 'Well—straight A's.' And he said, 'Too bad.' His remark confused me, so I said, 'Too bad? What do you mean?' And he said, 'Well, if you had bad grades, at least you'd know what you're feeling upset about. But with straight A's it's much more difficult to know what your problem is.' And with that he turned and walked into his office.

"I've thought about this from time to time, and even now I'm still not sure of everything he was trying to tell me, because often there were several layers of meaning in what he said."

In my view, Bettelheim meant his remark to be provocative but not too baffling. It's a fact that we have moods and can't always give a satisfactory account of them, even to ourselves. This is a stubborn reality of the human condition, and Wyatt's mood at that moment had to be fathomed, if at all, by himself. A passing remark, one that seemed casual but was not, showed that Bettelheim would not help, that nobody would follow Wyatt out into the world and watch over him. He had grown stronger at the School, and now he had to carry the burden of individuality that all are born with.

Bettelheim had also offered Wyatt a large but simple truth, one that could last a lifetime: if you can't name the cause of your distress and thus begin to objectify it, then some conflict in your identity has screened itself off from you. At all costs, Wyatt now had to try to advance his self-knowledge as a precondition for earning the authentic self-esteem of an adult.

"More than anything else," Wyatt said, "Dr. B. was concerned with how I felt about myself, and on that point, he would never give an inch."

Bettelheim eschewed pro forma sympathy and so responded by leaving Wyatt with a little dilemma; this treated him respectfully by implying that he would have the wit to look for an answer, as well as the moral stamina to go on even if he didn't find it at once. Bettelheim underscored his point when he held back from intervening with more questions. Intervention would have meant that he felt Wyatt was still too much of a child to bear unhappy feelings. Restraint meant the opposite. Bettelheim knew, better than most, that sympathy at the wrong moment can mislead a young person and weaken his resolve to rely upon himself. Wyatt's academic performance showed a certain strength suggestive of inner resources, and so Bettelheim removed himself from the equation.

In the total therapeutic milieu, counselors gave children much love and care, whereas Bettelheim did not. He dared to declare that *love is not enough* and then show his caring in another way; he toughened the children by demanding strength. His manner carried conviction, the belief that they could find an inner unity, the morale, courage, character, and flexibility to survive.

When a counselor's undemanding love filtered past a child's defenses, the mutual feeling that grew up between them could slowly erode the child's rocklike attitude that denied the possibility of love and caring; and when the moment came for the child to face Bettelheim in all his furious authority, it took the tenuous resilience of self-love to do so, just as it would take inner strength later in life to face demoralizing setbacks and the despair aroused by failure and loss. Even if a child had not felt Bettelheim's wrath directly, he saw it happening to others, feared it, and lived with its possibility. A child first needed to know a steady love in order to *want* to live, to grow, to take a place in the world; but he needed steady strength to survive in the struggles ahead, where love alone was not the answer.

Bettelheim had survived the demoralizing milieu of the camps by tending to his inner life. He came to see that what happens inside us can be at least as painful and destructive, if not more so, than what happens externally, and that both inner and outer realities make up the human condition. The School milieu was the large outer envelope of loving care that let a child begin at last to look at the workings of his own personality and thus grow stronger. For his part, Bettelheim modeled strength; he had been humiliated repeatedly for almost a year, and he knew that only inner strength can stand up to the kind of humiliation that is always possible in our imperfect world.

Counselors, teachers, cooks, and housekeepers embodied the pleasure principle at the School, and Bettelheim became the reality principle. We use both to survive in life, because reality is not always pleasurable, and our drive for pleasure is not always realistic. Bettelheim's overarching idea in structuring and running the School was to balance the demands and pressures of Freud's Eros and Thanatos, since he believed that only through such balance could the student hope to find satisfaction and build an autonomous life.

Bettelheim's insight owed much both to Goethe and to Freud, but for me the marvel is his strength of purpose in the School's slow creation through the interplay of the pleasure principle and the reality principle. I can only hope that others see, as I do, this complex achievement as a contribution to our understanding of how children — especially troubled children — may best be cared for and educated to find their own best selves.

CHAPTER 24

The Last Years at the School

BETTELHEIM'S chief job every day was to teach and train his staff, and his sensitivity never let down, even toward the end of his tenure, at a time when the School was mature and when he knew he had to pass his job on to the next generation.

Episodes in the careers of several workers in the 1960s show how Bettelheim taught personally to benefit staff, students, and School. Steve Herczeg, a counselor, told me of a surprising incident when he became angry at Bettelheim over a boy with poor bodily coordination who "could barely walk without stumbling over his own feet." One day in the gymnasium the boy threw a ball that ricocheted off two walls, then hit another child in the head.

"When something like this happened, we'd tell Dr. B. the next time he made rounds, so I told him, and he went over to the boy and gave him absolute hell for hitting the other boy. He said he knew that this boy knew what he was doing and that he meant to do it. I was furious, because the boy didn't have the coordination to carry out a sophisticated shot like that. When we had tea that night, about eleven o'clock, I asked Dr. B. why he had given the boy a hard time. He said, 'Well, the boy wanted to do it, that's why,' and I told him I disagreed. I was very vehement and said it was impossible, and Bruno said, 'Well, that's the way it is. Eventually he will tell you.' "

Steve knew the boy much better than Bettelheim did and knew that the idea was absurd. However, Steve also saw the boy in therapy, and a few days later the teenager surprised him. "He told me he had been thinking, 'What if I threw the ball and it hit this part of the wall, would it ricochet off the other wall and hit the kid?' And he figured out, yes, it would. So I told Dr. B. he was right, and he said, 'Yes, I told you so.' He always liked to be right, but he *really* enjoyed being right on that one.

"It didn't matter how disturbed the person was, he had to be held accountable, and not just to equalize things by punishment or retribution. It's a matter of respecting a person enough to hold him responsible. That was Bettelheim's principle of respect, and I've held on to it. If you don't focus on a disturbed child's responsibility, then he has less chance to learn to take responsibility for his actions, and even less chance to know who he is."

In telling this story, Steve's point was also to show how firmly Bruno held to his rule that if a person did something, he had a reason and was responsible. For me, the story shows Bettelheim in action, teaching by a timely intervention, which an incredulous counselor was forced to live with and resolve.

Steve also commented on the evolving effect of giving a child love and earning his trust. "The kids I worked with had very little separation, or 'individuation,' to use Margaret Mahler's term. First you had to merge with the kid's sanity—for lack of a better word—and after you became melded together with him, the trust grew. You trusted the child, you trusted your impulses, the child trusted you, so that the better you knew yourself, the better you got to know the child."

One boy in Steve's group wore a big plastic button that said DO NOT DISTURB. He was angry all the time, locked in a rigid personality—"and he had a lot of murderous fantasies. When we sat around the table for snacks or to play games, he was always tapping his finger, and after some weeks— after I got to like him—it occurred to me that the finger-tapping expressed his desire to kill me. When we finally began talking about that feeling, my insight proved to be right on the money, and after a while the tapping subsided. By the way, this kid turned out very well indeed."

Steve's background was unusual for a counselor, but Bettelheim obviously came to feel that he had long-range potential at the School. As a brawny teenager Steve had worked on the Chicago docks, then got a football scholarship to a small college, where he became a strong player because he enjoyed the physical violence of football. After college, he took a series of jobs in the mental-health field, ultimately as director of athletic programs for adolescents at a major state hospital. Unhappily married but hoping to make a better career for himself, he enrolled at the University of Chicago for a Ph.D. and applied for a job at the School.

He showed up an hour late for his interview, and of course Bettelheim's first question was, "Why are you late?" Steve mentioned the heavy traffic, which was partly true, but he also admitted that he doubted he could hold a job and study for a degree at the same time. Bettelheim's probing led Steve to reveal the state of his marriage, and it took several interviews before he was hired as a "research assistant," with his salary drawn from a research grant even though he was actually a counselor.

Steve believed he had a below-average intellect, which his grades at college seemed to confirm. "I was truly repressed, and to play football violently the way I did, I had to restrict my sensitivity and thought processes. I didn't think about what I was doing on the football field, I just had to do it, and I guess Dr. B. used his forcefulness to get me to think about it. He intimidated me, because I saw that he knew me better than anyone I'd ever met. He knew my strengths, my weaknesses, and I felt vulnerable around him, but he made me use my intellect, which is the best thing that could have happened."

Steve pursued the Ph.D., although still so unsure of himself that he got written excuses from the preliminary exams, which he planned to use in case he failed. When he passed, he ran into Bettelheim's office in great excitement and said, "I passed my prelims!" Bettelheim looked up and said, "Well, what did you expect? Now, I'm doing something, get out of here and leave me alone."

"He treated it as a matter of fact," Steve said, "as if he expected me to pass. He was gruff, but in a nice way he was showing his confidence in me."

Soon after he came to the School, Steve realized he wanted a divorce, and for a time he treated the place "like a monastery" by withdrawing from everything else and throwing himself into his work with a group of boys. In due course he noticed a young counselor named Joan Deutsch, who had started at the School three years earlier than himself, and after Steve's divorce they became interested in each other. They married while still at the School, and I interviewed them together. Like several counselors, Joan had been drawn to the work by Bettelheim's books. She exchanged several letters with him, but when she came to Chicago for an interview he was away in Israel, having left Jacqui Seevak (by now assistant principal) in charge. Instead of an interview, she had three days of intense work, and despite disturbingly mixed feelings, she took the job.

Some weeks later Bettelheim came back, and Joan got into a serious argument with him almost at once. He insisted that she move into the School, where she would have to share a room. Needing privacy, she stood her ground, and he gave way when he saw how strongly she felt.

Later, she moved into the School, but only after she could have her own room. I asked Steve why Bruno had given in to a stubborn newcomer hired in his absence, and Steve said, "Dr. B. was an exceedingly good judge of people, and I believe he looked for those with a core resilient enough to withstand what you find in self-examination. I saw children grow and become healthier as a reflection of growth their counselors made."

DURING Joan's first year, Karen Zelan left the School, and Joan worked with Karen's group. It was a rocky transition, she said, because Karen had cared for everyone so long and so superbly. The girls went into shock at Karen's loss, and one of them attacked Joan's co-counselor. Still in her first year (she was only twenty-two), Joan froze — "I couldn't react because I denied the violence of it, and later when I thought about what my non-reaction meant, it shattered me."

The co-counselor handled the incident well, as did the girl, but Joan came to realize that she could not integrate the experience and get past it. She shrank from what she might find if she looked into herself. She interpreted the incident several times in staff meetings, where Bettelheim and others gave friendly support. Toward the end of her first year, she began to recognize deep contradictions in her attitudes, and Bettelheim suggested she take time off to make up her mind about staying at the School.

For the next three weeks Joan stopped being a participant-observer, as all counselors were, and became simply an observer—mainly of herself. She had never admitted to having problems, believing herself "sunshiny and nice," able to listen to everyone else's troubles. Now, she could not go on forcing sympathies she did not feel; she had to test her inner strength, the capacity to deal with her impasses. When she finally felt more sure of herself, she told Bettelheim, who reassigned her to a group of boys. "It took me another year before I felt I had the job under control," she said, "but those three weeks to think quietly were very important to me."

Bettelheim had given Joan a time-out because he valued her and saw she had run up against a major resistance. Her decision did not have to be rushed; it merited careful study by one who knew the work but needed to know the depths of her commitment, which she could see more clearly only if not assailed by the daily tensions of her job. She might reject the School decisively, or she could make a well-informed commitment of the kind most valuable to him, to the children, and to herself. Impulse and heart had brought Joan to the School, and now her head found reasons for knowing her heart was right.

SOME YEARS later, after Bettelheim retired and Bert Cohler was named director, Steve became assistant director for a time. Eventually he had a falling-out with Cohler and was fired. By that point he and Joan had married, and both left the School at about the same time.

"For a while I was at home having children," Joan said, "and then I wanted to go back to work when I was around forty." She was surprised to find that her experience at the School meant nothing in the job market, and so she took a social-work degree.

"In social work, the person who does the casework with children is low man on the totem pole. It's not even considered a therapeutic relationship," she said. "In Bettelheim's model, the counselor was the most important person in the child's life. I couldn't get used to having a supervisor, the way it's done in regular social work. All of a sudden I was being told what to do, which is not the way I had learned it with Dr. B."

She found this kind of teaching offensive and demeaning. "It's one of the things wrong with the social-work model. Dr. B. didn't do it that way at all. He got you to analyze yourself, which isn't demeaning. Of course, you find things in yourself that you don't like, but you could live with the way he did it. It's impossible when you're told, 'This is what you're doing and this is what you mean.' He didn't do that. By the time I came to the School, in 1964, he had so much confidence in what he was doing that he didn't keep a tight rein on everybody, telling people how to do things step by step, which is what you find in institutions."

When I interviewed Joan, she had worked in one unhappy job—her first after going back into professional life. Luckily, this experience did not set a pattern: she soon found an organization where the supervisor was more in sympathy with her approach to children. In the last fourteen years she has had only two jobs, and, she said, "My supervisors have been wonderful, giving me the freedom to use all I learned from Dr. B. and at social-work school."

AT THE time I saw the Herczegs, Steve worked in private practice and also taught courses at Northwestern University Medical School. He always offered a course in milieu therapy, but students were not interested. "As for my course on adolescent development in the life cycle, I use readings from Blos, Winnicott, Mahler, Freud, Aichhorn, and Bettelheim. But the Ph.D. students I work with just don't know about Bettelheim, and it bothers me that the School as he ran it isn't seen for the remarkable place it was."

Steve happened to be on hand when Anna Freud toured the School and gave Bettelheim her opinion about it in 1966. "She said something like, 'If my father had had a picture of what he wanted for disturbed children, this would be it.' I don't know whether that's true, but that's what she said. I could see Bruno was pleased, but he didn't make anything of it later."

I asked Joan why she thought Bettelheim had so little acceptance among psychologists. "I believe the reason is that he really does put the kids first, and I don't think that's true of many people in our profession, sad to say. Secondly, he always taught that there's not much difference between the person who is psychotic and ourselves. A lot of psychologists will say that, but they don't really believe it. Actually, he rarely used the word *psychotic*—he talked about people who were disturbed. Other psychologists may *say* we're all basically alike, but Dr. B. practiced it."

Steve added, "Sometimes he would handle a situation wrong, but he believed he was right, so it worked out eventually. If the child feels you really believe you're right, he can survive your mistakes. Being sincere has a value all its own for a disturbed child."

CHAPTER 25

The Personal Teacher

BETTELHEIM'S forcefulness as a teacher came from the intensity of his approach to each staffer, but some who knew him believed that his narrow focus was also a weakness. He had a practical reason for this, since only by dealing with a counselor as troubles arose could he help clarify work problems and emotional impasses.

"His teaching was very much devoted to the personal development of the staff," Bertram Cohler said. "He would argue that personal education is the highest form of teaching, but affective education like that doesn't help people enough. It doesn't encourage mastering and understanding."

Cohler was unique at the School in that he arrived in 1950 as an eleven-year-old disturbed child, lived there until he left for college, then returned in 1969 as codirector when Bettelheim was planning, reluctantly, to retire. For the next three years Cohler was in charge, while Bettelheim traveled more than usual and took a sabbatical year in California. Ultimately Bettelheim could not let go, and in 1972 Cohler resigned; in the mid-1990s he returned as director for two years.

I interviewed him after his first stint running the School but before his second; we were in his psychoanalytic office on the ground floor of a small building on the Hyde Park campus. The casual air of his office put me at ease, no doubt in the same way it reassured the children he saw in treatment. I noticed stuffed animals scattered about, as well as a rag doll, a dollhouse, and a wooden boat with a loading crane that really worked. Wherever a child might look, his eye would fall on an object that invited play: toys lying on tables and chairs, on the sofa, on shelves, window ledges, and Bert's desk. Yet the room felt neither "arranged" nor disorderly; rather, it seemed both casual and interesting.

Before I met him, I took it for granted that Bert would not wish to go into detail about his troubled emotions or his years as a student, and in fact he said so when we were about to start taping. Nevertheless, toward the middle of the interview some impulse overcame my conscious intent, and I suddenly asked why he was sent to the School. "Because I was an obnoxious kid," he said, "and everybody couldn't stand me."

How was he obnoxious? "Well, I kicked my gym teacher in the balls," he said with a slight smile. His answer startled me; my impression of him up to that point (we'd had lunch together) was of a man with a strong personality but dominated by and immersed in intellectual concerns. I reacted by saying that he must have had a good reason to kick the teacher.

"For reasons that were good to me, but you can't go around kicking your teachers. From the time I was a kid at the School," he said, redirecting the conversation, "I was determined to be a psychoanalyst when I grew up." The fascination of the School had taken over, and he learned mostly from the staff rather than from Bettelheim.

"Bruno would make cursory rounds and keep us under control—he was law and order—but the excitement for me came from the staff and from trying to figure out what was going on."

When Bert commented on Bruno's lack of theory in his personal teaching, I said that in a clinical context he always guarded against looking at a child theoretically, which keeps the therapist from entering into the child's world. Bert agreed and added, "The irony is that Bruno was so theoretical himself. I think *Freud and Man's Soul* is a very important book. But Bruno, who had this ambivalence about theory, more than anybody else translated theory into practice.

"But he did have a funny attitude toward theory. One time I read the Rapaport seminars in the School's library and saw what Bruno did, his textual exegesis to Rapaport's work. Rapaport was one of the major figures in American psychoanalysis and along with Heinz Hartmann one of the leading ego-psychologists of the twentieth century. Bruno had annotated the seminars Rapaport gave at Yale, and his comments were just awesome. I mean, Bettelheim was easily Rapaport's master in psychoanalytic theory. He had read every page of those twenty-four volumes of Freud and could tell you what Freud said about a particular subject at a particular time."[1]

Bert believes that Bettelheim's contributions to American intellectual life have not been appreciated—vagina envy, for instance, and his influence in anthropology and education, including the "subjective curriculum." I had not noticed the term in Bettelheim's writings, so I asked Bert to explain.

"The notion is that the child is tracking in his own mind his subjective response to what's being taught him, the objective curriculum. The curriculum takes on a personal meaning for the child, and teaching has to attend to that meaning. I remember the staff meeting about a girl who was having trouble learning the multiplication tables, especially the number eight. So Bruno pointed out that 'eight' is also 'ate.' Then everybody understood that her fantasies about swallowing people up—this was a somewhat obese girl—were connected in a way that made it hard for her to learn the curriculum."

Bert said that when he took over the School, he found the staffers unable to think for themselves. "Counselors would tell me what they thought Bruno would do in a given situation, and I would say, 'Why do you think Dr. B. would have done it that way?' They didn't know, but they could parrot what he did."

I said I had gotten a different story from several former counselors, like Fae Tyroler, Gayle Janowitz, and Kathy Lubin, all of whom said Bruno had forced them to think about how to deal with the children.

"I think that was true in the earlier days," Bert said, "and also true with those particular people"—but when he returned to the School in the fall of 1969, it seemed very different to him. "It's an irony that this man who was probably the leading Freud scholar of our times should have so actively discouraged scholarship among his coworkers. With rare exceptions—and Karen and Jacqui are exceptions—counselors ended up as housewives or at most minor figures in some child-care institution rather than carrying forth the School's tradition of leadership in residential treatment.

"Relatively few out of the several hundred who were there have taken positions of leadership in child care or become educators, significant educators, in their own right, which is strange considering his own personal magnetism and clarity, and I think it's because people gained from him at the School mostly in terms of their personal education."

MUCH LATER in my thinking about Bettelheim as I worked on this book, I realized that if he had allowed any of his ambitions, and he certainly had them, to supplant the children as a motive, if he had looked beyond them to personal celebrity, to his influence on residential treatment, to taking on disciples (as Freud had done) whom he expected to become missionaries for his methods, then the atmosphere and purpose of the milieu would have changed, to the detriment of the children. They would not have been there for themselves—the promise of the milieu—but for his ambitions.

If his attention to the children in the here and now, through the methods of the School, could help them learn and grow, then that was enough; and if the example of the School (as described in his books) showed that these methods worked, then *that* was enough. Perhaps his self-circumscribed horizon lessened his worldly significance as an educator, but it left him with clarity about the children in his care.

Bettelheim might have sought foundation money to create a movement, disciples and all, but this would have taken his attention into another sphere and put the School on a different path. This path might have turned him into a kind of Maria Montessori with psychoanalytic insights, but what would it have done for the children already in the School?

His personal teaching style was a shining facet of his clarity insofar as he induced staffers to respond more deeply to themselves and more genuinely to the children. After all, he said and believed that improvement would come only within a personal relationship. He could protect the milieu and teach the staff, but a counselor had to enjoy, understand, and respect her youngsters to work toward better feelings and, eventually, their strength. That was the whole point.

BRUNO came into Bert's office one day when Bert was working on a paper and said, "You'll never make it as the School's director if you spend your time writing."

"I said, 'Well, that's ludicrous. That's exactly how you made it as director.' I think he meant he was concerned I would spend too much time in the office and not enough out with the kids, which was really not a worry, I used to take them on outings and go swimming with them and such.

"But when I look at his work as a whole, the School seems the least interesting part. He had a singular genius for understanding children in institutions, but my argument is that just like Freud—Freud did not care about his patients— I mean, yes, of course, he cared about them, yes, he was a superb clinician, yes, he helped people, but Freud's heart was not just in helping people but in the theory of human nature, or wishes. Bettelheim, of course, he cared about children and wanted to make their lives better, but he had a larger agenda, a statement of man's relation to his world."

Although I had not worked out my thoughts at this point, I said that Bert's characterization of Bruno was so much at odds with my sense of him that I would ask him if he saw himself in this way. "Tell him that you and I talked about it," Bert said. "Feel free to tell him that and that I thought he had a singular genius and that he taught me some of it. I mean, I'm a better analyst for it—though my patients will sometimes say I don't understand them. Lots of times I *don't* understand them, but I would have been even worse off without the training both as a kid and as a staff member at the School."

While they were codirectors, Bettelheim several times emphasized to Bert that although the School was therapeutic, he conceived of it as a school rather than a children's psychiatric institution and that he saw himself in that setting as an educator rather than a psychoanalyst. As a summing up of the Bettelheim he knew, Bert said, "It's enough to say that he was a caring man who understood the inner lives of children. He had a way, a window into the soul; he would look at a kid and tell the kid what was wrong. That's genius, just sheer genius."

BY HIS personal teaching, I believe that Bettelheim held staffers steady in his orbit and drew them closer with the gravitational tug of a transference; but he did not become close to most of the children. When I first told him I wanted to interview teachers and counselors who had worked with him, he looked into his address book and suggested I call Betsy, whom I have mentioned earlier. He would not call former counselors himself, but if I asked Betsy to introduce me to others in the Chicago area, this would dispel their reluctance to talk to an outsider. Before meeting her, I didn't understand why Bruno had singled her out; in later conversations I saw that he trusted her deeply and felt a lasting attachment—feelings she reciprocated.

Bettelheim had hired Betsy as a teacher in 1964; she needed no orientation, because, like Bert Cohler, she had already lived at the School. Understandably, she would not talk about her disturbed childhood and her time as a student, although she did say that she had been a patient of Emmy Sylvester's before entering the School. On Karen Zelan's first day, in 1956, Betsy, by then an "old child," was among those who had given Karen a hard time for not knowing how to do anything. Later, Karen left Betsy in charge of the group when Elsie ran away.

Betsy worked at the School for ten years as a teacher and therapist and then worked elsewhere as a teacher. On a hot summer afternoon we sat in the living room of her home, a large brick house with plenty of lawn in a small Midwestern town. We talked, and she was the calm and careful center in a noisy scene, with half a dozen children (not all hers) running in and out of the house and up and down the stairs. Once, a child suddenly wailed outside because the bigger kids didn't want to play with him, and Betsy interrupted our conversation to go out and remedy the injustice. He was her youngest child, and a little while later he came inside happy and excited, to show her a lucky Popsicle stick he'd just found, and she admired it. Also, her mother called. I noticed Betsy's eyes and face as she responded to all these realities of family life, and I saw that she kept a firm fix on everyone in her world even while answering my questions about the world of the School—the world of her troubled past, where she had become, through the people and methods of the milieu, the person who would teach some children and mother others.

BETTELHEIM gave Betsy a class of six girls, ages six to eighteen; one was autistic. Despite Betsy's familiarity with the workings of the School, her days proved to be so hard that for a month she wondered how she could get up in the morning and make it to the job. She had "played around" for five years in college, and now the disturbed children exhausted and frightened her. It was July, so she spent most of the time outdoors, getting acquainted with the girls rather than attempting classroom work. One of the girls had been diagnosed as learning disabled. "She was also hyperanxious, and her parents thought she was hopeless. However, I got very close to her, and of course she started to learn." Like Bettelheim, Betsy saw "learning disabled" as a label, and if you ignored the label you'd find ways to help.

"The autistic girl would scream and scream and scream, and at first I couldn't control her. She was nine years old but only just developing language and basic skills, like reading and math. When she'd start to go wild, I'd calm her down by sitting next to her."

Betsy knew the girl had a reason for screaming at that moment, and working from this attitude she could at least start relating to her.

"When you're in charge of a group like mine, you made sure you never had your back to anyone. You can't let anybody drop off your radar. I learned to do this, and toward the end of my first year I was very proud of myself because I had rapport with everybody. The class became a cohesive group."

Just as she was feeling great, Bettelheim asked her to take in another child. "I almost shrieked. Why did he have to change my class when it was all under control? Of course, that's why he did it, and he brought in a hyperactive boy." Her classroom was being remodeled just then, and she was using the playroom with the piano—"Karen's piano, as a matter of fact." The boy had been given many medications to calm him down, but nothing worked. Bettelheim stopped all medication, as was his rule, and the boy kept jumping. He jumped over the couch, he jumped on the piano, he bounced around the room—and Betsy got exhausted all over again.

A week later Bettelheim and the staff interviewed an extremely withdrawn girl; Betsy went into the reception room and talked with her for a few minutes. At the staff meeting, Bettelheim asked for opinions: could the school help this eight-year-old? Betsy spoke up and said yes, she should be admitted.

"The next day I came into the staff room at three o'clock, ready to collapse—this hyperactive boy was still jumping all over the place—and Dr. B. comes over to me and says, 'Well, you've got another one. Will you take her?' I didn't say anything, but I thought, 'Oh, no, I just can't do it.' He must have read my face, because he looked at me and said, 'Yes, you can. You can do it very well.'

"I was sitting on the couch in the staff room, totally wiped out, and he's telling me I have to take another kid. But he said, 'Go in and talk to this girl one more time. Do you really think you can say no to someone who needs help you can give?' So I talked to her again, and five minutes later I said, 'I'll take her.' So I did, and as it turned out, she became someone I really loved. I still see her even though she doesn't live in this part of the country. Her family is part of my extended family, and mine is part of hers. But what I find interesting is that at first I felt very clearly that I couldn't do it, and then Dr. B. was easily able to convince me I could."

In fact, Bettelheim did not convince Betsy. He had seen her dismay, voiced his confidence in her, and then asked a question that engaged her in the girl's fate. With a little nudge, and a question whose answer carried emotional commitment, Betsy convinced herself. It was personal teaching.

I ASKED Betsy to describe her teaching day, which began when the children were brought to the auditorium by the counselors after breakfast.

Her classroom had two couches, and everyone first sat down and talked for a while. "The kids all brought up things that had happened to them since three o'clock the day before. It was a little like group therapy—one might say, 'I got a terrible letter from home,' or another would say, 'I had an awful dream last night.' You can't expect kids to do classwork, intellectual activity, if a bad dream is dominating them. The teacher's first job is to understand the children, and that means talking about what's on their minds."

Two of the girls Bettelheim put in Betsy's class were six-year-olds with no schooling at all, and two others were eighteen and often absent, attending classes at Roosevelt University, in downtown Chicago. The younger ones had to be taught to read, write, and count, and one other girl, of high school age, had to learn algebra, which Betsy remembered only vaguely herself.

"I didn't have the slightest idea how to teach it, so I got a book and we learned algebra together. The girl was anorexic and resented authority, but since I wasn't telling her what to do, we shared the experience. The fact that I learned algebra with her meant more to her than the algebra itself."

What kind of behavior did she cope with in a typical class? "Oh," she said, "I could have an autistic girl sitting in a chair, rocking back and forth, playing with her fingers, totally in her own dream world. Another time I had an autistic girl who was very happy in class, but she'd become violent in the dorm. Sometimes she would pull up her dress and masturbate. Then maybe a wandering kid, walking in circles and talking to himself."

Later, she had two boys who retreated into paranoid explanations about poisons or government. "They developed elaborate ways to evade bad feelings about themselves. Maybe their father never wanted to see them, or their mother was never home, and their feelings were intolerable, so all their energy went into paranoid constructions, but they were actually very smart kids."

Given such a range of disturbance among students (as well as their age differences) classroom teaching at the Orthogenic School had to meet each child's unique needs. The staffer who got personal teaching from Bettelheim could, in turn, give a similar intensity of attention to the child.

Now and then Betsy had a student who was withdrawn, and she mentioned Cindy,* who, at twenty, was the oldest person Bettelheim had admitted at that point. Cindy sat on the steps of the fireplace with her chin on her knees for hours without speaking. "She could spend half a day withdrawn like that, her emotions frozen, totally depressed."

Betsy knew her description of the class sounded strange—"but you shouldn't think the classroom was a circus; I'm only showing the variety of behavior. I was there to settle kids down and bring them together, and I did it. Individual attention was the key, so it helped if I sat down beside the autistic girl when she was screaming, and it helped to set limits for the hyperactive boy and yell at him. When Dr. B. came in and yelled at him, that helped, too. But again, you have to discover what's on the kid's mind."

Later the staff found that the boy had been afraid of being controlled by tranquilizers and so tried to jump even more frantically when forced to take them. "After we pointed out that he didn't have to take drugs at the School, he started to ease off."

When Betsy established rapport with a child, she looked for ways to make it stronger. "I had such a relation with the anorexic girl that sometimes all I had to do was give her a look. If I served some food and she resisted eating, I'd catch her eye, and she knew darned well from the way I looked at her that she'd better eat or there'd be trouble. I'd yell at her, or Dr. B. would yell at her, and she couldn't stand being yelled at."

Betsy first created a tie with each child and then worked to create a tie between children. "The adult has to spot interests and encourage them to establish the major tie, and when you can give something to all the kids at the same time, then you've brought them together." She took it as on-the-job training, discussing each child and making the right plans. "Also, you had to supply direction all the time. They couldn't function without it."

It may sound odd for children with radically different behaviors to sit in the same class, but Betsy said that a sharp divergence between symptoms might help one child relate to another. "It can be good for a withdrawn child to be with one who acts out. Each has a characteristic the other can use, and Dr. B. was very aware of this when he was putting a class together. I remember Cindy became interested in one of the autistic children and stirred out of her withdrawn state. That was a good beginning for her."

Betsy has seen other institutions, and she said that the School under Bettelheim had remarkable stability because of his skill in handling groups. "When you took in someone, the whole group changed and everybody had to readjust, but if they had been stable for a while, they could do it." The adult had to be stable, too. "I was in collapse from one readjustment when Dr. B. gave me the new child, but I could do it because I felt his confidence. If he believed in you, you felt it."

BETSY had agreed to teach for only a year, but as the time neared, she began to have doubts. The workings of personality fascinated her, and when Bettelheim suggested that she become the therapist for a girl in her class, she decided to stay. "We were always investigating, talking to the kids. It was like taking a puzzle apart and then fitting the pieces back together, making a wonderful new thing with it. Some staffers just wanted to help the children, and others were more drawn to the intellectual puzzle of understanding them. For me it was both, and I believe it was also both for Dr. B. When I left the School for a while, I really missed the puzzle element, the intellectual stimulation of it." Later, as her family grew, Betsy stopped teaching and worked only as a therapist, which took less time.

"Some of the children were really impossible. I remember after Marcia left, I asked Dr. B., 'Why did you take on a child like that?' And he got really angry with me and said, 'Well, if I didn't, she would have gotten nothing. At least we've given her some worthwhile years so that the rest of her life can be a little better.' He said this with such meaning and passion that I can still remember his face as he said it."

BETSY had told me that she stopped the hyperactive boy from running around and made him sit down, and later I asked Bettelheim about this. "Well," he said, "she might try to sit him down and talk to him. We always tried to talk with the children, most of all to show our understanding that they were upset, or that their behavior was reasonable and justified, at the same time suggesting that maybe there was a better way for the child to cope with the problems that beset him. I will not say that nobody ever said, 'Stop it!,' because with children like these, some people just cannot help themselves. 'Stop it!' is a kind of built-in reaction. But generally our purpose was to talk with the child about what upset him, to find ways to satisfy needs of the moment and to make him more comfortable." He added that most teachers, understandably, want children not to make *them* uncomfortable. "However, at the Orthogenic School we—the adults, the therapists, the teachers—took the stance toward the children that our task was to 'make things more comfortable for you, and you have to help find out how to do that.' "

I mentioned that Paul said Bettelheim would seize him by the arms and shout, "What are you doing? Stop it!," and this was very impressive to him.

"He would get too excited," Bettelheim said. "If I told him to stop it, by that time I knew what was bothering him, and I was setting limits. Being called in to settle something is part of the father's job."

Betsy had spoken of a girl who masturbated in class, and Bettelheim had written in *Love Is Not Enough* about a girl who masturbated with flashlight batteries. I talked about both of them and asked how he would handle this kind of behavior, particularly in front of other children. He had no specific memory of either girl but was willing to discuss such a situation hypothetically.

"The other children sometimes ignored disturbing behavior," he said, "but also sometimes they would stop the child, or say to us, 'Why don't you stop her?' And our answer usually was, 'Stopping her is not going to solve the problem. We have to find out why she does this.' Or, 'You don't like it, and maybe I don't like it either, but we have to understand why she's doing it, because only then can we help her find better ways to solve these problems.' The other children will feel ambivalent, because to some degree they dislike the way they want us to act in stopping her.

"On the other hand, our attitude is reassuring to them, because it means that when they engage in some behavior that others disapprove, we're not going to force them, but we will also try in their case to understand them. At the immediate moment it's annoying, but over the long run it's very reassuring. As for the flashlight batteries, one question is, why does she use them? It's not the most natural way to masturbate, no? And if it's in front of others, why does she have the need to advertise it, so to say?

"After all, most people at one time or another in their lives masturbate, but they do it privately, so why does she want to arouse the other children's sexual feelings—or angry feelings, or embarrassed feelings—as a by-product? Why does she need *that* to have satisfaction? Essentially, she must feel that her genitalia are entirely unacceptable, and she does it either to prove something, or to demonstrate to herself that they are not as unacceptable as she believes. What she does is really an act of aggression, not just an act of sexual gratification, and so we must try to separate in her mind the sexual gratification which she can have in private, where nobody will object, and the public act of aggression.

"But why does she use her sex aggressively and provocatively? What is she trying to gain? What kind of reaction do you really want from other people when you do that? What do you expect from them? Obviously, she expects them to be shocked. I can't ask her why, because at this moment my greater interest is not *that* she does it, but *how* she does it. Of course, the main thing you need is that she's willing to communicate with some-body. That's the really big thing. Once you have such a child willing to communicate, you have already won the most difficult battle.

"To begin with, we must give this child the feeling that we are on her side. A child who masturbates openly is at war with the whole world. So we try to show her that she is not at war with us. Then when she talks, we can ask, 'What reaction do you expect from others?' and she will more or less admit that she wants to shock them, and we might say, 'So what does it gain you?' "

I wondered whether the teacher might offer the girl a piece of candy or direct her attention to something else, but Bettelheim erupted, "No, no, no, no! I wouldn't try to distract her, because that is to belittle what she does. She has engaged in behavior that is very important to her—surely socially unacceptable, but to her extremely important, and to try to distract her means that I pay no attention to it, or I don't *want* to pay atten-tion to it. I know this is usually advocated—'Pay no attention to it'—but that doesn't work, because such a child wants to achieve specific goals, and this we have to recognize and accept. When we know the goals, then we can offer better ways than obscenity to reach them."

But what if the other children object? "We may say, 'Well, she has these problems, you have other problems, we all have problems. Let's not get excited about it.' At that point we don't interpret *why* she does it, because we can't be sure. The girl hears the adult saying that everybody has problems, and so she knows we are not blithely stopping her without being interested in what she's trying to gain, and that eventually permits establishing a relationship.

"To everybody else her behavior is unreasonable, but to such a girl it is reasonable because she had a certain goal in mind. So whatever a person does he does because he thinks it's the best thing he can do. That's the principle I tried to explain in my book on child rearing—that's what the whole book is based upon. We have to realize that no matter how outra-geous the child's behavior appears to us, he does it for reasons that are good to him. And we have to understand these reasons before we can know what to do about his behavior."

I HAD asked Betsy about the autistic girl who had been violent in the dorm but so easy in class. Betsy said that she was an abandoned child who had been found as an infant in a vacant house and had lived in various foster homes for six years. "She never really developed an ego. I think I might have been the first one who ever established a genuine relation with her. In the dorm she had a series of new counselors who couldn't control her, and she got more and more wild with them, because their lack of control frightened her. In class she knew I could control her, and she was a sweet, wonderful little girl." Betsy had no special formula, but she empathized with the girl and could talk to her. Also, the dorm group itself was problematic because it was unbalanced by having other autistic children in it. "The group didn't have much chance to work. I did what I could in the classroom, but after I left they couldn't keep her in the School. We wouldn't often have a child like her; most kids were able to stay until they could manage some kind of life, either in a home setting or to go out into the world, to high school and college."

When I interviewed Betsy in 1985, the novel *The Pelican and After* by Thomas Lyons had recently been published. It portrayed a school like the Orthogenic School, with a director (obviously based on Bettelheim) who was cruel and hit children. Publicity material said that Lyons had been at the School for some years, and in newspaper and other interviews he spoke freely about Bettelheim as someone who hit children frequently. It was meant to be a portrait, and those associated with Bettelheim recognized it as such.

I borrowed Betsy's copy of the book and read it but somehow could not develop a sympathetic or vicarious interest in the boy and his story. The subject matter intrigued me without the story ever taking on the kind of fictional life that would make me want to keep turning the pages. By the end, I felt that the lead character did not understand what was happening to him, in him, or around him. When I asked Bettelheim about it some months later, he said he thought the novel rather well done but that an ordinary reader like myself might be put off because the action was shown through the mind of a paranoid adolescent.

He disliked the monstrous sketch of himself, but he felt he understood the reason for it, and in his opinion the book was an effective and accurate rendering of its point of view. However, he did not believe it was true to life in any larger sense, and he thought that Lyons had semidemonized him because this helped his inner stability in some way. Bettelheim had refused to discuss the matter of hitting with at least one reporter who called to ask about the book, and he told me very little about Lyons.

"TOMMY was angry," Betsy said, "as some of the children were and are. But I believe he was also showing how much he needed Dr. B. to control him at that stage." She thought a stronger point was the novel's account of the "hang-ups" that adolescent boys felt around female counselors. "I'm very sympathetic with this. It was the beginning of their sexual awakening, and some were disturbed by being constantly confronted with females who were not mother figures. It aroused fantasies, but of course, there could be no acting out."

Betsy added that the children at the School were raised as brothers and sisters and were careful not to get carried away sexually, even though they lived in close proximity. "They did pair themselves off as they reached later years, but the institution had enough control in this area—at least as far as I saw, and there wasn't much I didn't see in the twenty years I was there, first as a child, then teacher and therapist."

To Betsy, Bettelheim was unique in that he took almost all kinds of disturbed children into the School in the belief that they could become better and grow. She said that the School was a world apart from institutions "where they work from the premise, 'We're going to keep you here and take care of you and give you this and that.' Dr. B.'s attitude was, 'We're not going to *keep* you here, but as long as you're here we'll help you reconstruct your personality and grow up, so that you can develop your own self-controls and go out and be whatever you want, with a life meaningful to yourself.' " Betsy firmly believes that any therapist who begins with this attitude will see a favorable influence on the whole course of a child's therapy.

"Dr. B. *assumed* that the kids would be able to control themselves eventually, and so this is what he got, to a good degree. Everything he did was in line with this. Even if he was controlling a child, the child's self-control was the ultimate purpose. If one kid slugged another—it didn't happen often, but if it did—he'd immediately punish the kid who did the slugging. He told the counselors not to touch kids in that situation, but he came right away and slapped the kid so the guilt didn't build up. The guilt is destructive if the child becomes defensive about it and creates a crazy rationalization for his act. After he's hit, he can cry and be unhappy, but maybe he can deal with the reason he was so angry that he hurt another kid."

Betsy said that the School would not have worked unless someone with Bettelheim's firmness and insight kept the children's inner chaos from taking over. "He always punished for the child's own good, and in doing this he protected others. However, he couldn't protect others without protecting the child from his own worst impulses. A lot of people don't like Bettelheim because they can't accept his view of the human personality as having terrible depths. It says something they can't face about the human race, very much including themselves. They don't see how hopeful and positive he was about the kids, but he also saw and guarded against the destructive depths."

Betsy knows a number of Orthogenic School children who hate Bettelheim. "But," she noted, "I believe they feel that he never accepted them. Or they have other reasons I wouldn't go into. The School was set up so that we were always being challenged to figure out what was going on in ourselves. Dr. B.'s attitude was, 'If you don't want to work and get better, get out! Go! If you don't think it's good here, leave, goodbye! We don't need you!' I think some of the kids who are most bitter are those whose counselors were ambivalent about them—or about Dr. B., or about the School. He couldn't always get the counselors he needed, and he made some mistakes on those he kept. It's too bad that it was like that, but the School worked well for a lot of kids. You just don't hear about them because they've put it behind them and made real lives."

The previous weekend a dozen or so of Betsy's "kids" had come back for a get-together, and some began to weep when they tried to say how much the School meant to them. Bettelheim consciously encouraged children to discover their own interests and values, as these had done, and Betsy also took this lesson into her life as a mother.

"I let my children make personal decisions in situations where nothing terrible is going to happen if they make a mistake. But *they* decide. If they decide wrong, they'll be unhappy, but the next time they'll make a different decision. They've got to know they're in charge if they're going to learn what it's like to make a decision and live with the consequences, without excuses."

I asked Betsy if she ever saw a child actually developing a conscience, and she said, "Maybe you could say that you were helping develop a conscience, but you couldn't actually see that. You do see the kids begin to get an awareness that they're not just acting to act, that behind everything we do there's a reason—a reason they need to understand. If you mean that kind of thing as conscience, then you could see it, but it's not like a 'guilty conscience.' Our job was to help the child become conscious of *why* he was doing something, so that he could decide *whether* he would do it and so have control of his life. Then he wouldn't need a Dr. B. authority figure to come along and go *bang!*"

BETSY was the first staffer I interviewed from the School, and I was just beginning to understand something Bettelheim refers to only briefly in his books and had not said in conversation with me—that he had taken the authority-figure role both to run the School and to offer an organizing element for chaotic and troubled personalities. Students feared Bettelheim, even those who liked him as much as Betsy obviously did. I asked about Bettelheim's possible influence on a child's superego and wondered if Betsy could tell me how he had affected her in this regard, but she ignored the thrust of my question (or perhaps not?) and said simply, "He loved me."

This startled me, and my instant unspoken reaction was that her certainty must be mostly in her mind, that she had magnified Bettelheim's kindness over the years into something parental and personal, a feeling of having been loved with warmth and protection, as a father loves a daughter. I knew enough at this point to realize that the School would have suffered had Bettelheim shown open preferences among the children; but on the other hand, he had deep personal responses to people, so it was possible. (One male former student said that Bettelheim was more involved with the girls than with the boys, and Bettelheim himself told me he supposed he was closer to female counselors than to males.)

I made a note to ask him about Betsy in our next interview, and I also had another matter that seemed related: a former staff member had criticized him for taking a female counselor on his lap, although the person would not say this on tape or name the counselor.

About a month later I saw Bettelheim again, and I raised the question of the female staff member on his lap. His eyes opened wide with astonishment, and he asked who had said this. I told him, and he seemed to take no offense, merely waving the matter away as "a jealous fantasy."

"But," I said, "some of the women who worked there believed that you loved them." I was thinking of Betsy, and also of Kathy Lubin. I had asked Kathy whether she felt Bettelheim loved her, and she had said yes.

"Well," Bettelheim said, "some I did love in my own way, but I want to make clear that if there had been any sex, the School would have exploded. Now I will say I occasionally put an arm around their shoulders—that, yes. But the only one I took on my lap was Betsy, because Betsy had been a child, my child, when she was six years old."

I said that Betsy was very clear in telling me that he loved her. Did he in fact love her? He hesitated only a second and said, "Yes."

It occurred to me later that I had put Bruno in a difficult position. Before answering my question, he perhaps weighed what his statement would mean both to her and to anyone else who had been at the School. For her sake, he could never deny loving her, but he may also have taken into account a retrospective jealousy that might be aroused in others.

I wondered how Betsy had come to have such a place in his affections, and though he did not wish to go into detail, he told me a little. He said that when she first came to the School he took her onto his lap, which was not his usual way. (He remembered her as a six-year-old, but she was actually eight; since she is a small adult, she was no doubt also small for her age as a child.) His practice was not to show affection in this way, but because of Betsy's particular need and his own feelings, he apparently made an exception. To understand why, we would presumably have to go into the relationship between Betsy and her father; however, neither she nor Bettelheim would discuss the circumstances that brought her to the School.

At the outset of our interview, I had asked Betsy to tell me her first impressions of Bettelheim, but she could recall nothing. By contrast, she said that Bettelheim remembered a great deal about her. He had started to talk about it when she saw him in the summer of 1985, but she did not wish to discuss it even with him, and so they talked of other things. Bettelheim's relation to her was exceptional in that he had paternal feelings toward her, feelings that she recognized and welcomed.

BETSY left the School shortly after Bettelheim did, and many of the staff also left. Losing his unique attention, insight, and personal support made this inevitable, she said. "Dr. B.'s strong convictions about what to do kept things on an even keel, and he understood the children, so he could give leadership all the time. Without that, and without his kind of staff training, it's chaos. He managed to show how to work with kids in a way that could let people feel better about themselves. If that's missing, then you can't take care of kids with such deep problems. You can do something, but it doesn't have the same scope."

She had more babies but took other jobs where she could use what she had learned. When I saw Betsy, she had just finished four years at a small private school, teaching four children who had emotional disturbances. Out of a class of twenty, all were normal except those she taught. Her students had graduated, and because of the lasting effect of her personal teaching they could be expected to continue to function on a semi-independent level and be mainstreamed into the public school system.

I ALSO interviewed Cindy, mentioned earlier in this chapter, who had come to the School after two suicide attempts. When Cindy was sixteen, she made her first attempt, in the aftermath of her mother's death; the second was a few years later, in college, from which she was expelled, not for trying to kill herself but for forging a prescription for diet pills. The legal charges would be suspended if she entered psychiatric treatment, and her father suggested that she go to Chicago to see Bettelheim.

After she talked with him for ten or fifteen minutes, Bettelheim said, "Would you like to come here?" This surprised her—she thought she had come only for a consultation.

"I said, 'I don't know, I'll have to ask my father.' Dr. B. got very angry and said, 'Zis is something that you have to do yourself! You can't ask your father!' After all, I was twenty years old. So I said, 'Okay, I guess I'll come.' Dr. B. was looking for a commitment and wanted to be sure *I* wanted to come, with no one in the family influencing or pressuring me."

Two weeks later Bettelheim went on a trip, and Cindy ran away. She had managed to hide some money and wanted to leave without having to face him. She also said she felt threatened because he wasn't there, that even students who were the most frightened of him felt his absence as a danger. And there was something else. "I wanted to get some cigarettes and start smoking again. You can't smoke at the School, and I was putting on a lot of weight, which upset me. So I ran away."

Her father heard almost at once and called the police in Chicago, who took Cindy from a train about to leave Union Station. When Bettelheim returned, he called her into his office, very angry. "He said again that if I wanted to leave, I could leave, but if I wanted to stay, he had to know *right then and there*. Was I going to stay and make a commitment to try and improve myself and my life? He was very serious, and there's no question that he *was* the School for me. I believe I agreed to stay because of him."

THE SELF-AWARENESS that Bettelheim demanded from a student almost always emerged in the relationship with a trusted counselor. However, Cindy's counselor did not grow as close to her as Betsy did (or as her therapist, Margaret Carey, did). In the nuclear family a child has at least two chances for a loving and protective relationship, to be understood, to identify with an adult. At the School, Cindy had four adults: two counselors, a teacher, and a therapist. Cindy's main counselor meant well, she said, but shared certain characteristics with her mother, which made Cindy uncomfortable. I said that Bettelheim must have been aware of the similarities between Cindy's mother and the counselor; could he have placed her with that counselor for that reason? Cindy doubted this, but at any rate in giving her to Margaret Carey he had put her with a therapist whose attitude and manner counterbalanced the counselor's.

"It was hard for me to leave class every afternoon and go back to the dorm, because I was so much freer and relaxed in class. With my counselors it was too intense, but I felt no pressure from Betsy." Bettelheim's demand for a commitment had also been a pressure on Cindy, one she came to accept because she felt that he and the School were not pressing her to be anyone except herself.

The effect of the milieu was cumulative for her, with no dramatic turning points. Change came so gradually that she could not put her finger on one incident and say that it had made her different. "You become more aware, a little bit at a time. It's like that student said, little things and time. And it's the relationships. For the first time in my life, I felt like someone cared how *I* felt and really understood me. Betsy says I was frozen when I came to the School, not relating to people, and I guess she and everybody else helped me defrost."

On Sundays Cindy filled in for the kitchen staff. "I liked bringing food out to the table and clearing up the dining room afterward. We washed the tables and chairs, swept the floor, made sure everything got into the dishwasher. I really liked the idea of serving and tried to do it the way Betsy did for us in class—making everything special.[2] It wasn't a chore, it was a privilege, and nobody supervised us. Then we'd sit and talk and have coffee, which we weren't as a rule allowed to do. I just loved it."

How did a young woman in her mid-twenties feel, living with children and going to sleep in a dorm where a counselor not much older than herself read a bedtime story? "It felt right at the time," Cindy said, "and I don't think anything else matters. When I was ready to leave, I left."

When that moment came, some at the School felt she wasn't ready, so she took an apartment nearby and saw Margaret Carey for therapy three times a week for two years. "I was a little nervous going out on my own, but things worked out well. Looking back, it's sad to think that everything nice in the School has to be done as rehabilitation. I'd rather think of parents doing things because they're happy to meet the needs of their kids.

"But Dr. B. always said, 'We're not interested in changing your parents; we're interested in changing you, helping you to have the kind of life you want. There's not much you can do about your parents, and if you keep hoping they'll change, you won't do anything about yourself.' I know that's true, but it's also true you can't help hoping your parents will change."

Cindy had come to the School in 1969, and I interviewed her in 1985. At that distance in time, what did she think about Bettelheim?

"To me he'll always be the person who took a chance on me, saw a possibility that could come out. He was very direct, and he asked questions that touched things you didn't want to think about, things hidden from yourself. That was the beauty of Dr. B. — he always knew where to poke to make you think. And he saved my life."

Even with the occasional provocative question, Cindy saw little of Bettelheim at the School. "My relation with Dr. B. was mostly in my head, because I had a hard time talking to him. He symbolized so much."

For Bettelheim and any student, this was as it should be: not only did he provide protection and order, he symbolized them. His relationship to a child may not have been therapeutic, but it made therapy possible. It also helped the child build up a mental structure, the superego, in which he was seen and felt as the ultimate authority. A student might love him or hate him, but either way he would have given the child's mind a polarizing force.

MORALLY, Bettelheim's stance with Cindy was the same as with the staff: an insistence on personal responsibility. And he expected everyone in the School to act on that principle. Sue Gottschall, a counselor who came in the mid-1960s, spent her first day observing with Kathy Lubin, where she saw a girl step on another girl's foot and then apologize for the "accident." Sue was surprised when Kathy sat the girl down and talked about why she had done it, holding her responsible. Later Sue asked Kathy, "Why were you accusing that girl?" and Kathy explained how our unconscious can influence us. Her words rang true for Sue, who went on to work at the School for ten years.

She said that Bettelheim had "yelled" at her only twice, both times over responsibility. (Bettelheim's yelling was, of course, a vivid moment of personal teaching.) The first time occurred when Sue had been there for about six months. She and her co-counselor, a psychiatrist who wanted a stint at the School before going into private practice, took their group of boys out onto frozen Lake Michigan to walk on the ice. Sue had grown up on Lake Ontario and had done this kind of thing all her life.

"When Dr. B. heard about it, he became furious and screamed at me in the staff meeting, 'Two counselors are worse than none!'—because both of us had ducked our responsibility by *not* making the decision *not* to do it. The issue wasn't physical danger—the ice was actually safe. But he yelled and pointed out that walking on ice could provoke anxiety in the kids because they weren't sure whether it would support them."

The other time Bettelheim exploded was four years later, when a friend of Sue's had just come back from Peru and she had to work on a Sunday. "So I made a mistake: somehow I left a pair of scissors, blunt scissors, in the dorm. I went back and got them later, there was no problem, but I confessed it to Dr. B. I told him the truth: I just didn't know whether I wanted to be there on Sundays—I was thinking about spending time with my boyfriend. Dr. B. yelled, 'Well, make up your mind!' and I did and stayed six more years."

In both incidents Bettelheim reacted partly to indecision. The second time he no doubt hoped Sue would stay but demanded only that she do one thing or the other and not vacillate. He expected mistakes, but he boiled over at mistakes that came from a person's agility in dodging a clear-cut decision. Counselors had to act, not dither; indecision disturbed the children by making them unsure of the counselor's feelings toward them.

SUE TOLD of another instance of Bettelheim's focus on responsibility, this time with a sixteen-year-old boy who had "the emotions of a much younger child." A black ghetto bordered the School on the south side, and one day a woman was murdered in the backyard that separated the ghetto houses from the School. The body lay in full view of the windows of Sue's dorm for hours while police worked at the crime scene.

"I closed the curtains because I didn't want kids hanging out windows and looking at her body all cut up and bloody. However, Dr. B. walked into the dorm and saw what I'd done, and he flipped open every curtain. He took this sixteen-year-old by the arm and went over to the window and said, 'Now, you look out there! That's what you're going to become if you don't change yourself!' It was astonishing, but later I understood why—that the boy had no superego, that Dr. B. was functioning as one by showing him he might come to a bad end if he didn't improve himself. For a long time I didn't know whether I should be doing things like that, but finally I realized I shouldn't—that I had to take care of the three-year-old needs and leave the superego needs to Dr. B."

When she drew the curtains, Sue had not made a mistake; quite the opposite. She was right to protect her boys from an ugly scene, but Bettelheim was equally right to open the curtains—in his case, to drive home a lesson to a particular boy. He shocked the boy, provoked his anxiety, tried to make him feel harsh reality. He wanted the boy to realize that taking responsibility for oneself always begins in the here and now. It was a superego warning about the reality principle and the consequences of behavior—and like a good superego, Bettelheim encouraged survival. He showed this acting-out delinquent boy a vision of death in order to point him toward life.

In this instance, Bettelheim intervened with an act that combined shock value with survival value, but at another juncture he threw the burden of guidance back on Sue. She told of an incident from her early years with a group of boys aged fourteen to eighteen.

"I had put them to bed, and I usually sat in the dorm until they went to sleep. The room was pretty dark—all the lights were out except for my reading lamp, and I was reading the kids to sleep. So I was reading away, and meanwhile two boys over in the corner were giggling. I paid no attention to them and had no idea anything was going on.

"But Dr. B. walked into the dorm and caught on immediately. He realized that the two giggling kids were masturbating together—not together, but simultaneously. He threw on all the lights and called all eight boys out of bed into a circle around the table in the center of the room. He said, 'Now you talk to Sue about this,' and with that he walked out of the room. I've told this story before, and people seem flabbergasted and ask, 'What did you say?' and I reply honestly, 'I don't remember.' "

Sue later thought about Bettelheim's intent, and she came to feel that he was telling the children, "This is the person responsible for you, she's taking care of you, and she's here to help you with those feelings."

I believe Sue is correct, but I also believe Bettelheim knew that sexual advice would be too highly charged if it came from his God-of-wrath throne. Sex was private, best discussed by someone emotionally close to the child, and his confidence in Sue helped her wing it.

"Of course, if he didn't react to a person in that way, the person usually left. Nine of the eleven prospective counselors who started about when I did left the School inside a year. Only two of us stayed any real length of time, but of course you had to turn your life over to the job."

I mentioned staff meetings, and Sue said they made her uncomfortable, but she couldn't do without them. To get what she needed, she had to reveal intimate details when examining her own reactions to the children—in front of twenty-five people. "It's not group therapy, it's a form of teaching, learning to deal with the kids by dealing with your own reactions. You're spilling your guts in front of everybody, and if you couldn't do that, the School didn't work for you, and sooner or later you left."

I ASKED Sue about her reaction when a young man kicked Bettelheim in the groin, and she recalled how frightened she was when she heard about it. "I was scared first, and then I got mad. I was angry with Dr. B. because he was supposed—in my mind—to be so in control that this kind of incident could never occur."

Attacks on the staff were common in the New York State facility where she had first worked, she said, but they were rare at the School.

"The methods of the milieu kept it from happening. If kids were well taken care of by their counselors, they didn't act out with violence. But then I was also angry at the counselors involved for not protecting Dr. B. I've forgotten—probably I'm blocking it—who was there at the time.

"By the way, the boy Dr. B. forced to look at the woman's body was finally able to leave the School. He's married and has a job, and he keeps in touch with me. Above all, you've got to remember what the alternatives were. Many kids improved enough to leave the School and lead normal lives, but others could only live at home. Of course, that's preferable to an institution. Many of my kids were able to finish college and hold jobs and live relatively comfortable lives, which I think is a good measure of success."

SUE WORKED with Bettelheim in his last years at the School, by which time he had detractors throughout the university. Many people she met would ask her how she could stand working for such a man.

"They'd ask the question," she said, "and then tell a story of something they saw in class that showed why Bettelheim was a terrible person. I took all his classes, because I got my master's at the university, and in all that time I saw only one example of the kind of thing that most people mean when they're telling you a 'horror story' about him.

"There was a young woman in class who raised her hand and said, 'I'm having a problem with my stepson. He's four years old, and he gets up at two in the morning and goes downstairs and out of the house. We live right next to the Illinois Central, and he goes up on the platform and takes the train downtown. What can I do about this?' And Dr. B. said simply, 'Lock the door.'

"Then she went into a long harangue about how she *couldn't* lock the door. But Dr. B. kept asking questions, and it was clear to me that he was trying to get her to see that she really *wanted* the boy to do what he was doing. However, she totally refused to understand her part in it. So Dr. B. got angrier and angrier until he turned red in the face and finally gave up on her. There's no punch line to the story—he just gave up.

"But that's the kind of thing people remember him for, without understanding one thing: that he got into a fury if you refused to look at yourself as being in any way connected with the problem. People who didn't know him will talk about his intolerance, and he certainly had it, but it was for those who refused to look at themselves, or who acted as if they had no guilt."

When I interviewed Sue, her job was training Head Start teachers. "It's just amazing to me—or perhaps I shouldn't be amazed, because it's the same old story—but there's no insight at all into the way the feelings of teachers affect what happens between them and the children they're working with. It's a struggle to get teachers just to look at what *they* bring to the classroom, as distinct from what the kids bring."

I asked whether she had found any shortcuts for teaching this, and Sue laughed, a little sadly. "No," she said. "Just like there's no way of curing disturbed kids quickly."

CHAPTER 26

An Unwelcome Retirement

IN 1970, at the age of sixty-seven, Bettelheim was forced to begin a painful separation from the world he had created. Pressed by the university to find a replacement even before he reached retirement age, he somehow could not do it. He had asked Ben Wright several times, but Wright wanted a private life and knew he could not run the School as Bettelheim had.

Ugo Formigoni, Robert Bergmann, and Peter Wolff all knew the School well, but they also knew themselves well enough to turn Bettelheim down. He used his powers of persuasion on Formigoni, a psychiatrist from Italy who had worked as a counselor for five years in the early 1960s, and Formigoni entertained the idea briefly but decided against it.

However, one possibility remained that tempted Bettelheim perhaps more than all the rest. Bert Cohler had gotten a Ph.D. at Harvard, and with a faculty appointment at Yale in the offing, he was beginning an academic career that promised to be highly distinguished. Also, he knew the School in a way nobody else did—as a student. The possibility of being succeeded by someone who had lived at the School as a student made Bettelheim's legacy seem self-perpetuating.

He went to see Cohler and concluded that Cohler actively wanted the job, wanted it enough to give up Yale. For Bettelheim, the force of innate desire was a huge factor in one's success, so if Cohler wanted it so much, then maybe it would work, and if it worked it would be ideal. Bettelheim dreaded leaving the School, but he was going away for a year, to the Center for Advanced Study in the Behavioral Sciences at Stanford University, to write a book.

In June 1970 he called me to talk about publishing and the possiblility that he might want me to represent him as an agent. He was going to leave the Free Press—another painful separation, since Jeremiah Kaplan was one of his oldest friends. But Jerry had been promoted "into the stratosphere," as Bruno put it, after Macmillan bought the Free Press, and he no longer had any direct responsibility for individual books, even those of a personal friend like Bettelheim.

Also, something very unpleasant had happened. An editor at Macmillan had sent Bruno the manuscript of Tom Lyons's *The Pelican and After*, seeking his approval. The book's unfavorable portrait was less angering than the fact that his own publishers would ask him to write a letter saying he would not sue if they published the novel. This insulted him, and he refused to write such a letter.[1] He had no intention of suing and could never have sued a former student, but the request made him feel betrayed in a relationship that had lasted twenty years; and so he called me. Incidentally, he asked, what did I think he should write next?

"A book on raising children," I said—a matter much on my mind just then. He said he would think about it and call again after his vacation.

BRUNO and Trude left Chicago at the end of June for a long vacation in Africa and Europe, and it was late summer before they rented a house near Stanford. He was given an office at the center in which to write, and he had nothing but free time, and he was totally miserable.

After twenty-six years, running the School had become as natural to him as breathing; deprived of this work, he was useless. Also, everything felt wrong: the house they had rented wasn't homelike, he couldn't find a comfortable chair for reading, the lighting was bad. But he knew it was more than that, and he wrote Ruth Marquis:

> Being out here with no other purpose but to write, I find writing nearly impossible, and I realize how closely all my writing was really connected with the daily clinical experience. Suddenly . . . nothing comes to mind.

Of course, he had to stay half a continent away from the School. Cohler needed to establish his own authority, and this could not happen if Bettelheim were in his office, where anyone could see him at a moment's notice. It was exile, and in exile he fell into a serious depression. Without the work of the School to occupy him, he could begin to ameliorate the depression only by becoming engrossed in a book, and so he continued to try.

In fact, he had already begun a book at the School, and this was the project he hoped to write at the center. Long before *The Empty Fortress*, he had talked of doing a book about the School's staff, and he had assembled much of the research and written sections of the manuscript, which he had left with his other papers in Chicago, to be shipped to California after his vacation.

However, he kept avoiding the staff idea because the subject brought feelings of finality he could not yet face. He told Ruth Marquis he would

like to [write] the book on children and how to raise them. . . . More and more I feel a need for it, and particularly of a book that sees the kid in contact—the [reciprocity] with the parent. . . . Essentially what I would like to do is what I shall try to do with the book on the staff: to show that if they understand what is involved in their own reactions to what goes on with the kids, they become able to handle the situation . . . so much better. . . . What do you think? And how does one go about doing it?

He told himself that he wouldn't begin the staff book until he could work with the staff again, which he would do in the following year. And then something else happened: the partial manuscript and all his papers were lost.

They shipped it fourth class uninsured, though I had ordered it railroad express, fully insured, and the package got lost in the mail. . . . What about that for getting even with me for leaving the School? Now I have to start from nothing, which infuriates me, but I also know that maybe that's best rather than to try to rework old stuff.

It was typical of him to find a benign possibility in his loss, to look beyond the disaster of his papers and fix on the goal of a good book.

Later in September, still unable to write, Bruno sent Ruth a list of previously published papers for a collection: what should he include, which should he drop? It was a stopgap idea, abandoned before long when he committed himself to the child-rearing book. In October he called to ask me to go ahead and find a new publisher; having written a personal letter to Jeremiah Kaplan about his move, he was now ready to start with someone else. Robert Gottlieb of Knopf made an offer, and Bruno signed a contract in November.

He expected to work in the usual way, with Ruth editing as he wrote. After all, she had read, discussed, edited, reread, and reedited most of his writing for over twenty years. However, differences—personal, political, and psychological—had grown up between them. She had kept her reservations to herself, and he did not guess how much she was changing. Then toward the end of her work on *The Children of the Dream,* a moment had come in which Bruno seemed slightly irritated by her intense and protracted editing.

"I remember," Ruth said, "just a little bit of that kind of exasperation at the end of *The Empty Fortress,* which was a terribly difficult book on the picky editing level. There were so many theoretical unknowns in that book, just doing it meant he was really sticking his neck out. But his impatience was more overt at the end of the kibbutz book, like I was making this process drag on too long. My own internal signals told me something was wrong, and I sensed in him an attitude that was new—a sort of annoyance. It wasn't exactly anger. I don't think Bruno in his whole life ever got angry with me."

The warning signal for Ruth came in one of their daily conversations, going over pages of *The Children of the Dream* that he had sent her for comment. It was their customary editing process, and she was asking for changes or additions, but this time he resisted.

"I heard in his voice a kind of irritation, like, 'Oh, god, let's get this done and off to the printer.' It wasn't so much 'I'm sick of this book' as 'This has been going on for too long.' The implied criticism was that I was too fussy, and I resented it because this was precisely what he had valued *most* in the early years. I had never felt the slightest constraint in editing that way, and I didn't care how many times the damn thing had to be retyped.

"And remember, when we started, there was no Xerox. Every blasted thing was typed and retyped and then typed again, and I marveled at the patience in his office. I'd see notes from him to a secretary that said, 'I want this clean, and I want two copies sent *immediately* to Ruth Marquis.' What should I say? It made me feel very important. I have a memo from one of the girls who used to do the typing—and my god, he had wonderful typists, they just never made mistakes, it was incredible. She wrote me a funny note—'Listen, around here if Ruth Marquis says something, we'd better do it, or off with our heads!' It made me laugh and think to myself,

'Boy! I ain't important in this world, but I sure am in *one* office!' It was a wonderful feeling."

Bettelheim's half-expressed impatience had brought her up short, and suddenly her reservations crystallized. "I realized he was getting older and more testy, but I didn't like it. Also, I'm sure that in my unconscious or preconscious I must have been thinking, 'Hey, girl, it's time to get out of this—both of you have had it,' or words to that effect. However, I never thought it consciously. In 1970 I had enough *feeling* reasons, and they all came together at that time, and I meant it."

When he called to talk about the new book, she stunned him by refusing to edit it. Nothing he could say would change her position. It was final.

Two matters troubled Ruth, starting in the 1960s. She felt Bruno retreated from, or at least did not pursue, the insights and positions that had made the "Generations" essay and "Growing Up Female" so exciting to her. Even as she found more meaning in the women's liberation movement, she saw that he found less. In the same vein, it disappointed her that his attitude toward mothers seemed to harden. Despite his words to the contrary in his writings, she felt that he held mothers too much responsible for the child's emotional well-being and did not think enough about the mother's feelings.

Her other major difference with him concerned the student unrest of the 1960s. Living in Ann Arbor brought Ruth into contact with the founders of Students for a Democratic Society, and she became close friends with one of them, whose political aims she shared. Bettelheim was an anathema to college rebels just then, and Ruth tried to maintain loyalties on both sides but felt torn and ill at ease. Something had to give, and it was her loyalty to Bruno.

In spite of her decision and his shock, they remained friends. "Bruno would still call and ask me to give him an opinion on something, and the call was a sort of thinly disguised hope that I would get involved again." He could not believe she would persist in denying him her unique help, and he may have tried to regain it by drawing her into a discussion of his ideas.

"He would talk about something, and I would say no, then I'd say yes in a limited way. I'd make conditions like, *Well, I'll look at it and tell you my opinion, but I am not going to fix anything;* that is, really edit."

THE LOSS of Ruth's genuine interest and friendly opposition left Bettelheim to struggle fitfully with the child-rearing book. His depression did not lift. Missing the work of the School, at odds with himself, at odds with Ruth for reasons he did not fathom — it was a wonder he could write at all. For years he had written in his office at the School, often late at night while still on call, relying on Ruth to challenge whatever she did not understand or what he had not properly expressed. Now, burdened and preoccupied with his emotional losses, he busied himself, with marginal satisfaction, in an office that would never be his own, hoping to heal his unhappy spirit by writing parts of the book for Knopf. He read, he reflected, and he wrote, but he still could not see what the book as a whole should be.

Meanwhile, calls from the School disturbed him, calls from members of the staff complaining about Bert Cohler — a development that brought his attention back to a scene his feelings had not left.

"He had people calling him every day about what Bert was doing," Margaret Carey said, "and I didn't think that was right. I don't know what Bert thinks, because we never talked about it, but I thought Bruno should have given him more of a chance. However, Bert had lots of ideas he wanted to try out, and he was doing it with his head rather than with his heart. That wasn't Bruno's way at all. By and large, Dr. B. and I got along fine, and I really only fought with him over Bert."

In a way, the problems inherent in handing over the School may have pointed Bettelheim toward work that lifted his depression. He set the child-rearing book aside long enough to look again at the book on the staff. Since he was leaving the School, he might be wise to describe it in a comprehensive way, and his account would always be there for future reference. So he dropped the idea of writing only about the staff and its training, in favor of telling how the School was organized to encourage youngsters in a long and sustained effort to reintegrate their personalities. To give the book an even larger relevance — always a goal in his writing — he planned it as a description of how any mental institution might be organized for this result. With the change of perspective, he shed the block that had been haunting him and began to work with his usual energy on his fourth book about the School.

In fact, for a time he worked on both books, but he knew he would finish the book on the School first, having asked several of those connected with the School over the years to help him with it. In the late summer of 1971 Bruno invited Joan (my wife and partner) and myself to have breakfast with him at the Algonquin, where he always stayed. Joan talked about raising a child and Bruno asked her to write him a letter with her ideas about what should be covered in the child-rearing book—"anything that comes to mind."

She did so, and in November he wrote back, saying that

> every one of your points, or problems, or issues (I do not know what to call them) is most timely and important, and I hope I shall be able to do them justice. The book I am working on—at this time mostly in my mind—seems to become ever more difficult and ever more important to write. I have not yet made as much progress as I hoped, but please tell Theron not to worry. It is my way of worrying my head off for a long time before the writing starts. You may also tell him—such are the vagaries of life—I have made very good progress on another book, my last summing up and, if I may call it, testament on the work of the Orthogenic School, something vaguely named a treatise of milieu therapy, or what a mental hospital really should be like. I trust Knopf won't mind if they get two books instead of one.

Bruno also invited Joan to jot down her ideas and write him again—"I do enjoy struggling with the problems of parents." If he didn't, he said, he would never have undertaken the book, but he needed to know as much as possible of how a parent saw a problem in order to involve himself in it.

As always, other people's problems stimulated Bettelheim to explore his reactions on a subject. He evolved no theoretical structure as a model for addressing such questions and offered, more often than not, a particular answer. He liked real-life examples, and when he asked a parent, "What are *your* problems?" he got responses that inspired him to examine his feelings as if he were the child or the parent in the situation. I am sure he asked many others besides Joan to talk about parenting, but he did not ask me, perhaps because he saw I was inexperienced.

Six months later, in May 1972, he signed a contract with Knopf for a book entitled *The Secular Cathedral*. He finished it before the end of 1972, with the help of a new personal editor, Joyce Jack. The final manuscript devoted less than half of the text to the staff, and the rest dealt with other aspects of milieu therapy and mental institutions. After Joyce's editing, Bettelheim again asked Ruth Marquis to read the finished manuscript; however, Ruth knew this would turn into a huge commitment, and she said no. Bettelheim wrote her from Israel in January 1973:

> Naturally I was disappointed that you don't feel inclined to read the manuscript. . . . I had wanted to get your reaction, and hopefully maybe even a sensible title based on its content.
>
> I feel it could have become a very good book, if you would again have been able to help me with it. This is said not to make you feel guilty, just an objective statement. Now that I am a month and 8,000 or more miles away from it, I fear it is not a good book. At the moment, engulfed by Israeli problems [he had been invited by the government to consult on education], I feel very distant from it, probably also part of the second and what I know must be the final separation from the School and what it meant in my life, wrote it most to free myself and not enough to communicate to others. I should have let it rest a couple of years, but I am too old to do so and was too anxious to get it out of my system. Only you could have restrained me and with your discussion of it made it a good book. I have no misgivings about the girl who edited it, she tried hard and meant well, and helped it some. But she does not understand what the issues are, not what I tried to do and so could never challenge my thoughts, only my diction. The same I fear will be true with the editors at Knopf. But I need somebody who can really question my ideas, and there is none around. If David Rapaport would still be alive, he might have been one, but I can't think of anybody who could and more important would want to do it. Karen made some good suggestions for additions for which I am grateful, but she did not question what I said, nor suggest what else needed to be said. Well, there just is no other like you for me.

He called her when he returned to Chicago, and she agreed to think about a title if he would send her the table of contents. In March 1973 he replied:

> You didn't expect me to be satisfied with sending you just the table of contents. Since the end is in the beginning, and the end is the end, I also enclose the first and last two pages. Maybe this will give you a better idea of what I was trying to do, and a sample of how bad the book is written, since you didn't bring it into this world. You would be amazed how many people are asking me whether we still work together, and how disappointed they are if I have to tell them that you no longer

want to have anything to do with me. . . . I probably will not be able to resist the temptation to call you soon again. In the meantime, of course, I have been thinking about what we talked about, only one of the issues I'll take up now. [Ruth had argued that books about raising children made parents feel guilty when they couldn't live up to what the books recommended.] The difficulty in dealing with the issue of parental guilt is that I cannot accept that psychoanalytic writings have created it. Sure, they have added to it, and gave it substance. But guilt comes from way back when, and way back deep down. If you are secure within yourself, nothing anybody writes is going to give you guilt feelings. Worry, yes, every parent worries about his kids, guilt about how and what he is doing is something else. . . . If you for some reason need to feel guilty, don't hang it on what you do with your kids. . . . The real problem: we, the analysts, have made it possible for parents, particularly mothers, to give content to their vague guilt feelings by what they are doing or not doing to their children. That's bad enough, I agree, and because we give this content to our guilt feelings, we resent our children because we think they caused it, which they did not, and that's where things go much more wrong than in regard to guilt. . . . I have been saying for years that the worst you can do is to feel guilty about what you did to your kid, because this is such a tempting weapon in their hands to act out all their oedipal resentments that they practically cannot help using it, and then they feel miserable for having done so, and you invited them with your guilt to do so. But here I go again making parents feel guilt, so what's the end? . . . I cannot help feeling that by feeling guilty about one's child one relieves one's guilt about having been a bad child to one's parent.

Bettelheim closed this letter with a cheerful dig:

But just imagine if you'll have to read this book once it's published and it'll have a stupid title? There I go making you feel guilty, as seems to be the job of the analyst. How else could he justify his fees?

At Ruth's suggestion, *The Secular Cathedral* became *A Home for the Heart.*

NOW THAT Ruth could look back on a friendship of almost forty-five years, what was the deepest divergence between herself and Bruno? I

asked because I had noticed in our conversations that the political differences were less. She seemed to have had second thoughts on the desir-
ability of "revolution," whereas the psychological differences remained.

"It was his attitude toward the mother," she said. "Okay, the development of the child doesn't happen in a vacuum; it's the mother who does
it. But the relation is a dyad, two individuals working as a pair. There's no
such thing as total devotion to the object of your care, so the mother
should not be expected to give *everything*. Well, yes, you give your life—I
carried my child out of a burning building and didn't care whether I got
hurt; that part of motherhood is true. But otherwise the mother half of the
dyad has needs just as important and subtle as the infant's. It wouldn't be
fair to say that Bruno never thought about this, but I felt he stopped facing
it, and I had to face it as a mother. He loved teaching, and he did it in his
books. He liked to teach motherhood, but he saw it mainly from the
child's point of view.

"He spent so much of his life trying to help us understand what children need to grow up decently, I wanted him to do the same kind of job
for mothers, who have to answer the child's needs. But I saw this wasn't
going to happen, first when he went on in the fairy tales, and then later
when he did it again in *A Good Enough Parent*. Anyhow, our separate
positions hardened, and I felt he retreated from where he once stood on
these questions. None of what I'm saying should take away by one inch
from the rest of what he gave the world. I think he's one of the great minds
of our time, I mean about a whole slew of things. But on that one issue I
disagree with him."

Later, she said, "I guess I feel that Bruno at his core was just not as
empathic with mothers as he might have been, given how much he knew.
Of course, he always said I expected too much."

RUTH'S disappointment might not have become a hard and final judgment if she had continued to edit and thus influence Bettelheim. He valued her conversation, with its trustworthy freshness of feeling and
commonsense reactions to his written ideas—ideas that, when at last set
down in a book, formed the best self he could discover and create. He
hoped to teach in his books but for a long time could not do so to his satisfaction without Ruth's patient questioning of his words. However, in 1970,
when she took a separate path, at her choice and with no apparent regret,
she was thinking too many things she could not say, and so her separation
from him was all for the best—for both of them.

I must add that her ultimate point about Bettelheim's "core" is valid; or, rather, almost valid, because it would have taken a drastic departure from his beliefs for him to adopt the positions she wished. Ruth might have drawn him in her direction, but I doubt she would have been happy with the final product, which would have fallen far short of her perception of a mother's need.

Bettelheim knew the problem, and he knew a solution, because he lived with Trude, a wife and mother who enjoyed her career as a social worker. He knew it could be done, and he approved; research would not have told him much more than this. Ruth was right in saying that Bettelheim thought first of the child, but this was natural in view of the reality that the child is the weak and dependent partner in the dyad.

Bettelheim had grown up at a time, in a place, and in a class where adults were expected to take care of children without cavil or question. This was not only a heartfelt value for him; it was a conviction and a position he would never have abandoned. As a commentator on the life he saw around him, he had been early to recognize that a woman isolated by motherhood faced a dilemma when her needs were at odds with those of her family; he had pointed to the problem but could offer no one-size-fits-all remedy. The individual mother, caught in the whirl of her agitated and unequal share of the dyad, had to find answers that were immediate, workable, and personal—as Trude had done. Bettelheim could not advise a generation of women on this point; solutions were idiosyncratic and perhaps most worthy if they took some features from the extended family.

The young Bruno's upper-middle-class life in Vienna was close to what we now call the nuclear family, but it also owed something to the extended family of its ghetto past. Aunts, uncles, and cousins (not to mention servants) all helped enlarge the household scene and relieve the mother in some ways, while bringing new problems to the fore. Bettelheim had hoped to find insights into the modern mother's dilemma when he went to Israel to study the kibbutz (organized to free parents from the daily burdens of child rearing), but he came away with reservations about patterns of personality in children who grew up fearing to differ from their peer group. Also, he saw the kibbutz child's need to conform as hampering creativity and individuality. In any event, a pure kibbutz life could not survive except in a closed society such as Israel had in some ways approached in its early years. The kibbutz fascinated him but offered no quick lessons for Americans with generational and family problems.

Bettelheim had another reservation about the emotional life in the kibbutz: the absence, as he saw it, of true intimacy. He made this point without idealizing intimacy, saying that the intimacy of traditional family life also created a chronic quandary, because a sustained close relation with another person, a deep attachment based on shared experiences, would entail discomfort and pain. He wrote about this in *The Children of the Dream* under the subheading, "The Hedgehog's Dilemma," referring to a passage in Schopenhauer in which the philosopher compared people to hedgehogs in winter. Their problem was to move close enough to each other to stay snug and warm, while keeping a distance from one another's quills. Bettelheim's experience in life had led him to conclude,

> Unfortunately, it seems that the distance that protects us from being pricked does not offer much warmth or creature comfort.[2]

We can see the hedgehog's dilemma hiding in the shadow of the estrangement between Ruth and Bruno: living far apart, they spoke almost every day for years, in wide-ranging conversations that kept them close in spirit. Ruth's spontaneous questions and independence of mind had helped Bruno develop ideas from their first rough forcefulness to eventual clarity, finding nuances that did not sacrifice conviction. However, when she began to guard her responses because of sympathies with feminists and college radicals, an unspoken barrier rose up within her. Complete candor would have led to an open break, which she did not want, and so she became less frank. With so much being left unsaid, she internalized her "quills" and suffered a discomfort that at last forced her to disconnect from him. It was, I believe, entirely reasonable for her to bow out and not undertake detailed, hands-on editing of Bettelheim's books when her spirit was no longer compatible with his.

Bruno may have sensed but did not grasp the depths of her alienation from him. He had trusted her too much and for too many years to guess what she did not say. Still admiring him, she wished to avoid the emotional stings, perhaps the angry astonishment that saying everything would provoke. So it was, at the moment when Bettelheim finally had total freedom to write and to teach with his writing, that he lost the one person who could question his sallies into truth in ways that made them stronger. For the books that followed *The Children of the Dream*, he had to rely, in accord with his values of self-knowledge and personal responsibility, upon himself to question his ideas.

BRUNO would not discuss Cohler with me, except to say that he was an honorable man and had resigned as director. In our 1983 interview, he also did not wish to comment on Jacquelyn Sanders, the next director, who had, a year earlier, banned him from visiting the School. He wrote and said, and I'm sure he believed, that anyone who ran a school had to do it in his or her own way. The blunt reality of being cut off from his life's work shocked him, but the work itself, with all the benefits that followed from the creation of milieu therapy, remained his own inimitable prize.

CHAPTER 27

The Film

IN JANUARY 1973, when Bettelheim was visiting Israel as a consultant, a television producer telephoned from Paris to say that he would like to make a film about the School. In years past, many others had asked permission for a documentary, and Bettelheim had always refused. Now, after a few minutes on the phone with Daniel Karlin, and with no pause for reflection, he said yes and felt convinced that his decision was natural and right.

Only later did he analyze the emotions of that moment, the isolation and depression that had led him to reverse a strict rule about filming at the School. His isolation in Israel had deepened his depressed mood as he faced the inevitable loss of his little world to the next director. His seventieth birthday, in August, would make the parting irreversible, and he dreaded his life without the School, where for so long he had found his own meaning in helping others find theirs.

He had led half his life in Austria, half in America; the Viennese life had been erased like chalk on a blackboard, and now he felt as if the same would happen to his American life. These feelings had dominated him in the weeks before Karlin called, but as the producer talked about the children and the film, his mood began to lift. Abruptly, the film became a promise of continuity: if Karlin made it the way he said, the meaningful half of Bettelheim's life would be saved. His impulsive consent contradicted a long-standing conviction and seemed out of character, but in helping children he had often looked for exceptions to a rule; now, without a second thought, he found an exception for himself.

Suddenly he agreed and invited Karlin to visit him in Chicago in June. Back at the School in March, however, he was brought up short when his codirector, Jacquelyn Sanders, objected strongly. Many staffers joined her, saying that Dr. B. was showing an odd disloyalty to his own work, because they feared the filming would disrupt the milieu and disturb the children. His impending departure had already upset many at the School; wouldn't the intrusion of a crew with camera, lights, and microphones make the transition worse?

This was a reasonable doubt, but Bruno found that he still wanted the film. He and the staff discussed it at length, the question was put to a vote, and a sizable majority agreed with him. However, the staff remained sharply divided, and he sensed that some went along with him simply as a parting gift.

Since the students had to be consulted, he explained the film to them and asked their permission. The film would not be shown in America, and nobody would be filmed who did not want to be. The students decided they should meet Karlin first, and when the producer arrived in June they talked with him; most liked him and voted to let him make the film.

In fact, filming had been done at the School for professional purposes, but there had been nothing to show a lay public the life and methods of the milieu. Several times Bettelheim had tried to write the narrative for a documentary on the School, but he'd always found that he lacked perspective. If he was too close, perhaps someone like Karlin might do better. Bettelheim had intended a short film made about the autistic girl Marcia for audiences like the one at Anna Freud's Hampstead Clinic in England, where he presented it with a running commentary. There, he did not bother to write down his narrative, because his sense of his audience allowed him to extemporize. However, he knew so much, and in such intimate detail, that the larger picture of the School eluded him. He decided that Karlin, a sympathetic outsider, would mirror the public mind in a way he could not. Readers could decide about milieu therapy from his books, but the audience in France who saw Karlin's film would grasp how the School worked, not through an author's words but with images of real people made by an independent observer.

WHEN BETTELHEIM saw the final version of *Une autre regard sur la folie* ("Another Look at Madness") about a year later in California, he liked it with one exception: he hated the way he looked and sounded on screen. The "horrible character of the old director" was pompous and seemed to believe he had all the answers.

He had known at the time that he felt self-conscious, and now he saw it on the screen. Part of the problem came from speaking without a sense of the audience he was addressing. In a lecture he kept those he faced clearly in mind—what they believed, who they were; but as he tried to play himself in the film, he was lost. At the School he knew everyone personally, and so he acted with a vigorous certainty of his duties and powers. However, lacking a feel for his standing with the film's viewers, not even sure who they would be, he had been filled with doubts about how to "play" his part. There is perhaps an irony in the fact that he habitually left himself out of his books, only to have the film also miss the authentic and true Bettelheim as director. When he'd agreed to making the film, he had not fully understood what he wanted to achieve and why. The reasons that came to mind in his first conversation with Karlin were like the first page of a book, with more to follow. For the final page, my guess is that he wanted to cut his ties to the School by dramatizing his departure to himself, but to the best of my knowledge he never quite said this.

UNE AUTRE REGARD was aired on French television over four nights early in October 1974.[1] Public television in France had been under attack, and many reviewers praised the first part of the series just before it was broadcast, urging their readers to watch it and think about the issues it raised. Each of the first three programs drew an audience of four million viewers, the last fewer; by chance when the second program was shown, a strike had taken regular French programming off the air, and the segment that included Bettelheim's film of Marcia, which Karlin had incorporated in his film, was carried on all three channels. Not every viewer liked what he saw, but the series was a success that gave Bettelheim a high profile in France for the rest of his life.

Some of the staff at the School never understood or accepted Bettelheim's reversal of his rule about filming, but his intuition that it would have a minimal effect on the milieu and the children proved correct. Some children may have tried to show off in ways undesirable for themselves, but no long-term problems emerged. In fact, the excitement surrounding the film probably helped the transition as an unprecedented event filling the weeks that led up to the unprecedented event of Bettelheim's retirement. Marking his departure with the film may also have made his loss more bearable to those most affected by it, since the turmoil and commotion of making the film became a kind of public celebration of the School's importance and involved almost everybody there. Treating his last days in this way, the School did not try to hide or gloss over the reality of Bettelheim's sad good-bye, but faced it.

CHAPTER 2 8

The Path to a
Useful Enchantment

IN 1973 Bruno and Trude bought a house in a country setting—in Portola Valley, near Palo Alto and Stanford. San Francisco was within easy reach, and Bruno, having disposed of thousands of books he no longer had room for, wanted access to the resources of a great university. Trude settled in by planting gardens on the slopes surrounding the house; it seemed that making a new home, taking care of Bruno, and tending her flowers was all the retirement she could have wanted. When I spoke with her during this time, I heard the voice of a woman peaceful and happy with the way her reality had turned out—even though the deer and rabbits sometimes found her plants to their taste.

As for Bruno, a quiet life in the countryside left him at loose ends. He had always lived in a big city and would have preferred the busy scene of San Francisco, but Trude chose the new home, and he owed it to her. For thirty years she had made possible his single-minded commitment to the School, and now it was her turn. Restless in retirement, he traveled frequently to lecture, returning to Chicago for classes and consultations. Still, he could find no way to replace his almost unlimited absorption in the School, and he cast about for more to do, another book or a grant study that would engage his mind and heart. He wrote Ruth Marquis that he would

> figure out what little kids think when they sit in classes and are being taught. In short, how does the preconscious of kids support or interfere with what goes on in class, and how should they be taught so that their preconscious will support the learning.[1]

He had started to analyze primary readers, whose empty stories, he believed, told the child "that there is no point at all in learning to read"—a conclusion that still held true for him nearly ten years later in the book he wrote with Karen Zelan, *On Learning to Read.*

With *A Home for the Heart* behind him, he went to work again to shape the book on child rearing and began to write a chapter on fairy tales. He sketched out a brief analysis of "Little Red Riding Hood" to show how the story would touch a child's hopes and fears, and having been asked to speak at a psychoanalytic meeting, he turned the sketch into a short talk. The warmth of the audience's reception surprised him; many people came up afterward to praise his insights and offer comments. This was the kind of reaction he valued most, because it suggested he had hit upon a topic with wide appeal. A few weeks later he mentioned to me in a phone call that he might try to write a book on fairy tales—the subject was too broad for only a chapter in the child-rearing book. I was mildly concerned about again delaying the book under contract but asked him to show me what he meant.

Writing and thinking about the meaning of fairy tales settled him down as nothing else had done, and it was a relief. It was deeply personal, it embodied the sense of larger purpose he had lost, and teaching through books was work he could do for the rest of his life. Although this work did not exactly replace the School, he was teaching again in a major way; he felt useful, doing something that mattered. With his retirement he had been in a dark woods, and now he was winding his way out, as if by an enchanted path.

BETTELHEIM sent me most of the fairy-tale book by early summer 1975. According to Ruth Marquis, "I remember him saying about it, 'This is so easy, I could do it in my sleep.' And it was true, he could spin it out by the yard." Ruth did not edit the book, though when Bettelheim asked her for ideas on a title, she obliged.

"A line from Shakespeare came into my head," she said, " 'Sweet are the uses of adversity,' and then 'enchantment' fell into place. I laughed when I saw Bruno on the *Dick Cavett Show*, and Cavett praised the title. Bruno said something like, 'Well, I'm not sure I like the title now—I'm sorry I called it that.' He was feeling annoyed with me again for not working with him."

Ruth gave the work a title without having read it, and when Bruno sent her a published copy, she hated the book. "The message for me is, 'This is how you can understand a fairy tale, and it's equally important *how* you tell it and *where* the child sits, whether in your lap or across the room. I felt like saying, 'Shut up and stop telling me how to read fairy tales to my child. I'll do it the way I damn please, spontaneously.' Actually, my son bought the book and loved it, but I didn't like the point of view I felt there."

I had heard objections like this, and I said to Ruth (as I had to others) that I didn't believe Bettelheim meant his book in the way some had taken it. Ruth said, "Of course he didn't! He would have *died* if he thought all his readers felt that way."

In the passage that roused Ruth's anger, he says that

it depends largely on the narrator's feelings about a fairy tale whether it falls flat or is cherished.[2]

He describes a grandmother holding a child on her lap while telling the tale and contrasts this with a parent who is bored by the story and reads it out of a sense of duty.

Is this a rule or an illustration to make a point? Maybe a little of both, and in Ruth's favor we should note that at the start of that section ("On the Telling of Fairy Tales") Bettelheim comes close to laying down a rule when he says that adults should *tell* the tales rather than reading them. However, he took care to soften his "rule" into a suggestion:

To attain to the full its consoling propensities, its symbolic meanings, and, most of all, its interpersonal meanings, a fairy tale should be told rather than read.[3]

In other words, if you want to get the most out of a fairy tale, tell it, don't read it; but he adds that if we read it, we need to do so with "emotional involvement in the story and in the child," and with empathy for what it means to the child. Not quite a rule, but warm advice.

To evaluate Bettelheim's intent in *The Uses of Enchantment*, it may be helpful to recall his teaching methods in different settings. At the School he was the lawgiver, the boss, the protector-supporter; in his professorial mode, he spoke in tones that were forthright, positive, and often abrasive. Exercising his authority either as director or teacher, he did not hesitate to set standards and profess truths; that is, to offer specific messages to the superego, often framed in questions that effervesced in the listener's mind. Memorable drama, rousing battles, scathing put-downs, probing questions—these made up his methods both in classroom and milieu.

However, his books teach in another way; he wrote to persuade, to stimulate, to convince—all for a lay reader and a general public. With Ruth's earlier help (and by dint of daily effort teaching the School staff to speak plainly) he had long sought to give up the special languages of psychoanalysis and psychology in order to reach a wider public. Bettelheim did not order his readers around; he engaged them, hoping to draw them to the point of view that had moved him to write the book in the first place.

It seems to me that a fiery reaction like Ruth's to a piece of writing— anger that interprets a suggestion as a disguised command—may hint that Bettelheim remained a strong presence for her, an influence by transference even after she rebelled. In some hidden part of her spirit, he stood like an icon; if not, why so much fire? Yes, she *felt* ordered around, unable to ignore the icon even though not directly aware of it, as we are unable to ignore any standard-bearer in our unconscious.

Interpretation invites interpretation, and hers of him invited mine of her. If my notion had come to me while Ruth was alive, I would have told her; and she would surely have disagreed, saying that she knew Bruno better than I did and that in his heart he wanted everybody to do things his way. Which of course might be true.

THE USES OF ENCHANTMENT was Bettelheim's most successful book and his second after Ruth stopped working with him. Some of it appeared in the *New Yorker*, thanks to an inspired excerpt-condensation by one of its staff members, William Whitworth, who had called me for a second chance at the manuscript after the magazine rejected it. The acceptance by the *New Yorker* was Bettelheim's first there, and it almost seemed to awe him. (His compliments to me were excessive, so much so that I felt obliged to point out that this particular bit of good luck came from the thoughtful perserverance of an editor he did not know.) John Updike reviewed the book favorably on the front page of the *New York Times Book Review*, and it went on to win the National Book Award and the National Book Critics Circle prize. However, I believe it was his appearance in the *New Yorker* that pleased Bruno most.

AFTER Bettelheim's death, a few passages in *The Uses of Enchantment* were cited as grounds for a sensational charge of plagiarism. Alan Dundes, a professor at the University of California, Berkeley, published a scholarly note entitled "Bruno Bettelheim's *Uses of Enchantment* and Abuses of Scholarship."[4] In the first two-thirds of a seven-and-a-half-page text, Dundes praises some of Bettelheim's insights into fairy tales, then dispraises him for "lack of familiarity with folkloristics."

Without question, the latter point is true. Bettelheim's book had 122 footnotes and a bibliography of 59 titles, but he was not a folklore expert. Those who practice folkloristics seem to comb through endless variations in fairy tales looking for everything except their magic and unfading relevance. Folkloristics has scholarly value, but Bettelheim was fascinated by the fairy tale's astonishing power to touch our depths, and so he wrote about that.

Dundes does not detail his charge until near the end of the text, where he uses the word "sin" three times in a four-line paragraph. Most of his effort to prove that Bettelheim copied from others yields thin fare, but one citation seems troubling; Dundes quotes a passage from a book by Julius E. Heuscher, who wrote:

> While one must never "explain" the fairy tales to the child, the narrator's understanding of their meaning is very important. It furthers the sensitivity for selection of those stories which are most appropriate in various phases of children's development and for stressing those themes which may be therapeutic for specific psychological difficulties.[5]

He then matches this with a quotation from *The Uses of Enchantment*:

> One must never "explain" to the child the meanings of fairy tales. However, the narrator's understanding of the fairy tale's message to the child's preconscious mind is important. . . . It furthers the adult's sensitivity to selection of those stories which are most appropriate to the child's state of development, and to the specific psychological difficulties he is confronted with at the moment.[6]

Similarities between the two excerpts abound, but in a second reading my eye caught Dundes's ellipsis in the quote from Bettelheim, and I looked

up the passage as Bettelheim wrote it. I found that Dundes had cut out
this sentence:

> The narrator's comprehension of the tale's many levels of meaning
> facilitates the child's deriving from the story clues for understanding
> himself better.[7]

To leave out this sentence is the same as cropping a photo to remove
something you don't want us to see. It is scholarly censorship to score a
deceptive point. Most of us take the critic's good faith for granted, without
wondering what difference deleted words would make. A casual glance at
the two passages gives a clear impression that one writer has copied
another; if, however, we add the sentence Dundes cut, we see that Bettelheim's idea is more intricate and detailed than Heuscher's, and more
complete. It shows exactly what Bettelheim hoped would happen with the
child—always his first thought—namely, that the child's self-knowledge
would grow if the adult grasped the story's many levels. Bettelheim's grand
theme, *the need to know ourselves*, was never far from his mind, and it
jumps out at us from the sentence Dundes cut:

> One must never "explain" to the child the meanings of fairy tales.
> However, the narrator's understanding of the fairy tale's message to
> the child's preconscious mind is important. *The narrator's comprehen-
> sion of the tale's many levels of meaning facilitates the child's deriving
> from the story clues for understanding himself better.* It furthers the
> adult's sensitivity to selection of those stories which are most appropri-
> ate to the child's state of development, and to the specific psychologi-
> cal difficulties he is confronted with at the moment.

I have added emphasis here to show that Dundes cut Bettelheim like Pro-
crustes forcing an unwary traveler to fit the legendary bed; his deletion
lops off half Bettelheim's meaning. Dundes trimmed in a way to fool the
casual eye, shaving Bettelheim down to a visual twin by quoting fifty-two
words from Heuscher, sixty-one from Bettelheim. The Bettelheim quote
would have been proper at eighty-three words, but then the similarity
would not have been so striking. The slur of plagiarism could only mask
itself in the color of truth by an editing that carefully conceals meaning
rather than bringing it into the mind's light.

Perhaps a less sensational charge could have been mounted on: 1) the
chain of reasoning in Heuscher, which Bettelheim follows (although with

a new and crucial link added in the middle); and 2) the word "explain," set off by quotation marks. These similarities show that Bettelheim knew Heuscher and agreed with him as far as he went; however, he sharpened and deepened the message by focusing it on the child's understanding of himself. What I find of positive value in comparing the two citations is seeing Bettelheim's mind at work, the connection he made as he extends Heuscher by suggesting that the insight of self-knowledge can start very early, with a child sitting on a parent's lap. A warm lap is one of the more comforting possibilities in the human condition, and, as Bettelheim notes elsewhere, it is a safe place in which to feel (in imagination) some of the fears of life.

THE PERSON usually most sensitive to plagiarism is the author who has been copied, but in the news stories I saw, Heuscher had not seemed at all concerned or offended. I wanted to get a fuller account of what he thought, in the event that he had reservations he had been too polite to express. He was past retirement age when we met, and since Bruno referred to Heuscher's book as "Jungian" and I knew he was born and brought up in Switzerland, I asked if he considered himself a Jungian analyst.

"Well, I suppose so," he said. "I have a very limited psychoanalytic training. It was close to Jungian psychology, but different—it's close to existential philosophy. I have applied a great deal of existential thought to psychotherapy—which I am not alone in—but I hesitate calling myself an existential psychotherapist because it's a sort of vague term. I'm a psychotherapist trying to cope with some of the ultimate concerns of human needs, and I use any insights that are valuable, from whatever source."

Heuscher had not known Bettelheim personally but had read several of his books and he commented on two of them: *The Children of the Dream* ("which I loved") and *Freud and Man's Soul* ("a very good contribution to psychiatry"). He had been called by newspapers and magazines after Dundes's scholarly note prompted a flurry of stories in the press.

"Why a person who is a professor at the University of California would waste his time with such a trivial thing," he said, "I cannot tell you. I haven't read his material—all I know is what the papers asked me. One of the calls I got was from Jeffrey Masson. Do you know who he is?"

I knew Masson as the author of a book accusing Freud of suppressing the truth about a major theory in psychoanalysis. I had not read his book but recalled seeing an excerpt in the *Atlantic* and thinking he had some valuable points, although I remained unpersuaded by his conclusions. Heuscher told me Masson was a friend of Dundes's and seemed to want to intervene on his behalf.

"Jeffrey Masson called me," Heuscher said, "and the way I understood his question was, Why was I not perturbed about the Bruno Bettelheim plagiarism? I said, 'I'm not even convinced that this should be called plagiarism.' Actually, I'm sure this idea was not original with me, either. It's an idea I have heard from several people that I like—it's not an original product, you know, that you have a claim on. Of course, I didn't copy it from anybody, and when I wrote it, I wouldn't have known where I got the idea, but by that time it had become my idea.

"By that I mean, when you express an idea with the full conviction that it is a real truth, you can dispense with having to give a reference. Bruno Bettelheim was a very busy gentleman, I assume, and he had, probably, some people collect material for him when he wrote. And probably somebody collected this, and he was not even aware that he was taking from somewhere. I think it's just an idea that many people have had—it has no proprietary rights. I'm sure it was not done deliberately, and I think it's ridiculous to make a thing about this."

IN HIS NOTE Dundes also says that not explaining fairy tales to a child is a "key" idea in Heuscher, and he accuses Bettelheim of a "wholesale borrowing of key ideas." He fails to list any other "borrowed" ideas but does say, a few paragraphs later, that Bettelheim's book is "infinitely superior" to Heuscher's. Curiously, Dundes neglected to mention that in Heuscher's revised edition of his book (1974), he dropped this "key" idea.[8] I know Dundes is a meticulous scholar who would not deliberately overlook a second edition so different from the first, and so I take this as a lapse or mistake that could have happened to anyone: an understandable and all-too-human error.

When I asked why Heuscher had not kept the idea, it surprised him because he didn't realize he hadn't. He checked the later edition to be sure, and then said, "Probably it didn't happen to fit in, but I still believe it's true."

I do too, and so did Bettelheim, but it is only a reminder of what *not* to do. The child wants the enchantment of a good story whose meaning thrills him as the tale carries him along, and if the adult condescends or teaches pointedly, it will kill the magic and arouse resistance.

HEUSCHER, a transparently decent man, had guessed correctly that Bettelheim often asked others for suggestions, and it is possible that a friend sent him the quote from Heuscher. But I believe the book was one he read himself, and he does refer to it.[9] He probably made notes, then mislaid or lost the reference and so did not realize he should have accounted for Heuscher more fully. In spite of similarities, the two passages are different because Bettelheim developed the thought and rephrased it, but even with fewer parallels he would have hastened to credit Heuscher if he had noticed them.

DUNDES ends the text of his note as follows:

> Whether it was a matter of laziness or outright intellectual dishonesty, Bettelheim's legitimate and worthwhile contribution in *The Uses of Enchantment* is permanently marred by his failure to observe conventional academic etiquette.[10]

I quote this, first of all, to show that Bettelheim's failure at "etiquette" is the ultimate charge in a scholar's note widely interpreted as proving that Bettelheim plagiarized. Dundes had chosen his words with care and did not call Bettelheim a plagiarist. This was done for him by the press on the basis of a neat aspersion: if an undergraduate turned in a paper that borrowed without attribution,

> he or she would almost certainly be accused of plagiarism.[11]

In its daily haste, the press jumped from Dundes's hypothetical wording to a flat accusation and so gave innuendo the instant status of fact. Perhaps Dundes tried to correct the media's error, but if so, the correction has not come to my attention.[12]

DUNDES took one final slap at Bettelheim in a footnote that refers to articles by Charles Pekow and Ronald Angres, published not long after Bettelheim's death, accusing him of having abused children at the School. At first glance this footnote seems tacked on, since it has no logi-

cal connection with the rest of the note. However, Dundes connects it by
mentioning Bettelheim's "stature and reputation"; then he footnotes the
word *reputation* and repeats the gist of the Pekow and Angres charges.
With this, I realized that these few pages, brimming with academic pretense and weighted down with scholarly apparatus, were actually crafted
as a smear on a dead man's reputation. The resonance between "abuse" of
children on the last page and the "abuse" of scholarship in the note's title
closes the circle nicely, with a wink and a nod. The desire to smear must
have been deeply felt, because it shows the only hint of stylistic life in an
otherwise barren exercise.

However, the exercise does not withstand serious examination. Dundes the scholar had fourteen years in which he could have published his
clever and hostile remarks—years during which he admits he recommended *The Uses of Enchantment* as a textbook for his students. Of
course, had he published his note earlier, he might have had to face Bettelheim himself, and he wisely chose not to do this.

DUNDES'S note was not the first occasion for a reviewer to accuse Bettelheim of borrowing. When *The Uses of Enchantment* came out, in 1976,
Alison Lurie wrote in *Harper's Magazine* that Bettelheim failed to credit
David Riesman with an analysis of a particular fairy tale. The charge
angered and upset Bettelheim, but it also mystified him because it was
untrue. He wrote to *Harper's* and quoted from the pages where he mentioned Riesman in connection with the tale. He added that part of a footnote with a reference to *The Lonely Crowd* had been inadvertently
dropped; however, since the book's index listed Riesman, and since Bettelheim named him twice in the text, the loss of a note did not explain the
reviewer's charge.

Another comment by Lurie also puzzled and disturbed Bettelheim—
that he was "determined to explain for once and all what folk tales, and
especially fairy stories, mean." Bettelheim had written,

> As with all great art, the fairy tale's deepest meaning will be different
> for each person, and different for the same person at various moments
> in his life.[13]

In the introduction and elsewhere, he emphasized that it was impossible to encompass *all* the meanings of fairy tales, which delight and
enchant us through art, not through psychological content. Nevertheless,

he wanted to show adults how fairy tales might help a child's emotional growth, and he organized the book with certain concerns in mind. Part One examines tales that deal with our need for inner integration, Part Two with tales involving oedipal problems. Parents need sensitivity to these matters, and Bettelheim hoped to teach adults how to pass on the magic of fairy tales to their children.

The Uses of Enchantment sprang in part from the same urge that animates *A Good Enough Parent*: Bettelheim's desire to influence the way parents see themselves in relation to their children. Since such relationships are often highly charged, I wish I had thought of telling Bruno he might have handed some readers a hot potato. Many reacted angrily, like Ruth Marquis (and certain reviewers), so I believe the comparison is apt. Of course, if you can hold the potato long enough to toss it from hand to hand, some of the heat will dissipate, and you can eat it.

PLAGIARISM is an apt topic also, because once when Bettelheim did borrow from another writer, he was upset to find he had done so, even in a small way. After *The Children of the Dream* (1969) had gone to press, he learned that the words of the title appeared in someone else's book. As usual, Ruth Marquis had been responsible for the title, and in glancing over a book Bruno consulted for research she noticed the phrase "children of the dream" in the book's last paragraph. She had read this much earlier, then forgotten it, and the words had come back to her, unreferenced, when she was thinking about a title. The book was *Children of the Kibbutz* by Melford E. Spiro, an anthropologist at the University of California, San Diego.

Oddly enough, the spark for *The Children of the Dream* had occurred more than ten years earlier, when Bettelheim had read *Children of the Kibbutz* and disagreed with it so strongly that he wrote an essay critical of it. The essay grew into a monograph, which he eventually destroyed, because, as he said in the first chapter of *The Children of the Dream*, "I realized when all was said, he [Spiro] had been there, and I had not."

> There could be no doubt either of Spiro's sincerity or intelligence. So if he had arrived at what to me seemed erroneous interpretations, they might still be the right ones, derived from a "feel" of things he had gotten on the spot. Though his findings did not always accord with his data, they might still be correct and represent a "higher" truth. After

all, he had lived with the problem, and with the kibbutzniks; he had not just observed. The only way to be sure if my objections were way off or not was to go and find out for myself. . . . In retrospect I am very glad I arrived at this conclusion. Because later, in Israel, my own observations taught me that he was more often correct than my untested judgments had allowed, even though, as the reader will see, the conclusions we arrived at differed in very important respects.[14]

Eager to apologize for borrowing the phrase that had become his title, and without mentioning that someone else had suggested it, Bettelheim wrote to Spiro:

I have no other excuse for not having acknowledged this but the fact that, while the way you stated it must have made a deep and lasting impression on me when I read it more than a decade ago, in the intervening years the thought that these were the children of a dream became entirely disconnected from my having received this idea from your book. . . . I guess that it must have been the beauty of your formulation that stuck in my mind. This is hardly an excuse for my not having consciously realized it. Nor do I think that the fact that you do not explicitly speak about "the children of the dream" can serve as an excuse for me not giving you credit for having used what essentially was one of your ideas as the title of my book.

All I can do now is to offer you my sincere apologies for not having given you the credit that belongs to you.

Spiro wrote back a week later:

I am delighted to learn from your letter of March 19, that you have just published a book on the Kibbutz. Although I appreciate your words of apology, I hasten to assure you that no apology was necessary. I look forward to reading the book.

In accord with his rule of personal responsibility, Bettelheim had taken upon himself total blame for the unconscious borrowing. Nor did he plead forgetfulness, since this would have been untrue to his psychological principle that in such matters there are no accidents. He had read Spiro's book closely enough to write a monograph about it, he had heartily approved of the title that turned out to be borrowed, and both actions brought him into the moral arena. Even to hint that another person had been involved in the borrowing would have been reprehensible. It was *his* book, and he alone owed the apology, and he made it.

The letter to Spiro typifies a man sensitive to the rights of others and honorable to a fault about his fault. From a factual point of view his account is misleading—somebody else was involved—but I have no doubt that he saw the entire borrowing as his own, believing that he should have recognized the phrase "the children of the dream," rather than simply taking Ruth's suggestion. It is refreshing to see how far he felt he should go when he had to beg someone's pardon, but for me the key to his conscious self (as well as the heart of his morality) is that he seems to have made no excuses for or to himself about himself.

Anyone who reads the Bettelheim-Spiro letters should be able to lay to rest any suspicion of plagiarism and understand how repugnant an act of plagiarism would have been to the spirit of my friend Bruno.

CHAPTER 29

The Father's Role

IN THIS book-as-portrait I have not set out to answer Bettelheim's army of critics nor do I expect to decrease their number. Rather, I hope to show a man for whom teaching was the most satisfying work he could find, work in which he felt singularly useful. The milieu of the School suited his restless nature and gave endless play to his urge to guide others, because he could teach, and teach, all day long and into the night. In the last chapter, I took a short detour to examine the plagiarism slander, in part because I thought his reputation had been unfairly handled. The media transmuted the original charge, then trumpeted exaggerations without checking the evidence. Bettelheim could not answer, so I have made his case. Perhaps my words will help restore his good name wherever an ugly impression lingers among those who recall the episode, which came and went quickly but left a bad odor behind.

Besides showing him as a teacher, my aim has been to draw the reader into the work and methods of the School and, as a friendly outsider, to shed new light on him as its head. Despite his personal renown, he is not fully recognized as the remarkable educator he became, and it may be that someone, somewhere will sometime wish to work with troubled children in a comparable way. For this, Bettelheim's books are priceless on the methods of the milieu—but with one omission: as long as he was connected with the School he held back in writing about himself, partly because he had to hit children. In a way it was his highest function, and knowing this, I have tried to place him within a panorama that would otherwise not extend to the breadth of his accomplishment.

After his death, in 1990, a few persons said that he had mistreated children at the School, and again there was only one-sided reporting. This failure of the press was, I believe, understandable: some of those accusing him did so under protection of confidentiality about their medical history. Questions can't be asked, but this does not make me doubt the truthful intent of Pekow and others, although the charges leveled after Bettelheim died could have been made earlier without fear of legal retaliation, because he did hit some of the children and could not have denied it.

In principle I do not believe anyone who attended the School owes the public (or myself, or the press) glimpses into his private life. Bettelheim never thought so either, nor did he think the children owed the School or himself a debt of gratitude. Now that he is dead, privilege leaves a gap in the story as it has been told, but I doubt he would have cared. He worked to help unhappy children find better lives for themselves as they grew and learned, and his reward when they succeeded was the way he felt about himself when he saw their success.

Leaving aside individual stories of hitting, Bettelheim's reasons for the practice must be spelled out if we want to understand him, and I hope to put his use of physical discipline within the framework of its need as he saw it.

If this were a portrait on canvas, in the background we would see a small but recognizable figure of a man slapping a child. A painting could make us feel the child's shock without conveying the fullness of the man's motive, but the fact that I can offer this chapter to get the latter idea across is one advantage of writing over painting.

As MENTIONED earlier, a published account of Bettelheim hitting children at the School appeared in *The Pelican and After*, the 1983 novel by Thomas Lyons. Lyons writes of a student in an institution modeled on the School, and the demonic director looks like Bettelheim. Lyons not only dedicated the book to him, but in television and newspaper interviews he made a point of connecting the novel with his life at the School. Bettelheim disliked Lyons's portrayal but noted the adolescent's viewpoint was well done. When a reporter called to ask if he actually hit students, he said that the matter was between himself and the children, and he refused an interview.

Jacquelyn Sanders also wrote about hitting in *A Greenhouse for the Mind* (1989), where a chapter entitled "Discipline (Does It Have to Hurt?)" covers her reasons for having stopped the practice.[1] Neither her book nor Lyons's novel aroused much comment, despite their disclosures.

A mention of "spanking" in a 1970 article in the *New York Times Maga-zine* also passed without journalistic follow-up.

Although I knew of Lyons's book, I did not get around to examining it until 1985, after my interview with Betsy, who urged me to read it. Betsy and I talked a little about Bettelheim slapping some of the children, and I told her I would ask him why he did it. Gayle Janowitz, whom I inter-viewed the next day, said that she had never seen Bettelheim hit a child in the early years but had heard of it happening later.

By the time Bruno and I got together for another interview, I had come round to seeing the slap or hit as a need of the moment in the milieu but not a major concern.[2] At that point I knew just enough about the School to guess that sometimes Bettelheim had to restore order quickly, and it seemed reasonable that a slap would do the job. If I had foreseen the furor after his death, I would have spoken with him at greater length about the hitting, because he was quite willing to talk about it for this book, which we both expected to be published in his lifetime. How-ever, I believe that his remarks, though not extensive, go to the heart of his motives.

My conclusion that he was doing it for the milieu was quickly cor-rected when I learned from him that "restoring order" was secondary and that the first order he wanted to reestablish was in the child's inner world, not in the little world of the School.

As it happened, our discussion began with a contradiction I thought I had found between a statement in *A Home for the Heart* and some-thing I had heard. In the book Bettelheim says that no child ever tried to commit suicide at the School. However, a former staffer said (off the tape) that a boy had tried to hang himself in a closet and that Bettelheim had hit him very hard. I asked Bruno whether he recalled the child's suicide attempt.

He looked startled and said, "No child ever really tried seriously to commit suicide. It's entirely possible that somebody went through the motions to get a reaction—partly to provoke, partly to find out what the reaction would be. Several children threatened it—that was by no means a rare occurrence."

I insisted that someone had told me, I couldn't remember who, about a boy trying to hang himself in a closet. I had no description of him and no name, but, I said, "After somebody got him down, you really hit him—hard."

"Well, I don't know, I have no recollection, and probably I repressed it if I did it, and that's why I can't remember. If I would know who the child was, I might be able to recollect."

But what would he have been doing?

"I think my action was partly my own upset, and *should be* my own upset. I wanted to show him how terribly upsetting it was to me, and nothing else would have convinced him of that."

"You couldn't just say you were upset?"

"No, that wouldn't work."

"Because they've heard so many words?"

"That's right, words were a dime a dozen. But I really would be interested to know who it was, and I can't remember."

After we talked, it occurred to me that a boy so angry and despairing that he wanted to kill himself would never be consoled by a hug or softened by soothing words, nor reassured by a mild emotion; but Dr. B.'s heavy hand carried conviction—proof that the "father" cared.

I recalled a lesser type of physical discipline with Paul: Bettelheim would seize him by the arms and shout, "What are you doing? Stop it!" Paul said this was very impressive, as mentioned earlier, and I asked Bruno why he did it. He said that Paul tended to get overexcited and simply had to be calmed down, but even when he intervened in a mild way, he was doing what the staff couldn't.

"I put myself on the line. I was always called in when things got out of hand, to settle the issue, and that is partly why I got respect from the staff. This is a part of the father role, you know."

How often did he have to intervene?

"Oh, I would say there was daily something—some bigger, some smaller—but practically daily something had to be settled."

We talked about Shelton Key's experience when he slapped a child and one of the boys said, "Wait'll Dr. B. finds out."

"That's the most important thing," Bruno said, "that the children have the feeling that I would protect them against unfairness. Of course, when I slapped, I never did this unless I had a very strong relation with the child, because it had to be an emotional act in an emotional context; otherwise it's punishment or brutality."

SOME COUNSELORS had given me the impression that slapping was mainly for adolescents and that he did less of it with the smaller children.

"I touched them only when it was therapeutically indicated. Sometimes they had to see that you are upset and sometimes you had to demonstrate that you can control them. But you don't have to do it to small children. Most of the time it is enough if you take them by the arm or by the hand or whatever. Counselors were not supposed to hit the children. As a matter of fact, with Harry [described in *Truants from Life*], it was a turning point when I fired the counselor, and the reason was not that he might have slapped him, but he turned him over and spanked him, you know, and that was a deliberate act of punishment, rather than an emotional response. An emotional response can take many ways, one can live with it, but if somebody thinks they have the right to punish you, you can't live with it."

I was looking for a moment in the development of the School when Bettelheim saw that he had to use physical discipline stronger than taking Paul by the arms, but I did not phrase the question precisely enough. I asked at what point he began to think of slapping as part of therapy, and he said, "I never considered it an important part of therapy. It's not part of therapy at all. It was terribly important for them that if they cannot reestablish self-control that somebody can control them, because the anxiety of not being in control becomes too great. Secondly, it is important for somebody to have a strong emotional reaction. Sometimes you can do this with your voice.

"Well, I always said that if I can't control these children with my voice, then I can't control them. But sometimes one would get so out of control, so out of bounds, that some radical measure was needed as a shortcut. It's an undesirable shortcut. It was against all my principles to hit the children, but I learned that sometimes it's a shortcut that is important for the person—to feel that they can be controlled, because the anxiety of their getting completely out of control is very great.

"I think also the fact that I was in control of the situation was very important for the staff. And I would say in my favor I don't recall I ever slapped a child when somebody else hadn't started it up, and then I had to protect a counselor, or another child. Whenever I was there at the beginning of the interaction with the child, it was never necessary."

But what about the fact that many children, especially in the later years, were afraid of him?

"Well," he said, "I think that in a way they were afraid of me, and it served a useful purpose. Why? Because it kept their disintegrating tendencies in balance. These tendencies could become very destructive, and the children needed some authority figure."

He added later, "A school needs a head—any educational institution needs one head who is very sure in himself what he is doing, where his actions are not authoritarian but authoritative because he feels himself really in command and carries the responsibility. And I think that some of the staff and the children really profited a great deal because there was somebody who felt in command."

MARGARET CAREY, the longtime Orthogenic School therapist, had seemed such a gentle person that I went back to see her after Bettelheim's death, to ask what she thought of his slapping children and when she first saw it. She had known him for fourteen years and had worked part-time during that period without ever suspecting that he sometimes hit a child. She first saw it in 1961, just after she started full-time, in a general meeting following a holiday.

"An adolescent girl, she was fourteen or fifteen, had bought some earrings while she was home on a visit and brought them back to the School. She'd had her ears pierced also, and Bruno wouldn't give permission for any abuse of the body. Kids were not supposed to wear earrings, but she sidled up to him and showed him these earrings in front of the whole school. She was defying him utterly, and he slapped her. Then he looked at me as if to say, 'What are you going to think of me?' Well, I was very surprised.

"I was never slapped as a child, so I could never really accept the idea of hitting. It took the girl aback, of course. I didn't understand what was going on, but I gave Bruno the benefit of the doubt and thought there must be some meaning I had missed. Another time I saw Dr. B. slap a boy, and he said to me right afterward, 'Now Jimmy* knows who to hate.'

"We must have discussed this kind of thing in staff meetings, though I don't have a specific memory of it. I think the idea was that the child could hate Dr. B. and in that way get a more organized personality. And emotions. But I never got used to it. Recently a therapist friend of mine said that if Bruno had had more of a sense of humor, these children could have been handled in a different way, rather than letting them hate him."

Several others told me that Bettelheim usually discussed an incident in the next staff meeting and gave precise reasons for his action. The remark of Margaret's friend implies that Bettelheim should have wanted to be liked by the children; but, as discussed earlier, he had to avoid that temptation. Good humor and reason may guide children within the family, and perhaps did so in some orphanages, but the School was not a family or an orphanage. Counselors had to be tolerant and loving, whereas Bettelheim stood (in part) for the harshness of the real world, which often surprises us, limits us, disappoints us, and disregards our view of ourselves.

CHAPTER 30

The Autocrat

ETTELHEIM AND Sylvester had conceived a school without hierarchy or status, where he and she would be two among equals, and their progressive notion of educational democracy worked, but not as well as it might have. (Redl tried it in Detroit and failed.) When Bettelheim saw that the School might do better with a single head who had a strong hand and convictions to match, he also saw that he could do it partly in the style of his *gymnasium* headmaster almost forty years earlier: combining emotional distance with managerial closeness, in a manner decisive, stern, and self-assured. Remarkably, there was a consilience of needs that made his idea possible. The children's parents needed therapeutic help so desperately that they gave him free rein; helping the children was inherently fascinating and also filled an emotional need in him in a unique way; and the children needed love within a firmly managed milieu, a school dominated by the presence of an insightful and unambivalent autocrat.

AN AUTOCRAT rules without dispute and settles questions on his word alone, which Bettelheim did for years. However, he was an autocrat with a difference—one who wanted to teach by stimulating others and whose power had narrow limits. An autocrat in politics or in the family is not the same as an autocrat in a school, where actual power does not extend beyond the school's walls or reach the student who has left (although it does color the student's imagination and influence the structure of his psyche).

Another important difference was that Bettelheim delegated power to his staff and expected his own function to be circumscribed and complemented by theirs and by their autonomy. He hired people who had to achieve autonomy at the School if they were to do the job, people whom he would guide more than dominate. When he did dominate, it would be by authenticity of insight and mastery of crisis. In teaching at the School his ideal was to demonstrate solid authority so that no staffer need obey blindly, as with an authoritarian.

Bettelheim objected to Jules Henry's conclusion that he permitted autonomy to the staff, because autonomy *permitted* is not real autonomy. In fact, autonomy was *required*; a counselor made her own mistakes and had her own successes, even with guidance from all sides. Bettelheim hired and fired at will, but he praised the counselors' autonomy as the School's greatest strength. When he pointed out mistakes and helped at an impasse, he aimed toward more autonomy, not less. The child's healing never began without trust in a caring adult, and only a sincere adult could build up personal trust. However, because of Bettelheim's resolute distance, the child's trust in him perhaps remained more institutional than personal.

Bettelheim reached his goals through real people, not puppets, and the counselor who succeeded did so because of her genuine responses. Bettelheim's two deepest insights into the work and organization of the School were that it needed an autocratic head and that therapy did not take a "professional." A friendly amateur, willing to learn, could do it.

Bettelheim's forceful personality—*he meant what he said*—gave him the autocrat's upper hand. Diana Kahn remarked that the mere fact that he did not want children to hit counselors deterred their violence.

"Somebody, somehow," she said, "had to reassure us that we weren't in danger, or else we couldn't do our jobs. And if the kids felt the staff was safe, they felt safe from attack by each other."

A child sometimes reported a new counselor's mistakes to Bettelheim when he made rounds, and he usually reprimanded the adult in front of the children. If Diana had made a child feel unsafe (for instance, by not respecting his person or possessions) Bettelheim upbraided her publicly. She hated it, but when it happened she was relieved because the School operated with such clarity.

"It felt clean," she said, "and it gave you clarity about yourself."

But how thoroughly did the staff learn the lessons of autonomy?

Bert Cohler has said that when he took over in 1969 and Bettelheim was not on hand, counselors were always asking, "What would Bruno do?" Bert pushed them to think for themselves, and I have no doubt that Bettelheim would have done the same thing by posing a question or with a cutting comment, if a staffer seemed to be trying to pick his brain or anticipate his response. A counselor did not learn autonomy in one lesson or overnight, and wherever the weed of dependency sprang up, it had to be pulled out.

DIANA drew the distinction (as others also did) between the staff's duties and the director's. On her very first shift, when she knew next to nothing, a ten-year-old boy kicked her and she kicked him back.

"I thought I had behaved appropriately, so I reported the incident to Dr. B. He became very angry and almost shouted at me, 'If you think it's right to kick children, you should become a jailer! You should not work here.' This shocked me and made me ashamed, because I suddenly saw how wrong I was."

Later she understood why: "If a counselor was unsympathetic, or harsh and judgmental, Dr. B. would put a stop to it by saying, 'It's my job to be the superego—the children don't need that all day; they need more support from you.'"

AS MASTER of the School, Bettelheim decided instantly what level of force to use. Margaret Carey recalled once seeing him make his point not by hitting but by shouting. One day an adolescent boy in treatment with her had the duty of serving in the dining room, and he came up to Bettelheim's table and dropped a butter dish. Bettelheim exploded at him.

"Dr. B. absolutely roared, 'You're not an idiot! You don't need to do that! You don't have to act the fool!' And then he roared some more. I felt sorry for the boy—to me he was just a little frightened rabbit, and here was Bruno making things worse. But later, as we went on in treatment, I understood what Bruno was trying to do. The boy's father had an attitude that the child was a fool, and Bruno was fighting against that attitude, which the kid had internalized. Bruno looked like he was terribly angry, but I don't believe he was actually angry at the boy. He wanted to stop him from putting on an act of being incompetent, and he was backing him as an adequate and competent person. Bruno knew what the child needed at that moment, and he used the roar to bring the point home."

In this intervention the reader can see that Bettelheim attacked an attitude that was a serious flaw in the boy's superego. Bettelheim meant to cancel, if possible, the father's degrading judgment and replace it with his own. Hitting would not have made the point in a fair way, but perhaps a sudden giant roar would be memorable enough to stop the boy the next time he felt impelled to act out his and his father's belief that he was clumsy.

Children often came to the School with an unfinished or poorly formed inner guide, "a superego full of holes," as Bettelheim put it. To fill in the holes he offered—besides the counselors' love—his own standards, plus himself as the watchful power to be feared and obeyed. Whether a child had too much or too little superego, Bettelheim loomed as the menacing reality he might have to face, acting with speed, with conviction, and without ambivalence to carry off his duty as the School's autocrat.

BETTELHEIM wrote no rationale for hitting, and I doubt that he ever worked his insights into a theory. However, he knew what he was doing at the School and discussed specifics with the staff. Also, he had practical reasons for hitting and practical reasons for not writing about it.

To explain hitting in his books about the School would have completed the picture, but at the cost of a public quarrel with those sure to disagree with him. Any defense of hitting would seem like self-justification, and no matter how cogent and consistent his arguments for a timely use of force, he could not expect the world to applaud. If psychologists, scandalized by the spectacle of a slap in a "benign" milieu, raised a cry against the School, it would not survive; children would be taken away, to suffer new mischief. Further, if he wrote about himself as the milieu's reality principle and superego, it would sound arrogant, even to many who understood Freud, or thought they did.

Many readers would see his point, but too many would not, and some patrons of the School, unable to answer the doubts of their friends, would desert it.

When Bettelheim made hitting a practice, he was in a trap but not in a quandary: if he did not use the shortcut of a slap, youngsters who needed a sharp limit, a humiliating rebuke, would go on their way, id-driven, valuing their hostile acts, sanctioned by a flawed superego; and if he told the world the whole story, he might as well resign. I suspect it was an easy choice.

He had always been irked by half-truths often repeated about the School, such as calling its methods "permissive"—a chronic distortion made by people determined to believe that a single attitude, *love*, answered all needs. He knew better, but at some point he chose to live with a half-truth himself, one that let the School, his work, and the children's lives go forward.

Another motive for living with less than the truth was the probability, which he mentioned to me, of supporters repeating a less-than-half truth: "Bettelheim says it's okay to slap kids." Rather than courting misjudgment on all sides, he chose to act for the children and leave the world in the dark.

THE WORK of the School proceeded empirically, by trial and error, as the staff and Bettelheim found new methods in daily experience. No one could say when he had first slapped a child, and if I had asked him directly I doubt he would have remembered, but we need to look further to see why it worked well enough in his hands to become a method.

A big reason, of course, was the benign milieu. Everything in the environment, especially the staff, made it possible for him to slap a child and then walk away, leaving a shocked youngster to be comforted *at once* by his counselor. But did this work for the child?

Karen Zelan said that the child usually calmed down, as if something had been released, or perhaps put back together. Slapping almost never happened in her group, but Bettelheim told the staff that when he shaped up a child with a slap, that child would become open to the good impressions of the counselor's nurturing as she stepped in with her affection and empathy. Bettelheim also reminded them that a slap would pave the way for the counselor to teach the child something new and important *about himself.*

Karen said that after an intervention, Bettelheim later tried to deal with the child's central problem. "He did this all the time. For instance, he'd walk into the dorm and say to a child, 'Your problem is so-and-so'— always on the money, of course—and then he'd go out and leave the counselor to help the child understand what had been said. That was one of our jobs, that was the therapy, and Bruno didn't do it."

On one occasion, she said, Bettelheim began to talk quietly with Vivienne: he brought her close to a girl with blue eyes and had the two youngsters stand face to face and stare into each other's eyes. Karen later asked why he did this, and he replied, "So they could see they weren't going to destroy each other." Vivienne did not try to scratch the girl again.

While this episode was going on, Bettelheim commented to Karen, "You don't want to get your hands dirty." In fact, Karen knew she could not nurture and hit, and she didn't *want* to hit, so any physical discipline was left to him. All the times he had to slap or reprimand Vivienne occurred when the girl was with someone else, not Karen. Vivienne sensed the depths of Karen's feelings for her and so did not act out. However, when a child did act out, Bettelheim was clear in his certainty that it was right to hit *that* child at that moment. Curiously, the "dirty hands" remark suggests a lingering reservation about hitting, and at some level Bruno may have remained at odds with himself. However, he stood firm in what he had to do for the child and the milieu.

Of course, dirty hands carried a risk for him, because some students he hit in the later years towered over him and could have fought back. In fact, I asked him about being kicked in the testicles, and he said he didn't recall the incident. I didn't believe him but saw he wouldn't budge.

No former staff member acknowledged seeing the assault, but by piecing together hints from several sources I was able to conclude that the attacker may have been a boy about Bettelheim's own size who was strong enough to make his kick count. For some reason he had slapped the student, who retaliated by kicking him where it would hurt most. The attack took Bettelheim by surprise and went on long enough for the adults nearby to intervene, but they all froze.[1]

In the aftermath, I gather that Bettelheim felt less disturbed by his attacker, whose motive was obvious, than by the staffers who did not move quickly to help. If he parsed their irresolution, as I'm sure he did, he would have been vexed and dismayed to feel that their slow response meant they unconsciously approved the assault.

The event was a crisis that challenged both Bettelheim and the milieu, and so he spoke the next day at the three o'clock meeting, in part to spell out the psychology and symbolism of the incident, such as why he was kicked where he was kicked. His unruffled presence was more eloquent than his words; he stood unchanged before the whole School, his dignity untouched, his resolve and strength as clear as ever. All saw that he was still the Dr. B. who protected the School, the director they were attracted to, whom they respected and sometimes feared, a man fully in command of himself and their world.

NOT EVERYONE gained from Bettelheim's sense of command, but as he said, *some* did. When he hit a child, all children saw his convictions about their behavior; a public slap warned them and perhaps added a prickle of fear to their superego in the kind of internalization that made Bettelheim a presence even in his absence. It was a lesson in reality, there for the learning.

As the School's superego figure he used force, but he did not think it best in family life, where a fed-up parent's "Go to your room" or "Get out of my sight" should do the job. His resort to a slap was meant for youngsters too troubled to live at home.

In ordinary family life, an hour's banishment would prompt guilt or unconscious separation anxiety in a child, followed by a return to the family fold. In the milieu, where the child's sense of belonging depended on his trust in his counselor and (by extension) in the world of the School, deliberate use of separation anxiety would push him out of reach. On the other hand, when a child defied the rules, Bettelheim guarded the School's boundaries of behavior, judged the child's motive, and shook him up with a slap, relying in the next moment on the support of the counselor's active warmth and the milieu's passive but steady indulgence.

THE MILIEU also had warmth and support for adults.

"If he badgered someone," Karen Zelan said, "he took it for granted that the others would close ranks and help the one who'd just gotten the brunt of his anger. Personally, I couldn't stand it when he turned on me, and once in my first two years I got up and ran out of the meeting. My coworkers were supportive afterwards, which was really necessary."

Karen added that Bettelheim's slap cleared the air for the counselor who had been having a problem. The child often picked up the counselor's relief at the sudden change of atmosphere when Bettelheim defused the hostility and dispelled any guilt the child might have felt for his aggression. The counselor, getting the benefit of a slap and grateful that she didn't have to do it, felt freer to make new beginnings with the child.

TO UPHOLD authority in this way, Bettelheim had to be sure not only of his goals but of the purity of his motives in the running of the School, which I see as threefold:

1. to help the children;
2. to show the world what could be done with deeply troubled youngsters; and
3. to satisfy his yearning for work that mattered.

Without the third motive he could not have given his life to the first two. He could not have helped children by developing residential therapy in the form of a school, and by creating a place where children always came first, even when he had to bring them down to earth with a slap.

Guilt does not invariably function as a firm voice of conscience or guide to behavior; fear also has a role to play. Primitive feelings called for primitive barriers, and if guilt did not block a child's hostility, fear might. The iron in Bettelheim's spirit gave weight to his hand in raising barriers of fear, and his insight into a child's motives told him the moment to do what he did.

The girl with the earrings had offered such a moment. She defied Bettelheim's authority in front of the assembled students, and he jolted her vanity and their latent defiance when he slapped her face. She alone took the blow, but the whole room felt it. As a Freudian realist, he did not try to wish away the potential for hostility in youngsters, and he reacted to her insolence in a flash, with swift justice.

THOUGH he didn't write about his hitting at the School, Bettelheim did publish an essay on the value of fear in a child's superego. In "Education and the Reality Principle" he argues that a young child must learn right and wrong in black and white terms to internalize a sense of order—that is, to develop a useful superego. In turn, the shape of his superego determines whether or not he *can* be educated, because only the superego will support a stubborn commitment to the reality that education takes a long time and does not always give pleasure. Children with poorly formed superegos simply cannot meet the demands of school. Bettelheim dismisses the popular notion that it is enough for teachers merely to make classwork fun, saying that

> for education to proceed, children must have learned to fear something *before* they come to school.[2] [Emphasis added.]

By this he does not mean a child's fear of being hit at home or hurt in the neighborhood, but the fear that occurs within conscience. Many underprivileged children cannot readily apply themselves to studies, because, he says, they reach school without the beginnings of a middle-class morality to shape their conscience. Many middle- or upper-class children also came to the Orthogenic School with malformed superegos, and for that reason they and poor children alike needed to experience a world of pleasure before "any learning to live by the demands of reality."[3]

He stresses that young children must feel satiated over and over with emotional and physical pleasure (*fun!*) before conscience can take root. A child's steady enjoyment of instinctual pleasure—such as in food, fantasy, play, and warmth from an adult—encourages him to internalize standards in his superego that will later guide him toward the reality principle, where he can postpone an instinctual demand in favor of a long-range goal.

Bettelheim focuses this essay upon underprivileged children, but it is obvious that many of his points apply to some in the School, where a child could learn about himself, do schoolwork, and improve his social behavior.

Growing and learning in the School required a sequence in the child's life: as a precondition to everything, he had to have self-respect; and as a precondition to self-respect, he had to enjoy and value himself in the nurturing milieu; but to enjoy or like himself there, he first had to be liked by someone else, in most cases a counselor. Once this chain of psychological purpose had been set in process by the counselor, the pleasures and problems of sustained effort in learning allowed the child to earn self-esteem based on his competence. The pleasures of living had to precede the pleasures of formal education, because, as Bettelheim said, it was not all pleasurable; and the superego had to be strong enough to postpone instinctual satisfaction. Education based only on the pleasure principle could help a child begin but never go very far; the reality principle and its mainstay, an adequate superego, had to underlie and oversee the educational process.

Bettelheim says that the mature morality a child needs if he is to profit from years of schooling must itself evolve from a

> once-rigid belief in right and wrong based on a fear of *perdition* that permits no shading or relativity.[4] [Emphasis added.]

As the School's autocrat and superego, he displayed right and wrong in a superbly clear light, without shadows, and by "perdition" he meant any fear that motivates action or restraint, from a religious "damnation in hell" to a personal "loss of parental affection." He notes that it seems to make little difference what the fear is, so long as the adult sets standards that help the child distinguish right from wrong. The parent must also

have cared for the child well enough to foster a conscience that can correct behavior that deviates from internalized standards. He warns, however, that a parent's approval of the child cannot be unconditional.

> If, as modern middle-class parents are often advised, affection and
> approval are guaranteed to the child no matter what, there will be no
> fear—but neither will there be much morality.[5]

Here we see one of his reasons for dealing sharply with children and
not relying upon the counselor's love alone. With no separation anxiety in
the milieu, the main source of fear was Bettelheim, willing to get his
hands dirty on behalf of youngsters whose foreshortened sense of social
and personal reality often did not moderate their aggression.

We can guess that the submission or compliance of some students
went only skin deep. Anyone who resisted inwardly and pretended to
yield might leave the School without absorbing the values Bettelheim
tried to exemplify. He had to prove his strength many times over before
his moral force could become an internal authority for a child—if it ever
did. Everyone knew that the ethos of the milieu was to encourage the
growth of individuals, not indoctrinate them, and as they gained their own
strength, some were sure to harbor deep resentments against Bettelheim
forever.

In the essay he also says that an "irrational superego anxiety" had to
exist in a child's conscience to ensure traits of

> diligence, concentration and perseverance. . . . Only when such traits
> have become an inseparable part of the personality is the anxiety no
> longer necessary for learning.[6]

In this context he points out that anxiety can have positive effects, such as
helping make the child a social being. It should be remembered, of
course, that many at the School had severe problems in this regard.

BETTELHEIM'S autocratic control modeled firmness for any superego
capable of being re-formed. As the strongest person in the School, he
commanded respect, inspired admiration, invited some measure of identification, and aroused fear. His scrutiny of the often discordant forces of
emotions came into play to help others reach firm inner ground, but he

wanted all to fear his disapproval, even as he hoped they would, later in life, fear self-disapproval.

In Freud's concept, the chief function of conscience or superego is to limit our instinctual satisfactions. Bettelheim held himself answerable for children separated from their parents and so took on the job of inhibiting them by enforcing limits on their behavior. By redirecting aggressive impulses and correcting hostile acts, and by not tempting children to fantasize about him as a father, he avoided creating an attachment with unreal expectations.

Bettelheim had a clear agenda: he wanted the child to become the kind of person who valued his inner life and the feelings of others, who held himself accountable for his acts and feelings, and who developed the resilience he would need for life on his own. Bettelheim sometimes told the staff they might not like the person a child became, but that was not the point. At the end of all their work, the child belonged to himself.

Some readers may feel that Bettelheim overreached, that he arrogated power to himself too boldly as the milieu's superego. However, in this he was both Freudian and traditional. Teachers have long wielded parental authority, as Freud recognized:

> The superego is the successor and representative of the individual's parents (and educators) who had supervised his actions in the first period of his life; it carries on their functions almost unchanged.[7]

Freud conceptualized the superego as autocratic by nature and spoke of the "autocracy of conscience" that "rules the anarchy of id." Bettelheim objectified this function by ruling the School with a sharp autocratic edge.

Steve Herczeg was one of the former counselors who called Bettelheim the School's superego, adding that the counselors were like the ego, and the children, with their chaotic impulses, like the id. "It is the interaction between all three forces that allows growth and development," he said, "but without a superego that leads the way to health, I don't think you could make it work. The School needed a figure like Dr. B. to be organized around. I can't see a place like that being run by a committee."

Bettelheim solved the basic problem of control of the milieu and in the child, but that was not the whole story. "Some of the children who came to us were overcontrolled," he said, "and when that was the case we were anxious because they might become utterly destructive, or self-destructive, when the controls were lifted. In fact, this is a well-known phenomenon, that in treating a really disturbed individual, one has to be very careful. When self-control is removed from a person like this, he can become homicidal or suicidal, so one has to go slowly and carefully in the lifting of overcontrols."

Another wrinkle in the control problem was the child who *wanted* to be controlled. Paul (described in *Truants from Life*) threw wild tantrums and resented it when Bettelheim only stood and watched. This surprised Paul, who admitted later that he had wanted adults to restrain him because he dreaded the long process of developing inner controls. Bettelheim had intuited Paul's motive and knew that intervention to control the tantrum would keep Paul from learning to control himself.

"It takes a lot of energy to develop self-control, most of all simply to *have* self-control," Bettelheim said. "It's different when somebody else controls you; you can rage against them. But when you control yourself, you can't express your anger quite so easily. Also, if another person controls you, you can always find a way to escape their control. With self-control there's no way to escape it. If you control me, I don't have to control myself, no? If you lock me up, there's no danger that I can do anything wrong, and in this circumstance I don't have to develop self-control. Also, I can hate you."

In our 1983 interview Bettelheim had said of his attitude toward the children, "It was not to my purpose that they should think they were monsters." Later I learned that he let himself become a monster in the minds of some, in part to help them restrain their hostility.

Bettelheim wanted a child to develop a favorable self-image based on reality, including the reality of the counselor's empathy and love. The child could think the worst of Bettelheim, but Bettelheim could not view the child as a little monster and do what he had to do. (If your superego thinks you're a hopeless case, you'll think so too.) For his purpose, the child had to *believe* he was capable of getting better, and Bettelheim led the way with his own conviction, which he conveyed to the counselor, who in turn conveyed this feeling to the child.

He saw the children as utterly human in emotions and behavior, not set apart from the rest of us. Yes, they were disturbed and disturbing, but to him they were souls in trouble, children he could help. They were human nature in its extremity, not examples of a "bad seed." He also saw what was good in them, and he sometimes restored a counselor's balance by reminding her, "These kids are fun!" He could say it because it was true: a child at the School was always far more than the sum of his disturbances.

However, if the child got away with a hostile act, if he saw the "monster" in him dare and win, nothing could be worse for his inner life, because a vicious success encouraged viciousness, not conscience and a better feeling about himself. A vigilant Bettelheim hit children to demolish self-esteem gained in the wrong way. No doubt he sometimes dealt unjustly, but because everyone knew he acted out of conviction, even injustice could have a good side effect in the minds of others, in the way a rumble of thunder warns of a distant storm. Since the slap was also an act of protection, he could rely on most children's trust of him to override resentment if he made a mistake; and anyhow, it was never a mistake to warn the whole School.

BETTELHEIM insisted that slapping was not therapy, so the question arises, how could he say it was therapeutically indicated? Perhaps the best way to clarify the point is to compare him to a lifeguard who saves someone from drowning; getting a swimmer out of deep water is not therapy, but artificial respiration is. In the same vein, a person trapped in a fire needs first to be rescued; burn treatments come later. When a slap worked, it put out the behavioral fire, brought the child back to the milieu, and left him ready for love and the little steps of therapy.

Bettelheim shook up children for many reasons: vanity, defiance, lying, a tirade, arrogance, deviousness—any act that pitted the child against others in his environment or set his worst impulses against his better self. The slap was not "punishment" for a "crime," nor was it like a penalty that society imposes for breaking the law. The fact that many interpreted it in this way is understandable, but Bettelheim's business was rescue, not jail, and when he slapped he was striking at a child's mischievous sense of himself.

At the moment of impact the youngster felt humiliation and rage but often had no perspective on Bettelheim's intent. Reality overwhelmed him with the message *You can't do that here.* Most students would not have been sent to the School unless they had earned this response, many times over, before Bettelheim became their larger reality and demonstrated the world of rules they would have to live in as adults. As suggested earlier, a gentler version of his message came from the counselor, along with the warmth that made its meaning bearable. The children needed this warmth to reclaim their self-respect, to be reconciled to a world less than perfect and to a self not so grand as they thought. Counselors could lead them to understand Bettelheim's intent and its meaning for themselves, but nothing good would happen unless he first rescued them from the shallows of vanity or the fires of arrogance. Holding on to their flaws for dear life (as we all do), they had to be shaken loose; and Bettelheim, embodying the reality principle, did the shaking.

OUR SENSE of self is complex but does not seem so: an effortless stream of consciousness fills my inner eye with a vision that feels clear and trustworthy, and all the while an unwilled infusion of unconscious defenses color and shape the "reality" I think I know. If I am asked my reason for anything, simple desire (*I like it*) often comes to mind, but this explains nothing. No one can be expected to recall the forming of his conscience or to remember just how he began to value whatever he values. A time or a place may come to mind, but *why* and *how* are elusive. Nothing influences the course of our life more insistently than our sense of self, yet nothing is harder to pin down.

Nevertheless, this was Bettelheim's target as he aimed to redirect emotions, defenses, and attitudes in the children. Mental habits are dyed into personality and express (or suppress) feelings hidden from ourselves, interpretations we are not aware of, based on a life history both real and imagined. This held true for the youngsters Bettelheim rescued when he caught attitudes that kept a child from living in relative peace with others and with himself. Slapping was the shortcut he took to let therapy resume; it was crude, but somehow in the darker corners of personality development, his sincerity made the shortcut work.

AT ALL times, the children aroused sympathies in him that he could not put on display. Their needs moved him, but more than this, he was moved by his belief that they would benefit from the love and guidance the School offered. His self-knowledge told him he could help, and his self-respect demanded that he do it. Freud theorized that we have aggression as an inherent drive, balanced with the equally intrinsic drive of love. Bettelheim structured the School to take both into account, dealing with children every day in ways he believed would advance their growth as long as they felt loved and also found satisfying ways to control and use their aggressive tendencies.

THE QUESTION remains: could a residential school have been created in another form, without the need for slapping or hitting? The answer, of course, is yes and no, as we can see in the other school Bettelheim wrote about—Summerhill.

CHAPTER 31

The Other School

A S I HAVE described, Bettelheim divided responsibilities between himself and the staffers so that they did all the nurturing and left the physical discipline to him. In a residential school for troubled children it seemed impossible to combine both aspects of care in the same person. However, at least one man did it—after a fashion. I am referring to A. S. Neill, the educator who founded and wrote about the school in England named Summerhill. Bettelheim published an admiring essay on Neill, and although he calls Neill's philosophy "charmingly naive," he praises his work as being "rich in psychological wisdom."[1]

It is easy to see why Neill was able to nurture children and discipline them, if we compare the level of disturbance in children at the Orthogenic School with the level at Summerhill. Neill's students were not the hard cases Bettelheim accepted year after year; their emotional disorders were far milder. Even so, Neill had to hit them on occasion—not often, but still he could not do his job at all times with warmth, good humor, and reason.

Bettelheim retells an incident in which Neill dealt with a boy who hit and threatened other children and then bit and kicked Neill. Neill hit back at once, and since he was twice the child's size, the boy "soon gave up the contest and rushed from the room." An attack like this was nearly unheard of at Summerhill; Neill rarely had to use force, and when he did, it worked, with no backlash. Why could he do it as a simple corrective? Why was it wrong for Diana Kahn to kick a child but right for Neill?

The answer to both questions is the same: Neill's relationship with the children, plus the less intense level of their needs. The fashion in which he ran Summerhill was that of a good enough father whose children needed extra attention and understanding to get through an unhappy

time. Being only moderately disturbed, they accepted him without needing years to build up trust; and because he genuinely liked them, a relation was formed in which they usually got over whatever had brought
them to Summerhill. Affection was their lot much of the time, physical
discipline almost never.

Neill had no problem acting as superego, protector, role model, and
nurturer, and in this he was doing what good parents do—naturally, and
with the results good parents get. Neill was perhaps the warmest, most
poised, and reliable adult the children had met, and he was probably the
perfect teacher for troubled youngsters who had not reached the depths of
unhappiness Bettelheim's students had. Otherwise, Neill's common sense
and love would not have been enough.

> Since the changes Neill produced in his children were based on iden-
> tification, he succeeded only with those who could identify with him.
> And many could, because he was simply one of the grandest men
> around. Most of all, Neill was all of a piece, with hardly a flaw in his
> personality—excepting always his naiveté. In a great man, this is
> rather an asset. But what a liability it becomes in smaller men![2]

Bettelheim so obviously admired Neill's personal qualities, including
his ability to empathize with children, that I once asked if he thought
Neill could have run the Orthogenic School. He hesitated for a moment
but finally said he did not think so. The reasons can be found in this same
essay, where Bettelheim writes that Neill

> remained unaware that while anxiety causes neurosis, anxiety is also
> what keeps society going. Anxiety is one of the mainsprings of creative-
> ness, invention, and progress, particularly in its sublimated form. Yes,
> anxiety about loss of self-respect is even the wellspring of Neill's own
> success, which can only be described in terms of another pair of old-
> fashioned virtues: personal honesty and common decency.
>   He failed, however, to take account of the existential anxiety
> which, according to some psychoanalysts, originates in separation anx-
> iety. Nor did he talk about our deep inner conflicts or our
> psychosocial crises: he took no note of the continuous battle between
> id and superego, of eros against the instinct of aggression, to mention
> only two of these conflicts. His naive optimism stands here in stark
> contrast to Freud's pessimism about human nature. Neill remained

unaware of the reasons why the things he did worked. He believed they worked because he was on the side of the children, which indeed he was. Since he believed children were born without sin, and that their difficulties come not from within themselves but from a bad society, his solution was to protect children from society, to take their side against it. Would that things were that simple![3]

Bettelheim could sketch Neill deftly because he liked him, even though Neill held naïve convictions about human nature. Since both ran residential schools for troubled children, it was easy for Bettelheim, always prone to delve into why he thought what he thought, to write about a likable man doing worthy work in a manner quite different from his own.

There is, of course, great social value in having two such schools in some ways alike but also strikingly different. If one was wrong for a child, the other school might be better. For mildly neurotic children with workable superegos and a need to get away from home, you could choose Neill's model of a therapeutic milieu, ideally with a director like Neill. But for the deeply troubled child, you would want Bettelheim's Orthogenic School milieu, directed by an autocrat who knew his mind.

BETTELHEIM'S wary pessimism about our nature came not only from the depths of psychoanalysis but also from insights that ranged far beyond Freud—reflections on Dachau and Buchenwald, ideas tested in the fires of self-discovery. Unshakable convictions derived in this way made him a shrewd caretaker for extremely disturbed children, whom he did not idealize, romanticize, or see simplistically, and toward whom he felt no guilt for laying down the law with an angry slap.

The confirmed pessimist Bettelheim was a never-say-die optimist when he wanted to help a child: we are who we are, but *knowing* who we are will lead to better choices in the ever-changing scene we call life.

Perhaps Bettelheim could not have caught the glimmer of his hopes except against the dark backdrop of an austere skepticism, deepened and distilled after the camps. In the tension between his pessimism about human nature and his optimism about helping an unhappy child, he found meanings that made him look forward each day to his hours at the School. Those like Neill who see sunlight everywhere tend not to look into life's shadows or to think about the bedevilment that overcomes so many, the inward plague that in one sense is the sufferer's own creation but in another not his fault.

The true ambivalence in Bettelheim's heart was about life—to be, or not to be. As long as he could be useful, he came down on the side of being. When a child succeeded, Bettelheim won a battle against himself in his unending war to quell his own worst fears about our fate and the depravities of the human soul. But he could not have the School forever.

CHAPTER 32

Death and . . .

IN THE last decade of Bettelheim's life, a series of misfortunes left him sad, anxious, and often depressed. "Bruno believed that his old age was secure," Ruth Marquis said, "because as he declined, Trude would always be there to look after him." He was nine years older than Trude, and both took it for granted that she would outlive him. Then in 1979 Trude learned she had cancer; the treatments brought mixed results, so the worry was always there, but hope was there as well because she had many good days.

Despite the shadow of Trude's up-and-down health, she and Bruno enjoyed their retirement together. In 1982, Jacquelyn Sanders wrote a letter that cut him off from the School. He had half expected it, but it was another exile, one in which his books, travels, and lectures helped him adjust to the reality that the School was no longer his, even at the abstract level of an occasional consultation. His accomplishment remained, and that had to be enough.

During my visit in 1983, Trude showed few signs of illness and kept a neat and comfortable home, as I imagine she had always done. Only the garden seemed neglected, because she did not have the energy for outdoor work. Still, when Bruno and I first came up the steep driveway, I saw a row of beautiful leafless irises standing in full bloom against the foundation of the house. Bruno noticed my gaze. "They're called 'naked ladies,' " he said.

Trude got up early every morning to make breakfast and lay out Bruno's medicines at his place on the table. Until midweek I saw nothing in her manner to suggest that she was not feeling well, and on that Wednesday we drove to San Francisco for a meeting at the offices of the law firm in which Eric worked. He showed us into a large conference room with a long gleaming table, where Bruno and Trude looked surprisingly small as they sat and waited to sign new wills.

Eric left us (for reasons of legal propriety), and one of the partners of the firm came in with an assistant, who brought the wills. At the sight of the papers Trude suddenly became subdued and almost withdrawn. It occurred to me later that she had fallen silent on the brink of a formality whose meaning for her was as heavy as a tombstone. Yet she had to do what was expected of her so that the business of the world could proceed in a dignified room with a wall of windows and a majestic view of the bay.

The partner, making small talk, said something about "next year," and Trude murmured a few words, almost to herself. I caught only part of what she said but heard enough to know that she thought she might not live until next year. The windows and the long polished table and the eagle's-eye view would all be as impressive as ever next year, and the business of the world would still be pressed forward, with all the importance that we attach to it, but the document she was about to sign tied up her hopes in a neat bundle and put them away. As if she had no future.

Bruno looked startled at her words about next year, and then distress came over his face. He leaned toward her, put his hand on her arm, and seemed to reassure her in a low voice, and after a moment everyone got down to the formalities.

In GOOD weather San Francisco sparkles, and since it was a bright August afternoon, Bruno suggested that we drive up Telegraph Hill before going home, so I could see the spectacular view. The detour took less than an hour, but as we drove back down the hill I noticed that Trude, in the back seat, seemed not to feel well. Five or six hours up and about had tired her noticeably. When we reached the house she apologized for neglecting me but said she had to go to her room to lie down. Then I realized that earlier in the week she had been resting in the hours when I interviewed Bruno. Today there had been no rest.

It was late afternoon, and I went into the living room to read, a room with tall windows and views west to the Santa Cruz Mountains and north to the hazy towers of San Francisco. An hour later Trude came in and offered me a glass of wine before dinner, and we sat and talked about Bruno (elsewhere in the house, at his desk, working) and admired the sunset and listened to Kiri Te Kanawa singing the four last songs of Richard Strauss. Trude had become a hostess again, and I was her guest.

TRUDE had surgery and started radiation therapy in 1980, and in the first year the treatments seemed to help. Then late in 1981 a serious relapse sent her back to the hospital. When she came home, she and Bruno began to gather information on how to prepare for an assisted suicide. This was simply a precaution, since they still hoped that her condition could be stabilized. However, if terminal illness threatened prolonged suffering or helplessness for either of them, they wanted to know the alternatives. Both understood what it meant to be trapped, and both found the prospect intolerable.

Bettelheim's emotional reserves and intellect had helped him fight off death feelings in the camps, where suicide was always an option; later, at the School, he had faced a crisis that agitated and depressed him when he needed surgery for both eyes, a procedure he feared would leave him blind.

Going blind would rob him of the priceless stimulus he needed for his inner eye. With years of practice, he had made a habit of looking closely at little things—a counselor's slight gesture, the fleeting expression on a child's face, a door hinge with dust. And if he lost his eyesight, he would lose the School, would become a burden to himself and others by being cut off from the work that gave his life meaning.

Just before the operation he called Ruth Marquis from his room in the hospital and told her he had put a dose of cyanide in the drawer of a table at his bedside. If the operation failed, he would take it.

"That was the first time I heard him speak in a purposeful way about suicide," Ruth said. The finality of his words and the determination in his voice left her in shock, unable to speak. She sat for a long time at her desk not moving, trying to sort out her silent turmoil. She knew Bruno well enough to feel his desperation, and she hoped he would change his mind, but she knew he wouldn't. Luckily, the surgery was a complete success.

"There was another thing," Ruth said. "For some time after his sixtieth birthday, Bruno was convinced that he would suddenly die from a coronary. I don't know who he told besides me, but he cleared his desk, started getting rid of things, finished all his projects, and got ready to die with no loose ends left dangling. When nothing happened, the feeling gradually went away."

IN 1982 Bruno and Trude heard about a group in Scotland called EXIT and another in France, La Sui Fei. Both advocated that anyone who wanted to end his life for good reasons (such as incurable illness or a hopeless physical situation) should be allowed to do so. Bruno wrote to EXIT asking for their literature, but the organization had just been outlawed and could not send the book he wanted. EXIT referred him to the Hemlock Society, a new organization started in the United States by Derek Humphry, an English journalist and author who had left England after narrowly escaping prosecution on a charge of assisting his wife's suicide.

However, on October 9, 1982, Bruno wrote Ruth Marquis that he could not find the Hemlock Society. He also said,

> All this has become a real problem for me for a variety of understandable reasons, but I still couldn't make up my mind how I'll really feel when it comes to it. I know what I'd want, but as often in life there is a gap between what one wants and does. Well, enough of that.

On November 6, he wrote to Ruth again:

> I finally got some news from Hemlock, including their new address. I am sending you the material they sent me. Naturally I have some slight hesitation to send it to you, for obvious reasons. But since I feel as strongly as you that the most important decisions in one's life should be left to the person himself, including whether one wants to go on with it, I am letting you have this material.

Toward the end of this letter he said:

> Nobody should live so long, least of all me, but as long as I am not in too much pain, just the normal aches and pains, arthritis, etc. which are to be expected for an old broken down Jew at my age.

Ruth had no problems on the horizon that called for this information, but the right to suicide was a matter of principle with her. Nine years earlier *Ms. Magazine* had published a letter from her on living wills, which instruct doctors not to use extreme life-support measures. She and Bruno had talked several times about how to escape the indignities that may occur at the end of our life, and this was the context for the information he sent.

ABOUT a year later, in September 1983, Bruno and Trude took a long-planned trip to Europe, which Bruno had told me would be their final visit. They spent a week in London with Eric (who had just left San Francisco to live and work in England), then went to Venice and treated themselves to a week in the luxury hotel Danieli's. The third week took them to Basel to see Emmi Vischer Radanowicz-Harttmann and her husband. As mentioned earlier, Trude and Emmi had become close friends at the Montessori school in Vienna, and Emmi's family had helped Trude after her escape across the border in 1938. In Basel a crisis suddenly developed, about which Bruno later wrote Ruth Marquis,

> On the second day there, Trude collapsed with a congestive heart failure and was for nine days in intensive care in the hospital in Zurich.

Trude's condition was so serious that Bruno called the children, and all three flew to Zurich.

> Seeing them helped Trude greatly because from the moment they arrived did she begin to improve.

It was a close call, he said, but Trude was flown back to California with a doctor and a nurse. Soon afterward, she collapsed again:

> She had another congestive heart failure, requiring another hospitalization. Since then she has made some progress, she is not stabilized but can do very little, so our lives have become very restricted.

In the same letter (dated January 19, 1984) he explained that he had delayed writing Ruth because he'd had the flu, and

> together with everything else . . . was kind of depressed and I did not want to write you in such a bad mood.

The letter has a sad tone that suggests Bruno was still depressed; he regrets that the children cannot come as often as he and Trude would like:

Things are really as well as they can be, given our state of health and age. It is difficult to have the children so far away when one is relatively speaking incapacitated. . . . Well, children have to come into their own, and live their own life, but when I think how it was in the old country, when my mother visited her old and sick parents every day, one wonders whether all the progress is really worth it.

Ruth said that Trude's illness desolated Bruno; he could not change it, of course, and being useless around the house made things worse. "He hated to cook and really didn't know what he was doing in the kitchen," she said. "If you're used to someone preparing food for you, as he was, and then it stops, you feel abandoned. He got people to come in, but he felt terrible about what was happening."

Much later in 1984 Bruno wrote to Ruth again:

What a lovely surprise to receive your letter! And you even remembered my birthday! Well, I am by now 81 and feel it in every one of my bones. No good to be so old and to live so long. As you know, one has a choice on this matter, but to take it is also dismal for a variety of reasons, although the thought of choosing it is never far from my mind. But at this moment I have no choice, because I must take care of Trude. And although I know that she thinks much more often and more persistently of this choice because she suffers much and is terribly weak, I cannot share my thoughts with her, because she already fears too much that she is a burden on me, and so I must avoid anything which would or could support this view.

He explained that Trude also had diabetes in addition to cancer.

By now it is impossible to say what role the medication for both illnesses play into her condition, but they certainly complicate matters. . . . Trude's illness is foremost in my mind, to the exclusion of nearly everything else.

Later in that letter he wrote:

Did I tell you that when Trude was so ill last September in Zurich and flying her back in the hospital plane, etc. was costing a fortune that suddenly Sandy Lewis stepped in and took care of it all. This must have given him some thought that I could have ill afforded these expenses, and so starting some four months ago he arranged for me to receive a pension the rest of my life. . . . So small miracles of gratitude do happen. While I did not need this pension desperately, what with the continuing expenses—we need help to take care of Trude, and this, out here, is practically impossible to get and very expensive, so the pension he gives me takes care of a significant portion of these added expenses. But it is not the money that touches me, but that one of my kids from the school wishes to take care of me, as I took care of them, which gives me much satisfaction.[1]

IN OCTOBER Trude grew so weak that she was hospitalized again; she died on October 23, about a year after her collapse in Zurich. Gayle Janowitz had not spoken to the Bettelheims for some weeks when a friend told her of Trude's death. She called the next day, and Bruno answered the phone, but she could not make out his words because he was weeping and distraught.

He and I did not talk about Trude's death at the time; however, a month later he told me that in the last weeks of her life, he had kept hoping she would stabilize. "You always hope for another month," he said. And then he added, in a soft, heavy voice, "It was fifty years."

ON HIS next visit to New York, toward the end of 1984, Bruno called to ask me to meet him for lunch at the Algonquin. I arrived a little early and waited for him at the table. He came down from his room but did not greet me with his usual, *How are you? How are things?* Instead, his first words were, "Well, I am afraid I will live three years."

I protested, but as we talked, I saw he was not making a prediction; he was referring to his unhappy state of mind, which he did not expect to get better, and to his physical condition, which he was sure would get worse. For one thing, he had tolerated a growth in his throat that triggered spasms of coughing. He could not swallow solid food, but for years he refused to consider an operation because the growth was too near his vocal cords and he might lose his voice.

At lunch we talked: he felt lost without Trude—missed her all the time—still had his children and his work—his energy level was much lower now—he just couldn't work the way he used to—he needed a good title for the parenting book—he'd sent off a final draft to Joyce Jack (his personal editor)—a meeting of the Jewish Board of Guardians— a car would pick him up at five o'clock to go upstate for a speaking engagement—back at midnight—catch a plane tomorrow morning . . . and so on.

I knew he was doing his rational best to keep busy and not give in to his sadness, and so his day was longer than mine. For the life of me I couldn't see the lower energy level, though I'm sure he felt it. Later, I told Joan, my wife, that if his health held, he would stay active for a very long time.

IN 1985 Bruno went to Vienna for two weeks. His daughter Naomi's husband had been posted there by the State Department, and after their first child was born, they invited Bruno for a visit. At the same time they also invited Gina Weinmann, whom Naomi kept in touch with.

Gina and Bruno revisited some scenes of their life in Vienna, such as the house they were forced to leave in 1938. Naomi has a snapshot of them in front of the house. Bruno stands ill at ease in his raincoat, his face glum, his body stiff, looking every day of his eighty-two years, like the "old broken down Jew" he told Ruth Marquis he was. Gina looks spirited and almost regal as she smiles brightly into the camera.[2]

ALL THREE children had asked Bruno to live with them, but he continued to fear being a burden and so lived alone in the house in Portola Valley for nearly two years after Trude died. The only genuine satisfaction in his nominal association with nearby Stanford University had been Alvin Rosenfeld's seminar for child psychiatrists in training (and other mental health professionals).

Bruno and Rosenfeld met often, discussed cases, and grew closer as friends. Rosenfeld's respect and warmth made up for the coolness in the rest of department, but in time it became clear that the feelings against Bettelheim had also worked against Rosenfeld. He resigned in 1983, and after a year or so, Stanford dropped the seminar, leaving Bettelheim with less of the work he valued most.

Bettelheim always wanted to go on teaching, but somehow nothing came along to replace the weekly drama of young therapists presenting cases that puzzled them. A senior psychiatrist who had sat in on the sessions (and also presented cases) asked him to consult at a unit of San Jose Hospital, which helped his morale a little. However, it did not stimulate him like the interplay with younger therapists to whom he could pass on his vision of children and whom he taught with the bold theatrics that made the seminar exciting.

BRUNO and Trude had grown even closer in their retirement; a year after her death he told me that their opinions had become "strangely parallel—not necessarily identical—simply because of the respect we had for each other. Very few people understood our relation."

Several times he had said that Trude gave him courage and freedom to run the School and also that they had the most harmonious marriage of anyone he knew. (As noted earlier, this was true later but not at first, when the School's unrelenting dominance may have come close to overwhelming their relationship.)

He told Celeste Fremon, who interviewed him for the *Los Angeles Times*, that he and Trude had grown together in marriage, whereas he and Gina had grown apart. He spoke in Freudian terms of his loss of interest in life after Trude's death—of the waning of the life drive (Eros) and the ascendancy of the death drive (Thanatos), saying that "it can also reach a point in old age where one must accept that one withdraws the libido from the world because otherwise one couldn't face death. . . . As long as our sex drives are still active, we are going to find women beautiful—some, anyway—and worth living for. It's as simple as that. The less erotic life there is left, the greater the tendency toward death. . . . I [have] watched in myself the withdrawal of my libido from those things in which they were invested in the past."

Celeste Fremon asked, "Is the waning of the libido a consequence of a loss of love in one's life?"

"Loving and being loved," he said. "The two work together."

Fremon noticed that a quick wave of emotion flooded Bettelheim's face when he said this, and she guessed he was thinking about his life with and without Trude. A moment later he changed the direction of the interview, saying, "Well, maybe we could talk about some other topic."[3]

YEARS earlier Bettelheim had written a definition of "a unique love relation" that balances head and heart:

I love you because you meet my needs and desires as nobody else can—love me because I am uniquely worthy of your love, or shall try to be so.[4]

Here, the balance may seem weighted more to the head than to the heart, so that the definition owes more to reason than romance. However, it is Bettelheim's picture of love as a long-term relationship—a sketch, formed by three strong lines:

> *A declaration of love;*
> *a plea to be loved in return;*
> *and a promise.*

I believe this definition described his relation with Trude, which in the course of their lives stretched across fifty years of work and family. He knew that love by itself was not enough to help disturbed children, nor was it the be-all and end-all in marriage, as his marriage to Gina had proved. The fidelity of each partner to the feelings of the other, their fitting together and honesty within marriage, their self-respectful efforts to be worthy of each other, and the complex realities they had to face when having children and raising them to be themselves—all this took far more than love, even though love was indispensable. I asked Bruno if he wanted to add to his definition of love or change it in any way, and he said that he remained very satisfied with it.

BETTELHEIM had hoped to keep his independence by living at home, but the Portola Valley house, shared with Trude for the last ten years, now felt vacant, with the dreadful emptiness of familiar things. His was an abiding loss, not to be put out of mind by work and travel. Then, in 1986, at San Jose airport, he fainted and fell. It was a mild stroke, from which he recovered quickly, and, having no impairment, he decided not to upset his children by telling them. However, it was a warning for him to begin to think seriously about a retirement home.

Eric came from London to go with him to look at places around Palo Alto, but Bruno hated what he saw; besides, he thought he might leave the San Francisco area altogether. Gina was calling him, and although he still loved her in a way, he felt uncomfortable with the idea of seeing more of her. She had not changed; she was still "too bossy."[5]

After talking things over with his daughter Ruth, a psychotherapist in Pasadena and recently divorced, they agreed that he should move in with her and her two children. At this point, both Eric and Naomi doubted that the arrangement would work; they and several others, including Gina, advised against it. However, he thought it worth a try, that it would be better than living alone or in a retirement home, and he went ahead, selling the house in Portola Valley to buy a larger one in Santa Monica.

He moved to Santa Monica in September 1986, settled in with Ruth and her children, and went on with his usual schedule. He traveled, he lectured, he gave interviews about A *Good Enough Parent*—living a busy public life while growing more troubled in private. He did not tell me he was depressed, perhaps because I was working on this book, but once in the summer of 1987 he called and said in a terrible voice, "Theron, I am sinking." He sounded so agitated and distressed that it alarmed me, but he hung up before I could ask what was wrong. I called back, got no answer, and left a message on his machine. When I didn't hear from him by evening, I called Ruth, whom I barely knew; she said only that Bruno was out at the moment, had been depressed for some time, and was seeing an analyst. A few days later he called, sounding more like himself, and apologized for having troubled me.

In November 1987, while he was in Florida for a lecture, a second stroke left him partly paralyzed in his right arm and leg. Now he was seriously disabled, with a depression that he struggled to master for the rest of his life. His physical impairment and unhappy frame of mind made it almost too much effort to find a new home, but it was also obvious that he had to do it. A retirement home was not a home in his meaning of the word, and so he resolved to try once more to live by himself. Much later he told me in an offhand way that he'd had doubts about living in the same house with his daughter but thought he'd know in six months. "I knew sooner than that," he said, "but I couldn't face it, and that's why I got depressed." This was as far as he wanted to go with me in talking of something very private.

Ruth Marquis knew his side of the story and would not tell me, which I thought right and proper. In fact, I felt no curiosity because I believe (as I think Bruno did) that a respect for privacy—one's own and that of others—is a fundamental decency too often flouted in our time.

From a practical point of view, I felt that this family quarrel had no relevance to the theme I was developing of Bettelheim as an educator. Yes, self-knowledge could have saved him the grief that others in the family circle foresaw, but we can already guess this truth about his mistake and don't need the sad details. Like the rest of us, he had blind spots and sometimes expected too much, as was clear in his foolish hopes about Gina after Buchenwald, when he thought he could resume his life with her.

He once remarked that a friend is someone who sees your world the way you do, and although he differed with Ruth Marquis on politics, in private matters she was a friend worthy of his confidence. He spoke to several friends in Los Angeles, without, so far as I know, going into details about himself and his daughter Ruth. He told David James Fisher that he felt no conscious anger toward her, which was possibly true when he said it, but he changed his will to exclude her, then changed it back because Naomi wouldn't stand for it.

After another illness early in 1988, he at last moved out of the house with Ruth and took a small apartment in Santa Monica. The woman he eventually hired to clean, shop, cook, and housekeep was so limited in English (she spoke Polish) that it frustrated him constantly. Also, he hated to be a cripple, especially hated needing help to take a bath and get dressed.

Since he couldn't work as before, he collected the essays that would become *Freud's Vienna*. He did continue to collaborate on the book he had begun with Alvin Rosenfeld, *The Art of the Obvious*, based on disguised material from transcripts of the teaching seminar at Stanford. For more than a year Rosenfeld shaped the chapters and came from New York with pages for Bettelheim to read. Bruno could no longer type quickly, as he had done all his life, so he offered suggestions verbally, which Rosenfeld worked into the text. His depression was never far away, but when he focused on a goal and did something positive, like working on a book, his mood was manageable.

IN THE summer of 1988 I arranged to visit Bruno in Santa Monica for an interview during the Labor Day weekend. Shortly before I left New York, he called: the diverticulum in his throat was worse, and the doctors had recommended an operation. It might be three or four months before his voice came back, if it ever did, and he urged me not to make the trip. I said I'd see him in the hospital.

In Santa Monica three days after the operation, I checked the hospital's visiting hours and went over after lunch without calling ahead. There was no point in taking my tape recorder; I'd had a good session with Karen Zelan in Oakland the day before, and perhaps I would tell him about that. He wouldn't be able to talk, but I would.

At the hospital I went up to the floor where I would find him, and as I walked down the hall I suddenly thought I could hear his voice; this seemed unlikely, but as I came near the doorway of his room, it was true: I could hear him speaking in a normal tone. He was busy and forceful on the telephone, and it sounded so good that I must have gone in with a slightly foolish grin on my face.

He had surprised everybody by recovering his voice almost at once. He was still very weak, and the doctor had ordered him to get out of bed and walk around to strengthen himself. On that day and the next, he and I took slow walks in the hallway; he supported himself with a cane in his good hand while resting his paralyzed hand on my arm. We talked about everything, including the other patients whose stories he had learned, but somehow a taped interview was not something we wanted to do. With both a successful operation and his eighty-fifth birthday just behind him, he seemed in remarkably good spirits.

I DID not see Bruno again for about a year and a half, although we often spoke on the phone. Late in 1989 he told me he was thinking of moving to the Washington, D.C., area and at some point mentioned that a house near Naomi was vacant. I suggested that he rent it and get a housekeeper. No, he said, he'd turn into a burden if he were so near, and Naomi had two young children.

He found a two-bedroom apartment in The Charter House, a retirement home in Silver Spring, Maryland, and I determined to take the Metroliner on several weekends to see him and get back into the book. But for my first trip, we planned to spend the afternoon taking care of business that had piled up while he was moving and getting settled. Then we would have dinner and a friendly visit until he went to bed. No interview just yet.

Bruno greeted me at the door of his Charter House apartment in his stocking feet, an informality that startled me. Later I saw why: to put on his shoes he had to struggle like a child. He showed me into a book-lined study that also had a desk, a stereo, and most of the record collection I had seen at Portola Valley. He said he had played only one or two since he moved in; it was just too awkward for him to put records on the turntable. A word processor Naomi had bought sat on the desk unused. He could not type except by pecking with his left hand, and Naomi thought a word processor would be easier than his typewriter. Bruno said he had tried to follow the instructions that came with the machine, and when he couldn't, he gave up.

I sat down in a low leather chair and eased off my shoes to keep him company, pleasantly surprised by how cushiony the carpet felt. It was so soothing that I told myself how well he had done in getting this clean and comfortable place. We talked about various matters, and then I took several foreign contracts from my briefcase and described each in turn. His bank had asked him not to sign checks anymore because his signature had changed, but I knew he could do well enough for foreign publishers. He said, "Oh, why don't you sign them for me?" I insisted he do it, and he sat at the desk and signed them slowly as I turned the pages.

When I put them back in my briefcase, Bruno took a chair opposite me and suddenly said, "It was a mistake to move here."

He gazed at me steadily, waiting, and when I hesitated he said, "I have decided to take my life."

He must have seen the shock in my face, because he quickly added that he had not decided *when* to do it, only that he *would* do it. I sat stunned and numb, because I knew he was totally serious.

A year earlier he had spoken about suicide, telling me almost in a casual way that he had hoped to go with a doctor friend to the Netherlands, where assisted suicide was legal, but the doctor had died.[6] He had then asked Eric to go with him.

"What did Eric say?"

"He wouldn't do it. He got very angry with me."

Back when he told me this, he had mentioned the idea of suicide as if it were a thing of the past, and he hadn't mentioned it since. I thought perhaps Eric's anger had somehow reassured him, that the suicidal feelings had subsided. What could I say now that would stop him, get him to rethink his decision?

"What about your children?"

It was a reasonable question, but as I should have guessed, he had already gone down that path.

"Well, I know," he said, then added, "I'm not going to do it soon."

"What about the children from the School? You're still very important to them. They've told me so."

He nodded and said, "I've thought about that." Again, he was far ahead of me. Knowing himself as the prime mover in the moral development of children at the School, convincing them that life was worth living, he also knew that his self-imposed death might strike at that belief in a shocking way. Later I reasoned that he may have felt they would see his choice as realistic when they understood his circumstances. At any rate, at this unique moment in his life, his needs came first, not theirs.

It had been naïve of me to hope I could change his mind, but I tried again, talking to him about himself, for this book. When we had begun, more than six years earlier, perhaps he was concerned how the world would see him; but no more. I sensed that helping me know him better and find the shape of my book held no interest for him. He had lived his life and did not need to relive it.

I can now appreciate the bleakness of his inner landscape at that moment: he had lost Trude, he could no longer speak with the child who had been in some ways his favorite, his body had betrayed him by rendering him unable to write new books or essays. He could not manage to write (as several of us had suggested) by dictating into a tape recorder and then revising; he had to pour out his thoughts on the typewriter, had to feel his way through his ideas with his hands as he wrote and rewrote. He could still speak impromptu, but this was less satisfying, because he had always tried to write up a fresh idea for a lecture so he could give the audience something new to think about. And now he couldn't.

The telephone rang six or seven times as we talked. An old friend was coming to Washington, and he asked her to visit him; other callers wanted him for a dinner or a reception, but his status as the latest social lion in the nation's capital bored him, and he made excuses. Only one call raised a spark of interest: Eric, who had just given a lecture in Florida on his legal specialty, was flying back to London and called from the airport to see how Bruno was doing. They talked for a few minutes and then Bruno handed me the phone.

Eric said, as to a fellow conspirator, "Keep him busy! We've got to keep him busy!" I said I'd try.

In fact, that had been my first thought when I tried to bring up my book in progress an hour earlier, but I didn't get far discussing his past life. The conversation had come round to his health, and this was the moment when he said he'd had two strokes and hadn't told anybody about the first one. Now he had congestive heart failure and took Ritalin; fluid constantly collected in his lungs, and he took Lasix to drain it. This sent him to the bathroom frequently, which embarrassed and annoyed him when he had a visitor like myself.

Had the psychoanalyst in Los Angeles helped?

"A little," he said.

Why not more?

If a person has not experienced the ravages of old age, he said—the sadness, the debility—it is impossible to grasp what someone in his position is feeling. The analyst had given him a prescription for Prozac to combat his depression, and he was still taking it.

Did it help his mood?

"No, not really," he said. "It doesn't do anything."

Later in the conversation he said that what he feared most was a stroke that would leave him paralyzed but still aware. He had visited his friend Fritz Redl several years earlier, when Redl was bedridden and helpless, drifting in and out of consciousness, sometimes recognizing Bettelheim, sometimes not. In clear moments, I asked, did Redl know what was happening to him? Bruno considered the question briefly and then said, "I think so."

He also spoke of his former analyst Richard Sterba, living in a coma for over a year with round-the-clock nursing care. Monica Schneider, Sterba's daughter, told me that Bruno had said to her in a telephone conversation while he was still living in California that he would never allow himself to suffer her father's fate, that he had prepared for such an eventuality.

To me he said that there were two possibilities in his situation: to have a wife who took care of you, like Redl; or to have plenty of money for total care, like Sterba. Now Trude was gone, and care like Sterba's would waste what he wanted to leave to his children.

I asked if he was in pain from his heart condition; he looked uncomfortable at the question and hesitated but said, "Yes." His failing heart could bring death at any time. After the second stroke the doctor had told him he was a good candidate for a third and massive stroke that would either kill him or leave him helpless but alive. He was not afraid of death, but the living death of Redl and Sterba appalled him.

After a while he had talked enough about his poor health, and toward the end of the afternoon he remarked that the books lining the walls were not in any kind of order. The movers had shelved them haphazardly right out of the packing boxes, without regard to subject matter or the alphabet, and their disarray irritated him.

"I can't find my books," he said, meaning the books he had written.

"Let me look for them," I said and then walked back and forth, scanning the shelves for the familiar spines. In ten minutes I had all his titles on one shelf. When I sat down, Bruno got up from his chair, still not wearing shoes, and stood before the shelf that held his books. "Well," he said, "at least I have my books arranged now. That's something."

ON OUR way out for dinner that evening, I saw a sign in the elevator announcing a memorial service for a resident, dead only a few days. It had a cheerful tone that disconcerted me. I pointed and said, "Do they do this often—announce a service?" Bruno nodded, looked away from the sign, and gave the slightest of shrugs. Others were in the elevator, and he didn't want to speak. In the lobby a moment later I noticed a group of residents passing the reception desk, walking with the slow and careful movements of the very frail. Bruno caught my glance and remarked in his casual, blunt manner, "Everybody here is waiting to die."

When I left at the end of the evening, I said I'd be back in two weeks to tape an interview and would plan to stay overnight in the neighborhood so we could have more than an afternoon's session.

"You shouldn't go to so much trouble," he said, but I promised to come.

BACK HOME the next day, I told Joan of Bruno's feelings, and almost before I finished, she picked up the phone and called him. She said she'd just heard he was talking about suicide, and she had to call to say we didn't want him to do it—we were upset that he was so sad.

"Look," he said, "I don't want to be a burden to everyone. I can't walk, or work, or tie my shoelaces."

"You know," she said, "I see people here in New York, while I'm walk-ing the dog. They use these electric chairs, and some even have dogs with them. They get around very well, they go everywhere. You could do that, too, Bruno."

"That's fine for them," he said, "but it's not for me. I don't want to live like that."

"It's not the worst thing in the world," she said, and he fell silent. She spoke again of how we wanted him to go on living, but afterward she said, "He really wasn't listening."

ON MY second trip to Silver Spring we spent most of the afternoon talk-ing about the School. Bruno looked tired but seemed not as depressed as before; he said he had stopped taking Prozac and didn't miss it. When Joan phoned in midafternoon about several agency matters, I whispered (at the end of our conversation) that Bruno was feeling better.

The telephone kept interrupting us. Among others, Jacquelyn Sanders called, and when Bruno hung up he said, "She'll be in Washington for a conference and may come to see me. I think she wants to make amends."

One of the last calls of the day came from a woman with whose organization I had corresponded. They wanted to sponsor a seminar with mothers, like the group in Chicago forty years earlier. It could give us the material for another *Dialogues with Mothers*, but I wanted it principally to occupy Bruno, who would enjoy grappling with the problems of the latest generation of mothers. Now he learned the organization could sponsor only four meetings, not a weekly group running for several months. He had hoped for an open-ended series—and a small reason to go on. Four meetings felt like nothing.

I saw the disappointment in his face, as if another door on life had slammed shut. He craved the tonic of real work to lift his mind and spirit, and a chance for this had just fallen through. During one of Celeste Fremon's interviews with him in 1989, she noticed a vivid change in his manner when a former patient called. He became animated, his voice grew stronger as he helped someone through a difficulty. At that moment he felt useful; now in this new place, no one was using him except as a celebrity.

In fact, Washington had given him almost a hero's welcome, a social whirl far surpassing anything in San Francisco or Los Angeles. However, he was bitter. A ringing telephone, engraved invitations, and being lionized by people who knew little and cared less for his ideas was not his notion of a useful life. He told Ruth Marquis that no one was really interested in *him*—they wanted his celebrity. "They love you," she said, but he corrected her: "They love my famous me."

IN LOS ANGELES Bruno had become seriously committed to an odd group of therapists who asked him to lead a seminar, and he now felt that cutting these new ties was his single worst mistake in moving to Washington. For the first time in his life he had led a group in which all the therapists were ministers or church members. The fact that they were religious and he was not became irrelevant as he worked with them and saw the depths of their sincerity. For him nothing could be more to the point, because he valued sincerity at least as much as a disturbed child did.

Also, psychoanalysis in America had always troubled him by its emphasis on money. An analyst needs money to live, but Bettelheim believed that too many—not all—thought too soon about the patient's ability to pay, whereas their first question should be, *Can I help this person?* Before committing to a patient, the analyst needed to look into himself for hints of his therapeutic sincerity. Curiously, the sincerity Bettelheim sensed in the church group made him feel closer to them than he felt toward many orthodox analysts. In hindsight he saw that he should not have given up these people just when they were bringing the satisfaction of useful work into his life once more. He knew it wasn't going to happen in Washington.

On that Friday afternoon I returned to some of the themes that had emerged when I reviewed what Bruno and others at the School had told me. We talked briefly about what he looked for when he interviewed a would-be counselor, and this time he said he tried to find genuineness.

Why, I asked?

Because disturbed children were often acute on this point.

And why was genuineness so important to them?

"Because they had, in the past, most of them, been surrounded by people who didn't act genuine with them," he said.

"When you put it that way, you seem to be blaming the parents."

"Well, the parents couldn't help themselves. They acted out of their own needs. They're human beings, too, and human beings with great difficulties." (And the parents' parents had *their* problems, he said.)

Was the trouble more in the child or in the parents' expectations of the child?

"Well, it was both," he said. "You know, if the child doesn't respond normally, or up to our expectations, it's very upsetting to the mother. And the mother responds then with her own pathology. Her own pathology is aggravated and activated by the child's absence of normal responses."

We also talked of why family life seems to be losing its genuineness (one of the topics in *A Good Enough Parent*). "Parents and children no longer live really together and work together," he said. "Instead, they spend their free time together. It's a change in the intensity and nature of the relationship between parent and child."

I suggested that it also required a change in the nature of what the family had to do to survive.

"That's right, that's right," he said. "In order to survive in the past, parents and children had to work together. And this working relationship was a very strong bond between parents and children." Now keeping the genuineness when the family does not work together toward a common goal becomes harder to achieve. For many people, love is not enough to hold the generations together comfortably.

I asked about the School's demands on his time and suggested that he had managed to have a private life despite the hours. He surprised me by saying, "Kind of. I try to keep the two things separate, my private life and the School. But I have really very little time for private life."

Saturday had been as demanding as weekdays. Why? "Because the children were there, there was no school, so they were the whole day with counselors, who needed my support even more than on school days." They needed him on Sundays as well, but then he tried to spend a few more hours at home.

I asked what he was paid, and at first he could not recall. He finally said that he did not think it was ever more than $28,000 a year and that many other professors on his level got as much as $50,000.

"Why didn't you ask for a raise?"

"Because I felt I couldn't ask for money for me and for the School, and I preferred to ask for the School. And since I was satisfied with a very low salary, I could expect my teachers and counselors to be satisfied with relatively low salaries."

"But you had to send three kids to college."

"I managed," he said. "Well, my wife was working too, don't forget." (His writing income helped, but as noted earlier, it was modest in the years with me until near the end of his life.)

Bettelheim had always argued that the cost of the School was cheaper than custodial psychiatric care. His strongest point was that he helped many very troubled children have a life on their own (or with minimal care), whereas their fate elsewhere might have been unhappier. However, money was a side issue for him; even if the School had cost more than custodial care, he would have done it his way because his way was kinder. I wondered if his residential milieu could work for adults, as *A Home for the Heart* suggested.

"Well, of course, the whole thing has to be changed, because children are children and adults are adults. But the approach, my approach, would be the same." He felt certain it would be less expensive to do things his way; for instance, psychiatric nurses cost far more than his counselors.

"Most of them were graduate students. I think it was possible for the Orthogenic School to run on such a small budget because it was part of a university. You have the supply of bright graduate students eager to learn to develop themselves. And it's a good cause, a cause they can embrace." He thought the Peace Corps was a fair analogy to the School and said later, "It takes young people who are not yet settled in life, who are still developing, and who want to develop themselves."

I said Bert Cohler saw the School as a means to a larger end for Bettelheim, such as research and books.

"No, not really. The Orthogenic School was the center of my life. Otherwise I couldn't have done it. It's the other things, the things I wrote, that were incidental."

So it wasn't a laboratory, a place to collect data?

"No. The university saw it as a laboratory."

"And you allowed them to see it that way?"

"That's right."

TOWARD late afternoon Bruno felt very tired, and so we turned off the tape recorder and he went into the bedroom to lie down. He invited me to follow him and sit and talk, and I took a chair at his bedside. He had hung an oil portrait of Trude where it would face him in bed, a painting that brought her back as I remembered her, with an alert gleam in her deep-set eyes. "It's a good likeness," I said, and Bruno, resting on the bed, agreed. He looked up at Trude's face and murmured, "Well, she left me."

Stupidly, I almost said, *She didn't leave you, she died.* Then I understood, he was telling me not a fact but a feeling, as a child might but not in a childish way, that her death left him lonely and abandoned.

AFTER a while Bruno dozed off, and I went into the study to read. He napped until dinnertime, then said we should go out to a restaurant. He hadn't liked the Charter House menu at lunch, which he said was often reprised at dinner. We walked to the restaurant across the street, but it was noisy and crowded, so we set off down the hill to the Holiday Inn where I was staying. He and Eric had gone there for dinner a few weeks ago; it would be adequate and not noisy, he said.

Bruno walked slowly, with a cane, but even a hundred yards downhill took serious effort. At the table, our waitress brought menus and warm crusty rolls. Bruno looked at his roll without touching it, and I knew something was wrong.

"I can't eat this," he said, "I'm sorry." His dental bridge was so painful that he had stopped wearing it, and so he couldn't chew the roll. I sent back his roll for sliced bread, and we took up our menus. Bruno liked swordfish steak but wondered aloud whether it might be too tough for him; the waitress thought not, so he ordered it. I had wondered the same thing and asked for crab cakes, which I knew would be soft.

We talked, our dinners came, and Bruno's face fell. He poked at the fish with his fork, then put down the fork and sighed. He hated to make a fuss, but his choice had been a mistake; grilling made the swordfish hard and stringy. He turned to look for the waitress, and in that moment I reached over and switched our plates. If I'd asked, his lifelong Viennese sense of decorum would have taken charge. He protested but gave in, and the crab cakes were quite soft. About halfway through the first one he touched it with his fork, looked up, and said, "For future reference, what is this?"

I told him and smiled; if he was thinking of future dinners, he was not about to commit suicide, and since his mood seemed lighter, perhaps talking about the School in our interview had helped.

WE CAME out into a gentle rain drifting down like a passing spring shower; it wouldn't drench us, but I didn't want Bruno's bald head to get wet. I told him to wait, that I'd go back to The Charter House for an umbrella. No, he wouldn't hear of it, and he set out across the street ahead of me. I caught up with him and we walked up the hill, his cane tapping the damp sidewalk. Just before we reached the Charter House entryway, he suddenly stopped. His hand went to his heart, and he said, "Oh my god," in a low voice.

"Is something wrong? Are we walking too fast?"

I thought we had walked slowly, but the slight rise of the hill must have been a strain.

After a long moment he said, "I'm all right," and began walking again. Upstairs at his apartment we agreed to meet after breakfast the next day, and I said I'd come at ten o'clock.

"No," he said, "make it ten-thirty. I think I need a little more rest."

ON SATURDAY morning we discussed, among other things, the concentration camps. When I had tried to write that section of the book, something kept holding me back; later, I realized I'd been unconsciously afraid to put myself in Bruno's place, to imagine what he had felt. Now if he was willing, I wanted to find out more, to learn details he had left out of his writings and the earlier interview; but I soon saw that he still seemed tired from the night before, and his answers grew short. I said I'd write some pages about the camps and that if I had them by the following Friday, and if he was free, I'd come back.

"Well, I hate you to promise you will make this trip," he said.

"Well, I don't hate it," I said, and he laughed.

I unhooked the microphone from his shirtfront and put the tape recorder away, and he moved to a chair in which he could lean back and rest. For a while we discussed his dislike of the retirement-home environment. Suddenly I realized what he needed: I said how much better it would have been for him if he lived in the Orthogenic School now, surrounded by everything he knew so well. It was too bad he couldn't have made his home there after Trude's death. He might have lived in two rooms and gone on helping students and staff—on call, as needed. It would have been a retirement, but a useful one.

Bruno had been sitting with his eyes nearly closed, his head resting on the back of the chair. He opened his eyes wide, sat up straight, and said, "That would have been ideal."

LATER we had lunch in the Charter House dining room, then went upstairs to his apartment and talked a while longer. Finally I prepared to leave, and Bruno stood in his shirtsleeves and stocking feet, looking on as I took my briefcase and raincoat from the hall closet.

I turned at the door and said I hoped to see him next week. He nodded hesitantly and said, "Well, you don't have to."

"Oh, I want to, but I'll call you first."

He nodded again, and we said good-bye.

THAT WAS after lunch on Saturday, March 10, and less than three days later he drank some alcohol, swallowed sleeping pills, and put a plastic bag over his head.

About a year later I spoke with Ruth Marquis for the first time, and she told me of Bruno's long-standing resolve to have a *passport,* a way out of life if life somehow threatened to trap him. She also said that after he joined the Hemlock Society, "He did more than simply think about suicide. He got himself a cache, a supply of drugs."

His passport was Seconal, but in his last weeks he was terrified that the pills were too old. Ruth had researched the shelf life of drugs and knew how to increase dosages beyond the expiration date. "I knew a lot more about it than he did. They don't deteriorate that fast, as I told him."

Bettelheim's Seconals probably came from the doctor he had asked to go with him to Holland. About fifty one-hundred-milligram tablets would work for most people, but the method he chose calls for fewer if used with a plastic bag. The Hemlock Society recommends enough to cause sleep but not death, plus a loose-fitting plastic bag over the head, secured tightly at the neck. As the sleeper breathes, the trapped air gives up its oxygen and slowly smothers him. If the bag is the right size, about two hours of drug-induced sleep will bring a peaceful death.

Sadly, the method did not work peacefully for Bettelheim, whose body was found just outside his bedroom.

A PERSONAL note: I did not hear that Bruno had committed suicide until a day later, and for the next four nights I had screaming nightmares about him. When Joan told me she couldn't stand it anymore and that if I kept having nightmares I'd have to sleep in another room, I stopped.

For some days a regret gnawed at me, a feeling that I had let Bruno down by not responding in a more heartfelt manner to his distress when he first told me of his decision. Instead, I had fallen silent and gone numb—understandable from my point of view but sad for him. Moments later, I had disappointed him with reasonable questions rather than feeling an instant empathy that might have eased his desolation.

But before I got to the point of feeling all this about his suicide, the timing of it began to puzzle me. Why had he picked *that* day for his last act of self-assertion? Those who knew him best have often said that he usually had good reasons for what he did and could list them. Would he not have thought through his suicide in some detail, including the detail of when he would do it? Was there a symbolic meaning in the date?

Some have pointed to March 13 as the anniversary of the *Anschluss,* the day that changed Bettelheim's life forever. I entertained this notion several times, but it always felt alien to the man I knew and have come to know better since his death. True, he gave intense scrutiny to gestures, but he rarely made grand gestures himself—especially about himself. Rather, he explained himself as plainly as he could, and people could make of him whatever they wished. I do not believe he meant to contrive a ponderous irony, or that he chose a sad anniversary for his final act.[7]

Some have said, and I agree with them, that if Bettelheim had planned to end his life on Monday night or Tuesday morning, he would not have made a lunch date Tuesday with Judith Viorst, who intended to write about him for the Style Section of the *Washington Post*; nor would he have told someone from Boston (who called on Monday) to come and see him the next day. It would have been easy to put off both with a simple excuse, which the courtly thoughtfulness in his character would have demanded, even as he neared his last hour.

A FEW days after Bruno's death, I asked Joan what she thought about the timing of it. Why had Bruno acted, why did he do it *then*? I had spent many hours with him Friday and Saturday and was sure his suicidal feelings had let up. I was wrong, but did she see anything I didn't?

Joan thought for a moment and then said, "Something happened."

Something happened? What could have happened? I tried to visualize something, anything, but drew a blank—until I remembered Friday night in the rain, walking up the hill. I told her of Bruno stopping, putting his hand to his chest, and saying, "Oh my god." I said perhaps his heart had skipped a beat at that moment, or raced for a few seconds.

"So what do you think happened?" Joan asked.

And then I realized how plainly Bruno had stressed his fear of being left alive and helpless by a stroke, in a state like Redl's or Sterba's. He was unhappy about much in his life, but this was a present danger, a fate he wanted to preempt. He had said it more than once, he had given it weight, whereas I had not given it the same weight, because I didn't see it from his point of view. But now I did. He feared the third stroke, and he must have had a fresh incident. He needed no memories of a lost past to darken his mood and trigger suicide; he had a practical reason right there in his chest.

A moment later, I answered Joan. "I think he had another warning from his heart, something that made him feel he had waited long enough, that he'd better do it while he could."

"You can never know that," she said.

She was right, of course. I was trying to fill in a blank, find a near motive, something decisive just before he killed himself, something I would never *know*, as she said, and could only guess through empathy. Later I recalled the accident in Austria, when Bruno wrecked his roadster and could hear but not speak. Back then, he feared being buried alive, and in his declining days a little accident in an artery might almost do the same.

As I was writing the last draft of this chapter and came to the timing of the suicide, Naomi's husband called to ask a question about their taxes, and when we finished I asked him a question about Bruno. Naomi had said that her husband and Bruno took a short walk on his final visit and that something happened that hinted his suicide was imminent.

For some reason I had not thought to raise the subject in previous conversations, but now I did. The two men had gone for a walk before dinner, and Bruno had suddenly put his hand to his chest and said he had a pain. That instant on Sunday was nearly identical to the moment with me two days earlier, and it is reasonable to suppose that in Bruno's failing condition he must have felt his heart jump or threaten to stop a number of times. Hearing that he had used the word "pain" on that Sunday prompted me to ask myself why he had hesitated when I had asked if his heart was painful. Now I believe he hesitated because he wanted to tell me the truth but not the whole truth: yes, he had pain, but the significance of the pain for him was its intensity, which would serve as a cue to his final act. His timing.

ALTHOUGH I still can't know this for sure, the explanation does well enough to let me stop wondering about it. It has also freed me to imagine Bruno's last hours, and so I offer the reader a scenario that has formed itself in my mind.

HE IS ALONE; his heart has been erratic and suddenly beats with a pain longer and sharper than before; abruptly he decides he must end it all.

He catches his breath, summons his strength, and laboriously pecks out a short note to Naomi and Eric.

He pours a glass of Scotch or brandy and drinks it down, then pours another.

He has abhorred the taste of hard liquor ever since he was a teenager, when he made a fool of himself and got ridiculously sick; but these drinks will not give him a hangover, nor will their oblivion prove brief.

He has kept the Seconals close at hand, no need to hide them.

He swallows them with more alcohol.

He takes off his glasses; he sits on the bed, not tipsy yet, which is good; he needs the last of his strength and the best of his poor coordination for the plastic bag.

He takes the bag, which Ruth Marquis said he asked her about because he was so unaccustomed to doing anything for himself that he had no idea where to shop for it.

His half-paralyzed right hand makes him clumsy as he struggles to pull the bag over his head and secure it at the neck to keep fresh air out and carbon dioxide in.

At last he lies on the bed, his head swimming from so much liquor. The whole world has come down to the awkward bubble of the bag, which brings the sound and rhythm of his breathing into his ears.

The sound irritates him, but the liquor takes the edge off and the rhythm is soothing. The warm air from his lungs makes him uncomfortable, though he can endure it, waiting in the dark, because he knows that each breath takes away a little oxygen.

He is drowsy, and soon he will fall asleep under the gleam of Trude's eyes, which he saw facing him for the last time just before he put on the bag.

He dozes restlessly and wakes sometime later, he doesn't know when; he is drunk, still alive, panting and stifling. When he inhales, his face feels the touch of the bag, slick with the wetness from his breath.

He is awake and not yet too far gone. He becomes angry, almost indignant, at the treachery of pills and alcohol that did not bring peace and oblivion as promised.

Stubbornly and against his will, his body struggles to live, craves to breathe, demands oxygen.

But he will not give in.

He fights back a rising panic; his heart pumps harder as the breath of life is slowly removed from his bloodstream.

He is alarmed that he may fail in what he most wants to do.

He lies there angry, almost angrier than he has ever been in his life, because he wants to leave life and cannot.

His anger gives him strength, the will to withstand the brute force of life that grips him. He wants to hurry up and die, and his anger tells him that if he moves his body, he can meet death sooner.

He pushes himself up, and his good hand clutches the glasses he had laid aside; he rolls or falls off the bed, crawls or rolls or perhaps staggers across the carpeted bedroom floor, out into the foyer not far from the closet and the apartment's front door. He does not think of where he is; he thrashes about with all he has left, a swimmer against the stream of life, until at last he can struggle no more. His body is stilled. He is drained of all heart, all hope, except the hope to die.

The darkness of the bag that snugs his head is now at one with the dark place of his mind. He does not know his breathing has stopped, that the room is silent, that his body, still warm, has gone soft and limp. He is not aware that he has at last elbowed his way into the house of death.

BETTELHEIM faced a hard choice, and my thoughts about this have come slowly, against much resistance and not in an orderly way. But the more I have tried to grasp his point of view, the more reasonable he appears in choosing death. The result for me was his loss, and I still feel it, but the result for him was peace, relief from the fear that in one unwilled second he might turn into a human vegetable.

If he had changed his mind, he could have pulled the bag free with his left hand, even in a moment of panic, but his last struggle was to die, not live. His shortcut to death ran into a roadblock, and, true to character, he forced his way past it to his destination.

I now regard his suicide as an act typical of him in its clarity, courage, and rationality. His manner of death seems as memorable and meaningful as the way he lived, and I feel an admiration that is also sad.

When I spoke with Eric just after Bruno's death, he ended his side of the conversation with the words, "Master of his fate to the end!"—which I believe is true. Bruno simply would not continue to risk a massive stroke that might condemn him to a life without meaning. He had prepared to act when the time came; and when the time came, and with whatever warning it came, he made his exit from life's scene as the unmistakable Bruno Bettelheim.

CHAPTER 33

. . . *Transfiguration*

A FTER HE died, Bettelheim's public status went through a startling transfiguration. If he had seemed distinguished and somehow benign in life, in death he became a figure of malice and cruelty. Seeing the change was like watching a mime pass his hand in front of his face and turn a smile into a scowl. At the time I was astonished, although I understood what was happening. Bettelheim had ceded a power to those he angered, the power to damage his name because he had failed to give a full account of his function at the Orthogenic School—an obligatory defect if he was to go on helping those who benefited from his guidance. No doubt some were not helped when he functioned as superego and reality principle, but I believe others were.

Beyond this, he had taken positions on public questions that angered many whose opinions differed from his; however, he told disturbing truths to correct and discomfit conventional wisdom, in much the same way as he shook up misguided students at the School. He held fast to his attitude that the world could be a better place than he knew it was—a small hope that had a large meaning for him.

He may have foreseen the bitterness that would erupt once he passed from the scene, but if he did so, he showed no concern and made no plea for the world's pardon. He was satisfied to have done his work, including the books he wrote.

By its nature, this narrowly focused account of him has dramatized a partial view of the man, but I hope readers will find here a fresh perspective on the meaning of Bettelheim's life. He held his convictions firmly and expressed them forcefully, often behind a screen of careful questions that made his listeners question themselves and what they *thought* they knew. That was the teacher's job. Rarely has a public figure's reputation fallen so suddenly and dramatically after his death. That it should have happened in this way was understandable, but also unfair and unrealistic. In this book I hope I have told his story in a way that may begin to *retrans-figure* him in the world's opinion and to restore a reasonable balance in our view of Bettelheim as a psychologist and teacher who did work worthy of our attention.

CHAPTER 34

Ripples

BETTELHEIM left behind a solid body of work that I now think of as his permanent self—work that I expect will touch anyone looking for insights into psychology, therapy, or the human condition. However, there was more to him than the milieu and his books; the fact is, like many teachers he affected and changed the lives of people in surprising ways. In my 1985 interview with Gayle Janowitz, she had said that I should meet two women whose activities showed "Bruno's ripple effect."

Gayle introduced me first to Sue Duncan, who in 1961 had started a children's center in the empty basement of a church in a South Chicago neighborhood. Sue invited me to her home in Hyde Park, and when we sat down for lunch, she asked her youngest son, Owen, to say grace. During lunch she told me that in college she had been drawn to the Quaker religion; later, as I thought about her, I concluded that she was the kind of person I would call a practicing Christian of no strict denomination. She had set up the center with yearly financial support from her father and the moral support of Trude Bettelheim, her friend and neighbor, who occasionally volunteered to work and play with the children at the center.

At the outset Sue wondered whether to teach a few children intensively or to bring together a large group. Trude suggested she talk to Bruno, who recommended the group approach and urged her to take in children as families. This proved good advice, because as she taught older children to read, they taught their younger brothers and sisters. Over the years, hundreds learned to read at the center, including some who joined the Blackstone Rangers, the street gang then dominant in the neighborhood.

For Sue, blacks living in a ghetto so near her own home in Hyde Park were to be treated as neighbors, and gang members responded by treating the children's center as off-limits, thus giving her protection. She worked there through three pregnancies, nursed her babies in the church basement, and did not hesitate to take her children along when they were older. Friends warned her that it was dangerous, and again she consulted Bruno, who said he thought she could do it. I imagine he saw her sincerity and openness as her best protection. And it almost was.

Once when Owen was ten, a ring of fifteen-year-olds surrounded him and began hitting him to see how much punishment he could take. When I met Owen he was fifteen himself, about six feet tall and very well put together. I asked how much could a ten-year-old do against so many bigger boys.

"Not much," he said, smiling, "but I did my best."

"He was a good talker," Sue said. "He talked his way out of things."

The ten-year-old had faced a ghetto ritual and survived; also, he knew his mother's rule of no fighting at the center. She would expel the bullies, so he came back the next day without worrying about it.

WHEN SUE'S father fell ill and could no longer send her money, she talked to Trude, who asked Bruno to help. By that time the Bettelheims were living in California, but he found anonymous donors who eventually made up the $20,000 a year Sue needed.

I ASKED Sue what she had learned from Bettelheim, and she said it was not so much a matter of specific advice but what she picked up when she audited his lectures and went to the Saturday-morning seminar for mothers. Of the "dialogues" she said, "I could never pick a bone with him. He was so on target with whatever problems people were bringing up, and that was good for me, because I was running my school by that time."

How did she see him in the classroom? "Scary, terrifying, and sometimes he could be very rough on a person — but he would *engage* the class. He'd ask questions, and then someone responded, and if it was an ignorant response he would let the person know it."

And as a teacher? "Just enormous insight," she said, "sensitivity, compassion, and clarity of thought. He's clear and logical, with no psychological language. He sees through the child's eyes, feels how the child feels.

He asks lots of questions, and I do that myself; I'm interested to get responses. That's how you find out where somebody is."

She added, "Dr. B. always said, when you're with children, protect them, and that's been basic with me, but that's from the heart, too." The advice Sue said she remembered best was Bettelheim telling teachers to start where the child is. "Each child is at a different place, and if you start above or below, it's very destructive. You don't want to bore the quick child, lose his interest, lose his concentration, lose his respect."

As a way of teaching children to read, Sue insisted that they begin to write. Each child had to write a story every day in the notebook she had given them, and three- or four-year-olds dictated their stories to an older sibling or a teacher. (Sue hired volunteer college students at a dollar a day and paid her own children the same whenever they taught at the center.)

Every student's quota was to write one page a day, and they had to show Sue their page before they could go into the gym to play. If she was too busy to look, she would tell an older student to read to a smaller child for fifteen minutes. "I think that the older child always learns something from reading to a younger person."

Sue had one final comment that recalled Bettelheim's influence on setting up the center to take in children as families: "I believe you should build on the family, give them strength, because they'll be there when you're not there."[1]

THE OTHER person Gayle Janowitz suggested I meet was her next-door neighbor Barbara Stein, a longtime public school teacher in Hyde Park. She had been intrigued by Bettelheim and had taken his courses while working for her master's in education. I asked her to recall an example of his singling out a student and giving him a rough time—a practice I had come to see as a strong teaching technique that also suited his irascibility.

Barbara told of a young man who always sat in the front row and often raised his hand to answer or ask a question. One day Bettelheim asked a question, and the class was silent. (Barbara felt intimidated in this class-room, and no doubt others did as well.)

Seeing no hands, Bettelheim looked at the young man in the front row and directed the question to him. The answer came back stiff and vague; Bettelheim turned caustic, demanding simple words, not such *fancy* lan-guage as "unsatisfactory interpersonal relationships." Barbara thought the student had, in a way, been inviting Bettelheim's assault and got it.

"Obviously there was something going on between them. You know, this was part of his reputation. The kid stopped coming to class after that."

Barbara remembered a second incident and described it. "Again, there was a young man doing the same kind of thing, getting Bettelheim to pay attention to him and trying to answer all the questions correctly in order to be rewarded." She said that Bettelheim "picked on him" with questions like "What do you mean by such-and-such?" and "Is that the best you can say?" This went on for perhaps ten minutes, and then an older woman (someone in her fifties, who stood out because most others were under thirty) raised her hand.

"Bettelheim called on her, and she said, 'Dr. Bettelheim, I'm a teacher. I come here after working all day'—it was winter and very bad weather—'I come here all the way from Evanston because I want to take a course with you, and I have sat here and listened to you go through this with various people who make a bid for your attention. You respond in this bombastic way, then you assault this person, take him apart in front of everybody, never put him back together again, make the person feel like two cents. I pay a lot of tuition, I spend a lot of time, I didn't come here to listen to that. I came here to learn something from you that I can use in my classroom. I didn't come here to learn how you go about assaulting people.'

"And the room was deathly silent. And he hesitated and everybody expected him to take out after her, and instead he said, 'Thank you, madam. You're absolutely right in your comments. I apologize to you, and I will not do that again.' And he didn't—in that course." She added that even though the woman had a point, they were all fascinated watching him when he attacked a student.

As shown earlier, Bettelheim dealt harshly with naïve, ignorant, jargon-prone, or hostile students in order to rivet and ready the class for his message, and his response here might look as if he had been chastened; however, my guess is that he recognized a serious teacher, one who wanted to improve herself. He tormented a young man who wished, in his transference, for a symbolic father's approval, but he felt instant respect for a woman who hoped to learn something she didn't already know about her profession.

Many regarded his harshness as unkind, but I wonder how kind it is *not* to extinguish a student's illusions about himself and the teacher? (I include the student's illusion that he speaks well when he parrots the jargon of psychology.) Bettelheim's rejection of such students, called "abuse" by some, can also be seen as the opposite, that he was not abusing the student but disabusing him of stupid notions and unrealistic attitudes. He apologized to a woman in whom he saw a commitment to the honorable profession of teaching; he saw no such commitment in the young man who, out of his inner confusion and as a defense against personal emptiness, had begged for attention. I consider students who ran up against Bettelheim's verbal ax as part of the "ripple effect," if in fact they were turned away from a calling for which Bettelheim judged them unsuited.

BETTELHEIM'S toughness could also have a happy result for a student, depending upon his or her character. Bruno once told me of having returned to the university for a visit; across the dining room of the Quadrangle Club, where he and Trude were having lunch, there was a table of young women, one of whom stopped to speak to him on her way out. They were teachers attending a conference at the university, and this young woman, who was black, said she wanted to thank him.

Why?

Because he had given her an F on a paper she wrote for his class.

But why thank him for an F?

Because, she said, it was her first failing grade in college, and it shook her up. She had been getting good grades for work she knew was poor, and she suspected teachers were passing her on race alone. Bettelheim's F shocked her into seeing that she should study diligently to earn her degree. (I doubt the F would have had its bracing effect without the spontaneous reaction of her character: she respected Bettelheim, with an attitude intrinsic to her own sense of self-worth—and conscience—which demanded that she adhere to clear standards of learning.)

At that point she buckled down; she studied hard, got grades she knew she deserved, graduated—and found a teaching job she liked. Now she had worked long enough to know that teaching was right for her, and she thanked Bettelheim for having brought her up short with an honest F.

Of course, he congratulated her and wished her well, but he admitted to me that she had been in one of his larger classes and that when he gave the paper an F he had no idea who he was grading. If he had known, he said, he was not sure he could have failed her. His remark came with a touch of sadness that seemed to render a little judgment against himself, a passing regret in the complex irony of life that he might not have been as good a person as the young woman thought.

In any event, I see her success as a ripple.

BARBARA STEIN had taken other courses with Bettelheim, the most memorable one being a small class given at the Orthogenic School. At the time, she had started teaching in a South Shore neighborhood in transition, a place where whites were moving out and blacks moving in. She heard that Bettelheim was offering a government-sponsored course for a limited number of teachers in neighborhoods like this, and she signed up.

She said that it was not the big classroom scene with a huge audience drawn by Bettelheim's international reputation; everyone here had come to ask practical questions. "This was a small room with a pot of coffee and tea, with only ten people who came to just sit and talk to him about their problems in dealing with their school and the children in such a school." In this setting where he was teaching one-on-one, she found Bettelheim warm and inspiring, not the overwhelming figure in the large classroom.

Barbara added that there were none of the famous assaults in this class, perhaps because everyone there was a working teacher. "He seemed to have a great deal of respect for people who were out there doing it instead of just talking about it."

Rather than lay out abstract principles or lessons, Bettelheim asked the teachers to describe specific situations. Barbara brought up the problem of eating in class. She told him her classroom smelled from pickles and chewing gum, and this disturbed her when she was trying to teach reading. Bettelheim advised not telling the children to throw the gum away or get rid of the pickles or to say, "I'm going to tell your mother"—the usual things teachers do. "Why don't you just talk to them about why it bothers you," he said, "and see if that helps?"

She did, and it helped in an important way that she always remembered, by creating "a kind of rapport between me and these kids on a level that I hadn't approached before." Not all the eating in class stopped, but the youngsters began to see her as a real person with her own needs, not just another adult telling them what to do.

"I suppose the thing I learned most from him is to talk to the people you're trying to deal with and open up a little bit yourself." She recalled substituting in a library: "These were seventh- and eighth-grade kids, again in a school not even in transition anymore; it had already become a black school, and there were some really tough boys, and I was afraid of them. I was in my twenties, and they were bigger than I was."

In effect, the students had been dumped in the library for a forty-minute period when they had no class, and they were bored. Barbara knew nothing of library science and was only expected to keep them quiet. Almost at once they became noisy and restless, and she didn't know what to do to quiet them down. She thought, *How am I going to deal with this? I'm in over my head.* Finally she decided to try what she had learned from Bettelheim and to tell them she was afraid of them. She did so and also pointed out that she was young and new—" 'and you're doing all these rowdy things.' And it worked; they got quiet, they settled down.

"I said, 'You're not interested in library and books, and I'm not trained to do this, so why don't we just use this as a talking period, but talking to each other, not talking among yourselves.' "

The students were happy to talk to her, to complain, to tell her what was wrong with the school, with the system, with the teachers. It proved to her that she could take charge just by following Bettelheim's idea of addressing her real concerns. "It was fun, I enjoyed it. They did too. They didn't learn a thing about using the library, but I didn't care, and no one else cared either. The point is, they were right, because no one cared what they did in the library."

Of course, that was only good for the first day. Many of the youngsters were teenagers who could not read, and so Barbara decided to read children's books to them, books with very simple messages or themes—*Stone Soup,* for instance. After reading aloud for ten minutes, she would ask what they thought a little child would like or dislike about the book. In this way, she said, the fighting, pushing, and screaming died down as the young people listened to the story and then began to talk to her and one another. A good story, plus honesty and respect in the way Barbara presented herself, brought the class to order.

BARBARA also thought that Bettelheim's feeling for children had touched her as a mother. One day he came to visit the Janowitzes, next door to the Steins, and walked in through the Janowitz back gate at a moment when Barbara and her daughter happened to be out in their backyard next door.

"My daughter was a baby, and she was sitting in one of those plastic swimming pools. She was cute and pretty, and she was sitting there dumping water back and forth from a pail."

Barbara had been in Bettelheim's classes, but of course he did not recognize her. For the baby girl splashing in the plastic pool, things could hardly have been busier, but for adults it was a serene and time-less moment on a hot afternoon. Bettelheim stopped at the fence, arrested by the innocence, the single-minded artlessness, of a baby at play.

"He just stood there and looked at her, and he said, 'That's so beautiful,' and then he went in the Janowitzes' house. And I didn't even answer him."

ONE OF the last Orthogenic School workers I interviewed was also one of the last to join the School during Bettelheim's tenure. Marci Enos was taking one of his classes in 1969 when she was approached by Bert Cohler to join the School under a new program for hiring graduate students who would work as counselors part-time. Marci was hired without an inter-view, perhaps because Bettelheim had a sense of her from the class. She always sat in the first row—"plunked down right in front of him"— and was noticeable because she was an attractive young woman of mixed black and American Indian heritage. Also, she always spoke up in class and took part in discussions.

On Marci's first day at the School, just before starting, she made the acquaintance of Betsy, now a teacher, in the staff room, and Betsy asked how she felt.

"I'm really, really scared."

Betsy laughed and said, "Well, so are they." Betsy's attitude somehow pushed Marci past her fear, and when she went in and sat down with the group of girls at snacktime, she forgot herself and focused on them. She had memorized their names before the first meeting—a standard practice at the School—but she soon learned that more than names had to be fixed in mind.

"If the kids were going away on trips you had to memorize when they were going, what flight, so you could discuss it with them without reading from a piece of paper. It was incredible training." Years later in private practice, she found that the memory habits she learned at the School had become almost automatic.

Marci's relationship with Bettelheim was an easy one. She took her dorm group for a walk one day, and a girl threw a tantrum right outside his office—"pulling up her dress and that kind of thing"—while the other girls accused Marci of losing control. She thought, *If he looks outside his office, I'm dead.* After she got the group back to the dorm, she went to talk to him.

"He listened, and he said, 'Vell, why don't you just stay in for a little while? Maybe you need to stay in, but I don't think it was bad. You learned something, nobody came to grief, you were embarrassed.' I thought, *That's true, somehow I managed it. I kept control of the situation, I got them all in.* And I felt very good about it."

Marci became friends with Betsy, whom she thought of as Bettelheim's "psychological daughter." Betsy was the one person, she said, who could "strike terror" into the heart of younger counselors. "Betsy really did see everything, and she really did know everything. The kids adored her and looked up to her, because she was, in a sense, one of them."

Marci felt the reassurance many have mentioned when Bettelheim made rounds. The dorm quieted down when he walked in, and she sensed he was backing her up as he tried to speak to everyone. "But what's surprising to me is that the same thing would happen when he'd walk into the auditorium at Judd Hall." She said he walked down the aisle in a room full of people busy talking to one another, and although he said nothing as he approached the rostrum, a wave of silence spread through the room. "I hear that when he went to faculty meetings it was the same—there would be a kind of hush."

TOWARD the end of her first year as a counselor, Bettelheim called Marci into his office and asked if she would take a full-time job as a teacher. She had two young children at home, and it would have been hard to work full-time as a counselor, so she became a teacher. Bettelheim was phasing himself out, but Marci continued to look to him as someone from whom she could learn.

An important trait she felt she had in common with him was trying to sense what another person feels about you—"especially emotionally disturbed teenaged kids, to adjust to be empathic with them, to see why they don't like you. I think that takes a real strange thing in your head. It's not so much that I wanted them to like me, but that I was aware of their discomfort. And I think that's what Dr. B. does, to some extent. He has a sense of what people are thinking, how they are responding to him, and sometimes he gets angry at it, sometimes he just explodes, but sometimes he's gentle and tries to help that person work with it. And I think that's what he saw in me, and why he knew I could make it at the School.

"I don't think he would have liked me if he thought I was just some conciliatory, passive black person trying to pretend I was white. I think he tested that out when racial things came up in class, but at the same time there was a genuine interest in me and how I was going to handle that. By the way, if someone was just too totally wholesome and normal, they didn't usually make it at the School. You have to have acknowledged and worked with your own stuff to see someone else's."

Marci believes that Bettelheim respected her ability to work without defensiveness in the School, and with a minimum of fear. In turn, she saw him as "an enormously strong man"—but vulnerable. He wasn't there merely for her and others; in and for himself, he needed love and care. She got an insight into this when he came in one day, still frail from a leg operation. That afternoon Trude called to make sure he didn't overdo things, and he left. Marci left a little later to go shopping at Marshall Field's, where she happened to take an escalator that carried her up past the book department—"and there was this little man! I almost fell off the escalator!"

Her jaw dropped; she stared at him in shock, almost outraged: he shouldn't *be* there, he should be at home resting! Bettelheim must have felt her gaze, because he glanced up at her on the escalator, rising out of sight. When she came back down, he was still there, browsing among books. ("Next to the Orthogenic School, Marshall Field's was the place he loved," she said.) Passing an hour in a bookshop was so clearly what he needed at that moment, she couldn't tell anyone at the School she had seen him playing hooky. When she met him the next day, she simply smiled at him—"and he understood."

Marci also said (like several others) that she felt his confidence in her, his trust that she could deal with the children, that he would not have to come to her rescue. Having learned to value this attitude, she was later able to convey a similar confidence to many in therapy with her.

AN EXPERIENCE she took away from Bettelheim's smaller classes, with their intense and personal moments, was his technique for evoking insights.

"He had a way of coming at you, of saying something two or three steps ahead, and some people got confused or upset. He was hard to track or to follow, and I think he did that deliberately. He'd say something that would shock you, and you'd think, *Where did he get that?*" She said that Bettelheim often did not deal with the manifest content of a student's remark; if he caught the emotion behind it, he would address that.

His ability to synthesize also fascinated Marci, and she found herself doing the same thing, suddenly making points that surprised her. She would go home and say to her husband, "I had one of those oracular days again"—exhilarated because she had reacted to Bettelheim with new ideas. "I would put something together and just say it—and find myself exactly where he was. I mean, there were times when we were able to kind of meet in midair."

MARCI had gone to college at sixteen and at seventeen was absorbed in Freud, a precociousness perhaps due in part to early reading. Her grandmother had taught her to print the alphabet at four, and before learning to form words and sentences, Marci would scribble letters at random. If she saw her grandmother writing a letter to someone, she would insist on sending her own letter along—a page of scribbles, which her grandmother carefully enclosed. Soon she was making words and sentences and could write a real letter, but still only by printing. Even writing no more than a sentence was laborious, and she at last rebelled, saying, "I don't want to do this, it's too hard. I can't write—I want to scribble."

Her grandmother agreed, and Marci began to scribble quickly at random as before, then suddenly burst into tears. Her grandmother asked what was wrong, and Marci said, "I can't scribble anymore."

"That's the story of my life, right there. I can't scribble anymore. Once you know how to write, your ego doesn't let you." She recalls sitting in a little chair and using the seat of a big chair as her desk, printing slowly but making sense. "And in a way, that's how I was at the Orthogenic School, and that's the way Dr. B. is; that's what he wants of people. Once you understand your own issues and how they interfere or how they can help you as you delve into things—if you can tap into that, then you can't scribble anymore."

WHEN SHE was still very young, Marci came home one day and told her mother some white children in the neighborhood had insulted her about her skin, which is light brown. Her mother responded with level-headed advice Marci believes has helped her at the School and elsewhere:

> Some people have a real problem about that, and it's very sad, and you can't let it upset you. You just have to go ahead and do what you have to do, and not be nasty or mean to them. You might not want to talk to them, because when people are being mean, no matter what they're saying, you don't want to be around them.

Marci felt the truth of this attitude, especially after her mother went on to name white neighbors—adults—who liked her and were nice to her. Her mother's matter-of-fact common sense helped Marci remember that not all whites wanted to insult her; and somehow, over the years, she has never thought of herself primarily in racial terms.

A troubling moment had come on her first day at the School just before she met the children. They would all be white, and she had suddenly thought of herself as "black"; this had added a new fear to her anxiety as a beginner, but Betsy had brightened her mood with a casual remark.

ONE AFTERNOON Marci's younger daughter was scheduled to meet her at the School but came late because of a mix-up. There wasn't time for Marci to take her home and return, so the girl had to come along to a Bettelheim lecture.

Marci's daughter was a Brownie (wearing her uniform that day) and happened to have Girl Scout cookies with her. "I wonder," she said, "if Dr. Bettelheim would buy some cookies." Marci told her they had to wait outside the classroom and get Dr. B.'s permission for her to attend the lecture. When he came, the girl asked permission and also said shyly, "And you might like to buy some cookies."

Bettelheim took it all in stride. "He said, 'Well, I'm sure I would like to buy some cookies. Of course, you may come. I hope you don't get bored.' And she said, 'No, I think it will be very interesting.' So in we went," Marci said, "and the discussion got onto something about where babies come from, why children think that the stork brings babies.

"She whispered to me, 'I think I know why,' and I whispered back, 'You can raise your hand.' "

She did, and Bettelheim acknowledged her, saying, "Oh, this young lady has something to contribute."

"She stood up," Marci said, "and a hundred pairs of eyes turned and looked, and she said, 'Because it has that big, big beak. And people think that beak means that it could carry a baby. And the big beak makes it look strong.'

"And it was great, he loved it, he just went bananas!

"He said, 'You see, it's absolutely right—you see, out of the mouths of babes! Of course, it's the big beak! The masculine! The strength!" Bettelheim went on to point out the nurturing message in the image, that the stork could feed and carry, and also that the beak was both fierce and protective.

"Afterward everybody came up, praising her, saying, 'Gosh, you have so much courage, you stood up,' and she felt really terrific. I think it did something for her life, too. He was wonderful with her, she never forgot that. And he bought some cookies."

RIPPLES follow a splash, and Bettelheim made many splashes, both as a writer and as an educator. However, the School that he developed and guided for almost three decades has faded from public view in the nearly thirty years since he left it. His version of milieu therapy was never a quick fix but *is* an alternative to the drugs that now dominate psychotherapy for young people.

PERHAPS rescuing youngsters in Bettelheim's milieu can be compared to raising children in the traditional family, because both milieu and family are cottage industries. Hands-on care, a close eye for a child's feelings and needs, the stabilizing force of long-term trust, the child's maturing recognition of reality (and deepening awareness of the human condition), the testing of talents and interests—all these seem to require a small and personal setting. To grow strong within themselves, children need first to believe that the world revolves safely around them, long before they step onto the moving platform of a world that doesn't. Many things that count in the idea of growing up seem tied to a nurturing milieu, itself surrounded by a larger reality; and for such a milieu to help a child toward mastery, a strong and strongly motivated director like Bettelheim seems called for.

Nevertheless, as remarkable as he was, it is impossible for me to believe that of all the people on earth, only Bruno Bettelheim could maintain a therapeutic milieu. Louis Harper had hoped to make a similar environment in Milwaukee but found that the authorities to whom he reported could not accommodate the long-term needs of children in the milieu. Perhaps it can only be done securely in an academic setting that gives a director time and freedom to produce the benefits of milieu therapy, plus access to a pool of graduate students who learn about themselves as they care for disturbed children. ("Zee children get better as zee serapist gets better," was the way Bruno often put it.)

In any event, Bettelheim showed that milieu therapy would work. Only slowly did he come to a full understanding of what he had to do for troubled children to help them find some measure of inner poise and outer peace. Now others can take up where he left off, and I think he hoped this would happen. Tested methods are there, along with the totally human problem of the therapist's (or director's) own "issues."

Of course, there is also now the problem of Bettelheim's damaged reputation. He reached the general audience he had hoped for but remained an outsider in the psychoanalytic profession and was enthusiastically discredited soon after his death — unfairly but understandably so, as I hope I have shown. Psychoanalysts who sent him their children fell silent about him where they might face disapproval from the colleagues. This is also understandable, and I note it not to lay blame but merely as a fact of group dynamics, a swimming with the stream.

One question Bettelheim would never address or allow me to dwell upon in our conversations was the seeming unwillingness of analysts and psychologists to credit his contributions. Whenever I asked, he might shrug and say he didn't know why, that he wasn't a good union member and so on; however, this was the man who modified Freud with the concept of vagina envy; who argued that circumcision was not symbolic castration; who introduced the term *extreme situation* to signify external conditions that can change a person's inner life; who did for fairy tales what Freud had done for dreams; who made shrewd observations on the relationship between Jung and Freud in his review of a book about Jung and Sabina Spielrein, the gifted young woman known for contributions to Jung's and Freud's thinking; and, finally, Bettelheim perfected, over many years of practical care, sophisticated but commonsense methods for a new approach to treating mental illnesses.

I spoke with Steve Herczeg, who had worked at the School and who had researched the history of milieu therapy for a college course he offered.

"It's weird," he said, "but when you look into the subject you find there's no recognition of the fact that Bettelheim invented milieu therapy. He worked it out first with Emmy Sylvester, and then kept refining it with the staff and changing it as long as he was at the School. But in the books I've seen, the creation of milieu therapy is attributed to a couple of psychiatrists or to Maxwell Jones, who had some kind of hospital program. Those now credited with inventing it wouldn't have lasted a week trying to run the School. Well, maybe a bit longer if they could keep the staff. But I get pretty hot about it, because I see that Bettelheim's work has been so thoroughly disregarded."

While I was writing this book I happened to read an article about milieu therapy in a major newspaper. It surprised me, because the reporter did not mention Bettelheim's name. Curiosity got the better of me, and I called to ask why he had left out Bettelheim. He seemed genuinely puzzled and said, "What does Bettelheim have to do with milieu therapy?"

I began to explain the Orthogenic School, but then I sensed he thought he was talking to a crank, and so I thanked him and hung up. In fact, he was a good writer and exceptionally well qualified to cover psychology, but he had earned a graduate degree in psychology from an Ivy League university without ever hearing of the Orthogenic School's successful milieu. It was clear to me that group opinion and conventional wisdom in the academic world had turned Bettelheim, even before his death, into a nonperson in that milieu.

HAVING drawn (as it were) to the end of this portrait, perhaps I owe the reader a word more about my relation to Bettelheim. After he became a client, I found myself advising someone whose work continued to gain in my esteem the more I understood of it. In all our dealings, he was reasonable, unfailingly courteous, and businesslike. As time passed we spoke more often on the phone and usually saw each other for a breakfast or a lunch when he came to New York. His way of expressing interest in me felt genuine and so led to a reciprocal affection that was somehow never tested by his natural irascibility.

To the world at large he was an authority figure (perhaps also to me, in some ways), but our relationship took form with an imperceptible and unlikely role reversal: I came to be an authority for him on his books, the work that filled his retirement. Not that I was a *figure*, but still he looked to me for advice and followed it almost without question. I now believe that being trusted implicitly solidified my motives in working on his behalf.

However, Bettelheim wanted more than business advice from me—he wanted to be taken care of. I first glimpsed the deeper shades of this feeling when he was living in California and I had told him to call me at home in the evening if his schedule ran past our regular office hours. I often took work home, and one evening I was sitting in the easy chair where I usually read manuscripts. Whenever our English bulldog noticed me there, he took it as a signal to climb onto my lap and settle down for a nap, snoring peacefully while I turned pages over his back.

Bruno called one evening, and Joan told him it would take a moment for me to come to the phone because Buck was on my lap. Bruno had met Buck and could visualize this highly domestic scene, and he said to Joan, "Ohhhh, to be Buck!"

It was wistful, funny, and sincere, a wish for safety, comfort, reassurance, protection. I can guess that he never got enough of a safe lap himself—who does?—and that he created the benign milieu for others so that it met some of the same needs as a lap. Before Ruth Marquis would discuss Bruno with me in any detail, she wanted to know my feelings about him, and I told her how he instantly identified with Buck on my lap. She said, "Well, he knew who loved him."

In this story I also see the emotional starting point of Bettelheim's extraordinary insight into children—his quick self-knowledge, his willingness to tell himself of a weakness as well as to let a trusted friend in on the secret. Honesty like this opened him to quick empathy with children, to sense the content of their feelings about themselves. Imagining what the other person felt by imagining what you would feel in a similar situation was also Bettelheim's chief rule in practicing psychotherapy. When I pointed out to him an almost identical idea in Adam Smith's *The Theory of Moral Sentiments*, Bruno was amazed, amused, and gratified.[2]

BETTELHEIM was at heart a teacher, but first he was a learner who had absorbed the value of discipline in schoolwork as a way of dealing with the world at large—a lesson and prelude to the more difficult discipline of psychoanalysis as a way of dealing with one's inner world. His formal analysis was replaced, in time, by an informal self-analysis that was perhaps even more rigorous and self-humbling than his hours and years with Sterba.

In one of his last interviews, he spoke of analysis never coming to an end, and that was true of the way he lived. He respected his feelings and used them, as when his anger at a student's self-oblivion set the stage for a memorable drama. Why should Bettelheim have been angry at a foolish student for transferring troubled feelings about a father to himself, a forceful teacher? Obviously, among other reasons, because he had made transferences he later recognized as stupid, and with this self-knowledge he could focus his anger and give that student a lesson in reality. The rest of the class got the same lesson but from a safer perspective, as spectators.

IN QUIET moments Bettelheim's face often looked mournful, even before Trude died. Afterward, as long as he could write and travel, useful work let him put her loss aside for hours at a time, but her companionship and the reality of her love were sadly missed. Joan happened to speak to him on a related topic, and he made a remark she has always remembered, that *mourning has no end.* He knew mourning was a crucial step in making the best of life afterward, but this concept belies a loss that lingers even as life goes on. In any event, it was clear to me that he never stopped mourning Trude.

Sometimes the expression on Bettelheim's face also told of his months in the camps, when he was taught the reality of life without mercy. Against this background, he projected positive attitudes in the School, where he made an astonishing success by staying true to his insights and convictions. However, he could never deny having seen ordinary people, fellow humans, perpetrate and enjoy immense cruelties. Only by setting himself to think his way past this ugly truth and proving that he could create a better truth did he earn reprieve from bitter moods ever ready to rise within him. Even so, in his last year he admitted he was still puzzled about why it was so hard to put the camps behind him, and he said, "As far as I can figure out, it is an experience that makes one lose one's belief in mankind as such."[3]

Although he could not sustain an unclouded belief in the human race, he could make choices to help unhappy children. In the camps Thanatos ran wild, but thanks to the total milieu, a child's innate potential for pleasure could take root and flower.

In time, however, I came to sense in him an almost bottomless pessimism, a hidden fear that he managed to neutralize only by risking defeat in work he found priceless. And whatever he did, he had to do more. A child might fail, might fade away into a life without hope, but he could not stop to mourn that failure; the School had to go on, for the sake of all who grew stronger there. His hopes for the goodness of life took on solid form when he modeled confidence for staff and children, and all the while the School's good work allowed him to defend himself, temporarily, against his grim conclusions about humanity.

The School stood at the center of his life, but life itself was too vast, too varied, too surprising to be one thing only; it had to have balance, and so he balanced school with family, work with love, Eros with Thanatos, the dry light of intellect with the heart's hopeful warmth.

Firmly held and firmly balanced values, not rigid rules, gave him the inner poise to go on mastering the crises of his complex little corner of the world, where he also had to find a balance between the good and the hostile in a child, to fight for the child's better self by confronting the worse. This aspect of his protector's role, slapping a child, calls to mind Hamlet's words to his mother: "I must be cruel only to be kind."

When Bettelheim hit a child, his hand ruled the School as an incarnation of the reality principle; but his hand could serve reality for only a brief moment: other directors had to follow, if the School were to go on. Yet he could not let go of it; he needed to help it, could not turn his back on a creation that was fated to go the way of all institutions, which evolve, or devolve, into something else. In his heart he knew that he *knew* better than anyone else; that he could *help* more than anyone else; that he *cared* more than anyone else. Now, unhappily, he was too old, and all these feelings and facts left him burdened with an ache to act, but no authority. Helpless, he could not use what he knew, and I have come to believe that the settled sadness of his face said what he could not: that the School, his treasure for so long, was not the School anymore.

CHAPTER 35

Pessimism and Hope

ONE MEASURE of a man is the kind of person he holds in the highest esteem. For example, Bettelheim admired Freud's powerful and original mind, his stubbornness in pursuing ideas across whole decades, his honorable flexibility in reversing himself when wrong—and yet he had reservations about Freud that narrowed the scope of his admiration. Bettelheim was pessimistic like Freud, but toward the end of his life he wrote of two people whose humanity and integrity added a dot of bright color to his pessimism, a faint glimmer of hope for the human race. They were a woman and a man who acted with uncommon decency in terrible times and at peril to themselves.

The man was Janusz Korczak, a doctor and writer who oversaw a Jewish orphanage in Warsaw for thirty years and who in 1942 chose to accompany the orphans in his care to the gas chambers at Treblinka, knowing that their trust in his presence would spare them the worst terrors of their last hours. He could do no more than reassure the orphans until the moment he died with them, although he might have done less, because a friend had given him new identity papers for his escape. He is reported to have said, "One does not leave children at a time like this."

A fellow Pole, John Paul II, declared Korczak a symbol of religion and morality, but Bettelheim found a different meaning: righteousness without religion.[1] His point is implicit but clear, even though he could make it only by citing the Talmud:

> Up to the last, he lived according to what the rabbinical fathers once wrote. When asked, "When everyone acts inhuman, what should a man do?" their answer was, "He should act more human." This is what Korczak did to the very end.[2]

Bettelheim concludes by noting that of the 840,000 Jews murdered at Treblinka, Korczak's name alone has been honored with an inscription:

JANUSZ KORCZAK (*Henryk Goldszmit*) AND THE CHILDREN

THE OTHER person whose courage and decency inspired Bettelheim as he neared the end of his life was the woman who hid Anne Frank's family for two years. Miep Gies survived to write a book, *Anne Frank Remembered*, and it was the subject of Bettelheim's last book review.

Her simple story made a deep impression on him because of Miep Gies herself—the person he felt her to be. Bettelheim had seen the demons in ordinary men swarm out and overwhelm all decency, and he admired Miep Gies, an Austrian gentile living in Holland, because of her empathy for young Anne Frank. Miep had risked her life rather than turn away from the mild and worried man who sought her help. Otto Frank asked her to hide him and his family, and she said, "Of course." Out of his own decency he started to remind her of the possible consequences of her act, but she cut him off.

"When I said, 'Of course,' I meant it."

At that moment she chose to defy a world of men whose unexamined anger ruled most of Europe, men who bullied others and made themselves feared for known cruelty; but her heart had a landscape better than theirs, and she would not submit.

This stirred Bettelheim and gave him hope, though not merely because of her brave kindness in going against the tides of her time; for him, the supreme meaning in Miep Gies was the fact that she was ordinary. In her book, she wrote: "There is nothing special about me, I was only willing to do what was asked of me and what seemed necessary at the time."[3]

She was an average person, she was simple, she had nothing unusual about her, no special brilliance of any kind that would have made anyone notice her; but her square and upright nature, her ordinary human good sense and warmth of feeling that guided her in a crisis, made her stand as high as anyone could in Bettelheim's eyes.

There is an echo here of the way he staffed the School. Now and then he got an exceptional recruit, but he took it for granted that an ordinary, average, decent person could learn his methods and respond with personal parallels—empathies—to a child whose unhappy feelings crippled him. In the broadest sense, the ordinariness of Miep Gies heartened Bettelheim; it wiped away some touch of the human stain left by average and ordinary men whose mark in history is an indecency from which we turn away.[4]

The fact that people are not all alike is sometimes hard to hold in mind, but in thinking about Janusz Korczak and Miep Gies, Bettelheim found a small respite from what he had felt and seen of the worst of life. They were good.

BETTELHEIM had left instructions for his body to be cremated, and five days after his suicide his ashes were buried in a grave next to Trude's. Rabbi David J. Meyer began his eulogy with a Talmudic reference, noting that whoever teaches his child does not teach that child alone but also his descendants, down to the end of all generations.[5] Bettelheim never spoke of himself in cosmic terms, but I can imagine him giving a quick nod in partial agreement and adding the reminder that teaching can be for better or worse, depending on *what* is being taught and *how*. This image came to mind because Bruno once told me that it usually took three generations to make a child ready for the Orthogenic School.

Rabbi Meyer closed his eulogy with a tale about a student who spent many years with a teacher so devoted to teaching that he wanted to make even his death a lesson. On the night he knew he would die, the teacher took a torch and went into the forest with his student. In the midst of the dark woods, the teacher suddenly put out the torch. The student exclaimed, "What's the matter?" and the teacher answered, "This torch has gone out." His voice faded as he moved on, and the student cried, "But will you leave me here in the dark?"

The teacher's voice came back faintly: "No, I will not leave you in the dark; I will leave you searching for the light."

BETTELHEIM's voice is silent now, but the man I have come to know by working on this portrait strove above all else to teach therapists, especially therapists, to think independently and to imagine their way into the patient's heart by looking into themselves. He knew that when the teacher was no more, the student would always face, alone, a darkness in the patient's soul; and he knew that enlightenment, the human connection, could come only from the spark of human empathy that makes a sudden glow in one's own darkness.

The Bruno Bettelheim I knew made himself strong by struggling against the unremitting currents in our stream of life, a task of exceptional subtlety because those currents also flow at all times within our selves. This was how the teacher fought to the bottom of his convictions, and only by so doing could he reach the inner state he prized, the learner's gladness that he is rising to the light.

Schizophrenia

I have used the term *schizophrenia*, with reservations and as convenient shorthand, but mostly without the popular connotation of a "split personality," where Dr. Jekyll and Mr. Hyde take turns in a single body. In 1911 a Swiss psychiatrist, Eugen Bleuler, coined *schizophrenia* to replace an older term, *dementia praecox* ("early or premature insanity"). He meant to highlight a disorder in the working of the mind, a lack of coordination (and therefore a splitting) between the mind's various psychological functions—in other words, a disruption of the mind's own dynamic. The *Encyclopaedia Britannica* comments that "neither the old term nor the new is entirely satisfactory . . . to cover the various patterns of disturbance usually included in the group" (vol. 19, p. 1161).

Brief dictionary definitions of schizophrenia refer to psychotic reactions, withdrawal from reality, disintegration of personality, and loss of contact with the environment. *Webster's Third* gives a longer account, but all such efforts to define are necessarily impersonal and detached, whereas Bettelheim's approach was personal and empathic as he sought to understand a particular child. It is obviously more therapeutic to start a relationship with a child like Wyatt by seeing him as he sees himself—not "schizo" but deeply unhappy.

Bettelheim's experience on the train to Dachau and Wyatt's "wall of glass bricks" both show similar states of mind: emotional numbness, and a withdrawal from external realities as a way of coping internally and avoiding panic. The adult Bettelheim (he was thirty-five) survived by getting emotional distance and using his intellect about his predicament, but a child like Wyatt needed a casually benign new milieu that included caring adults, if his self-knowledge and integration were to grow.

Finally, Bettelheim's own comment on the inadequacy of psychiatric terms as applied to children was that "the categories all come from adult psychiatry. In a child, these things are much more confused, much vaguer, because the child's grasp of reality is tenuous at best."

APPENDIX B

Defense and Autonomy

In *Freud and Man's Soul* Bettelheim argues that *defense* is not a wholly satis-factory translation because it suggests that we defend ourselves against outside attack, whereas the "attack" actually comes from within. We are disturbed or "attacked" by feelings we cannot allow into our awareness, and so we push them back into the unconscious. If the unconscious threatens to bubble up with something out of character for the person we think we are, we evade it in some way, leaving the unacceptable thought still safely locked within.

Such a defense protects us from the truths our passions tell us and masks the depths of our hostility and frustration. Although tucked out of sight, our aggressive feelings remain an urgent aspect of ourselves. Moreover, a clever defense (and our unconscious is clever, as Freud showed) that bans a feeling gives us the illusion of controlling that feeling; and, in a way, this actually happens. But even as our defense succeeds, the forbidden feeling is not defeated, merely repulsed. The defense has parried the attack with a move too quick for our inner eye, and the idiosyncratic power of our unconscious has invented a defense that becomes a part of a stable, conscious self.

Taking all this for granted, Bettelheim taught his staff to understand that a child's defense was evidence of creativity and autonomy, that our defenses spring up spontaneously within us as we seek to preserve what we believe and wish to be our authentic self. In other words, we do it to ourselves, and any-one who tells himself that he has no choice and therefore no autonomy has autonomously created a defense that relieves him of responsibility by falsely denying his autonomy.

Because a defense is also a form of self-government, Bettelheim always spoke of a child's symptomatic behavior as an achievement and saw it as a key to the child's world. In Wyatt's case, the conviction that he was superior to adults allayed his anxiety about their power over him, but his defense was illu-sory. In time, as he let go of his defenses, he built up other aspects of his per-sonality, with better results for himself in adapting to life.

APPENDIX C

Superego and Id

Freud did not develop his concept of the superego in final form until over twenty years after he began practicing psychoanalysis. For decades he referred to the unconscious as if it were a single entity, the *es* (it or, in Latin, id). Eventually he drew a distinction between its two main features: the *id*, all impulses and repressed feelings; and the *Über-ich*, or "over-I" (superego), which seems to take charge of the mind. It shields the ego against the demands of the id and also guides us in life, sometimes by bossing us around.

This invisible mentor is apparently made up of rules, fears, advice, warnings, punishments, and anything that comes into our awareness propelled by *ought* and *should*. It includes the ordinary activities of conscience, such as guilt and self-judgment, although superego and conscience are not the same thing: I hear the voice of my conscience, but my superego is silent, known only by inference.

At various times Freud called the *Über-ich* a structure, a province, and an institution. However, such words bring to mind images of blueprints, maps, and bureaucracies, and these do not quite fit. Perhaps it is better to speak of the superego simply as a mental force that acts swiftly and remains unseen, with a logic we can grasp and a coherence we take for granted.

Somehow it keeps track of our hierarchy of values that helps bring order to our feelings, and its presence strongly suggests our absolute need for enough inner orderliness to attain a measure of control in life. It internalizes norms of personal and social behavior and remembers all that is "over" us, including not just morality but cultural and artistic standards. It says, *Do this* and *Feel that* and sometimes checks us with a *Don't!* Besides the highest values, it also knows the lowest and often feels infallible as it registers what we most admire and most despise. It has been called both a storehouse and a theater of values, but in my view it is more pointedly dynamic than that: it is our inner director, whose version of reality perhaps enables us to survive.

As mentioned above, Freud at first believed that our unconscious is a single vast psychic realm with a hidden life of its own, but he later concluded that one of its parts has dominion over the others. In his final view, the chaos of the id involuntarily submits to the unseen ordering power of the superego, which is every bit as much *Über-es* as it is *Über-ich*. The interplay between superego and id influences the course of our conscious life, and in turn the conscious self may modify some aspect of the superego if a defensive impasse is dissolved.

Speaking of the id, Freud called it "a cauldron of seething excitement," and he found in it no negation, no sense of time, no change in its own processes despite the impact of experience and the passage of time. He saw it as sheer will, incoherent because of the many violent impulses that live side by side with all their contradictions intact, all shouting in voices that we do not hear but cannot escape. It has been likened to a prison where forbidden and repressed desires exist as angry inmates, forever clamoring to break out. The superego is the warden of this prison of id.

Once, at the end of a long conversation, I asked Bruno to characterize the id in his own words, but he did not care to do so, except to say, with typical understatement, "It's not very nice."

Also, in an apparent quest to mark out a clearer place for autonomy in the mind's structure, Bettelheim sometimes threatened to abandon the Freudian frame of reference. For instance, in writing about the effect of social change, he tried to explain superego and id as static institutions that are disintegrated by a fast rate of social change unless the individual has a strong and autonomous ego. He wrote in a letter to Ruth Marquis:

> But since I no longer believe that the tripartite division of the mind has any validity or usefulness, I can't put it in these terms and I have to wait until I develop my own conceptual structure, which I probably shall arrive at in about a hundred years. (3/26/57)

In fact, in *Freud and Man's Soul*, twenty-five years later, he remains staunchly Freudian.

Eidetic Memory and False Memory
(and Autism)

In 1986 I heard Ralph Tyler, who had given Bettelheim his first job in America in 1939, speak of him as having been plucked out of the camps by the Rockefeller Foundation and brought to Chicago. Given Tyler's close relations both with the foundation and with Bettelheim, he should have recognized the impossibility of his statement, so I asked Bruno a few hours later why Tyler had said something I knew was absurd.

"Eidetic memory," Bruno said. We were walking down the stairs in the Quadrangle Club, about to meet someone else, and I never got around to asking Bruno for a definition, but I understood him to mean that Tyler had a fixed image, a clear picture-memory of something that never took place. A neurologist friend of mine remarked that there can be *any* degree of imprinting from reality and also any degree of imprinting from the activity and force of the mind itself; this is simply how we work.

In a study called *The Seven Sins of Memory*, Daniel L. Schacter makes the familiar point that "hindsight bias" is all too common: "People seem almost driven to reconstruct the past to fit what they know in the present. In light of the known outcome, people can more easily retrieve incidents and examples that confirm it" (p. 146). Schacter also says that visual imagery adds to suggested memories: "If imagery is a kind of mental signature of true recollections, then embellishing a false memory with vivid mental images would make it look and feel like a true memory" (p. 125).

Since this image-embellishment no doubt happens within all of us, I take it for granted that Bettelheim was not immune to it and that some of his stories from Vienna (family legends, for instance) got better as the years passed. Schacter describes a fascinating instance of the construction of a specific false memory in the Oklahoma City bombing investigation. He demonstrates convincingly that one witness unintentionally constructed a false memory of

John Doe #2 and that further investigation showed there was no such person (John Doe #1 being Timothy McVeigh).

In any event, I believe some of the discrepancies Richard Pollak had pursued in *The Creation of Dr. B.* can be attributed to false memory.

However, it seems only fair to mention the one area in which Pollak may have a legitimate point, namely in the résumés that Bettelheim began writing in 1939 when he came to the States and desperately sought work—résumés that claimed a range of credentials he did not have and never suggested in any interview or conversation with me. In those job applications he made statements about his life in Vienna that were not true and described his background in ways that often departed from reality. Be that as it may, when I think of a man who had lost everything and sought a foothold in a new life, I cannot find it in my heart to condemn him (or anyone else) in that extremity. Also, as Pollak notes, Bettelheim invented credentials needlessly, because, among other things, a person "with wit and drive could get ahead in the land of opportunity."

My disagreements with Pollak would add up to a book longer than this one, and so I will touch upon only one topic where I regard his account of Bettelheim as both tendentious and wrong—his effort to claim that Bruno played fast and loose with data about the Orthogenic School's results for autistic children. Karen Zelan worked with many such children at the School, and in private practice she has treated more than forty autists. At my request she wrote a note on Bettelheim's description of the "cure rate" of autistic children at the School (pages 413–16, *The Empty Fortress*):

> To confirm or disconfirm Bettelheim's assertions, you'd have to know who the forty autistic children were. Then you'd have to gather a panel of experts who'd look at the children's histories, referring information including their diagnoses by other physicians, reports by staff including the consulting psychiatrists, and a sample of staff process notes. Only then would you have a reliably diagnosed autistic group. Also, the panel would have to know the current literature on autism's diagnosis, i.e., what "autistic spectrum" and "Asperger's syndrome" are.
>
> It's heartening that Bettelheim used other investigators' attempts as a context for his analysis, notably that of Leon Eisenberg. So Bettelheim's format for reviewing his data did not come out of the blue.
>
> Bettelheim not only compares Eisenberg's outcome data to his own but compares his and Eisenberg's speaking versus nonspeaking autists in an attempt to tease out what may be important for a positive

therapeutic outcome. (I come to the same conclusion as Bettelheim did, that the autistic child's ability to speak makes a difference in the prognosis.) Bettelheim also discusses length of psychotherapeutic treatment and, not surprisingly, finds that Eisenberg's lower "cure rate" is correlated with fewer psychotherapeutic interventions (i.e., fewer treatment hours).

I don't believe that Bettelheim overestimated or inflated the number of autistic kids at the O.S. In the eight years I was there some twenty-five students seemed either classically autistic or to have Asperger's syndrome. Of course, there may have been autistic students I didn't know before and after my time.

I'd say that there were probably more students on the autistic spectrum during his thirty-year tenure than Bettelheim reports. In any case I believe he was prescient in that he had an intuitive understanding (way back then) of the overlap between the classically autistic group and the Asperger's group. We still don't know whether the neurological substrate will turn out to be the same or similar for all children on the spectrum.

There are two points to remember about Bettelheim's results at the Orthogenic School. First, he objected to follow-up studies because they violated the understanding—the covenant—the School had with the children. The School was for them. Period. It had no other purpose, and they owed it nothing. If they were required to take part in follow-up studies, or even to be grateful, the School's promise would be a sham. As Karen Zelan put it in a letter to me,

> The problem is the getting of the data, because this would be an intrusion that could undo the therapeutic work. Bettelheim did not want to threaten the children's therapy by pressing former students to respond. Even if some did volunteer information on how they were doing, we don't know why *they* did and others didn't. So the resulting data is of necessity unsystematically culled.

For Bettelheim, helping the child took precedence over everything else, including trying to convince doubters. The child had to be convinced that life was worth living, and those readers yearning for the cold reassurance of a statistic would have to shore up their opinions elsewhere. If the internal coherence of his work did not bring conviction, then he would rather live with the public's doubt than a broken promise.

The second point to remember is what one considers as a "cure." Many at the School (both counselors and students) said to me that to move a child from a back ward to a front ward was a great improvement. If living at home with limited freedom was the "cure," then this was still better than custodial care in a mental institution. Bettelheim could shrug off doubts to the contrary.

NOTES

Introduction: A Personal Note

1. *The Informed Heart*, pp. 78–79.
2. *The Informed Heart*, p. 79.
3. *The Informed Heart*, p. viii.
4. At the same time I wrote Bettelheim, I also wrote a letter to Max Lerner (whom I had just met) with the suggestion about Eichmann. Lerner wrote back to say it was not a good idea.
5. I met Ruth and Naomi, Bettelheim's daughters, only after his death.
6. At first I had suggested to one of my clients that Bettelheim would be a likely subject for a *New Yorker* profile, but William Shawn, the magazine's editor at the time, would not offer an assignment, and the writer could not work "on spec."

Chapter 1: Young Bruno—Infancy, Background, and Early Adolescence

1. I have not tried to replicate Bruno's accent except on occasions when he had trouble with a "th" or a "w." Usually he spoke very clearly, and I realized after a while that at least part of his problem came from dentures that were painful or needed refitting; his teeth had been damaged when he was taken to Dachau in 1938. The mispronunciations I sometimes show are ones I heard myself or were reported by someone else quoting him. Usually when he said "Oedipus," there was an umlaut or "r" in there somewhere, making the name sound like "Erdipus," and despite other oddities he tried his best to be understood. It was an ongoing problem that seemed to become more troubling in his last years. In my final interview with him (he couldn't wear the dentures that day) he said, "Zat's where zees sings all started." He was referring to the course of his life after the camps, but that obviously includes his problems in speaking clearly.
2. The two previous books on Bettelheim say that Moritz Bettelheim was born in Budapest rather than Bratislava, but they give differing dates of birth. I did not happen to ask Bruno's sister about family legends, but many families have them, and they are often not strictly accurate. I doubt that Bruno ever tried to research his family background, and I do not think it crucial in this account of his life. For Bettelheim's own version, see *Freud's Vienna*, pp. 132–34. I did confirm that there is no record of Jacob Moritz Bettelheim in Bratislava.
3. Bruno mistakenly recalled the region of Seidler's birth as Moravia, which in the nineteenth century was still more of a backwater than Bohemia in the empire.
4. "About the value of three dollars," according to Bettelheim.
5. For a good account of Adolf Seidler, see *Bettelheim: A Life and a Legacy* by Nina Sutton (New York: Basic Books, 1996), pp. 24–25. Bruno did not speak to me of Seidler's sharp business practices, possibly because he hated to be associated, even remotely, with

such behavior. However, he showed his dislike of Seidler in other comments on his personality.

6. Again, Bettelheim was mistaken. Jacob was actually his grandfather's first name. I have chosen to use Moritz rather than Jacob, because this was how Bruno thought of him and referred to him. I have also chosen to follow the affectionate and intimate form of first names as used in everyday conversation; for example, Paula rather than Pauline and Grete instead of Margarethe. On the stage and in America, Grete called herself Margaret.

7. The only Yiddish word I recall Bruno using: "Superb housekeeper."

8. In modernizing Vienna, authorities also took the occasion to disperse the various departments of the university so that students (potential rebels) would be less likely to form a spontaneous mob. In the same spirit, planners made the Ringstrasse too broad for impromptu barricades, because in 1848 the rebels had successfully defended their cause for a brief time in the narrow streets of the old city. Perhaps not incidentally, this was also the age of boulevards in many European cities.

9. *Gymnasium* is pronounced with a hard g. As used in this book, the German word refers only to a school and never to a place for exercise.

Chapter 2: Gymnasium *and Wandervogel*

1. Bettelheim remembered the number of students as a hundred.

2. One who cares for children on the kibbutz.

3. *A Good Enough Parent*, p. 113.

4. The clubroom was called the Heim (the home, or nest).

5. For a fuller account, see *Freud's Vienna*, pp. 24–29.

6. P. 58. See Walter Laqueur's *Young Germany* (New York: Basic Books, 1962) for a full account of the Wandervogel. A few commentators have been understandably troubled by the fact that some Wandervogel groups (not the one in Vienna) displayed the swastika; but this prehistoric emblem linked youngsters to an ancient past in a vague symbolic way and only became charged with hateful meaning by the Nazis. Nonetheless, it is true that many German Wandervogel clubs were highly nationalistic and excluded Jews. Depending on local prejudice, French, Danes, Slavs, and Italians were also excluded. Membership reflected the biases and beliefs in German-speaking countries. Hans Willig told me that discussion of racial or religious differences was absolutely forbidden in the Vienna club. On the occasion of a Wandervogel convention, everyone agreed on two propositions: that the movement should not condone prejudice, and that any club could make any rule necessary about its membership. Small wonder that the movement never became more than a stimulating escape for adolescents, but in this it was of great value to many. It also inspired some members to become teachers.

7. In *A Good Enough Parent*, pp. 80ff.

8. Bettelheim recalled him as a respected scholar who taught history, Latin, and introductory philosophy. After the government collapsed in November 1918, the new regime dismissed Rebhahn and appointed a more liberal headmaster.

9. *A Good Enough Parent*, p. 81.

Chapter 3: The University; the Business; Gina

1. Hochschule fur Welthandel; literally, High School for World Commerce, perhaps better translated as International Trade School. It was not a high school but a college with aims similar to our graduate business schools.

2. Some details of this aspect of Bettelheim's education are from *Bettelheim: A Life and a Legacy* by Nina Sutton (New York: Basic Books), pp. 71–74.

3. *Anschluss* is "union" or "joining," and it refers to the joining of Austria to Germany in 1938. The third largest political party in the 1920s (the German Nationalists) advocated this, as did early leaders among the Social Democrats (Austria's largest party). It was an idea supported by Austrians from many walks of life.

4. Bettelheim would sometimes make a general point about sexual behavior in Vienna, saying that before men had effective methods of contraception, a husband might go to a brothel, in part to protect his wife from an unwanted pregnancy. Of course, this was not likely to be true of less affluent men.

5. This anecdote comes from an interview with Marilyn and Larry Levy, friends in Los Angeles.

6. Bettelheim's sense of Jewishness was not a topic I ever raised. The vague self-doubt implied by dwelling on that question was not in the Bruno I knew. He had known he was Jewish before he was old enough to realize that the world had prejudices toward Jews, and in adulthood he came to see his cultural heritage as both honorable and valuable. Also, since he had a penchant for swimming against the tides of popular opinion, being a Jew in a gentile society suited him temperamentally. I believe he would have seconded Freud's comment that being Jewish freed him from many biases that limited others intellectually, and that as a Jew he was prepared to go into opposition.

7. The house also stood two doors away from the summer villa of Frau Katharina Schratt, the mistress of Emperor Franz Josef. Her garden shared a wall with the palace grounds, a wall with a discreet doorway through which the emperor could slip unnoticed.

8. Gina Weinmann told me a somewhat different story about the girl who had lived with them. She said that Anna Freud referred the woman and her child to the Sterbas for analysis, and the Sterbas suggested that the girl enter a small private nursery school started by Anna Hatschek. Gina became a partner with Hatschek, an arrangement Bruno financed. "We had no contact with Anna Freud," Gina said. "This was a very small experimental school for a few nursery school children who had some disturbances, but it was not a model for the Orthogenic School. It was a totally different thing."

Gina also said that the girl "could not function normally, but she was a pretty child, a very pretty child, and she was sickly, she was autistic." When I questioned the word *autistic* to make sure that Gina meant it in a formal way, she said she could not be certain that the girl was "absolutely autistic," but that she was both "very fragile" and "withdrawn."

The nursery school was in Hatschek's apartment, and the girl also lived in the apartment. Gina saw her every day during the week, but the weekends became a problem, because the girl was lonely and missed Gina. Hatschek suggested that Gina take the girl home on weekends.

"She developed a very strong attachment to me, very personal, as it should have been, so I took her along on weekends and brought her back to school on Monday." The girl continued to live in the Hatschek apartment, but "when she became so depressed, besides being withdrawn, I decided to keep her in the house."

The details of the two accounts of how the girl came to the Bettelheims cannot be reconciled, although both stories show a certain fortuitousness. In Bruno's version, Gina meets the mother by chance, feels sorry for her, and invites her to dinner. Later, after seeing the girl, both Bruno and Gina discuss taking her in and mutually decide to try it. In Gina's version, the referral runs through proper channels, and she eventually makes the decision to have the girl live with them. In each account, Gina is the first and principal contact; both indicated that Gina took care of the girl, and Bruno saw her at lunch and in the evening. Later in the girl's seven-year stay, Trude worked with her in the Montessori school. However, for me the most telling fact in the picture here is that the girl did not keep in touch with Gina but with Bruno. Bruno had told me that the girl wrote to him occasionally over the years and that he always wrote back. Gina confirmed this and said that the girl was not in touch with her.

9. A *Good Enough Parent,* pp. 199–200.

10. A *Good Enough Parent,* p. 200.

11. Some schools called themselves "Montessori" but were casual about the methods recommended by Maria Montessori; Trude's school employed the Montessori methods.

12. The quotations I have used are from tapes Trude made for the Bettelheim children shortly before she died.

13. For some reason, Gina did not attend the party, and Bruno substituted for her.

14. Gina consistently refused to speak to me over the telephone about Bruno and in fact at first refused to give me any interview at all. I called several times, and she finally agreed to see me if I came to San Francisco but said I should not come solely to see her, because she might change her mind. When I made my plane reservation I called again and told her the date; she remained reluctant, but in the next phone call she said she would see me. However, she did not wish our interview to be taped. Because of this restriction, my verbatim quotes from Gina are very few. She would not explain why she did not want a taped record of her comments.

I went to San Francisco and saw Gina, but the interview did not last long. From the start, her anger toward Bruno and her coldness toward me were all too apparent. After a half hour or so of questions, she made the point that Bruno should not have called himself a psychoanalyst, and my reply unfortunately made her so angry that she terminated the interview. I said that in his *Who's Who* entry he identified himself not as an analyst but as a psychologist and educator; I added that in our conversations over the years he did not often speak of himself as a psychoanalyst.

Gina got up from her armchair and took one of Bruno's books off a shelf and thrust it at me, pointing to the note about the author on the book jacket, which indeed referred to him as a psychoanalyst. Then she told me I was "too close" to him to write about him, and the interview was over.

My definition of a psychoanalyst at that time was, vaguely, someone who saw a series of patients individually, doing in-depth analysis by interpreting dreams, and so on. I had never thought about who was an analyst and who wasn't and so was ready to agree with Gina that we should not, officially, call Bruno an analyst. In any event, my thoughts about him had always been primarily as an educator. Just to be on the safe side, I suggested to Bruno's publisher that future book jackets should not refer to him as a psychoanalyst.

I have now concluded, however, that Gina was not quite correct. It is true that Bruno did not conduct (as far as I know) traditional psychoanalysis to help patients with dreams and to uncover the unconscious sources of their unhappiness, and it is also true that when the Chicago Psychoanalytic Society admitted him as a member in 1946, it specified his status as "non-clinical." The Society then recommended that he be accepted by the Chicago Psychoanalytic Institute, an independent organization that supervised training analyses, but the head of the Institute, Franz Alexander, refused.

It seems likely that Alexander had a change of heart later, because Bettelheim led a training seminar at the institute for four years (1951–55) for analysts of children. Ruth Marquis, who sat in on some of the sessions, told me they were incredibly exciting as Bruno asked questions about the cases the analysts presented. Also, Alexander gave high praise to *The Informed Heart* in the *New York Times Book Review,* one of his themes being (as Sutton correctly noted) the author's self-analytical approach (Sutton, p. 254). If Bettelheim was qualified to *train* analysts in several years of seminars, then I believe the argument about the use of the word *psychoanalyst* becomes a quibble, a distinction without much of a difference.

15. Vienna also had "ghetto" families in the sense that they did not live in luxury and met with open hostility in their surroundings. However, much of the "decorum" of the upper middle class also prevailed.

Chapter 4: A Bearable Moratorium; a Ph.D.

1. Some traditions change very slowly. In 1972 our travel agent tried to book us into the Sacher and was told the hotel was full. We stayed elsewhere but on our first evening in Vienna went to the Sacher for dinner. The dining room was almost empty, and I asked our waiter why. He said that everyone had just gone off to Salzburg for the Mozart festival. "Oh, does the hotel have rooms?" I asked, and he said it did. When I told Bruno this story years later, he asked if my travel agent was Jewish. In fact he was, and several other friends gave the same explanation as Bruno's, that a Jewish travel agent in New York City would be expected to have a mostly Jewish clientele. However, three decades have now passed, and perhaps our travel agent, Mr. Simon, if he were still alive, would not encounter in our enlightened time a veiled excuse from a very fine hotel like the Sacher.

2. Erik Erikson, *Identity: Youth and Crisis*, p. 157. Some observers also refer to the moratoriums simply as prolonged adolescence.

3. Erikson has written about moratoriums in the lives of Martin Luther, George Bernard Shaw, Hitler, Freud, and others.

4. *The Informed Heart*, p. 8.

5. "The Problem of the Beautiful in Nature and Modern Aesthetics." For a good discussion and summary, see Nina Sutton's *Bettelheim*, pp. 541–44.

6. Neither Sutton (p. 553) nor Pollak (p. 50) believe that this meeting with Freud took place or that Bettelheim applied to the Vienna Psychoanalytic Institute. There is no record in the files of the institute, but I do not believe that the evidence, or the lack of it, is the full story. See the discussion of eidetic memory in Appendix D.

7. The training analysis came at a relatively late date in the development of psychoanalysis as a profession. Most analysts in the first generation around Freud did not undergo analysis at all. Instead, they gathered in his apartment for the Wednesday-night meetings that began in 1902 and turned into the Vienna Psychoanalytic Society six years later (the institute was founded in 1925). They also read Freud's books and papers, wrote and delivered treatises on analytic subjects, and attacked one another with the weapons that Freud had put into their hands. Colleagues pounced on one another's slips of the tongue with glee, and their sparring often became hot and hostile. Freud undertook short-term analytic sessions with a few of his adherents, but for the most part he treated patients rather than would-be analysts.

As late as 1914 Freud still believed that a "normal" person could take up the profession of analyst once he gained an insight into his own dreams, which he might do through self-analysis, by reading the literature, and by talking with other members of the society. Nobody in the early years thought of a training analysis as a prerequisite to work in the field (Reuben Fine, *A History of Psychoanalysis* [New York: Columbia University Press, 1979], p. 90).

By 1930 the requirement of a training analysis had been adopted by psychoanalytic societies around the world. Gina and Bruno would have known of the "didactic" as an interesting new development, but most of the analysts they knew would not have had such training.

8. I spoke to Kronold (he had changed his name in America) after Bettelheim's death, and he had no recollection of Bettelheim beginning a training analysis with him. He said he had heard from someone that Bettelheim had a second analysis with Ernst Kris, but he could not be sure. He recalled having met Bettelheim in Vienna on social occasions.

Chapter 5: *The* Anschluss; *Dachau*

1. For details of the crisis, see *The Rise and Fall of the Third Reich* by William Shirer (New York: Simon and Schuster, 1960), pp. 325–47. There is some disagreement on whether German troops crossed the border late on March 11 or early on March 12.

2. Protective custody was already legal under the German constitution when the Nazis came to power, and it was meant to protect the state, not the prisoner.

3. In the SS, the expenditure of a bullet had to be reported to superiors. A beating did not.

4. By his "personal integration," Bettelheim meant the self he knew and trusted because he had developed it with some success throughout his life. He felt that his ego, built up by dealing with reality, would have failed (lost its integration) in the face of a reality as shocking as the experience on the train; his self-protection occurred in the form of detachment from his ego.

5. *Surviving*, p. 52.

6. At this time the SS did not yet tattoo the prisoner's number on his arm.

7. *Surviving*, p. 13.

8. *The Informed Heart*, p. 148.

9. *The Informed Heart*, p. 290–92.

10. *The Theory and Practice of Hell* by Eugen Kogon (New York: Berkley Books, 1980).

11. Kogon, p. 313; *The Informed Heart*, p. 186.

12. *The Informed Heart*, p. 187.

13. *The Informed Heart*, p. 180.

14. *The Informed Heart*, p. 187.

15. Typically, Bruno did not tell me this about himself, probably because he did not wish to seem to spotlight his virtues. However, in Trude's tape she says that a man in the camps with Bruno said he gave talks about psychoanalysis. See also Sutton, pp. 195–96, and Pollak, p. 77.

16. *The Informed Heart*, p. 115.

17. *Surviving*, p. 13.

18. *The Informed Heart*, p. 15.

19. *The Informed Heart*, pp. 17–18.

20. *The Informed Heart*, pp. 19–20.

21. *The Informed Heart*, p. 157.

22. *The Informed Heart*, p. 158.

23. *The Informed Heart*, p. 160.

24. The historian Raul Hilberg (*The Destruction of the European Jews* [New Haven: Yale University Press, 2002]) found this figure interesting as a considerable overestimate. I believe it is another example of the limitations of memory.

25. *Surviving*, p. 241.

26. *Surviving*, p. 241.

27. Sons of the Archduke Ferdinand, who was assassinated in Sarajevo in 1914.

28. I have been told that the Venetian Republic punished military disobedience in this way and that the practice may date back to the Roman legions.

29. *The Informed Heart*, p. 154.

30. *The Informed Heart*, p. 155.

31. *The Informed Heart*, p. 155.

32. *The Informed Heart*, p. 210.

33. *The Informed Heart*, p. 211.

Chapter 6: From Bad to Worse

1. *The Theory and Practice of Hell* by Eugen Kogon, p. 108.

2. Martin Sommer survived the war and was tried and sentenced to life imprisonment in East Germany. However, he was eventually released for reasons of health, and he died in an old-age home in 1988. (Private communication from Raul Hilberg.)

3. *The Informed Heart*, p. 174.

4. *The Informed Heart*, p. 141.

5. *The Informed Heart*, p. 207.

6. *The Informed Heart*, p. 132.

7. *The Informed Heart*, p. 135.

8. *The Informed Heart*, p. 181.

9. *The Informed Heart*, p. 182.

10. Ibid.

11. *Surviving*, p. 292.

12. *Surviving*, p. 65.

13. *The Informed Heart*, p. 138.

14. Kogon, p. 80.

15. *The Informed Heart*, p. 138

16. *The Informed Heart*, p. 228.

17. *The Informed Heart*, p. 193.

18. *The Informed Heart*, pp. 164–65.

19. Francis van Gheel Gildemeester was a religious Dutch philanthropist who had gained the confidence of Austrian Nazis by helping Nazis imprisoned in Vienna after the murder of Dollfuss in 1934. In 1938 authorities allowed him to help Christians emigrate, and some Jews converted in order to qualify for his aid.

Chapter 7: The Worst Moment; the Release

1. This was not the same Richard mentioned in Bettelheim's letter to his mother from Dachau.

2. Marilyn Levy.

3. *The Informed Heart*, p. 150.

Chapter 9: Trude; Bruno's First Job

1. From Trude's account, we know that her relationship with Bruno did not go smoothly at first. Pollak (pp. 103–4) says that Bruno proposed to another young woman in Chicago, perhaps partly in anger at Trude for her affair in Australia. However, he gives no date for the possible proposal, which may have occurred (if it did) before Trude's arrival

from Australia. In any event, Bruno and Trude took an apartment together about a year after Trude arrived.

2. *Freud's Vienna*, p. 214.

3. The information about Frieda Weinfeld comes from *Memorial to the Jews Deported from France, 1942–1944* by Serge Klarsfeld, pp. 259–60 and 266. "Frieda" was the diminutive for her given name, Frederika, and so I have referred to her here as her family did and as she appears on the convoy list.

Chapter 10: Getting a Foothold; Starting a Family

1. The Midway is a heavily traveled avenue on the site of the "Midway Plaisance" of the 1893 Columbian Exposition. The roadway is lined with wide lawns and also has a broad, treeless stretch of grass turf in the middle, between lanes.

2. Michael Jenuwine, "A History of the Orthogenic School of the University of Chicago from 1912 to 1990" (unpublished paper).

3. A century ago, *orthogenic* was an accepted psychiatric term for the treatment and correction of abnormalities in children but is not now in general use.

4. *Apperception* in this context is understanding in terms of one's previous experience. Rorschach was a Swiss psychiatrist who had created an "Experiment in the Interpretation of Forms," which was not in fact a test. "It could not be quantified," Bettelheim said, "and it offered nothing that could be ascertained for certain, but in the English-speaking world it became the Rorschach test, and it has been quantified."

5. "The Self-Interpretation of Fantasy." *American Journal of Orthopsychiatry*, vol. 17 (1947), pp. 80–100.

6. Ibid.

7. Ibid.

8. Ibid.

9. Sylvester also worked at the School under Bettelheim's predecessor.

10. *Love Is Not Enough*, p. 35.

Chapter 11: The Orthogenic School: Taking Charge

1. *A Home for the Heart*, p. 123.

2. When the object of our transference helps us see our flaws and mistakes and still accepts us in spite of them, this inspires loyalty and seems lovable.

3. *A Home for the Heart*, p. 388.

4. *A Home for the Heart*, pp. 388–92.

5. *A Home for the Heart*, p. 217.

Chapter 12: Writing

1. *Freud and Man's Soul*, p. 50.

Chapter 13: Making the Milieu

1. Jenuwine, "A History of the Orthogenic School."

2. Bettelheim did not like to use the word *patient* but never found a good alternative.

3. One of Freud's most famous sayings, "To love and to work," is apocryphal. The words do not occur in this form in his writings and first appeared in print in Erik Erikson's *Childhood and Society* (1963). Erikson told an interviewer that he had heard it in Vienna

and that it impressed him. Freud may well have said it, and it certainly resonates as a useful summary of his hopes for a good life, but this formulation perhaps owes more to Erikson's reasonable and optimistic outlook than to Freud's often pessimistic context. See "Apocryphal Freud: Sigmund Freud's Most Famous 'Quotations' and Their Actual Sources" by Alan C. Elms (*Annual of Psychoanalysis*, vol. 21, 2001. Analytic Press: 2001). My thanks to Dr. Jerome Kavka for bringing this essay to my attention.

4. How the boys came to enter the office because of a counselor's ambivalence is a fascinating story and can be found in *A Home for the Heart*, pp. 92–93.

5. Paul's diagnosis was institutionalism, a condition in which the child fails to develop normally and may even deteriorate from lack of human contact.

6. One reason for the bars was that the neighborhood just south of the School had become a ghetto, with an increase in crime.

7. As does the image of the person to whom we have transferred unconscious emotions.

Chapter 14: Transference; Therapy; Staff Meetings

1. Bettelheim said that Franz Alexander told him he tried to analyze Anna Freud later but "couldn't make a dent."

2. "Little Hans." When Freud saw Hans again at age nineteen, he remarked how well the young man had turned out.

3. Gina went for her next analysis to Editha Sterba, who also analyzed the American girl—Gina's patient—and Trude.

4. See discussion of Bettelheim's paper on the TAT, earlier.

5. Countertransference occurs when a patient influences a therapist's unconscious feelings. It is similar to a patient's transference of unconscious feelings to the therapist and complicates relations between patient and therapist.

6. Freud said, "Transference is merely uncovered and isolated by analysis. It is a universal phenomenon of the human mind, it decides the success of all medical influence, and in fact dominates the whole of each person's relations to his human environment" (Reuben Fine, *A History of Psychoanalysis*, p. 424).

7. Here it seems likely that Steve Herczeg was feeling something (in transference) toward Bettelheim that had to be worked through.

8. Toward the end of the seminar, after the major issues had been dealt with, Bettelheim suddenly began to denounce himself, sounding quite angry for having overlooked the implications of a detail in Frank's presentation. It was an important detail, but he expressed no anger at Frank for missing the point, while seeming thoroughly annoyed with himself. He also upbraided Rosenfeld for not "reminding" him, which Rosenfeld took in good humor. In thirty seconds of fuming, Bettelheim managed to label himself and Rosenfeld as failures and to leave the students untouched. I believe he faked this "failure" for reasons given in his letter to me.

9. Letter from Bruno Bettelheim to Theron Raines.

Chapter 15: The First Book

1. Gina Weinmann, who knew Sylvester in both Chicago and San Francisco, confirmed to me that the break between Bruno and Emmy resulted from her insistence on writing in orthodox fashion for a strictly professional audience. In fairness to "Dr. Emmy," I should add that many of the counselors (Gayle Janowitz, for instance) liked and admired

her. In 1990 I went to the nursing home in San Rafael where Dr. Sylvester had moved after Alzheimer's made it impossible for her to live alone. I had hoped to get at least a word or two from her about her side of the break with Bruno, but it was not to be. I met her in the nursing-home lobby in the presence of a nurse and several other people. She and the nurse were tossing a toy basketball back and forth, and she said twice, in a sad and toneless voice—never looking at me—"I'm not supposed to talk to anybody."

2. Another example of transference.

3. Freud learned to listen to his analysands with an "evenly hovering" attention, which Peter Gay calls "alert passivity" (*Freud: A Life for Our Time,* New York: W. W. Norton, 1988, p. 73).

4. Bettelheim coauthored *The Dynamics of Prejudice* with Morris Janowitz, and it was also published in 1950, the same year as *Love Is Not Enough.* However, the latter was his first solo performance. Ruth Soffer edited both books. Bruno liked Morris and invited him to the ice-cream sessions at the School, where Gayle and Morris first met. Everyone understood that Bruno was trying to make a match, and the other counselors soon took up the cause. They would catch Gayle just before she went into the room where Bruno and Morris were, saying, *"He's* in there! Take off that ratty sweater and put on something nice."

5. The North Shore Hospital Lecture Series on the Normal Child. A transcript of the speech was kindly supplied by the Menninger Foundation.

Chapter 16: A Growing Reputation; the Next Stage for the School

1. As seen in the photographs in *Love Is Not Enough.*

2. Philip Pekow Hall, named after a major benefactor of the school, housed adolescents two to a room and also provided recreational facilities, including a "pub" used as a game room. A dormitory room typically accommodated six to eight children, but Bettelheim wanted more space and privacy for teenagers. The 1952 addition had brought the School's capacity up to forty with longer therapy terms, and Pekow Hall raised it to fifty-two. Bettelheim himself later (after he left the School) came around to the view that perhaps the addition of Pekow Hall made the School too big. However, in his last years there he still hoped for one more expansion and ordered a set of plans for a facility that would take children under the age of one year. If he had been able to carry this through, the School would have spanned the entire range of development, infancy through adolescence. Jacqui Sanders told me that she saw the plans when she came back to the School to succeed Bettelheim. Bruno never mentioned this idea to me.

3. This was often true of innovations at the School. Bettelheim felt that the School would be best developed by many minds and hands working toward a common goal, as medieval cathedrals had been built.

4. From "My Life at the Orthogenic School," a speech given by Josette Wingo at the 1986 Festschrift for Bettelheim at the University of Chicago.

5. They married seven years later, the first of several couples who met and married at the School. I interviewed them together at their home in South Shore, a suburb south of Chicago on the lake shore.

6. Fae's account of the incident is slightly different from Bettelheim's. Hers was based on memory about thirty-five years after the event, whereas Bettelheim wrote, probably from notes, about fifteen years afterward. The differences are not significant.

7. Involuntarily, spontaneously, unconsciously.

8. Just for an allegorical touch in the portrait, I might add the likeness of an ovenbird in flight; its characteristic call is *teacher teacher teacher.*

Chapter 17: The Next Books; a Knack for Controversy

1. *Symbolic Wounds*, p. 16.
2. *Symbolic Wounds*, p. 58.
3. *Symbolic Wounds*, p. 149, 150.
4. *Symbolic Wounds*, p. 150.
5. Letter from Bruno Bettelheim to Ruth Marquis, September 20, 1956.
6. I have not been able to locate the article referred to, and Ruth Marquis had no memory of it.
7. *Symbolic Wounds*, pp. 10, 11.
8. Nina Sutton, *Bettelheim: A Life and a Legacy*, p. 562, note 29.
9. Jules Henry, "Types of Institutional Structure," *Psychiatry*, vol. 20, 1957; and "The Culture of Interpersonal Relations in a Therapeutic Institution for Emotionally Disturbed Children," *American Journal for Orthopsychiatry*, vol. 27, 1957.
10. *Surviving*, p. 250.
11. *Surviving*, p. 255. Here, Bettelheim used "death instinct"—a formulation he corrected in *Freud and Man's Soul*.
12. *Surviving*, p. 247.
13. For an impeccable account of the reception of the diary and play, see "Who Owns Anne Frank?" in *Quarrel and Quandary* by Cynthia Ozick (New York: Knopf, 2000). This essay first appeared in *The New Yorker*.
14. *Freud's Vienna*, p. 270.
15. *Freud's Vienna*, p. 267.
16. *Freud's Vienna*, pp. 270–71.
17. *The American Heritage Dictionary* (1970), under "error."
18. *Freud's Vienna*, p. 257.
19. *Freud's Vienna*, p. 252.

Chapter 18: The Indispensable Other

1. Inge Fowlie had no recollection of this. Almost invariably, when I asked a second participant about an incident someone else had recalled, the second person did not remember it at all. The reason for this, in my opinion, is that we recall moments that are important to us, and they may not have the same weight in another person's mind. Inge said she might have noticed Karen's hesitancy in taking off her coat and would have expected the children to notice this also. The same would have applied to leaving the candy, especially since each child had a personal box with candy in it.
2. Inge Fowlie does not recall the moment in this way. The prospect of losing Marcia upset her because she wanted to continue the work that might help the girl, and so she went to see Bettelheim. She found he had made up his mind that Karen would be a better primary person in Marcia's life, that Inge's personality was perhaps too active and forward—that Karen related more slowly to Marcia, which Marcia needed at that point. Inge said she believed he may have been right.

Chapter 20: A Boy's Conscience

1. The school's psychiatrist at that time.
2. See Appendix A for a discussion of *schizophrenia*.
3. *Freud and Man's Soul*, pp. 58–59.

4. *Webster's Third New International Dictionary* (G. & C. Merriam Co., 1966) has a curious lapse. Page 1165 has a heading that shows *inner voice* as the last listing on the page; but the last word is actually *innerve*, and the first word on the next page is *inness*. Somehow a proofreader's inner voice (or silent superego) told him to leave out *inner voice*. Readers who dislike Freud are allowed to think it was merely a mistake. (See discussion of *mistake* on pp. 254–55.)

5. This incident probably took place while Bettelheim was in Israel, leaving Jacquelyn Seevak (Sanders) in charge. He had named her the School's assistant principal, and he authorized her to carry out his role as disciplinarian.

Chapter 22: The Three Things — and Empathy

1. *A Home for the Heart*, p. 314.
2. *A Home for the Heart*, p. 315.
3. *A Home for the Heart*, p. 313.
4. *A Home for the Heart*, p. 315.
5. *A Home for the Heart*, p. 314.
6. Ibid.
7. *A Home for the Heart*, p. 242. Bettelheim quoted T. H. Huxley's definition of science and applied it to the milieu.

Chapter 23: Helping Someone Else, Helping Yourself

1. Founded by John Dewey.

Chapter 25: The Personal Teacher

1. Bettelheim did not remember the "subjective curriculum," and he also said he had not annotated the Rapaport seminars. I believe he simply forgot both matters. When Bert returned to the School for his second term as director, the Rapaport book had vanished, as had many other books in the School's library, apparently stolen.

2. This shows the power of personal teaching and personal tradition at the School. Betsy did for Cindy what Karen Zelan had done for Betsy — made "everything special."

Chapter 26: An Unwelcome Retirement

1. For a good description of Bettelheim's problem with Lyons (and vice versa) see Sutton, pp. 567–69. After about a year, Bettelheim dropped all his objections and signed a letter to Lyons authorizing publication.

2. *The Children of the Dream*, p. 271.

Chapter 27: The Film

1. Bettelheim wrote an introduction to a book on the film. Some of my narrative is taken from his account there; *Une autre regard sur la folie* (Stock, 1975).

Chapter 28: The Path to a Useful Enchantment

1. Letter from Bruno Bettelheim to Ruth Marquis.
2. *The Uses of Enchantment*, p. 155.
3. *Uses*, p. 150.

4. Alan Dundes, "Bruno Bettelheim's *Uses of Enchantment* and Abuses of Scholarship," *Journal of American Folklore*, vol. 104, no. 411, Winter 1991.

5. Julius E. Heuscher, *A Psychiatric Study of Fairy Tales* (Springfield: Charles Thomas, 1963.) p. 186.

6. *Uses*, p. 155.

7. Ibid.

8. Heuscher, 2nd ed., 1974.

9. *Uses*, p. 314.

10. Dundes, "Bruno Bettelheim's *Uses of Enchantment* and Abuses of Scholarship."

11. Ibid.

12. Pollak cites another scholar as charging Bettelheim with plagiarism in *The Uses of Enchantment*. In 1978 Joan W. Blos published a review, "The Emperor's Clothes," that praises the book briefly for allowing "adult readers to recover the value of what the tales convey," then quickly condemns it as "not deserving of accolades for its scholarship." She adds that the book should have been "shorter and more careful."

At this late date I must admit that when Bruno submitted the manuscript, my pleasure in it may have blinded me to its flaws. The same might have been true of Bruno's personal editor and of Robert Gottlieb, who published the book so successfully. Bettelheim acknowledged Gottlieb and singled him out as a "rare publisher" who was "finely perceptive" and who had a "sound critical attitude." (I agree on all counts.)

All the same, I grant that agents and editors may be at fault for not noticing a need of footnotes which, presumably, would have warded off the censure of scholars. However, when I take the book from my shelf from time to time, I rarely wish for more footnotes than I see there. More than 7½ percent of the text is in notes, bibliography, and index—ample for the popular audience Bruno sought. He might have added a few notes had he seen the parallels his detractors have overstressed, but the occasion did not arise.

As for Blos's specifics, like Dundes she loads her critic's guns with a spattering of elliptical dots that knock words out of juxtaposed quotes to make them near equals, while neglecting any other meaning Bettelheim had added. Blos's charge is: "Assimilation without attribution is not the scholarly thing to do." I won't argue the point but will add that in her comparisons of Bettelheim's text to Heuscher's she may have wished to call Bettelheim a plagiarist but did not do so. Both Dundes and Blos weighed their words carefully, words that Pollak turned into flat-out charges of plagiarism.

Even with more footnotes, I doubt the book would have had a better verdict from Blos, who ended her review by saying that the "Emperor" was "wearing a stuffed shirt." (*Merrill-Palmer Quarterly of Behavior and Development*, vol. 24, no. 1, 1978.)

Both Pollak and Sutton note other similarities between Heuscher and Bettelheim, but I believe Heuscher was correct that Bettelheim did not realize he was "taking from somewhere" (p. 354).

For an intelligent account of how even a careful author may inadvertently copy another person's work, see "How I Caused That Story," by Doris Kearns Goodwin, *Time* magazine, 4 February 2002.

13. *Uses*, p. 12.

14. *The Children of the Dream*, pp. 16–17.

Chapter 29: The Father's Role

1. Jacquelyn Seevak Sanders, *A Greenhouse for the Mind* (Chicago: University of Chicago Press, 1989).

2. October 1985.

Chapter 30: The Autocrat

1. I wrote this account before reading in Sutton's book that the student was Charles Pekow. Wyatt did not tell me that he witnessed the attack, but he did remark in passing that he thought Bettelheim was wrong in slapping the student.
2. *Surviving*, p. 133.
3. *Surviving*, p. 141.
4. *Surviving*, p. 130.
5. Ibid.
6. Ibid.
7. Sigmund Freud, Standard Edition, vol. 23, p. 117A (Moses and Monotheism).

Chapter 31: The Other School

1. *Surviving*, p. 170.
2. *Surviving*, p. 173.
3. *Surviving*, pp. 172–73.

Chapter 32: Death and . . .

1. Salim ("Sandy") Lewis has been mentioned earlier as both a student and a counselor at the School. His success as a financier and his openness in crediting Bettelheim and the School have made him perhaps the best known of its graduates.

Bettelheim's pension of $24,000 a year was modest even by 1980 standards, and Lewis gave the University of Chicago funds to increase it. Only in the last three years of his life did Bruno begin to make the kind of money from his books that he had made in Austria as a businessman. However, he never seemed to invest any emotion in the making of money, although he was a meticulous bookkeeper. He called me on three occasions in twenty years because my year-end accounting differed from his. Twice he was right. Starting in 1988 we computerized our accounts, and when he called with a question about the total for that year, I said I could show him with a printout that the computer had the correct figure.

Suddenly it was a sad moment. I could hear the distress in his voice when he saw that he could no longer keep track of the money from his writing. "The accountant has to do it," he said; and after that, I sent all checks and reports to his accountant.
2. Naomi had written Bruno and Gina separately, inviting them to Vienna for a visit. By chance, and without speaking to each other, both picked the same date. "It was hilarious," Naomi said.

Ever since childhood, Naomi had felt close to Gina, almost as if she were an aunt. Gina's daughter was the same age as Naomi, and Gina had often brought her over to the Bettelheims' so the two children could play together. When Gina told her daughter that she had been married to Bruno in Vienna, Trude and Bruno sat their three children down and also broke the news—before they received the information from someone else at some point in the little enclave of Hyde Park.
3. Interview tape made by Celeste Fremon.
4. *The Informed Heart*, p. 94.
5. Ruth Marquis said he told her this. In my opinion, Bruno retained remnants of the "love at first sight" transference he experienced when he saw the sixteen-year-old Gina at her father's graveside. However, by the age of eighty-three, he was able to be more rational about her.

6. Bruno was mistaken. Visitors *may* have been assisted in this way, but it was legal only for Dutch citizens. Of course, his doctor may have had a friend in a Dutch hospital.

7. I cannot believe that Bettelheim chose a "momentous" date to end his life. On the other hand, I can speculate that the date chose him. Given the psyche's power to express itself somatically, I think it possible that an unconscious prompting ruffled his heart and brought him to a moment of decision.

Bruno's sister, Grete, also committed suicide, less than a year after my interview with her. She had great difficulty breathing when we spoke, and she could not keep enough oxygen on hand in the retirement home where I saw her. About two months after Trude died, Grete took an overdose of pills.

Chapter 34: Ripples

1. I called Sue Duncan while this book was in galleys, because I had heard that her older son, Arnold, was recently named head of the Chicago school system—at thirty-eight, the youngest in its history to hold that position. We talked about his twelve-hour days on the job, and her pride was unspoken but obvious. She asked about my book, and in the course of our conversation volunteered that she had raised her children very much under the influence of Bettelheim's ideas. Now every child in Chicago's schools, she said, is getting a little of Dr. B. through Arnie.

For me, her words resonated with Rabbi Meyer's comment (Chapter 35) that one's teaching goes down through the generations, and I reflected later on how Bruno might have responded to Sue's remark. It would have pleased him immensely, but I believe he would have disagreed with her and have told her that her child's adult behavior, the tenor of his approach to life, how he deals with his own feelings and the feelings of others, was in large measure the result of having protectors and models like Sue and Starkey Duncan.

Incidentally, one of Arnold Duncan's chief assistants in the school system is a lawyer who is the daughter of Morris and Gayle Janowitz, and so perhaps the ripple effect goes on.

2. Adam Smith, *The Theory of Moral Sentiments* (Indianapolis: Liberty Classics), p. 47.

3. Celeste Fremon tape.

Chapter 35: Pessimism and Hope

1. Righteousness (if that's the right word) without religion is obviously based on autonomy, personal standards, and choice.

2. *Freud's Vienna*, p. 206.

3. *Freud's Vienna*, p. 208.

4. *Ordinary Men* was the title of a 1992 book by Christopher R. Browning about one aspect of the Final Solution.

5. The Talmud, Tractate *Kiddushin* 30a.

BIBLIOGRAPHY

Works by Bruno Bettelheim

"Self-Interpretation of Fantasy." *American Journal of Orthopsychiatry*, vol. 17 (1947), pp. 80–100.

Love Is Not Enough: The Treatment of Emotionally Disturbed Children. Glencoe, Ill.: Free Press of Glencoe, 1950. (I used the seventh printing, New York: Free Press, 1966.)

The Dynamics of Prejudice: A Psychological and Sociological Study of Veterans (with Morris Janowitz). New York: Harper & Brothers, 1950.

Symbolic Wounds: Puberty Rites and the Envious Male. Glencoe, Ill.: Free Press of Glencoe, 1954.

Truants from Life: The Rehabilitation of Emotionally Disturbed Children. Glencoe, Ill.: Free Press of Glencoe, 1955.

The Informed Heart: Autonomy in a Mass Age. Glencoe, Ill.: Free Press of Glencoe, 1960. (I used the sixth printing, New York: Free Press, 1967.)

Dialogues with Mothers. New York: Free Press of Glencoe, 1962.

Symbolic Wounds. New York: Free Press of Glencoe, 1962. (This is the revised edition. I used the Collier Books reprint of this edition, 1970).

Social Change and Prejudice (with Morris Janowitz; this book includes *The Dynamics of Prejudice*). New York: Free Press of Glencoe, 1964.

The Empty Fortress: Infantile Autism and the Birth of Self. New York: Free Press, 1967.

The Children of the Dream: Communal Child-Rearing and American Education. New York: Macmillan, 1969. (I used the ninth printing of the Avon edition, first published in 1970.)

A Home for the Heart. New York: A. A. Knopf, 1974.

Une autre régard sur la folie (with Daniel Karlin). Paris: Stock, 1975.

The Uses of Enchantment. New York: A. A. Knopf, 1976. (I used the Vintage Books edition, 1977).

Surviving, and Other Essays. New York: A. A. Knopf, 1990.

On Learning to Read: The Child's Fascination with Meaning (with Karen Zelan). New York: A. A. Knopf, 1981.

Freud and Man's Soul. New York: A. A. Knopf, 1982.

A Good Enough Parent: A Book on Child-Rearing. New York: A. A. Knopf, 1987.

Freud's Vienna and Other Essays. New York: A. A. Knopf, 1990.

The Art of the Obvious: Developing Insight for Psychotherapy and Everyday Life (with Alvin A. Rosenfeld). New York: A. A. Knopf, 1993.

Other References

Browning, Christopher R. *Ordinary Men: Reserve Police Battalion 101 and the Final Solution in Poland.* New York: HarperCollins, Aaron Asher Books, 1992.

Dundes, Alan. "Bruno Bettelheim's *Uses of Enchantment* and Abuses of Scholarship." *Journal of American Folklore,* vol. 104, no. 411 (Winter 1991).

Encyclopaedia Britannica, 1969.

Erikson, Erik. *Identity: Youth and Crisis.* New York: W. W. Norton, 1968.

Fine, Reuben. *A History of Psychoanalysis.* New York: Columbia University Press, 1979.

Frank, Anne. *Anne Frank's Diary: The Critical Edition.* New York: Doubleday, 1989.

Freud, Sigmund. Standard Edition, vol. 23. London: Hogarth Press, 1953–74.

Gay, Peter. *Freud: A Life for Our Times.* New York: W. W. Norton, 1988.

Henry, Jules. "The Formal Social Structure of a Psychiatric Hospital," *Psychiatry* 17 (1954).

——. "Types of Institutional Structure," *Psychiatry* 20 (1957).

——. "The Culture of Interpersonal Relations in a Therapeutic Institution for Emotionally Disturbed Children," *American Journal of Orthopsychiatry,* vol. 27 (1957).

——. *Pathways of Madness.* New York: Random House, 1971.

Heuscher, Julius E. *A Psychiatric Study of Fairy Tales: Their Origin, Meaning, and Usefulness.* Springfield, Ill.: Charles Thomas, 1963.

——. *A Psychiatric Study of Fairy Tales,* 2nd edition. Springfield, Ill.: Charles Thomas, 1974.

Hilberg, Raul. *The Destruction of the European Jews.* New Haven: Yale University Press, 2002.

Jenuwine, Michael. *A History of the Orthogenic School of the University of Chicago from 1912 to 1990.* Unpublished paper.

Klarsfeld, Serge. *Memorial to the Jews Deported from France 1942–1944.* New York: The Beate Klarsfeld Foundation, 1983.

Kogon, Eugen. *The Theory and Practice of Hell.* New York: Berkley Books, 1980.

Laqueur, Walter. *Young Germany.* New York: Basic Books, 1962.

Lyons, Tom Wallace. *The Pelican and After: A Novel About Emotional Disturbance.* Richmond: Prescott, Durrell, 1983.

Marcus, Paul. *Autonomy in the Extreme Situation: Bruno Bettelheim, the Nazi Concentration Camps, and the Mass Society.* Westport, Conn.: Praeger, 1999.

Morton, Frederic. *A Nervous Splendor: Vienna 1888–1889.* New York: Penguin, 1981.

——. *The Rothschilds: A Family Portrait.* New York: Atheneum, 1983.

Ozick, Cynthia. *Quarrel and Quandary.* New York: A. A. Knopf, 2000.

Pollak, Richard. *The Creation of Dr. B.: A Biography of Bruno Bettelheim.* New York: Touchstone, 1998.

Sanders, Jacquelyn Seevak. *A Greenhouse for the Mind.* Chicago: University of Chicago Press, 1989.

Schacter, Daniel L. *The Seven Sins of Memory.* Boston and New York: Houghton Mifflin, 2001.

Schorske, Carl E. *Fin-de-Siècle Vienna: Politics and Culture.* New York: A. A. Knopf, 1980.

Shirer, William. *The Rise and Fall of the Third Reich: A History of Nazi Germany.* New York: Simon and Schuster, 1960.

Smith, Adam. *The Theory of Moral Sentiments.* Indianapolis: Liberty Classics (no date).

Sutton, Nina. *Bettelheim: A Life and a Legacy.* New York: Basic Books, 1996.

INDEX

PERMISSIONS ACKNOWLEDGMENTS

GRATEFUL acknowledgment is made to the following for permission to reprint previously published and unpublished material.

Alfred A. Knopf: Excerpt from *Surviving and Other Essays* by Bruno Bettelheim. Copyright © 1979 by Bruno Bettelheim and Trude Bettelheim as Trustees. Excerpts from *Freud's Vienna and Other Essays* by Bruno Bettelheim. Copyright © 1990 by Bruno Bettelheim. Reprinted by permission of Alfred A. Knopf, a division of Random House, Inc.

American Orthopsychiatric Association, Inc.: Excerpt from "Self-Interpretation of Fantasy" (*American Journal of Orthopsychiatry*, vol. 17, 1947). Copyright © 1947 by the American Orthopsychiatric Association, Inc. Reprinted by permission of the American Orthopsychiatric Association, Inc.

Ruth Bettelheim, Naomi Pena, and Eric Bettelheim: Material from letters of Bruno Bettelheim, from Trude Bettelheim's audiotapes, and from the lecture of Bruno Bettelheim. Copyright © 2002 by Ruth Bettelheim, Naomi Pena, and Eric Bettelheim. Excerpts from *Symbolic Wounds* by Bruno Bettelheim. Copyright © 1956 by The Free Press, copyright renewed 1982 by Bruno Bettelheim. Revised edition copyright © 1962 by The Free Press of Glencoe, Inc., copyright renewed 1990 by Ruth Bettelheim, Naomi Pena, and Eric Bettelheim. Reprinted by permission of Ruth Bettelheim, Naomi Pena, and Eric Bettelheim.

The Free Press: Excerpts from *The Informed Heart: Autonomy in a Mass Age* by Bruno Bettelheim. Copyright © 1960 by The Free Press, copyright renewed 1988 by Bruno Bettelheim. Reprinted by permission of The Free Press, an imprint of Simon & Schuster Adult Publishing Group.

Robert B. Silvers: Excerpts from a letter of Robert B. Silvers. Reprinted courtesy of Robert B. Silvers.

Dr. Melford E. Spiro: Excerpt from a letter dated 3/26/1969 from Dr. Melford E. Spiro. Reprinted courtesy of Dr. Melford E. Spiro.

A NOTE ON THE TYPE

THE TEXT of this book was set in Electra, a typeface designed by W. A. Dwiggins (1880–1956). This face cannot be classified as either modern or old style. It is not based on any historical model, nor does it echo any particular period or style. It avoids the extreme contrast between thick and thin elements that mark most modern faces, and it attempts to give a feeling of fluidity, power, and speed.

Composed by Stratford Publishing Services, Brattleboro, Vermont
Printed and bound by Berryville Graphics, Berryville, Virginia
Designed by Irva Mandelbaum